Dreamweaver MX
THE MISSING MANUAL

*The book that
should have been
in the box*

Dreamweaver MX
THE MISSING MANUAL

David Sawyer McFarland

POGUE PRESS™
O'REILLY®

Beijing · Cambridge · Farnham · Köln · Paris · Sebastopol · Taipei · Tokyo

Dreamweaver MX: The Missing Manual

by David Sawyer McFarland

Copyright © 2002 Pogue Press, LLC. All rights reserved.
Printed in the United States of America.

Published by Pogue Press/O'Reilly & Associates, Inc.,
1005 Gravenstein Highway North, Sebastopol, CA 95472.

November 2002: First Edition.
April 2003:   Second Printing.
June 2003:   Third Printing.

ISBN: 0-596-00349-8

Table of Contents

Part Three: Bringing Your Pages to Life

Part Four: Building a Web Site

TABLE OF CONTENTS

The Missing Credits

About the Author

David Sawyer McFarland is president of Sawyer McFarland Media, Inc., a Web development and training company in Portland, OR. He's been building Web sites since 1995, when he designed his first Web site: an online magazine for communication professionals. He's served as the Webmaster at the University of California at Berkeley and the Berkeley Multimedia Research Center.

In addition to building Web sites, David is also a writer, trainer, and instructor. He's taught Dreamweaver at Intuit, UC Berkeley Graduate School of Journalism, the Center for Electronic Art, the Academy of Art College, Ex'Pressions Center for New Media, and the Art Institute of Portland. He's also written articles about Dreamweaver and the Web for both *Macworld* magazine and CreativePro.com.

He welcomes feedback about this book by email: *missing@sawmac.com*. (If you're seeking technical help, however, please refer to the sources listed in Appendix A.)

About the Creative Team

David Pogue (editor) is the weekly computer columnist for the *New York Times* and the creator of the Missing Manual series. He's the author or co-author of 25 books, including six in this series and six in the "For Dummies" line (including *Magic, Opera, Classical Music,* and *The Flat-Screen iMac*). In his other life, David is a former Broadway show conductor, a magician, and a pianist (*www.davidpogue.com*).

He welcomes feedback about Missing Manual titles by email: *david@pogueman.com*.

Nan Barber (co-editor, copy editor) co-authored *Office X for the Macintosh: The Missing Manual* and *Office 2001 for Macintosh: The Missing Manual.* As the principal copy editor for this series, she has edited the titles on iPhoto, Mac OS 9, AppleWorks 6, iMovie, Dreamweaver 4, and Windows XP. Email: *nanbarber@mac.com*.

Rose Cassano (cover illustration) has worked as an independent designer and illustrator for twenty years. Assignments have ranged from the nonprofit sector to corporate clientele. She lives in beautiful Southern Oregon, grateful for the miracles of modern technology that make living and working there a reality. Email: *cassano@cdsnet.net*. Web: *www.rosecassano.com*.

Phil Simpson (design and layout) works out of his office in Stamford, Connecticut, where he has had his graphic design business since 1982. He is experienced in many facets of graphic design, including corporate identity, publication design, and corporate and medical communications. Email: *pmsimpson@earthlink.net*.

Danilo Celic (technical editor) picked up Dreamweaver 1.2 as a demo version on the cover CD of some imported magazine, and soon realized that hand coding everything was not at all what it was cracked up to be. Today, he often comes to the aid of struggling developers in the Macromedia newsgroups, where he serves as a Team Macromedia volunteer for Dreamweaver. While the languages may change, the wee hours stay the same—unfortunately for his lovely new wife, Melissa.

Acknowledgments

Many thanks to all those who helped with this book, including my students, who always help me see technical issues through beginners' eyes, and Danilo Celic, whose technical edits provided a comfortable safety net to protect me from any embarrassing gaffes.

Of course, without the hard work of the Dreamweaver team, this book wouldn't have been possible. A special thanks to David Deming, Jay London, Sho Kuwamoto, and Wanda Huang from Macromedia for providing quick and informative answers during the writing of this book.

Finally, thanks to David Pogue whose unflagging enthusiasm and endurance is inspiring; my wife, Scholle, for always being there; my mom and Doug; Mary and David; and Phyllis and Les, whose enthusiasm for this project never failed to encourage me.

—David Sawyer McFarland

The Missing Manual series is a joint venture between Pogue Press—the dream team introduced on these pages—and O'Reilly & Associates, one of the most respected publishers on earth. It's only because Tim O'Reilly and his team had the vision to take a gamble on this concept that this book came into existence.

Thanks, too, to agent David Rogelberg, the Missing Manuals' first believer; David Sawyer McFarland, who was not only a dream author but who performed an eleventh-hour "beta read" of his own; Johnna Dinse for her masterful indexing talent; and the other Pogues—Jennifer, Kelly, and Tia—who make this series, and everything else, possible.

—David Pogue

The Missing Manual Series

Missing Manuals are designed to be authoritative, superbly written guides to popular computer products that don't come with printed manuals (which is just about all of them). Each book features a handcrafted index; cross-references to specific page numbers (not just "See Chapter 14"); RepKover, a detached-spine binding that lets the book lie perfectly flat without the assistance of weights or cinder blocks; and an ironclad promise never to use an apostrophe in the possessive word *its*.

Recent and upcoming Missing Manual titles include:

- *Mac OS X: The Missing Manual,* Second Edition, by David Pogue
- *iPhoto: The Missing Manual* by David Pogue, Joseph Schorr, & Derrick Story
- *Photoshop Elements 2: The Missing Manual* by Donnie O'Quinn
- *Switching to the Mac: The Missing Manual* by David Pogue
- *Mac OS X Hints* by Rob Griffiths
- *Office X for Macintosh: The Missing Manual* by Nan Barber, Tonya Engst, & David Reynolds
- *AppleWorks 6: The Missing Manual* by Jim Elferdink & David Reynolds
- *iMovie 2: The Missing Manual* by David Pogue
- *Mac OS 9: The Missing Manual* by David Pogue
- *Windows XP Home Edition: The Missing Manual* by David Pogue
- *Windows XP Pro: The Missing Manual* by David Pogue, Craig Zacker, & Linda Zacker

Introduction

The World Wide Web continues to evolve, growing in scope and complexity, with new technologies popping up every year to make the Web look and work better. Even people building personal Web sites now employ several programming languages and server technologies to dish up content. Throughout its history Dreamweaver has managed to keep pace with this changing technological landscape with each new version.

Dreamweaver MX is no exception—it's capable of working with more technologies than any previous version. Whether you're creating database-enabled Active Server Pages, using Cascading Style Sheets for cutting-edge design effects, or simply sticking to straightforward HTML pages, Dreamweaver has just about all the tools you need.

Any enterprising designer can create Web pages, Cascading Style Sheets, and even JavaScript programs with a simple text editor. In fact, Dreamweaver MX provides powerful text-editing abilities to create a basic text file or a complex Java server page. But why go to all that trouble when Dreamweaver's *visual* page-building approach makes your job of creating beautiful, complex, and useful Web sites much easier? Whether you're new to building Web pages or a HARD-CORE, hand-coding HTML jockey, Dreamweaver is a powerful tool that lets you build Web sites quickly and efficiently, without compromising the quality of your code.

What's New in Dreamweaver MX

If you've never used Dreamweaver before, see Chapter 1 for a grand tour and welcome. If you're upgrading from Dreamweaver 4 or some other version, you'll find that Dreamweaver MX offers a host of new features aimed at both the novice Web designer and the seasoned HTML guru:

- Dreamweaver MX offers **improved support for Cascading Style Sheets** (Chapter 8). Dreamweaver can now display most CSS properties, while a revised CSS Panel simplifies the process of applying and editing styles to text, images, and links.

- New **template features** offer more flexibility than ever before. You can now add complex logic to templates so they can be modified from page to page—giving added subtlety while still maintaining design integrity and control. (See Chapter 18 for more.)

- Building Web sites that meet the needs of physically disabled Web surfers is a worthwhile challenge. If you develop sites for most government agencies, it's also the law. You'll find many tools for building **accessible Web pages**. By adding Dreamweaver's accessibility tools to your Web pages, more of your visitors can enjoy HTML objects such as images, tables, and forms.

- Want to make sure your site is up to snuff? In addition to the site wide reporting features introduced in Dreamweaver 4, the new **validation tool** (Chapter 15) will clean up the HTML, XHTML, or XML syntax of your entire site.

- If you need help using Dreamweaver, look no further than the new **Answers panel** (Appendix). You'll find tutorials, articles, technical notes, and more, right at your fingertips. Best of all, new content is continually downloaded from the Macromedia Web site (without any marketing messages or ads).

- Tired of having to add the same code over and over? Do you have a favorite table design that you use frequently, for instance? The new **Snippets panel** (Chapter 17) can help. Here you can store and reuse common bits of code—HTML, JavaScript, CSS, and so on—or take advantage of the many code snippets that ship with the program.

- If you're a hand-coding junkie, Dreamweaver MX aims to please. In addition to the powerful text-editing abilities introduced in Dreamweaver 4, you'll find support for **code coloring**, a **tag library editor**, and **tag hints**, which provide pop-up access to tags and tag properties.

- An **improved interface** organizes the many panels that used to float in an almost uncontrollable mass. Windows users also can take advantage of an integrated interface similar to those used in programming software.

- Dreamweaver 4 was a great program for building static Web pages. But if you wanted to build a database-driven site, you had to shell out the extra bucks for Dreamweaver's more powerful sibling, UltraDev. Dreamweaver MX now does it all. Using its **dynamic Web site features** (Part 6), you'll be building pages to add, edit, and delete database information in no time.

- If you were an UltraDev user, you'll find that Dreamweaver MX offers **more server models** to work with, including ASP, ASP.NET, JSP, Cold Fusion MX, and PHP.

Cold Fusion developers will be pleased as well; Dreamweaver MX uses a new approach for writing cleaner, more professional Cold Fusion code.

Tip: Macromedia occasionally issues updates to Dreamweaver. To make sure you're using the latest version, visit the Macromedia Web site at *www.macromedia.com/support/dreamweaver/ downloads_updaters.html.*

HTML 101

Underneath the hood of any Web page, whether it's your Uncle's "Check out this summer's fishin'" page or the home page of a billion-dollar online retailer, is nothing more than line after line of ordinary typed text. With its use of simple commands called *tags*, HTML (Hypertext Markup Language) is still at the heart of most of the Web.

The HTML code that creates a Web page can be as simple as this:

```
<html>
<head>
<title>Hey, I am the title of this Web page.</title>
</head>
<body>
Hey, I am some body text on this Web page.
</body>
</html>
```

While it may not be exciting, the HTML shown here is all that's needed to make a Web page.

Of Tags and Properties

In the example above—and, indeed, in the HTML code of any Web page you examine—you'll notice that most commands appear in *pairs* designed to surround a block of text or other commands.

These bracketed commands constitute the "markup" part of the Hypertext Markup Language and are called *tags*. Sandwiched between brackets, tags are simply instructions that tell a Web browser how to display the information on a Web page.

The starting tag of each pair tells the browser where the instruction begins, and the ending tag tells it where the instruction ends. Ending tags always include a forward slash (/) after the first bracket symbol (<), which tells the browser that this is a closing tag.

Fortunately, Dreamweaver can generate all of these tags *automatically* behind the scenes. By no means will you ever have to memorize or type out these commands (although many programmers enjoy doing so for greater control). It's important to understand that at its heart, Dreamweaver is a program that converts your visual designs into underlying codes like the following.

- The **<html>** tag appears once at the beginning of a Web page and again (with an added slash) at the end. This tag tells a Web browser that the information contained in this document is written in HTML, as opposed to some other language. All of the contents of a page, including other tags, appear between the opening and closing <html> tags.

If you were to think of a Web page as a tree, the <html> tag would be its trunk. Springing from the trunk are two branches that represent the two main parts of any Web page: the *head* and the *body*.

- The *head* of a Web page, surrounded by **<head>** tags, contains the title of the page. It may also provide other, invisible information (such as search keywords) that browsers and Web search engines can exploit.

In addition, the head can contain information that's used by the Web browser for displaying the Web page and for adding interactivity. *Cascading Style Sheet* information, used for formatting text and other elements, may be defined in the head of the document (see Chapter 9). In addition, JavaScript scripts, functions, and variables can be declared in the head of the document. In fact, Dreamweaver Behaviors (Chapter 11) achieve their interactive effects with the help of JavaScript code placed in the head of the page.

- The *body* of a Web page, as set apart by its surrounding **<body>** tags, contains all the information that appears inside a browser window—headlines, text, pictures, and so on.

In Dreamweaver, the body area is represented by the blank white area of the document window (see Figure I-1), and resembles the blank window of a word-processing program.

Figure I-1:
The document window displays your page as you build it. You can add text, graphics, and other elements to it, and—thanks to Dreamweaver's visual approach— see a close approximation of how the page will appear in a Web browser.

Title: [   ]

Untitled-3.htm *

<body>

606 x 316   1K / 1 sec

Most of your work with Dreamweaver involves inserting and formatting text, pictures, and other objects in the body of the document. Many tags commonly used in Web pages appear within the <body> tag. Here are a few:

- You can tell a Web browser where a paragraph of text begins with a <p> (opening paragraph tag), and where it ends with a </p> (closing paragraph tag).

- The <b> tag stands for bold. If you surround some text with it and its partner tag, </b>, you get boldface type on the Web page. The HTML snippet <b>Hello</b> would tell a Web browser to display the word "Hello" in bold type on the screen.

- The <a> tag, or anchor tag, creates a link (hyperlink) in a Web page. A link, of course, can lead anywhere on the Web. How do you tell the browser where the link should go? Simply give the browser more instructions inside the <a> tags; for instance, you might type <a href="http://www.missingmanuals.com"> Click here!</a>.

  The browser knows that when your visitor clicks the words "Click here!," it should go to the Missing Manual Web site. The *href* part of the tag is called, in Dreamweaver, a *property* (you may also hear the term *attribute*) and the URL (the Universal Resource Locator or Web address) in this example, *http://www.missingmanuals.com* is the *value* of the *href* property.

Fortunately, Dreamweaver exempts you from having to type any of these codes, and provides easy-to-use window called the Property inspector for adding properties to your tags and other page elements. To create links the Dreamweaver way (read: the easy way), turn to page 95.

XHTML, Too

Like any technology, HTML is showing its age. Although it has served its purpose well, it's always been a somewhat sloppy language. Among other things, it allows uppercase, lowercase, or mixed-case letters in tags—<body> and <BODY> are both correct. HTML also supports unclosed tags: you can use a single <p> tag (without the closing </p>) to create a paragraph. While this flexibility may make writing pages easier, it also makes life more difficult for Web browsers, PDAs, and other technologies that must interact with data on the Web. Additionally, HTML doesn't work with one of the hottest up-and-coming Internet languages: XML, or Extensible Markup Language.

To keep pace with the times, an improved version of HTML, called XHTML, is finding its way into more and more Web sites. Once again, Dreamweaver MX is right on the cutting edge: it can create and work with XHTML files. If you only understand HTML, don't worry; XHTML isn't a revolutionary new language that will take you hours to learn. In essence, it's HTML with more strict guidelines applied. For example, the HTML page code listed above would look like this in XHTML:

```
<?xml version="1.0" encoding="iso-8859-1"?>
<!DOCTYPE html PUBLIC "-//W3C//DTD XHTML 1.0 Transitional//EN"
"http://www.w3.org/TR/xhtml1/DTD/xhtml1-transitional.dtd">
<html xmlns="http://www.w3.org/1999/xhtml">
<head>
<title>Hey, I am the title of this Web page.</title>
</head>
<body>
Hey, I am some body text on this Web page.
</body>
</html>
```

Notice that everything below the <head> is *exactly* the same as the HTML page. The information that begins the page, however, is how the page identifies which standards it conforms to. In this case, it merely says that the page is a type of XML document, in particular, an XHTML document. (Dreamweaver will automatically write all of this code when you create a new XHTML page.)

As you can see, the real code used to make the page is much like HTML. To make an XHTML file comply with XML, however, there are a few strict rules to keep in mind:

- **Begin the page with a document type declaration and namespace.** That's the first few lines in the code above. It simply states what type of document the page is.

- **Tags and tag attributes must be lowercase.** Unlike in HTML, typing the tag <BODY> in an XHTML file is incorrect.

- **Quotation marks are required for tag attributes.** For example, a link written like this <a href=http://www.missingmanual.com> is valid in HTML, but won't work in XHTML. You have to enclose the value of the hreg property in quotes: <a href="http://www.missingmanual.com">.

- **All tags (even empty tags) must be closed.** To create a paragraph in XHTML, for example, you must begin with <p> and end with </p>. Some tags don't come in pairs. These tags, called *empty tags,* have no closing tag. The line break tag is one example. To close an empty tag, you must include a forward slash at the end of the tag, like this: <br />.

If all this seems a bit confusing, don't worry. All of these strict XHTML rules are built into Dreamweaver, so creating an XHTML page using Dreamweaver's visual design tools won't feel one bit different from creating an old-style HTML page. (For more information on creating an XHTML page in Dreamweaver see page 31.)

The Very Basics

You'll find very little jargon or nerd terminology in this book. You will, however, encounter a few terms and concepts that you'll encounter frequently in your computing life:

- **Clicking.** This book gives you three kinds of instructions that require you to use your computer's mouse or trackpad. To *click* means to point the arrow cursor at something on the screen and then—without moving the cursor at all—to press and release the clicker button on the mouse (or laptop trackpad). To *double-click,* of course, means to click twice in rapid succession, again without moving the cursor at all. And to *drag* means to move the cursor while pressing the button continuously.

- **Keyboard shortcuts.** Every time you take your hand off the keyboard to move the mouse, you lose time and potentially disrupt your creative flow. That's why many experienced computer fans use keystroke combinations instead of menu commands wherever possible. Ctrl+B (⌘-B), for example, is a keyboard shortcut for boldface type in Dreamweaver (and most other programs).

  When you see a shortcut like Ctrl+S (⌘-S) (which saves changes to the current document), it's telling you to hold down the Ctrl or ⌘ key, and, while it's down, type the letter S, and then release both keys.

- **Choice is good.** Dreamweaver frequently gives you several ways to trigger a particular command—by selecting a menu command, *or* by clicking a toolbar button, *or* by pressing a key combination, for example. Some people prefer the speed of keyboard shortcuts; others like the satisfaction of a visual command array available in menus or toolbars. This book lists all of the alternatives, but by no means are you expected to memorize all of them.

About This Book

Despite the many improvements in software over the years, one feature has grown consistently worse: documentation. With the purchase of most software programs these days, you don't get a single page of printed instructions. To learn about the hundreds of features in a program, you're expected to use online electronic help.

Until version 4, in fact, Dreamweaver still came with a printed manual. With MX, however, all you get is a *Getting Started* booklet. You'll find the real information only in the program's online help screens.

But even if you're comfortable reading a help screen in one window as you try to work in another, something is still missing. At times, the terse electronic help screens assume you already understand the discussion at hand, and hurriedly skip over important topics that require an in-depth presentation. In addition, you don't always get an objective evaluation of the program's features. (Engineers often add technically sophisticated features to a program because they *can,* not because you need them.) You shouldn't have to waste your time learning features that don't help you get your work done.

The purpose of this book, then, is to serve as the manual that should have been in the box. In this book's pages, you'll find step-by-step instructions for using every Dreamweaver feature, including those you may not even have quite understood, let alone mastered, such as Libraries, Layout view, Behaviors, and Dreamweaver's dynamic Web site tools. In addition, you'll find clear evaluations of each feature that help you determine which ones are useful to you, as well as how and when to use them.

Dreamweaver MX: The Missing Manual is designed to accommodate readers at every technical level. The primary discussions are written for advanced-beginner or intermediate computer users. But if you're a first-timer, special sidebar articles called Up To Speed provide the introductory information you need to understand the topic at hand. If you're an advanced user, on the other hand, keep your eye out for similar shaded boxes called Power Users' Clinic. They offer more technical tips, tricks, and shortcuts for the experienced computer fan.

Macintosh and Windows

Dreamweaver MX works almost precisely the same in its Macintosh and Windows versions. Every button in every dialog box is exactly the same; the software response to every command is identical. In this book, the illustrations have been given even-handed treatment, rotating among the three operating systems where Dreamweaver is at home (Windows XP, Mac OS 9, and Mac OS X).

One of the biggest differences between the Mac and Windows versions is the keystrokes, because the Ctrl key in Windows is the equivalent of the Macintosh ⌘ key.

Whenever this book refers to a key combination, you'll see the Windows keystroke listed first (with + symbols, as is customary in Windows documentation); the Macintosh keystroke follows in parentheses (with - symbols, in time-honored Mac fashion). In other words, you might read, "The keyboard shortcut for saving a file is Ctrl+S (⌘-S)."

About the Outline

Dreamweaver MX: The Missing Manual is divided into six parts, each containing several chapters:

- Part 1, **Building a Web Page,** explores Dreamweaver's interface and takes you through the basic steps of building a Web page. It explains how to add text and format it, how to link from one page to another, and how to spice up your designs with graphics.

- Part 2, **Building a Better Web Page,** takes you deeper into Dreamweaver and explains how to gain greater control of the design of a Web page. You'll learn how to use more advanced features such as tables, layers, Cascading Style Sheets, and frames. In addition, you'll get step-by-step instruction in using Dreamweaver's Layout view, as well as how to view and work with the underlying HTML code of a page.

- Part 3, **Bringing Your Pages to Life,** helps you add interactivity to your site. From using forms to collect information from your site's visitors, to easily adding complex JavaScript programs, this section guides you through adding animation, multimedia, and other interactive effects.

- Part 4, **Building a Web Site,** covers the big picture: managing the pages and files in your Web site, testing links and pages, and moving your site onto a Web server connected to the Internet. And since you're not always working solo, this section also covers features that let you work with a team of Web developers.

- Part 5, **Dreamweaver Power,** shows you how to take full advantage of such time-saving features as Libraries, Templates, and History panel automation. It also covers Dreamweaver's Extension Manager, a program that can add hundreds of new, free features to the program.

- Part 6, **Dynamic Dreamweaver,** presents a gentle introduction to the often confusing and complex world of database-driven Web sites. You'll learn what you need to build a dynamic Web site; how to connect Dreamweaver to a database; and how to use Dreamweaver to build pages that can display database information, as well as add, edit, and delete database records.

At the end of the book, an appendix provides a list of Internet resources for additional Web-design help. At the Missing Manual Web site, you'll find a free, downloadable bonus appendix: a menu-by-menu explanation of the Dreamweaver MX commands, in both Windows and Macintosh versions.

About→These→Arrows

Throughout this book, and throughout the Missing Manual series, you'll find sentences like this one: "Open the System Folder→Preferences→Remote Access folder." That's shorthand for a much longer instruction that directs you to open three nested folders in sequence, like this: "On your hard drive, you'll find a folder called System Folder. Open that. Inside the System Folder window is a folder called Preferences; double-click it to open it. Inside *that* folder is yet another one called Remote Access. Double-click to open it, too."

Similarly, this kind of arrow shorthand helps to simplify the business of choosing commands in menus, as shown in Figure I-2.

Living Examples

This book is designed to get your work onto the Web faster and more professionally; it's only natural, then, that half the value of this book also lies on the Web.

As you read the book's chapters, you'll encounter a number of *living examples*—step-by-step tutorials that you can build yourself, using raw materials (like graphics and half-completed Web pages) that you can download from *www.sawmac.com/dwmx/*. You might not gain very much by simply reading these step-by-step lessons while relaxing in your tree hammock. But if you take the time to work through them at the computer, you'll discover that these tutorials give you an unprecedented insight into the way professional designers build Web pages.

You'll also find, in this book's lessons, the URLs of the finished pages, so that you can compare your Dreamweaver work with the final result. In other words, you won't just see pictures of Dreamweaver's output in the pages of the book; you'll find the actual, working Web pages on the Internet.

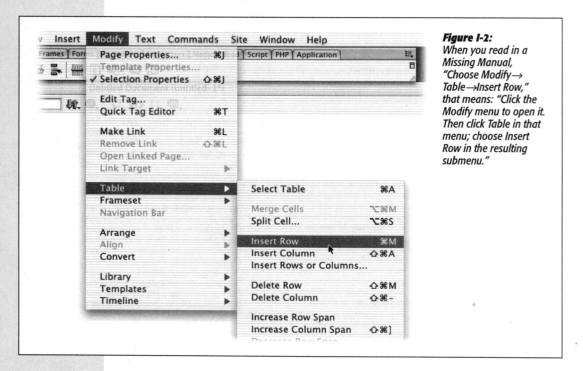

Figure I-2:
When you read in a Missing Manual, "Choose Modify→ Table→Insert Row," that means: "Click the Modify menu to open it. Then click Table in that menu; choose Insert Row in the resulting submenu."

About MissingManuals.com

At the *missingmanuals.com* Web site, you'll find articles, tips, and updates to the book. In fact, you're invited and encouraged to submit such corrections and updates yourself. In an effort to keep the book as up-to-date and accurate as possible, each time we print more copies of this book, we'll make any confirmed corrections you've suggested. We'll also note such changes on the Web site, so that you can mark important corrections into your own copy of the book, if you like. (Click the book's name, and then click the Errata link, to see the changes.)

In the meantime, we'd love to hear your own suggestions for new books in the Missing Manual line. There's a place for that on the Web site, too, as well as a place to sign up for free email notification of new titles in the series.

Part One: Building a Web Page

1

Dreamweaver MX Guided Tour

Welcome to Dreamweaver MX

Dreamweaver MX is a program for producing and managing Web sites. Whether you need a simple five-page Web site to let your friends know about your upcoming dance party, or a thousand-page e-commerce system with database connections and dynamically generated content, Dreamweaver MX can help. It lets you build Web pages and sites quickly and maintain them with ease. It also lets you add interactive behavior and advanced Web technologies like Cascading Style Sheets, and Dynamic HTML.

What MX is All About

The MX version of Dreamweaver is really two programs in one.

First, it's the latest version of Dreamweaver itself, complete with all of the fabulous layout, design, and productivity tools that made a hit of Dreamweaver 4 and its predecessors.

Second, it incorporates the program formerly known as Dreamweaver UltraDev. This program, once sold separately, offers advanced programming technology for data-driven Web sites.

These two newly merged programs add up to a serious tool for creating dynamic, database-driven Web sites. You can now turn your company's database of products into a dynamic online catalog—or turn that cherished recipe collection into an on-line culinary resource for an adoring public. You can even create Web pages for updating and deleting database records, meanwhile keeping designated areas of your site secure from unauthorized visitors. Most reassuring of all, Dreamweaver MX does the programming for you.

If you've never used Dreamweaver before, but have already built one or more Web sites, you won't have to start from scratch. Dreamweaver happily opens Web pages and Web sites that were created in other programs without destroying any of your carefully handcrafted code. While Dreamweaver has always prided itself on leaving HTML code you write exactly as you wrote it, Dreamweaver MX offers greater support for hand-coded Web pages. In fact, many of the new features in MX are aimed specifically at people who like to work in the raw code.

Why Dreamweaver?

There are other Web-page design programs—dozens of them, in fact. But Dreamweaver has become one of the leading programs thanks to key benefits like these:

- **Visual page building.** If you've spent any time using a text editor to punch out the HTML code for your Web pages, you know the tedium involved in adding even a simple item like a photograph to a Web page. When your boss asks you to add her photo to the company home page, you launch your trusty text editor and type something like this: *<img src="images/staff/bigcheese.gif" width="100" height="150" alt="The Boss" border="0">*.

  Not only is this approach prone to typos, but it also separates you from what you want the page to *look* like.

  Dreamweaver, on the other hand, takes a visual approach to building Web pages. If you put an image on your page, Dreamweaver shows you the picture on the screen. As in a word processor, which displays documents on screen as they should look when printed, Dreamweaver provides a very close approximation of what your Web page will look like in a Web browser.

- **Complex interactivity, simply.** You've probably seen Web pages where a graphic (on a navigation bar, for example) lights up or changes appearance when you move your mouse over it.

  Dynamic effects like this—mouse *rollovers,* alert boxes, and navigational pop-up menus—usually require programming in *JavaScript,* a programming language that most Web browsers understand. While JavaScript can do amazing things, it requires time and practice to learn.

  But Dreamweaver relieves you of having to learn JavaScript for these purposes; the program makes it easy to add complex interactivity with just the click of the mouse. Chapter 11 explains how you can use these *Behaviors* (ready-made JavaScript programs in Dreamweaver) to bring your pages to life.

- **Roundtrip code.** Every now and then, even in Dreamweaver, you may sometimes want to put aside the WYSIWYG (what-you-see-is-what-you-get) view and look at the underlying HTML code of a page. You may feel more comfortable creating some of your HTML by hand, for example, or you may want to tweak the HTML that Dreamweaver produces.

Macromedia realized that many professional Web developers still do a lot of work "in the trenches," typing HTML code by hand. In Dreamweaver, you can edit the raw HTML to your heart's content. Switching back and forth between the visual mode—called the Design view—and the Code view is seamless and, best of all, nondestructive. Unlike many visual Web page programs, where making a change in the WYSIWYG mode stomps all over the underlying HTML code, Dreamweaver respects hand-typed code and doesn't try to rewrite it (unless you ask it to).

In addition, Dreamweaver can open many other types of files commonly used in Web sites, such as external JavaScript files (.js files), so you don't have to switch to another program to work on them.

See Chapter 9 to learn more about how Dreamweaver handles writing and editing code.

• **Site management tools.** Rarely will you build just a single Web page. More often, you'll be creating and editing pages that work together to form part of a Web site. Or you may be building an entire Web site from scratch.

Either way, Dreamweaver's site management tools make your job of dealing with site development easier. From managing links, images, pages, and other media to

---

UP TO SPEED

Hand-coding Versus WYSIWYG Editors

Creating Web pages in a text editor was long considered the best method of building Web sites. The precise control over HTML available when code is written by hand was (and often still is) seen as the only way to assure quality Web pages.

Hand coding's reputation as the only way to go for pros is fueled by the behavior of many visual page-building programs that add unnecessary code to pages—code that affects how a page appears *and* how quickly it downloads over the Internet.

But hand coding is time-consuming and error-prone. One typo can render a Web page useless.

Fortunately, Dreamweaver brings solid code writing to a visual environment. Since its earliest incarnation, Macromedia has prided itself on Dreamweaver's ability to produce clean HTML *and* its tolerance of code created by other programs—including text editors. In fact,

Dreamweaver includes a powerful built-in text-editing mode that lets you freely manipulate the HTML of a page—or any other code, including JavaScript, Visual Basic, or Cold Fusion Markup Language.

But the real story is that the code produced from working in the visual mode is as solid and well written as hand coding. Knowing this, you should feel free to take advantage of the increased productivity that Dreamweaver's visual-editing mode brings to your day-to-day work with its one-click objects, instant JavaScript, and simplified layout tools. Doing so won't compromise your code, and will certainly let you finish your next Web site in record time.

Besides, no Web-design program is *really* WYSIWYG—what you see is what you get. Because every browser interprets the HTML language slightly differently, Web design is more like *WYSIRWYGOAGD*: what you see is roughly what you'll get, on a good day.

---

working with a team of people and moving your site onto a Web server, Dreamweaver automates many of the routine tasks every Webmaster faces. Part 4 of this book looks at how Dreamweaver can help you build and maintain Web sites.

- **Database-driven Web sites.** Data makes the world go round. Whether you're a human-resource records manager or a high-school teacher, you probably keep track of a lot of information. Today, companies and individuals store reams of information in database systems like Microsoft Access or Oracle 9i. Dreamweaver MX can help you bring that information to life on the Web without having to learn a lot of programming along the way. From accessing information—such as the latest items in your company's product catalog—to updating and editing databases online, Dreamweaver MX can help you build database-driven Web sites. Part IV of this book offers a gentle introduction to building *dynamic* Web sites.

- **Have it your way.** As if Dreamweaver didn't have enough going for it, the engineers at Macromedia have created a software product that is completely customizable, or as they call it, *extensible.* Anyone can add to or change the menus, commands, objects, and windows in the program.

Suppose, for example, that you hardly ever use any of the commands in the Edit menu. By editing one text file in the Dreamweaver Configuration folder, you can get rid of any unwanted menu items—or even add new commands of your creation. This incredible flexibility lets you customize the program to fit your work methods, even add features that Macromedia's programmers never imagined. Best of all, the Macromedia Exchange Web site includes hundreds of free and commercial extensions to download and add to Dreamweaver. See Chapter 20 for details.

The Dreamweaver MX Interface

Dreamweaver's windows let you add and modify elements of a Web page. Macromedia refers to most of these windows as *panels,* and Dreamweaver has an almost overwhelming number of them.

Many of these windows are used to assist with specific tasks, like building style sheets, and are described in the relevant chapters. But you'll frequently interact with four main groups of windows: the document window, the Insert bar, the Property inspector, and panel groups.

Note: The look of these windows depends on what kind of computer you're using (Windows or Macintosh) and what changes you've made to the program's preference settings.

Even so, the features and functions generally work identically no matter what your situation. In this book, where the program's operation differs dramatically in one operating system or the other, special boxes and illustrations (labeled "For Macs Only" or "For Windows Only") will let you know.

The Document Window

You build your Web pages in the *document window*. As in a word processor, you can simply click inside the body of the document window and type to add text to the page. You'll work in this window as you build a page, and you'll open new document windows as you add or edit pages for your site.

Several other screen components provide useful information about your document. They may appear in different locations in Windows or on the Mac (see Figures 1-1 and 1-2), but work the same. For example:

Figure 1-1:
In Windows, you switch between documents by clicking a document tab that appears immediately below the document window. In this example, clicking the banner.html tab brings that page to the front. (This nifty feature works only if the document window is maximized.) You can also hide the Panels (the stack at the right edge of the window) by clicking the Hide Panels button (circled). To show the panels, click the button again.

Insert bar

Document window

Property inspector

Panel groups

FOR WINDOWS ONLY

The Dreamweaver MX Interface for Windows

Dreamweaver for Windows opens with a window configuration Macromedia calls the Dreamweaver MX *Workspace* (see Figure 1-1), in which all the different panels and windows are fused together, filling the screen edge to edge and top to bottom. You may be familiar with this arrangement, known as the *multiple document interface* (MDI), from programs like Microsoft Outlook.

If you're a longtime Dreamweaver user and prefer the traditional layout of Dreamweaver 4, choose Edit→ Preferences. In the Preferences dialog box, click General in

the list of categories on the left, and then click the Change Workspace button. Select Dreamweaver 4 Workspace. (The other option here, HomeSite/Coder-Style, gives you a window design that resembles HomeSite, a Macromedia text-editing program.) Click OK.

For the purposes of retaining sanity (and keeping the book's length below that price-sensitive 2,500-page barrier), this book assumes that you're using the standard Dreamweaver MX Workspace.

• **Title bar.** The title bar shows the title of the Web page you're currently working on, and, in parentheses, the name of the underlying *file* and what folder it's in. For instance, in the example shown in Figure 1-1, the Web page called *When Cabbages Attack!* is saved as an HTML file called *title.html* in a folder called *cabbage*. (In Windows, the title bar appears on the top of the screen; on the Mac, it's at the top of the document window.)

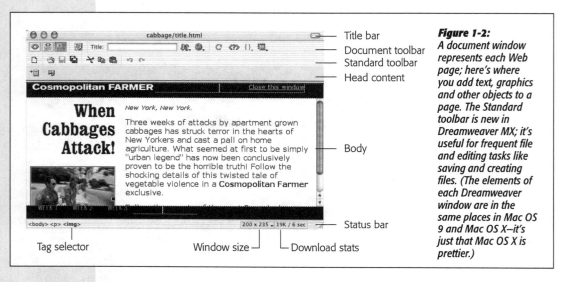

Title bar

Document toolbar

Standard toolbar

Head content

Body

Status bar

Tag selector

Window size

Download stats

Figure 1-2:
A document window represents each Web page; here's where you add text, graphics and other objects to a page. The Standard toolbar is new in Dreamweaver MX; it's useful for frequent file and editing tasks like saving and creating files. (The elements of each Dreamweaver window are in the same places in Mac OS 9 and Mac OS X–it's just that Mac OS X is prettier.)

• **Document toolbar.** The *Document toolbar* lets you change the title of a page, switch between Design and Code views, preview and debug the page in different Web browsers, access a context-sensitive reference (help) system, and change the look of the document window. You'll be reading about its various buttons and menus in the relevant chapters of this book. (To make the toolbar visible if it's not already, choose View→Toolbars→Document.)

• **The Standard toolbar.** The *Standard toolbar*, new in MX, includes buttons for frequent file and editing tasks like creating a new page, opening a page, saving one or all open documents, cutting, copying, pasting, and undoing and redoing actions. (This toolbar is hidden until you summon it by choosing View→Toolbars→Standard.)

• **Head content.** Most of what you put on a Web page winds up on the *body* of the page, but some elements are specific to the region of the page called the *head*. Here you put things like the title of the page, *meta tags* (keywords) that provide information for some search engines and browsers, JavaScript scripts, and Cascading Style Sheet information (Chapter 8).

None of this information is actually visible on your Web page once it's "live" on the Internet. But while working in Dreamweaver, you can have a look at it by choosing View→Head Content. You'll see a row of icons representing the different bits of information in the head.

- **The status bar** provides useful information about your page. It appears at the bottom of the document.

The tag selector (shown in Figure 1-2) is also extremely useful. It provides a sneak peek at the HTML codes that, behind the scenes, compose your Web page. It indicates how tags are nested in the document, based on what you've selected or where the insertion point is. You can also use the tag selector to select an HTML tag and all of the information nested inside it. For instance, clicking the <p> selects the paragraph and everything inside it. This feature is very useful when you want to set *properties* (see the Property inspector below), add *behaviors* (Chapter 11) or precisely control the application of *styles* (Chapter 8).

You'll make good use of the tag selector in the tutorials to come. For experienced Dreamweaver users, it's one of the program's most used tools.

GEM IN THE ROUGH

The Window Size Pop-Up Menu

Creating pages that look good on different monitors set to a wide range of resolutions is one of the most difficult tasks facing Web designers. After all, not everyone has a 21-inch monitor or views Web sites with the browser window maximized to fill the whole screen. Nothing is more dispiriting than spending a solid week designing the coolest looking Web page, only to have your client call up to say that your design doesn't fit his 15-inch monitor (a painfully common story).

You can simulate browser windows of different sizes by dragging the resize handle at the lower-right corner of the document window, of course. But Dreamweaver has a better tool for such experiments: the Window Size Pop-Up Menu on the status bar at the bottom of your document window. Clicking the black arrow next to the window-size stats lets you choose a different setting for the document window, as shown here. Use this feature to test how your page will look inside different-size browser windows. The numbers indicate the width and height in pixels.

(Windows note: If your document window is maximized and you're using the standard Dreamweaver MX Workspace, this feature doesn't work. Choose Window→ Cascade to "unlock" the document window from its space on the screen. Now you're free to resize the window—and to use the Window Size Pop-Up Menu.)

The first pair of numbers indicates the amount of usable space in the document window; the numbers in parentheses indicate the resolution of the monitor. The third option shown here, in other words, indicates that if someone has a 640x480 monitor and maximizes the browser window, there are 600 by 300 pixels of space to display a Web page. (Even though a monitor's resolution is, say, 800 x 600, after you subtract the space required to display the browser's toolbar, location bar, status bar, and other "chrome," 760x420 pixels of space will be visible when a Web page is opened.)

In any case, note that the window size pop-up menu doesn't actually set the size of your *Web page;* Web pages are usually fluid, and can grow or shrink to the size of each visitor's browser window. For techniques that let you exercise greater control of your page presentation, see Chapter 6.

591 x 279	
592w	
536 x 196	(640 x 480, Default)
600 x 300	(640 x 480, Maximized)
760 x 420	(800 x 600, Maximized)
795 x 470	(832 x 624, Maximized)
955 x 600	(1024 x 768, Maximized)
544 x 378	(WebTV)
Edit Sizes...	

Tip: Clicking the <body> tag in the tag selector is the same as pressing Ctrl+A (⌘-A)—it selects everything in the document window. After selecting everything this way, for example, you could press the Delete key to quickly get rid of everything in your document.

The Insert Bar

If the document window is your canvas, the Insert bar holds your brushes and paints, as shown in Figure 1-3. (It was called the Objects panel in Dreamweaver 4.)

While you can add text to a Web page simply by typing in the document window, adding elements like images, horizontal rules, forms, and multimedia elements is simplified by the click-to-add approach of the Insert bar. Want to put a picture on your Web page? Just click the Image icon.

Note: Adding elements to your Web page this way may feel like magic, but the Insert bar is really just a quick way to add code to a page, whether it's HTML, XHTML, JavaScript, or server-side code like Visual Basic (see Part 6 of this book). Clicking the horizontal rule icon, for instance, simply inserts the <hr> tag into the underlying HTML of your page. Of course, Dreamweaver's visual approach hides that messy code, and cheerfully displays a gray horizontal bar on the page.

When you first start Dreamweaver MX, the Insert bar is open (see Figure 1-3). If you ever close it by mistake, you can open it again by choosing Window→Insert or by pressing Ctrl+F2 (⌘-F2). On the other hand, if space is at a premium on your screen, you can close the Insert bar and use the Insert *menu* instead. Its commands duplicate all of the objects available from the Insert bar.

Figure 1-3:
See the arrow next to the word Insert? When the arrow points down, the Insert bar (shown split in half to fit the page) displays all the tabs and available objects. When the arrow points to the right, the window is reduced to a thin bar, with only the word Insert visible.

The strange-looking button at the top-right corner is actually a menu that lets you access a Help screen, close or maximize the window, or even rename the window. (If you don't like the name *Insert,* you can change it to *HTML thingies,* for all Dreamweaver cares.) On the Mac, you have the added option of displaying this window vertically at the side of your monitor, exactly as in Dreamweaver 4; just click the Orientation icon (circled in Figure 1-3).

Twelve different sets of objects are available from the Insert bar, each under a different tab. Click one of these tabs to see the corresponding category of objects worth inserting:

- **Common objects.** In addition to objects like images, tables, and horizontal rules, which you'll use frequently in everyday Web design, this tab of the Insert bar offers objects that may not be part of your daily routine: Flash files or Web pages produced by Macromedia's Web graphics program, Fireworks.

- **Layout objects.** The objects in this tab help you control the layout of a Web page by organizing a page's contents using *HTML tables* or *layers*. In addition, this tab lets you use Dreamweaver's Layout View—a customized approach to building complex table designs that's covered in Chapter 6.

- **Text objects.** For formatting type, making it bold or italic, for instance, you can turn to the Text tab. Most of the buttons on this tab aren't technically objects; they don't insert new objects onto the page. Instead, they format text already present on the page. For the most part, the Property Inspector offers the same formatting options and is a more common tool for formatting text.

Tip: Using the Text Objects tab can be disorienting. Some "text objects" create incomplete HTML and actually dump you into the raw HTML of the page, leaving the nice visual design view behind. In general, the Property inspector and Text menu let you do everything in this tab—more quickly and more safely.

- **Table objects.** If you like to hand write the code that produces HTML tables, this tab is for you. It inserts HTML tags for creating tables, table captions, table heads, and other table-related tags. With one exception—the table object, which you can also find on the Common Objects tab—these objects only function when you're in Code view. Truth is, you'll probably find it easier to create tables using the tools in the Common objects tab *or* the Layout tab, as described in Chapter 6.

- **Frame objects.** It's possible to display several Web pages in one browser window at the same time, thanks to an HTML mechanism called *frames;* see Chapter 7 for complete details.

- **Form objects.** Want to get some input from visitors to your Web site? You'll use *forms* when you want to receive visitor feedback, collect credit card information for online sales, or gather any other kind of data on your Web site. The Forms tab lets you add form elements like radio buttons, pull-down menus, and text boxes. (For more on forms, see Chapter 10.) You'll also use this tab a lot when building the *dynamic* Web pages discussed in Part 6.

- **Template objects.** Dreamweaver's Templates feature lets you build basic Web page designs that you can use over and over again in your site, speeding up your production process and facilitating easy updates. In Dreamweaver MX, the Templates tab also offers advanced features for building complex logic into your templates that let you easily modify the look and content of template pages. See Chapter 18 for details.

- **Character objects.** These are special symbols, like copyright and trademark symbols, that you can pop onto your page.

• **Media objects.** Use the Media tab to insert multimedia elements like Shockwave, Java applets, plug-ins, Active X controls, and Dreamweaver's own Flash objects (Flash Text and Flash Buttons). Multimedia objects are discussed in Chapter 13; you'll find more info on Flash Text and Buttons on page 128.

• **Head objects.** The Head tab lets you insert objects that don't actually appear on your Web page: what alphabet the browser should use to display the page (Cyrillic or Japanese, for example), or a description of the page for use by search engines.

• **Script objects.** This tab lets you add *server-side include* files (files that a Web server merges into a Web page before delivering it to the browser) as well as your own JavaScript programs.

• **Application objects.** Dreamweaver MX makes connecting your Web pages to databases as easy as clicking a few buttons. (OK, *almost* that easy; see Part 6.) The Application tab adds many powerful tools for building dynamic pages: controls that add records to your database, for example, or update information already in a database.

The Property Inspector

After dropping in an image, table, or anything else from the Insert bar, you can use the Property inspector to fine-tune its appearance and attributes. Suppose, for example, that your boss has decided he wants his picture centered in the middle of the page. After highlighting his picture in the document window, you would then use the Property inspector to change its alignment.

The Property inspector is a chameleon. It's aware of what you're working on in the document window—a table, an image, some text—and displays the appropriate set of properties (that is, options). You'll use the Property inspector extensively in Dreamweaver.

Tip: Double-click any blank gray area in the Property inspector—or striped area in Mac OS X—to hide or show the bottom half of the palette, where Dreamweaver displays an additional set of advanced options. (It's a good idea to leave the inspector fully expanded most of the time, since you may otherwise miss some useful options.)

Close box   Quick tag editor   Help

Expand/Collapse
the Property inspector

Figure 1-4:
The Property inspector changes depending on what's selected in the document window, but certain options are always available.

The Property inspector appears the first time you run Dreamweaver MX. But if you don't see it, you can reopen it by choosing Window→Properties, or by pressing Ctrl+F3 (⌘-F3).

Tip: At its heart, the Property inspector is simply a display of the attributes of HTML tags. The *src* (source) attribute of the *img* (image) tag, for instance, tells a Web browser where to look for an image file. The best way to make sure you're setting the properties of the correct object is to click its tag in the tag selector (see page 19).

Panel Groups

So far, this chapter has described the Insert bar, Property inspector, and document window—but those are just the beginning of Dreamweaver's windows. In Dreamweaver 4, in fact, it was easy to wind up with window sprawl: multiple floating windows cluttering up your screen. In Dreamweaver MX, most of the remaining windows—called *panels*—sit in tidy groups on the right edge of your screen.

For example, a panel group named Design harbors panels for working with Cascading Style Sheets, HTML Styles, and Dreamweaver Behaviors (see Figure 1-5).

Tip: To view the panels in a group, click the expander arrow or the panel group's name; to hide the panels, click the arrow (or name) again.

Figure 1-5:
To open a panel, click the arrow next to the panel group name (Application or Files, for example). Clicking a tab brings the corresponding panel forward. Each panel group has its own Context menu button (circled). Clicking the button reveals a contextual menu that lets you move a panel to another group, create a new panel group, rename a group, or completely hide a group of panels.

The various panels and their uses will come up in relevant sections of this book. But a few tips concerning Dreamweaver's panels are worth noting here:

- Double-click anywhere in a panel group's gray title bar to open that panel group *and* expand it to fill the maximum space available.

  This is really the best way to open a panel group. Not only is the title bar a larger target, but most panels contain a lot of information. You'll want to see as much of it as possible.

- You can even rename a panel group. Maybe the name Code doesn't make sense as the name of a panel group; after all, there are plenty of different kinds of codes involved in building Web sites.

  To rename a group, open its contextual menu, either by clicking the context menu *icon* (see Figure 1-5) or by right-clicking (Windows) or Control-clicking (Mac) the title bar. In the contextual menu, choose Rename Panel Group. Type the new name into the resulting window—*HTML,* in this example—and then click OK.

- If you want to hide all windows *except* documents, choose Window→Hide Panels (or press F4)—a useful trick when you want to maximize the amount of your screen dedicated to showing the actual Web page you're working on. To bring back all of Dreamweaver MX's administrative windows, press F4 again, or choose Window→Show Panels.

Tip: Dreamweaver for Windows includes a button for hiding only the panel groups. See Figure 1-1 for this handy trick.

- If you've really made a mess of your screen, having dragged Dreamweaver windows all over the place, you can make them snap back into a tidy arrangement by choosing Window→Arrange Panels. (Unfortunately, this command arranges only tool panels and inspector windows. It doesn't arrange your document windows or, on the Mac, the Site window.)

Where Did the Property Inspector Go?

Occasionally, one of the floating windows—the Property inspector, for example—simply disappears. Yet when you visit the Window menu, you still see a checkmark next to the window's name. In other words, that window is actually still open…somewhere.

This problem can result from accidentally dragging a window off the screen or from choosing a smaller screen reso-

lution. Either way, simply choosing the window's name from the Window menu won't help you; you're just hiding or showing a window that's beyond the boundaries of your monitor. Even quitting and restarting Dreamweaver is no use.

To get out of this predicament, choose Window→Arrange Panels to make the windows snap back to their default—and visible—locations on the screen.

The Dreamweaver Test Drive

Although reading a book is a good way to learn the ins and outs of a program, nothing beats sitting in front of the computer and taking a program through its paces. Many of this book's chapters, therefore, conclude with hands-on training: step-by-step tutorials that take you through the creation of a real, working, professionally designed Web site for the fictional online magazine *Cosmopolitan Farmer*.

The rest of this chapter, for example, introduces Dreamweaver by taking you step by step through the process of building a Web page. It shouldn't take more than an hour. When it's over, you'll have learned the basic steps of building any Web page: creating and saving a new document, adding and formatting text, inserting graphics, and adding links.

If you're already using Dreamweaver and want to jump right into the details of the program, feel free to skip this tutorial. And if you're the type who likes to read first and try second, read Chapters 2 through 5, and then return to this chapter to practice what you've just learned.

Note: The tutorial in this chapter requires the example files from this book's Web site, *www.sawmac.com/ dwmx/*. Click the Tutorials link to go to the tutorials page. Download the files by clicking either the Tutorial 1 Mac files or Win files link, depending on the kind of machine you're using (Mac or Windows).

After you've downloaded and decompressed the files, you should have a DWTutorial1 folder on your computer, containing the Web pages and graphics needed for this tutorial. If you're having difficulties, the Web site contains detailed instructions for downloading the files you'll be using with this book.

Phase 1: Creating a Web Site

Whenever you build a new Web site or edit an existing one, you must begin by introducing Dreamweaver to it—a process called *defining a site*. This simple process is the most important first step when you start using Dreamweaver, whether you plan to work on a five-page Web site, build a thousand-page online store, or edit an existing Web site.

Whenever you want to use Dreamweaver to create or edit a Web site, your first step is always to show the program where the *root folder* is—the master folder for all your Web-site files. You do it like this:

1. **Choose Site→New Site.**

   The Site Definition wizard appears, new in Dreamweaver MX (see Figure 1-6). Make sure the Basic tab is selected.

2. **Type** *Tutorial 1* **in the Site Name field. Click Next.**

   The name you type here is solely for your own reference, to help you identify the site in Dreamweaver's Site menu. It won't appear on the Web.

In the next step, you'll tell Dreamweaver whether you plan on building (a) regular Web pages or (b) pages that require a special server for creating the dynamic, database-driven Web sites discussed in Part 6 of this book.

3. **Click "No, I do not want to use a server technology." Click Next.**

     In this tutorial, you'll be building a basic Web page.

    In the next steps, you'll tell Dreamweaver how you want to work on the files in your site and where you store those files. In this example, you'll use the folder you downloaded from this book's Web site; in other situations, you'll choose (or create) a folder of your own.

4. **Click "Edit local copies on my machine."**

    Understanding why you made this choice takes a bit of explanation.

    The most common method of working on the files of a Web site involves having two sets of files: the *local site* on your hard drive and the *remote site* on the Web (see the box below).

    But there are other ways to work on Web sites. For example, if you work at a company with its own Web server in-house, you may want to work directly on

---

UP TO SPEED

Three Folders Worth Knowing About

During the tutorial in these pages—and, indeed, everywhere in Dreamweaver—you'll encounter a few terms frequently heard at Web-designer luncheons:

Root folder. The first basic rule of Web design is that every piece of the site you're working on—Web-page (HTML) documents, graphic images, sound files, and so on—must sit in a single folder on your hard drive. That master folder is the *root folder* for your Web site—in fact, it's the *local* root folder. ("Local" means *on your computer*, as opposed to the copies of these Web pages that will ultimately hang on the Internet. "Root" means "the master, outer, main folder, in which there may be plenty of sub-folders.")

Local site. The usual routine for creating Web pages goes like this: You first create the page on your own computer, using a program like Dreamweaver; then you upload it to a computer on the Internet called a Web server, where your handiwork becomes available to the masses. In other words, almost every Web site in the universe exists in two places at once. One copy is on the Internet, where every-

one can get at it. The other, original copy is on some Web designer's hard drive.

The copy on your own computer is called the *local site* or the *development* site. Think of the local site as a sort of staging ground, where you build your site, test it, and modify it. Because the local site isn't on a Web server and can't be accessed by the public, you can freely edit and add to a local site without affecting the pages your visitors are viewing, meanwhile, on the remote site.

Remote site. When you've added or updated a file, you move it from the local site to the *remote site*. The remote, or *live*, site is a mirror image of the local site. Because you create it by uploading your local site, it has the same organizational folder structure as the local site, and it contains the same files. Only polished, fully functional pages go online (to the remote site); save the half-finished, typo-ridden drafts for your local site. Chapter 16 explains how to use Dreamweaver's FTP features to define and work with a remote site.

---

the live, online Web files over the corporate network. In fact, there's a third method: you can even edit your Web pages directly on the Internet.

But the first method is by far the best one. Working directly on the live version of the site—the one anyone with a Web browser can see—exposes your half-finished pages, complete with typos and missing pictures, to your audience. It's a much better idea to perfect a page on your own computer, and then, when it's finished, move it to the Web server.

Figure 1-6:
The Basic tab of the Site Definition window—new in Dreamweaver MX—takes you step by step through the process of setting up a new site. Each stage of the process—Editing Files, Testing Files, and Sharing Files—is clearly labeled. Depending on the type of site you're building, and which Dreamweaver features you plan on using, you'll be taken through a series of simple questions that help you set up your site.

5. **Click the folder icon next to the label, "Where on your computer do you want to store your files?"**

   The Choose Local Root Folder window opens, so that you can choose a folder on your hard drive that will serve as your *local root site folder*—the folder on your computer where you'll store the HTML documents and graphics files that make up your Web site.

6. **Browse to and select the DWTutorial1 folder.**

   The Mac and Windows versions of Dreamweaver handle this ritual a bit differently; see Figure 1-7.

   If you were starting a Web site from scratch, you could also create a new empty folder at this point. You would then save your Web pages and graphics into this folder as you built your site.

For more on root folders and organizing Web sites, see Part 4. For now, the fact to burn into your brain is that all the files that will constitute your Web site must live, while you're working on them, in a single folder—the *local root folder.*

7. Click Next.

Now Dreamweaver asks how you want to connect to your *remote server*—the computer that will dish up the finished Web files to your adoring public.

Figure 1-7:
When it comes to selecting a local root folder, the Mac and Windows versions of Dreamweaver differ slightly.

Top: In Windows, the folder name appears in the Select field at the top of the Choose Local Folder window. You click Select to define that folder as the local root.

Bottom: On the Mac, you highlight the folder in the list in the middle of the window, and then click Choose to set that folder as the local root.

8. **Choose None from the first menu; click Next.**

   Dreamweaver can move your files to a Web server automatically, as you'll learn in Chapter 16.

   After clicking the Next button, you see a summary of your settings. If you made a mistake, click Back to move back to the appropriate step in the process to make changes.

9. **Click the Done button.**

   A dialog box appears, letting you know that Dreamweaver is about to create a *site cache* for your Web site. That's a small database (cache) that tracks pages, links, images, and other components of your site. The cache helps Dreamweaver's site-management tools avoid breaking links, warn you when you're about to delete important files, and help you reorganize your site quickly.

Tip: This dialog box will appear each time you define a new site. When it gets old, just turn on "Don't show me this message again."

Defining a site doesn't actually do anything to your computer; it doesn't create a home page or add a folder, for example. It merely prepares Dreamweaver for working on a site.

Tip: Dreamweaver lets you define *multiple* Web sites, a handy feature if you're a Web designer with several clients, or if your company builds and manages more than one site. To define an additional site, choose Site→New Site and follow the steps on page 25. You can then switch from one site to another using the Site List in the Site window (see Figures 14-5 and 14-6).

Phase 2: Page Properties

As noted at the beginning of this chapter, Dreamweaver has many different windows that help you build Web pages. For this tutorial, though, you'll need only three: the Insert bar, document window, and Property inspector (see Figure 1-2). (If you don't see the Insert bar, choose Window→Insert; if the Property inspector isn't visible choose Window→Properties.)

Before beginning the Web site construction in earnest, though, you'll help yourself greatly by adjusting a few Dreamweaver preferences like this:

1. **Choose Edit→Preferences.**

   The Preferences dialog box opens (see Figure 1-8).

2. **In the Category list on the left side of the Preferences dialog box, click Invisible Elements. Make sure the fourth option, Line Breaks, is turned on.**

   In the coming steps, you'll see why this option is useful.

---

3. **Click OK.**

The dialog box closes; you're ready to start building a Web site.

Figure 1-8:
Dreamweaver's Preferences dialog box is a smorgasbord of choices that let you customize the program to work and look they way you want. In this step, you're making the normally invisible Line Break tags visible. As you'll see, this makes importing and formatting paragraphs of text a much simpler process.

Phase 3: Creating and Saving a Web Page

"Enough already! I want to build a Web page," you're probably saying. You'll do that in this phase of the tutorial.

1. **Choose File→New.**

Although you may already have a blank document open, you should get to know the New Document dialog box—a new element in Dreamweaver MX (see Figure 1-9).

Tip: If you don't want to deal with this window every time you create a new page, click the Preferences button. In the Preferences dialog box, turn off the "Show New Document Dialog on Control-N" checkbox.

While you're at it, you can also specify what kind of file you want Dreamweaver to make whenever you press Ctrl+N (⌘-N). For example, if you most commonly create plain HTML files, choose HTML. But if you most often create dynamic pages (like the ASP.NET pages described on page 620), you can choose a different type of file—ASP.NET VB, for example.

With these settings, pressing Ctrl-N (⌘-N) will instantly create a new blank document. (Choosing File→New, however, will still open the New Document window.)

---

2. Click inside the document window, and then choose File→Save.

The Save As dialog box opens.

3. Save the page as *advertise.html* in the DWTutorial1 folder.

Make sure you save this page into the correct folder. In Phase 1, you defined the DWTutorial1 folder as the root of the site—the folder that holds all the pages and files for the site. If you save the page outside of this folder, Dreamweaver will get confused, and its site management features won't work correctly.

Tip: Most operating systems let you save files with long names, spaces, and characters like #, $, &, and ⌘. But some browsers and servers have trouble interpreting anything other than letters and numbers; for example, Netscape 4.x can't "see" any files with spaces in their names. Play it safe: use only letters, numbers, and—if you want a good substitute for a space—the underline or underscore character, like_this (Shift-hyphen).

Your Web-page documents also need a file name extension at the end of the file name, such as *index.html*. Web servers rely on extensions like .htm, .html, .gif, and .jpg to know whether a file is a Web page, graphic, or some other type of file. Windows automatically adds the extension to your saved document names. But on the Mac, where you can save files without extensions, make sure its name ends in the suffix *.html* or *.htm* when you save a Dreamweaver document.

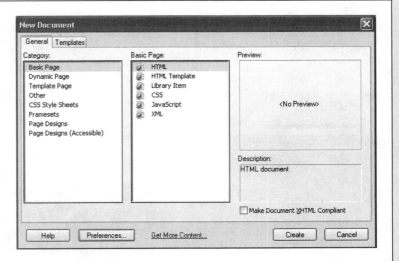

Figure 1-9:
The New Document dialog box appears whenever you choose File→New or press Ctrl+N (⌘-N). It lets you create a whole range of different types of documents including basic Web pages, dynamic pages (see Part 6), templates (Chapter 18) and style sheets (Chapter 8), to name a few. Furthermore, it lets you change the default language for creating your pages from HTML to XHTML, the newer standard described on page 5. Just turn on Make Document XHMTL Compliant (lower right).

4. If the document window toolbar isn't already open (see Figure 1-2), choose View→Toolbars→Document to display it.

The toolbar at the top of the document window provides easy access to a variety of tasks you'll perform frequently, such as titling a page, previewing it in a Web browser, and looking at the HTML source code.

---

5. **Click in the Title field in the toolbar; type** *Advertise with Cosmopolitan Farmer.*

   The Title field lets you set a page's title—the information that appears in the title bar of a Web browser. The page title is also what shows up as the name of your Web page when someone searches the Web using a search engine like Yahoo or Google.

Tip: Try this simple experiment: Go to *www.altavista.com* and search for *Untitled Document.* You'll find that the Web is strewn with thousands upon thousands of Web pages without titles, many of which were created with Dreamweaver.

That's because when you create a new Web page, Dreamweaver assigns it the not-so-glamorous title "Untitled Document"–and all too many people forget to change that dummy text to something more meaningful. Not only does "Untitled Document" look very unprofessional on a Web page, but an untitled page looks terrible in the results list of a search engine.

---

6. **Choose Modify→Page Properties.**

   The Page Properties dialog box opens (see Figure 1-10), in which you can define the basic attributes of each Web page you create. It's a good idea to do this as soon as you create and save a page.

   You'll notice that the title of the page is already set. You typed it into the toolbar in the previous step.

Figure 1-10:
The Page Properties dialog box lets you set general properties of a Web page, such as the color of text and links. Clicking a color box opens the color selector. You can choose one of the colors in the palette or even use the eyedropper to sample a color from your document window. You can even sample colors from anywhere on their screen— even from open documents in other applications.

7. **Click the small gray box next to the word Background. Using the eyedropper cursor, click a black square on the pop-up color palette.**

   When you create a new document in Dreamweaver, the page background is white, just as in a word processor. But if white pages don't inspire your design sense, you're not stuck. Using this pop-up palette, you can choose any background color you want (or, if you're an HTML guru, you can type in the hexadecimal number of the color you want). Both the palette and the hexadecimal color-specifying field reappear fairly often in Dreamweaver.

   In this case, you've just set the background color of the Web page to black.

Tip: You can even fill the background of your page with a graphic—to add a subtle pattern for texture, or to put the company logo in the background as a "watermark."

To choose a background image, click the Browse button shown in Figure 1-10. This opens a window that lets you search for the graphic you want to use. Be careful with background images, however. If there's a lot of contrast and detail in your background image, it can easily obscure the rest of the content on the page.

---

8. **Click the small black box next to the Text label. From the pop-up color palette, choose white (or type #FFFFFF into the box beside the palette square).**

   Unless you intervene, text appears in black on a Web page. But since you just set the background of this page to black, the text needs to be a light color—white, in this case—to be readable. (White will just be the proposed color. You'll be able to override this color on a case-by-case basis, as you'll see later in this tutorial.)

9. **In the Links color field, type #FFCC00; in the Visited Links field, type #FF9900; and in the Active Links color field, type #FFFFCC.**

   These are hexadecimal codes that specify specific Web-page colors; more on this notation on page 33.

   Links come in three varieties: regular, visited, and active. An *active* link is one you're clicking at this moment; a *visited* link is one you've already been to, as noted in a browser's History list. And, finally, a *regular* link is a plain old link, unvisited, untouched. You can choose different colors for each of these link states.

   While it may seem a bit like overkill to have three different colors for links, the regular and visited link colors can provide very useful feedback to Web visitors by indicating which links they've already followed and which remain to be checked out.

10. **Check the margins. Adjust them, if you like.**

    Most browsers put a little bit of space between the contents of your Web page and the top and left sides of the browser window. The exact amount of this margin varies from browser to browser.

If you like, you can change the default setting so that the browser adds more space to the top and left side of the page—or eliminates the margin altogether.

Using Dreamweaver's Color Box

The innocent-looking gray box shown here is called the *color box*. You can use it choose a color for the selected Web-page element in any of three ways.

First, you can click one of the colors on the pop-up palette of color choices that appears when you click the box.

Second, you can use the eyedropper cursor that appears when you click the color box. This cursor is "loaded"; you can click any color visible on your screen—even outside the dialog box you're in—to select a color, a trick that comes in handy when you want to use a color from a graphic you've placed in your document. You can even sample a color from another application's window: just click with the eyedropper. (This click may take you out of Dreamweaver; just return to Dreamweaver to see that the color has been applied.)

Color box   Default color   Color picker

Palette options

✓ Color Cubes
Continuous Tone
Windows OS
Mac OS
Grayscale

✓ Snap to Web Safe

Finally, you can click the Color Picker icon, identified here, to launch the Mac or Windows color-picker dialog box.

If you decide you don't want to add color, or you want to remove a color you've already applied, click the Default Color button on the pop-up color palette. Without a specific color setting, Web browsers will use default colors for the element in question (black for text, for example).

Next to the color box in any Dreamweaver dialog box is a blank text field. If you know your Web colors, you can type their *hex codes* into this box, which is sometimes faster and more precise than clicking the rainbow palette.

In a hex code, a Web color is represented by a six-digit code like this: #FF0000. (Hexadecimal notation is a system computers use for counting; it's what you'd use for counting, too, if you had 16 fingers. In this system, you count like this: 0, 1, 2, 3, 4, 5, 6, 7, 8, 9, A, B, C, D, E, F..) The best way to learn a color's hex value is to choose it in the palette, and then look at the code that Dreamweaver writes into the text box next to it.

You can choose a different set of colors in the palette, too, using the Palette Options pop-up menu. You can choose Color Cubes, Continuous Tone, Windows OS, Mac OS, or Grayscale. The first two contain the *Web-safe* color palette (colors that most machines will reliably display in the same shades you pick) in different arrangements. The Windows OS and Mac OS palettes display the colors available on those respective operating systems when in 256 color mode. Finally, the grayscale palette offers 256 somber shades of gray; you'll find them useful primarily when building Ingmar Bergman tribute sites.

Finally, when you use the eyedropper to sample a color, Dreamweaver uses the nearest Web-safe color—one of only 216 colors. When people surfed the Web with old monitors and old video cards, sticking to Web-safe colors was a good idea. Today, however, most computer screens can show thousands or millions of different colors—many more than are available from the Web-safe palette. In short, consider turning off the "Snap to Web Safe" option in the Palette Option menu. You'll have a much wider range of colors to choose from—and all of them, these days, are safe.

Unfortunately, Internet Explorer and Netscape Navigator use different terms for the top and left margins, so you need to set all four of the Margin boxes here if you want to see the same size margins in the two browsers. In Internet Explorer, the numbers you put into Dreamweaver's Left Margin and Top Margin boxes define the distance between your page contents and the left and top of the browser window, measured in pixels. In Netscape browsers, Dreamweaver's Margin Width box defines the space from the *left* edge of the window, and Margin Height for the space from the *top*.

Tip: To completely eliminate margins, type *0* in each margin field. That's a useful setup when you want a graphic, such as a banner, to butt directly up to the top and left edges of the browser window.

Setting all four of these options won't cause any problems with the different browsers. Internet Explorer simply ignores the Netscape-specific code, and vice versa.

For this tutorial, you don't need to set any margins, but keep this discussion in mind when you start building your own pages.

11. **Click OK to close the window and apply these changes to the page.**

    You return to your document window (see Figure 1-11). If you see an asterisk next to the file name at the top of the document window, Dreamweaver is trying to tell you that you've made changes to the page since you last saved it.

Figure 1-11:
Don't confuse the title *(what appears in the title bar of a Web browser) with the* file name *(the name of the file saved onto your hard drive, ending in .htm or .html).*

12. **Choose File→Save (or press Ctrl+S [⌘-S]).**

    Saving your work frequently not only prevents a serious headache if the power goes out as you finish that beautiful—unsaved—home page, but also ensures that you won't have problems setting up links later. (Links are often dependent on where a page is saved in the folder structure of a site.)

Phase 4: Adding Images and Text

Now you'll add the real meat of your Web page: words and pictures.

1. **Under the Common tab of the Insert bar, click the Image button (Figure 1-14).**

Alternatively, choose Insert→Image. Either way, the Select Image Source dialog box opens.

2. **Browse to the *images* folder in the DWTutorial1 folder; double-click the graphics file called *banner.gif*.**

   The banner picture appears at the top of the page, as shown in Figure 1-12. A thin border appears around the image, indicating that it's selected. The Property inspector changes to reflect the properties of the image.

Figure 1-12:
When an image is selected in the document window, the Property inspector reveals its dimensions. In the top-left corner, a small thumbnail image appears, as does the word Image—*to let you know an image is selected—and the image's file size (in this case, 10 K). The other image properties are described in Chapter 5.*

3. **In the Alt field in the Property inspector, type *Advertising Information*.**

   An image's *Alt* property is a text description of the graphic. It's important to add a text label for each graphic on your Web page; two populations will thank you. First, there are the people who deliberately *turn off* pictures in their Web browsers, in exchange for a dramatic speed-up in the appearance of Web pages. Second, visually impaired people often use software that reads the text of Web pages out loud. In both cases, the Alt label you give each picture is all these visitors will have to go on.

4. **Deselect the image by clicking anywhere in the document window outside of the image. Press Enter to create a new paragraph. Type *Ad Sizes and Rates*.**

   The Property inspector now displays text-formatting options.

Note: The key called Enter on a Windows keyboard is called Return on some Macintosh keyboards. On the Mac, you can press either Return or Enter.

---

5. **From the Format pop-up menu in the Property inspector, choose Heading 1 (see Figure 1-13).**

   This Format pop-up menu offers a number of different paragraph types. Because you're about to type a heading for your page, you've used the Heading 1 style, which makes text big and bold.

6. **Press Enter to create another new paragraph. Type this:** *Cosmopolitan Farmer offers 3 sizes and rates for advertisements.*

This text is smaller than the headline above it. When you press Enter or Return at the end of a headline-formatted paragraph, Dreamweaver MX automatically formats it as a paragraph. (Want proof? Look at the Property inspector's Format pop-up menu. It says "paragraph.")

Figure 1-13:
If you don't see font, size, and color options, click the HTML/CSS button (circled). See page 241 for details on its use.

This new text is a bit dull, so you'll spice it up like this:

7. **Highlight the entire sentence you've most recently typed.**

You can do so by dragging carefully across the entire line. (Unlike the Format pop-up menu, which affects an entire *paragraph* at a time, the Font pop-up menu, which you're going to use next, only applies to *selected* text.)

8. **From the Font pop-up menu in the Property inspector, choose "Arial, Helvetica, Sans-Serif."**

The sentence is now displayed in another font. (Why is more than one font listed for each choice in the Font pop-up menu? Turn to page 80 to find out.)

Next, you'll want to italicize the name of your publication:

9. **Select the words "Cosmopolitan Farmer," and then click the button labeled *I* in the top row of the Property inspector.**

The *I* button, of course, means *italics*. Dreamweaver italicizes your selection.

For added attractiveness, you can now add a horizontal line—a *rule,* as designers call it—underneath the text you've typed so far:

10. **Click at the end of the last sentence to place the cursor there. Press Enter to create a blank line, and then click the Horizontal Rule button in the Insert bar (see Figure 1-14).**

Dreamweaver inserts a line across the page. It's highlighted, meaning that the Property inspector is showing its characteristics.

11. **With the horizontal rule still selected, type *580* in the W field of the Property inspector. Press Enter.**

The width of a freshly minted horizontal line is 100%—meaning that it spans the entire width of a browser window, no matter how wide the window is. You've just changed your selected line's width to 580 pixels wide.

12. **From the Align pop-up menu in the Property inspector, choose Left.**

Normally, a horizontal rule is centered in the middle of a page. Now the line is aligned to the left, to match the alignment of the text and graphics on the page.

Next, you'll add a subhead to the page, a graphic, and a set of bulleted information points.

E-mail link   Image   Horizontal rule

Figure 1-14:
The Email link, Image button, and Horizontal Rule button are just three of the objects you can insert.

13. **Click below the horizontal rule and type** *Square Button*. **From the Format pop-up menu in the Property inspector, choose Heading 2.**

The text for Square Button (one of the online ad sizes your Web site will be offering) changes style. It's now bigger and bolder, though smaller than the first paragraph—the Heading 1—at the top of the page. Now add some additional formatting to this text:

14. **Select the text you just typed; choose "Arial, Helvetica, Sans-Serif" from the Font pop-up menu in the Property inspector.**

A quick way to select a paragraph is to click the <h2> that appears in the lower left-hand corner of the document window (the tag selector, which lets you quickly and accurately select HTML tags—in this case, the Heading 2 tag).

To add some visual variety to the page, you'll color this heading.

15. **With the text still selected, click the Color box in the Property inspector. From the pop-up palette, choose a light yellow color.**

The text changes to the color you selected.

16. **Click at the end of the line of text; press Enter.**

Although the new line is formatted as a "paragraph" and not Heading 2, it still retains most of the formatting of the previous paragraph: same font, yellow color. You don't want those settings for this paragraph, so you need to get rid of them.

17. **From the Font pop-up menu in the Property inspector, choose Default Font.**

Doing so doesn't actually assign any font information to the paragraph. It simply erases whatever fonts had been assigned, leaving it up to a visitor's browser to determine the font to use.

Now you'll get rid of the color.

18. **In the Property inspector, delete the hex number for the yellow color you selected earlier.**

It begins with a # sign and looks something like this: #FFFFCC.

Alternatively, you could use the color box and select the Default Color swatch (see the box on page 34). However, you'll find simply deleting a value from a field in the Property inspector is a quick way to get rid of an unwanted property.

Now you'll add another image—a sample advertisement—to the page.

19. **Click the Image button on the Insert bar (or choose Insert→Image). Browse to the *images* folder in the DWTutorial1 folder; double-click the file called *square_ad.jpg*.**

A square ad for *Cosmopolitan Farmer* appears. It would look better if it were indented a bit.

20. **Click to the right of the image to deselect it.**

A tall, blinking insertion point should appear just to the right of the image.

21. **Click the Indent button on the Property inspector (see Figure 1-15).**

Dreamweaver indents the picture.

Figure 1-15:
Many of the Property inspector text formatting options are similar to tools you'd find in a word processing program.

Outdent — ⌐ Indent

Bulleted list

22. **Hit the Enter key to create a new paragraph. Click the Bulleted List button in the Property inspector.**

Next, you'll be adding a series of bulleted items that explain the size and cost of a Square Button ad in *Cosmopolitan Farmer*.

23. **Type *$100 for one month*; hit Enter. Type *Dimensions: 125 x 125* and hit Enter. Click the Bulleted List button again to end the list.**

You can also click the Outdent button to do the same thing.

You've just added a list with two bulleted items and reset the formatting to a regular paragraph—no indent and no fancy formatting. Next, you'll add another horizontal rule.

24. **Click the Horizontal Rule button in the Insert bar.**

    Dreamweaver inserts a line across the page. It's highlighted, meaning that it is selected.

25. **Click in the W field of the Property inspector; type *580*. From the Align pop-up menu in the Property inspector, choose Left.**

    As you did once before, you just created a horizontal rule of a specified width and aligned against the left edge of the window.

    Your Web page in progress should now look like the one shown in Figure 1-16.

26. **Choose File→Save.**

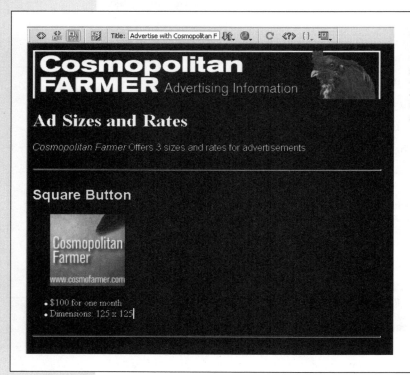

Figure 1-16:
The Web page is starting to come together. You've added graphics, text and horizontal rules, as well as played with some of the text formatting options available in the Property inspector.

Phase 5: Preview Your Work

Dreamweaver is as close as a Web-design program can be to a WYSIWYG application, meaning that for the most part, What You See in the document window Is What You'll Get on the Web.

At least that's how it's supposed to work. But Dreamweaver may display *more* information than you'll see on the Web (including "invisible" objects, table borders, and other elements that you won't see in a Web browser), and may display *less* (it sometimes has trouble rendering complex designs and Cascading Style Sheet information).

Furthermore, much to the eternal woe of Web designers, different Web browsers display pages differently. Pages viewed in Netscape don't always look the same in Internet Explorer. In some cases, the differences may be subtle (for example, text may be slightly larger or smaller). Other times, the difference is dramatic; Layers, for example, an advanced design technology discussed in Chapter 12, are notoriously finicky in Netscape, while much more predictable in Internet Explorer. Throughout this book, you'll find tips and techniques to deal with this problem.

If you're designing Web pages for use on a company intranet, and only have to worry about the one Web browser your IT department has put on everyone's computer, you're lucky. But most of us have to deal with the fact that our sites must withstand scrutiny by a wide range of browsers; it's a good idea to preview your Web pages using whatever browsers you expect visitors to your Web sites to use. Fortunately, Dreamweaver lets you preview a Web page using any browser you have installed on your computer.

Before you can preview a page, you need to set up your list of browsers in the program's preference window, like this:

1. **Choose File→Preview in Browser→Edit Browser List.**

   The Preview in Browser preferences window opens (see Figure 1-17).

2. **Click the + button.**

   The Add Browser or Select Browser window opens.

3. **Click the Browse button. Search your hard drive to find the browser application you most frequently use and select it.**

   Dreamweaver inserts the browser's default name in the Name field of the Add Browser window. If you wish to change its name for display purposes within Dreamweaver, select it and type a new name. (Don't do this *before* selecting the browser, however; Dreamweaver erases anything you might have typed after you select a browser.)

4. **Turn on the Primary Browser box. Click OK.**

   You've just designated the browser as your *primary* browser while working in Dreamweaver. You can now preview your pages in this browser with a simple keyboard shortcut: F12.

   If you like, you can also choose a secondary browser, which you'll be able to launch by pressing the Ctrl+F12 (⌘-F12) key combination.

Now you're ready to preview your document in a real, bona fide Web browser. Fortunately, Dreamweaver makes it easy:

5. **Press the F12 key (or choose Edit→Preview in Browser and select a browser from the menu).**

   The F12 key is the most important keyboard shortcut you'll learn. It opens your Web page in your primary browser, letting you preview your work.

Tip: The Document toolbar also has a preview button—the icon that looks like a globe. Click it to open a menu listing all the browsers you've set up in the Preview in Browser dialog box (Figure 1-17).

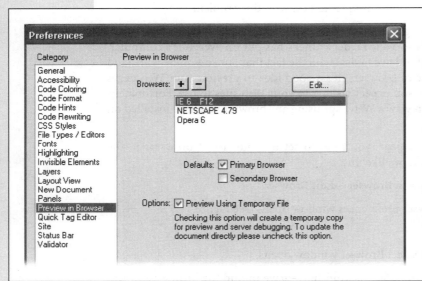

Figure 1-17:
In the Preferences window, you can tell Dreamweaver which browsers you wish to use for previewing your Web pages. You can set the browser to be your primary browser, accessible by the F12 key, or your secondary browser, accessible by Ctrl+F12 (⌘-F12). To preview a page with a browser other than the primary or secondary, choose File→Preview in Browser and select the appropriate browser from the submenu.

6. **When you're done previewing the page, go back to Dreamweaver.**

   Do so using your favorite way to switch programs on your computer—by using the Windows taskbar, the Dock in Mac OS X, or the Mac OS 9 Application menu.

WORKAROUND WORKSHOP

When F12 Doesn't Work on the Mac

In Mac OS 9, the F12 shortcut in Dreamweaver may not work. Mac OS 9's "hot keys" function (which lets you launch favorite programs by pressing your F keys) intercepts Fkey presses in other applications, including Dreamweaver.

To turn off this feature so that you can use the predefined function-key commands in programs like Dreamweaver,

choose ⌘→Control Panels→Keyboard. Turn off the Hot Function Key Settings checkbox and click OK.

(In Mac OS X, the F12 key is often the same as the Eject key—but Dreamweaver commandeers the keystroke for the Preview in Browser function.)

Phase 6: Finishing the Page

You've covered most of the steps you'll need to finish this Web page. All you need to do now is add the rest of the ad sizes and rates, add some contact information, and add a copyright notice:

1. **Click below the last horizontal rule in the document window; type** *Full Banner.*

   Notice that there's no formatting. Since the text is a heading of the same importance as the "Square Button" paragraph above it, it would be nice to make it look the same.

2. **Follow the formatting instructions in steps 13, 14, and 15 in Phase 4 of this tutorial.**

   This formats the text as a Heading 2 using the font combo of "Arial, Helvetica, Sans-serif" and the yellow color you selected earlier. You can also use the eye dropper tool to sample the yellow color straight from the first headline on the page as described on page 32.

   Now it's time to add another graphic—a sample full banner ad—and a set of bulleted information points, just as you did for the "Square Button" section of the page.

3. **Click at the end of the paragraph and press Enter to create a new paragraph and repeat steps 16 and 17 in Phase 4.**

   Doing so strips away all formatting in this paragraph, creating a clean slate for adding and formatting new text or images.

4. **On the Insert bar, click the Image button (or choose Insert→Image).**

   The Insert Image dialog box appears.

5. **In the DWTutorial1→images folder, double-click the file** *full_banner_ad.gif.*

   A full banner ad for *Cosmopolitan Farmer* appears. It would look better if it were indented a bit.

6. **Click to the right of the image to deselect it and place the insertion point at the end of the line.**

   Whatever settings you change on the Property inspector, in other words, will now affect the paragraph that contains the graphic.

7. **Click the Indent button on the Property inspector.**

   Dreamweaver indents the paragraph by a preset amount.

   Finally, you're ready to add the last bit of information about this advertising option.

8. **Hit Enter to create a new paragraph; click the Bulleted List button in the Property inspector.**

   You've just added a bullet at the beginning of the paragraph.

9. Type *$560 for one month,* and then press Enter; type *Dimensions: 468 x 60,* and then press Enter.

You've just created two bulleted items.

10. Click the Bulleted List button again to end the list.

To wrap up, you'll insert another horizontal line beneath your ad rates:

11. Click the Horizontal Rule button in the Insert bar.

Dreamweaver inserts the line; you'll need to make it look like the other lines on the page.

12. With the horizontal rule still selected, click in the W field of the Property inspector and type *580.* From the Align pop-up menu in the Property inspector, choose Left.

The line moves to the left edge of the window, just like the other lines you inserted.

13. Choose File→Save.

You're now ready to add the last elements to this page and finish this tutorial.

14. Click below the last horizontal rule in the document window; type *Half Banner.*

15. Repeat steps 2-12 above to add and format the final ad size and rates.

You'll use the graphic called *half_banner_ad.gif* located in the *images* folder. The two bulleted items of text should read: "$230 for one month" and "Dimensions: 234 x 60."

16. Click below the last horizontal rule on the page; type *Contact Information.* Choose Heading 1 from the Format pop-up menu in the Property inspector.

You've just created a big, bold heading.

17. Press the Enter key; choose Paragraph from the Format pop-up menu in the Property inspector. Choose "Arial, Helvetica, Sans-Serif" from the Font pop-up menu.

You've set up the formatting in advance for the typing you're about to do:

18. Type *The sales staff at Cosmopolitan Farmer would be happy to take your money. Contact us and we'll make it so. Call us at 555-768-9090 or email our* (don't type a final period).

Web pages can contain email links—a link that opens your visitor's email program, and automatically adds an email address to a new message. Dreamweaver has a built-in function for adding this type of link.

19. Click the Insert Email Link button in the Insert bar (see Figure 1-14), or choose Insert→Email Link.

The Insert Email Link dialog box opens.

20. **Type *Advertising Department* in the Text field.**

    This is the text that will appear on the Web page.

21. **Type *adsales@cosmofarmer.com* in the EMail field, and then click OK.**

    Notice that "Advertising Department" appears on the page underlined and in yellow. This is the formatting for links on this page. The email address adsales@cosmofarmer.com, however, is embedded into the link of the page. It may be invisible to your audience, but a Web browser knows it's there.

22. **Press Enter to create a new paragraph.**

    A blank line appears. You'll add some text and a link to another Web site.

23. **Type *For more information on online advertising, visit the Internet Advertising Bureau.***

24. **Select the words "Internet Advertising Bureau."**

    You'll turn these words into a link that, when clicked, will send your visitor to another Web site.

25. **In the Link field in the Property inspector, type *http://www.iab.net* and press the Enter key.**

    You've just added an *external link*. When you preview this page and click that link, you'll be taken to the home page for the Internet Advertising Bureau.

26. **Press Enter and add another 580-pixel horizontal rule to the page.**

    In other words, repeat steps 11 and 12 above. This line, like the other ones you've added, helps break up the page into distinct sections.

27. **Click below that last line and type *Copyright 2002, Cosmopolitan Farmer*.**

    No page is complete without stamping your legal rights onto it. But that doesn't mean you have to rub it in anyone's face, so you'll make the text a little less noticeable, like this:

28. **Select your copyright-notice text; from the Size pop-up menu in the Property inspector, choose 2.**

    The text shrinks one size. (See page 83 for an explanation of why Dreamweaver doesn't offer the traditional list of font point sizes.)

29. **Choose File→Save. Press the F12 key to preview your work in your browser.**

Congratulations! You've just built your first Web page in Dreamweaver, complete with graphics, formatted text, and links. If you'd like to compare your work with an actual, Internet-posted version of the same page, visit the tutorial page for this book, *www.sawmac.com/dwmx/tutorials*.

Much of the work building Web sites will involve using many of the procedures covered in this tutorial—defining a site, adding links, formatting text, and inserting graphics. The next few chapters cover these basics in greater depth and introduce other important tools, tips, and techniques for using Dreamweaver to build great Web pages.

Adding Text to Your Web Pages

True, broadband Internet media like streaming video, audio, and high-quality graphics continue to grab the headlines. After all, it's exciting to speculate about the Web replacing your telephone, or tapping your keyboard to get movies on demand.

But the Web is primarily woven with *words*. Stephen King novellas, Sony PlayStation 2 reviews, and tour dates for Britney Spears's upcoming concerts still drive people to the Web. As you build Web pages and Web sites, you'll spend a lot of your time adding and formatting *text*. Understanding how Dreamweaver works with text is vital to getting your message across effectively.

This chapter covers the not-always-simple act of getting text *into* your Dreamweaver documents. In Chapter 3, you can read about formatting this text so that it looks professionally designed.

Adding Text in Dreamweaver

In many ways, Dreamweaver works like a word processing program. When you create a new document, the blinking cursor appears at the top of the page, ready for you to begin typing. When you finish a paragraph, press Enter or Return to start a new one. Text, as well as anything else you add to a Web page, starts at the top of the page and works its way to the bottom.

Adding Special Characters

Many useful special characters—such as copyright or trademark symbols—don't appear on your keyboard, making them difficult or impossible to type. The Characters tab of the Insert bar lets you use a variety of symbols and international characters quickly by clicking an icon.

To open this panel:

1. **Choose Window→Insert to open the Insert bar (Figure 2-1, top).**

   The keyboard shortcut Ctrl+F2 (⌘-F2) works, too.

2. **Click the Characters tab.**

   The palette shown in Figure 2-1 appears, offering a wide range of symbols and international characters. Unlike regular Western characters, such as *a* or *z*, these special characters are represented in HTML by a code name or number. For instance, a trademark symbol (™) is written in HTML as *&#153*.

3. **On the Characters tab, click the symbol you want.**

   Dreamweaver inserts the appropriate HTML code into your Web page. (Alternatively, you can click the rightmost symbol, the Other Characters button, to bring up the wider ranging Other Character dialog box shown at bottom in Figure 2-1.)

Figure 2-1:
Clicking the Other Characters button on the Characters tab (top) brings up the Insert Other Character dialog box (bottom). However, there are even more characters in the Western alphabet than are listed in this dialog box. You can find a table listing these characters and their associated entity names and numbers at www.ramsch.org/ martin/uni/fmi-hp/iso8859-1.html. *To add a character not available from the Insert Other Character window, type the character's name or number in the Insert field and click OK.*

Caution: If you set the encoding of your Web page to anything other than Western in the Page Properties window (Modify→Page Properties), you can reliably insert only line breaks and nonbreaking spaces. The other special characters available from the Character category of the Objects panel may not work.

Line breaks

Pressing Enter creates a new paragraph, exactly as in a word processor. Unfortunately, Web browsers automatically insert a blank line's worth of extra space above and below paragraphs—which can be a real nuisance if you're trying to create several single-spaced lines of text, like this:

702 A Street
Toadsuck, AR 98789
USA

Each part of the address is on its own line, but it's still just a single paragraph (and shares the overall formatting of that paragraph, as you'll learn in the next chapter).

To create this effect, you need to insert a *line break* at the insertion point, using one of these techniques:

- Click the line break icon on the Characters tab of the Insert bar (the very first symbol at top in Figure 2-1).
- Choose Insert→Special Characters→Line Break.
- Press Shift-Enter.

Tip: When you place a line break in Dreamweaver, you may get no visual hint that it's even there; after all, a regular paragraph break and a line break both create a new line of text. At times, this can be a big problem. Copying and pasting text from email, for instance, sometimes adds unwanted line breaks. A line break may also go unnoticed, if it occurs at the end of a long line.

Fortunately, you can bring those line breaks out of hiding. Choose Edit→Preferences (or Dreamweaver MX→Preferences in Mac OS X), or press Ctrl+U (⌘-U). Click the Invisible Elements category. Make sure the Line Breaks checkbox is turned on. Now you'll see each line break appear as a small gold shield (⊞).

Nonbreaking spaces

You may have noticed that if you type more than one space in a row, Dreamweaver ignores all but the first space. This isn't a glitch in the program; it's standard HTML. Web browsers ignore any spaces following the first one.

Therefore, a line like "Beware   of   llama," which contains ten spaces between each word, would appear on a Web page like this: "Beware of llama." Not only do Web browsers ignore multiple spaces, but they also ignore any spaces that aren't *between* words. So if you hit the Space bar a couple of times to indent the first line of a paragraph, you're wasting your time. A Web browser won't display any of those spaces.

This feature makes good sense, because it prevents Web pages from being littered with extraneous spaces. However, there are times when it's useful to add a space before the beginning of a word. For instance, adding spaces at the beginning of a paragraph can simulate a first-line indent, which is otherwise impossible to create using HTML.

There may be times, too, when you *need* more than one space in a row. Consider the text navigation bar at the bottom of a Web page, a common Web-page element that lists the different sections of a Web site. Visitors can click one of the section titles to jump directly to a different area of the site. For clarity, many designers like to add multiple spaces between the text links, like this:

<u>News</u>   <u>Classifieds</u>   <u>Jobs</u>

In all these cases, a *nonbreaking space* can save the day. It looks just like a regular space, but it acts as glue that prevents the words on either side from being split apart at the end of a line. (That's why it's called a nonbreaking space.)

But when designing Web pages, you'll probably be interested in this fascinating cousin of the regular Space bar for a different reason: it's the only "text spacer" you can use in HTML text.

To insert a nonbreaking space, click where you wish to add the space, and then do one of the following:

- On the Characters tab of the Insert bar, click the Non-Breaking Space icon. (It's the second button shown at top in Figure 2-1.)
- Choose Insert→Special Characters→Non-Breaking Space.
- Press Ctrl+Shift+Space bar (⌘-Shift-Space bar).

Tip: If you add multiple spaces often, Dreamweaver MX offers a new shortcut. Choose Edit→Preferences to open Dreamweaver's Preferences window (in Mac OS X, choose Dreamweaver MX→Preferences instead). Click the General category. Then turn on "Allow Multiple Consecutive Spaces" under "Editing Options." Now, whenever you press the Space bar more than once, Dreamweaver inserts *nonbreaking* spaces.

In fact, MX is even smarter than that. It inserts a regular space if you press the Space bar just once, a nonbreaking space followed by a *regular* space if you hit the space bar twice, and multiple nonbreaking spaces followed by a final regular space if you hit the Space bar repeatedly. Since nonbreaking spaces act like glue that keeps words stuck together (see the box on the facing page), the extra regular spaces allow the lines to break normally, if necessary.

Adding a Date to Your Page

The Common tab of the Insert bar offers an icon called Date. Clicking this icon (📅) or choosing Insert→Date opens the Insert Date dialog box (Figure 2-2). Either way, Dreamweaver inserts today's date, as your computer understands it, onto your Web page in progress. You can also specify whether to include the day of the week and the current time.

Select the format you wish from the Date Format list. There are thirteen different formats to choose from, such as March 7, 1974 or 3/7/74.

You may wonder why Dreamweaver includes an insert date function anyway. How hard is it to type *Thursday, July 12?*

Actually, the real value of the Insert Date feature lies in the Update Automatically on Save checkbox. Choosing this option forces Dreamweaver to *update* the date each time you save the document.

Many designers use this feature to stamp their Web pages with dates that indicate when the contents were last updated. For example, you might type *This page was last revised on:* ; then choose Insert→Date and select the Update Automatically on Save option. Now, each time you make a change to the page, Dreamweaver will automatically change the date to reflect when you saved the document. You never again have to worry about it.

Figure 2-2:
When you insert a date object (a placeholder for the actual date) onto a Web page, you have several additional options: If you want to add the day of the week, choose the format you want from the Day Format pop-up menu (top). You may also choose to add the current time in hours and minutes—in either military time (22:18) or regular time (10:18 PM)—from the Time Format pop-up menu (bottom).

UP TO SPEED

Keeping Headlines Together

You can use nonbreaking spaces as invisible glue that keeps two or more words together on a single line. That's a very useful tactic when you're dealing with headlines, for example, in which a single word, if forced onto its own line, would create unappealing white space and confuse the headline's meaning, as shown here.

Cabbage Attacks Bull Terrier Librarian Says

Cabbage Attacks Bull Terrier Librarian Says

Adding a nonbreaking space between the words "Librarian" and "Says" in this example ensures that those words won't get split across a line break, and helps clarify the presentation and meaning of this headline. You can use any of the three methods described on the facing page to do so.

Copying and Pasting Text

If you're building Web sites as part of a team or for clients, your writers are likely to send you their copy in word processing documents—from Microsoft Word, for example. Unfortunately, Dreamweaver falls a bit short when it comes to handling text from other programs. Unlike publishing programs such as Quark XPress or Adobe PageMaker, Dreamweaver can't import a word processing document.

"Importing HTML from Word" on the facing page offers a workaround that helps you bring Word documents into Dreamweaver. For text in other formats, however, you'll need to resort to copying and pasting, like generations of Web designers before you.

Open the document in whatever program created it—Word Perfect, AppleWorks, or whatever. (If the content you need is contained in a plain-text file, you can open it directly in Dreamweaver.) Select the text you want (by dragging through it, for example), or choose Edit→Select All (Ctrl+A [⌘-A]) to highlight all text in the document. Then choose Edit→Copy, or press Ctrl+C (⌘-C), to copy it. Switch to

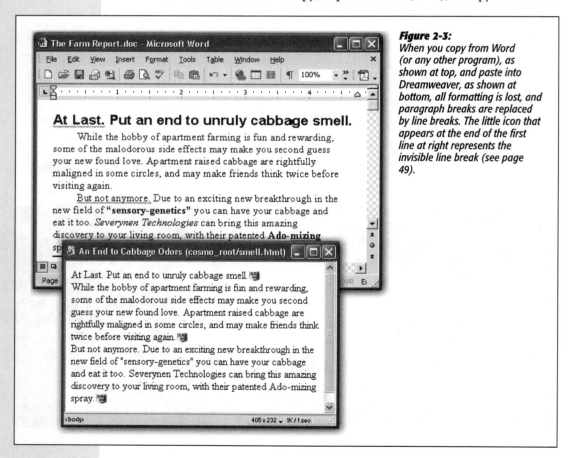

Figure 2-3:
When you copy from Word (or any other program), as shown at top, and paste into Dreamweaver, as shown at bottom, all formatting is lost, and paragraph breaks are replaced by line breaks. The little icon that appears at the end of the first line at right represents the invisible line break (see page 49).

Dreamweaver, click in the document window where you wish the text to go, and choose Edit→Paste (Ctrl+V [⌘-V]).

This routine pastes the text into place. Unfortunately, you lose all text formatting (font type, size, color, bold, italic, and so on) in the process, as shown in Figure 2-3.

Furthermore, you'll find pasted paragraphs separated by line break characters, not standard carriage returns. Strangely enough, this means that when you paste in a series of paragraphs, Dreamweaver treats them as though they were one gargantuan paragraph. These line break characters can pose problems when trying to format what you *think* is a single paragraph.

Tip: You *can* make Dreamweaver paste separate paragraphs correctly—but only in Windows. The trick: In the word processor, before copying the text, add a blank line by pressing the Enter key an extra time between paragraphs. If you'll be cutting and pasting a lot of text from other programs, ask whoever is writing the text for your Web site to use a double Return to separate paragraphs. If it's too late for that, just use your own word processor's Replace command to replace single Returns with double ones. (Dreamweaver sometimes doesn't format the *first* paragraph you paste as an HTML paragraph. That is, it doesn't wrap the text in the first paragraph with the <p> tag. You may have to format this as a paragraph yourself, as described on page 65.)

If you work with spreadsheets or need to present numbers and other information in a table, you can import such information directly into a table in Dreamweaver, as described on page 179.

Importing HTML from Word

Pasting text from another program into your Dreamweaver document works just fine, but it's not the most elegant or efficient method for getting text onto a Web page. Not only do you lose formatting, but the resulting line breaks are a real annoyance.

WORKAROUND WORKSHOP

Pasting HTML

Suppose you've copied some HTML code, maybe out of the Source view of an actual Web page in a Web browser, or from a "How to Write HTML" Web site. You'll notice that when you paste it into Dreamweaver, all the HTML tags appear in the document window, complete with brackets (<>) and other assorted messiness.

To avoid this mess, choose Edit→Paste HTML. This command adds the code to the HTML of your page, making visible only the text you'll want the public to see, just the way things should be. Similarly, if you want to copy the

HTML code *and* the visible text from your document window, use the Edit→Copy HTML command—a handy technique when you want to paste your work into another Web authoring program.

By the way, you don't have to use these commands when copying and pasting *within Dreamweaver*. The regular Copy and Paste commands are smart enough to keep all of the formatting—and HTML tags—when copying and pasting within a Dreamweaver document.

A better alternative is to use Microsoft Word to save documents as Web pages, which then act as an intermediary between Word and Dreamweaver. All recent versions of Word (97, 2000, and 2002/XP for Windows; 98, 2001, and X for Mac) can save files in HTML format, with formatting like fonts, text colors, and text sizes intact.

The drawback to this method is that Word produces hideous HTML code. One look at it, and you'd think that your cat fell asleep on the keyboard. So that it will be able to reopen the document as a Word file when the time comes, Word injects reams of information adding greatly to the file size of the page. This is a particular problem with the latest versions of Word, which add loads of XML and Cascading Style Sheet information. Fortunately, Dreamweaver can strip out most of that unnecessary code and produce leaner Web pages, as described below.

Exporting HTML from Word

From Word 97 (Windows) and Word 98 (Mac), you save a Word document as a Web page by choosing File→Save As HTML. Word 2000, 2001, and 2002/XP users do the same by choosing File→Save as Web Page.

Importing the HTML into Dreamweaver

Once you've saved a Word Web page onto your hard drive, bring it into Dreamweaver using either of the following methods.

The Open command

You can open a Word HTML file just as you would any other Web page: by choosing File→Open. Once the file is open, choose Commands→Clean Up Word HTML.

The Clean Up Word HTML dialog box opens; Dreamweaver automatically detects whether the HTML was produced by Word 97/98 or Word 2000/2001/2002/XP, and then applies the appropriate rules for cleaning up the HTML.

Note: If Dreamweaver doesn't recognize the version of Word you used, a warning box pops up. Select the correct version from the pop-up menu.

There are two tabs in the dialog box: Basic and Detailed (see Figure 2-4). The Basic tab is the same regardless of whether the HTML was created by Word 97/98 or Word 2000/2001/2002/XP. It lists the actions Dreamweaver can perform on the document when opening it.

The first four options, for example, fix problems that Word introduces to the HTML it creates. It's usually best to leave these options turned on.

The last three options of the Basic tab work like this:

- **Set background color.** This option lets you choose what color you want for the Web page. By default, Word produces Web pages with no background color— which some browsers display as a dull gray. Dreamweaver sets it to #ffffff (white), but you can change this value to another hexadecimal color value (see the box on page 34).

- **Apply Source Formatting.** To make the HTML of the page look more like other pages produced by Dreamweaver, turn on this checkbox, which makes Dreamweaver rewrite the HTML to fit Dreamweaver's style (which you can define, as described on page 82).

- **Show log on completion.** This option generates a report describing all of the changes Dreamweaver made to the Word HTML.

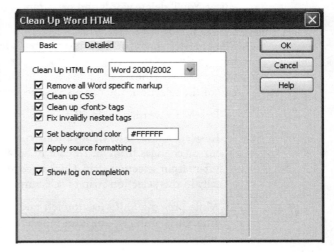

Figure 2-4:
You can access advanced options on the Detailed tab of the Clean Up Word HTML dialog box. Since Word 97/98 and 2000/2001/2002/XP write such wildly different HTML, the options available in the Detailed tab vary depending on which version of Word created the page. Dreamweaver's factory settings do the best job at producing lean pages.

The Import Word HTML command

Another approach to bringing Word HTML into Dreamweaver involves using the Import command.

To make it work, open any Dreamweaver document. Even a blank, unsaved document will do. (Your text won't go here—you're just working around a Dreamweaver bug.)

Choose File→Import→Word HTML. In the dialog box that appears, navigate to and select the Word HTML file you wish to import. You'll then be presented with the same Clean Up Word HTML dialog box described in the previous section. After you make your choices and click OK, Dreamweaver presents a new, unsaved document that bears at least a passing resemblance to your Word original.

The Cleanup Word HTML feature of Dreamweaver is quite an achievement. Considering the complexity of the code generated by Microsoft Word, it's amazing that Dreamweaver can cut through most of the chaff to get to the wheat.

Unfortunately, it's not perfect. While Dreamweaver does a good job of fixing the HTML produced by Word 97 and 98, the extensive use of Cascading Style Sheets in Word 2000, 2001, 2002/XP, and X is often more than Dreamweaver can handle. Even after cleaning up Word 2000 HTML, a Web page may still be filled with unnecessary junk. (On the other hand, if you plan on using Cascading Style Sheets in your site, Word 2000/2001/2002/XP/X can play a useful role in your Web production workflow. To see how, see the box on page 247.)

Selecting Text

After you get text into your Dreamweaver document, you'll undoubtedly need to edit it. You'll delete words and paragraphs, move sentences around, add words, and fix typos.

The first step in any of these procedures is learning how to select text, which works much as it does in word processors. You drag across text to highlight it, or just click where you wish the selection to begin and hold down the Shift key as you click at the end of the selection. You can also use shortcuts like these:

- To select a word, double-click it.

- To select a line of text, move your cursor to the left of the line of text until the cursor changes from an I-beam to an arrow, signaling that you've reached the left-margin selection strip. Click once to highlight one line of text, or drag vertically in this selection strip to select multiple lines.

- While pressing Shift, use the left and right arrow keys to select one letter at a time. Ctrl+Shift (⌘-Shift) and the left and right arrow keys select one *word* at a time.

- Ctrl+A (⌘-A) selects everything in the body of the page—text, graphics, and all.

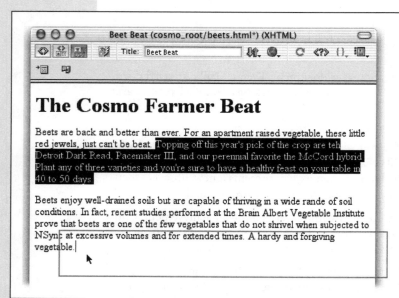

Figure 2-5:
You can move a blob of selected text simply by dragging it to another location in the document window. Point to a spot inside your high-lighted selection; the cursor changes from an I-beam to an arrow; you can now drag the selection. Let go of the mouse button to drop your selection at the spot indicated by the vertical bar, as shown here. This technique works with graphics and other objects you've selected in the document window, too. You can even move a copy of the selection by pressing Ctrl (Option) as you drag-and-drop the selection.

Once you've selected text, you can cut, copy, or delete it. To move text to another part of the Web page, or even to another Dreamweaver document, use the Cut, Copy, and Paste commands in the Edit menu. You can also move text around by dragging and dropping it, as shown in Figure 2-5.

Once copied, the text remains on your Clipboard and can be placed again and again (until you copy something else to the Clipboard, of course). When you cut (or copy) and paste *within* Dreamweaver, all of the formatting you have applied to the text stays intact. So if you copy a headline in bold green type and paste it into another document window in Dreamweaver, it stays bold and green.

To delete any selection, press Delete or choose Edit→Clear.

Spell Checking

You spend a lot of time perfecting your Web pages, making sure the images look great, that the text is properly formatted, and that everything aligns to make a beautiful visual presentation. But one step is often forgotten, especially given the hyperspeed development process of the Web—making sure your Web pages are free from typos.

Spelling mistakes give an unprofessional impression and imply a lack of attention to detail. Who wants to hire an "illustraightor" or "Web dezyner"? Dreamweaver's spell checking feature can help you.

About Dictionaries

Before you start spell checking, you should make sure that the correct *dictionary* is selected. Dreamweaver comes with fourteen dictionaries for eleven different languages, plus three English variations and both Iberian and Brazilian Portuguese. When it checks your spelling, the program compares the text in your document against the list of words in one of these dictionaries.

To specify a dictionary, choose Edit→Preferences (Dreamweaver MX→Preferences in Mac OS X)—or press Ctrl+U (⌘-U)—to open the Preferences dialog box. Select the General category, and then choose a language from the Spelling Dictionary pop-up menu.

Performing the Check

Once you've selected a dictionary, open the Web page whose spelling you wish to check. You can check as much or as little text as you like, as follows:

1. **Highlight the text (which can be even a single word).**

   If you want to check the *entire* document, make sure that nothing is selected in the document window. (One good way to make sure nothing is selected is to click in the middle of a paragraph of text.) Unlike spell checkers in other programs, you don't have to place the cursor at the beginning of the document. Dreamweaver always checks spelling starting at the beginning of the document, no matter where the insertion point is.

2. **Choose Text→Check Spelling (or press Shift-F7).**

   The Check Spelling dialog box opens (see Figure 2-6). If the selected word is not in Dreamweaver's dictionary, it appears in the top field of the box, along with a list of suggested alternative spellings.

   The first suggestion is listed in the Change To field.

3. **If the Change To field is correct, click Change.**

   If Dreamweaver has correctly flagged the word as misspelled, but the correct spelling isn't in the Change To field, double-click the correct spelling in the list. If the correct spelling isn't in the list, type it yourself in the Change To box.

   Then click the Change button to correct this one instance, or click Change All to replace the misspelled word everywhere it appears in the document.

   Dreamweaver makes the change and moves on to the next questionable spelling.

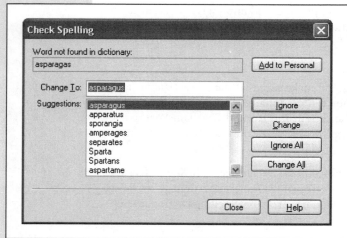

Figure 2-6:
Dreamweaver's spell checking feature checks words only in the document window. It can't check the spelling of comments, Alt tags, or any text that appears in the head of the document. Nor can you spell check an entire Web site's worth of pages with a single command; you need to check each Web page individually.

4. **If the word is actually correctly spelled (but not in Dreamweaver's dictionary), click Ignore, Ignore All, or Add to Personal.**

   If you want Dreamweaver to ignore this word *every* time it appears in the document, rather than just this instance of it, click Ignore All.

   On the other hand, you'll frequently use some words that Dreamweaver doesn't have in its dictionaries. You may, for instance, use a client's name throughout your Web pages. If that name isn't in Dreamweaver's dictionary, Dreamweaver will consistently claim that it's a spelling error.

To teach Dreamweaver the client's name so that the Check Spelling dialog box won't pop up each time you spell check, click Add To Personal. Dreamweaver adds the word to your personal dictionary, which is a special dictionary file that Dreamweaver also consults when checking your spelling.

After you click Ignore or Change, Dreamweaver moves on to the next word it doesn't recognize. Begin again from step 3.

5. To end spell checking, click Close.

Undo, Redo, and the History Panel

One of the great consciousness-altering moments of the twentieth century was the introduction of the Undo command. After a long day in front of the computer, the ability to undo any action seems quite natural. (Unfortunately, reaching for the Ctrl+Z keys after spilling grape juice on Grandma's antique tablecloth still doesn't work in the real world.)

Fortunately, most steps you take in Dreamweaver can be reversed with either the Undo command or the History panel.

Undo, Redo

Like most computer programs these days, Dreamweaver lets you undo the last step you took by pressing Ctrl+Z (⌘-Z), or by choosing Edit→Undo. (This command changes to reflect your most recent action. If you just deleted some text, for example, it says Edit→Undo Delete.) When you're feeling indecisive, you can *redo* the action you just undid by choosing Edit→Redo or by pressing Ctrl+Y (⌘-Y).

Tip: Jumping back and forth with the Undo/Redo commands is a good way to compare a change you made to a Web page with its previous appearance. For instance, suppose you're having trouble deciding on a background color for a Web page. You could set it to dark blue, then set it to dark purple, and then choose Edit→Undo Set Page Properties to return to the dark blue background. Choose Edit→Redo Set Page Properties to see the purple background again. This before-and-after toggling feature of the Undo/Redo combo can be a great addition to your Web-building arsenal.

You're not limited to a single undo, either. You can undo multiple steps, up to 50 of them, or whatever number you specify in Preferences. Choose Edit→Preferences (in Mac OS X it's Dreamweaver MX→Preferences) to open this dialog box; click the General category from the Category list; and change the number in the Maximum Number of History Steps box. (Note, however, that the more steps Dreamweaver remembers, the more memory the program needs. If you set this preference very high, or your computer doesn't have a lot of memory, you may find your computer acting sluggish.)

Tip: You can even undo actions *after you have saved* a document (although not after you've closed it). Unlike many programs, Dreamweaver doesn't erase the list of actions you've performed when a page is saved. This means you can feel free to save as often as you want—a wise safeguard against crashes and other mishaps—without losing the ability to undo what you've done.

History Panel

You may wonder why the Preferences setting for the Undo command refers to "History Steps." It's because Dreamweaver creates a *history* for a document as you work on it. Each time you add text, insert a graphic, change the background color of the page, or do anything else to a document, Dreamweaver adds a new step to a list of previous actions.

All of these steps are listed in the History panel. To see it, choose Window→Others→History, or Shift-F10.

Each row in the panel represents one action or step, and includes a description. For instance, hitting Return or Enter while typing in the document creates a step called New Paragraph. Steps are listed in the order you perform your actions, with the latest actions at the bottom and earliest action at the top of the list.

But the History panel isn't just a dull document to pore over—it's a living, multiple-step Undo command. Use the History slider to move to any step in the history list. To undo one action, for example, drag the slider up one step. When you do this, you'll notice that the slider's previous position step is grayed out. Steps that are dimmed represent future steps, so moving the slider down one step is the equivalent of choosing Edit→Redo.

You can undo or redo multiple steps by moving the slider up or down the list. Alternatively, you can click on the track to the left of a step to move the slider to that step.

If you want to eliminate all of the history steps for a document—to free up some of your computer's memory, for example—select Clear History from the History Panel's context menu. But be careful: this is the one action you can't undo.

Figure 2-7:
The History panel can do a lot more than undo actions. It can also be used for automating many routine tasks that you perform while building your Web pages. To find out how to use this feature, see Chapter 19.

Text Formatting

Getting text onto a Web page (Chapter 2) is a good start, but effective communication requires effective design, too. Large, bold headlines help readers scan a page's important topics. Colorful text focuses attention. Bulleted sentences crystallize and summarize ideas. Just as a monotonous, low-key voice puts a crowd to sleep, a vast desert of plain HTML text is sure to turn visitors away from the important message of your site. In fact, text formatting could be the key to making your *Widgets Online 2003 Sale-a-thon* a resounding success instead of an unnoticed disaster.

To help you get your point across, Dreamweaver provides the tools you need to format your text in compelling and eye-catching ways (see Figure 3-1 for examples of good and bad text formatting).

Paragraph Formatting

Just as you use paragraphs to help organize your thoughts into clear, well-structured, and cohesive units when you're writing a paper or letter, you organize content on Web pages into blocks of information within HTML tags (see page 3 for more on tags). The most basic block of information is a simple paragraph, indicated in HTML by a *paragraph tag,* like this:

```
<p>Hello. This is one paragraph on this Web page. </p>
```

To a Web browser, everything between the opening <p> and closing </p> tags is considered part of the same paragraph. Many Dreamweaver formatting options—headlines, lists, indents, and alignment, for example—can apply only to an entire paragraph at a time, as opposed to individual words. In a word processor, you'd call this kind of formatting *paragraph* formatting; in Web design, it's called *block-level* formatting. The idea is exactly the same: These characteristics affect an entire paragraph (that is, a *block* of text, whether that's just one sentence or several sentences) at a time.

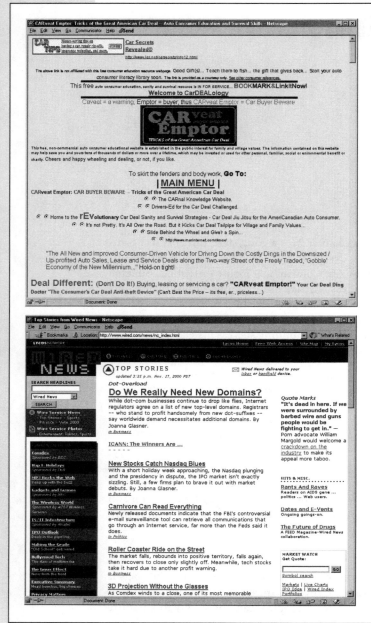

Figure 3-1:
Both of these pages use different fonts, colors, and sizes to display text, but the one at bottom uses a consistent arrangement of styles to organize the text and guide the reader through the page. Notice how the headline "Do We Really Need New Domains?" with its larger type size draws your eye to it immediately. Below that, the supplementary articles and their summaries are easy to identify and read. In the page at top, by contrast, the largest type element, "Main Menu," sits in the middle of a scattered, randomly formatted sea of text.

(*Character-level* formatting, on the other hand, can be applied to individual words or even letters. Bold and italic fall into this category, as described later in this chapter.)

Figure 3-2:
The choices labeled in italics apply to an entire paragraph; the other options represent inline, or character-level, formatting options. Click the CSS/HTML mode button to toggle between basic formatting (top) and Cascading Style Sheet formatting (bottom).

Paragraphs

When you create a new document in Dreamweaver and start typing, the text you type has no paragraph formatting at all, as indicated by the word None in the Format pop-up menu at the left side of the Property inspector. (*None* isn't an HTML tag; it just means that there are *no* tags at all surrounding your text.)

When you press Enter or Return, you create a new paragraph, complete with opening and closing <p> tags, as shown above, but your newly born paragraph still has no formatting tags. When your Web site visitors look at it, the font and size of your type are determined by their own Web-browser preference settings. It may not look anything like the typography you saw in Dreamweaver.

You can add the Paragraph format to any block of text. Since this formatting option affects all of the text in the block, you don't need to select any text as a first step. Simply click inside the block of text and do one of the following:

• In the Property inspector, choose Paragraph from the Format pop-up menu.

• Choose Text→Paragraph Format→Paragraph.

• Press Shift+Ctrl+P (Shift-⌘-P).

Tip: Much to the chagrin of Web designers, Web browsers display a line's worth of blank space before and after block-level elements like headings and paragraphs. This visual gap can be distracting, but unfortunately, you can't get rid of it with regular HTML.

However, many of the formatting limitations of HTML, including this one, go away when you use Cascading Style Sheets. See the Tip on page 260 to fix this problem.

Headlines

Headlines announce information (**The Vote is In!**) and help organize content. Just as this book uses different levels of headings to introduce its topics—from chapter titles all the way down to subsections—the HTML heading tag comes in a variety of sizes used to indicate importance.

Headlines range in size from 1 (largest) to 6 (smallest), as shown in Figure 3-3. HTML's creators intended these headings to be an outlining aid for Web authors, but these days, Web designers use them more frequently simply for basic text formatting.

To turn a paragraph into a headline, click inside the line, or block, of text and then do one of the following:

- In the Property inspector, select one of the heading levels (Heading 1 through Heading 6) from the Format pop-up menu.

- Choose Text→Paragraph Format→Heading 1–6.

- Press Ctrl+1 (⌘-1), for the Heading 1 style, Ctrl+2 (⌘-2) for Heading 2, and so on.

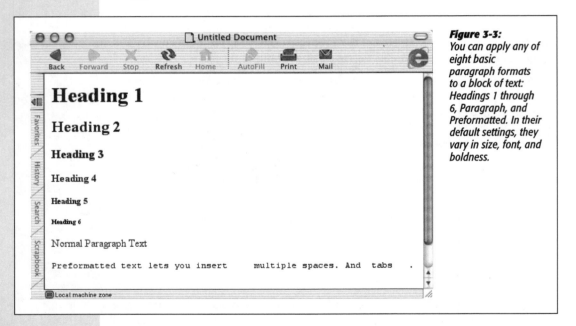

Figure 3-3:
You can apply any of eight basic paragraph formats to a block of text: Headings 1 through 6, Paragraph, and Preformatted. In their default settings, they vary in size, font, and boldness.

Preformatted Text

Web browsers normally ignore extra spaces, tabs, and other blank-space characters when displaying a Web page. However, using the Preformatted paragraph format, you can override this behavior. Preformatted paragraphs display *every* text character in a paragraph, including tabs, multiple spaces, and line breaks, so you don't have to resort to multiple nonbreaking space characters (see page 49) to insert more than one space in a row.

The original idea behind the Preformatted format was to display tabular data—as in a spreadsheet—without the use of tables. That's why preformatted paragraphs show up in a *monospaced* font like Courier. In monospaced fonts, each letter of the alphabet, from *i* to *w,* is the same width and takes up the same horizontal space on a page, making it easy to align letters in columns. That's also why, when you use this paragraph style, you can use tabs to align text in columns. (When you use any other paragraph format, Web browsers ignore tabs.) These days, however, Dreamweaver's table feature is a much superior method of creating columns; see Chapter 6.

Note: Unlike in version 4, Dreamweaver MX doesn't let you just type multiple spaces or tabs, even when using Preformatted formatting. To get around this limitation, you can edit directly in the Code view (see Chapter 9), or turn on the program's multiple-spaces feature. Choose Edit→Preferences. Make sure the General category is selected and turn on Allow Multiple Consecutive Spaces.

This limitation doesn't apply to text you *paste,* however. Choosing the Preformatted option for pasted text containing multiple spaces and tabs leaves all extra space intact.

Nonetheless, the Preformatted format can still be useful—when displaying sample HTML or programming code, for example. You can add the Preformatted format to any block of text. Simply click inside the block of text and then take one of these two steps:

- Choose Format→Preformatted in the Property inspector.

- Choose Text→Paragraph Format→Preformatted Text.

Keep in mind that preformatted text appears exactly as you enter it. Unlike normal paragraph text, lines of preformatted text don't automatically wrap if they're wider than the window. To end a line of preformatted text and create another, you must press the Enter or Return key to create a manual line break.

Paragraph Alignment

All text in a Web page starts out aligned with the left edge of the page (or, in the case of tables, to the left edge of a table cell). But there are times when you may want to center text in the middle of the page—perhaps an elegantly centered title—or to the right side. You can even create nice straight margins on both sides of a paragraph using the justification option. Although justified text looks elegant—simulating the typography of a fine book—the formatting doesn't show up in some older browsers (Internet Explorer 4, for example). While there are many ways to align text in Dreamweaver, the Property inspector's word processor–like controls make this a snap (or, rather, a click).

To change a paragraph's alignment, click inside a paragraph and do one of the following:

- In the Property inspector, click one of the alignment icons in the upper-right corner (see Figure 3-2).

- Choose Text→Align→Left, Center, Right, or Justify.

- Use one of the following keyboard shortcuts:

  Left: Ctrl+Alt+Shift+L (Shift-Option-⌘-L)

  Centered: Ctrl+Alt+Shift+C (Shift-Option-⌘-C)

  Right: Ctrl+Alt+Shift+R (Shift-Option-⌘-R)

  Justify: Ctrl+Alt+Shift+J (Shift-Option-⌘-J).

After you align a paragraph, the Property inspector displays a depressed button for the alignment option you chose, indicating what kind of alignment you've applied.

You can remove an alignment by reapplying the *same* alignment. For instance, if you've right-aligned a paragraph, clicking the right-align button in the Property inspector removes all alignment information and returns that paragraph to its default setting. (This is a better solution than clicking the left-align button, which adds extra lines of HTML code to do the same thing.)

Indented Paragraphs

Indenting a paragraph can set it apart from the paragraphs before and after it. It's perfect for adding a small amount of space on either side of a paragraph, and it's frequently used to present a long quote or passage from a book or other source. In fact, an indented paragraph is called a *blockquote* in HTML.

To indent a paragraph or block-level element like a heading, click it and do one of the following:

- Click the Indent button on the Property inspector (see Figure 3-2).

UP TO SPEED

Keep Your Pages Lean

Many of the things that contribute to slow Web page downloads—congestion on the Internet, for example—are out of your control. But you can do your part by making sure your pages are as compact as possible. For instance, keep the file size of graphics down and eliminate extraneous lines of HTML code. The more HTML you include in a page, the larger the file, and the slower the download.

For example, text on a Web page aligns to the left of a page *by default*. You'd be pointlessly bloating your Web page, therefore, by specifying left alignment of your text using a paragraph's alignment property. In fact, when you encounter the phrase "by default" describing an HTML property in this book, it's a safe bet that you can get that effect without adding any HTML.

Other ways to keep your pages lean and fast are highlighted throughout this book, but remember this rule of thumb: The less HTML code you create, the faster your Web page will download, and the happier your audience will be.

- Choose Text→Indent.

- Press Ctrl+Alt+] (Option-⌘-]).

Unfortunately, since indenting a paragraph simply nests that paragraph in a basic HTML <blockquote> tag, you don't have any control over how *much* space is added to the margins of the paragraph. Most Web browsers insert about 40 pixels of blank space on the left and right side of a blockquote.

You can add additional space to the margins of a paragraph by applying *another* indent, thus creating a nested set of blockquotes. To do so, click an already indented paragraph and repeat one of the indenting procedures described above. To add multiple indents, continue in this way.

Note: Unfortunately, you're still deprived of the ability to specify exactly how much more indentation you're getting. For the ultimate in margin control, therefore, use Cascading Style Sheets for pixel-level accuracy as described on page 259.

But what if you want to remove indents from a paragraph? Use Dreamweaver to *outdent* it, of course. (Yes, *outdent* is a real word—ever since Microsoft made it up.) To remove a paragraph's indent formatting—that is, remove a <blockquote> tag—click inside the paragraph and do one of the following:

- Click the Outdent button on the Property inspector (see Figure 3-2).

- Choose Text→Outdent.

- Press Ctrl+Alt+[(⌘-Option-[).

You can continue to outdent a paragraph using one of these methods until the paragraph returns to the left edge of the page; at that point, the outdenting commands have no further effect.

Lists

Lists organize the everyday information of our lives: to-do lists, grocery lists, top ten lists, and so on. On Web pages, lists are indispensable for presenting groups of items such as links, company services or employees, or a series of instructions.

HTML offers formatting options for three basic categories of lists (see Figure 3-4). The two most common types of lists are *bulleted* (called *unordered lists* in the HTML language) and *numbered* lists (called *ordered* in HTML). The third and lesser-known list type, a *definition* list, comes in handy for creating glossaries or dictionary-like entries.

Bulleted and Numbered Lists

Bulleted and numbered lists share similar formatting. Dreamweaver automatically indents items in either type of list, and automatically precedes each list item by a character—a bullet, number, or letter, for example.

- Unordered or bulleted lists, like this one, are good for groups of items that don't necessarily follow any sequence. They're preceded by a bullet.

- Ordered lists are useful when presenting items that follow a sequence, such as the numbered instructions in the paragraph below. Instead of a bullet, a number or letter precedes each item in an ordered list. Dreamweaver suggests a number (1, 2, 3, and so on), but you can substitute Roman numerals, letters, and other variations.

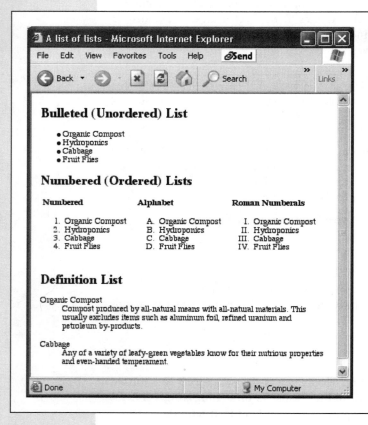

Figure 3-4:
HTML has several predefined list formats, including bulleted lists and definition lists, which let you organize information into orderly units. Once you've told Dreamweaver that you intend to create a bulleted or numbered list, it adds the bullets or the numbering for you automatically.

You can create a list from scratch within Dreamweaver, or add list formatting to text already on a Web page.

Creating a new bulleted or numbered list

When making a list in Dreamweaver, you start by choosing a list format, then typing the list items:

1. **In the document window, click where you wish to start a list.**

   See Chapter 2 for full detail on adding text to a Web page.

2. **Apply the list format by clicking the Ordered or Unordered List button in the Property inspector.**

Alternatively, you can choose Text→List→Unordered List or Ordered List. Either way, the first bullet or number appears in your document automatically.

3. **Type the first list item and then press Return. Repeat until you've added all items in the list.**

The text you type appears (*Organic Compost,* for example, in Figure 3-4) after the bullet or number. When you press Return, a new bullet or number appears, ready for your next item. (If you just want move to the next line *without* creating a new bullet, insert a line break by pressing Shift-Return.)

4. **When you've finished the list, press Enter or Return twice.**

The double carriage return ends the list and creates a new empty paragraph.

Formatting existing text as a list

You may have several paragraphs of text that you've already typed in or pasted from another application. It's a simple process to change any such group of paragraphs into a list.

1. **Select the text you wish to turn into a list.**

The easiest way to select text is to drag from the first list item straight down into the last item of the list. Lists are block-level elements; each paragraph, whether it's a headline or regular paragraph, becomes one bulleted or numbered item in the list. In other words, you don't actually need to select all of the text in either the first or last paragraph.

FREQUENTLY ASKED QUESTION

When Not to Approach the Insert Bar

Should I use the Insert bar's Text tab for formatting text?

In a word, no. Unlike most of the other tabs in the Insert bar, you use the Text tab mainly when working in Code view (see Chapter 9). It contains many of the same formatting options as the Property inspector—the h1, h2, h3 in this figure, for instance, are the same as Headings 1, 2, and 3 in the Property inspector's Format pop-up menu. However, using some of the options can generate invalid HTML if not used correctly. And despite its usual tidiness, Dreamweaver doesn't clean up code produced this way.

In fact, some of these options, when you use them in Dreamweaver's Design view, actually split the document window in two, showing the HTML code on top and Design view on bottom. This arrangement can be confusing if you're not accustomed to seeing—or are just uninterested in—the raw HTML code.

All of the major text-formatting options are available from the Property inspector and Text menu. If you stick to these two tools, you can safely avoid the Text tab.

---

2. **Apply the list format.**

As when creating a list from scratch as described above, click either the Unordered or Ordered List button in the Property inspector, or choose from the Text→List submenu. The selected paragraphs instantly take on the list formatting, complete with bullets and automatic numbering.

Whichever way you started making a list—either by typing from scratch or by reformatting existing text—you're not stuck with the results of your early decisions. You can add onto lists, add extra spaces, and even renumber them, as described in the following section.

Reformatting Bulleted and Numbered Lists

HTML tags define lists, just as they define other Web-page features. Making changes to an existing list is a matter of changing those tags, using Dreamweaver's menu commands and Property inspector tools.

Adding space between list items

Usually there isn't any blank space between items in a list, which makes for nice, compact lists. However, sometimes a long list of unspaced, bulleted items can look too congested, especially when each item is itself several lines long.

Fortunately, you can take advantage of the spacing provided by the paragraph tag. To add space between one list item and the item below, click the item and change the paragraph formatting from None to Paragraph. To add space between *all* items in a list, simply select the entire list—click on the <ul> or <ol> tag in the tag selector (see Figure 3-5)—and apply paragraph formatting in the Property inspector. Note

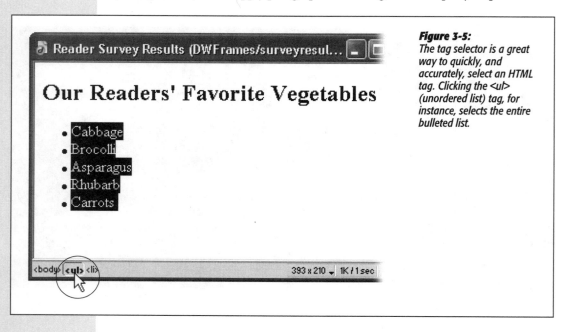

Figure 3-5:
The tag selector is a great way to quickly, and accurately, select an HTML tag. Clicking the <ul> (unordered list) tag, for instance, selects the entire bulleted list.

that the display in Dreamweaver MX may look a little funny—the items in the list don't match up with the bullets or numbers. This is just a Dreamweaver quirk; press the F12 key to preview the page in a browser to see how the list will actually appear.

Tip: Another method of adding space between lists items involves using the Cascading Style Sheets *margin* property as described on page 259. By controlling the top and bottom margins of a list item, you can add space before or after each item in a list.

Adding new items to a list

Once you've created a list, it's easy to add additional items. To add an item at the beginning of a list, click before the first character of the first list item, type the item you wish to add, and press Enter or Return. Dreamweaver makes your newly typed item the first in the list, adding a bullet or number accordingly (and renumbering the other list items, if necessary).

To add an item at the middle or end of a list, click at the end of the *previous* list item and press Enter or Return. The insertion point appears after a new bullet or number; type your list item on this new line.

Figure 3-6:
The List Properties dialog box lets you set the type and style of a list. It offers five styles: Number (1, 2, 3), Roman Small (i, ii, iii), Roman Large (I, II, III), Alphabet Small (a, b, c), and Alphabet Large (A, B, C).

Changing bullets and numbers

Bulleted and numbered lists aren't limited to just the default round black bullet or the numbers 1, 2, or 3. You can choose from two bullet types and a handful of different numbering schemes:

1. **Click once inside any list item.**

   Strangely enough, you can't change the properties of a list if you've first selected the entire list, an entire single list item, or several list items.

2. **Open the List Properties dialog box.**

   To do so, either click the List Item button in the bottom half of the Property inspector or choose Text→List→Properties. (If the list is inside a table cell, your only choice is to use the Text menu. In this situation, the List Item button doesn't appear in the Property inspector.)

3. **Choose a type from the List Type pop-up menu.**

In this way, you can turn a numbered list into a bulleted list, or vice versa. You should avoid the two other options in the menu—Directory List and Menu List. These are old list types that won't work in Web browsers of the future.

4. **Choose a bulleting or numbering style.**

Bulleted lists can have three different styles: default, bullet, and square. In most browsers, the *default* bullet style is the same as the *bullet* style (a simple, solid, black circle). As you might guess, the *square* style uses a solid black square for the bullet character.

Ordered lists, on the other hand, have a greater variety of style options. The default is a simple numbering scheme (1, 2, 3…), but you can choose from any of five styles for ordered lists, as shown in Figure 3-6.

5. **Set the starting number for the list.**

You don't have to begin a numbered list at 1, A, or the Roman numeral I. You can start it at another number, if you wish—a trick that can come in handy if, for example, you're creating a Web page to explain how to rebuild a car's engine:

As part of each step, you want to include a photograph. You create a numbered list, type in the directions for step 1, hit Return, and insert an image (as described in Chapter 5). You hit Return again and type in the text for step 2. Unfortunately, the photo, because it's technically an item in an ordered list, now has the number 2 next to it, and step 2 is listed as 3!

When you remove the list formatting from the photo to get rid of the 2, you create one list above it and another below it (as described on page 76). Step 2, *below* the photo, now thinks it's the beginning of a new list—and starts over with the number 1!

The solution is to make it think it's a *new* list that begins with 2.

To start the list at something other than 1, type the starting number in the Start Count field (Figure 3-6). This must be a number, even if you choose to display the list using letters. So to begin a list at D instead of A, type *4* in the Start Count field.

In fact, you can even change the style of a *single* list item. For instance, you could change the third item in a numeric list from a 3 to the letter C. (Of course, just because you can, doesn't mean you should. Dreamweaver is very thorough in supporting the almost overwhelming combination of options available in HTML, but, unless you're building a Dadaist revival site, how often do you want a list that is numbered 1, 2, C, iv, 5?)

6. **Click OK to apply the changes.**

Tip: Once again, you can access more advanced formatting options for lists using Cascading Style Sheets. For example, you can use a graphic of your own creation to begin each bulleted list item, instead of choosing from the same boring set of square or circular bullets. See page 261 for the details.

Nested lists

Some complex outlines require multiple *levels* of lists. Legal documents, for instance, may list major clauses with capital letters (A, B, C, and so on) and use roman numerals (i, ii, iii, and so on) for subclauses (see Figure 3-7).

It's easy to create such nested lists in Dreamweaver; Figure 3-7 shows the steps.

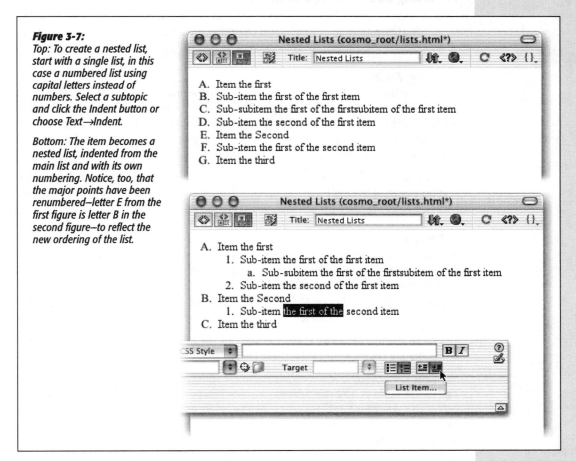

Figure 3-7:
Top: To create a nested list, start with a single list, in this case a numbered list using capital letters instead of numbers. Select a subtopic and click the Indent button or choose Text→Indent.

Bottom: The item becomes a nested list, indented from the main list and with its own numbering. Notice, too, that the major points have been renumbered—letter E from the first figure is letter B in the second figure—to reflect the new ordering of the list.

Definition Lists

Definition lists can be used to display items in a dictionary or glossary, or whenever you need to present a term and its definition. Each item in a definition list is composed of two parts: a word or term, and a definition.

As you can see in Figure 3-4, definition lists aren't as fancy as they sound. The first item in the list—the word or term—is presented on its own line with no indent, and the second item—the definition—appears directly underneath, indented.

You can't create a definition list using the Property inspector. Instead, start by highlighting the paragraphs that contain the terms and definitions you wish to include in the list; then choose Text→List→Definition List.

To turn a definition list *back* to regular paragraphs, select it and choose Text→List→None, or click the Outdent button in the Property inspector.

Removing and Deleting List Items

Dreamweaver lets you take items out of a list in two ways: either by removing the list *formatting* from an item or items (and changing them back into normal paragraphs) or by deleting their text outright.

Removing list items

To remove list formatting from one or more list items (or an entire list), highlight the lines in question and then choose Text→List→None (or just click the Outdent button on the Property inspector). You've just removed all list formatting; the text remains on the screen, now formatted as standard paragraphs. (For nested lists, you'll need to click the Outdent button several times.)

If you reformat an item in the middle of a list using this technique, it becomes a regular paragraph. Dreamweaver turns the items above it and below it into separate lists.

Deleting list items

A simple way to delete a list or list item is to use the tag selector in the status bar of the document window (see Figure 3-5). To delete an entire list, click anywhere inside the list, then click its tag in the tag selector—<ul> for a bulleted list or <ol> for a numbered list—and press Delete. You can also, of course, drag through all the text of the list and then press Delete.

To delete a single list item, click that item in the document window, click the <li> tag in the tag selector, and then press Delete.

Tip: You can rearrange a list item by dragging it to another position within the list. If it's an ordered list (1,2,3…), Dreamweaver automatically renumbers the list. For example, if you select an item numbered 4 (or D, if it's an alphabetical list) and drag it to the second position in the list, Dreamweaver changes the item to 2 (or B) and renumbers all items that follow.

However, selecting a list item can be tricky. If you simply drag to select the text, you don't actually select the list item itself, with all its formatting and numbering. To be sure you've selected a list item, click the <li> tag in the tag selector in the document window's status bar (see Figure 3-5). Now, when you drag the selection to a new position in the list, the number (or bullet) follows. You can also select a list item in this way, copy or cut it, and paste it back into the list in another position.

Character Formatting

The simple formatting applied by a paragraph format is not much to write home about, much less to advertise on a résumé. Heading 1, for instance, is generally displayed in black and bold using a large Times New Roman font. (Yawn.)

To really make your Web pages stand out, you may want to apply different fonts, colors, sizes, and styles to your text. Unlike paragraph formatting, which applies to an entire HTML paragraph, you can apply character formatting to any selection of text, whether it's a single word, one sentence, an entire paragraph, or your whole Web page.

In general, you apply character formatting just as you would in a word processor: Select the text (using any of the methods described on page 56) and then apply a format using the Property inspector or Text menu.

The remainder of this chapter describes this approach to text formatting, which is a simple and quick way to add color and variation to the text on a page. However, this method is becoming quickly outdated. Technical organizations like the World Wide Web Consortium recommend against the kind of character-level formatting discussed here, since it relies on old HTML tags like the <font> tag.

But more importantly, professional Web designers—who not only want to keep up with technical trends but also must build functional Web sites that work for and please the vast audience of Web surfers—are steadily moving to the more sophisticated typographic controls offered by Cascading Style Sheets, as discussed in Chapter 8.

Using the instructions in the rest of this chapter, you can still build professional-looking Web pages that work in most Web browsers today and still will, well into the future. These techniques are fast and easy to learn. However, if you'd rather enjoy

---

UP TO SPEED

When Bold and Italic Are Neither

If you're familiar with previous versions of Dreamweaver, you may be confused by the HTML code that Dreamweaver MX produces when making text bold or italic. Instead of using the <b> tag—the traditional HTML code for bold—Dreamweaver now uses the <strong> tag. And instead of <i> for italics, clicking the I button on the Property inspector gets you <em>, or the emphasis tag. In Dreamweaver MX, Macromedia has decided to follow industry practices rather than stick to an old tradition.

For most purposes, <strong> and <em> behave identically to <b> and <i>. They look the same—bolded or italicized—in most browsers. However, when encountered by *screen*

readers (software or equipment that reads Web pages aloud for the benefit of the visually impaired), the <strong> tag triggers a loud, strong voice. The <em> tag also brings an emphasis to the voice of screen readers, though with less strength than the <strong> tag.

Since most Web browsers simply treat the <strong> tag like the <b> tag, and the <em> tag like the <i> tag, you'll probably never notice the difference. However, if you prefer the simple <b> and <i> tags, choose Edit→Preferences. Select the General category and turn off the box labeled "Use <strong> and <em> in place of <b> and <i>."

---

the many visual and technical benefits of more professional formatting techniques, turn to Chapter 8 and learn how to use CSS for formatting your Web pages.

Text Styles

To add emphasis to your words, you can choose from several text styles. You can apply the two most common emphasis effects, bold and italics, from the Property inspector. For less frequently used styles choose from the Text→Style submenu (see Figure 3-8).

To add bold or italic formatting to text, select the word or words you'd like to make bold or italic, then click the Bold or Italic button on the Property inspector.

Tip: Use italics with care. While italics are frequently used in printed material to add *emphasis* or for referencing a book title, they can be difficult to read on a computer screen, especially at small type sizes.

Figure 3-8:
While the Property inspector lets you apply bold and italic styles to text, the Text→Style menu (top) offers a larger selection of text styles.

As you can see (bottom), the many different style options are usually displayed in bold, italics, the browser's monospaced font (usually Courier), or some combination of the three. (In real life, you'll rarely use any of these additional styles.)

As shown in Figure 3-8, HTML offers a host of different text styles, some of which fulfill obscure purposes. For instance, the Code and Variable styles are intended for formatting the display of programming code, while the Sample style represents the output from a computer program—not exactly styles you'll need often in promoting, say, your Cheeses of the World mail-order company.

In general, you're better off avoiding such styles. But if you think one of them might come in handy, you can find more about these styles from Dreamweaver's built-in HTML reference; see Chapter 10 for details. In particular, stay away from the underline and strikethrough styles: Both have been deprecated in the HTML 4 standard and may produce no effect in future browser versions. (You can, however, turn to Cascading Styles Sheets text formatting abilities to put lines through and under any text you'd like. See page 253 for more.)

Fonts

Formatting fonts for the Web is very much like using fonts in a word processor. Sadly, it carries some of the same drawbacks. For example, if you create some beautiful document in Microsoft Word, using fancy fonts you just bought from a small font company in Iowa, you're in for a rude surprise when you email the document to your boss. He won't see anything resembling what the memo looked like on *your* screen. Because he doesn't own the same fonts you used, he'll see some default font on his computer—Times, perhaps. Fonts show up in a distributed document only if each recipient happens to have the same fonts installed.

On the Web, you're in the same predicament. Although you're free, as a Web designer, to specify any font you want in a Web page, it won't show up on a viewer's computer unless she's installed the same font in her system. Otherwise, your visitor's Web browser will show your text in a default font, which is usually some version of Times or (if you used the Preformatted format) Courier.

UP TO SPEED

Knowing Your Font Types

You can literally find tens of thousands of different fonts to express your every thought: from bookish, staid, and classical type faces to rounded, cartoonish squiggles.

Most fonts can be divided into two categories: *serif* and *sans-serif*. Serif fonts are best for long passages of text, as it's widely believed that *serifs*—small decorative strokes ("hands" and "feet") at the end of a letter's main strokes—gently lead the eye from letter to letter, making text easier

to read. Examples of serif fonts are Times, Times New Roman, Georgia, and Minion, the font in the main body paragraphs of this book.

Sans-serif fonts, on the other hand, and are often used for headlines, thanks to their clean and simple appearance. Examples of sans-serif fonts include Arial, Helvetica, Verdana, and Formata, which you're reading now.

There are several solutions to this dilemma. One is to use Flash Text, which is described on page 132, or to convert your text into graphic images (page 111). Another is to specify the font you'd *like* to use; if your viewer's computer has the specified font installed, that's what she'll see. You can specify secondary or tertiary font choices if the preferred font isn't available. In fact, Dreamweaver offers prepackaged lists of such "first choice, second choice, third choice" fonts, as you'll find out in the following section.

Applying font formatting

Dreamweaver's approach to font formatting is straightforward:

1. **Select the text whose font you want to change.**

   As in a word processor, you can also click somewhere and then choose a font for text that you're *about* to type. (If you're pasting text from another application, paste first, then select it and apply a font.)

2. **Select the font from the Property inspector or from the Text menu.**

   Choose a font from the Font pop-up menu in the Property inspector, or choose Text→Font and select a font from the submenu.

   You'll soon discover that Dreamweaver's font menus aren't quite what you're used to. When you apply a font to text, you have to choose a little *list* of fonts like "Arial, Helvetica, sans-serif." You can't just choose a single font, such as Helvetica.

Note: If you don't see the Font pop-up menu in the Property inspector, you've probably clicked the toggle CSS/HTML mode button (see Figure 3-2). Click the button again to leave the CSS formatting mode and to display the font, color, size, and alignment buttons.

That's because, as noted on page 81, in order for your viewer's computer to display a font correctly on a Web page, it must have the same font installed. If the font's not there, the browser simply replaces the font specified in the Web page with the browser's default font.

In order to gain some control over this process, you can specify a list of fonts that look similar to your first-choice font (Arial, for example). Your visitor's Web browser checks if the first font in the list is installed on the computer. If it is, that's what your visitor sees when viewing your Web page.

But if the first font isn't installed, the browser looks down the list until it finds a font that is. Different operating systems use different fonts, so these lists include one font that's common on Windows and another, similar-looking font that's common on the Mac. Arial, for instance, is found on all Windows machines, while Helvetica is a similar font for Macs.

Tip: While Mac and Windows used to come with very different sets of preinstalled fonts, there's been some convergence in the past few years. These days, you can count on the average Mac or PC having the following fonts:

Arial, Arial Black, Comic Sans MS, Courier, Courier New, Georgia, Impact, Monotype Sorts, Times New Roman, Trebuchet MS, Verdana, Webdings, Wingdings.

If your audience includes Unix or Linux users, all bets are off. In this case, you should stick to these three fonts: Helvetica (make sure to also specify Arial for Windows users), Times (Times New Roman for Windows), and Courier (Courier New for Windows).

That's it. You're just applied one of Dreamweaver's preinstalled fonts. If you'd like a greater degree of control of what fonts your page displays, read on.

Creating custom font lists

Dreamweaver comes with six preset "first choice, second choice, third choice" font lists, which incorporate fonts that are standard on both Windows and Mac. But you can easily stray from the pack and create your own font lists for use in your Web pages. If you proceed with the custom approach, make sure you know what fonts your visitors have—easily done if you're designing a corporate intranet and know what computers are used in your company—and always specify one font that you *know* is installed. In this way, your page may not look exactly as you intended, but it'll at least be readable.

Here's how you create a new "first choice, second choice, third choice" font list.

Note: Technically, you can specify any number of fallback fonts in one of these lists, not just first, second, and third choices. Your list can specify only a single font, or a long list arranged in order of preference.

1. **Open the Edit Font List dialog box.**

   Choose Edit Font List from the Property inspector's Font pop-up menu, or choose Text→Font→Edit Font List. Either way, the Edit Font List dialog box appears (Figure 3-9).

2. **Select a first-choice font from the list of Available Fonts, or type in the font name.**

   All fonts on your computer are listed in the Available Fonts menu. Simply click to select the font you wish to add.

   Alternatively, you can type a font's name into the box that appears directly below the list of available fonts—a handy trick if you want to include a font that *isn't* installed on your computer (a Windows font when you're working on a Mac, for example).

3. **Add the font you've just specified to your new, custom font list by clicking the << button (or just double-clicking the font name).**

   Your first-choice font appears in the Chosen Font list.

4. **Repeat steps 2 and 3 for each font you wish to include in your custom list.**

   The order in which you add the fonts is the order they appear in the list. These become the "first choice, second choice, third choice" fonts.

   Unfortunately, there's no way to change the order of the fonts once you've added them. So if you accidentally put the fonts in the wrong order, you must delete the list by clicking the – button (at the upper-left corner of the dialog box) and start over.

5. **Add a generic font family.**

   This last step isn't strictly necessary, but it's a good idea. If your Web-page visitor is some kind of anti-font radical whose PC doesn't have *any* of the fonts you've chosen, her browser will substitute the generic font family you specify here. On most systems, for instance, the monospaced font is Courier, the serif font is Times, and the sans-serif font is Arial or Helvetica.

   Generic fonts are listed at the bottom of the list of Available Fonts and include Cursive, Fantasy, Monospace, Sans-Serif, and Serif. Select a generic font that's similar in appearance to the fonts in your list. For instance, choose Sans-Serif if your list consists of sans-serif fonts like Helvetica or Arial; choose Serif if you specified fonts like Times or Georgia.

6. **Click OK.**

   Your new font package appears in the Property inspector's Font pop-up menu, ready to apply.

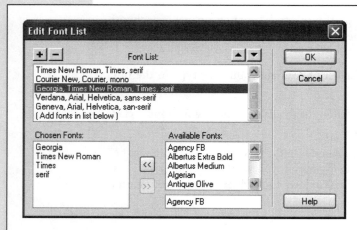

Figure 3-9:
Not only can you create your own font lists, but you can also edit, remove, or reorder the current lists in this dialog box. When you click a list in the Font List, the "first choice, second choice, third choice" fonts appear in the lower-left corner. To remove a font from that list, click the font name and then click the >> button. To add a font to the list, select a font in the Available Fonts menu and click the << button. Finally, to reorder the font lists as they appear in the Property inspector or Text→Font menu, click the arrow keys near the upper-right corner of the dialog box.

Font Size

Varying the sizes of fonts on a Web page is one way to direct a viewer's attention. Large type screams "Read Me!"—excellent for attention-grabbing headlines—while small type fades into the background—perfect for necessary but unexciting legal mumbo jumbo like copyright notices.

Unless you specifically define its size, text in a regular paragraph appears at the default size specified by your visitor's Web browser, such as 12 points. (A *point* is a typographic measurement equal to 1/72 of an inch.)

In theory, 12-point lettering is roughly 1/6 of an inch tall. In practice, however, the resolution of the monitor, the font itself, and the operating system drastically affect the size of type on the screen. To the eternal frustration of Web designers who are used to, say, PageMaker or Quark XPress, text on a Web page viewed in Netscape Navigator for Windows, for instance, appears substantially larger than when viewed in Navigator on a Mac. Add to this the fact that people can change their browsers' default text size to any size they like, and you'll quickly understand that Web design requires a Zen-like acceptance of factors beyond your control.

However, HTML does provide a modicum of control. You can choose from seven different "virtual" font sizes, ranging from 1 (smallest) to 7 (largest). Each size is *relative* to the default text size defined in each visitor's Web browser. (Now you know why Web-design programs don't simply offer a font size menu with commands like 12 Point, 14 Point, and so on.)

FREQUENTLY ASKED QUESTION

Changing Sizes

Why can I apply font sizes like -1 or +2, and what does the Size Change menu do?

Here's another example of Dreamweaver's drive to give you access to almost every possible HTML tag and property setting ever created. Yes, if you select Text→Size Change, you can choose from options from -3 up to +4. In addition, the Property inspector's font size menu offers positive and negative values ranging from 1 to 7.

These settings let you specify a text size that's relative to what is called the *basefont* size of a Web page. That basefont size, unless you indicate otherwise, is equivalent to a text size of 3. So, if you applied the size of -1 to some text, it would appear as size 2 text.

You can, if you so desire, change the basefont size of a Web page, although Dreamweaver doesn't provide an easy way to do it. You need to enter the code by hand in Code view (see Chapter 9) by adding the following tag to the <head> tag of a Web page: *<basefont size=3>*. Replace the number 3 with any number from 1 to 7; now all text defaults to that size. So if you set the basefont to size 7 and then set some text to a size of -3, it shows up as size 4 text.

Confused by all this math? Don't worry about it; the <basefont> tag is an old HTML tag. It won't be included in future definitions of the HTML language, and may not work in new versions of the popular Web browsers. In other words, don't bother using these relative size options; stick to the standard numbering, 1 through 7, or better yet, check out the much more refined size control that Cascading Style Sheets offer (Chapter 8).

"Standard" text on a Web page is considered size 3. Each size increment represents a 20 percent change in the font's size: size 4 is 20 percent bigger than size 3, while size 2 is 20 percent smaller than size 3. So, for example, if the Web browser's default text size is 12 point, size 3 text is 12 points, size 2 is 10 points, and size 4 is 14 points.

To specify one of these relative text sizes, first select it and then do one of the following:

- In the Property inspector, choose a font size, 1 through 7, from the Size menu (see Figure 3-2).

- Choose Text→Size, and select a size from the submenu.

Tip: Since size 3 is the default size of text anyway, it's a waste of time and precious file size to set text to size 3. Better to just leave the font size set to None, which requires no additional HTML tags.

Font Color

Most color formatting you do in Dreamweaver, whether it's for text or for a table cell, makes use of Dreamweaver's *color box*. For more information on applying color in Dreamweaver and using the color box, see page 34.

To set the color of text, first select it and then take your pick:

- In the Property inspector, click the color well and select a color.

- In the Property inspector, click the Font Color field and type in the *hexadecimal number* (page 34) of the color you want. (Clearly, this is the option for hard-core HTML geeks. After all, surely you've memorized the hex number of that light shade of blue you always use; #6699FF, isn't it?)

Remember, as part of the properties for a Web page, you can choose a default color for all text on the page—see page 33 for details. This is a useful shortcut for when you want all or most of the text on a page to be a color other than black.

POWER USERS' CLINIC

The <font> Tag: Use at Your Own Risk

For years, font faces, sizes, and colors have been specified using HTML's <font> tag. As of HTML 4.0, however, the W3C (World Wide Web Consortium) officially *deprecated* the font tag, meaning that it will no longer be used in future versions of HTML. In the long term, this means that future browser versions may not recognize formatting that relies on the <font> tag.

In reality, since so many Web pages have been built using this tag, browsers will continue to support it for several years at least. However, it's becoming increasingly common to use Cascading Style Sheets—the state-of-the-art formatting standard—to define the look of text and other objects on a Web page instead. To learn how to create and use CSS, see Chapter 8.

HTML Styles

Adding formatting options to text can require many clicks of the mouse and many trips to the Property inspector. Suppose, for instance, that you want all of the major headings on a page to be formatted as Heading 1, using the Arial font, in red, italic, and centered. If your page has many headings, this could add up to a lot of formatting work.

To streamline such situations, use Dreamweaver's HTML Style feature. HTML Styles provide a single-click method for applying multiple text formatting options.

Note: Bear in mind that HTML Styles are not an "official" Web technology like Cascading Style Sheets or JavaScript. They're purely a Macromedia creation, a shortcut for completing multiple formatting tasks in one step.

The control center for HTML Styles is the HTML Styles panel. To open it, choose Window→HTML Styles or press Ctrl+F11 (⌘-F11). The panel lists all styles defined for the current site (see page 25 for full detail on creating sites in Dreamweaver) and lets you create, apply, edit, and delete HTML Styles.

Figure 3-10:
In order to edit, delete, or duplicate a style, you need to select it. Unfortunately, selecting a style while the Auto Apply box is turned on applies that style to any text you've selected, whether you want it to or not. For this reason, make sure this box is not checked when you edit or delete an HTML Style.

Remove formatting

A Paragraph style

A Character style

Auto apply

Context menu

Add style   Delete style

Creating HTML Styles

You can create an HTML Style either by formatting some text by hand first, or from scratch.

Here's how to create an HTML Style based on text you've already formatted:

1. **Select the text.**

   You can, if you like, create an HTML Style from scratch. But you save a lot of time by preformatting some text in your document, and then telling Dreamweaver to base its new style on *that*.

Make sure the HTML Styles panel is open, as described above.

2. **On the HTML Styles panel, click the Add Style button (the button marked with the +).**

You can also choose Text→HTML Styles→New Style or select New from the context menu on the HTML Styles panel.

In any case, the Define HTML Style window opens, as shown in Figure 3-11.

3. **In the Name field, type a name for your new style.**

For example, you might call it Author Name or Copyright.

The name you type appears only in the HTML Styles panel; it won't become part of the Web page itself.

4. **Specify whether the style should affect a selected piece of text or an entire paragraph.**

If you want the style to apply to a single word or a selection of text, not a whole paragraph—in other words, its *character* formatting—choose Selection. For instance, if you want your company's name to appear in a different font face and color, create a selection style. If you choose this option, the Paragraph options—alignment and paragraph formatting—are dimmed and unavailable.

A *paragraph* style, on the other hand, affects an entire paragraph or block-level element, such as a heading. (See page 63 for more on the character/paragraph formatting distinction.)

A small character symbol appears in front of your style's name in the HTML Styles list, indicating how the style will be applied. If you chose Selection, a character symbol (a) appears before the name. If you chose Paragraph, a paragraph symbol (¶) appears. (Both are shown in Figure 3-10.)

5. **Choose how to apply the style to already formatted text.**

If you apply an HTML Style to text that you've already formatted, Dreamweaver could easily become confused. Should it remove all previous formatting and *then* apply the HTML Style? Or should it *add* the HTML Style formatting to any formatting that already exists?

You decide how Dreamweaver handles this dilemma using the *Add to Existing Style* and *Clear Existing Style* options. For example, say you've selected some blue, bold text, and you've created a paragraph HTML Style with the Arial font set to size 4.

If you turned on the Add to Existing Style option, when you apply the style to the blue, bold paragraph, the entire paragraph would take on the Arial, size 4 formatting. The blue and bold text would get the same paragraph formatting, but remains blue and bold.

However, if you chose the *Clear* Existing Style option when you created the HTML Style, the entire paragraph would be formatted as Arial, size 4, but the blue color and the bold style would be removed from the text. In fact, all formatting *except* that specified by the HTML Style would be removed.

6. **Click OK to finish creating the style, or Cancel to close the dialog box without creating the style.**

Since you're basing this style on already formatted text, the Font and Paragraph attributes are already defined.

Figure 3-11:
The Define HTML Styles window lets you define the various font and paragraph attributes of an HTML Style. The options are the same as those in the Property inspector or the Text menu. If you need help, you can click Help to activate Dreamweaver's Help system. In addition, if you don't like the font and paragraph attributes you've set for the style, you can click Clear to reset all attributes of the style to None.

To create an HTML Style from scratch, use the HTML Styles panel (Figure 3-10); click the Add Style button. (The long way is to choose Text→HTML Styles→New Style or select New from the context menu on the HTML Styles panel.) In any case, the Define HTML Style window opens, as shown in Figure 3-11.

Name and set the basic properties of the style, as described in steps 3–5 above, then set up the font, size, color, and type style. If it's a paragraph style, you can also specify a paragraph format—Heading 1, Paragraph, Preformatted, and so on—and an alignment option—left, centered, or right. (HTML Styles can't include list formatting—bummer.) Finally, click OK.

Applying HTML Styles

Of course, *creating* a style is just the first step in using HTML Styles. Once you've defined a style, you *apply* it to text just by selecting the text and then using the HTML Styles panel.

Tip: If you're about to apply a paragraph-level style, you don't have to select the whole paragraph. Simply clicking anywhere inside the text block is enough.

If the Auto Apply checkbox is selected (see Figure 3-10), a single click on the style's name applies it. If Auto Apply is not turned on, you have to click the name of the style to select it, and *then* click Apply.

And if all of this is too confusing, you can always apply a style by choosing its name from the Text→HTML Styles submenu.

Editing styles

Editing a style is just as easy. With the Auto Apply checkbox turned off, double-click a style name. The Define HTML Styles window opens (Figure 3-11). Make any changes you like to the style, and then click OK.

Although HTML Styles may remind you of styles in, say, Microsoft Word, they're not the same thing. Editing a style, for example, affects only *subsequent* applications of the HTML Style; Dreamweaver doesn't automatically update text that you'd *previously* formatted with the style. You have to tell Dreamweaver to update them, as described next.

GEM IN THE ROUGH

Anti-Styles

Even if you don't plan to use HTML Styles, two default styles listed in the HTML Styles panel (Figure 3-10)—and the Text→HTML Styles submenu—can be very useful: Clear Selection Style and Clear Paragraph Style.

Actually, these aren't styles at all. They're more like anti-styles. Both come in handy when you want to remove a bunch of formatting from a selection or paragraph of text.

Suppose you highlight some text that includes both paragraph styles and character styles, as shown here at top. If you click the Clear Selection Style button, Dreamweaver removes all character formatting from the selec-

tion, including font face, color, size, and type style (center). But it preserves paragraph formatting, such as alignment, and doesn't affect any other formatted text in the paragraph.

If you click Clear Paragraph Style, however, Dreamweaver removes all text *and* paragraph formatting from a block of text as shown here at bottom. It also converts headings and preformatted text to plain paragraphs.

These may not seem like earth-shattering tools, but imagine the alternative: selecting each piece of formatted text and removing text and paragraph attributes one at a time from the Property inspector.

As noted above, editing a Dreamweaver style doesn't change the formatting of text to which you'd already applied that style. If you create a style called Footer with a font size of 2 and a color of red, editing the style to make its text purple doesn't affect any Footer text you've already typed—that text stays red. You have to manually reselect the text and reapply the style to update the formatting.

Tip: On the other hand, Dreamweaver *can* make a formatting change that ripples through and updates all corresponding formatting on a Web page (or even a Web site)—but not with HTML Styles. The trick is to use Cascading Style Sheets instead, as described in Chapter 8.

Removing HTML Styles

If you want to remove an HTML Style that you've defined, make sure the Auto Apply checkbox is turned off, and then select the style you wish to edit from the HTML Styles panel. (If Auto Apply is turned on, clicking a style doesn't mean "I want to edit this style"—it means "I want to apply this style to selected text.") Click the Trash can icon in the lower-right corner of the HTML Styles panel or choose Delete from the panel's context menu to banish the style. (Doing so has no effect on text to which you've already applied that formatting.)

With an understanding of paragraph and character formatting options, as well as a working knowledge of HTML Styles, you're ready to bring your message to the Web in colorful and attention-grabbing ways. To take your designs further by introducing graphics to your Web pages, see Chapter 5.

DREAMWEAVER MX: THE MISSING MANUAL

Links

The humble hyperlink may not raise eyebrows anymore, but the notion that you can easily navigate a whole sea of information, jumping from one piece of information to another with a simple click, is a very recent and powerful invention. Interested in a particular band? Go to Yahoo.com, type in the band's name, *click* to go to its Web site, *click* to go to the page that lists its upcoming gigs, *click* to go to the Web site for the club where the band's currently playing, and *click* to buy tickets.

Although links are a basic part of building pages, and although Dreamweaver, for the most part, shields you from their complexities, they can be tricky to understand. The following section provides a brief overview of links, including some of the technical distinctions between the different types. If you already understand links, or are just eager to start using Dreamweaver, jump to "Adding a Link" on page 95.

Understanding Links

A link is a snippet of computer code that gives a Web browser directions for how to get from one page to another on the Web. What makes links powerful is the fact that the distance those directions take doesn't matter. A link can just as easily lead to another page on the same site or to a page on a Web server halfway around the globe.

Behind the scenes, a simple HTML tag called the anchor (<a>) tag generates each and every link. Links come in three different flavors: absolute, document relative, and root relative. See page 94 for some examples of each link type in practice.

Absolute Links

When people need to mail you a letter, they ask for your address. Suppose it's 123 Main St., New York, New York 12001. No matter where in the country your friends are, if they write *123 Main St, NY, NY 12001* on an envelope and mail it, their letters will get to you. That's because your address is unique—just like an absolute link.

Similarly, every Web page also has a unique address, called a *URL* (most people pronounce it "You Are El"), or Uniform Resource Locator. If you open a Web browser and type *http://www.sawmac.com/dwmx/index.html* into the Address bar, the home page for this book opens.

This URL is an *absolute link*; it's the complete, unique address for a single page. Absolute links always begin with *http://*, and you'll use them anytime you link to a Web page *outside of your own site*. Absolute links always lead to the same page, whether the link to it is on a page in the current site or an entirely different site.

The bottom line: Use absolute links when you want to link to a page on another Web site.

Document-Relative Links

Suppose you, the resident of 123 Main Street, drop in on a couple who just moved into the neighborhood. After letting them know about all the great restaurants nearby, you tell them about a party you're having at your place.

When they ask you where you live, you could, of course, say, "I live at 123 Main St., NY, NY 12001," but your neighbors would probably think you needed a little psychiatric help. More likely, you would say something like, "Just go across the street and turn left. I'm the second house on the right." Of course, you can't use these instructions as your mailing address, because they work relative only to your neighbors' house.

When you want to create a link from one Web page to another within the same Web site, you can use similar shorthand: a *document-relative* link. In essence, a docu-

---

UP TO SPEED

Parts of a URL

Each chunk of a URL helps a Web browser locate the proper Web page. Take the following URL, for instance: *http://www.sawmac.com/dwmx/index.html.*

http—This portion specifies the *protocol*—the method the Web browser must use to communicate with the Web server. HTTP stands for hypertext transfer protocol. For what it's worth, HTTP specifies a connection to a Web page, as opposed to protocols like *ftp* (for transferring files) and *mailto* (for email addresses).

www.sawmac.com—This portion specifies the exact computer that's dishing out the Web site in question—that is, it's the address of the Web *server*.

/dwmx/—This is the name of a folder (sometimes called a directory) on the Web server.

index.html—This is the name of the actual document or file that the Web browser is supposed to open—the Web page itself. It's these HTML documents that Dreamweaver creates.

---

ment-relative link—like the directions you give your neighbor—simply tells the browser where to find the linked page *relative to* the current page. If two pages are in the same folder, for instance, the path is as simple as "Go to that page over there." In this case, the link is simply the name of the file you wish to link to: *index.html.* You can leave off all that *http://* and *www.sawmac.com* business, because you're already there.

Document-relative links can be finicky, however, because they're completely dependent on the location of the page containing the link. If you move the page to another part of the site—filing it in a different folder, for example—the link won't work. That's why working with document-relative links has traditionally been one of the most troublesome chores for a Web designer, even though this kind of link is ideal for linking from one page to another in the same site.

Fortunately, Dreamweaver makes working with document-relative links so easy, you may forget what all the fuss is about. For example, whenever you move a page into a different folder—a maneuver that would normally shatter all document-relative links on the page—Dreamweaver quietly *rewrites* the links so they still work. Even better, using the program's site management tools, you can cavalierly reorganize your Web site, moving folders and files without harming the delicate connections between your site's files. Dreamweaver's site management features are discussed in depth in Part 4.

Root-Relative Links

Root-relative links describe how to get from one page to another within the same site, just like document-relative links. However, in this case, the path is described relative to the site's *root folder*—the folder that contains the home page and other pages, folders, and files that make up your site. (For a detailed description of the root folder and structuring a Web site, see Chapter 15.)

Imagine you work in a big office building. You need to get to a co-worker's office for a meeting. You call him up for directions. Now, he may not know the precise directions from your office to his, but he can tell you how to get from your building's entrance to his office. Since you both know where your building's front door is, these directions work well. Think of the office building as your site, and its front door as the *root* of your site.

Root-relative links always begins with a slash /. This slash is a stand-in character for the root folder—the front door—of the site. The same root-relative link always leads to the same page, no matter where it is on your Web site.

Although the principle behind them makes sense, there are some major drawbacks to using root-relative links in Dreamweaver. The most apparent is that they don't work when you test them on your own computer; clicking a root-relative link in a Web browser *on your own machine* produces only a "file not found" error. Such links work only after they're moved to a Web server. Web servers understand root-relative links, but your local computer doesn't.

Stick to document-relative links for your pages, but keep this discussion in mind. You'll see later that Dreamweaver's site management features use root-relative paths to track your site's files behind the scenes.

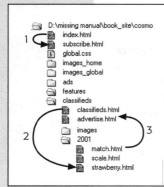

Figure 4-1:
Here are a few examples of links for a fictitious Web site located at www.cosmofarmer.com. Notice that although the root folder (cosmo) is nested inside several other folders—book_site and missing manual—it's still the top level folder for the site, since it holds the home page and all of the other files that go on the site. Keep this distinction in mind: The site root is not the same as the top level of your hard drive.

Link Types in Action

Figure 4-1 shows a Web site as it lies on a hard drive: folders filled with HTML documents and graphics. Here's a closer look at some links you might find on the pages there, and how they might work:

Links from the Home page (index.html) to the Subscribe page

The home-page document is usually called *index.html*. (The exact name depends on the configuration of your Web server. Contact your Web host, or the person in charge of your Web server, to confirm.) You could create the link from it to the subscribe.html page—identified by the number 1 in Figure 4-1—using any of the three link types:

- **Absolute.** *http://www.cosmofarmer.com/subscribe.html.* What it means: Go to the Web site at *www.cosmofarmer.com* and download the page *subscribe.html.*

- **Document Relative.** *subscribe.html.* What it means: Look in the same Web site and folder and download the page *subscribe.html.*

- **Root Relative.** */subscribe.html.* What it means: Go to the top level folder of this site (called *cosmo*, in this case) and download *subscribe.html.*

Tip: If you can write an absolute URL, you can easily create a root-relative URL. Simply strip off the *http://* and Web server name. In the above example, erasing the *http://www.cosmofarmer.com* in the absolute address leaves */subscribe.html*—the root-relative path.

Links from the Classifieds page to the Strawberry page

Now imagine that you're building a Web page that's in a folder inside another folder. Here's how you'd use each of the three link types to open a document that's nested in a subfolder (called 2001, in this case), as identified by the number 2 in Figure 4-1:

- **Absolute.** *http://www.cosmofarmer.com/classifieds/2001/strawberry.html.* What it means: Go to the Web site at *www.cosmofarmer.com,* look in the folder *classifieds,* and then in the folder *2001;* download the page *strawberry.html.*

- **Document Relative.** *2001/strawberry.html.* What it means: From the current page, look into the folder *2001* and download the page *strawberry.html.*

- **Root Relative.** */classifieds/2001/strawberry.html.* What it means: Go to the top level folder of this site, look in the folder *classifieds,* and then in the folder *2001;* download the page *strawberry.html.*

Links from the Match page to the Advertise page

Now suppose you're building a Web page that's in a deeply nested folder; you want it to link to a document that's *outside* of its folder, a link labeled 3 in Figure 4-1:

- **Absolute.** *http://www.cosmofarmer.com/classifieds/advertise.html.* What it means: Go to the Web site at *www.cosmofarmer.com,* look in the folder *classifieds,* and download the page *advertise.html.*

- **Document Relative.** *../advertise.html.* What it means: Go up one level—outside of the current folder—and download the page *advertise.html.* In links, a slash / represents a folder or directory. The two dots (..) mean: Go up one level, into the folder that *contains* the current folder.

- **Root Relative.** */classifieds/advertise.html.* What it means: Go to the top level folder of this site; look in the folder *classifieds,* and download the page *advertise.html.*

The executive summary

To summarize all of this discussion: Use absolute URLs for linking *outside* of your site, use document-relative links for links *within a site,* and avoid using root-relative links altogether.

Adding a Link

If all that talk of links got you confused, don't worry. Links *are* confusing, and that's one of the best reasons to use Dreamweaver. If you can navigate to a document on your own computer or anywhere on the Web, you can create a link to it in Dreamweaver, even if you don't know the first thing about URLs and don't intend to learn.

Figure 4-2:
Here are three ways to add links on a Web page: the Link field, the Point-to-File icon, and the Browse-for-File icon.

Format Paragraph ▲ Default Font ▲ Size None ▲

Link http://www.missingmanual.com ▲ ⊕ ▢ Target

Link field   Point to File ⌐ ⌐ Browse for File

Browsing for a File

To create a link from one page to another on your own Web site, use the Browse for File button on the Property inspector (see Figure 4-2) or its keyboard shortcut (see the steps below). Browsing for a file in Dreamweaver uses the same type of dialog box that you already use to open or save a file, making this the easiest way to add a link. (To link to a page on another Web site, you'll need to type the Web address into the Property inspector. Turn to page 99 for instructions.)

Note: Before you add any links, *save your Web page.* Not only is saving often good computer common sense, but saving a document means that you've settled on a folder location for it—a requirement if you hope to use document-relative links.

1. **In the document window, select the text or image you want to use for the link.**

    You can select a single word, a sentence, or an entire paragraph. When this process is over, the selected words will show up blue and underlined (depending on your visitors' Web-browser settings), like billions of links before them.

    In addition, you can turn a picture into a link—a great trick for adding attractive navigation buttons.

2. **In the Property inspector, click the folder (Browse for File) icon.**

    Alternatively, choose Modify→Make Link or press Ctrl+L (⌘-L). In any case, the Select File dialog box opens (see Figure 4-3).

3. **Navigate to and select the file you'll want the link to open.**

    The file should be a Web page that's part of your Web site. In other words, it should be in the local root folder (see page 26), or in a folder therein.

    If you try to link to a file outside the root folder, Dreamweaver alerts you to this problem, and offers to copy the file into the root folder. Accept the offer. Remember: For a Web site, the root folder is like the edges of the known universe; nothing exists outside it.

4. **From the Relative To menu, choose the type of link—Document or Site Root.**

    As noted earlier in this chapter, document-relative links are the best choice. Root-relative links (which is short for Site Root–relative links) don't work when previewing the Web site on your own computer.

Note: Get in the habit of double-checking this pop-up menu. As discussed in Figure 4-3, Dreamweaver remembers your selection and uses it the next time you create a link. If you inadvertently choose Site Root here, Dreamweaver will quietly continue to use Site Root–relative paths for creating hyperlinks and inserting graphics. Furthermore, you won't realize your mistake, because root-relative links work just fine when you press F12 to preview your pages in your Web browser. However, if you were to open your Web site directly using your Web browser's Open command, the same root-relative links and graphics would suddenly stop working. To avoid such confusion, use document-relative links in Dreamweaver.

5. Click Select (Windows) or Open (Mac) to apply the link.

The text or image now links to another Web page. If you haven't yet saved the Web page, Dreamweaver doesn't know how to write the document-relative link. Instead, it displays a dialog box saying that it will assign a temporary path for the link until you save the page—see the box on page 102.

Figure 4-3:
The Select File dialog box looks slightly different in Windows (top), Mac OS X (middle), and Mac OS 9 (bottom), but all of them let you browse your computer's file system to select the file you wish to link to.

From the Relative To pop-up menu, you can choose what type of link to create: Document or Site Root relative. Since root-relative links don't work when you preview your pages on your computer, choosing Document from the pop-up menu is almost always your best bet.

Whichever you choose, Dreamweaver remembers your selection and uses it the next time you create a link. Keep this quirk in mind if you suddenly find that your links are not working when you preview your pages. Odds are you accidentally selected Site Root at some point, and Dreamweaver continued writing site root-relative links.

After you apply a link, graphics don't look any different, but linked text appears underlined and colored (using the color defined by the Page Property window, which is described on page 32). If you want to take the link for a spin, press F12 to preview the page in your browser, where you can click the link.

Using the Point-to-File Icon

You can also create links in Dreamweaver by dragging icons, which is one great use of Dreamweaver's Site window (shown in Figure 4-4). If your site involves a lot of links, learning the Point-to-File tool will save you time and energy.

To use this trick effectively, position your document window and Site window side-by-side, as shown in Figure 4-4.

1. **In the document window, select the text or image you want to turn into a link.**

   Make sure that both the Property inspector and Site window are open. To open the Property inspector if it's not on the screen, choose Window→Properties. To open the Site window, choose Window→Site Files. (Before using the Site window, you need to first create a local site, as described on page 25.)

Figure 4-4:
In this figure, the text "more –>" is selected in the document window to the left. To link to another page, drag from the Point-to-File icon in the Property inspector to a Web page in the Site window shown at right. In this example, Dreamweaver creates a link to the Web page called mowers.html. Another method would be to press Shift and drag from the text "more –>" to the page mowers.html in the Site window.

2. **Drag the Point-to-File icon from the Property inspector *onto* a Web page in the Site window (see Figure 4-4).**

   Alternatively, you can Shift-drag the selected text or image in the document window to any Web page in the Site window—a method that bypasses the Property inspector altogether.

3. **After dragging over the correct Web page, release the mouse button.**

   The selected text or image in your Web page turns into a link to the file you just pointed to.

Typing (or Pasting) the URL or Path

If you need to link to another Web site, or you feel comfortable with how document-relative links work, you can also simply type the URL or path to the page in the Property inspector. Note that this is the *only* way to add a link to a page outside of the current Web site.

1. **In the document window, select the text or image you want to make into a link.**

2. **In the Property inspector, type the URL or path to the file in the Link field (see Figure 4-1).**

   If the link leads to another Web site, type an absolute URL—that is, a complete Web address, starting with *http://*.

Tip: An easier approach is to copy a complete URL—including the *http://*—from the Address bar in your browser window. Then paste the address into the Link field.

To link to another page on your own site, type a document-relative link (see page 94 for some examples). You'll be less prone to error if you let Dreamweaver write the correct path using the browsing or point-to-file techniques described above; but typing the path can come in handy, for instance, when you want to create a link to a page you haven't yet created.

Tip: If you're adding an absolute link to a Web site without specifying a Web page, always add a final / to the address. For example, to link to Yahoo, type *http://www.yahoo.com/*. The final slash tells the Web server that you're requesting the default page (home page) at Yahoo.com.

Although leaving out the slash works too (*http://www.yahoo.com*), the server has to do a little extra work to figure out what page to send back, resulting in a slight and unnecessary delay.

Also include the slash when you provide a link to the default page inside a folder on a site like this: *http://www.sawmac.com/dwmx/*.

---

3. **Press Enter (Return) to apply the link.**

   The text or image now links to another Web page.

Using the Hyperlink Object

Dreamweaver MX provides yet another way to add a link. The Hyperlink object on the Insert bar (see Figure 4-6) lets you insert a link with many optional properties.

Unfortunately, only the latest browsers—Internet Explorer 6, Mozilla, Netscape 6, and later versions of these—actually understand these additional properties, and you can only use the hyperlink object to create a *new* text link. You can't use it to add a link to an image or to text you've already placed on the page.

If you want to give this feature a spin anyway, here's how it works. Start by clicking on the page where you wish to insert a new link. Then:

1. **Choose Insert→Hyperlink or click the icon on the Insert bar.**

   The Hyperlink dialog opens (see Figure 4-5).

2. **Type the text you want to appear in the Text box.**

   This is the text that you'll see on the page, and that your audience will click to follow the link.

Figure 4-5:
To apply these optional properties to an image or existing text, you have a couple of options. You can always go into Code view (as described in Chapter 9) and hand-edit the HTML, but it's easier to use the Tag inspector, new in Dreamweaver MX, to access all the properties available to a particular link. (For details see page 288.)

3. **Click the folder icon and search for the page you want to link to.**

   Alternatively, you can type a URL in the Link box.

4. **Set the target for the link.**

   If you want the link to open in the same window, like most links, don't select anything. The targeting option works just like a regular link (see page 98).

   The last three options are more interesting.

5. **In the Tab Index box, type a number for the tab order.**

   In some newer browsers (notably Internet Explorer), you can press the Tab key to step through the links on a page (and boxes on a form). This feature not only provides useful keyboard control of your Web browser, but is also important for people who can't use the mouse due to disability.

Normally when you press Tab, the browser highlights links in the order in which they appear in the HTML of the page. The Tab Index, by contrast, lets you *control* the order in which links light up as a visitor tabs through them.

For example, you can make your main navigation buttons the first things to highlight when someone presses Tab, even if the buttons are not the first links on the page.

For the first link in order, type *1* here; number other links in the order you want the Tab key to follow. If you aren't concerned about the order of a particular link, leave this option blank or type *0*. The Web browser will highlight that link after the visitor has tabbed through all links that *do* have a Tab index.

6. **Type a title for the page you're linking to.**

    This property is optional. The latest versions of Internet Explorer display this property in a small tooltip window when you move your mouse over the link.

7. **Type a key to define an access key.**

    An access key provides a way to trigger a link from the keyboard. Internet Explorer, Netscape 6 and later, and Mozilla understand this property in conjunction with the Alt key.

    For example, if you type *h* in the Access Key box, a visitor to your page could press Alt-H to mouselessly open that link. (Of course, unless those who visit your site are psychic, it's a good idea to provide instructions by adding the access key information to the link: *Home Page (Alt-H).)*

Adding an Email Link

Whenever you want to invite your visitors to email you, an *email link* is the perfect solution. When someone clicks an email link, her email program launches automatically, and a new message opens with your email address already in the To field. She can then just type her message and send it off.

An email link looks like this: *mailto:bob@cosmofarmer.com.* The first part, *mailto:,* indicates the type of link, while the second part *(bob@cosmofarmer.com)* specifies the email address.

Figure 4-6:
The Common tab of the Insert bar includes three link-related objects: The Hyperlink for adding text links, the email link for adding links for email addresses, and the Named anchor for adding links within a page.

Note: Email links work only if the person who clicks the link has an email account and an email program. If someone visits your site from a computer at the public library, for example, he might not be able to send email. If this drawback troubles you, remember that you can also collect information using a *form* (as discussed in Chapter 10), a feedback method that has neither the limitations nor the easy setup of an email link.

You can create an email link much the way you'd create any other Dreamweaver link: by selecting some text or an image and typing the mailto address, as shown above, into the Link field in the Property inspector. To simplify this process, Dreamweaver has a quick method of inserting an email link:

1. **On the Common tab of the Insert bar, click the Email Link icon, which looks like an envelope (see Figure 4-6).**

   Alternatively, choose Insert→Email link. In either case, if you've already typed the text *(Email me!)* on your Web page, select it first. The Email Link dialog box opens (see Figure 4-7).

FREQUENTLY ASKED QUESTION

The Mysterious Triple Slashes

Why do my links start with file:///*?*

Links that begin with file:/// (as in this example: *file:///D:/ missing manual/book_site/cosmo/subscribe.html*) aren't valid links on the Web. Rather, they are temporary addresses that Dreamweaver creates as placeholders for links to be rewritten later. (A file:/// path tells Dreamweaver where to look on your computer for the file.) You'll spot these addresses when you add document-relative links to a page that hasn't been saved, or when working with files that are outside of your site's local root folder.

Suppose you're working on a Web page that will contain your company's legal mumbo-jumbo, but you haven't yet saved it. After adding a document-relative link that links to your home page, you notice that the path displayed in the Property inspector's Link field begins with file:///. Since your legal page hasn't yet been saved and therefore doesn't yet have a folder location, Dreamweaver can't create a link telling a browser how to get from it to the home page.

So Dreamweaver creates a temporary link, which helps it keep track of what page to link to. Once you save the page

somewhere in the site, Dreamweaver rewrites the link into a proper document-relative format and the file:/// disappears.

Likewise, when you work with files that are outside of the local root folder, Dreamweaver can't write a proper link. (Any folder outside of the local root folder isn't part of the Web site; and there's no way to write a correct link from nowhere to somewhere.) So, if you save a page *outside* of the local root folder, Dreamweaver writes all document-relative links on that page as file paths beginning with file:/// To avoid this invalid-link problem, always save your Web pages in either the local root folder or a folder *inside* of the local root folder. To learn more about root folders and Web sites, see Chapter 14.

When you *link* to a page—or add an image (Chapter 5)—that's stored outside of the local root folder, Dreamweaver has the same problem. However, in this instance, Dreamweaver gives you the option of copying the out-of-bounds file to a location of your choosing within the root folder.

---

2. **In the Text field, type the text that you'll want to appear on the Web page.**

This should give visitors some indication of what the link does. For instance, *Email the Webmaster.* (If you selected text in the document first, it automatically appears in the Text field.)

Figure 4-7:
The Email Link dialog box lets you specify the text that appears on the Web page and the email address for a mailto link. You can also select some text you've already added to the document and click the Email Link icon on the Insert bar. The text you selected is copied into the Text field in this dialog box.

3. **Type an email address into the E-Mail field.**

This is the address that appears in the user's email program when she clicks the link. (You don't have to type *mailto:*—Dreamweaver adds it to the email address automatically.)

4. **Click OK.**

Dreamweaver adds the text to the page, complete with a mailto link.

Linking Within a Web Page

Clicking a link usually loads a Web page into the browser window. But what if you want to link not only to a Web page, but to a specific *spot* on the page? See Figure 4-8 for an example.

Introducing the *anchor link*, a special link type that's designed to auto-scroll to a particular spot on a particular page.

Phase 1: Creating an anchor

Creating an anchor link is a two-step process: First add and name an anchor, thus identifying the destination for the link; then add a link that goes to that named anchor. For instance, in the Answers page example of Figure 4-8, you would place a named anchor at the beginning of each answer.

To create a named anchor:

1. **In the document window, click where you want to insert the named anchor.**

The named anchor is the place where you want the link to jump to.

2. **Insert a named anchor.**

You can do so using any of three methods. *Using a menu:* Choose Insert→ Named Anchor. *From the keyboard:* Press Ctrl+Alt+A (Option-⌘-A). *In the In-*

sert bar: Select the Common tab and click the Named Anchor icon—see Figure
4-6.

3. **Type the name of the anchor in the Insert Named Anchor dialog box.**

   Each anchor on a page should have a unique name, something short and easy to
   remember. No spaces are allowed, however. Punctuation is illegal, too; stick to
   letters and numbers. If you violate any of these regulations, Dreamweaver will
   remind you with an error message.

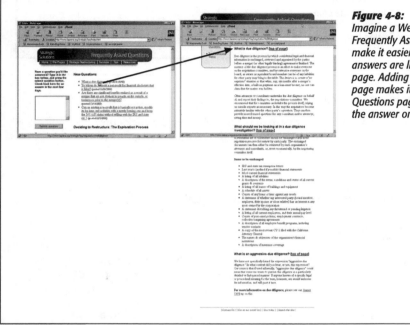

Figure 4-8:
*Imagine a Web page with a list of
Frequently Asked Questions (right). To
make it easier to update, all of the
answers are listed together on a single
page. Adding anchors to the Answers
page makes it possible to jump from the
Questions page to the precise location of
the answer on the Answers page.*

4. **Click OK to insert the named anchor.**

   You'll see a gold shield with an anchor on it at the point where you created the
   anchor. Click this icon to show the anchor's name in the Property inspector. (If
   you don't see it, refer to page 106 for details on hiding and showing anchors.)

   The anchor icon is the key to removing or editing the anchor later: Just click the
   icon and press Delete to get rid of it, or click it and change its name in the Property inspector. (Deleting the name in the Property inspector deletes the anchor
   from the page entirely.)

Phase 2: Linking to an anchor

Creating a link to a named anchor is not all that different from linking to a Web
page. Once you've created and named an anchor, you can link to it from within the
same Web page, or from a different page.

To link to an anchor on the same page:

Linking Within a Web Page

1. **In the document window, select the text or image you want to make into a link.**

   For example, drag across some text, or highlight a graphic.

2. **In the Property inspector, type #, followed by the name of the anchor into the Link field.**

   Alternatively, use the Point-to-File icon, as shown in Figure 4-9.

   The # sign indicates that the link goes to a named anchor. In other words, if you wish to link to an anchor named *directions,* the link would be *#directions.*

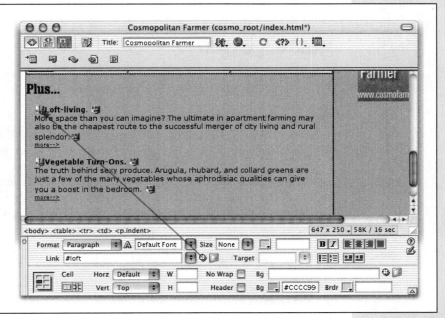

Figure 4-9:
You can use the Property inspector's Point-to-File icon to link to a named anchor on a page. Simply select some text or an image in an open page. Then drag the Point-to-File icon to an anchor on any other open document to set the link. If you can't see the shield icons that mark anchors, see page 106 for instructions on how to make them visible.

You can also link from one Web page to a particular location on another Web page in your site. The process is the same as linking to an anchor on the same page, except that you have to specify both the path to the Web page and the name of the anchor:

1. **In the document window, select the text or image you want to turn into a link.**

2. **In the Link field of the Property inspector, type or choose the URL or path of the page you wish to link to.**

   You can use any of the methods described above: browsing, point-to-file, or typing the path.

   Unfortunately, if you browse to select the linked file, Dreamweaver doesn't display any anchors on that page, so you need to perform one extra step to link to the anchor:

3. Click at the end of the URL or path. Type #, followed by the name of the anchor.

What you see in the Link field should something look like this: *contact.html#directions*.

Viewing and hiding anchors

A named anchor isn't visible in a Web browser; it's represented in Dreamweaver as an anchor-on-a-gold-shield icon. As with other invisible elements—line breaks, for instance—you can make named anchors show up by choosing View→Visual Aids→Invisible Elements, or choosing Visual Aids→Invisible Elements from the Options menu in the toolbar (see page 18). (If anchors still don't appear, visit the Preferences window and make sure the Anchor box is turned on, as shown in Figure 1-8.)

Modifying a Link

At some point, you may need to change or edit a link. Perhaps the URL you were linking to has changed, or you simply no longer need that link.

Changing a Link's Destination

As you'll read in Part 4, Dreamweaver provides some amazing tools for automatically updating your links so your site stays in working order, even if you move files around your site. But even Dreamweaver isn't smart enough to know when a page on someone *else's* Web site is moved or deleted. And you may decide you simply need to change a link so that it points to a different page on your own site. In both of these cases, you'll need to change the links on your Web pages by hand.

1. Select the text link or picture link.

Do so by clicking anywhere inside the text link, or clicking once on the link image.

The existing link path appears in the Link field in the Property inspector.

FREQUENTLY ASKED QUESTION

Anchors Away

When I click on a link to an anchor, the Web browser is supposed to go to the page and display the anchor at the top of the browser window. But sometimes the anchor appears in the middle of the browser. What's that about?

Web browsers can't scroll beyond the bottom of a Web page, so an anchor near the bottom of a page sometimes can't move to the top of the browser window. If one of your own Web pages exhibits this problem, the fix is simple: just add a bunch of empty lines—press the Enter key repeatedly—below the last item on the page. You've just added space at the bottom of the page, so the browser can scroll the page all the way to the anchor.

---

2. **Use any of the techniques described on page 95 for specifying the link's target.**

   For example, click the Browse-for-File button in the Property inspector and locate a different Web page in your site.

   The destination of the link changes to the new URL, path, or anchor.

Removing a Link

Sometimes, you want to stop a link from linking—when the Web page you were linking to no longer exists, for example. You want the text or image on your Web page to stay the same, but you want to remove the disabled link. In that case, just select the link text or image, and then use one of these tactics:

- Choose Modify→Remove Link.

- Press Ctrl+Shift+L (Shift-⌘-L).

- Delete the text in the Link field of the Property inspector and press the Enter or Return key.

The text or image remains on your Web page, but it no longer links to anything. If it's a text link, the color changes from your site's link color (see page 32) to the normal text color for the page.

Of course, if you're feeling particularly destructive, you can also delete the link text or image itself; doing so also gets rid of the link.

FREQUENTLY ASKED QUESTION

Link Colors

How can I change the color of my links?

To help Web visitors identify links, Web browsers usually display linked text in a special color (blue, for example).

If you'd prefer a different hue, you can control which color the browser uses from the Page Properties dialog box. Choose Modify→Page Properties to open it. For more information, see page 32.

While we're on the subject, I'm already using a different color for my links to make them stand out from the other text. Can I get rid of the underline that Dreamweaver automatically puts under links?

Yes, but not with HTML alone. By default, all text links show up with underlines, and no HTML code can change that. However, Cascading Style Sheets provide a lot more formatting control than plain HTML—including, yes, the ability to remove link underlines. To find out how, see Chapter 8.

DREAMWEAVER MX: THE MISSING MANUAL

Images

Nobody believes that a picture is worth a thousand words more than today's Web designers, as evidenced by the increasingly visual nature of the Internet. In fact, it's not difficult to stumble onto a home page these days composed of nothing but graphics (see Figure 5-1).

Even if you don't want to go that far, understanding how to use graphics effectively is invaluable. Whether you want to plop a simple photo onto your page, cover it with clickable "hot spots," or design an interactive set of buttons that light up when the cursor passes over them, Dreamweaver makes the job—and the underlying JavaScript programming—easy.

Adding Images

If you were writing out the HTML instructions for your Web page by hand, you'd insert an image into a Web page using the image tag—<img>. The primary *property* of an image is called the *source* (Src), which is the URL or path to the graphics file.

Dreamweaver does all of this coding for you automatically when you insert a picture into your fledgling Web page:

1. **Save the Web page that will contain the image.**

   In order to insert an image, Dreamweaver must determine the path from your Web page to that image, which could be anywhere on your hard drive. As with links (see page 95), saving the page before you proceed enables Dreamweaver to correctly determine the path from the image to the page you just saved.

2. In the document window, click where you want to insert the image.

This might be at the beginning or end of a paragraph, or within a cell in a table (see Chapter 6). To set a graphic apart from other text, press Enter, creating a blank line, before inserting it.

Figure 5-1:
Some Web sites rely almost exclusively on graphics for both looks and function. The home page for the PBS Kids Web site, for instance, uses graphics not just for pictures of their shows' characters, but also for the page's background and navigation buttons.

3. Choose Insert→Image.

Alternatively, you can click the Image button in the Common tab of the Insert bar (see figure 5-2). Or, if you're a keyboard nut, press Ctrl+Alt+I (Option-⌘-I).

Figure 5-2:
The Common tab of the Insert bar has three tools for adding graphics to your pages.

Insert Image —   └─ Insert Placeholder Image   Insert Rollover Image

In any case, the Select Image Source dialog box opens. This box is identical to the Select File window that appears when adding a link to a page. The only difference is the Preview Images checkbox—turning it on shows a thumbnail of any selected image in the Preview window.

4. **Browse to and select the graphics file you wish to add to the page.**

The file must be in one of the formats that work on the Web: GIF, JPEG, or PNG.

The file should be stored somewhere in the local root folder of your site (see page 26) or in one of its subfolders. If it isn't, Dreamweaver can't add the correct path to your Web page.

That's why, if you select a graphic for insertion that's not already in your site folder, Dreamweaver offers to add a *copy* of it there. If you choose Yes, a Copy File As dialog box opens, so that you can save the file in your local root folder, renaming it if you wish. If you choose No, Dreamweaver uses a file-relative path (beginning with *File:///*) for the image's Source property (see page 102). But clicking No is usually a bad idea: While it allows the graphic to be displayed while you work with Dreamweaver on your computer, the graphic won't appear once you move the document to the Web.

5. **Choose the type of path to create: Document or Site Root.**

When you insert an image into a Web page, you don't actually add the graphics file to the HTML file. Instead, you create a *path* to the image, a coded description of where a computer can find the relevant graphics file, so that a Web browser knows where to look for and download the graphic.

UP TO SPEED

GIFs, JPEGs, and PNGs: The Graphics of the Web

Computer graphics come in hundreds of different file formats. The assorted acronyms can be mind-numbing: TIFF, PICT, BMP, EPS, Amiga IFF, and so on.

Fortunately, graphics on the Web are a bit simpler. There are only three graphics formats—two established formats and one exciting newcomer. All three provide good *compression;* through clever computer manipulation, they reduce the graphic's file size so it can travel more rapidly across the Internet. They differ only in the details.

GIF (Graphics Interchange Format) files provide good compression for images that have areas of solid color: logos, text, simple banners. GIFs also offer single-color transparency, meaning that one color in the graphic can be made to disappear, permitting the background of a Web page to show through part of the image.

A GIF image can only contain a maximum of 256 shades, generally making photos look blotchy. That radiant sunset photo you took with your digital camera won't look so good as a GIF.

JPEG (Joint Photographic Experts Group) graphics, on the other hand, pick up where GIFs leave off. JPEG graphics can contain millions of different colors, making them ideal for photographic images. Not only do JPEGs do a better job on photos, they also compress much better than GIFs, because the JPG compression algorithm considers how the human eye perceives different adjacent color values. When your graphics software saves a JPEG file, it averages the colors of adjacent pixels.

Finally, the **PNG** (Portable Network Graphics) format holds great promise for the future. These files can be compressed even smaller than GIF format, can contain millions of colors, and offer 256 levels of transparency, which means that you could actually see through a drop shadow on a graphic through to the background of a Web page. Only the most recent Web browsers recognize this format, so you'd be well advised to avoid PNG graphics for the moment.

In general, Document is the best choice. Site Root–relative paths don't always work when previewing a page. (See page 92 for detail on the difference between document- and root-relative links.)

6. **Click OK (Windows), Choose (Mac OS X), or Open (Mac OS 9).**

The image appears on your Web page.

Tip: Dreamweaver also permits several drag-and-drop techniques for quickly adding images to your pages.

Make sure you've defined a site as described on page 25. Then open the Site Files window (press F8). You can drag any graphic file from that window right into an open Dreamweaver document. You can also drag graphics in from the Assets panel, as described on page 444.

Dreamweaver even lets you drag a graphic from your desktop onto a page. If you do this, Dreamweaver will dutifully copy the file into your site folder, so that the image will show up properly on the Web page.

Adding an Image Placeholder

It's not uncommon to find yourself working on a Web site without all the pieces of the puzzle. You may start building a page, even when your client has yet to give you all the text she wants on the page. Or you may find that a photograph hasn't been shot, but you want to get the page ready for it. Other times, you may be responsible for building the Web pages, for example, while another designer is creating the banners and navigation buttons.

To help out in these kinds of situations, Dreamweaver MX introduces the Image Placeholder button. It lets you insert a placeholder—called an *FPO* (For Placement Only) image in publishing—so that you can stake space on the page for a graphic that isn't ready yet. This way, you can lay out the basic structure of the page without having to wait for all the graphics to arrive in their final form.

To insert a placeholder, do one of the following:

• Choose Insert→Image Placeholder

• On the Insert bar, click the Image Placeholder icon in the Common tab (see Figure 5-2).

In the window that appears (see Figure 5-3), type a width and height for the image, which determines how much space the placeholder will take up on the page. The Name and Alternate Text fields are optional. (If you fill them out, they'll appear in the Name and Alt boxes of the image's Property inspector, as discussed next.)

The Color box lets you specify a color for the placeholder—presumably to make the placeholder more colorful than the default gray color. However, this option has some drawbacks. Behind the scenes, Dreamweaver inserts a little extra code in the <img> tag for the placeholder color. Unfortunately, even after you replace the placeholder with a real image, the extra code that supplies the color isn't erased from the <img> tag, and you can no longer erase it with the Property inspector. As a result, if the image you finally use is a transparent GIF or PNG file, the color you selected when adding the placeholder will show through in the transparent areas of the image.

To eliminate the now-extraneous placeholder color, you'll need to go into Code view (see Chapter 9), find the correct tag for the image, and remove a property that looks like this: *style="background-color: #99CC66"*. (The actual color number depends on which color you picked.)

To avoid all of this hassle, just don't use the color option when inserting an Image Placeholder.

Figure 5-3:
The values you type for Name, Width, Height, and Alternate Text appear in the Property inspector after inserting an Image Placeholder. You may be tempted to use the Color field to give your placeholder an eye-catching shade, but because it can interfere with transparent images and can be removed only in Code view, don't use this option.

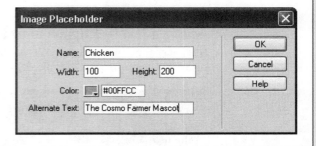

Of course, using a placeholder doesn't do you any good if you don't eventually replace it with a real image. Once you've got the image that should finally appear on the page, just double-click the placeholder on the Web page. The Select Image Source window appears. Follow steps 4–6 on page 111 to insert the new image.

If you also own Fireworks MX, Dreamweaver's Web graphics companion program, there's an added benefit to the Image Placeholder. When an Image Placeholder is selected in the document window, the Property inspector includes a button called Create. Clicking this button launches Fireworks MX and opens a new, blank graphics document set to the exact dimensions you specified earlier. You can then create your graphic in Fireworks MX. After you save the file, Fireworks will export it to whatever folder you specify and automatically insert it into your document—replacing the placeholder.

Modifying an Image

After inserting a graphic, you can work on it in several ways: by attaching a link to the image, aligning it on the page, or adding a border and margin to it, for example. As with most objects on a Web page, you set image properties using the Property inspector (see Figure 5-4).

Naming an Image

Just to the right of an image's thumbnail on the Property inspector is a small field where you can type a *name* for that image. Most of the time, you'll leave this field blank. However, if you plan to add interactive effects to it, such as the rollover effect discussed on page 126, or your own JavaScript programming, you *must* name your picture. Whatever name you choose should only use letters and numbers—no spaces or other punctuation. (When you do this, Dreamweaver adds both a *name* property and an *ID* property to the image tag. The name tag is still used by most browsers, but the more recent ID tag is fast becoming the standard way that JavaScript identifies an object on a page.)

Note: JavaScript uses the image name or ID that you type here for its own reference; no one actually sees this name in a Web browser. In other words, this isn't the place to give your graphic a text label that shows up when your reader has graphics turned off. For that purpose, read on.

Adding a Text Description to an Image

Not everyone who visits your Web site gets to see those stunning photos of your last summer vacation. Some people deliberately turn off graphics when they surf, en-

---

UP TO SPEED

Making Accessible Web Sites

Many people using the Web have disabilities that make reading, seeing, hearing, or using a mouse difficult. Visually impaired people, for example, may be unable to benefit from images on the screen, even though they have software that can read aloud a Web page's text.

Dreamweaver MX introduces a number of new features for making your Web sites more accessible. That's good news if you're building a Web site for the federal government or one of the many states that support Section 508 of the Workforce Investment Act. This law requires Web sites built for or funded by the government to offer equal or equivalent access to everyone. Throughout this book, you'll find tips for using Dreamweaver MX's accessibility features, and on page 472 you'll learn how to use a new tool to find out if your site is compliant with Section 508.

The Alt property described on these pages is an important first step for assisting visually impaired Web surfers. For complex images, such as a graph that plots changes in utility rates over time, you can also supply a more detailed description on a separate Web page. The *longdesc* (long

description) property of an image lets you specify a link to a page containing a text description of the image. Some Web browsers understand this property, allowing visually impaired visitors to jump to a page with a text description that screen-reading software can read aloud.

While you can't find the Longdesc property in the Property inspector, you can turn on an accessibility option in Dreamweaver that lets you add it every time you insert a graphic. Choose Edit→Preferences to open the Preferences window, and select the Accessibility category.

Turn on the Images checkbox.

Now whenever you insert a graphic, the window shown here will appear, so that you can quickly set the Alt text and select an HTML page containing a long description.

Note that you're not *required* by Section 508 to use the long description property when inserting images. It's merely recommended if the image is particularly complex or includes information that can't be explained in the Alt property—for example, graphs or images that include a lot of text information.

---

joying a Web without the wait, since graphics-free Web pages appear almost instantly. Other people have vision impairments that prevent them from enjoying the visual aspects of the Web. They rely on special software that reads Web-page text aloud, including any labels you've given your graphics.

Figure 5-4:
The Property inspector displays all the properties of a selected graphic, including its width, height, source, border, and even a tiny preview at upper-left.

To assist Web surfers in both situations, make a habit of setting the *Alt property* of the image. Short for *alternative text,* the Alt property is a text description that Web browsers use as a stand-in for the image (see Figure 5-5).

Figure 5-5:
The Alt property can be an important aid for those surfing without graphics. In the top figure, graphics denote the different sections of the site, such as Features, Site of the Week, and Insights. With graphics turned off (bottom), that information is still available, thanks to the alt text.

However, graphics without an Alt property simply disappear or display the generic label IMAGE. In the case of an important identifying graphic like the site logo (the "design interact" banner in the first figure), a missing <alt> tag leaves visitors wondering where they are.

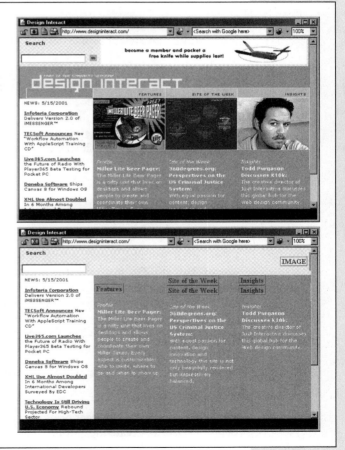

To add a text description to an image, type it in the Alt field in the Property inspector. If you're naming graphics that will be navigation buttons, you could just use the same text that appears on the button, such as *Home* or *Products*. For images that carry greater meaning—such as a photo of the product itself—you might use a more detailed description: "Photo of the Anodyne 3001—the most powerful apartment gardening tool ever devised."

Note: In some cases, however, a description can be more of a distraction than a help. For example, a common technique in laying out a Web page involves using invisible 1-pixel images—often called *spacer images* (page 154). Because these images serve as a layout aid and don't convey any meaningful information, a description isn't necessary.

In this instance, you can use the pop-up menu that appears to the right of the Alt field. This menu, new in Dreamweaver MX, lets you choose one option: <empty>. Use the <empty> Alt property to make your pages meet accessibility requirements without adding distracting and unnecessary descriptions (see the box on page 114).

Changing the Size of an Image

The Width and Height properties of a graphic do more than determine its screen size; they also help Web browsers load it quickly and efficiently. Since the HTML of a Web page downloads before any graphics do, a Web browser displays the text on the page first, and then adds the images as they arrive. If width and height attributes are missing, the browser doesn't know how much space on the page to give each image, so it has to redraw the page after each image is downloaded and its dimensions are determined. The stuttering appearance of this redrawing is disconcerting, makes Web pages appear slowly, and shatters your reputation as a cool, competent Web designer.

Fortunately, you don't have to worry about specifying the picture's dimensions yourself: Whenever Dreamweaver inserts an image into a Web page, it automatically calculates its width and height and enters those values into the W and H fields in the Property inspector (see Figure 5-4).

You can, if you like, shrink a graphic by typing smaller values into the W and H fields, but doing so won't do anything to speed up the download time. You'll make the picture *appear* smaller, but the Web browser will still have to download the entire graphics file. To make your graphic smaller both in appearance and file size, do it in an image-editing program like Fireworks, Photoshop, or ImageReady. Not only will you get an image that's exactly the size you want, but you'll also trim a few bytes off its file size, and maybe even save a second or two in download time.

On the other hand, setting width and height values that are *larger* than the actual dimensions of the graphic merely distorts the image by stretching it, creating an undesirable pixellated effect. If you want a larger image without distortion or pixellation, start with a larger original image: return to your digital camera or stock photo CD, or re-create the graphic at a larger size in Photoshop or Fireworks.

Tip: You can use the image-distorting properties of the Property inspector's width and height fields to your advantage when working with solid-color shapes. Say you want to insert an orange line, 580 pixels wide and 4 pixels tall, to separate two paragraphs on a page. Sure, you could insert a GIF graphic with an orange background that's 580 pixels wide by 4 pixels tall.

But the clever Web designer would save on file size by creating an orange GIF graphic that's only 1 pixel by 1 pixel, inserting it into the page, and using Dreamweaver to change its size to 580 x 4. After all, stretching a solid-color graphic doesn't break it up; it just makes more of the solid color. And the 1-pixel GIF is a far smaller file than the 580 x 4 one. Even better, you can reuse it to make lines of other sizes and take advantage of a Web browser's download-saving cache (see the tip on page 476).

Aligning an Image

Images, like text, appear in the normal flow of HTML in a page. In other words, a picture can appear as a paragraph by itself, or within a sentence or paragraph of text.

The Property inspector has two sets of alignment controls that affect images (see Figure 5-6). Only the Align pop-up menu, however, controls alignment specific to an image. (The second set of alignment options applies to the entire paragraph, as discussed on page 67.)

WORKAROUND WORKSHOP

Watch Those Resize Handles!

After you insert an image in the document window, a thin black border appears around it, indicating that it's selected. Three small black squares—the resize handles—appear on the right edge, bottom edge, and lower-right corner, as shown here.

Dragging these handles changes the width and height of the graphic—or, rather, the Width and Height *properties* in the Property inspector. The graphic file itself remains unchanged.

As noted on page 116, however, dragging one of these handles to make the picture appear bigger is almost always unsuccessful, resulting in distortion and ugly pixellation.

But those pesky resize handles are far too easy to accidentally grab and drag. In fact, sometimes you might resize a

graphic and not know it. Perhaps you accidentally dragged the left resize handle a few pixels, making the graphic wider, but not enough to notice.

Fortunately, the Property inspector provides some subtle feedback to let you know if your graphic is distorted. A boldfaced number in the W or H field tells you that the Width or Height property now differs from the actual dimensions of the graphic.

Clicking the letter W or H in the Property inspector *resets* the Width or Height property back to that of the original graphic file, undoing your little slip of the mouse. Clicking the Reset Size button in the lower-right corner of the Property inspector resets both properties.

If you've inserted a graphic into a text paragraph, you can specify exactly how the image relates to the words around it. The Align pop-up menu in the Property inspector lets you select ten different options (see Figure 5-7). However, only six of them work in all browsers. Avoid the other four, as noted below, which work only in a few certain browsers.

Image alignment — Paragraph alignment

Figure 5-6:
Only the Align pop-up menu provides options specific to the image. The alignment icons affect the entire paragraph—not just the image. If you just want to center-align a graphic, however, without affecting any text around it, put the image in its own paragraph and click the center align button.

To set a graphic's vertical alignment, click the image to select it. Then choose one of the options from the Align pop-up menu at the right side of the Property inspector. You can see each illustrated in Figure 5-7:

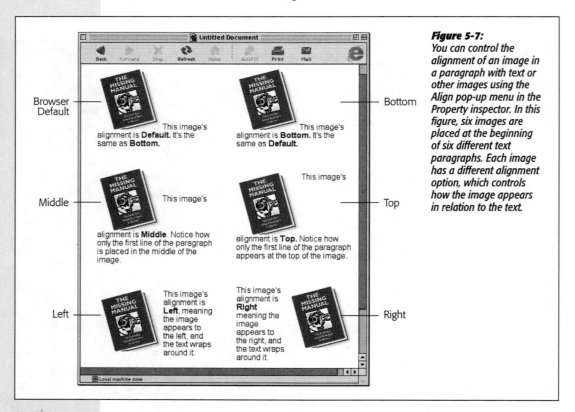

Figure 5-7:
You can control the alignment of an image in a paragraph with text or other images using the Align pop-up menu in the Property inspector. In this figure, six images are placed at the beginning of six different text paragraphs. Each image has a different alignment option, which controls how the image appears in relation to the text.

- **Default** means that the graphic will sit on the baseline (the bottom of the line of text on which the graphic appears). The effect is identical to choosing **Bottom**.

- **Middle** aligns the text on the current line with the middle of the graphic, but may add an awkward-looking complication. Subsequent lines of text move *below* the graphic—a problem you can solve by using either of the two wrap alignment options, as described below.

- **Top** alignment aligns the image with the top of the line of text in the paragraph. Again, because top alignment can create a gap between the first line and the rest of the text, consider using the Left or Right wrapping options described below.

- **Left** places an image to the left of any text, which then wraps down the right side.

- **Right** moves the image to the right and wraps text along its left edge.

- **Baseline, TextTop, Absolute Middle,** and **Absolute Bottom** are not part of the official HTML standard and only work in a few browsers, so avoid them.

Adding a Margin Around an Image

When you place an image into a paragraph, text butts right up to the edge of the graphic—an invasion of the picture's personal space that's often visually unappealing. Fortunately, you can add a margin of space around your images with the Horizontal Space and Vertical Space properties.

Figure 5-8:
The horizontal margin setting is particularly useful in combination with an image's Left or Right alignment option (see page 117). When using either of these two wrap alignment options, a horizontal margin setting adds much needed space between an image and any text wrapping around it. (To turn on the onscreen rulers shown here, choose View→Rulers.)

You add a margin around an image by telling Dreamweaver how many pixels of space to add on each side. As shown in Figure 5-8, about 20 pixels makes an attractive amount of space. To add a margin above and below a graphic, type a number of pixels in the V Space field in the Property inspector. To add space to the left and right of an image, type a number in the H Space field. (Sorry, you can't specify independent values for each of the four margins—at least not without using the Margin property of Cascading Style Sheets, as described in Chapter 8.)

Adding a Border

Dreamweaver offers a quick, easy way to add a border around a graphic using the Border field on the Property inspector (see Figure 5-4).

To add a border, click the image to select it and then type a width, in pixels, into the Border field. One pixel creates a fine, almost invisible border; ten pixels makes a fat one. Press Enter or Return to apply the new border. Click anywhere on your page to remove the selection border and resize handles, the better to see the results of your work.

Tip: The color of a border you create this way depends on what browser your visitor's using. For some, such as Netscape Navigator 4, Opera 6 (on Windows), and Internet Explorer 5 (on the Mac), the color is the same as the text color you chose in the Modify→Page Properties dialog box (see page 32). Internet Explorer 6 and Opera 6 (on the Mac), on the other hand, draw a black border. (However, if you add a link to an image with a border, the color changes to the link colors specified for the page, as discussed on page 34).

To avoid all that confusion, use the Cascading Style Sheet *Border* property. Using CSS as described on page 260, you can individually control the size, style, and color of each of the four borders.

It's worth noting that if you don't specify *any* border for an image that you've defined as a link (by leaving the Border box empty), most Web browsers add a border around the image anyway. This automatic border is two pixels wide and colored with the link colors defined in the Page Properties dialog box. To remove this distraction,

---

EASTER EGG HUNT

Meet the Geeks Behind Dreamweaver

Hidden throughout Dreamweaver are amusing diversions programmed by Dreamweaver's engineers: so-called *Easter Eggs,* a computer-industry term for buried credits screens that appear only when you stumble onto the secret and unusual combination of words, keystrokes, and mouse-clicks.

One of these is hidden in the Property inspector. Select an image in the document window. Then Ctrl-double-click (⌘-double-click) the thumbnail of the graphic in the left side of the Property inspector. A picture of one of Dreamweaver's programmers appears, along with his name. Ctrl (⌘)-double-click the thumbnail repeatedly to cycle through the names and pictures of other members of the Dreamweaver team.

give the image a Border value of 0 (as opposed to leaving the box blank). Dreamweaver usually adds the 0 automatically when you add a link to an image, but occasionally, you may need to do this by hand.

Editing Images

Nothing's ever perfect, especially when you're building a Web site. Corrections are par for the course—not just to a Web page, but to the pictures on it, as well: "Hey, can you change the text on that button from 'Now Firing' to 'Now Hiring'?"

In the hands of less-capable software, you'd face quite a tedious switching-and-opening task each time you wanted to open a graphic. You'd have to open Photoshop, Fireworks, or whatever graphics program you prefer; choose File→Open; navigate to your Web site folder; find the graphic that needs touching up (if you can even remember its name); then open it to make your changes.

Dreamweaver proves much more considerate of your time, because it lets you specify your favorite graphics program. Thereafter, using that program to edit a picture on your Web site is as easy as a couple of clicks.

Setting Up an External Editor

Before you can take advantage of this timesaving feature, you need to tell Dreamweaver which graphics program you want to use.

1. **Choose Edit→Preferences (Dreamweaver→Preferences in Mac OS X).**

   The Preferences dialog box opens, as shown in Figure 5-9.

2. **In the left pane, click File Types/Editors.**

   The Preferences box now shows your current settings for the editing programs you prefer for editing different types of files. Two columns appear in the bottom half of the box: Extensions and Editors.

3. **Select a graphic extension from the Extensions list.**

   Three types of graphic files are listed: GIFs, JPEGs, and PNGs. You can choose a different editing program for each type of file, if you like. You can add file name extensions for file types not shown by clicking the + button above the Extensions list.

4. **Click the + button above the Editors list.**

   The Select External Editor dialog box opens.

5. **On your hard drive, find the program you wish to assign as an editor for the selected type of graphics file.**

   It might be Photoshop, AppleWorks, ImageReady, or whatever.

6. **If you wish to make this program the primary program for editing this type of file, click Make Primary.**

This *primary* editor will be the one Dreamweaver opens when you choose to edit the graphic. (You can define other, less frequently used editors as well. See the Tip on the facing page.)

7. **Repeat steps 3–6 for each type of graphics file that you work with.**

   Dreamweaver treats GIFs, JPEGs, and PNGs as separate file types, so you need to assign an editor to each. Of course, most people choose the same program for all three file types.

8. **Click OK to close the Preferences dialog box.**

Figure 5-9:
You can select external editors for various types of Web files—including graphics formats such as GIFs, JPEGs, and PNGs— from the File Types/Editors category of the Preferences dialog box.

From now on, whenever you need to touch up a graphic on your Web page, just select it and then click Edit on the Property inspector (see Figure 5-4). Alternatively, right-click (Control-click) the image and choose the Edit With Fireworks (or Edit With Photoshop, if you set that as your primary editor) from the contextual menu. In any case, your graphic now opens in the graphics program that you set as your primary editor in step 6 above.

Now you can edit the graphic and save changes to it. When you return to Dreamweaver, the modified image appears on the page. (If you're a Fireworks user, you're in even better shape; read on.)

Tip: You aren't limited to just one external editor. For instance, if there's some Fireworks feature you need even though Photoshop is your primary editor, you can still jump to it directly from Dreamweaver.

The trick is to right-click (Control-click) the image you want to edit, whether it's in the document window or the Site Files window. Choose Edit With→Browse from the contextual menu. Then, in the resulting dialog box, choose the editing program you want to use. That program opens automatically, with the graphic you clicked open and ready to edit.

Editing Images with Fireworks

Fireworks is Dreamweaver's companion graphics program—a powerful image-editing program made specifically to create and optimize Web graphics. You can get it as a stand-alone product, or included with Dreamweaver as part of its Studio MX package.

The engineers at Macromedia have made sure that these sibling programs play well together. You can switch back and forth between them with a single click, for example. And instead of simply opening a GIF or JPEG file when you click the Edit button in the Property inspector, Fireworks can open the original Fireworks file.

That's good, because most Web graphics don't start life as compressed GIF or JPEG files. Very often you'll have a higher quality image in your image editor's native format—.psd for Photoshop or ImageReady, for example, or. png for Fireworks. This source file may contain lots of additional information that doesn't need to be in the final image you use on the Web. For example, in most image editing programs, text can remain editable, so that it's easy to modify the link description on a button, say. In other words, most often you'll want to make changes to the original Photoshop or Fireworks file and *then* export it as a GIF or JPEG. If you're using Fireworks, Dreamweaver makes this process easier.

When you export a GIF or JPEG graphic from Fireworks, save it into your Web site folder—into a subfolder called Images, for instance. (See page 422 for strategies to help you organize your site's files.) When you do so, Fireworks creates a folder called _notes in the same folder. This folder contains small files whose names end in .mno—for Macromedia Note—that tell Dreamweaver where to find the original Fireworks PNG file on your computer.

When Dreamweaver opens a Web page, it checks for this folder and any notes that are associated with the graphics on the page. When you select an image created with Fireworks, Dreamweaver displays this information in the Property inspector (see Figure 5-10).

To edit a Fireworks graphic, just click it in the document window, and then click Edit in the Property inspector. Or, if you're in a hurry, just Ctrl (⌘)-double-click the image; or right-click (Control-click) it and choose Edit With Fireworks MX from the contextual menu. Either way, Dreamweaver launches Fireworks. (You may be prompted to choose whether to open the source file of the exported GIF or JPEG, depending on how you've set up your Fireworks preferences.)

In Fireworks, make any changes you wish to the image. When you're finished, click Done. Fireworks exports the image, closes the file, and returns you to Dreamweaver. The updated graphic appears on your page.

Figure 5-10:
You see special logos (circled) and options when you're working with a graphic created in Fireworks.

Image Maps

As Chapter 4 makes clear, it's easy to turn a graphic into a clickable link. It's also possible to add *multiple* links to a single image.

Suppose your company has offices all over the country, for instance, and you want to provide an easy way for your visitors to locate the nearest state office. One approach would be simply to list all of the state names and link them to separate pages for each state. But that's boring! Instead, you could use a map of the United States—one image—and turn each state's outline into a hotspot that's linked to an appropriate page, listing all of the offices in that state.

The array of invisible link buttons (called *hotspots*) responsible for this magic is called an *image map*. An image map contains one or more hotspots, each leading somewhere else.

Here's how to go about creating an image map:

1. **Select the graphic you wish to make into an image map.**

   The Property inspector displays that image's properties and, in the lower left corner, the image map tools, shown at bottom in Figure 5-11. (These appear in the lower half of the Property inspector, which appears only if the Property inspector is fully expanded [page 22]).

2. **In the Map field of the Property inspector, type a name for the map.**

   The name should contain only letters and numbers, and can't begin with a number. If you don't give the map a name, Dreamweaver automatically gives the map the ingenious name *Map*. If you create additional image maps, Dreamweaver will call them Map2, Map3, and so on.

3. **Select one of the image map tools.**

   Choose the rectangle tool, the circle tool, or the polygon tool depending on the shape you have in mind for your hotspot. For instance, in the image in Figure 5-9, the polygon tool was used to draw each of the oddly shaped hotspots.

4. Draw the hotspot.

To use the rectangle and circle tool, click directly on your picture; drag diagonally to form a rectangle or circle. To make a perfect square, press Shift while dragging with the rectangle tool. (The circle tool always creates a perfect circle.)

To draw an irregularly shaped hotspot using the polygon tool, click once to define one corner of the hotspot. Continue clicking until you've defined each corner of the hotspot. Dreamweaver automatically joins the corners to close the shape.

Dreamweaver fills in the inside of the hotspot with a light blue tint to make it easy to see. (Your Web visitors won't see the blue highlighting.)

If you need to adjust the hotspot you've just drawn, click the arrow tool on the Property inspector. You can drag the light blue square handles of your hotspot to reshape or resize the area, or drag inside the hotspot to move the whole thing. If you change your mind about the hotspot, press Delete to get rid of it altogether.

Figure 5-11:
Individual links on an image map—called hotspots—show up in transparent blue in Dreamweaver. When you select a hotspot, the Property inspector displays its Link, Target, and Alt properties. The lower half of the inspector displays the name of the map as well as tools for selecting and drawing additional hotspots.

5. Add a link to the hotspot.

After you draw a hotspot, that hotspot is selected; its properties appear in the Property inspector (see Figure 5-11). Use any of the techniques discussed on page 95 to link this hotspot to another Web page or anchor.

6. If necessary, set the Target property.

Most of the options in the Target pop-up menu are useful only when you're working with frames, as discussed in Chapter 7. The _blank option, however, can be useful any time: It forces your visitor's Web browser to load the linked page into a *new* browser window. The original page remains open, underneath the new window.

7. **Set the Alt property of the hotspot.**

By typing a label into the Alt box in the Property inspector, you provide a written name for this portion of the graphic. As noted on page 114, Alt tags are extremely important to people who surf the Web with graphics turned off, or who use text-to-speech reading software.

8. **Repeat steps 2–7 for each hotspot you wish to add to an image.**

As you work, you can see the light-blue hotspots filling in your image map.

Editing a hotspot's properties

As noted in step 4 above, you can change a hotspot's shape by dragging its tiny square handles. But you can also change its other properties—which Web page it links to, for example.

To do so, click to select the image map. Using the black arrow tool—the hotspot selection tool—on the Property inspector (see Figure 5-11), click the hotspot you wish to edit. Then use the Property inspector controls to edit the Link, Target, and Alt properties.

If you're having a fit of frustration, you can also press Delete or Backspace to delete the hotspot altogether.

Rollover Images

Rollover images are among the most common user-interface elements on the Web, especially when it comes to navigation buttons. You've almost certainly seen rollovers in action, when your mouse moves over a button on some Web page and the image lights up, or glows, or turns into a frog.

This simple change in appearance is a powerful way to inform a visitor that the graphic is more than just a pretty picture—it's a button that actually does something. Rollovers are usually used to show that the image is a link (see Figure 5-12).

Figure 5-12:
Rollover graphics appear frequently in navigation bars, like the one shown at top. As your cursor touches a rollover button (top), the button changes appearance (bottom) to indicate that the graphic has a functional purpose—in this case, "I'm a link. Click me."

Behind the scenes, you create a rollover by preparing *two different* graphics—"before" and "after." One graphic appears when the Web page first loads, and the other appears when your visitor's mouse moves over the first. If the cursor then rolls away without clicking, the original image pops back into place.

This dynamic effect is achieved with the use of JavaScript, a programming language that most Web browsers use to add interactivity to Web pages. Fortunately, you don't need to be a programmer to take advantage of this exciting technology. Dreamweaver's many prewritten JavaScript programs, called Behaviors, let you add rollover images and other interactivity to your pages. (More about Behaviors in Chapter 11.)

Figure 5-13:
The Insert Rollover Image dialog box lets you set up the rollover effect. Turning on Preload Rollover Image forces the browser to download the rollover image file with the rest of the page. (If you turn preloading off, the browser doesn't download the file until the mouse moves over the original image, causing a disorienting delay.)

To insert a rollover image, start by using a graphics program to prepare the "before" and "after" button images. Unless you're going for a bizarre distortion effect, they should be exactly the same size. Store them somewhere in your Web site folder.

Then, in the document window, click where you want to insert the rollover image. Frequently, you'll use a table to lay out your rollover buttons (Chapter 6), and insert the image within a table cell.

Choose Insert→Interactive Images→Rollover Image (or click the Rollover Image button on the Common tab of the Insert bar). Either way, the Insert Rollover Image dialog box appears (see Figure 5-13.) Fill in the blanks like this:

- **Image Name.** Type a name for the graphic, if you like. JavaScript requires *some* name for the rollover effect. If you leave this blank, Dreamweaver gives the image an unimaginative name—for example, Image2—when you insert a rollover. However, if you plan to later add additional interactive effects (Chapter 11), you might want to change it to something more descriptive, to make it easier to identify the graphic later.

- **Browse button #1.** When you click the top Browse button, a dialog box appears prompting you to choose the graphic you want to use as the "before" button—

the one that first appears when the Web page loads. (See page 111, step 4, for more on choosing graphics.)

Browse button #2. When you click the second Browse button, Dreamweaver prompts you to choose the "after" graphic images—the one that will appear when your visitor's mouse rolls over the first one.

- **Alternate Text.** You can give a text description for a rollover button just as you would for a graphic, as described on page 114.

- **When Clicked, Go to URL.** Rollover images are most commonly used for navigation elements that, when clicked, take the user to another Web page. In this box, you specify what happens when your visitor actually falls for the animated bait and *clicks* the rollover button. Click the Browse button to select a Web page from your site (see page 96) or, if you wish to link to another Web site type an absolute URL beginning with *http://*.

When you click OK, you return to your document window, where only the "before" button image appears. You can select it and modify it just as you would any image. In fact, it's just a regular image with a link and a Dreamweaver Behavior attached.

To see your rollover in action, preview it in a Web browser by pressing the F12 key or using the File→Preview in Browser command.

Flash Buttons

While adding graphic rollovers to a Web page is a breeze, DreamweaverMX's *Flash button* feature is even easier. Without any additional image-editing or animation software, you can bring your pages to life with interactive buttons that include animation and sound.

Flash buttons are predesigned buttons, to which you can add your own labels and links. They can do much more than just change from a "before" look to an "after" look. For example, they may have *three* different looks (a third being a "pushed down"

EXTENSION ALERT

InstaGraphics Extensions for Dreamweaver

Ever get tired of the limited number of fonts you can use on your Web pages? How about the appearance of those boring bullets in unordered lists? No problem. Dreamweaver lets you add new commands—called *extensions*—to the program. This great feature makes it possible to add literally hundreds of additional features.

Many are available for free from a Macromedia's Web site in a section called The Exchange—*www.macromedia.com/exchange/*.

Go there and search for InstaGraphics, a nifty extension that can convert headings and other text in a page to a GIF file using any font you installed on your computer. In addition, this extension can replace HTML bullets with a nicer looking graphic. (Fireworks is required to make this feature work.)

For more on using the Macromedia Exchange, see Appendix A.

---

look that shows up when the button is clicked). They may also play a sound or trigger a little animation.

You can download additional button styles from the Web, and, if you have Flash 5, you can even create your own (see the box on page 132).

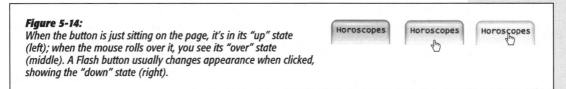

Figure 5-14:
When the button is just sitting on the page, it's in its "up" state (left); when the mouse rolls over it, you see its "over" state (middle). A Flash button usually changes appearance when clicked, showing the "down" state (right).

A Warning About Flash

It's important to understand, however, that Flash buttons (and Flash text, as discussed on page 132) are based on Macromedia's Flash Web animation technology. Flash is quickly becoming the standard format for Web animation, thanks to its small file size, crisp graphics, and interactive effects. But Flash files (called Flash movies) require special software to view; they won't work on your Web page unless each of your Web site visitors has installed the Flash plug-in.

Most Macintosh and Windows browsers now come with the Flash plug-in already installed, but Unix browsers and many older browsers may not have the plug-in. (Macromedia says that nearly 98 percent of the Web browsers worldwide have at least the Flash 3 plug-in installed—which is fortunate, since Dreamweaver's Flash buttons work with the Flash plug-in version 3 and above.)

The point is, though, that if you want to ensure that *everyone,* regardless of computer type, can savor your Web site to the same degree (without having to scurry off to another Web site to download the Flash plug-in), steer clear of Flash buttons. Furthermore, Flash movies can pose problems for disabled Web surfers.

Figure 5-15:
In MX, the Flash button and Flash text icons are on the Media tab of the Insert bar.

Adding a Flash button to a Web page

If you're still undaunted by the fact that not all of your audience may be able to enjoy Flash buttons, you're ready to proceed.

When you add a Flash button to a Web page, Dreamweaver creates and inserts a Flash movie file, ending in the extension .swf, into your Web page. You can preview the button within Dreamweaver and edit it at any time.

You perform most of the work in a single dialog box (Figure 5-16), which appears when you choose Insert→Interactive Images→Flash Buttons. You can also click the Flash Button object in the Media tab of the Insert bar. (Dreamweaver 4 users: notice its new location!) The object now is to choose the correct settings for the lively button you're about to create.

- **Style.** When you click a style name, an interactive sample appears at the top of the window. Try pointing to each sample as well as clicking it (and holding down your mouse button) to see all of its different looks. Stop when you find one you like.

- **Button Text.** Most button styles have space for a short piece of text that will appear as a label, right on the button. Into this box, type something informative about the button's function *(Buy Now!)* or its link *(Home)*. Buttons have limited space; Dreamweaver ignores letters that don't fit on the button.

Figure 5-16:
The Insert Flash Button window lets you select a style, set text, and add links and formatting to a Flash button. You can also go on the Web and collect lots more button styles by clicking the Get More Styles button. When you do, your Web browser launches and opens the Macromedia Exchange Web site. To go to the section of the Exchange where you can find additional styles, choose Flash Media from the Browse Extensions pop-up menu. See page 606 for more detail on using Macromedia Exchange.

- **Font, Size.** You can select a font from the Font pop-up menu and specify a size (in points) in the Size field. You can use any TrueType font you have installed on your computer; unfortunately, Flash buttons can't handle Postscript fonts.

- **Link.** If you want your button to link to another page when clicked, you can add either an absolute link or document-relative link (see page 92). Type an absolute link starting with *http://* in the Link field. Alternatively, you can click the Browse button and select a page from your site to create a document-relative link.

One thing to keep in mind about document-relative links in Flash buttons: the link information is embedded inside the Flash file. As a result, if you save the page you're working on to a different folder, the link won't work any more.

That's why, if you hope to create one set of Flash navigation buttons and use them over and over on all the pages of your site, you should use *absolute* links. These work regardless of the location of the Flash button file or the Web page the button is on. (*Site root–relative links* [see page 93] don't work at all in Flash movies.)

Tip: For a more advanced solution to this problem, see page 407.

- **Target.** If you want the linked page to open into a new browser window when clicked (leaving the current page in the current window), select the _blank option. The other Target pop-up menu choices are useful when working with frames (Chapter 7).

- **Bg Color.** Use this pop-up palette to choose a background color for your button.

  Flash buttons can't be transparent and, like all Web page graphics, can be only square or rectangular. In other words, if your Flash button is rounded (as most are), some areas around its corners will obscure the background of your Web page. What you're specifying here is a color for these exposed corner areas.

  By default, the background of a Flash button is white, but if you plan to use a button on a page with a different colored background, set the button to match the page's own background color.

- **Save As.** Dreamweaver automatically gives the button a file name—something like *button1.swf*—but you can change the name, if you like, by typing it into this box. Flash button files must end in the extension .swf (the file extension used by Flash movies), even on a Macintosh.

  If you like to keep your graphic files in a separate folder, you can click the Browse button to save the file into a folder of your choice. But be careful: Thanks to the varying ways different browsers work, a button to which you've given a document-relative link may not work unless you save the file into the same folder as its Web page.

When you click OK, Dreamweaver creates the Flash movie and saves it in the location you specified. Dreamweaver also inserts the movie into the Web page, with all of the appropriate properties set in the HTML of the page.

Editing Flash buttons

Once you've added a button to a Web page, you can edit it by double-clicking it (or by selecting it in the document window and clicking Edit in the Property inspector). The Insert Flash Button dialog box (see Figure 5-16) reappears. Make any changes you wish to the button, and then click OK.

And since Flash buttons are simply Flash movies, you can change any of the movie properties, such as height, width, or background color, using the Property inspector (see Chapter 13 for more on using Flash movies in Web pages).

Previewing Flash buttons

You can see the button in action by previewing the page in a Web browser by pressing F12. Or, if you just want to see the different looks for the button, you can preview the button without leaving Dreamweaver MX. The procedure may sound a little peculiar, but only until you remember that a Flash button is actually a little movie: select the button and then click Play on the Property inspector. The Flash button is now "playing." You can move your mouse over it, click it, and so on, savoring its animated smarts. To stop the button, click Stop in the Property inspector. (You can't double-click the button to edit it when it's playing.)

Flash Text

As noted in Chapter 3, Web browsers simply don't offer a lot of font choices. Even though it's possible to specify *any* font for your text, unless your visitors have the same font installed on their systems, they won't see the font you intended.

For this reason, Web designers either stick to the handful of fonts that are commonly installed on Windows and Macintosh computers, or they render type *as graphics* and insert them in the page. This workaround has its own downsides, of course: graphics take longer to download, and you can't edit the text once you've frozen it into a picture.

In an effort to give designers greater choices, Dreamweaver MX offers Flash text. Based on Macromedia's successful Flash technology, Flash text is a text-only Flash movie on your Web page that maintains the shape and quality of any True Type font you have installed on your computer. It offers a number of benefits:

POWER USERS' CLINIC

Behind Flash Buttons

You may be a little dismayed by either the limited number of styles available for Flash buttons, or the quality of the buttons' designs. You may decide that none of the buttons match your site's look, so why bother?

Fortunately, Flash buttons, like most features in Dreamweaver, are completely customizable. Each Flash button style is actually a *Generator* template. (Generator is a Macromedia product that can incorporate dynamic data, such as the time or weather, into a Flash movie, providing cutting-edge animation with up-to-the-minute information.)

You can create these buttons using the Generator authoring extensions of Flash 5. Unfortunately, the latest version of Flash, MX, doesn't have this feature, so you'll need to dig up an old copy of Flash 5 to do it. For information on creating your own Flash Buttons for Dreamweaver, check out Macromedia's Web site at *www.macromedia.com/support/ dreamweaver/assets/flashbutton.*

- Your visitors see exactly the same fonts you used when you created the Web page, even if they don't have the same fonts on their machines.

- The resulting Flash file is usually much smaller and of higher quality than the same text rendered as a graphics file.

- Since Flash uses *vectors*—mathematical formulas—to describe an image's shape and color, you can resize Flash text without degrading its quality.

Unfortunately, Flash text has a downside, too: like Flash buttons, Flash text requires the Flash plug-in. As discussed on page 129, some visitors may not be able to enjoy your handiwork.

Adding Flash text to a Web page

Inserting Flash text is a combination of adding text and creating a Flash movie. Because you have so many choices, working with Flash text takes longer than most Dreamweaver processes, although it's no harder. Once again, it all happens in a single dialog box (see Figure 5-17).

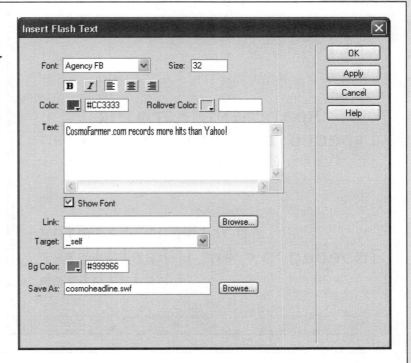

Figure 5-17:
The Flash text tool creates small text-only Flash movies that you can include on your Web pages. As with Flash buttons (see page 128), you can make the Flash text link to another Web page when clicked, either in your site or elsewhere on the Web.

To create Flash text, choose Insert→Interactive Images→Flash Text (or click the Flash Text icon on the Media tab of the Insert). Now make your settings.

- **Font, Size.** You can select any TrueType font you have installed on your computer. As noted earlier, Flash text doesn't work with Postscript fonts. Type a font size, measured in points, in the Size field.

   Unlike text in a Web page, which, thanks to the quirky HTML language, comes only in *relative* font sizes (1, 2, 3, 4, and so on), Flash text uses the traditional typographic units of measurement, points. 24 points is good for headlines, but you can specify a much larger size if you'd like.

- **B, I, alignment.** Using the tools just below the Font pop-up menu, you specify type-style attributes. For example, you can apply bold or italics by clicking the B or I buttons. You can also set the alignment of the text—left, right, or centered—by clicking one of the three alignment buttons (see Figure 5-18).

Figure 5-18:
You can align the text within a Flash text file. The alignment you choose here doesn't affect how the text is aligned on your Web page; it determines how the text is aligned inside of the finished Flash movie. If you think of each Flash text file as its own paragraph, the alignment options—shown here, from top to bottom, with Left, Middle, and Right alignment—make more sense.

- **Color.** Use this pop-up palette to choose a color for your text. (See page 34 for details on using the Dreamweaver color picker.)

- **Rollover Color.** Flash text can have one basic dynamic effect: it can change color when a viewer moves his mouse over it. This effect can be particularly useful if you wish to use the text as a link, because rollover effects are commonly used to indicate links. Use the Rollover Color pop-up palette to specify the color the text will become when the cursor points to it. If you don't want any rollover effect, leave this option blank.

- **Text.** The Text field displays your words in whatever font you've chosen. (If you turn off Show Font, on the other hand, you'll see only some generic font as you edit the text, but the software may feel more responsive as you edit.)

  As you type, you must manually enter a line break—by pressing Enter—wherever you want a line of text to end and a new line to begin. If you don't, Dreamweaver will create one wide (perhaps very wide, depending on how much text you have) Flash text movie. That's one reason it's usually better to use Flash text for short pieces of text like headlines or links.

- **Link.** You can use Flash text as a navigational element by attaching a link to it. In conjunction with a rollover color, you can use this feature to create simple dynamic navigation. In other words, if your Flash text says *Home,* you can set it up so that it's a button link back to your home page.

- **Target.** If you decide to turn your Flash text into a link, you can choose a *target* for that link using the Target pop-up menu, if appropriate. (As noted earlier, select the _blank option if you want the link to produce a new browser window when clicked. Otherwise, use this pop-up menu only when working with frames, as described in Chapter 7.)

- **Bg Color.** The Flash text you're creating is a rectangular text block, but the spaces between your lettering and the edge of the block aren't transparent; in fact, they start out white. The result—a bunch of white rectangles—can be pretty goofy-looking if the background of your Web page is, say, fuchsia.

  To make it look like the Flash lettering is sitting directly on your Web page's background (without the white rectangles), choose the background color that matches your Web page's background.

- **Save As.** Type a name for your Flash-text movie here. The Flash text tool stores the Flash movie in your site folder, within the folder that contains the Web page it's on. If you wish to save it in some other folder (an Images folder, for example), click the Browse button and navigate to it. If you've added a link to the text, however, save the Flash-text movie in the same place as the Web page. If you don't, the link may not work in all browsers.

- **Apply.** The Apply button creates the Flash file and shows you the text on the Web page, while leaving the dialog box open. The advantage here is that you can make adjustments before exiting the dialog box.

When you click OK, Dreamweaver creates a Flash file and inserts it on your Web page.

Editing Flash text

To edit Flash text you've created, open the Insert Flash Text dialog box using any of these procedures:

- Double-click the Flash text block in the document window.

- Select the Flash text and then click the Edit button in the Property inspector.

- Right-click (Control-click) the Flash text and choose Edit from the contextual menu.

Once the dialog box is open, you can make any changes you wish to the settings or text.

Resizing Flash text

You can freely resize Flash text in the document window, without ever worrying that it won't look good at one point size or another. Just select the Flash text block, and then use either of these techniques:

- Type new dimensions into the Width and Height fields in the Property inspector. You can set the size using either pixels or percentages.

- Drag one of the square handles on the edges of the Flash object. To avoid distorting the text as you resize the Flash object, Shift-drag the lower right handle.

You can always return the Flash object to its original size by clicking the Reset Size button on the Property inspector.

Tutorial: Adding Rollovers

Adding interactive elements to a Web page can be quite a chore. Unless you're a programmer, learning and using the JavaScript programming language can be time-consuming and frustrating. Fortunately, Dreamweaver does most of the work for you, with its powerful yet easy-to-use Behaviors.

In this tutorial, you'll add dynamic rollovers to the page you created in the first chapter.

Note: The tutorial in this chapter builds on the page you created in Chapter 1. If you no longer have that page handy, or you'd rather start fresh, you can download the example files from *www.sawmac.com/ dwmx/*. Click the Tutorials link. Download the DWImages–Mac files link or DWImages–Win files, depending on the kind of machine you're using (Mac or Windows).

After you've downloaded and decompressed the files, you should have a DWImages folder on your computer, containing the Web pages and graphics needed for this tutorial. If you're having difficulties, the Web site contains detailed instructions for downloading the files you'll be using with this book.

---

1. **Define the DWImages folder as your root folder.**

   If you're working on the page you completed in Chapter 1, use the local site you defined for that tutorial. That is, choose Cosmo Farmer from your Site menu.

   If you're starting fresh, see page 25 for complete instructions on defining a folder as your site folder. In short, this step involves choosing Site→New Site to open the Site Definition window; typing any name you like into the Site Name field; clicking the folder icon next to the Local Root Folder field; and choosing the DWImages folder as your local root folder. Click OK.

   Now the Site window (Figure 14-5) should be open on your screen.

2. **In the Site window, double-click the file called advertise.html.**

   The Advertise with *Cosmopolitan Farmer* page opens. You'll add rollover images to create a navigation bar.

3. **Click just to the right of the banner at the top of the page.**

   You may first need to widen the document window or scroll right until you see blank space next to the banner. Since the navigation bar will go directly below the banner, as part of the same paragraph, you'll insert a line break.

4. **Press Shift-Enter (Shift-Return) to insert a line break.**

   The insertion point now blinks just below the banner, and a gold shield, representing the line-break character, appears just to the right of the banner. If you don't see the gold shield icon, make sure you turned on invisible characters in the Preferences window, as described in Figure 1-8.

   Remember this Shift-Enter trick. It's a great way to make two images—one on top and one below—touch. When you're done with this tutorial, the banner will look like one solid image even though you're creating two separate rows of images.

Figure 5-19:
The Insert Rollover Image window lets you define the name, graphics, and link for a rollover. Make sure the Preload Rollover Image checkbox is turned on.

5. **Choose Insert→Interactive Images→Rollover Image.**

   If the Insert bar is open, you may prefer to click the Insert Rollover Image button there. Either way, the Insert Rollover Image dialog opens (see Figure 5-19.)

6. **In the Image Name field, Type *home*.**

   In order for this effect to work, each button must have its own name, which the JavaScript program will use to communicate with and control the graphic. Dreamweaver MX gives the graphic a generic name like Image1, but using a more descriptive name will make it easier for you to edit this effect later on.

7. **Click the first Browse button.**

   The Original Image dialog box appears. In the next step, you'll select the image for the button that will appear on the page.

8. **Browse to the DWImages→images folder; double-click the graphics file called home.gif.**

   The path to that graphic, *images/home.gif,* appears in the Original Image field. Next stop: choosing the graphic that will appear when a visitor moves the cursor over the button.

9. **Click the second Browse button; this time, double-click the file called home_f2.gif.**

   Now, you'll make the button more accessible to people who have turned off their graphics, or who are using screen-readers to read the page.

10. **Type *Home* in the Alternate Text box.**

    Now all you need to do is add a link to turn the graphic into a navigation button.

11. **Click the third Browse button (next to the When Clicked, Go To URL field)**

    The On Click, Go To URL dialog box opens, awaiting your selection of a Web page that will open when you click your rollover button.

    In this case, your button will link to the home page of the site.

12. **In the DWImages folder, find and double-click the file index.html.**

    At this point, the dialog box should look like Figure 5-19.

13. **Click OK.**

    You're back at your Web page document, where your new, rectangular button, called COSMO FARMER HOME, proudly appears.

    Congratulations! You've made your first rollover. To try it out for yourself, press F12 to preview the page in your Web browser. When you move your cursor over the button, the button should glow. When you click the button, it should open the home page.

14. Return to Dreamweaver.

Do so however you switch programs on your computer—by using the Windows taskbar or the Mac OS X Dock, for example.

If you like, you can finish up the navigation bar by adding the six other rollover images. Simply click next to the Home button, and then repeat steps 3–10 above. Here are the names, graphics, and pages you should use:

- Name: *features*
  Graphics: *features.gif* and *features_f2.gif*
  Alternate Text: *Features*
  Page to Link to: *features.html*

- Name: *projects*
  Graphics: *projects.gif* and *projects _f2.gif*
  Alternate Text: *Projects*
  age to Link to: *projects.html*

- Name: *horoscopes*
  Graphics: *horoscopes.gif* and *horoscopes _f2.gif*
  Alternate Text: *Horoscopes*
  Page to Link to: *horoscopes.html*

- Name: *quiz*
  Graphics: *quiz.gif* and *quiz _f2.gif*
  Alternate Text: *Quiz*
  Page to Link to: *quiz.html*

- Name: *reviews*
  Graphics: *reviews.gif* and *reviews _f2.gif*
  Alternate Text: *Reviews*
  Page to Link to: *reviews.html*

- Name: *classifieds*
  Graphics: *classifieds.gif* and *classifieds _f2.gif*
  Alternate Test: *Classifieds*
  Page to Link to: *classifieds.html*

When you're finished, choose File→Save, and then preview your new navigation bar (Figure 5-20) in your Web browser. Move your mouse over the buttons to see whether they change; click to jump to another page.

Tip: If you like, you can compare your work with the professionally completed version at *www.sawmac.com/ dwmx/tutorialsf/*.

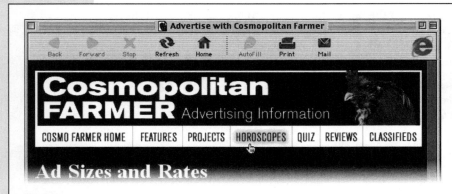

Figure 5-20:
Adding interactivity to your site using Dreamweaver's rollover objects is a breeze. No messy JavaScript programming to learn!

Part Two:
Building a Better Web Page

2

Tables

The Web was invented to help scientists exchange information, not to compete with the sophisticated design of newspapers, glossy magazines, or TV. Controlling a page's layout remains one of Web design's greatest challenges. The increasing expectations of the Web's users, however, have forced designers to push HTML into new territories, and the primary weapon in this battle has been the HTML <table> tag.

Though originally intended to display tables of data, today most Web designers use the <table> tag primarily for arranging elements on a Web page, as shown in Figure 6-1.

Figure 6-1:
Underneath many Web pages is an invisible skeleton that gives the page form and structure. HTML tables let you control the placement of graphics, text, and other elements on a Web page with accuracy. Without tables, Web content would simply flow from top to bottom on a page— boring!

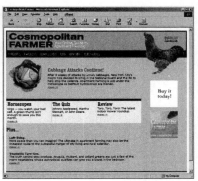

Of course, trying to force a round peg into a square hole isn't always easy, and creating complex designs with tables often requires clever tricks and workarounds. Fortunately, Dreamweaver MX's advanced table tools anticipate those needs and let you build beautiful table-based layouts. With these tools—and this book—you'll soon be gliding through HTML minefields along the path to attractive, effective Web pages. (If you can't wait to get started using Dreamweaver to create advanced layouts, jump to page 184 and follow the tutorial.)

Table Basics

A table is a grid of rows and columns that intersect to form *cells,* as shown in Figure 6-2. A cell acts like a mini document window, in which you can place images, text, and even additional tables. And because a cell can have a fixed width and height, you can place these items with precision. For example, you can build a table with three cells in a row and fill each cell with a single column of text, thus simulating the column layout of a print publication such as a newspaper.

Tables are also the key to building more complex designs. For instance, you can merge cells together to create larger cells that span columns or rows, nest tables for added versatility, and create flexible designs that expand to fit the browser window. (This should all sound familiar to anyone who's used, for example, the table tool in Microsoft Word.)

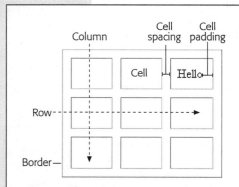

Figure 6-2:
Rows, columns, and cells make up a table. Cell spacing *specifies how many pixels of space appear between cells. Cell* padding, *on the other hand, is the space from the edge of a cell to the content inside the cell. It provides a margin between the four sides of the cell and the cell's content, as described on page 149.*

Since tables were not originally intended for layout purposes, many people find working with them counterintuitive. For starters, creating tables usually involves thinking in terms of rows and columns—but having to determine the number of rows and columns you'll need just to place an image at a particular position on a page is not a natural way to design.

That's why Dreamweaver offers two separate tools for achieving the same ends: *Standard view* and *Layout view.* Both of these tools are available from the Insert bar's Layout tab (see Figure 6-3). Layout view and Standard view both produce the same results—an underlying grid of tables and cells that let you control the layout of a page (see Figure 6-1)—and nearly the same HTML code. (Layout view adds a little extra code, HTML comments that help Dreamweaver display and manipulate tables).

But although they produce the same table structures, the two views offer different approaches to building them.

Note: When you first enter Layout view, the Getting Started in Layout View window may appear, offering a quick overview of the layout tools. Turn on "Don't show me this message again" to prevent this window from opening every time you switch views. Otherwise, it'll get old quick.

Figure 6-3:
The Layout Table and Layout Cell tools work in Layout view only; they're dimmed in Standard view. Likewise, the standard Table and Layer tools (see Chapter 12) are available only in Standard view.

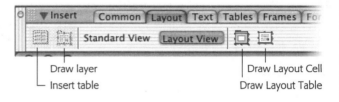

Draw layer
Insert table
Draw Layout Cell
Draw Layout Table

GEM IN THE ROUGH

Layers for Layout

As you can see by reading this chapter—and by building a few Web sites—tables aren't the most user-friendly method for creating layouts. Compared to the sophisticated tools you'll find in print-layout programs like PageMaker, Quark XPress, or InDesign, tables are a rather roundabout method for making pages look good.

The solution lies in the Layer tool, available under the Layout tab of the Insert bar. Layers—an example of Cascading Style Sheets in action (see Chapters 8 and 12)—are intended to be the perfect replacement for tables. Layers are box-like containers for text, graphics, or other content. Unlike table cells, layers can be placed anywhere on a page with pixel-perfect precision. A layer can even overlap another layer.

As with most promising technologies, however, layers don't have the foothold they should. Older Web browsers don't do an adequate job of displaying them. You may find what looks like a beautifully orchestrated graphic design in In-

ternet Explorer 5 for Macintosh crumbles to an unreadable mess in Netscape Navigator 4 for Windows. In fact, there are some designs you can do with tables that you simply can't yet duplicate using layers in *any* browser. Alas, such is a Web designer's lot.

Nevertheless, the future is bright for layers, and as more people out there grab the latest browsers, you may want to start experimenting with what is surely going to be the future of Web layout.

To get started, check out these sites dedicated to fighting the good fight for using CSS to design your pages:

CSS Layout Techniques: *http://www.glish.com/css/*

The Layout Reservoir: *http://www.bluerobot.com/web /layouts/*

Practical CSS Layout Tips: *http://www.alistapart.com/sto-ries/practicalcss/*

Standard view requires you to envision most of your design in advance, answering questions like: Where will items go on the page? How many table rows and columns will this require? What size should the table be? In essence, you need to know what the table will look like *before* beginning.

Layout view, on the other hand, lets you work at either the smallest level—a table cell—or the largest—a table. If you use the Cell drawing tool to draw a cell in the document window, Dreamweaver creates the underlying table structure. If you move the cell, resize it, or delete it, Dreamweaver rewrites the code to create a table to fit your design.

This flexibility makes the Layout view a very good place to start when creating a page's design. The changes that Dreamweaver can make to a table's HTML code in Layout view take fractions of a second, while comparable modifications in Standard view could take you much longer. Though it's certainly possible to revise a table's structure in Standard view, it can be more difficult (see page 163 for more on modifying tables).

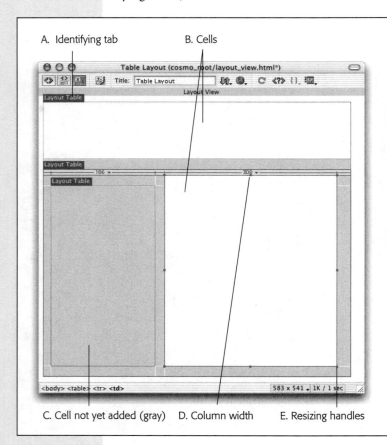

A. Identifying tab   B. Cells

C. Cell not yet added (gray)   D. Column width   E. Resizing handles

Figure 6-4:
Dreamweaver's Layout view may take some time to get used to. Tables are identified by small tabs on their top left corners labeled Layout Table (A). You can include more than one table per page, and even put a table inside of another table. Until you add cells to a table (white areas, B), you can't add text, graphics, or anything else. Areas of a table without cells have a gray background (C). The width of each column is shown along the top of the table (D). When you select a cell (E), eight resizing handles appear, which you can drag to change the dimensions of that cell.

Once the basic design of a page is complete, there's little difference between a page viewed in Layout view and a page viewed in Standard view. In fact, you may well switch to Standard view for good once the basic page design is complete. Standard view not only hides many of the visual aids included in Layout view (because they sometimes obscure text, images, and other elements on a page), but also lets you access tools that are unavailable in Layout view, such as the basic Table object and Layer tool. Furthermore, you can set up some properties of a table, like the background image, *only* in Standard view.

The first part of this chapter introduces the Layout view and its associated drawing tools; for a tour of Standard view and its techniques, see page 158. Just keep in mind that, whichever approach you take, you're still only creating basic HTML tables.

Layout View

In Layout view, you can start creating a table-based design using either of the two drawing tools—the Layout Cell drawing tool or the Layout Table drawing tool. Both tools await on the Layout tab of the Insert bar (see Figure 6-3).

How to Draw a Table in Layout View

Drawing a table is as simple as dragging. Click the Layout Table tool in the Insert bar's Layout tab (see Figure 6-3). The cursor changes to a + sign when you move it over the document window. Drag diagonally to create a rectangular box—the outline of the table. When you release the mouse button, a gray box appears, complete with green borders and a tab in the upper left labeled Layout Table (see Figure 6-4).

Note: Although Dreamweaver uses the words Layout Table and Layout Cell, they're still just HTML tables and cells. In other words, a Layout Table is simply a table viewed in Layout view, and a Layout Cell is just a table cell viewed in Layout view. In Standard view, the same items are just called tables and cells. In this book, you'll see the terms Layout Cell and Layout Table appear when referring to actions you perform while in Layout view.

This Layout Table tool may be a bit confusing until you learn some of Dreamweaver's rules for drawing tables:

- If the document is blank when you draw a table, the table appears in the upper-left corner of the page.

- You can't draw a table over anything that's already on the page. If you move the Table tool over text, the cursor changes to a forbidden (⊘) symbol, and nothing happens when you drag. If there's anything on the page—text, images, tables, even an empty paragraph—you must move the cursor to the bottom of the page in order to draw a table. For this reason, it's usually best to start with a blank document, draw your tables and cells, and only then add content.

- Tables can't overlap. The Table tool won't create a table if you drag over the edge of an existing one.

- You can draw a Layout Table *inside* another Layout Table, a technique called nesting tables (see page 178). However, you can only draw the second table inside the gray area of the Layout Table. In other words, you can't draw a Layout *Table* inside a Layout *Cell*.

Tip: To draw a number of tables one after another, without having to keep reselecting the Table tool, hold down the Ctrl (⌘) key when drawing a table. The Table tool remains selected between drags.

Tables are made of rows and columns, a structure Dreamweaver helps maintain by making the edges of tables snap against nearby tables or cells as you draw. If the cursor comes within eight pixels of the edge of a cell or another table, the table edge you're drawing snaps to the other table or cell's edge. This behavior helps you accurately align the borders of your tables. But if it bothers you, turn this snapping feature off by pressing the Alt (Option) key as you draw the table.

Layout Table Properties

After drawing a Layout Table, you'll see a rectangular gray square in the document window. A tab labeled Layout Table appears in the upper-left corner of the table indicating the table's width, in pixels, at the top. The Property inspector lists additional properties, such as table height, width, and background color (see Figure 6-5).

Figure 6-5:
These table controls are described in the following pages.

Table dimensions

The width and height of the table appear in the Property inspector. You can adjust these values by typing new pixel-measurement values in the Fixed and Height fields. Alternatively, to resize a table, you can drag one of the three handles that appear on the bottom edge, lower-right corner, and right edge of the table in the document window.

Instead of having a fixed width, a table can automatically adjust to fit the available space of your visitor's browser window. To activate this feature, click the Autostretch radio button in the Property inspector. (See page 153 for full detail on flexible layouts.)

Tip: If you find the table tabs that appear at the top of a layout table distracting, you can turn them off. Choose View→Table View and turn off the Show Layout Table Tabs option.

Background color

You can give your table a background color that's independent of the page color. To pick a background color, click the Bg color box in the Property inspector and select from the pop-up palette. (You can actually select any color on your screen using the eyedropper; see page 34.)

After you click, you may wonder if Dreamweaver has gone colorblind—the table's color doesn't match the color you selected. Tables in Layout view have a light gray background to indicate empty areas of the table (places where no cells have yet been drawn). Dreamweaver *mixes* this gray with the color you selected, creating a muddy blend. That gray is just for showing you the table's boundaries in Dreamweaver and doesn't appear in a Web browser.

Tip: You can modify this color. Choose Edit→Preferences (Dreamweaver→Preferences in Mac OS X) and click the Layout View category. You can modify colors for the table and cell outlines as well as the cell highlight and table background colors.

Cell padding and Cell spacing

When you add a background color to the cells in a table, you may sometimes want to create a visual gap between them, like the grout between tiles (but without the mold). To add this kind of space between cells in a table (see Figure 6-2), type a pixel value in the CellSpace field.

To add margins around all four edges inside a cell, type a pixel value in the CellPad field. This space keeps the text or graphics *inside* a cell from touching the edges of the cell. By default, both the CellSpace and CellPad values are set to 0, which is appropriate for a design that requires graphics to meet at the edges of cells.

Notice, for example, that the chicken in Figure 6-1 is actually made of four different graphics, each in its own cell. Chopping up a graphic in this way is a typical Web-design trick that lends special flexibility. In Figure 6-1, for example, the chicken graphic appears to jut straight down into the text area of the Web page—a feat that would be impossible if the chicken were a single rectangular image. In this case, if either the Cell Space or CellPad were set above 0, there would be visible gaps between the segments of the image.

How to Draw a Layout Cell

With the Layout Cell drawing tool, you can add cells to any Layout Table on the page. However, you don't need to draw a table before using the Cell drawing tool. In fact, many people use the Cell tool to sketch out the content areas of their pages, drawing boxes freehand on the screen and letting Dreamweaver create the rest of the table to fit.

For example, suppose you have a banner ad that must be placed in the upper-right corner of the page. First, you could select the Cell tool in the Layout tab of the Insert bar (see Figure 6-3); the cursor changes to a + sign when it's over an empty area of a

Layout Table or an empty area of the document window. You create a new cell just by dragging diagonally in the document window or inside an existing Layout Table. (If you draw a cell inside an existing Layout Table, Dreamweaver creates a rectangular cell. If you draw a cell in an empty document window, Dreamweaver creates a cell *and* a Layout Table that encloses it.)

Because tables are organized like a grid, Dreamweaver must organize cells in rows and columns. To indicate this underlying grid, Dreamweaver displays white lines projecting from the sides of a cell to indicate the rows and columns of the table (see Figure 6-6). In addition, as you add more cells to a table, the cursor snaps to these guidelines, as well as to table edges, when it's eight pixels away or closer. This snapping feature helps you accurately align the edges of your cells. Once again, you can temporarily override this feature, gaining complete dragging freedom, by pressing Alt (Option) as you draw the cell.

Tip: After drawing a cell, the insertion point blinks patiently inside the newly created cell, awaiting the text or graphics you're about to type, paste, or import. Creating another cell requires another click on the Layout Cell tool.

As in the previous Tip, however, you can draw several cells in sequence without having to reclick the Layout Cell tool after each just by pressing the Ctrl (⌘) key while drawing a cell. The Layout Cell tool remains selected when you release the mouse, ready to draw another cell.

As with Layout Tables, there are some limitations to drawing Layout Cells:

- You can't draw a cell over already existing content. If you move the Cell tool over text, images, or other content on a page, the cursor changes to a ⃠ symbol and won't draw over that area.

- Cells can't overlap each other.

- You can't draw a cell within a cell.

Layout Cell Properties

Like a table, a cell has its own width and height, and can have its own background color. You set these properties in the Property inspector.

To see the properties for a Layout Cell, first select it by clicking any highlighted edge of the cell (the edges appear highlighted in red when your cursor approaches). Resize handles appear around the cell, and the Property inspector displays its attributes (see Figure 6-6).

Alignment

By default, content added to a Layout Cell aligns with the left side of the cell, and rises to the top of the cell vertically. You can change either or both of these alignment options by setting the horizontal and vertical properties of the cell (see Figure 6-6).

To align the content horizontally inside a cell, select the cell, and then choose an alignment option from the Horz (Horizontal) pop-up menu in the Property inspector (see Figure 6-7):

- The **Left** and **Right** options align a cell's contents with its left or right walls. (Since Left is the default, choosing Left here only adds unnecessary code to your page.)

- The **Center** option centers the cell contents between the left and right walls of the cell.

The vertical alignment property works the same way; use the Vert (Vertical) pop-up menu of the Property inspector:

- The **Top** and **Bottom** options makes the cell contents rest against the cell's top or bottom edge, respectively.

- The **Middle** option makes the cell contents float in the vertical center of the cell. (This is the default behavior of a cell. Choosing Default instead will give the same results without adding any additional code.)

- The **Baseline** option aligns the bottom of the first line of text in the cell with the baseline of text in all the other cells in the row (see Figure 6-7).

Figure 6-6:
Turning on No Wrap (at the right of the Property inspector) prevents the contents of a cell from wrapping to the next line, usually with unattractive results. If you insert a long sentence into a cell that has the No Wrap setting, the cell grows to fit the entire length of the sentence. Keep No Wrap turned off to avoid such wildly expanding cells.

Moving and Resizing Layout Cells and Layout Tables

Once you've drawn cells and tables, you're not locked into that one design. Dreamweaver's Layout view provides several ways to adjust the size and position of cells and tables. As usual, Dreamweaver makes a pleasant task out of a normally time-consuming and error-prone job.

To move a cell, drag one of its edges. (Avoid grabbing one of the eight resize handles, however, or you'll change the cell's size instead of move it.) Dreamweaver lets you move the cell anywhere within the table. However, you can't move it outside of its Layout Table, into or overlapping another cell, or into another Layout Table. If you try, Dreamweaver displays the ⊘ symbol.

Tip: You can nudge a selected cell by 1 pixel at a time by pressing the arrow keys. Hold down the Shift key, too, to nudge the cell 10 pixels per press of the arrow key.

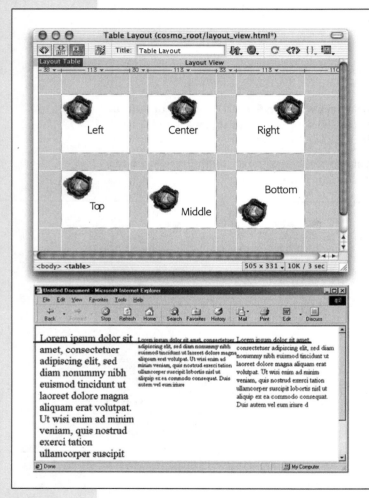

Figure 6-7:
Top: A cell's horizontal (top row) and vertical alignment properties (bottom row) affect how contents are aligned within a cell.

Bottom: The baseline option aligns the bottom of the first line of text in one cell with the other cells in the row. In other words, the first line of text in each cell rests on an invisible line called the baseline—represented in this figure by the black underline.

Once you've moved the cell, Dreamweaver redraws the underlying table to accommodate this change.

Resizing a table or cell is easy: For numerical precision, select the table or cell and use the Property inspector to adjust the Width and Height values. You can also resize a table or cell by dragging the handles that appear when you select it. However, since cells can't overlap each other or extend outside of a table, you can't drag the edge of a cell over another cell or out of a table.

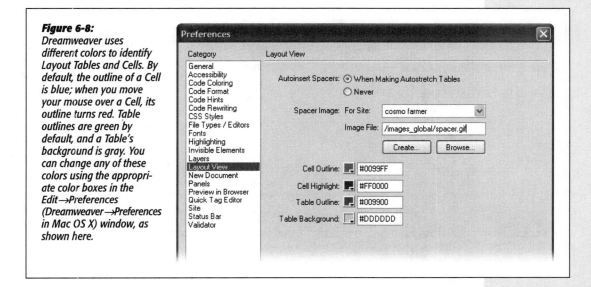

Figure 6-8:
Dreamweaver uses different colors to identify Layout Tables and Cells. By default, the outline of a Cell is blue; when you move your mouse over a Cell, its outline turns red. Table outlines are green by default, and a Table's background is gray. You can change any of these colors using the appropriate color boxes in the Edit→Preferences (Dreamweaver→Preferences in Mac OS X) window, as shown here.

Building Flexible Page Layouts in Layout View

When you set a fixed width for a Layout Table, as described on page 148, it remains the same width regardless of your visitor's browser window size. This level of certainty and control is great for making sure elements go where you want them. On the other hand, fixed-width designs leave large areas of empty space when viewed on larger monitors (see Figure 6-9 for an example).

One solution is to build flexible tables with Dreamweaver's Autostretch option. Flexible tables, sometimes called *liquid HTML,* expand or shrink to fit a browser window's available display area. In this way, your design can accommodate 15-inch *and* 21-inch monitors. (Imagine if newspapers grew or shrank to fit a reader's arm span!)

Creating a flexible-width table

Instead of being a certain number of pixels wide, a flexible table always fills the entire window. To achieve this effect, you must set *one* column in the table to Autostretch; that column will expand to fill the page. For instance, in the example in Figure 6-9, the column containing the headline "Pisces" expands, while the left-hand column, containing the navigation bar, remains a fixed width.

To create a flexible column, click the down-pointing triangle next to the pixel width number in the column header (see Figure 6-10) and choose Make Column Autostretch from the contextual menu. You can also select the *cell* you wish to make flexible and click the Autostretch button on the Property inspector. (Although you can also create a flexible table by selecting the *table* and setting its width to Autostretch, it's not necessary to do so. Dreamweaver automatically sets it to Autostretch when you create a flexible column.)

Figure 6-9:
Flexible table widths provide one solution to Web designers' greatest challenge: designing pages for different monitor and window sizes. A layout that uses a fixed width often has unwanted and distracting white space when viewed on larger monitors.

The top two images, for example, show the same fixed-width table viewed on a small screen (left) and a wider one (right). Flexible tables, on the other hand, can shrink or grow to fit the browser window, as shown in the bottom two images.

If you want to change the column back to a fixed width size, use the same menu, shown in Figure 6-10, to choose Make Column Fixed Width.

Adding spacer images

In order for the Autostretch function to work, Dreamweaver uses a transparent image—an actual, see-through GIF file called a *spacer*—to control the spacing of the columns that *don't* stretch.

Understanding why Dreamweaver adds these invisible spacer images requires some understanding of the way it "thinks." When you ask it to make the autostretch column grow as necessary to fill a browser window, Dreamweaver uses a little trick. It sets the column's width to *100 percent*. In other words, the column attempts to take up *all* the space available, even space used by other columns. This greedy behavior, of course, would ordinarily squish the table's other columns into hyper-thinness. That's why Dreamweaver inserts a spacer image (of the width you've specified) into each *fixed*-width column. The image acts like a steel beam across the walls of the fixed-width column, reinforcing it and preventing it from shrinking smaller than the size of the spacer image (see "Do the math" on page 172).

The first time you make a column an autostretcher, Dreamweaver opens a Choose Spacer Image dialog box. It offers you three choices:

- **Create a spacer image file.** If you choose this option, Dreamweaver will create a 1-pixel by 1-pixel, transparent GIF image and prompt you to name the file and save it into any folder of your Web site.

- **Use an existing spacer image file.** If you're already using a 1-pixel by 1-pixel transparent GIF (a standard Web-design tool), choose this option. Dreamweaver then lets you browse to and select the GIF file in your site folder. (To learn one use for such an image, see "Shrinking Down to a Pixel" on page 173.)

- **Don't use spacer images for autostretch tables.** This is not a wise choice if you want to use the Autostretch feature; it also doesn't work in Netscape 4. Most likely, your fixed width columns will appear much smaller than you intended.

Figure 6-10:
If you see two numbers in the column header of a Layout Table—like this "516" (495)—the first is the actual width of the cell as it appears on the screen. The second is the width specified in the HTML for that cell. You probably inserted something into a fixed-width cell that's wider than the cell itself. To resize the column to the larger size, choose Make Cell Widths Consistent from the column header menu.

Note: If you've used this feature in Dreamweaver 4, you may notice one nice change in MX. You can now use document-relative paths for spacer images. After you've set the spacer image for the site, Dreamweaver continues to use that file whenever you need one. You can select a different file at any time from the Edit→Preferences→Layout view tab (Dreamweaver MX→Preferences→Layout view in Mac OS X). (See Figure 6-8).

While Dreamweaver automatically inserts spacer GIFs, you can also add them manually by choosing Add Spacer Image from the column header menu (see Figure 6-10). This command is grayed out if you turned on the "Don't use spacer images" option in the Choose Spacer Image dialog box.

Removing spacer images

To remove a spacer image from a column, choose Remove Spacer Image from the column header menu. You can also remove *all* of the spacer images on a page by choosing Remove All Spacer Images from the column header menu, or by clicking the Remove Spacer Images button on the Property inspector when a table is selected (see Figure 6-5).

Using a Tracing Image

Layout mode lets you draw your designs directly in the document window, which is a wonderful feature. However, unless you can visualize the layout you want, you may feel that you're just aimlessly drawing boxes on a blank canvas.

Dreamweaver's Tracing Image feature helps you find your way around the dreaded blank screen. With it, you can import a graphic representation of your finished page design—a sketch you've created in a more art-oriented program like Fireworks or Photoshop—and use it as a pattern for tracing the table and cells of your page. In fact, it's very common in the Web-design biz to work up, in a program like Photoshop, a graphic that *looks* like a finished Web page—but it's one giant image, without individual buttons, tables, or editable text (see Figure 6-11).

To add a tracing image to your page, choose Modify→Page Properties (or choose View→Tracing Image→Load); the Page Properties dialog box opens (see Figure 6-11). Click the Browse button near the bottom of the window (next to the Tracing Image field); find and open a GIF, JPEG, or PNG file to use as the background image.

WORKAROUND WORKSHOP

Where Does the Spacer Image Go?

When inserting a transparent, 1-pixel-tall spacer image in a column, Dreamweaver creates a new table row at the bottom of the table. The spacer image is inserted in each fixed-width cell in that row.

Keep this behavior in mind if you try to place one table on top of another. If the two tables need to touch seamlessly—for example, if they share a color that needs to appear connected—that 1-pixel tall row created by the spacer images creates a 1-pixel gap between the two tables. To make matters worse, if you set one column to Autostretch, the row created at the bottom of the table is actually about 15 pixels tall! Quite a large gap.

Unfortunately, you can't solve this dilemma in Dreamweaver's visually oriented Design view. You must delve into the HTML code. After consulting Chapter 9, choose View→Code to open Dreamweaver's Code view.

You'll need to locate the closing </table> tag for the of-fending autostretch table. Directly above that, you'll find a single table row composed of an opening <tr> tag, several lines of <td> (table data or cells) tags, and a closing </tr> tag. First, looking for the <td> tag that contains the following code: . This is the HTML code for a nonbreaking space. Delete . Next, select the entire row, cut it, and paste it directly after the *opening* <table> tag. This essentially moves that bottom row (containing the spacer) to the *top,* and allows the table to rest seamlessly on any table directly below it.

And what if you also want to prevent a gap at *both* the top and the bottom of an autostretch table? Go to the page's HTML source code and locate the last row of the table, the one containing only spacer images. Delete it. Then, back in Design view (View→Design), click inside one cell in each fixed width column, insert a spacer image (see page 154), and set its width to match the desired width of that column. (These cells probably contain text or images. Insert the spacer image *after* any content in the cell.)

Last row — Spacer images

Now use the Image Transparency slider shown in Figure 6-11. To fade the image into the background of the page, move the slider toward the transparent setting, making it easier to distinguish between the tracing image and the actual content on the Web page.

When you click OK, you return to your Web page with the tracing image in place. (The tracing image appears only in Dreamweaver, never on the Web.)

Figure 6-11:
Top: You can hide or show the tracing image using the View Options menu icon at the top of the document window.

Bottom: In addition to setting the title and color of your page, the Page Properties window lets you add a tracing image to your document and fade it into the background as much as you want. In this example, the tracing image represents a Horoscopes page for the Cosmopolitan Farmer Web site. As you can see by the Transparency slider, it's been faded over 50 percent into the background of the page.

Tracing image

Tracing image file

Transparency slider

Hiding a tracing image

If you want to temporarily hide a tracing image, choose Tracing Image in the toolbar's View Options menu (shown at top in Figure 6-11); choose the same command again to show it. (The long way: Choose View→Tracing Image and turn off the Show option.)

Moving a tracing image

When you first select a tracing image, it appears against the top and left margins, if you've specified them (see page 33, step 10). If you didn't specify margins, Dreamweaver places the tracing image several pixels from the left and top edges of the document window—just where it would put text or graphics into a new Web page.

You can't just drag the tracing image elsewhere on the page. If you need it anywhere other than the upper-left corner, choose View→Tracing Image→Adjust Position. Type pixel values in the X and Y fields in the Adjust Tracing Image dialog box. (The X value is the distance from the left edge, and the Y value is the distance from the top edge.)

You can also align the tracing image to a selected object on the page, which comes in handy when you want to use a tracing image to create a portion of a Web page—a footer or sidebar element, for example. Select the element on the page and then choose View→Tracing Image→Align with Selection. The tracing image's upper-left corner aligns with the upper-left corner of the selected element. (In the case of a table cell, however, Dreamweaver isn't so smart. It aligns the tracing image with the top-left corner of the table containing the cell, not the cell itself.)

Note: To reset the tracing image to the upper-left corner of the page, choose View→Tracing Image→Reset Position. Unfortunately, this command doesn't place the image in its original position, at the margins of the page; it merely places it at the very corner (the 0,0 position) of the document window. You'll probably need to adjust it by choosing View→Tracing Image→Adjust Position. (To restore the default values, use 8 pixels along the X axis and 11 pixels along the Y axis.)

Once you've finished building the Web page, it's a good idea to remove the tracing image. Not only is it distracting when you view the page in Dreamweaver, but Dreamweaver introduces extra lines of Dreamweaver-specific HTML to accommodate it. These bandwidth-hogging extra bytes are unnecessary once the page is complete.

To remove a tracing image from a page, open the Page Properties dialog box once again, and then select and delete the file name in the Tracing Image field.

Tip: Tracing images aren't just for the Layout view. You can use a tracing image anytime—a handy feature when you're using Dreamweaver's Layers tools (see Chapter 12).

Inserting a Table in Standard View

While the Layout view is a great way to lay out a page, it can't do everything. You can't, for instance, add a background image to a table or cell in Layout view. Nor can you add color to a row of cells, or even insert a simple table for displaying data. Likewise, if you're already comfortable visualizing table-based layouts in your head (or if you find the Layout tools cumbersome), you may prefer the basic approach offered by the Table drawing object. In fact, even if you're sold on the Layout view, it's a good idea to familiarize yourself with these steps so that you can troubleshoot tables more easily.

To insert a table, first switch to Standard view by clicking the Standard View button on the Layout tab of the Insert bar (see Figure 6-3) or by choosing View→Table View→Standard View. Then proceed as follows.

1. **Place the insertion point in the document window where you'd like to insert a table.**

   You can add a table anywhere you can add graphics or text. You can even add a table to another table, by clicking inside a table cell.

2. **Choose Insert→Table.**

   You can also click the Table button on the Insert bar. It appears under both the Common tab and the Layout tab. You can also press Ctrl+Alt+T (Option-⌘-T). Either way, the Insert Table dialog box opens (see Figure 6-12).

3. **Using the Rows and Columns fields, specify how many rows and columns you want your table to have.**

   If you're using the table for layout purposes, you might only want two or three columns. If you plan to create a spreadsheet, you could create many rows or columns. (Don't panic about your estimate, since you can always add or remove rows or columns later.)

4. **Type the amount of cell padding, in pixels, you want for the table.**

   Cell padding is the margin—the space from the edge of a cell to its contents (see Figure 6-2). Unfortunately, this property applies to *every* cell in a table. You can't add margins to an individual cell in a table unless you use Cascading Style Sheets as described on page 259.

5. **Type the amount of cell spacing, in pixels, that you want for the table.**

   Cell spacing specifies how many pixels of space separate one cell from another (see Figure 6-2). Again, this property applies to every cell in a table. (Note that leaving these fields empty isn't the same as setting them to zero; see Figure 6-12.)

6. **Using the Width field, specify how wide you want the table to be (in units that you specify using the pop-up menu).**

   Tables can have either a specified, fixed minimum width, or they can take up a specified percentage of the space available on the page. To set a fixed width, choose Pixels as the unit of measurement and type a pixel amount in the Width field. Fixed-width tables remain the same size regardless of size of the browser window.

   Percentage widths let tables grow or shrink relative to the space available. In other words, the size of a table that's 100 percent wide stretches all the way across your visitor's browser window, no matter how wide or narrow. (You achieve a similar effect with the Autostretch feature in Layout view, as described on page 153.)

Note: Due to differences in the way browsers interpret HTML, the exact pixel dimension of percentage-based tables may differ from browser to browser. In some cases, a Web browser leaves room at the right edge of the browser window for scroll bars—even if the page isn't long enough to require scroll bars!

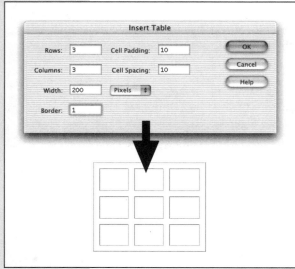

Figure 6-12:
The Insert Table dialog box lets you define the properties of the table. Leaving the Cell Padding and Cell Spacing fields empty isn't the same as setting them to 0. If these properties are empty, most Web browsers insert 1 pixel of cell padding and 2 pixels of cell spacing. If you notice unwanted gaps between cells in a table or between content in a table and the cell's edges, empty settings here are the most likely culprit. To truly leave zero space, set Cell Padding and Cell Spacing to 0. (Dreamweaver remembers the settings you use. When you use the Insert Table dialog box again, it starts with the same settings you entered previously.)

UP TO SPEED

Accessible Tables

Some table properties, like the table header described on page 167, can help make Web pages more accessible to people with disabilities. Dreamweaver MX includes the ability to add several accessibility elements to tables.

Choose Edit→Preferences (Dreamweaver→Preferences in Mac OS X) to open the Preferences window, and then select the Accessibility category. Turn on the Tables checkbox. With this option on, the box shown here appears after you insert a table in Standard view (it doesn't appear when creating tables in Layout view).

Use this feature when creating full tables of data, spreadsheet style, not when using tables to lay out the design of a page. Type information identifying the table in the Caption box; it will appear above the table on the page. From the Align pop-up menu, choose how to align the caption over the table. Use the Summary box to provide a detailed explanation of the table. Finally, the header option inserts a <th> tag, used to indicate a heading within a table. You could, for example, specify a heading that announces the type of information in a column or row.

For more information on these options, and to get a complete rundown on table accessibility, visit this page: *www.w3.org/TR/WCAG10-HTML-TECHS/#tables.*

7. Type a number, in pixels, for the border.

   If you don't want a border, type *0*. Dreamweaver uses dotted lines to help you identify rows, columns, and cells whose border is 0. (The dotted line won't appear on the finished Web page.)

8. **Click OK to insert the table.**

Once you've added a table to a page, you can begin filling the table's cells. A cell works like a small document window; you can click inside it and add text, images, and links using the techniques you've already learned. You can even insert a table inside of a cell (see page 178).

To move the insertion point from one cell to the next, press Tab. When you reach the last cell in a row, the Tab key moves the insertion point to the first cell in the row below. And if the insertion point is in the last *cell* of the last row, pressing Tab creates a new row at the bottom of the table.

Shift-Tab moves the cursor in the *opposite* direction—from the current cell to a cell to the left.

Selecting Parts of a Table in Standard View

Tables and their cells have independent properties. For example, a table and a cell can have different background colors. But before you can change any of these properties, you must first *select* the tables, rows, columns, or cells you want to affect.

Selecting a Table

There are a number of ways to select a table in the document window:

- Click the upper-left corner of the table, or anywhere on the bottom edge of the table. (Be careful using the latter technique, however. It's easy to accidentally *drag* the border, resetting the height of the table in the process.)

- Click anywhere inside the table, and then select the <table> tag in the document window's status bar (see page 19 to learn about the tag selector).

- Click anywhere inside the table, and then choose Modify→Table→Select Table.

- Right-click (Control-click) inside a table, and then choose Table→Select Table from the contextual menu.

- If the insertion point is in any cell inside the table, pressing Ctrl+A twice selects the table.

Once selected, a table appears with a thick black border and three tiny, square resize handles—at the right edge, bottom edge, and lower-right corner.

Selecting Rows or Columns

You can also select an entire row or column of cells by using one of the following procedures:

• Move the cursor to the left edge of a row, or the top edge of a column. When it changes to a right- or down-pointing arrow, click (see Figure 6-13).

• Click a cell at either end of a row, or the first or last cell of a column, and then drag across the cells in the row or column to select them.

• Click any cell in the row you wish to select, and then click the <tr> tag in the tag selector. (The <tr> tag is how HTML indicates a table row—this method doesn't work for columns.)

When a cell is selected, it has a dark border around it. When multiple cells are selected, each cell has a dark border (see Figure 6-13).

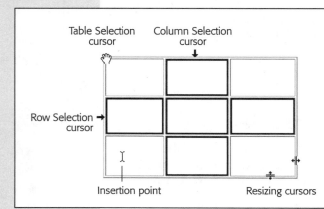

Figure 6-13:
When you're working with tables, the cursor can take on many different roles. The Table selection cursor lets you select the entire table (in Windows, this looks like a compass). When the cursor turns into an arrow (pointing either down or to the right), you can click to select a column or row of cells. The insertion-point cursor lets you click to insert content into a cell. When you pass the cursor over a resize handle, it becomes a resize icon, which you can drag to resize rows, columns, or the entire table.

Selecting Cells

To select one or more cells:

• Drag over adjoining cells. A solid black border appears around a cell when it's selected.

• To select several cells that aren't necessarily adjacent, Ctrl-click (⌘-click) them one at a time. (You can also Ctrl-click (⌘-click) an already selected cell to deselect it.)

• Click a cell, then Shift-click another cell. Your two clicks form diagonally opposite corners of an imaginary rectangle; Dreamweaver highlights all cells within it.

• Use the tag selector (page 19) to select a cell. Click inside the cell you wish to select, and then click the <td> tag in the tag selector. (The <td> tag stands for Table Data, which is how the HTML language refers to a cell.)

• If the insertion point is inside the cell you wish to select, press Ctrl+A.

Formatting Tables

When you first insert a table, you set the number of rows and columns, as well as the table's cell padding, cell spacing, width, and borders. You're not stuck, however, with the properties you first give the table. You can change any or all of these properties, and set a few additional ones, using the Property inspector.

When you select a table in Standard view, the Property inspector changes to reflect that table's settings (see Figure 6-14). You can adjust the table by entering different values for height, width, rows, columns, and so on in the appropriate fields.

In addition, the Property inspector lets you set alignment options and add colors or a background image, as described next.

Aligning Tables

In the normal flow of a Web page, a table acts like a paragraph, header, or any other block-level element. It's aligned to the left of the page, with other elements placed either above it or below it.

But you can make several useful changes to the way a table interacts with the text and other elements around it. After selecting the table, use one of the three alignment options in the pop-up menu at the right of the Property inspector:

- The **Left** and **Right** options align the table with the left or right page margins. Anything you then add to the page, including paragraphs, images, or other tables, wraps around the right or left side of the table.

- The **Center** option makes the table sit in the center of the page, interrupting the flow of the elements around it. Nothing wraps around the table.

Clearing Height and Width Values

Six tools hide behind the obscure-looking buttons in the bottom half of the Property inspector (see Figure 6-14).

- Clicking the Clear Height Values button removes the height properties of the table and each cell. Doing so doesn't set the heights to zero; it simply deletes the property altogether.

- Clicking the Clear Width Values button accomplishes the same purpose for the width properties of a table and its cells (see "Setting Cell Dimensions" on page 170).

When creating complex table designs, it's easy to get yourself into a situation where width and height measurements conflict and produce unreliable results. For example, it's possible to set one cell to 300 pixels wide, and later set another cell *in the same column* to 400 pixels wide. Since a Web browser can't do both (how can one column be both 300 *and* 400 pixels wide?), you'll get unpredictable results.

In tables with many cells, these kinds of problems are tough to ferret out. That's when you'll find these timesaving tools handy. You can delete the width and height measurements and start from scratch (see "Tips for Surviving Table Making" on page 170).

Four additional buttons let you convert pixel-based measurements to percentage measurements and vice versa. In other words, if a table is 600 pixels wide, and you click the Convert Widths to Percentages button, Dreamweaver assigns percentages to the table and each cell whose width is specified using pixels.

These percentages depend on how much of the document window your table takes up when you click the button. If the document window is 1200 pixels wide, that 600-pixel-wide table changes to a 50 percent width. Because you'll rarely do this, don't waste your brain cells memorizing such tools. (See "Resizing a Table" on the facing page.)

Clear width values —
Convert widths to pixels
Convert widths to percentages

Convert height to percentages
Clear height values —
Convert height to pixels

Figure 6-14:
When you select a table, you can do everything from adjusting its basic structure to fine-tuning (bottom row) its appearance in the Property inspector.

Decorating a Table

To spruce up a table, you can add color to its background and borders, and even add a background image. As usual in Dreamweaver, you make these changes in the Property inspector. First select the table (page 161), then click the appropriate box in the Property inspector—Bg color (background) or Brdr color (border)—and select a color from the color palette. (See page 34 for more on choosing colors in Dreamweaver.)

FREQUENTLY ASKED QUESTIONS

Floating Images

I want to create a Web page with a single image that floats right in the middle of a browser window, no matter what size the window is on the screen. What's the secret?

This little trick is a snap, and it's ideal for giving your Web site an introductory or splash screen page. Insert a one-row, one-column table into an empty document; make sure it has no cell padding, cell spacing, or border. Set the width of the table to *100%* and the height to *100%*.

Now set the horizontal alignment of the cell to Center, and the vertical alignment to Middle. Insert an image into the cell.

When visitors load the Web page, no matter what size their browser window is, the table fills the space, and the image floats right in the middle. Of course, you can put anything you want into the cell, including text or even another, smaller table.

To add a graphic image to the background of a selected table, click the folder icon next to the Bg field in the Property inspector. Browse to and open an image in your Web site folder; it appears immediately as a background image for the selected table.

Note: Be careful with these properties. Background images for tables work only in 4.0 or later browsers. Early versions simply ignore this property and display no image.

Resizing a Table

While you define the width and height of a table when you first insert it, you can always change your mind and modify the width or height later. To do so, first select the table, and then take either of these steps:

- Type a value into the W (width) or H (height) box on the Property inspector and choose a unit of measurement from the pop-up menu—either pixels or percentages.

- Drag one of the three resize handles on the right edge, bottom edge, or right corner of the table. The corner resize handle adjusts the height and width of the table simultaneously.

You can also, in theory, convert a table from a fixed unit of measurement, such as pixels, to the stretchy, percentage-style width setting—or vice versa—using four buttons at the bottom of the Property inspector (see Figure 6-14).

These options depend on the size of the current document window in Dreamweaver. For example, suppose the document window is 700 pixels wide, and you've inserted a table that's 100 percent wide. Clicking the Convert Widths to Pixels button sets the table's width to around 700 pixels (the exact value depends on the margins of the page). However, if your document window were 500 pixels wide, clicking the same button would produce a fixed-width table around 500 pixels wide. Two buttons let you control this separately for the height and width of the table and its cells (see Figure 6-14).

POWER USERS' CLINIC

The Dawn of Columns

As far as the standard HTML language is concerned, there really isn't any such entity as a column. Tables are created with the <table> tag, rows with the <tr> tag, and cells with the <td> tag—but there's no column tag. Dreamweaver calculates the columns based on the number of cells in a row. If there are 7 rows in a table, each with 4 cells, then the table has 4 columns. In other words, the number of cells in each row *determines* the number of columns.

But times are changing. Two new tags introduced in HTML 4—the <colgroup> and <col> tags—let you control various attributes of columns in a table. At present, not all Web browsers understand these tags, and Dreamweaver provides no easy way to add them. You can find out more about them, however, in Dreamweaver's built-in HTML reference (see page 288).

The Convert Width to Percentages buttons take the opposite tack. They set the width or height of a table and its cells to percentages based on the amount of the document window's width and height they cover at the moment. The bigger the window, the smaller the percentage.

Because the effects of these buttons depend upon the size of the document window, you'll find yourself rarely, if ever, using these two tools.

Modifying Cell and Row Properties in Standard View

Cells have their own properties, separate from the properties of the table itself. So do table *rows*—but not columns (see the box on page 165).

When you click inside of a cell, the top half of the Property inspector displays the cell's text formatting properties; the bottom half shows the properties for that particular cell (see Figure 6-15).

A cell is selected

Background color   Background image   Border color

A row is selected   Row formatting   Cell formatting   Row formatting

Figure 6-15:
Rows have their own distinct properties that you can set independently of a cell. For example, a row can have its own, independent background color and border color. (However, not all of the properties visible in the inspector apply to a row. When a row is selected, the Width, Height, No Wrap, and Header options affect the individual cells in the row.)

Alignment Properties

At the outset, a cell's contents hug the left wall of the cell and float halfway between the top and bottom of the cell. After selecting a row, a cell, or several cells, you can change these alignments using the Property inspector. For example, the Horz (Horizontal) pop-up menu in the Property inspector (see Figure 6-15) offers Left, Center, Right, and Default alignment options. (Default produces the same effect as Center without adding any extra HTML code.)

Note that these options are distinct from the *paragraph* alignment options discussed in Chapter 3. In fact, you can mix and match the two. Suppose, for example, that you have a table cell containing four paragraphs. You want all but one paragraph to be center aligned; you want the last paragraph to be right aligned. To do so, you could set the alignment of the *cell* to Center, then select just the last paragraph and set its alignment to Right. The paragraph's alignment overrides the alignment applied by the cell.

You can set the vertical alignment property in the same manner. Select the cells and then use one of the five options available in the Vert (Vertical) pop-up menu of the Property inspector: Default (the same as Middle), Top, Middle, Bottom, or Baseline.

(The Baseline option aligns the bottom of the first line of text in the cell to the baseline of text in all the other cells in the row. This option works only in Netscape browsers, so avoid it if you want your Web pages to look the same on all browsers.)

Table Header

If you're actually using a table for its intended purpose—to display a grid of information—you'll find the *Header* property useful. It converts the HTML tag used for the cell (<td>) into a <th> tag—a table header tag—which indicates that a cell is a *headline* for a column or row of data. You'd use this, for example, to announce the purpose of the table: *"Apartment Farmers by City: 1980 – 2003."*

The only visible change is that, in most Web browsers, the text appears in a header cell in bold type, center aligned. However, it can also be useful for screen readers to identify the purpose of the cell, and is considered an important part of making any informational table more accessible.

FREQUENTLY ASKED QUESTION

Suddenly Jumbo Cells

When I added some text to a cell, it suddenly got much wider than the other cells in the row. What gives?

It isn't Dreamweaver's fault. This is how HTML works.

Web browsers (and Dreamweaver) display cells to match the content inside. In the example shown here, the first cell of the first row has a little text, the second cell is blank, and the third cell has a 125-pixel-wide image. Since the image is the biggest item, its cell is wider than the other two. The middle cell, with nothing in it, is given the least amount of space.

Usually, you won't want a Web browser making these kinds of decisions. By specifying height and width for a cell (page 170), you can force a Web browser to display a cell with the dimensions you want.

You may also notice that Dreamweaver isn't always terrifically prompt about changing a cell's width as you add to its contents. You may add some text to a cell, click another cell, and add an image—but the cells don't change. However, if you save the file or click outside the table, suddenly the table goes crazy, and *all* of the cells resize.

Actually, Dreamweaver thinks it's doing you a favor. In the interest of speeding your editing along, the program doesn't automatically redraw the table with each change you make.

If you find this behavior disconcerting, choose Edit→Preferences (Dreamweaver→Preferences in Mac OS X) to open the Preferences dialog box. Make sure the General category is selected, and turn off "Faster Table Editing (deferred update)" under Editing Options.

A Property to Forget

The No Wrap options is of such little value that you'll probably go your entire Web career without using it.

But for thoroughness' sake—and in case you may actually find a use for it—here's a description. The No Wrap property prevents a Web browser from wrapping a line of text within a cell onto multiple lines. The browser instead widens the cell so that it can include the line without line breaks. The result is almost never useful or attractive. Furthermore, if you specify a width for the cell, this property doesn't work at all!

Cell Decoration

Cells needn't be drab. As with tables, you can give individual cells background colors or even background graphics (see Figure 6-16).

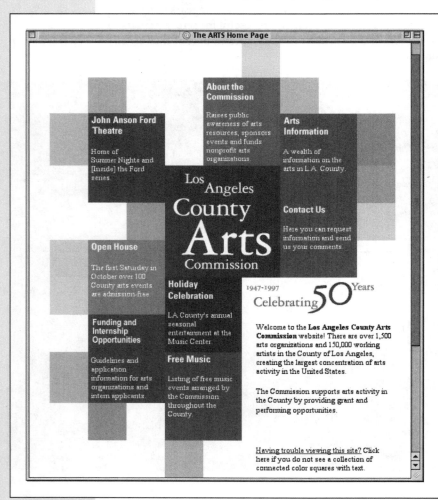

Figure 6-16:
Add impact with background color. The home page for the Los Angeles County Arts Commission (www.lacountyarts.org) makes a big visual statement without being a bandwidth hog. The trick? There are only a few graphics on this page. The colorful squares are simply table cells with a variety of background colors.

Adding cell background colors

To set the background color of one or more selected table cells or rows, do one of the following:

- Click the Bg color box in the Property inspector, and then select a color from the pop-up palette.

- Type a hexadecimal color value into the Bg color field.

You also have the option to set a color for the cell's border using the color box or Brdr field in the Property inspector. However, only Internet Explorer recognizes this property, and, since it is not officially part of HTML, it's unlikely that other browsers will ever support it.

Tip: Cascading Style Sheets do allow colored cell borders. In fact, you can set each of the four borders to a different color, if you're in that kind of mood.

Adding cell background images

You can also add an image to the background of a cell. In this instance, the cell acts much like a miniature document window; the graphic tiles (repeats endlessly) within the cell to completely cover the cell's background.

To add a background image to selected cells, try either of these steps:

- Click the Browse for File icon (the folder icon) to the right of the Bg field in the Property inspector (see Figure 6-15). In the resulting dialog box, navigate to and open the graphics file you want.

- Type the file path or URL of the graphic you want in the Bg field in the Property inspector.

WORKAROUND WORKSHOP

Beware the Resize Handles

Dreamweaver provides several techniques for resizing tables and cells while in Standard view. Unfortunately, the easiest method—dragging a cell or table border—is also the easiest to do by mistake. Because moving the cursor over any border turns it into the resize tool, almost every Dreamweaver practitioner drags a border accidentally at least once, overwriting carefully calculated table and cell widths and heights.

On occasions like these, don't forget the undo feature—

Ctrl+Z (⌘-Z). And if all is lost, you can always clear the widths and heights of every cell in a table (using the buttons in the Property inspector) and start over by typing new cell dimensions (see Figure 6-14).

Note that this problem rears its ugly head only when you're resizing a table in Standard view. Layout view provides another, superior method of resizing cell and tables by dragging (see page 151).

You can also set a background image for a table *row* (<tr> tag) using Dreamweaver, but it involves some coding that isn't officially part of HTML. In fact, only Netscape versions 4 and higher can display a background image for a table row at all.

Setting Cell Dimensions

Specifying the width or height of a particular cell works just as it does when you set the width or height of a table: select one or more cells and type a value in the W (width) or H (height) field in the Property inspector. This value can be specified either in pixels or a percentage. For instance, if you want a cell to be 50 pixels wide, type *50*. For a cell that you want to be 50 percent of the total table width, type *50%*. See below for detail on the business of controlling cell and table dimensions.

You can also resize a column or row of cells by dragging a cell border. As your cursor approaches the cell's border, it changes shape to indicate that you can begin dragging.

Dreamweaver MX is much better at calculating and writing the HTML code for tables than previous versions, which added lots of extraneous code whenever you dragged to resize a table or cell. However, if you mix and match the two approaches—dragging a cell border and typing a value in the Property inspector—you might end up in trouble. For example, suppose that you drag the border between two cells in a row, changing their widths to 100 pixels and 50 pixels, respectively. Dreamweaver sets the width value of the cell in the first column to 100 pixels, and the cell in the second column to 50 pixels. Previous versions of the program changed the width value of *every* cell in a column. By contrast, Dreamweaver MX uses complex rules to determine which cell it's actually going to modify.

So far, so good. But now suppose that you click in a cell in the first column and change its width value to 200 pixels. The HTML in your page now has a value of 200 pixels set for this cell, but it could also have 100 pixels set for another cell in that same column. Since all cells in a column must be equally wide, this conflict can lead to random results in different browsers. Therefore, it's best to avoid mixing the two approaches of setting cell widths and heights. (When madness like this strikes, don't forget you can completely clear the width and height of cells as describe on page 163.)

Tips for Surviving Table Making

Nothing can be more confounding than trying to get your tables laid out exactly as you want them. Many beginning Web designers throw their hands up in despair when working with tables, which often seem to have minds of their own. The Layout view eliminates many of the hassles associated with using tables for page layout, but here are a few problems that often confuse designers—and some tips to make working with tables more straightforward.

The contents take priority

You've created a 300-pixel-wide table and set each cell in the first row to 100 pixels wide. You insert a larger graphic into the first cell, and suddenly…Kablooie! Even though you set each cell to 100 pixels wide, as shown in Figure 6-17, the column with the graphic is much wider than the other two.

That's because a cell can't be smaller than the largest piece of content inside it. In this case, although you told the cell to be 100 pixels wide, the image is 174 pixels wide, and forces the first column to grow (and the others to shrink) accordingly.

Figure 6-17:
Because a Web browser can't shrink the image or hide part of it, the cell has to grow to fit it. That first column of cells is now 174 pixels wide; the other two columns must shrink in order to keep the table 300 pixels wide.

Original width settings:

Whole table: 300 pixels

Set each column manually

Suppose you've created a 580-pixel-wide table with three columns. You've set the width of a cell in each of the first two columns to 150 pixels and 50 pixels. You assume that the Web browser is smart enough to figure out what size the remaining

Figure 6-18:
In the top table, the designer set widths for the first two columns; the last column wound up with no width set. In the lower table, the designer manually set the width of the third column to 380 pixels; this time, the browser displays it correctly.

column should be: 380 pixels, of course, which is exactly what's left over if you subtract the first two column widths from 580. But you'd be wrong, as explained in
Figure 6-18.

Web browsers aren't so smart. As you can see in Figure 6-18, Netscape Navigator
needs more information to display a table correctly.

There is no such thing as column width, only cell width

To set the width of a column of cells, you have to set the width of only *one* cell in that
column. For example, in the second table in Figure 6-18, the first cell in the top row
has a width set to 150. You don't have to set the widths of the two cells below it.

This principle can save a lot of time, and, because it reduces the amount of code on
a Web page, and makes your pages load and appear faster. For consistency, it's a
good idea to pick either the first or last row of a table for width-setting.

The same holds true for the height of a row. You only need to set the height of a
single cell to define the height for its entire row.

Fortunately, Dreamweaver MX is much smarter than previous versions. When you
resize one or more cells, it adds width and height values only where they're needed,
without filling every cell with needless height and width values.

Do the math

Calculators can be really useful when you're building tables. Although you *could*
create a 400-pixel-wide table with three 700-pixel-wide columns, the results you'll
get on the screen can be unpredictable ($700 + 700 + 700 \neq 400$).

As it turns out, Web browsers' loyalty is to *table* width first, then column widths. If
you make the widths of your columns add up to the width of your table, you'll save
yourself a lot of headache.

The Spacer Image Revisited

Unfortunately, even if you explicitly set cell widths, some browsers still don't do a
good job at controlling the width of cells. Remembering that a cell can't be smaller
than the largest item inside it, as noted previously, is half the battle. For even more
control, use a spacer image, just as Dreamweaver does when you use the Autostretch
option in Layout view (see page 153).

For example, suppose you want to create a table that's 580 pixels wide, with two
rows and three columns. The widths of the columns will be 150 pixels, 20 pixels, and
410 pixels, respectively.

Specifying the widths of each cell in one of the rows would be a good start, but a
more reliable approach would be to use a *transparent GIF image* to reinforce the
column widths:

1. **In a graphics program, create a 1-pixel by 1-pixel transparent GIF graphic.**

   Dreamweaver can do this automatically if you use Layout view. See page 154.

2. **Create a new row at the bottom of the table.**

   One easy way is to click the lower-right cell of the table, and then press Tab.

3. **Click in the first cell; insert the spacer image by choosing Insert→Image and selecting the spacer file in your site folder.**

   Dreamweaver inserts the image and selects it in the document window.

4. **Using the Property inspector, change the width of the GIF to 150 pixels.**

   Since the first column in the table is 150 pixels wide, this graphic keeps the column from shrinking any smaller—which, in some browsers, it might otherwise do, thanks to an all-too-common bug.

5. **In the second cell in the row, insert another spacer GIF. Set its width to 20 pixels.**

   Like the previous image, this one helps maintain the 20-pixel width of the column.

6. **Finally, move to the third cell in the row, insert another spacer, and set its width to 410 pixels.**

   Your table is now rock-solid.

WORKAROUND WORKSHOP

Shrinking Down to a Pixel

Suppose you want to make an extremely short table cell. For example, one common trick for overcoming the drab gray quality of HTML's horizontal rule (see page 38, step 12) involves assigning a background color to a 1-pixel tall table cell that stretches the entire width of the page. When previewed in a browser, the cell looks like a colorful 1-pixel line. Make the cell 2 pixels tall, and you've got a 2-pixel-high line.

But sooner or later, almost every Dreamweaver student runs up against this one: Even when you set the height of an empty cell to 1 pixel, it's still a lot taller than it needs to be. No matter what you try, you can't get that cell any shorter.

When Dreamweaver inserts a table into a document, all of the cells of the table *appear* to be empty. However, Dreamweaver actually inserts a nonbreaking space (see page 49) into each cell, as a workaround for a particular display bug in Netscape browsers.

A nonbreaking space takes up space. Its height is based on the default font for the Web page. And because a cell can't be smaller than the largest item in it, Web browsers can't shrink the cell down to 1 pixel.

To get around this problem, create a 1-pixel by 1-pixel transparent GIF image and keep it in your site folder. If you insert that image into the cell, Dreamweaver graciously removes its unsolicited nonbreaking space (just as it would for any cell that's not empty). Repeat for each cell in the row. Now the row can shrink down to a single pixel.

Now you can see the advantages of Dreamweaver's Layout mode, which eliminates the need for many of these workarounds. It takes care of a lot of the headaches of building table-based layouts.

Adding and Removing Rows and Columns

Even after inserting a table into a Web page, you can add and subtract rows and columns from your table. The text or images in the columns move right or down to accommodate their new next-door neighbor.

Adding One Row or Column

To add a single row to the table, you can use any of these approaches:

- Click inside a cell. Choose Modify→Table→Insert Row, or press Ctrl+M (⌘-M), to insert a new row of cells above the current row. Alternatively, you can right-click (Control-click) a cell and choose Table→Insert Row from the contextual menu.

- To add a new row at the end of a table, click inside the last cell in the table and then press Tab.

The new columns inherit the properties (width, height, background color, and so on) as the column you originally clicked.

To add a single *column* of cells:

- Click inside a cell and then choose Modify→Table→Insert Column.

- Click inside a cell and then press Shift+Ctrl+A (Shift-⌘-A).

- Right-click (Control-click) a cell, and then choose Table→Insert Column from the contextual menu that appears.

In each case, a new column appears to the right of the current column.

Adding Multiple Rows or Columns

When you need to expand your table more rapidly, you can use a special dialog box that lets you add many rows or columns at once.

1. **Click inside a cell. Choose Modify→Table→Insert Rows or Columns.**

   The Insert Rows or Columns dialog box appears (see Figure 6-19).

2. **Click either Rows or Columns. Type the number of rows or columns you wish to add.**

   You can also click the tiny up or down arrow buttons next to the Number of Rows field.

3. **Indicate where you wish the new rows or columns to appear, relative to the cell you selected, by clicking Above or Below (for rows) or Before or After (for columns). Click OK to insert them.**

Using the dialog box gives you the advantage of choosing whether you want the new row or column to come *before* or *after* the selected information in your table, as shown in Figure 6-19.

Figure 6-19:
The Insert Rows or Columns dialog box lets you add multiple rows or columns to a table. The wording of the options changes depending on whether you're inserting rows or columns. Note that this dialog box offers the only way to add a column to the right edge of a table.

Deleting Rows and Columns

To delete a row from your table, you can use one of the following techniques.

Tip: When you remove a row or column, Dreamweaver also eliminates everything inside. So before you start hacking away, it's a good idea to save a copy of the page with the table.

- Select the row (see page 161). Press Delete to delete all of the cells—and everything in them—for the selected row.

- Click a cell. Choose Modify→Table→Delete Row, or use the keyboard shortcut Shift+Ctrl+M (Shift-⌘-M).

- Right-click (Control-click) inside a cell, and then choose Table→Delete Row from the contextual menu.

Deleting a column is equally straightforward.

- Select the column (see page 161), and then press Delete. You've just eliminated all the selected cells and everything in them.

- Click inside a cell and choose Modify→Table→Delete Column, or use the keyboard shortcut Shift+Ctrl+Hyphen (Shift-⌘-Hyphen).

- Right-click (Control-click) inside a cell, and then choose Table→Delete Column from the contextual menu.

Note: Dreamweaver doesn't let you delete a row if one of its cells is *merged* with a cell in another row. Nor can you delete a column if it contains a cell that's merged with a cell in an adjacent *column*. (Merged cells are discussed in the next section.)

Deleting a column in this way is actually quite a feat. Since there is no column tag in HTML, Dreamweaver, behind the scenes, has to select individual cells in multiple rows—a task you wouldn't wish on your worst enemy if you had to do it by editing the raw HTML code.

Merging and Splitting Cells

Cells are very basic creatures with some severe limitations. For example, all of the cells in a row share the same height. A cell can't be taller than the cell next to it, which can pose some serious design problems.

Consider Figure 6-20 at top, for example. In the top figure, the left cell (containing the gear graphic) is much taller than the top banner to its right. In fact, it's as tall as *both* banners to its right, as shown in the bottom figure. Ideally, you'd want the gear graphic cell to straddle the two cells to its right, as shown in the second banner example. In such situations, Dreamweaver provides several ways of persuading cells to work well together.

Figure 6-20:
You can create larger cells that span multiple rows and columns by merging adjacent cells. This trick can help solve some design issues and let you align items that normally would not align (top). The result can join multiple columns into one, multiple rows, or both at once (bottom).

The trick is to *merge* cells—combine their area—to create a larger cell that spans two or more rows or columns. In this example, the solution is to merge the two cells in the left column. This single cell holds the image of the gear, while perfectly aligning the two cells in the adjacent column. By using this technique, you can create some very complex designs. In fact, if you view tables created in Dreamweaver's Layout mode, you'll notice that Dreamweaver itself makes extensive use of this technique.

To merge cells, start by selecting the cells you wish to merge, using any of the methods described on page 162. (You can only merge cells that form a rectangle or square. You can't, for instance, select three cells in a column and only one in the adjacent row, as in an L shape. Nor can you merge cells that aren't adjacent; in other words, you can't merge a cell in one corner of the table with a cell in the opposite corner.)

Then, on the Property inspector, click the Merge Cells button (Figure 6-21), or choose Modify→Table→Merge Cells.

Tip: Better yet, use this undocumented keyboard shortcut: the M key. Just select two or more cells and press M. It's much easier than the keyboard shortcut listed in the online help: Ctrl+Alt+M (Option-⌘-M).

Dreamweaver joins the selected cells, forming a single new super cell.

Figure 6-21:
The Merge Cells button is active only when you've selected multiple cells. The Split Cells button only appears when you select a single cell or have clicked inside a cell.

Merge Cells ⌐ └ Split Cells

You may also find yourself in the opposite situation: you have one cell that you want to *divide* into multiple cells. To split a cell, click inside, or select, a single cell. Click the Split Cells button in the Property inspector. (Once again, you can trigger this command in several alternative ways. For example, you can choose Modify→Table→Split Cell. And if you prefer keyboard shortcuts, you can press

Figure 6-22:
The Split Cell dialog box lets you divide a single cell into multiple cells. You can choose whether to divide the cell into rows (multiple cells on top of each other) or columns (multiple cells side by side).

Ctrl+Alt+S [Option-⌘-S]. You can even right-click [Control-click] the selected cell and then choose Table→Split Cell from the contextual menu.)

When the Split Cell dialog box opens (see Figure 6-22), click one of the buttons to indicate whether you want to split the cell into rows or columns. Then type the number of rows or columns you wish to create; click OK.

If you split a cell into columns, everything in the cell winds up in the left column, with the new, empty column or columns to the right. When you split a cell into rows, the contents end up in the top row.

Nesting Tables in Standard View

By merging cells, you can create complex tables that offer precise control over your layouts. If you use Layout mode to create a detailed, handcrafted design, you'll see how Dreamweaver can generate complex tables using this technique.

But on the Web, simpler is usually better. Sometimes, instead of spending time and effort chopping up and merging cells to create a certain look, the best solution is to *nest* tables—placing a table within a table—instead of creating one complex table (see Figure 6-23).

Since a table cell acts just like a mini document, you can put anything that you'd normally place on a page inside a cell—graphics, text, links and, yes, even tables. Simply click a cell and use one of the techniques described above to add and format the table.

You can even place *more* than one table in a single cell. In Figure 6-23, for example, three tables are nested in the right-hand cell of the main table. They're in the flow of the cell contents, separated into individual paragraphs. By compartmentalizing and aligning information, nested tables make complex Web pages easier to both build and edit.

Be aware that there are some limits to nesting tables. For example, it's best not to nest more than three tables deep; in other words, a table inside of a table inside of a table. While most browsers can recognize and draw tables that are more deeply nested, such complexity can be difficult to render, resulting in pages that are slow to load, especially on slower computers.

Tabular Data

So far, you've learned about using tables for complex Web page designs, using tricks like merging cells, invisible spacer images, and Dreamweaver's Layout view. But what about the original purpose of a table—displaying data in an orderly manner? You can still do that, of course, and Dreamweaver provides a couple of tools to make the process of dealing with tabular data run smoothly.

Importing Data into a Table

Your boss emails you your company's yearly sales information, which includes data on sales, profits, and expenses organized by quarter. She asks you to get this up on the Web for a board meeting she's having in half an hour.

This assignment could require a fair amount of work: building a table and then copying and pasting the correct information into each cell of the table, one at a

Figure 6-23:
Top: This page at top looks complicated, but in Dreamweaver, it breaks down to a series of simple tables.

Bottom: The outside table (A) is a one-row, three-column table with a series of nested tables (B, C, D, E). The first cell contains another basic table (B), which has twelve rows and one column. Using alternating colors for each cell helps set off the information inside. The third column of the primary table holds the main content of the page; three tables (C, D, E) are placed within the flow of the cell.

One nice trick: Use the Align property of a table to create a "floating" sidebar within the normal flow of text. The announcements table here, for instance, is aligned to the right, while text in the cell wraps around it. Note that aligning a table like this is only possible in Standard view.

time. Dreamweaver makes your task much easier, because you can create a table and import data into the table's rows and columns, all in one pass.

In order for this to work, the table data you want to display must begin life in a *delimited* format—a task that most spreadsheet programs, including Excel, or database programs, such as Access or FileMaker Pro, can do easily. (Choosing File→Export or File→Save As in these programs usually does it.)

In a delimited file, each line of text represents one table row. Each line is divided into smaller units using a special character called a delimiter—most often a tab, but possibly also a comma or colon. Each unit represents a single cell in the row. In a colon-delimited file, for example, the line *Sales:$1,000,000:$2,000,000:$567,000:$12,500* would be converted by Dreamweaver into a row of five cells, with the first cell containing the word *Sales*.

Once you've saved your boss's spreadsheet as a delimited file, you're ready to import it into a Dreamweaver table:

1. **Choose File→Import→Tabular Data.**

   The Import Table Data dialog box appears (see 6-24).

Figure 6-24:
The Import Table Data dialog box lets you select a text file of data to import and choose formatting options for the table.

2. **Click Browse. In the Insert Tabular Data dialog box, find and open the delimited text file you wish to import.**

   A delimited file is no longer a spreadsheet, but a plain text file. Navigate to and double-click the file in the dialog box.

3. **From the pop-up menu, select the delimiter that was used to separate the data in the text file.**

   The choices are Tab, Comma, Colon, Semicolon, or Other. If you select Other, an additional field appears, in which you can type the character you used as the delimiter.

4. **Select a table width.**

   Choose Fit to Data if you want the table to fit itself to the information you're importing—an excellent idea when you aren't completely sure how much information the file contains. (You can always modify the table, if necessary, after importing the data.)

   On the other hand, if your Web page needs a table of a certain size, you can specify it by selecting the Set button and typing a value in the field next to it. Select pixel or percentage value (see page 159, step 6).

5. **Set Cell Padding, Cell Spacing, and Table Border, if you like.**

   See steps 4, 5, and 7 on pages 159–160 for details.

6. **Select a formatting option for the top row of data.**

   If the first line in the text file has column headings—Quarter 1 Sales, Quarter 2 Sales, and so on, for example—Dreamweaver lets you choose Bold, Italic, or Bold Italic to set this header row apart from the rest of the table. (No Formatting keeps the top row consistent with the rest of the table.)

7. **Click OK to import the data and create the table.**

If you'd like to jazz up your table a bit, but are short on time, you can apply one of Dreamweaver's preinstalled table designs (see Figure 6-25).

Figure 6-25:
Dreamweaver can apply canned designs to a table of data. Select a table in the document window, and choose Commands→ Format Table. You can then select one of the seventeen different designs from the list. You can even create your own design using the option menus. Unfortunately, you can't save a design you create. While these designs aren't useful when you're using tables to lay out a page as described earlier in this chapter, they are a quick way to spruce up a calendar or spreadsheet.

Sorting Data in a Table

If you have a table that lists employee names, you probably want to present that list in alphabetical order—or alphabetically *and* by department. Dreamweaver's Sort Table command takes a lot of the drudgery out of this task.

1. **Select the table you wish to sort.**

   See page 161 for some table-selection techniques.

2. **Choose Commands→Sort Table.**

   The Sort Table dialog box appears (Figure 6-26).

3. **Using the Sort By pop-up menu, choose the column you wish to sort by.**

   You can choose any column in the table. For example, suppose you have a table listing a bunch of products. Each row has the product name, number, and price. If you want to see the products listed from least to most expensive, you could sort by the column with the product prices.

4. **Use the next two pop-up menus to specify how you want the data sorted.**

   Data can be sorted alphabetically or numerically. To order the product list by price, choose Numerically from the Order pop-up menu. However, if you're sorting a Name column, choose Alphabetically.

   Use the second pop-up menu to specify that you want an Ascending sort (A...Z, 1...100) or Descending (Z...A, 100...1).

5. **If you like, choose an additional column to sort by, using the Then By pop-up menu.**

   This secondary sort can come in handy when several cells in the *first* sorting column have the same value. For example, if several items in your product list are all priced at $100, a sort by price would place them consecutively in the table. You could then specify a secondary sort that would place the products in alphabetical order within each price group. In this way, all of the products would be listed from least to most expensive, *and* products that are the same price would be listed alphabetically within their group.

6. **If the first row of the table contains data to be sorted, turn on Sort Includes First Row.**

   If, however, the first row of the table contains *headings* for each column, don't turn on this box.

7. **Choose whether to sort THEAD rows and TFOOT rows as well.**

   The <thead> and <tfoot> tags are intended to allow you to turn one or more rows into repeating headers and footers for long tables. However, since Dreamweaver doesn't give you an easy way to add these tags, and most Web browsers don't even understand them, what you do with these options probably won't have any effect on your sorting.

8. **Choose whether to keep row formatting with the sorted row.**

One way to visually organize a table is to add color to alternate rows. This every-other-row pattern helps readers to stay focused on one row of information at a time. However, if you sort a table that you had formatted in this way, you'd wind up with some crazy pattern of colored and noncolored rows.

The bottom line: If you've applied colors to your rows, and you'd like to keep those colors in the same order, leave this checkbox off.

9. **Click Apply to see the effect of the sort without closing the dialog box.**

If the table meets with your satisfaction, click OK to sort the table and return to the document window. (Clicking Cancel, however, does not undo the sort. If you want to return the table to its previous sort order, choose Edit→Undo Sort Table after closing the sort window.)

Figure 6-26:
The Sort Table command works well with Dreamweaver's Import Tabular Data feature. Imagine you're given a text file listing all of the employees in your company. You import the data into a table, but realize that the names aren't in any particular order. Use the Sort Table command, as described on page 182, to put the list of names into alphabetical order by last name.

Exporting Table Data

Getting data out of a table in Dreamweaver is simple. Just select the table and choose File→Export→Export Table. In the Export Table dialog that appears, select the type of delimiter (tab, comma, space, colon, or semicolon) and operating system where the file will be used (Mac, Windows, or Unix).

Finally, click OK. Give the file a name and save it onto your hard drive. You can then import this delimited file into your spreadsheet or database program.

Tables Tutorial

In this tutorial, you'll learn how to use Dreamweaver's Layout view to build a page for the *Cosmopolitan Farmer* Web site. You'll also practice adding tables using the Insert bar's Table object and gain experience with tracing images and Library elements.

Getting Started

Before you begin building the page, download the tutorial files. As always, you'll find them at *www.sawmac.com/dwmx/;* click the <u>Tutorials</u> link to go to the tutorials page. Click either <u>Tables Tutorial—Mac files</u> or <u>Tables Tutorial—Win files,</u> depending on the kind of computer you're using.

When the files have downloaded and decompressed, you should have a folder named DWTables on your computer, containing the Web pages and graphics needed for this tutorial. If you're having difficulties, the Web site contains detailed instructions for downloading the files you'll be using with this book.

1. **In Dreamweaver, choose Site→New Site.**

   The Site Definition window opens. Make sure the Basic tab is selected.

2. **Type *Tables Tutorial* in the site name field. Click Next.**

   This is the name that Dreamweaver will use while you are working on this tutorial.

3. **Select the "No, I do not want to use server technology" option and click Next.**

   In this tutorial, you'll be building a basic Web page. (The server technology referred to here is a far more complex, database-driven feature, as described in Part 6 of this book.)

   In the next steps, you'll tell Dreamweaver how you want to work on the files in your site and where you store those files. In this example, you'll use the folder you downloaded from this book's Web site. (In other situations, you'll choose or create a folder of your own.)

4. **Click "Edit local copies on my machine."**

   As mentioned on page 26, there are several ways to edit files and transfer them to a Web server. You'll be editing these right on your computer.

5. **Click the folder icon next to the label "Where on your computer do you want to store your files?"**

   The Choose Local Root Folder window opens.

6. **Browse to and select the DWTables folder.**

   Windows and Macs handle this slightly differently, as described on page 28. Selecting the DWTables folder makes it the local root folder—the folder that holds all the files, graphics, and other folders that are part of a single Web site (see page 26).

7. **Click Next.**

Next you'll be asked how you want to connect to a remote server—this is the computer (the Web server) that holds your finished Web files and dishes them out to the citizens of the Internet.

8. **From the pop-up menu, choose None.**

For this tutorial, you won't be connecting to a Web server. But, when building your own sites, you certainly will. For detailed instructions on transferring files to your Web server, see Chapter 16.

9. **Click Next.**

A summary of the options you selected appears. If you made a mistake, you can cycle back through the various screens by clicking Back.

10. **Click Done.**

Now you're all set to begin the tutorial.

Using a Tracing Image

In this tutorial, you'll be building the Pisces page in the Horoscopes section of the *Cosmopolitan Farmer* Web site. To get your page ready, follow these steps.

1. **Choose File→New.**

The New Document window appears. Here you'll tell Dreamweaver what kind of document you wish to create.

2. **On the General tab, select the Basic Page category.**

Dreamweaver can create many of the different file types used on the Web, but for most of these exercises you only need to create plain HTML pages.

3. **Click Create to open a new, blank Web page.**

Before getting started you should always save a new page.

4. **Choose File→Save; save this document as *pisces.html*.**

Save it into the DWTables folder.

5. **Click in the Title field in the toolbar; type *Pisces*.**

If you don't see the toolbar, choose View→Toolbars→Document.

6. **Choose Modify→Page Properties.**

The Page Properties window opens.

7. **Click the Browse button next to the Tracing Image field near the bottom of the window.**

   The Select Image Source dialog box appears.

8. **In the DWTables folder, double-click the file called *horoscope.gif*.**

   It's a GIF image of the design for this page.

9. **Move the Page Properties window so that you can see the document window underneath it, and then click Apply.**

   You should see the graphic appear in the document window (see Figure 6-27).

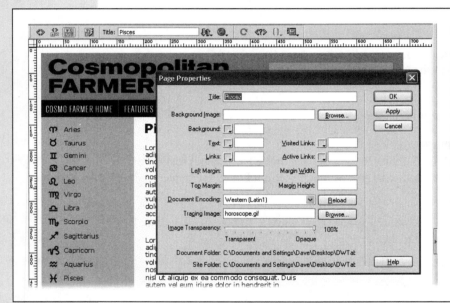

Figure 6-27:
You can use the Page Properties dialog box to change the page's background color, margins, link colors, and more. Call it up quickly by pressing Ctrl+J (⌘-J). (If you think you might find rulers helpful, as shown here, choose View→Rulers→ Show.)

10. **Move the Image Transparency slider to the middle—around 50%—and click OK to close the Page Properties dialog box.**

    The image fades into the background of the page. You've just inserted the *tracing image*—a GIF image that you prepared in some graphics program while brainstorming the design of your site, freed from the constraints of actually having to build the Web site while you played around with visual ideas. (You'll notice that the actual horoscope contains fake Latin gibberish. That's because the page is just a placeholder until your writing team comes up with the actual text for this Web page.)

    You'll use this graphic as a pattern for creating the page layout. This image won't show up in a Web browser; it only appears in Dreamweaver.

11. Choose File→Save.

Congratulations! You're well on your way to creating a beautiful new Web site. Next, you'll start to add the details.

Building the Banner in Layout View

You'll use Dreamweaver's Layout view to build a table-based page design.

1. **In the Insert bar, click the Layout tab (see Figure 6-3).**

   This tab contains useful tools for controlling layout and switching between Dreamweaver's two design views—Standard and Layout.

2. **Click the Layout View button.**

   Dreamweaver switches to Layout view.

   When you first switch to this view, the Getting Started in Layout View window may appear. This window explains how to use the layout tools. If you already get it, turn on "Don't show me this message again," and then click OK.

3. **On the Insert bar, click the Layout Table tool button (also shown in Figure 6-3).**

   The Layout Table tool lets you draw tables directly in the document window.

4. **Starting at the upper-left corner of the tracing image, drag diagonally down and to the right, creating a rectangle around the top banner of the tracing image.**

   The banner includes the orange and black portions at the top of the page.

   A light gray box with a green outline appears over the tracing image. The green tab in the upper left corner indicates that this is a Layout Table (see Figure 6-28).

   This page design has so many different areas, you'll need several different tables. While it would be possible to create a single table for the entire page, it's often a better idea to take a modular approach, dividing a page using multiple tables.

Figure 6-28:
If your Layout Table doesn't exactly fit the tracing image (the banner in this case), drag a resizing handle until the table is snug.

5. **On the Insert bar, click the Layout Cell tool button.**

   The Layout Cell tool lets you add cells to a Layout Table.

---

6. **Starting at the top-left corner of the Layout Table, drag diagonally to create a rectangle that includes the entire left half of the orange bar in the banner. Drag from the left edge to just past the word "to" and just above the black area, as shown in Figure 6-29.**

Cells are indicated by a light blue outline. This cell contains the site's logo.

When you release the mouse button, the insertion point blinks inside the cell you just drew. You're ready to fill it up with text or graphics.

Figure 6-29:
The Layout Cell tool lets you drag to create a rectangular cell within a layout table.

7. **Choose Insert→Image.**

Alternatively, click the Common tab of the Insert bar and then click the Insert Image button. Either way, the Select Image Source window appears.

8. **Browse to the *images* folder inside the DWTables folder. Then double-click the file called banner.gif.**

For a refresher on inserting images, turn to Chapter 5. You've just inserted an actual banner heading graphic over the sketch you made in your tracing image. In the event of an actual Web-creation experience, this is just what you would have done: placing actual graphics over the placeholders you had sketched in the tracing image.

By now, you'll notice that the image doesn't fit neatly over the tracing image, and it's hard to see what's happening on the page. You need to move the tracing image so that it sits directly under the graphics you're adding. Fortunately, Dreamweaver has a tool to do just that.

9. **Make sure the image you just inserted is still selected, and then choose View→ Tracing Image→Align with Selection.**

The tracing image aligns perfectly with the image.

Because the tracing image can sometimes obscure what you're doing on the page, it's useful to turn it off occasionally so you can see how your page is coming together:

10. **Choose Tracing Image from the View Options menu icon in the toolbar at the top of your document window (shown in Figure 6-11).**

The tracing image disappears. If there is no checkmark next to Tracing Image in the menu, the tracing image is already hidden. (You can also show or hide a tracing image by choosing View→Tracing Image→Show.)

11. **Move your mouse over the light-blue outline of the newly created cell until the outline turns red; click to select the cell.**

If you don't see any red outline, the cell is probably already selected. Eight handles appear around the edges of the cell when it's selected, and the Property inspector changes to indicate the properties of the cell (see Figure 6-30).

Figure 6-30:
The versatile Property inspector changes to show a number of settings for whatever you've selected on your Web page. In this case, a Layout Cell within a Layout Table is selected, as you can tell by the resize handles and the words Layout Cell in the inspector.

12. **In the Bg field of the Property inspector, type #FF9900.**

The graphic you imported was transparent and didn't include a background color of its own. You've just added an orange background color for the cell.

Everything looks good so far, so it's time to continue building the page's layout. You should turn the tracing image back on.

13. **On the toolbar, choose Options→Tracing Image.**

The tracing image reappears.

Next, you'll add an additional cell next to the banner image. This cell will hold an advertisement graphic.

14. **On the Insert bar, click the Layout Cell tool. Drag to draw a second cell that covers the rest of the orange area of the banner (see Figure 6-31).**

    Make this cell the same height as the other cell you drew. Notice that the cursor snaps to the top and right edges of the table. It also snaps to a line created by the bottom edge of the first cell.

Figure 6-31:
Adding additional cells to a table is as simple as dragging. The sides of a cell snap to other cells already in the table, making aligning the edges of cells…a snap.

15. **Choose Insert→Image.**

    Or, if you'd rather, click the Image button on the Insert bar's Common tab. In any case, the Select Image dialog box appears. You're about to choose a graphic that will fill the second cell. Because Web ads often change, the ad has a file of its own, rather than being part of your original logo graphic. This way, you'll be able to swap new ads in as necessary without disturbing the rest of your page.

16. **In the DWTables→*images* folder, double-click the file called ad.gif.**

    The image appears at the upper-left corner of the cell, but it would look better if it floated in the middle of the cell.

17. **Move your mouse over the light blue outline of the cell until it changes color to red; click to select the cell.**

    The next step doesn't change the *cell's* alignment—its placement on the page—only the alignment of its contents.

18. **In the Property inspector, choose Center from the Horz pop-up menu, and Middle from the Vert pop-up menu.**

    Now the ad floats in the center of its cell.

    Next up: Filling the ad cell with the same color orange as the first.

19. **Click the color box next to Bg in the Property inspector.**

    The color palette appears, but you're more interested in the cursor, which now resembles an eyedropper.

20. **Move the cursor over the orange in the left-side cell, and then click to "sample" that orange color.**

    The new, right-hand cell is now filled with the same orange color as the cell on the left. Although you already know the hexadecimal code for orange (because you typed it in a previous step), the eyedropper technique is handy when you don't know the code for a color that already appears in your layout.

21. **Click the Layout Cell tool in the Insert bar. Draw a cell that covers the entire bottom black bar in the banner.**

    This cell will contain a main navigation bar for the site. When you release the mouse button, the insertion point blinks inside the cell you just drew.

    In the next step, you'll insert a canned, ready-made navigation bar.

22. **Choose Window→Assets to open the Assets panel.**

    The Assets panel lets you quickly reuse elements contained in your site including graphics, colors, Flash movies, and more. The Assets panel is described in detail on page 442.

23. **On the Assets panel, click the last icon on the left—the one that looks like an open book.**

    This displays the site's Library. The Library lets you save and reuse frequently needed snippets of HTML (see Chapter 17 for much more detail).

24. **Select Main Navigation from the list in the Library window; click Insert (see Figure 6-32).**

    Dreamweaver drops in a row of navigation buttons. Notice that the Property inspector indicates that this is a special type of object called a Library item.

    To see how this page is shaping up, you'll temporarily hide the tracing image once again.

Figure 6-32:
Library items and other site elements such as colors and images can be found and reused from the Dreamweaver Assets panel.

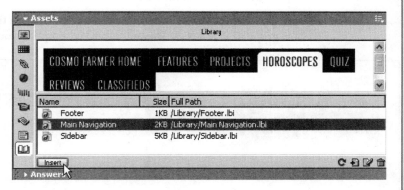

25. **Hide the tracing image again, as described in step 10.**

The tracing image disappears, and you see the nearly completed banner. But notice that the right part of the black row of navigation buttons is still white. To fix this anomaly, you need to give the cell a black background. Move your mouse over the light blue outline of the cell until it turns red; click to select the cell.

Next, you'll change the background color of the cell. Although the buttons themselves are black, the cell that extends to the right of the buttons has no color and thus lets the white of the page show right through.

26. **Using the Bg color box in the Property inspector, choose a black swatch from the pop-up color palette.**

If you're a hexy kind of person, you can instead type #000000, which means "black" in HTML.

27. **Turn the tracing image back on (see Figure 6-11). Now press F12 to preview the page in your browser.**

Maximize your browser window while viewing the page. If you have a high-resolution monitor, you'll notice that there's a large white margin to the right of the table. The page would look much better if the banner could automatically stretch to fill in the gap—a tricky bit of HTML programming, but an easy step in Dreamweaver.

28. **Return to Dreamweaver. Click the first column's header menu (see Figure 6-33), and then choose Make Column Autostretch.**

The Make Column Autostretch option makes one column in a table stretchy, as described on page 153, so that it can grow or shrink to fill the available space in a browser window.

As soon as you choose this command, a dialog box appears, asking if you're sure you want Dreamweaver to insert spacer graphics (page 154).

29. **In the dialog box, turn on "Create a spacer image file," and then click OK.**

Dreamweaver will use a special trick: it will create a tiny, 1-pixel transparent GIF graphic. That's what Dreamweaver is prompting you to save now.

Figure 6-33:
The width of a column is listed at the top of a column in Layout view. Clicking this number reveals a menu of options.

30. In the "Save Spacer Image" window, navigate to the DWTables→*images* folder. Save the image with the name spacer.gif.

Dreamweaver adds a 1-pixel tall row at the bottom of the banner table, and inserts the graphic into the right cell. The right column can now stretch to fit the browser window, since the spacer prevents the left cell from collapsing down to nothing. (See page 154 for more on this topic.)

31. Choose File→Save to save all your work so far.

Press F12 to view the final banner design in your default browser. It's looking extremely promising.

Building the Content Table

Now that you have the banner, it's time to turn to the actual contents of the page. An important feature of this page in the *Cosmopolitan Farmer* Web site is a second navigation bar that runs down the left side of the page, which lets your visitors click an astrological sign to read the appropriate horoscope.

1. On the Layout tab of the Insert bar, make sure the Layout view button is selected.

Figure 6-3 shows this button.

2. Click the Layout Cell tool on the Insert bar.

You don't have to start with the Table tool when working in Layout view. If you simply draw a cell, the program creates a Layout Table to fit.

3. While pressing the Ctrl (⌘) key, drag to create a cell the size of the beige sidebar in the tracing image.

When you draw a cell while pressing Ctrl (⌘), the Layout Cell tool remains selected—ready to draw another cell. Dreamweaver automatically creates a Table around this cell, causing most of your layout to turn light gray (to indicate table space where no cells yet exist).

Note: On the Macintosh, you'll smash right into a little Dreamweaver bug on this step. If you try drawing the cell from the bottom of the sidebar area upward to the bottom of the first table, Dreamweaver spits out a nasty error message. But if you draw the cell from just beneath the first Layout Table *downward,* you'll find that Dreamweaver is equally cranky; it doesn't let you draw a cell *exactly* below another table. (You have to begin the cell about ten pixels away.)

There's a quick workaround, however. Don't hold down the ⌘ key for this one. Draw the cell from the bottom up, but not all the way to the top—stop about Aries. Then select the cell by clicking carefully on its edge. Finally, drag the resize handle at the top of the cell upward until it touches the bottom of the first table. *C'est la guerre!*

You can release the Ctrl or ⌘ key for the next step.

4. **Starting at the top left corner of the P in the Pisces headline (but not all the way in the corner of its text area), draw a second cell that includes the Alert message (see Figure 6-34).**

If the cell continually snaps to the top of the table, hold down the Alt (Option) key when drawing this cell, which turns off the tool's habit of automatically snapping to the edge of nearby tables or cells.

This second cell will hold the main content for the page. Now you'll fill the new cell with text that was written by your crack team of astrologers.

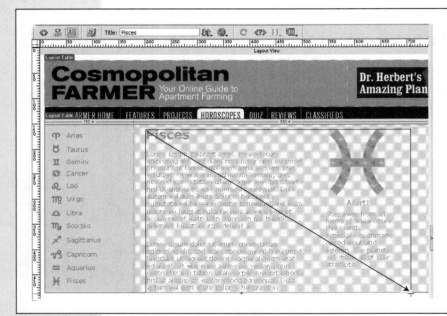

Figure 6-34:
To precisely place text on your Web page, draw a Layout Cell first; then you can paste text from a word processor.

If you did it right, there should be a little space between it and the sidebar, and between it and the top of the table. This small margin affords a little visual breathing room between the text and other elements around it.

5. **Choose File→Open. In the DWTables folder, double-click the file called text.html.**

This page holds the text for the horoscope page. Dreamweaver doesn't have an Import command like, say, PageMaker or QuarkXPress. Instead, you have to copy and paste text into your Web page, like this:

6. **Choose Edit→Select All to select all of the text on the page. Then choose Edit→Copy to copy it.**

Now you'll switch back to your layout and paste the copied text.

7. **Choose Window→pisces.html.**

A list of all currently opened Web pages appears at the bottom of the Window menu, so that you can switch between them by selecting their file names. Your Web page reappears.

Tip: The Windows version of Dreamweaver MX now includes small tabs for each open document. They appear at the bottom of the Document window; clicking a tab brings that page to the front.

8. **Click the large cell you just drew. Choose Edit→Paste to paste the text into the cell.**

   It may be hard to read, superimposed as it is over the dummy text in your tracing image; you'll take care of that in the following steps.

9. **Choose Modify→Page Properties. Select the file name in the Tracing Image field of the Page Properties window, and press Delete. Click OK.**

   Since you've finished creating most of the layout of the page, you no longer need the tracing image. Your page appears in all its glory, without the tracing image.

   Now you'll return to the cell you just added the text to and make it stretchy like the banner.

10. **From the column header menu above the cell with the Pisces horoscope, choose Make Column Autostretch.**

    This makes the cell flexible, as described in step 28 of the previous instructions. The cell now expands to fill the browser window, so that you can see all the text.

11. **Move your mouse over the light blue outline of the sidebar cell until it turns red, and click to select the cell. In the Property inspector's Bg field, type #CCCC99.**

    You've just set the cell's background color to a lovely shade of khaki.

    In the next steps, you'll insert a graphic into your navigation sidebar—the one that lists the zodiac signs.

12. **Click inside the beige sidebar.**

    If the Library window isn't open, choose Window→Assets and click the Library icon on the Assets panel.

13. **In the Library window, click the Sidebar item, then Insert.**

    Dreamweaver drops in a table that contains navigation for the Horoscopes section of the site. Notice that the Property inspector indicates that this—like the navigation banner you inserted earlier—is a special type of object called a Library item.

14. **Choose File→Save. Press F12 to preview your work in your browser.**

    It's a good idea to check your work in a browser every time you try something new, because Web pages can look slightly different in various browser windows.

Using the Table Object

Like the Layout Table, the Table *object* is a great tool for laying out Web pages. It's also the only way to achieve certain structures, like the nested table you'll be creating in these next steps. The Table object is available only in Standard view, not Layout view.

For the next steps, you'll need the *pisces.html* Web page you were working on in the previous steps. If it's not already on the screen, launch Dreamweaver and open the pisces.html file.

Tip: You don't have to choose File→Open; the bottom of the File menu lists the four most recently viewed documents. Choose a file's name to open it.

---

1. **Click the Layout tab on the Insert bar. Then click the Standard View button to switch out of Layout view.**

   The Layout Table tabs disappear, and the outlines of the tables and cells change to dotted lines. This is how Dreamweaver displays tables in Standard view.

2. **Click just before the P in the Pisces headline.**

   You've placed the insertion point at the beginning of the cell.

3. **Choose Insert→Table.**

   Or click the Insert Table button on the Insert bar. Either way, the Insert Table dialog box opens.

4. **Type the settings shown in Figure 6-35, pressing Tab to jump from box to box.**

   Don't forget to set the pop-up menu to Percent.

Figure 6-35:
Unlike Layout Tables, which you draw by dragging with the mouse, you create tables in Standard view by typing in dimensions and properties in the Insert Table dialog box. (This command, in fact, is available only in Standard view.)

5. **Click OK.**

   The two-row, one-column Table object appears in your Web page, outlined by transparent (but now highlighted) borders.

6. **With the table selected, choose Right from the Align pop-up menu in the Property inspector (see Figure 6-36).**

The table jumps to the right side of the Pisces horoscope area, and the text wraps around its left edge.

Figure 6-36:
When you choose Right in the Property inspector, the table will jump to the right side of the page. The gold shield that appears just before the "Pisces" heading—blue when it's selected—indicates where the table actually sits within the flow of the HTML code for the page.

7. **Ctrl-click (⌘-click) both cells in this new table, so that a black border surrounds both cells.**

Both cells are now selected. The Property inspector changes to reflect the properties of these cells.

8. **Choose Center from the Horz pop-up menu in the Property inspector.**

You've just center-aligned whatever you put into these cells. Now you're about to fill them up.

9. **Click the top cell; then choose Insert→Image.**

Of course, you can also click the Image button on the Insert bar's Common tab. Either way, the Select Image Source dialog box opens.

10. **Browse to the *images* folder in the DWTables folder. Double-click the file called pisces.gif.**

The Pisces symbol appears in the cell. (You may see most of the horoscope's text jump below the bottom of the new table you've inserted. Dreamweaver sometimes has trouble keeping up with your design on the screen. Don't worry; it'll look fine in a Web browser.)

11. **Click the bottom cell and type *Alert!* in it.**

Adding text to a cell is as simple as typing it, but there's much more you can do with text in Dreamweaver, as discussed in Chapter 3.

12. Press Enter to create a new paragraph within the cell, and then type: *Stay away from all forms of aquaculture this month, especially apartment-raised trout and salmon. The planets will doom all of your attempts.*

    Not the usual horoscope, perhaps, but you get the idea. You're almost done!

13. **Click either to the right or below, outside of the bottom table on the page.**

    You may need to scroll to the far right in order to see the right edge of the table. Clicking outside of this table positions the cursor outside the table.

14. **In the Library window (see steps 22 and 23 on page 191), click Footer, and then click Insert.**

    Dreamweaver drops in a table containing copyright information for the site.

15. **Choose File→Save. Press F12 to preview your work in your default browser.**

Congratulations: You've built a page with a precise layout and a flexible design. If you compare this page with the page you built in Chapter 1, you can see the greater control (and freedom) that tables offer the Web designer.

Feel free to compare your work with the finished Web page at *www.sawmac.com /dwmx/.*

Frames

The Web-page elements known as *frames* are both alluring and confusing. They're alluring because they can display multiple Web pages in a single browser window—one independent Web page per frame. Clicking a link may change the page in one frame, while leaving the contents of all the other frames untouched.

Frames offer an easy way to compartmentalize different elements within a single browser window. For instance, you can create separate pages for navigation, banners, and articles. Each can appear in its own frame, with its own scroll bars (see Figure 7-1).

At the same time, frames can be confusing to build, since they require a multitude of Web pages—including a special master page called a *frameset*—to work. People who create Web pages by typing pure HTML code into a text editor soon discover that building frames-based Web sites can be a frustrating exercise in file management. Dreamweaver MX, on the other hand, reduces much of this complexity by providing special Frames tools in the Insert bar's Frames tab and letting you preview exactly how the finished frames will look and work.

The Frame Page

What your Web-page visitor cares about is what's in the frames: the text and graphics. But for you, the biggest challenge is creating the special Web page—the frameset page—that gives the frames their structure. The frameset page itself usually doesn't contain text or graphics; it just describes the number, size, and placement of the frames. This page tells a browser which Web page should load into each frame, whether the frame has borders or scroll bars, and allows the visitor to resize the frame by dragging its border.

Figure 7-1:
Frames let you keep one element in place—the banner and navigation bars shown here, for example (www.mnh.si. edu/africanvoices/) while other contents of the Web page change. This way, the banner and the navigation bar remain visible in one frame, even as your reader scrolls to read a long page full of text or even reloads the page in another.

Note: You may have heard of another frame technology called *iframes.* The <iframe> tag lets you embed one Web page *within* another Web page. This way, you avoid having to use a frameset page while preserving the main benefits of frames.

Unfortunately, although the latest browsers can handle iframes, Dreamweaver MX doesn't provide any WYSIWYG tools for adding them to a page. Of course, if your HTML chops are sharp, you can jump into the document's Code view and write the <iframe> tags yourself. See Chapter 9 for more on working with raw HTML code.

Figure 7-2:
Frames can be obvious and ugly, or subtle and effective. Top: This fictional Web page has five frames. Notice the thick border between the frames and the unnecessary scroll bars that appear in the banner and sidebar.

Bottom: This page (bmrc.berkeley.edu/resources/) has three frames, but with borders turned off, the frames merge into a unified presentation. Only a single scroll bar appears in the content area (middle frame) of the page. This is your only clue that this page uses frames.

In this example, the advantage of using frames is that the site log and navigation (top frame) and the site tools (bottom frame) always remain visible even if you scroll to read the text contained in the middle frame.

The frameset page accomplishes all this with the help of two HTML tags: the <frameset> and <frame> tags. A <frameset> tag provides the superstructure of the layout: the number and size of frame rows and columns, as well as the overall border properties of all of the frames. Nested inside the <frameset> tag, a <frame> tag identifies the specifics for each frame: which page loads into the frame, and what visual elements—such as scroll bars—appear within the frame.

When your visitor's Web browser loads a Web page that contains frames, it first loads the frameset page and determines the number, size, and appearance of the frames, as described in the frameset. It then draws each of the frames in the browser window, and finally downloads the Web pages that appear in each frame.

Tip: Since a frameset page is just an empty structure, you must also create Web pages for each frame you wish to display. So if you add three frames to a page, you're actually creating *four* different Web pages: the frameset page, plus a page for each of the three frames. Because frames create more Web site files for you to manage, you may save yourself some headaches by keeping the number of frames in your site to a minimum.

Creating Frames

Before you begin creating frames, think about how they might best serve your Web site's structure. For instance, if you want a banner with the Web site's logo or name

When Frames Aren't the Best Solution

Frames are useful for banner logos, navigation bars, and so on. But if you look around, you'll notice that not many big-time Web sites use them. The reason: frames have serious drawbacks.

First, bookmarks and favorites don't always work with frames. When you click a link inside a frame, a new page loads inside it; if you click a link on *that* page, yet another page will load. Although it looks as if you are on a different page, the URL in the Address bar remains unchanged. That's because a Web browser uses the address of the *frameset* page.

In other words, suppose you follow several links within a single frame, and then use your browser's Add Bookmark or Add to Favorites command. Later, when you select the bookmark or favorite, you'll see the frameset page and the *original* pages inside it—you won't see the page you wound up on.

Printing a Web page with frames can be tricky, too. Since a frames-based page is composed of multiple Web pages, the browser doesn't know which page you want to print. Different browsers handle this dilemma so differently, novice Web surfers who don't understand the frames concept may get confused. For example, if you're using the Mac version of Internet Explorer 5 to view the second page in Figure 7-2, and you click one of the navigation buttons in the top frame, Internet Explorer thinks you've selected that frame. If you then choose Edit→Print, you'll print only that top frame—a useless row of buttons!

Still, used in moderation and in good taste (see Figure 7-2), frames can be an excellent addition to your bag of Web tricks. Small sites, where users aren't likely to print or bookmark the pages, can make good use of frames. And you needn't use frames everywhere on a site. You can effectively create small presentations within a site—such as an online portfolio—that benefit creatively from frames.

to appear at the top of each page, you could create a frame at the top to hold it. Or, to help your visitors get around, you might include a navigation bar in a frame at the left of the page consisting of a list of links to the site's main sections.

To create frames:

1. **Open or create a Web page.**

   This may be a new, blank page, or a page you've already created. This is the page you want to appear *within* a frame—for example, a page with a banner or a row of navigation buttons. Next, you'll create a frameset page around the current page.

   This may seem backward—you'd think you'd *start* with the frameset and then put pages into each frame. But you'll quickly get used to Dreamweaver's ways.

2. **Choose View→Visual Aids→Frame Borders.**

   You can also turn on the Frame Borders from the View Options menu in the document toolbar, as shown in Figure 7-3. A thick border appears around the edges of the document window, indicating that you're now working with frames.

Figure 7-3:
You can show and hide the frame borders that appear in the document window using the Options menu in the toolbar. Making them visible can be an enormous help when trying to understand what you've done with your frame layout.

3. **Create your frames within the window.**

   You can do so in any of three ways.

   First, you can drag one of the frame borders that now sit at the edges of the document window (Figure 7-4). To create a frame at the left edge of your page, for example, drag the left border inward toward the page center. To add a frame on top, drag the top border down.

Tip: You can create four frames at once—at the top, bottom, and both sides of the current page—by dragging one of the border corners.

Second, you can choose Modify→Frameset→Split Frame Left, Right, Up, or Down. This command may seem confusing at first, but it's worth learning if you want to make more complicated frame designs such as nested frames (see the facing page). Just remember to make your choice based upon where you want the *current* page to end up. If you want the current page to appear in the left frame, choose Left. If you'd like it to appear at the bottom, choose Down.

Finally, you may prefer to use one of Dreamweaver's one-click, canned frame designs. These options appear on the Frames tab of the Insert bar, as shown in Figure 7-5. (You can also get to them from the Insert menu by choosing Insert→Frames. The submenu lists the framesets available from the Frames tab, plus four other options: Frameset, Frame, Floating Frame, and NoFrames. These last four choices are available only when you're working in Code view [Chapter 9]. To add NoFrames content while working in Design view, see the Workaround Workshop on the facing page.)

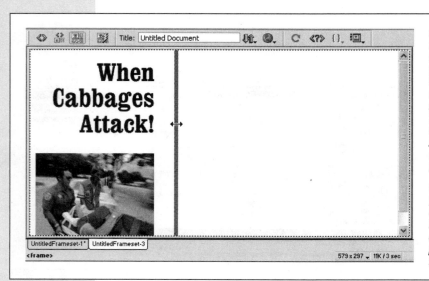

Figure 7-4:
Dragging a frame border is a quick way to create frames. When the cursor is positioned to begin dragging, it changes shape (as shown here). To create additional frames within the page, Alt-drag (Option-drag) one of the inner frame borders.

Of course, you can resize your frames by simply dragging the borders. But for greater precision, and to avoid some problems, see "Frame Size" on page 210.

When you finish splitting or dragging, borders appear around the frames you've just created. Behind the scenes, some strange things have just happened. First, Dreamweaver has created a frameset page—a new, untitled Web page that describes how a Web browser should draw the frames and which Web pages load into these frames—*around* the Web page you started with.

Second, Dreamweaver creates new, untitled documents for each frame you added to the page. For example, in Figure 7-4, one frame was added above the current page, and one below. In the process, Dreamweaver created three new documents: the frameset page, a blank document for the top frame, and a blank document for the bottom frame.

For proof, try this experiment: Click a visible portion of the original Web page you opened in step 1; note that the title bar of your window identifies its original name. Now, if you click inside one of the blank areas around your original document (that is, one of the other frames), the title bar changes to say *Untitled Document*. That's because you haven't yet saved or named the new Web pages that make up the new frames. You'll do that in a later step (see page 207).

Tip: To eliminate a frame, just drag its border back to the closest edge of the document window.

Nested Framesets

Although there's no limit to the number of frames you can have in a single frameset page, there are some restrictions on how you can arrange them. You can't, for instance, merge one frame into another, setting up a single frame that spans multiple columns or rows. In other words, a design like that pictured in Figure 7-6 is impossible using just a single frameset: the sidebar navigation spans the entire left side of the window, while the right side has two horizontal frames.

To overcome this limitation, you can insert a frameset *inside* a frame. Nesting framesets like this gives you much greater flexibility in your designs.

To nest one frameset inside another, just click inside the frame where you wish to insert a new frameset. Then choose Modify→Frameset→Split Frame Up, Down, Left, or Right.

WORKAROUND WORKSHOP

Don't Leave Anyone Out

Some very old, off-brand Web browsers can't display frames at all. For the unlucky people who use these, a Web site with frames is rather useless. In fact, a browser that doesn't understand frames simply displays a blank page when it loads a frameset.

You don't have to leave these visitors in the lurch, however. The <noframes> tag lets you add Web-page content that's especially for, and can be viewed by, these old browsers; frames-capable browsers simply ignore the <noframes> content. Choose Modify→Frameset→Edit NoFrames Content. The document window changes to an empty window, where you can add text, images, and other HTML.

Remember, what you put here is only for people who can't view frames, so don't feel you have to duplicate your entire Web site. One simple approach is to include a short message—"This site requires a frames-capable browser"—with a link to the Netscape, Microsoft, or Opera Web page, so the person can download a newer browser.

Alternatively, you could link to a non-frames version of your Web site; of course, in that case, you'd have to do the extra work of building an entire frame-free version of the site.

When you're finished adding content for the noframes page, choose Modify→Frameset→Edit NoFrames Content again to return to the document window.

Or, if you'd rather, you can use the Insert menu to insert frames. Choose Insert→ Frames and select the location (for example, left or top) where you want the new frame to go. (You can't drag frame borders to create a nested frameset.)

Tip: Dreamweaver offers some common, canned frame designs that you can apply with a click of the mouse. They're on the Frames tab of the Insert bar (Figure 7-5). Some of these designs include complex, nested framesets. (You can find additional frameset designs on the Macromedia Exchange described on page 606; just search for the extension called More Framesets.) Note that one frame in each button of the Frames tab is light blue; the blue frame shows where Dreamweaver will put the current Web page.

Figure 7-5:
Click a design to create the frameset, plus blank pages for additional frames.

The new frameset appears inside the original frame. (Because the borders of a nested frame look just like regular frame borders, use the Frames window, as shown in Figure 7-6, to keep track of what you're doing.)

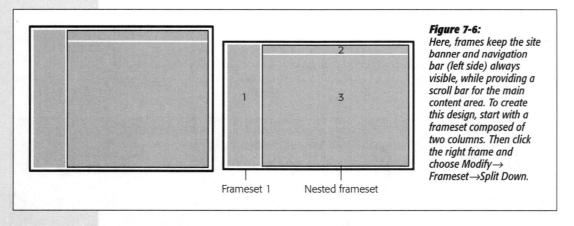

Frameset 1   Nested frameset

Figure 7-6:
Here, frames keep the site banner and navigation bar (left side) always visible, while providing a scroll bar for the main content area. To create this design, start with a frameset composed of two columns. Then click the right frame and choose Modify→ Frameset→Split Down.

Selecting Frames and Framesets

Think of a frame as a mini document window; each frame contains a separate Web page. When you click inside the frame, you can add images, text, and other elements to the page. Click inside another frame to edit *that* frame's Web page.

However, because framesets aren't *visible* elements of a Web page, Dreamweaver provides a special window—the Frames panel—that provides a simple visual overview of frames and framesets, making it easier for you to select and modify them. To open it, choose Window→Others→Frames or press Shift-F2 (see Figure 7-7).

Selecting a frameset lets you save it and modify its properties, such as frame size and whether or not there are borders, as described on page 209. There are several ways to select a frameset:

- Click the thick border around the edges of the frames in the Frames panel. The border becomes a solid black line to indicate that the frameset is selected.

- Move the cursor over a frame border in the document window, slowly if necessary, until it changes to a double-headed arrow; then click to select the border. (This works only if frame borders are visible on the page: choose View→Visual Aids→Frame Borders, or use the View Options menu in the document window's toolbar.) The gray frame borders acquire dashes to show that the entire frameset is selected.

Selecting a frame lets you save it and modify its properties, including margins and scroll bars, as described on page 214. To select a frame, do one of the following:

- Click a frame in the Frames panel.

- Alt-click (Option-Shift-click) a frame in the document window. (The <frameset> tag also appears in the tag selector, providing yet another way to select a frameset.)

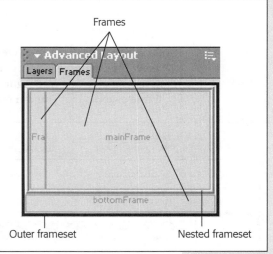

Figure 7-7:
The Frames panel shows a thumbnail diagram of the current document's frames. Thick 3-D borders represent a frameset, while thin gray lines represent the borders of frames. The thick black border—the outer frameset in this example—indicates a selected frameset, while a thin black border represents a selected frame. A name appears inside each frame to identify it, so that you'll know how to target links to this frame.

Frames

Outer frameset

Nested frameset

Saving Framesets and Frames

It's always a good idea to save Web pages as soon as you create them. For example, you must save them before you can make working links, as described in the note on page 96. Furthermore, you probably do some of your most important formatting, such as choosing a background color, right at the beginning, and you don't want to lose that in a crash or power failure. Finally, you need to save your frameset and all pages in it before you can even preview the frameset.

To save a frameset, select it using any of the methods just described. Then choose File→Save Frameset (or, to "spin off" a copy of the one you've opened, Save Frameset As). The first time you save a frameset, the Save dialog box opens. Name the frameset page and save it in your Web site folder. Although frameset pages have special properties, they're still just Web pages, and they still end in the appropriate extension (.html or .htm for regular Web pages, or one of the extensions—asp, .php, and so on—used for the dynamic pages described in Part 6 of this book). You can save them anywhere in your site folder (see Chapter 14 for some filing tips).

Saving a component page *inside* of a frame works just like saving regular documents: Click the frame in the document window and then choose File→Save Frame, or press Ctrl+S (⌘-S). You can also save all of your frames at once, as described next.

Saving multiple frames

One of the complexities of working with frames and framesets is the fact that you're dealing with many different Web pages at once, and, consequently, many different files. As you modify your frames and framesets and make changes to the pages in those frames, you'll be saving multiple files.

Fortunately, you don't have to plod through the document window, clicking inside each frame and saving it independently. To save all the pages in a frameset in one step, choose File→Save All.

Of course, just after you've created a frameset and frames, Dreamweaver doesn't yet know the component pages' names or folder locations. It therefore shows you the Save As dialog box (see Figure 7-8) *over and over again,* once for each component frame page, so that you can name and file each one.

Figure 7-8:
The File→Save All command is a powerful shortcut for quickly saving a frameset and all of its pages. The first time you save the frameset and frame pages, Dreamweaver places a fat, cross-hatched border around the frame you're about to save, so you can name each page individually.

Clearly, you need to know which frame you're saving each time the Save As dialog box appears. To help you, Dreamweaver provides a visual cue: A thick, crosshatched border appears around the frame you're about to save (see Figure 7-8). Type a name for that page and press Enter, repeating the process for all pages.

The same crosshatched border appears around the *entire* document window when you're saving the frameset itself.

Frame and Frameset Properties

After creating a frameset, it's time to take charge of the size, look, and contents of its frames. Dreamweaver treats framesets and frames as separate objects, each with its own set of properties. When you select a frameset or frame, using any of the methods described previously, you can view and modify its properties in the Property inspector (see Figure 7-9).

Tip: In general, it's better to set a *frameset's* properties before fine-tuning its *frames,* since some frameset properties affect the properties of individual frames.

Frameset Borders

Borders are intended to visually separate one frame from another, but professional Web designers generally shun their amateurish 3-D appearance and the boxy designs they create (see Figure 7-2).

If you're a professional Web designer (or just want to come across as one), consider eliminating frame borders entirely. Not only does this free up a few precious pixels of screen real estate, it also lets you create seamless frame designs, so that all your frames appear to be a single, unified Web page.

To control frameset borders, start by selecting the frameset itself (see page 206 for selection techniques). Now consult the Property inspector, where you'll find these options:

- **Borders pop-up menu.** Use this pop-up menu to indicate the visibility status of the borders. To turn off borders, choose No—a good idea, if for tastefulness' sake alone. If you must use borders, select Yes. (The Default setting has the same effect as selecting Yes on most browsers.)

- **Border Width.** Specify the thickness of your border by typing a number (in pixels) into the field. Type *0* if you want to completely eliminate borders. (You might think that choosing No borders would automatically eliminate any space between frames, but that's not the case. If you don't also set the Border Width to 0, a small gap will appear between frames on the page.)

- **Border Color.** Use this pop-up palette to choose a color for the border (see page 34). Of course, if you've turned off borders, you can leave this option blank.

The next time you save your document, Dreamweaver stores all of the new settings into the frameset file (see Figure 7-9).

Note: Nested framesets have their own border settings, but you don't have to specify them, since nested framesets inherit the border settings of the frameset they're in. For example, suppose you created a frameset and turned off the borders, and then you inserted another frameset into one of those frames (see page 205). The borders in the nested frameset are automatically turned off, having inherited the settings of the outer frameset. You can, however, assign completely different border settings for the nested frameset, overriding any setting inherited from the outer frameset.

Figure 7-9:
Even though framesets and frames are treated as separate objects, all of the frames' properties (size, border, etc.) are stored in the frameset file—not its page.

Frame Size

You can make your frames bigger or smaller simply by dragging the frame borders in the document window. But for more precise, numerical measurement, you'll need the Property inspector.

Start by selecting the frameset containing the frame in question (see page 206). Now consult the Property inspector's controls, which include:

- **Row/Column.** Dreamweaver thinks of a frameset as something like a table, with rows and columns. For example, if your frameset has two frames, one on top of the other, Dreamweaver thinks you have *two rows* of frames consisting of one "cell" each. Dreamweaver thinks of a frameset composed of three side-by-side frames as *three columns.* (Beyond this similarity, however, framesets are totally distinct from tables.)

  Use this control (or the thumbnail diagram next to it) to specify the row or column you want to work with. Figure 7-10 shows the details.

- **Value.** Here's where you specify the height or width of the row or column. This can be either a pixel value or a percentage, whichever you specify using the pop-up menu next to the Value field.

  If you set a row height or column width to a *percentage* value, its size will be a percentage of the browser window (or the parent frame, if the frameset is nested inside a frame). That's a handy design safeguard against the fact that every visitor to your Web page may be using a different-sized monitor. You might set up your left-side frame so that it always consumes, say, 25 percent of the window, no matter how big or small the window is.

Figure 7-10:
The Property inspector's Row and Column selector shows a thumbnail of the frameset's rows (top), columns (middle), or both (bottom). In the first example—one frame above another—you can only set the height of each row, since the width is the entire width of the browser window (or the parent frame, in the case of nested framesets). In the second example— two frames side by side—only the width of each frame can be modified. In the last example—four frames—you can set a mixture of the two: height for each row of frames, width for each column of frames.

- **Units.** Using this pop-up menu, you can choose Pixels, Percentage, or Relative.

  Relative is a special unit of measurement that you'll probably want to use for at least one column or row per frameset. To understand its use, imagine this setup: Three frames appear one on top of another. The top frame is a banner containing the Web site's name, the middle frame is the main text, and the bottom frame holds a navigation bar. If the heights of the top and bottom frames are 30 pixels, and the middle frame is 300 pixels, the page will look just fine if it's viewed in a browser window that's exactly 360 pixels tall (as shown at top in Figure 7-11).

However, if the visitor's browser is much taller, the top and bottom frames won't be the height you wanted (see Figure 7-11, bottom). You've told it that the total height of the frameset should be 360 pixels (30 + 300 + 30), but the window is actually much bigger—on the order of 900 pixels. In an effort to make the best of a bad situation, the browser just divides the remaining space among the three frames, adding a little height to each of the three frames.

A *relative* measurement, therefore, lets you give a frame a flexible size. It will grow and shrink to accommodate changes in the browser window. In addition, it lets you assign *absolute* (fixed) sizes to certain frames—banners and navigation bars, for example—that always remain fixed in size.

Tip: If the notion of freely reflowing Web-page contents doesn't sit well with your design sense, and you'd like a bit more control over your visitors' browsers, see page 345 for detail on how to make browser windows open to the exact height and width you want.

Frame Properties

Once you've set the border properties and frame sizes in the *frameset*, you can modify the properties of each *frame*. Select the frame and use the tools in the Property inspector, as shown in Figure 7-10.

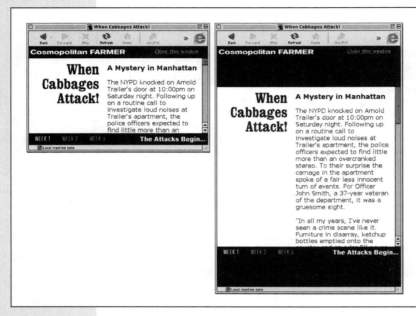

Figure 7-11:
You'll usually want to assign a relative width or height to one frame in each frameset, so that the frame grows or shrinks as the window is resized. If you don't, as seen here (before the window is resized, left, and after), all of the frames change size, creating undesirable space in some frames. Here, both the banner and bottom navigation bar would look much better if they remained the same height. Better, then, to give those frames a fixed height—say 30 pixels—and assign a relative height to the middle frame.

Name

Each frame can have its own name, but this isn't the name of the file (or the title of the Web page) that loads *into* the frame. A frame's name exists solely for identification purposes when working with links or JavaScript scripts—specifically, when you want to use a Dreamweaver Behavior (see Chapter 11) or target a link from one frame to another. You'll need frame names, for example, when you wish to use a navigation bar to load pages into another frame (see "Targeting Links, on page 215). Otherwise, frame names are optional.

Tip: If you create frames using the Frames tab of the Insert bar or the Insert→Frame command, Dreamweaver supplies generic names for the frames it creates. But if you use any of the other methods for creating frames, such as dragging frame borders from the edges of the window, you have to supply frame names yourself.

To set the name of a frame, select the frame by clicking it in the Frames window, and then type a name in the Frame Name field of the Property inspector.

Src

When you set a frame's *source* (Src) property, you're simply specifying the path to the Web page file that loads into that particular frame. You can change the path—and the Web page that appears in that frame—by clicking the folder icon and selecting a file from your site folder.

You can, if you like, link to a page that's on somebody else's site; just type the absolute URL here, beginning with *http://*. You won't, however, be able to see the other person's page within Dreamweaver. Instead, inside the frame you'll see only the words "Remote File," plus the URL. You have to preview the frameset in a browser connected to the Internet to see the remote file actually appear within the page. (If you do display someone else's Web page inside a frameset on your site, it's proper etiquette to ask for permission first. In fact, sites have been sued by companies whose pages have been "framed" this way.)

Note: Be careful using the Src property. One common mistake is to add the frameset page itself to one of the frames. In other words, it's possible to click the folder icon next to the Src field, and then select the current frameset page, thus creating a reference to itself.

When you preview the frameset, the browser loads the page—but when it attempts to load pages into each frame, it's trapped: It loads the frameset, which in turn has a frame, which loads the frameset again, which has a frame that loads the frameset again, and so on. This hall of mirrors continues until the browser crashes and your site's visitors curse your name!

Scroll

To create scroll bars for a frame—or hide them—use the Scroll property. You'll see four options in the Scroll pop-up menu in the Property inspector:

- Yes adds horizontal and vertical scroll bars to the frame, even if the frame doesn't contain enough material to require them.

POWER USERS' CLINIC

Frames from the Inside Out

The Src property provides an alternative method for building a frames-based design, preferred by some designers who learned to build frames-based pages before WYSIWYG programs like Dreamweaver came on the scene.

Imagine that you want to build a page with two frames: top and bottom. You could create a new page, add text and graphics, and then save it as, say, top.html. Now you create a second page called bottom.html, and save it for use as the bottom frame.

Finally, you need a third page, one that will serve to hold the first two; split this third page into two frames. Set the source (the Src property) for the top frame to *top.html*, set it to *bottom.html* for the bottom frame, and save the frameset using any name you like (like *frameset.html*, or if it will be the home page to the site, *index.html*).

Using this technique, you make and save the frame pages first, and *then* create and save the frameset page: two frames, three files.

• **No** prevents scroll bars from being added to a frame, even if that means some of its contents become inaccessible.

• **Auto** lets the browser determine whether to display scroll bars. If the contents don't fit inside the frame, the browser adds the appropriate scroll bar.

• **Default** works like Auto in most browsers. Since the effect of the Default option can vary from browser to browser, choose Auto instead.

In general, use the Auto option if you know your frame might require some scrolling, or No if it will not. For example, a frame containing a Web page with a lot of text will probably need a scroll bar, whereas a frame that simply contains the site's logo won't.

No Resize

Usually, your Web site visitors can resize the frames you've created just by dragging their borders right in the Web browser. But if you don't want people monkeying around with your designs, turn on the frame's No Resize checkbox in the Property inspector.

Tip: The No Resize option applies only to manual frame-edge dragging. In other words, even with No Resize turned on, your frames may still change size when the *browser window* is resized. If you want to prevent even that layout shift, see page 210.

Margin Width and Margin Height

You can adjust the top and left margins of a frame by setting its Margin Width and Margin Height properties. These settings control the position of the upper-left corner of a page in a frame, and they work exactly like page margins in a standard Web page do, as described in step 10 on page 33. (In fact, you can set both page *and* frame margins. Your margins will be the sum of the two. For example, a 10-pixel top page margin and a 10-pixel frame margin height will create a 20-pixel margin at the top of the frame.)

Margin *width* is the amount of space between the left edge of the frame's border and the left edge of the Web page; margin *height* is the space from the frame's top border and the top of the Web page. These margin settings apply to every page that loads into the affected frame.

Border and Border Color

Using these controls, you can assign a border and border color to each individual frame—giving one important frame a sky-blue border, say, but leaving all other frames borderless.

Unfortunately, Internet Explorer, Netscape Navigator, and Opera all handle this property differently, so you can't assume that it will work for all of your visitors. Furthermore, this option has no effect if you've turned off borders in the frameset (page 209).

Targeting Links

Normally, when you click a link, the Web browser replaces the current page with a new Web page, so that the entire browser window changes. But a browser treats each *frame* as an independent window, which offers some interesting and unique possibilities for linking. Clicking a link on a page merely replaces the contents of *that frame*, leaving the other frames in place.

Using the *Target* property of a link, you can choose, or target, which frame you want the linked Web page to load in. This option is extremely handy when you use one frame as a navigation bar whose links load pages into *other* frames.

To make a link open in a different frame, create the link as described on page 95, making sure that the link is highlighted. Then, in the Property inspector, choose the name of the frame where you'll want the page to appear, using the pop-up menu next to the Target field.

When you click the link on the finished Web page, the source Web page opens into the frame you just chose.

FREQUENTLY ASKED QUESTION

The Underscore Targets

What are the four choices in the Target pop-up menu that begin with the "_" character?

If you're working on a frameset page, the link target pop-up menu lists all named frames. But even when working in another kind of page, this pop-up menu always offers these four options for a link you've highlighted:

_blank opens a new, second browser window when your visitor click the link. The new window loads the linked page. The original window—the one containing the link— remains open. This feature lets you link to another site, for example, leaving your own Web site available in an open window. (To open a new browser window to an exact size, see page 345.)

_self loads the linked page into the same window or frame, replacing the current page. Of course, this is how links work normally, so there's little point in choosing this option unless you're trying to get extra exercise.

_top offers a specialized, but very useful feature. Suppose your Web page contains frames—and one of them contains a link to someone else's Web site. If a visitor clicks the link, the "foreign" Web site will appear trapped within one of *your* frames. This odd-looking effect is widely considered bad form.

To avoid this HTML social gaffe, choose the _top option for your link. This option forces your visitor's browser to load the linked page into the entire browser window, which overrides all frames and framesets, and avoids imprisoning someone else's Web site within your own.

_parent replaces the current frameset page with the linked page, exactly as the _top target does. The difference is visible only when the frameset page is itself loaded into a frame in *another* frameset page. In that case, this option will replace only the first frameset. (Beware: Netscape Navigator's support for this feature is notoriously flaky.)

Tip: Dreamweaver's Go To Url behavior lets you have a single link target multiple frames at once. Imagine loading four different Web pages with a single click! See Chapter 11 for more information on this powerful feature.

Inserting a Navigation Bar

One of the best reasons to use frames is to keep a *navigation bar* visible on the screen at all times. A navigation bar (called a "nav bar" in the trade) is a set of interactive buttons that let visitors jump to different pages or load pages into different frames. To make your life easier, Dreamweaver's Navigation Bar object makes quick work of adding complex interactive navigation bars to your frames.

Like the Rollover object described in Chapter 5, nav bar buttons use Dreamweaver Behaviors—JavaScript programs—to dynamically swap graphics files. Nav bar buttons also offer two additional styles that help your visitors know where they are in your site (see Figure 7-12).

Figure 7-12:
When a button first appears on a page, it's usually in its up state—untouched, ready to be clicked. But when the user moves her mouse over the button, it changes to its over state—useful for indicating that the button actually does something.

To create a navigation bar:

1. **Create graphics for the buttons in your navigation bar.**

   Each button in a navigation bar can have up to four different looks, or *states,* based upon an interaction with the user. You'll need to create multiple graphic files for each button, using a graphics program like Fireworks or Adobe Image-Ready. And, as with rollover images, make sure that each button graphic is *exactly* the same size. Otherwise, you'll get distortion (see page 126).

2. **Place the cursor in the frame where you'd like to add a navigation bar.**

   It's usually a sidebar, header, or footer.

3. **Choose Insert→Interactive Images→Navigation Bar.**

   Alternatively, from the Common tab of the Insert bar, click the Navigation Bar object.

Either way, the Insert Navigation Bar window opens (see Figure 7-13). Don't be overwhelmed. There are a lot of options in this window, but they're straightforward.

Just remember that a navigation bar is simply a collection of buttons. You add one button at a time to create a complete navigation system. Each button has a name, up to four different images, and a link.

The window starts out with a single element called *unnamed1*.

Figure 7-13:
This navigation bar has three buttons so far. The properties of the button w1—selected in the Nav Bar Elements list—are displayed, including the button's image files, alternate text, link, and target. This navigation bar will be laid out horizontally in the frame (see the Insert pop-up menu?). Unfortunately, the Insert pop-up menu and the Use Tables option are available only when you first insert the navigation bar. If you want to change the orientation after you've inserted the object, you'll have to do it by hand.

4. **Type a name for the first button in the Element Name field.**

   This name is just for behind-the-scenes use in the Web page. It won't appear on the button or anywhere on the screen. If you like, you can even skip this step and use Dreamweaver's default names: *unnamed1, unnamed2,* and so on.

5. **Click the Browser button next to the Up Image field to select a graphics file for the up state of the button.**

   This is the image you created in step 1.

6. **Choose graphics for one or more states for the button.**

   At a minimum, include an over image. But including images for the other two states of the button will add zing to your navigation bar.

   These different state images are good for helping your visitors understand where they are. For example, in Figure 7-12, the frameset loads the first of three pages covering a story about killer cabbages. The Week 1 button in the right corner is in its down state, meaning that "You are at this spot in the story." The Week 2 button is in its up state, meaning that it's clickable, and the Week 3 button is highlighted in its over state, since the mouse is hovering over it. Because these buttons consist of ordinary graphics files, you can make their different states look like anything you want.

7. **Type a text description for this button in the alternate text field.**

This optional step can be a help to those viewing the page with their graphics turned off or those who have vision impairments as described on page 114.

8. **Using the "When Clicked, Go to URL" field, specify the page you want the button link to open.**

Because this is a *navigation* bar, clicking the button should take your visitor to another Web page. You can click the Browse button to select a file from your site, type in a path to a page in the site, or, to link to a page outside of the current site, type an absolute URL beginning with *http://*.

9. **Select a Target from the pop-up menu.**

Since you're including the navigation bar in a frame of its own, the linked Web page should load into another frame, leaving the nav bar exactly where it was. Select the name of the frame from the menu. The Main Window option makes the Web browser replace the frameset and frames with the linked page.

(The names of the other frames in a frameset appear *only* if the current frameset is open and you're adding the navigation bar to one of the pages in a frame. If, for example, you've opened the navigation bar page by itself, Dreamweaver doesn't know the page is part of a frameset, nor does it know what the other frames' names are.)

Note: Take care not to turn off the Preload Images checkbox. As noted in Figure 5-13 on page 127, preloading images prevents a delay when a visitor moves the mouse over the navigation image.

---

10. **If you like, turn on Show "Down Image" Initially.**

The down image can function like a "You are here" sign, letting visitors know their location in the site. You should select this option for only one button in the navigation bar, and only if that button links back to the original frameset.

For instance, suppose your home page is a frameset, and one frame contains a navigation bar. Select this option for the Home button on the navigation bar. This way, when visitors peruse your page, that button is already highlighted—indicating where they are.

11. **Click the + button. Repeat steps 4 through 10 for each additional button in the
    navigation bar.**

    The -- button deletes the highlighted button. The up and down arrow buttons let
    you rearrange your buttons by shuffling a highlighted button up or down in the
    list.

12. **Choose the orientation of the bar from the Insert menu.**

    Navigation bars can run horizontally—perfect for headers and footers—or ver-
    tically—the right choice for a sidebar.

Tip: To help control layout, select the Use Tables checkbox. By containing your graphics within the cells of
a table, this feature keeps your graphics together on a page and prevents them from moving around if
someone resizes the browser window.

---

13. **Click OK to insert the navigation bar.**

You can insert only one navigation bar per Web page. Once inserted, you can edit it
only by choosing Modify→Navigation Bar. The Modify Navigation Bar dialog box
looks just like the one shown in Figure 7-13, so that you can edit, delete, and rearrange your navigation buttons.

To modify a button, select it in the Nav Bar Elements list. You can then assign new
images, settings, and links to it.

FREQUENTLY ASKED QUESTION

Nav Bars, No Frames

Can I use the Navigation Bar object without using frames?

Yes, but you'll lose most of the benefits of the Navigation
Bar feature and add unnecessary code to the page.

One of the cool aspects of a Dreamweaver nav bar is its
ability to indicate where the visitor is within the site, thanks
to the button's down state.

Imagine this scenario. You've built two frames: a top frame
for a nav bar and a bottom frame for the main content.
The buttons in the nav bar are all in their up states. Moving
your mouse over the first button causes it to glow, and
clicking it loads a new page in the bottom frame.

At the same time, the button you just clicked changes to its
down state, letting your visitor know which section of the
site he's seeing. Only the page in the bottom frame changes,
because the top frame with the nav bar simply uses a

Dreamweaver behavior to swap the graphics used for the
buttons.

Now imagine that you didn't use frames, so that you just
inserted the navigation bar on the same page as the main
content. When you click a button in the navigation bar, the
browser loads a new page, completely replacing the page
that had the navigation bar! You'd have to rebuild the navigation bar on every single page of your site.

Moreover, the down state of the button would never appear, because as soon as you click the button, a new page
replaces it.

In other words, there's not much point to using the Navigation Bar object in Dreamweaver unless you're also using frames. If you want to create a frame-free site, it's probably best to just stick with Rollover objects (see page 126)
for building navigation buttons.

Tip: For more advanced navigation bar features, see page 357.

Frames Tutorial

In this tutorial, you'll build an exclusive online story for *Cosmopolitan Farmer* magazine. In the process, you'll learn how to use Dreamweaver's frame-building features and add an advanced site-navigation toolbar.

Getting Started

Before you begin building the page, you'll need the tutorial files from this book's Web site. You'll also need to tell Dreamweaver a bit about the site you're creating.

1. **Download the files for this tutorial from the companion Web site.**

   Using your Web browser, visit *www.sawmac.com/dwmx/*. Click the Tutorials link to go to the tutorials page.

   Then click the link <u>Frames Tutorial—Mac files</u> or <u>Frames Tutorial—Win files</u>, depending on the computer you're using, to download the tutorial files.

   When the files are downloaded and decompressed, you should have a folder named DWFrames on your computer, containing the Web pages and graphics needed for this tutorial.

   Now launch Dreamweaver and begin:

2. **Choose Site→New Site.**

   The Site Definition window opens. Make sure the Basic tab is selected.

3. **Type *Frames Tutorial* in the box and click the Next button.**

   This is the Web-site name Dreamweaver will use while you're working on this tutorial.

4. **Check the "No, I don't want to use a server technology" radio button and click the Next button.**

   Dynamic Web sites and server technologies are covered in Part 6.

5. **Make sure the "Edit local copies on my machine" radio button is selected. Click the folder icon next to the field in the middle of the window. Navigate to and select the folder DWFrames; click Choose.**

   The path to this folder appears in the box. You've just told Dreamweaver where to find the files that make up your Web site.

6. **Click Next.**

   You arrive at the Sharing Files section of the Site Definition window. Since you'll be completing this tutorial on your computer and not moving it onto a Web server, you don't need to tell Dreamweaver how to connect to the server. If this were a real site that you planned to move onto a Web server so others could view it, you'd set up the Remote site information (Chapter 16) at this step.

7. **Make sure "I'll set this up later" appears in the pop-up menu. Click Next one last time.**

   A short summary of the settings for your site appears in the last panel of the Site Definition window.

8. **Click Done.**

   If a dialog box appears informing you that Dreamweaver is about to create a *cache* for this site (see step 9 on page 29), click OK. You *always* want Dreamweaver to create a site cache when you define a new site.

   You've now defined the site you'll be working on in this tutorial. Defining Web sites is described in more detail in Chapter 14.

Creating a Frameset and Frames

You'll create the online article by adding frames to a Web page that's already partly made.

1. **Choose File→Open, and then open the file in the DWFrames folder called** *title.html*.

   The Web page shows the article's headline. You'll start by creating a frameset and adding a single frame.

2. **Choose View→Visual Aids→Frame Borders.**

   If you prefer, you can instead use the View Options menu (the rightmost icon) in the document toolbar to choose Frame Borders (among other visual aids).

   A thin, gray border appears around the edges of the page.

3. **Drag the frame border at the top of the document an inch or so down to create a new frame.**

   In this one step, Dreamweaver creates a new, untitled frameset document and a new, untitled Web page in the top frame.

4. **Drag the bottom frame border upward to create a frame at the bottom of the window.**

   Dreamweaver creates a new, untitled Web page in the bottom frame and adds the necessary HTML code to the frameset document. Your screen should look something like Figure 7-14.

5. **Open the toolbar, if it isn't already open, by choosing View→Toolbars→ Document. Type** *When Cabbages Attack!* **in the Title field of the toolbar.**

   You've just replaced the default title, *Untitled Document*. The new page title appears in the title bar of the document window.

6. **Choose File→Save All.**

The Save As dialog box opens. Because you've just created several new, untitled documents, you'll need to save each one. The first document Dreamweaver saves, as shown by the crosshatched border in the document window, is the frameset page.

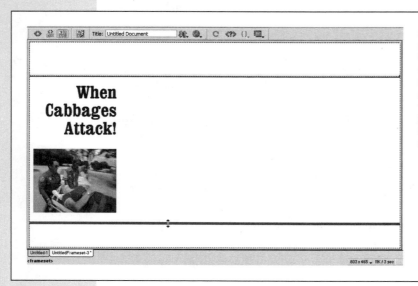

Figure 7-14:
Dreamweaver frees you from the confusing HTML required to build framesets and frames. Instead of messing around with <frameset> and <frame> tags, you can create frames quickly by dragging borders on the page.

7. **Type** *cabbages.html* **in the Name field. Click Save or press Enter to save the frameset page.**

Make sure that you save this page in the proper location—the DWFrames folder, which is the root folder of this site.

After you click Save, the Save As dialog box appears again. This time, it's prompting you to name and save the bottom page, which you'll later make into a navigation bar for the story.

8. **Save the bottom frame as** *navigation.html,* **also inside the DWFrames folder.**

The Save As dialog box appears once again, this time for the page in the top frame (see Figure 7-15). You've already downloaded the page that goes inside this frame, so you don't need to save a new page now.

9. **Click Cancel.**

Modifying the Frameset and Frames

Although you've got the basic structure of the page in order, each frame needs additional fine-tuning to make it look just right.

1. **Open the Frames panel, if it isn't already open, by choosing Window→ Others→Frames (or by pressing Shift-F2).**

   The small Frames panel opens, as shown in Figure 7-16.

Figure 7-15:
When saving multiple frame pages, one after another, how do you know which page you're saving? Dreamweaver uses a crosshatched border inside the frame to indicate which Web page it is saving.

2. **Select the frameset by clicking the thick border in the Frames panel.**

   To check what you've selected, look at the document window's status bar, where the <frameset> tag appears in bold.

Figure 7-16:
This panel lets you select framesets and frames to modify their properties. Thick, black borders indicate a selected frameset; a frame has a thin black border when selected. The name of each frame appears in the corresponding panel. In this case, none of the frames have been named yet.

3. **In the Property inspector, choose No from the Borders pop-up menu.**

As noted on page 209, frame borders are best avoided for professional-quality Web sites. Eliminating borders lets the frameset and all of its frames appear to be a unified whole.

4. **Type *0* in the Border Width field in the Property inspector.**

As explained on page 209, if you don't do this, Web browsers will leave space between each frame.

5. **In the Property inspector, click the top row of the row selector (see Figure 7-17).**

You've just filled in the Property inspector with the current settings for the top frame. Now you can modify them:

Figure 7-17:
You specify the size of each frame by selecting a frameset and then using the Property inspector.

6. **Type *30* in the Row Value field, and make sure Pixels is selected in the Units pop-up menu.**

When you press Enter, the top field shrinks.

7. **Click the bottom row of the row selector in the Property inspector, and type *30* in the Row Value field. Make sure Pixel units is selected.**

When you press Enter, the navigation field shrinks.

8. **In the Property inspector, click the middle row of the row selector and select Relative from the Units pop-up menu.**

The top and bottom frames have each been set to a fixed dimension of 30 pixels—they'll contain a thin banner and navigation bar. The middle frame, however, holds the article itself. Because you never know what size browser window your reader is using, you can't reliably specify a size for this middle row. Instead, you've set this row to Relative, meaning that it will take up whatever space is available.

9. **Click the top frame in the Frames panel to select it.**

The Property inspector displays the properties for that frame.

10. **Click the folder icon next to the Src field.**

The Select HTML File dialog box appears.

11. Select the file banner.html in the DWFrames folder, and then click Choose.

The page, with the Cosmopolitan Farmer logo, appears in the top frame of the document window.

12. Choose No in the Scroll pop-up menu and turn on the No Resize box.

Since this frame contains a simple static banner, scroll bars are unnecessary—and ugly.

13. Type *0* in the Margin Width field and *0* in the Margin Height field.

You've just eliminated all the space from the top and left edges of the banner.

14. Click the bottom frame in the Frames panel to select it.

This frame will contain the navigation bar for the story.

15. Choose No in the Scroll pop-up menu and check the No Resize box. Type *0* in the Margin Width field and *0* in the Margin Height field.

This frame will become your navigation bar. Because the nav bar fits completely within the frame, it doesn't need scroll bars or margins.

16. Choose File→Save All.

Because you've already named the files earlier in the tutorial, Dreamweaver simply saves them now.

Nesting Framesets

The middle frame of the Cosmopolitan Farmer design needs to be subdivided even further. The left side of the frame will hold a photo and title for the article, while the right side will contain the main text of the story. To prepare for this layout, you need to insert a frameset *into* this frame.

1. Click the middle frame in the document window.

2. Your cursor should now be in the document containing the title and photo. Choose Modify→Frameset→Split Frame Left.

Dreamweaver creates a new frameset with two frames side by side, inside the existing middle frame (see Figure 7-18). Keep in mind that although it *looks* like you've added the frameset to the middle Web page, the new frameset information is actually added to the original frameset page—cabbages.html.

3. Click the thick border of the nested frameset in the Frames panel, as shown in Figure 7-18.

You've just selected the frameset, so that you can change its settings.

4. In the Property inspector, click the left column of the column selector, and then type *200* in the Column Value field. Choose Pixels from the pop-up menu, as shown in Figure 7-19, and press Enter.

You've set the width of the left column to 200 pixels.

5. **Click the right column of the column selector in the Property inspector and choose Relative from the Units pop-up menu.**

   Once again, the Relative setting means that the width of this frame varies depending on the size of the visitor's browser window. That's the ideal setting for the frame that will contain the news story itself.

6. **On the Frames panel, click the left frame of this frameset to select it. On the Property inspector, choose No from the Scroll pop-up menu and turn on No Resize.**

   Since there's nothing in this frame but a title and photo, there's no reason to add scroll bars.

7. **Click the right frame on the Frames panel. Type *content* in the Frame Name field on the Property inspector, and then press Enter.**

   Unlike the other frames, you've named this one. Naming a frame lets you make it the target of links. In other words, you can make a link in another frame load a Web page into *this* frame. Because this frame holds the text of the article, it can vary in size and may need scroll bars.

   In the next steps, you'll add a Web page with the first part of the story.

Figure 7-18:
Dreamweaver denotes framesets with thick borders in the Frames panel. When selected, a frameset border turns solid black.

Figure 7-19:
The darkened panel in the thumbnail picture at the right of the Property inspector shows which frame you're currently working on.

8. Click the folder icon next to the Src field.

   The Select HTML File dialog box appears.

9. Double-click the file in the DWFrames folder called intro.html.

   The page appears in the right frame of the document window.

10. Choose File→Save All. To preview your work, press the F12 key (see Figure 7-20).

Figure 7-20:
Although this page contains four frames, there are no frame borders, so the page has a clean, unified look. The scroll bar only scrolls the text, leaving the banner, footer, title, and photo in place. The bottom frame is empty, but in the next section, you'll add a navigation bar to it.

Adding the Navigation Bar

The main page of the story is coming together well. But your hapless visitors are stuck here, with no way to view the other pages in the story. In the next step, you'll add a navigation bar to the bottom frame.

1. Click in the bottom frame of the document window. Choose Modify→Page Properties.

   The Page Properties dialog box opens, as shown in Figure 1-10 (page 32).

2. Set the background color to black.

   You can leave the page untitled, because only the title of the *frameset page* appears in the browser window's title bar. No one will ever see the title of this page.

3. **Click OK.**

You return to the document window.

4. **Choose Insert→Interactive Images→Navigation Bar.**

Alternatively, on the Common tab of the Insert bar, click the Navigation Bar object. Either way, the Insert Navigation Bar dialog box opens (see Figure 7-21). This navigation bar will have only three buttons—one for each week's story.

5. **In the Element Name field, type *w1*.**

The name of an element is only used as part of the programming of the page and is invisible to visitors. In this case, it's the button for week one.

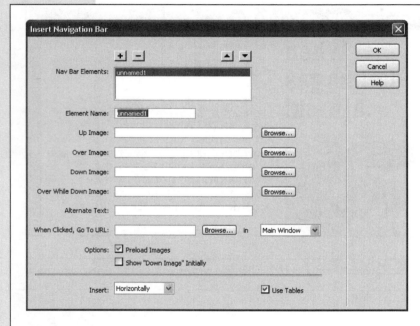

Figure 7-21:
From this one dialog box, you can create a navigation bar with any number of buttons. Just click the + button and type a name to add a new one to the list. You can reorder your navigation buttons anytime using the up and down arrows and delete unwanted ones by clicking the - button.

6. **Click the Browse button next to the Up Image field. In the images folder of the DWFrames folder, double-click the file called week1.gif.**

You've just told Dreamweaver what image to use for the up state of the button. In the next steps, you'll choose the over, down, and over while down images. (See step 6 on page 217 for details on button states.)

7. **Click the Browse button next to the Over Image field. In the Open dialog box, double-click the file called week1_f2.gif.**

Next stop: the button image in its down position.

8. **Click the Browse button next to the Down Image field. In the Open dialog box, double-click the file called week1_f3.gif.**

   Finally, you need to choose a graphic for the button's appearance when the mouse passes over it in its down state.

9. **Click the Browse button next to the Over While Down Image field. In the Open dialog box, double-click the file called week1_f3.gif.**

   In other words, there isn't any special graphic for this state. When a user moves the mouse over a button in its down state, it will remain unchanged. (If you don't specify a graphic at all, Dreamweaver will use the graphic you specified for the over image, in step 7, as the over while down image.)

10. **In the Alternate Text field, type Week 1.**

    This is the text that visitors will see instead of the button if they've turned off graphics in their browser.

11. **Click the Browse button next to the When Clicked, Go To URL field.**

    The Open file dialog box appears, prompting you to choose the HTML Webpage file that will open when the button is clicked.

12. **In the DWFrames folder, double-click the week1.html file.**

    This is the text for week one of the story—and it's what will appear when your visitors click the Week 1 button link.

13. **Choose "content" from the menu to the right of the URL field.**

    "content" is the name of the frame where each article in the story opens; it's the frame at right in Figure 7-20.

14. **Click the + button in the upper left of the dialog box to add an additional button. Follow steps 5 through 13 to add the Week 2 button.**

    Use the name *w2* for the button, and substitute *week2* where *week1* appears in the instructions.

15. **Click the + button in the upper left of the dialog box to add the last button. Follow steps 5 through 13 to add the Week 3 button.**

    Use the name *w3* for the button, and substitute *week3* where *week1* appears in the instructions. You're almost done.

16. **From the Insert pop-up menu, choose Horizontally. Turn on Use Tables.**

    Dreamweaver can automatically create a table to house the navigation graphics, which helps keep the graphics together and prevents possible display problems.

17. **Click OK to insert the navigation bar.**

    You return to your document window with the nav bar in place.

18. Choose File→Save All.

You've completed your masterpiece! Press F12 to view it and test it in your Web browser. If you like, you can visit *www.sawmac.com/dwmx/tutorials/* to compare your work with the finished one that's posted online.

Cascading Style Sheets

W hen you compare the formatting options discussed in Chapter 3 with the text styling in a magazine or book, the Web looks like the ugly duckling of the media world. The handful of options available in HTML—font face, size, and color—doesn't hold a candle to the typographic and layout control you get when creating a document in even the most basic word processing program.

But not anymore. A newer technology called Cascading Style Sheets has begun to address the shortcomings of HTML. Cascading Style Sheets (CSS) allow much greater control over the layout and design of Web pages. Using them, you can add margins to paragraphs (just as in a word processor), colorful and stylish borders to images, and even dynamic rollover effects to text links. Best of all, Dreamweaver's stream-lined approach lets you combine several of these formats into powerful style sheets with just a few mouse clicks.

Note: Cascading Style Sheets can be one of the most difficult Web-design concepts to grasp. As you read the following pages, resist the temptation to fling your monitor into the hallway until *after* you've followed the tutorial steps at the end of this chapter, which put all of the tech-talk into context.

Cascading Style Sheet Basics

If you've used styles in word processing programs like Microsoft Word or page lay-out programs like Quark XPress, Cascading Style Sheets (CSS) will feel familiar. A *style* is simply a rule describing how to format a particular piece of HTML. (A style *sheet* is a set of these canned styles.)

You might create a single style, for example, that formats text with the font Arial, colored red, and with a left margin of 50 pixels. You can also create styles specifically for working with images; for instance, a style can align an image along the right edge of a Web page and place 50 pixels margin between it and the surrounding text.

Once you've created a style, you can apply it to text, images, or other elements on a page. For example, you could select a paragraph of text and apply a style to instantly change the text's size, color, and font. You can also create styles for specific tags, so that all <h1> tags in your site, for example, are displayed in the same style, no matter where they appear.

Why Use CSS?

Although HTML alone provides basic formatting options for text, images, tables, and other Web page elements, Cascading Style Sheets have many advantages that make them a superior choice for many formatting tasks. In fact, the World Wide Web Consortium (W3C), the organization responsible for defining standards for the Web, plans to *phase out* the <font> tag in future versions of HTML in favor of CSS. In other words, upcoming Web browser versions may not even understand much of the text formatting you apply with the Property inspector. But they will understand CSS. (For a list of other obsolete tags, see *www.codehelp.co.uk/html /deprecated.html.*)

Even if the threat of obsolescence doesn't motivate you to use CSS, consider this: Style sheets offer far more formatting choices than HTML. With CSS, you can format paragraphs as they appear in a book or newspaper (the first line indented and no space between each paragraph, for example) and control the leading (the space

---

FREQUENTLY ASKED QUESTION

HTML Styles vs. Cascading Style Sheets

I think you've messed up in your book; I remember reading about this style-sheet business back in Chapter 3. Do I win anything?

Afraid not.

You're probably thinking of Dreamweaver's HTML Styles, which are indeed described on page 85.

CSS may sound like the same idea. However, several important differences separate the two. For example, when you update a CSS style, the changes you make are instantly applied anywhere the style is used. Your boss doesn't like the red color of the headings that appear on a page? Just change the style for that heading from red to blue, and all of the red headings suddenly turn blue. Dreamweaver doesn't, on the other hand, automatically update text you've formatted with HTML styles when you edit the HTML style. You must go back and individually apply the new style to your text.

Furthermore, while HTML Styles apply only to text, you can use CSS to format any HTML element, such as a table, image, or even the body of the page.

Most important, the underlying technology behind the two approaches is completely different. HTML Styles is simply a Dreamweaver tool that lets you quickly apply basic HTML formatting using paragraph formats and the <font> tag. CSS, however, is not HTML. Although CSS works with HTML (and XML), it has its own language with its own properties and syntax. (Fortunately, Dreamweaver's CSS tools hide all this complexity, so you may never know you're not working in HTML).

---

between lines of type in a paragraph). When you use CSS to add a background image to a page, you get to decide how (and whether) it tiles (repeats). HTML can't even begin do any of these things.

Even better, CSS styles take up much less space than HTML's <font> tag formatting. You can usually trim a lot of kilobytes from text-heavy Web pages using CSS while maintaining a high level of formatting control. As a result, your pages look great *and* load faster.

Style sheets also make updating your site easier. As mentioned previously, when you edit a CSS style, Dreamweaver immediately makes that change ripple through your site, *wherever* that style is used. You can thus completely change the appearance of a site by simply editing a single style sheet.

When Not to Use CSS

Cascading Style Sheets may sound like a cure-all for HTML's anemic formatting powers, but you may pay a price for their convenience.

The first consideration is compatibility. Although the CSS standard has been around for some time, not all Web browsers understand style sheets. And among those that do, some still don't always display style properties correctly (Netscape Navigator 4 is the main culprit here).

Internet Explorer 3 for Windows understood some style sheet properties, but not until Internet Explorer 4 and Netscape Navigator 4 could you count on consistent interpretation of CSS. The bottom line: If you worry that a substantial number of your visitors may still use pre-4.0 browsers, stay away from CSS.

UP TO SPEED

Getting to Know (and Love) CSS

Cascading Style Sheets are an exciting—and complex—addition to your Web building tool kit, worthy of entire books and Web sites on this topic alone. For example:

- For an excellent tutorial on CSS, visit Web Monkey's style sheet tutorial at: *http://hotwired.lycos.com/webmonkey/reference/stylesheet_guide/*.

- Ongoing discussions about CSS, and informative articles on this technology can be found at A List Apart: *www.alistapart.com*.

- For the ultimate source of information, turn to the World Wide Web Consortium's Web site: *www.w3.org/style/CSS/*. The W3C is the body

responsible for many of the standards that drive the Web—including HTML and CSS.

- If you just love to curl up by the fireplace with a good computer book, *Cascading Style Sheets: The Definitive Guide* by Eric Meyer (O'Reilly) can't be beat. Eric's Web site provides a lot of helpful information, too: *http://meyerweb.com/eric/css/*

Finally, you don't have to look any further than your own desktop for the ultimate reference to each CSS property. Dreamweaver's built-in Reference window provides instant access to concise information on Cascading Style Sheets (see page 288).

In fact, even if you're confident that only (or mostly) 4.0-or-later browsers travel to your site, you still need to test your pages thoroughly in a variety of browsers—especially Navigator 4, which tends to have the most trouble with CSS. (By contrast, if you only need to design for Internet Explorer 5 or later—or other CSS-capable browsers like Mozilla—you'll have a much easier time exploiting the powerful design potential of style sheets.)

Finally, as you'll become painfully aware, Dreamweaver's visual display doesn't always work when using Cascading Style Sheets. Although Dreamweaver MX displays CSS much better than in previous versions, you'll still find that some of the formatting properties described in this chapter—such as the border style—don't show up in the document window. You'll be forced to preview your pages in a browser frequently, just to get a clear view of how your pages are shaping up.

Internal vs. External Style Sheets

As you create new styles and add them to style sheets, you can then store these style sheets either internally, in the Web page itself, or in another file called an *external style sheet*.

Internal style sheets appear in the <head> portion of a Web page and contain styles that apply to that page. An internal style sheet is a good choice when you have a very specific formatting task for a single page. For example, perhaps you want to create styles to format the text and table of a chart that only appears on a single page.

An external style sheet, on the other hand, contains only styles—no HTML—and can be linked to numerous pages. You can create a single style sheet that affects many pages of your site, creating uniform formatting throughout. For instance, you can put a headline style in an external style sheet and link that sheet to every page in the site. Every headline on the site will then share the same look—instant design consistency! Even better, when the boss (or the interior decorator in you) calls up and asks you to change the color of the headlines, you need to edit only a single file—the external style sheet—to update hundreds or even thousands of Web pages.

You can create both types of style sheets easily in Dreamweaver, and you aren't limited to choosing one or the other; a single Web page can have both an external style sheet (for styles that apply to the whole site) and an internal style sheet (for page-specific formatting). You can even attach multiple external style sheets to a single page.

Types of Styles

Styles come in several different flavors. The two most common are *custom styles* and *redefined HTML tags*.

A custom style is one that you create, name, and attach manually to text or an HTML tag. Custom styles work the most like styles in word processing and page layout programs. For example, if you want the name of your company to be displayed in bold and red wherever it appears in the text of a Web page, you can create a custom style named Company with boldface and red text color formatting. You would then select your company's name on the page and apply this style.

The other major type of CSS style is called an *HTML tag style,* and it applies globally to HTML tags, as opposed to individual selections. For example, suppose you wanted to display every Heading 1 paragraph (see page 66) in the Arial font. Instead of creating a custom style and applying it to every Heading 1 on the page, you could create a HTML tag style for the <h1> *tag.* In effect, you redefine the tag so that it's displayed in Arial. The main benefit of redefining an HTML tag in this way is that you don't have to apply the style by hand. Since the new style says that *all* <h1> tags must use Arial, wherever a Web browser encounters a <h1> tag, it displays the text in Arial, the specified font.

These HTML tag styles are the easiest way to format a page. For one thing, there's no need to select the tag and apply the style; the page only needs to contain an instance of the tag—<h1> for example—that you've redefined.

Note: In the course of your Web-design career, you may well encounter alternate terms for custom and HTML tag styles. In the official terminology of Cascading Style Sheets, custom styles are actually called *classes,* and HTML tag styles are *type selectors.* Since *custom style* and *HTML tag style* are more descriptive terms (and the ones you'll see in Dreamweaver), you'll see those terms used in this book.

Nevertheless, there are times when only a custom style will do, such as when you want to apply different styles to various paragraphs on the same page. Simply redefining the <p> tag won't do the trick, because that would affect *all* paragraphs. Instead, you'd have to create a custom style for each paragraph format, and then apply the styles by hand.

Creating Styles

You start most CSS-related tasks in the CSS Styles panel, which is the command center for creating and using styles (see Figure 8-1). To open it, choose Window→CSS Styles (or press Shift-F11).

Phase 1: Set Up the CSS Type

To create a new style, click the New Style button on the CSS Styles panel (see Figure 8-1), or choose Text→CSS Styles→New CSS Style. The New CSS Style dialog box appears (Figure 8-2), where you begin the process of creating your new style:

- **Type.** Click the appropriate radio button for the kind of style you're creating: *Make Custom Style* (to create your own style from scratch) or *Redefine HTML Tag* (to create an HTML tag style that Dreamweaver will automatically apply to each occurrence of the tag). See the facing page for a discussion of these two types.

  The third type offered here, Use CSS Selector, lets you create a style for one of the four *pseudo-classes* Dreamweaver supports or for any valid CSS selector (see the box on page 239).

- **Name.** If you clicked the Make Custom Style button, type a name for the new style, to replace Dreamweaver's bland default name (*.unnamed1*). All custom styles begin with a period, according to standard CSS convention.

Tip: If you're in a desperate hurry, you can leave the period out. Dreamweaver adds it automatically when it puts the style in the style sheet.

Apply Styles View
Remove Style
Internal style
Style from an external style sheet
Edit Styles View
Attach external style sheet
New style
Delete style
Edit style sheet

Figure 8-1:
The CSS Styles panel lists the names of all custom styles available to the page from its internal style sheet as well as any linked external style sheets. Icons next to the name of each style identify its type—internal or external. You use the list to apply styles to selected objects on the page. As a result, only styles you apply yourself (custom styles) appear in the list. Dreamweaver doesn't list HTML tag styles here; they're automatically applied to HTML tags in the page. Turning on Edit Styles displays the formatting information contained in each style—including HTML tag styles.

Custom style names must *begin* with a letter, too, and can only contain letters and numbers. Dreamweaver lets you know if you use any invalid characters for the name.

If you chose Redefine HTML Tag instead, select the HTML tag you want to redefine from the Tag pop-up menu (which appears when you click the Redefine HTML Tag button).

Tip: If you're an HTML guru, you may find it faster to type the tag (minus the brackets) in the Name box. For example, if you want to create a style for all unordered (bulleted) lists, type *ul*.

If you clicked the Use CSS Selector button, Dreamweaver lets you select one of the four CSS pseudo-classes from the menu: a:active, a:hover, a:link, or a:visited (for definitions, see the box on page 239).

- **Define In.** Click This Document Only if you want the styles to apply only to the current Web page (creating an *internal* style sheet, as described on page 234). To create a new *external* style sheet, choose New Style Sheet File from the Define In pop-up menu. This option not only creates a new external CSS file (which you can save anywhere in your site folder), but also adds the necessary code in the current document to link it to that file.

If you've previously linked this document to an external style sheet (page 238), select that style sheet's name from the pop-up menu; you've just told Dreamweaver to store the new style into this external style sheet file.

Tip: If you create a bunch of internal styles in a particular page, and later realize you'd like to turn them into an external style sheet that you can use in other pages, you're in luck. Dreamweaver has a command for this very task. Open the page containing the internal styles you want to reuse and choose File→Export→Export CSS Styles. A dialog box opens, letting you save the file as an external style sheet. Don't forget to add the .css extension to the end of the file name.

Figure 8-2:
The New CSS Style dialog box is where you choose a type of style and give it a name. Depending on the type of style you choose, the label next to the naming box changes. In this example, since Make Custom Style is selected, the Name label appears. However, if you choose the Redefine Tag option, this changes to (not surprisingly) Tag; or Selector, if you're using the Use CSS Selector option.

If you indicated that you want to create an external style sheet, clicking OK makes a Save Style Sheet As dialog box appear. Navigate to your site's folder and type a name for the file new external CSS file. Just as HTML files end in .html, CSS files end in .css.

Tip: If you'll be using this style sheet for all of the pages in your site, you might want to save it in the root folder of your site and give it a general name like *site_styles.css* or *global.css*. (You don't have to type the .css file name extension, by the way. In this case, Dreamweaver adds it.)

No matter which Define In option you selected, clicking OK eventually brings you to the Style Definition window.

Phase 2: Defining the Style

The CSS Style Definition window provides access to all of the formatting options available to you and your Web-page text and graphics (see Figure 8-3). A blow-by-blow description of these various options begins on page 250.

Once you've defined the style, click OK in the Style Definition window. Dreamweaver adds the style to the specified style sheet, and, if it's a custom style, makes it appear in the CSS panel (Figure 8-1).

The real trick to creating a style is mastering all of the different properties available, such as borders, margins, and background colors, and *then* learning which ones work reliably in the different browsers.

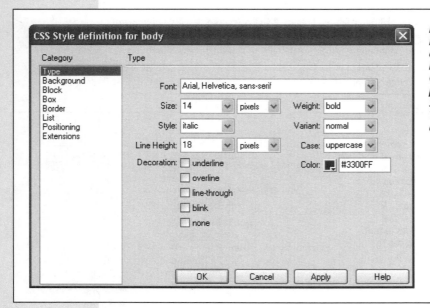

Figure 8-3:
For ultimate formatting control, Dreamweaver lets you set 71 different Cascading Style Sheet properties from the CSS Style Definition window. To learn about these options, see page 250.

Using Styles

Once you've created styles, applying them is easy. In fact, if you created HTML tag styles, you needn't do anything to apply them, because their selectors (see the box on page 239) automatically dictate which tags they affect.

Linking to an External Style Sheet

Whenever you create an external style sheet, Dreamweaver automatically links it to the current document. To use its styles in a different Web page, however, you must *attach* it to the page.

To do so, open the Web page to which you wish to add the style sheet. Click the Attach Style Sheet button (see Figure 8-1) on the CSS Styles panel. (If the CSS Styles panel isn't open, choose Window→CSS Styles or press Shift-F11.)

The Link External Style Sheet window appears. Click the Browse button. In the Select Style Sheet File dialog box that appears, navigate to and double-click the CSS (.css) file you wish to attach to the document. If Dreamweaver offers to copy the style sheet file into your site's root folder, click Yes.

The Link External Style Sheet window provides two other options: Link or Import. These two choices are nearly identical; they're simply two different methods of attaching an external style sheet to a Web page. The only real difference is that Netscape

Navigator 4 doesn't understand the Import method. For greatest compatibility, use the Link option.

Tip: Some sneaky Web developers take advantage of Netscape Navigator 4's inability to understand the Import method. Since Netscape 4 doesn't display many CSS properties correctly, some designers create *two* external style sheets: one with basic formatting that Netscape understands, and one with more complex CSS options that more advanced browsers can display.

First attach the Netscape style sheet using the Link option, and *then* attach the second style sheet using the Import method. Make sure to attach the linked style sheet first. Although Netscape will only read the linked style sheet, other browsers will read both. But because you attached the imported style sheet second, it appears below the other style sheet in the code of the page, and its styles will take precedence.

POWER USERS' CLINIC

Pseudo-classes and Other CSS Selectors

When you choose the Use CSS Selector option in the New CSS Style window (Figure 8-2), you aren't actually choosing a third type of style. You're entering the world of *CSS selectors,* where you can access even more advanced style types.

A CSS selector is simply the instruction that tells a Web browser *what* it should apply the CSS formatting rules to. In fact, HTML tag styles and custom styles are *types* of selectors. But there are other, more advanced selectors. For example, an ID selector (which always begins with a # symbol like this: *#menu1*) lets you create a style that identifies *one* element on the page. Most people apply it to an object that's controlled by a JavaScript program.

A *contextual selector* is yet another type of CSS selector. Contextual selectors let you create a "smart" style that applies only in certain contexts. For example, you could give a special design to the <b> (bold) tag, but *only* when it appears inside a <ul> (bulleted) list. In this case, the selector would be a combination of the two tags; you would type *ul b* in the Selector box.

You can even create contextual selectors that *combine* a custom style and an HTML tag. For example, you could create a special look for bold words that appear *within* text formatted with a custom style called *.sidebar.* (To create this setup, you'd type *.sidebar b* into the Selector box.)

Clearly, CSS selectors can add plenty of power, but also staggering complexity. To learn how to build them, see one of the references in the sidebar box on page 233.

In addition, Dreamweaver lets you select one of four *pseudo-classes* from the Selector menu. The first three (a:link, a:active, a:visited, and a:hover) correspond to the types of links described in step 9 on page 33.

For example, a:link represents the formatting state of an unvisited link on the page; a:active represents the look of the link as the visitor clicks it; a:visited is the link's look after the visitor has already been to the linked page; and a:hover describes the look of the link as the mouse moves over it. This last option works like a rollover image, but for text. (Note, too, that Netscape Navigator 4 doesn't recognize the a:hover style.)

To use these pseudo-classes, select each in turn from the Selector menu and set its formatting characteristics (font color, size, underscore, and so on).

You must create these pseudo-classes in a particular order. An easy mnemonic device for this is LVHA (for Link, Visited, Hover and Active). Using these styles, you could make your link text appear red and underscored before it's clicked, blinking when the mouse moves over it, purple boldface when clicked, and pale pink after it's been visited. (You might never be hired to do Martha Stewart's Web site, but you could do it.)

Dreamweaver adds the necessary HTML code to the head of the Web page and automatically formats any tags in the document according to the style sheet's HTML tag styles. You'll see the formatting changes take place in the document window immediately after attaching the external style sheet.

If the style sheet contains *custom* styles, on the other hand, you won't see their formatting effects until you apply them to an element on the page, as described next.

Applying a Custom Style

You can apply custom styles to any selection in the document window, whether it's a word, an image, or an entire paragraph. (You can apply any custom style to any element, although doing so doesn't always make sense. If you format a graphic with a style that specifies bold, red Courier type, it won't look any different.)

For example, suppose your company's name appears in a paragraph of text on a Web page that includes a custom style named .company. To format that text using

---

The Parts of a Style

Dreamweaver automatically handles the details of adding the proper CSS code to your pages, but if you're looking for something to read in bed, here's the behind-the-scenes scoop on how it works.

When you create an internal style sheet, Dreamweaver adds a pair of <style> tags to the head of the page. The opening <style> tag tells a Web browser that the following information is *not* HTML—it's CSS code. When the Web browser encounters the closing </style> tag, it knows the CSS style information has ended.

Each line inside the <style> tag is a single style. An HTML tag style for the Heading 1 tag (<h1>), for example, might look like this:

```
h1 {font-size: 24px; color:     o
#003399}
```

The first part—h1—is called a *selector* in CSS-speak, and indicates what the style applies to. In this case, wherever the <h1> (heading 1) tag appears, this style will apply.

The information between the braces—{ }—states what formatting the browser should apply. For example, the example above contains two formatting rules for the <h1> tag. Each rule is called a *declaration* and is composed of a

property and a *value*. For example, *font-size: 24 px* is one declaration with a property of *font-size* and a value of *24 px*. In other words, this rule tells a Web browser that text inside an <h1> tag should be 24 pixels tall. The second declaration in the example makes the text of all <h1> tags show up using the color #003399.

A custom style looks just like an HTML tag, except that instead of a tag, the selector is a name you've supplied preceded by a dot, like this:

```
.company {font-size: 24px; color:
#003399}
```

Styles stored in an external style sheet look exactly the same; the only difference is that external style sheets don't include the <style> tags. You can open a page in Code view (choose View→Code) and edit an internal style sheet, just as you would the HTML of the page (see Chapter 9).

In Dreamweaver MX, you can also look at the raw style information of an *external* style sheet by opening the .css file within Dreamweaver. Simply choose File→Open and navigate to the CSS file in the site. Click Open, and then edit away. You can change the hexadecimal color number, for example.

---

the custom style, you select the name in the document window and apply the style, as described below.

Similarly, to format larger selections, such as an entire paragraph, you'd select the paragraph and apply the custom style. In fact, you can apply a custom style to any HTML tag, such as the <p> (paragraph), <td> (table cell), or <body> tags.

When you apply a custom style (.content, for example) to a tag, Dreamweaver adds a special *class* property to the page's code, like this: <p class="company">. On the other hand, if you apply a class to a selection that *isn't* a tag—a single word that you've double-clicked, for example—Dreamweaver wraps the selection within a <span> tag like this: <span class="company">Cosmopolitan Farmer</span>. This tag, in other words, applies a style to a *span* of text that can't be identified by a single tag.

As you can see, it doesn't take much code to add a style to a Web page. A single application of a CSS style might add only 15 characters to your document (<p class="company">). When you compare that compact instruction with the equivalent HTML code required to produce the same formatted text (such as <font size="5" face="Georgia, Times New Roman, Times, serif" color="#999933">Cosmopolitan Farmer</font>), custom styles look downright petite.

To apply a custom style, select whatever it is you want to style—a single word or an HTML tag, for example. As always, the tag selector in the bottom of the document window is a great way to select a tag (see page 19). Then, in the CSS Styles panel, make sure the Apply Styles button is selected and click the name of the custom style you want (see Figure 8-1). You can also apply custom styles using the Property inspector (or remove them by choosing No CSS Style from the pop-up menu). This feature, new in Dreamweaver MX, lets you hide the HTML font formatting options in the Property inspector, and instead display a pop-up menu of custom styles (see Figure 8-4).

Figure 8-4:
The CSS/HTML mode button switches between HTML and Cascading Style Sheet formatting.

Finally, you can also apply a class from the document window's tag selector, as shown in Figure 8-5.

Tip: You've read it before, now read it again: Because Dreamweaver is limited in its display of some CSS properties, the only sure way to see how the page will look is to preview it in a Web browser. (See Figure 1-17 on page 42 for more detail on previewing.)

Un-Applying a Custom Style

To remove a style from an object on a Web page, simply select the element and click "(none)" in the CSS Styles list (see Figure 8-1). You can also choose Text→CSS Styles→None to accomplish the same thing.

Figure 8-5:
You can apply a custom style directly to a tag using the document window's tag selector. Just right-click (Control-Click) the tag you wish to format, and then select the custom style from the Set Class submenu. In addition, the tag selector lets you know if a tag has a custom style applied to it. If so, the style's name is added at the end of the tag. For example, in the bottom figure, a custom style named .photo is applied to a graphic (the <img> tag) on the page.

Tip: If you've applied a custom style to a selection of text, you don't actually have to select all of the text to remove the style. Just click anywhere inside it and click None in the CSS Styles list (or choose Text→CSS Styles→None). Dreamweaver is smart enough to realize you want to remove the style applied to the text. (If you applied the style to a tag, Dreamweaver removes the Class property. If you applied the style using the <span> tag, Dreamweaver removes the span tag.)

You can't, however, remove *HTML tag* styles from tags. For example, suppose you've redefined the <h1> tag using the steps outlined on page 235. If your page has three Heading 1 (<h1>) paragraphs, and you want the third heading to have a different style than the other two, you're out of luck. The only way to remove the formatting is to delete the <h1> style altogether (see page 245), which, of course, would remove the formatting from all three headings. In this case, you'd have been better off creating a custom style and applying it to the first two headlines only.

Manipulating Styles

As with anything in Dreamweaver, styles are easy enough to edit, duplicate, or delete; all you need is a map of the terrain.

Editing Styles

While building a Web site, you continually refine your designs. That chartreuse color you assigned to the background of your pages may have looked great at 2 a.m., but it loses something in the light of day.

Fortunately, one of CSS's greatest selling points is how easy it makes updating the formatting on a Web site.

Tip: Although this section talks mostly about text styling, you can also use CSS styles to add background colors, background images, borders, and accurate positioning that can apply to images, table cells, and other page elements. For an example of a CSS style applied to an image, see the tutorial on page 270.

Dreamweaver MX provides two main ways to edit styles: using either the Edit Styles view of the CSS Styles panel or the Edit Style Sheet window.

The quick, new way is to click the Edit Styles button on the CSS Styles panel (see Figure 8-6). You get a list of *all* styles available to the current Web page, including internal and external style sheets, and HTML tag styles. Double-click the name of

---

POWER USERS' CLINIC

A Time to Design

A new Dreamweaver MX feature called *Design Time style sheets* lets you "try on" different Cascading Style Sheets while developing your Web page in Dreamweaver—in other words, at design time. Using the simple dialog box shown here, you can hide the (external) style sheets you've attached to a Web page and try on new ones.

Design Time style sheets come in very handy when you're editing Library items that can't include style sheets, but can be formatted with CSS styles (page 521). You'll also use Design Time style sheets when you use the Tip on page 239 for dealing with Netscape Navigator 4. You can use this method to preview the page using the linked external style sheet, but hide the styles from the style sheet attached with the import method. It's a great way to get a glimpse of what your Netscape viewers will see.

Developers who use different style sheets for different Web browsers or different operating systems also use Design Time style sheets. This technique involves programming—using either JavaScript or one of the server-side languages

discussed in Part 6 of this book—to attach a style sheet to a page based on a visitor's browser or operating system.

To apply a Design Time style sheet to your page, choose Text→CSS→Design Time Style Sheets; the Design Time Style Sheets window appears. Click the top + button to select an external style sheet to display in Dreamweaver. Note that this doesn't *attach* the style sheet to the page; it merely selects a .css file to use when viewing inside Dreamweaver.

To view your page with this new style sheet, you may need to get an attached external style sheet out of the way. To do that, use the bottom + button to add it to the Hide list.

Design Time style sheets affect the look of the page only in Dreamweaver. They have no effect in an actual Web browser. That's both the good news and the bad news. Although Dreamweaver lets you apply custom styles that you take from a Design Time style sheet to your Web page, it doesn't actually attach the external style sheet to the page. You have to attach it yourself when design time is over, or else your visitors will never see the intended result.

the style to open the Style Definition window (Figure 8-3). This is the same window you used when first creating the style. Make your changes to the style, and then click OK.

Figure 8-6:
Internal styles are listed at the top under the name of the document—index.html, in this case. Styles contained in an external style sheet appear under the name of the CSS file: global.css. Unlike the Apply Styles view, which only shows custom styles, the Edit Styles view shows all styles, including HTML tag styles and other CSS selectors (see page 239). The formatting properties of the style are listed in the right hand column. For example, the HTML tag style for the <p> tag uses the font Verdana set to 12 pixels tall. Click the expand/collapse button to show or hide the styles for the internal or external style sheet.

When you click OK, you return to the document window, and Dreamweaver reformats the page to reflect any changes you made to styles used in the current document.

To edit a style, open the Edit Style Sheet window using any of the following techniques:

- Choose Text→CSS Styles→Edit Style Sheet.
- Click the Edit Style Sheet button on the CSS Styles panel (Figure 8-1).
- Press Shift+Ctrl+E (Shift-⌘-E).

Like the Edit Styles view of the CSS Styles panel, the Edit Style Sheet window lists *all* styles—custom, HTML tag, and CSS selector styles. (If you want to edit a style in an external style sheet, you'll need to select that file name in the list and click Edit before proceeding.)

Double-click the name of a style to open the Style Definition window (see Figure 8-3). Make your changes to the style and then click OK.

If the style belongs to an external style sheet, Dreamweaver returns you to that sheet's list of styles (see bottom image in Figure 8-7). Click Save to save the changes to the external style sheet and return to the Edit Style Sheet window.

If you're editing an internal style, Dreamweaver saves these changes to the style sheet and returns you to the Edit Style Sheet window.

When you click Done, you return to the document window; Dreamweaver reformats the page to reflect any changes you made to styles used in the current document.

Deleting a Style

At some point, you may find that you've created a style that you don't need after all. Maybe you redefined the HTML <code> tag, for example, and realize you haven't even used the tag in your site. There's no need to keep it around taking up precious space in the style sheet.

To delete a style, make sure the CSS Styles panel is open (Window→CSS Styles) and click the Edit Styles button. Click the name of the style you wish to delete, and then click the Trash can at the bottom of the panel (Figure 8-1). If you "trash" an *external* style sheet, you merely unlink it from the current document without actually deleting the .css file.

Tip: A faster way to delete a style is to right-click (Control-click) the name of the style in the CSS Styles panel and choose Delete from the contextual menu. This same technique works to delete custom styles in Apply Styles view of the CSS Styles panel.

You can also delete a style from the Edit Style Sheet window (Figure 8-7.) Open the window using any of the methods described on the facing page, click the name of the style in the window, and click Remove.

Figure 8-7:
When you open the Edit Style Sheet window, Dreamweaver lists all internal styles (styles added to the current document only) and each external style sheet attached to the page. External style sheets—global.css in the top figure, for example—are indicated by the word link *in parentheses. To edit the styles in the external style sheet, you must first select it in the Edit Style Sheet window and click Edit.*

Unfortunately, deleting a custom style *doesn't* delete any references to the style in the pages of your site. For example, if you've created a style called .company and applied it throughout your site, and you then delete that style from the style sheet, Dreamweaver doesn't remove the <span> tags or class properties that refer to the style. Your pages will still be littered with orphaned code like this—<span class="company">Cosmopolitan Farmer</span>—even though the text loses the styling. (See how to solve this problem using Dreamweaver's powerful Find and Replace tool on page 585.)

Duplicating or Renaming a Style

Dreamweaver makes it easy to duplicate a CSS style, which can be handy when you've created, say, an HTML tag style, and now decide you'd rather make it a custom style. Or you may want to use the formatting options from one style as a starting off point for a new style. Either way, you start by duplicating an existing style.

To duplicate a style, open the CSS Styles panel (Window→CSS Styles) and click Edit Styles (Figure 8-6). Right-click (Control-click) the name of the style you wish to duplicate, and then choose Duplicate from the contextual menu.

Tip: You can also duplicate a style in the Edit Style Sheet dialog box (Figure 8-7). Select the style's name, and then click Duplicate. Then read on.

The Duplicate CSS Style window appears (Figure 8-8), where you can give the duplicated style a new name, reassign its Type setting, use the Define In pop-up menu to switch it from an internal to an external style sheet, and so on.

Figure 8-8:
The Duplicate CSS Style dialog box looks and acts precisely like the New Style box (see page 237). You can select a new style type, name it, and add it to an external or internal style sheet. The only difference is that the duplicated style retains all of the CSS properties of the original style.

When you click OK, Dreamweaver adds the duplicate style to the page or external style sheet. You can then edit the new style, just as you would any other style (see page 242).

Tip: This procedure is the only way you can rename a custom style without actually editing the CSS code in Code view. After you select the custom style in the Edit Style Sheets window, click Duplicate and then type a new name in the Name box.

More About Styles

As you begin to pile styles onto your pages, you may start to notice some peculiar behaviors as styles start to interact. The rules governing these interactions can be complex, but boil down to two main concepts: *inheritance* and *cascading*.

Inheritance

Imagine that you've created a new style by redefining the paragraph tag (<p>). This style has a font type of Arial, is red, and is 24 pixels tall. Then you select a single word in a paragraph and apply bold formatting to it. When you use the Property inspector's bold button to do this, Dreamweaver quietly wraps that word in a pair of

---

POWER USERS' CLINIC

Using Microsoft Word to Prepare Content for CSS

It's easy enough to copy text from a word processing program, paste it into a Dreamweaver document, and then apply paragraph formatting and CSS styles. But when you need to create hundreds of Web pages, this time-consuming ritual can drive you quietly mad.

However, if your company or clients use Word 2000, 2001, or 2002/XP, and you use Cascading Style Sheets in your site, you can streamline this process. You take advantage of the fact that Word offers style sheets of its own, which it converts to CSS styles when you save a Word document as HTML (see page 53).

When Word exports the document, it records your style information as an internal CSS style sheet in the head of the HTML file. Once in Dreamweaver, you'll find that Word's built-in heading styles—like Heading 1, Heading 2, and Heading 3—turn into the appropriate HTML heading tags, <h1>, <h2>, and <h3>. Word's Normal style is converted to a plain paragraph—the <p> tag.

Custom styles you created in Word, on the other hand, become custom styles in Dreamweaver. What began life as Word paragraph styles are applied as custom styles to the paragraph tag (<p class="copyright">), and Word's character styles are applied as spans (<span class="company">). (One caution: When creating a character style in Word, don't specify the font. Changing the font of the style adds extra information to the Web page that Dreamweaver can't automatically remove.)

Often, however, the formatting that worked in Word (bold, red, whatever) isn't what you'll want on the final Web page. One way to redefine all of these styles is to edit them one at a time—but life's too short.

A better way is to create an external style sheet filled with styles whose names *exactly* match the style names from Word (and are formatted to your taste). Then *delete* the internal style sheet from the imported Web page (in Code view, delete the opening and closing <style> tags and all the style information between them). When you link the document to your new, external style sheet, you'll see your preferred formatting magically appear everywhere a Word style had been applied.

Here's an example. You have a Word document that includes one Heading 1–style paragraph and several paragraphs in a style called Content. You save it as a Word HTML document (page 54) and bring the page into Dreamweaver using the import Word HTML command (page 54). Then delete the internal styles and apply an external style sheet that includes a redefined <h1> tag style and a custom style called .content. Voila: instant formatting.

Using this trick, you free yourself from the tedious process of applying custom styles to every page. You also give the site's content producers—the people creating the text in Word—the responsibility of identifying the different text elements in each page, saving you many a weekends' worth of effort.

<strong> HTML tags (Dreamweaver MX doesn't use the <b> tag when making text bold—see the box on page 77).

When a browser loads the page, it formats all paragraphs in Arial, red, 24 pixels, because that's how you defined the <p> tag. But what happens when the browser suddenly encounters the <strong> tag? Since you didn't redefine the <strong> tag in red, Arial, 24 pixels, the browser scratches its little silicon head: Should the browser just resort to the *default* font, size, and color when it gets to the <strong> tag?

No, of course not. The bolded word should look just like the rest of the paragraph—Arial, red, 24 pixels—but be bold *too*. And indeed, that's how cascading style sheets work: the <strong> tag *inherits* the formatting of the surrounding <p> tags.

Just as human babies inherit traits—eye color, for example—from their biological parents, nested HTML tags inherit the properties of tags that surround them. A tag that's nested inside of another tag—that <strong> tag inside the <p> tag, for example—is called a *child*, while the enclosing tag is called the *parent*.

Inheritance passes from parent to child. So, in this example, the <p> tag (the parent) passes on the Arial font, red color, and 24 pixel size to the <strong> tag (the child). But just as children have their own unique qualities, the <strong> tag adds its own quality—boldness—to the properties of its parent.

Note: Inheritance applies to all styles, not just HTML tag styles. If you apply a custom style, for example, to a <td> (table cell) tag, all tags inside the cell—paragraphs, images, and so on—inherit the properties of the custom style.

Inheritance comes in quite handy at times. For instance, say you want to display *all* text on a page (paragraphs, headings, unordered lists, and links) using the Verdana font. You could, of course, knock off for the week and redefine *every* HTML tag used to format text—<h1>, <h2>, <p>, <a>, <ul>, and so on—or create a custom style and then manually apply it to all text on the page.

However, a better and faster technique would be to take advantage of inheritance. Every Web page contains a <body> tag, which contains all the elements of your page. The <body> tag, therefore, is the parent of *all* HTML you see in a page—images, paragraphs, headings, and so on. To quickly format all text, you could create an HTML tag style for the <body> tag using Verdana, or create a custom style using that font and apply it to the <body> tag. Every bit of text inside the body—all children—then inherit the Verdana font property.

Note: Actually, not *all* CSS properties are inherited. The Border property, for instance, is not inherited by child tags. Use Dreamweaver's built-in CSS Reference to see which properties are inherited (see page 288).

Cascading

At times, styles can conflict. Let's say you redefine the <h1> tag in an external style sheet, so that all <h1> tags will show up in red, using the Arial font. But now you attach this external style sheet to a Web page that already has an *internal* style sheet, whose <h1> tag style has been set to Times, 24 pixels.

When a Web browser has to display any text formatted as a Heading 1 paragraph, it runs into a little dilemma. The page has two different styles—two sets of formatting rules—for the *same tag*. So which does the browser choose: the style from the internal style sheet or the style from the external style sheet?

The answer is both. The browser merges the two styles into a sort of hybrid, following these rules:

- Properties that don't conflict are applied as usual. In the above example, the red color property only exists in the external style, while only the internal style specifies a font *size*. So far, the browser knows that, for this page, text inside <h1> tags should be both red *and* 24 pixels tall.

- When properties do conflict, a Web browser uses the property from the "closest" or more specific style. External styles (since they're in a separate file) are not as specific as the internal styles, which were created specifically to style this one page. In this case, the font Times (specified in the <h1> tag style in the internal style sheet) wins.

To summarize this example, then, the Web browser determines that text inside an <h1> tag on this Web page should be Times, red, 24 pixels tall.

This cascading effect applies to custom styles, as well. When there's a direct conflict between properties from a custom style and an HTML tag style, the custom style prevails. Because custom styles must be applied directly to a tag—<h1 class="specialHeadline">—they are considered more specific than the HTML tag style. After all, you added the style to a specific instance of the <h1> tag on the page.

Note: In the CSS version of "rock, paper, scissors," HTML text formatting beats CSS formatting. In other words, suppose you used the Property inspector to apply a size of 2 to some text and later apply a custom style, defined to have 48-pixel-tall text, to the same words. Web browsers will display the text as an HTML font size of 2, ignoring the CSS style.

These same rules apply when child elements inherit properties from parent elements, as described on page 247. For example, if you apply a purple, Arial-font custom style to the body of a page, then child elements (anything within the <body> tag) will inherit those properties. If you then redefine the paragraph tag so that paragraph text is green, paragraph text will inherit the Arial font from the body, but will ignore the purple color in favor of the green you specified when redefining its own—paragraph—tag.

If you're still reading, and haven't set this book aside in hopes that the swelling in your brain will subside, you've probably adequately absorbed the notion that the application of style properties can be quite complex. However, this information may come in handy. If you find that the styles you create don't seem to work the way you think they should, look to see if you've applied a style to a parent element, or whether you have two conflicting styles applied to the same text or object.

Style Properties

Cascading Style Sheets are a powerful and complex technology, providing *many* more formatting options than HTML alone, whose formatting options are few enough to fit, for the most part, onto the Property inspector. In fact, Dreamweaver lets you set 71 different CSS properties using the Style Definition window. The following pages cover each of the eight Style Definition categories and the properties available from each. (If you'd prefer an online reference, don't miss the built-in CSS reference available from the Window→Reference command; it's described more completely on page 288.)

Tip: As noted earlier, not all Web browsers can display the many different formatting options available through Cascading Style Sheets. Dreamweaver, in its zeal to give you access to as many options as possible, actually lets you set properties that don't work in *any browser at all* (such as the Page Break property described on page 262.) It can be frustrating to find a really cool style sheet property, only to realize that it doesn't work in most Web browsers.

There is hope, however. Webreview.com's invaluable Master Compatibility Chart saves you from groping around in the dark. This frequently updated Web page lists which CSS properties work on which browsers, broken down by Mac, Windows, and browser version. You'll find this indispensable guide at *www.webreview.com/style/css1/charts/mastergrid.shtml.*

Type Properties

As the name implies, the Type category of the Style Definition window lets you set formatting options that affect text (see Figure 8-9).

- **Font.** You choose a font for the style from the Font pop-up menu. As with the <font> tag (as described on page 79), you choose from *groups* of fonts rather than picking the specific one you have your heart set on. Unfortunately, your array of choices is no better than in HTML. Dreamweaver also lets you create your own "first-choice, second-choice…" font choices from this menu, exactly as described on page 81.

- **Size.** Unlike HTML, where font size is defined using a number from 1 to 7, CSS offers a dizzying array of size choices.

  If you want to make sure your text appears at the same size regardless of browser or platform, type a number in the Size box and select Pixels from the unit pop-up menu to its right. 12 pixels is a good size for regular type.

There's one downside to this approach: Pixel values prevent visitors from adjusting the size of text on the screen using their Web browsers' text size up/down controls. To give visitors more control, use one of the relative measurements on the bottom part of the pop-up menu (**small, large,** and so on), which are based on a Web browser's default font size (and *can* be adjusted by your visitors).

Figure 8-9:
You'll visit the Type category frequently while creating CSS styles. You set many different properties for formatting text—the most common use of CSS—and be assured that, unlike a lot of other CSS properties, type settings work well in almost all browsers that understand Cascading Style Sheets.

Figure 8-10:
The numeric values 100–900 are intended to work with fonts that have many different weights (ultrathin, thin, light, extra bold, and so on). 400 is normal; 700 is the same as bold. However, in today's browsers, you'll notice no difference between the values 100-500, and only slight changes in the thickness of the type at each higher level. The 900 option results in extra bold.

- **Weight.** Weight refers to the thickness of the font. The Weight pop-up menu offers thirteen different choices. Normal and bold are the most common, and work in all browsers that understand CSS. See Figure 8-10 for details.

- **Style.** In this peculiar instance, Style means **italic, oblique,** or **normal.** Technically, italic is a custom-designed, emphatic version of a type face, *like this*. Oblique, on the other hand, is just a computerized adaptation of a normal font, in which each letter is inclined a certain number of degrees to the right. In practical application, there's no visible difference between italic and oblique.

- **Variant.** This pop-up menu simply lets you specify Small Caps type, if you like—a slightly formal, fancy-looking type style much favored by attorneys' offices.

- **Line Height.** Line height, otherwise known as *leading,* refers to the space between lines of text in a paragraph (see Figure 8-11). To allow more space between lines, set the line height greater than the font size. (If you type a number without a % sign, Dreamweaver assumes you're specifying a line height in pixels. You can change the units of measurement using the pop-up menu to the right of the Line Height field.)

Tip: A good approach for line height is to type in a percentage measurement, such as *120%,* which is relative to the size of the text (see "Size" above); if your text is 10 pixels tall, the space from the base of one line of text to the next is 12 pixels (120% of 10). Now, if you change the size of the text, the *relative* space between lines remains the same.

Normal, the default setting (top paragraph in Figure 8-11), uses a line height that's slightly larger than the height of the text. You don't get access to the pop-up menu of measurement units (pixels, points, %, and so on) unless you choose **(value)** from this pop-up menu.

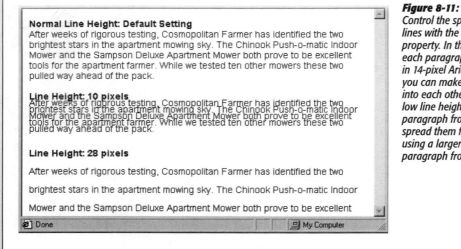

Figure 8-11:
Control the space between lines with the Line Height property. In this example, each paragraph's text is set in 14-pixel Arial. With CSS, you can make lines bump into each other by setting a low line height value (second paragraph from top), or spread them far apart by using a larger value (third paragraph from top).

- **Case.** From this pop-up menu, you can set up automatic capitalization of the text in this style. To capitalize the first letter of each word, choose **capitalize.** The **uppercase** option gives you all-capitals typing, while **lowercase** makes all letters lowercase. The factory setting is **none,** which has no effect on the text.

- **Decoration.** This strange assortment of five checkboxes let you dress up your text, mostly in unattractive ways. **Underline, Overline,** and **Line-through** add horizontal lines above, below, or through the affected text, respectively. Turning on **Blink** makes affected text blink on and off; unless you want to appear on one of those "worst Web site of the week" lists, avoid it. You can apply any number of decorative types per style, except **none.**

Tip: On certain forward-thinking Web sites these days, text links don't appear underlined. Instead, they show up in a different color.

You, too, can perform this trendy design stunt, just by redefining the <a> tag with Cascading Style Sheets, turning on the none option for the Decoration property. Voila! No more underlines.

Use this technique with care, however; most Web surfers have grown accustomed to associating underlines with clickable links. If you do remove an underline, use some other cue—bold and colorful text, for example—to indicate that the text is a link.

- **Color.** Set the color of the style's text using Dreamweaver's color box, which is described on page 34.

Background Properties

While you're probably familiar with changing the background colors of Web pages, tables, and table cells, Cascading Style Sheets provide even more options for adding colors and images to the backgrounds of your styles (see Figure 8-12).

Background Color

Any object can have a background color: a single word, a paragraph, or the Web page itself. Using this color box, you can redefine the <td> (table cell) tag, for example, using a light blue background color (every table cell on the page gets filled with that light blue color).

Background Image

Add a background image to the style by clicking the Browse button and selecting an image from your site. You can also type an absolute URL, starting with *http://*, to use an image off the Web. (Remember that Dreamweaver can't display images specified with an absolute URL. You'll have to preview the page in a Web browser connected to the Internet to see the effect.)

To fill your entire page background with some repeating graphic, you could either redefine the <body> tag using this property, or create a custom style with a Background Image property and apply it to the <body> tag as described on page 240.

Of course, you can also set up a background image using the Page Properties window (see the tip on page 33). The main advantage of the CSS method is that you can control how the image tiles (repeats) and where it's placed on the page (see below). Furthermore, using CSS, you can add background images to any *individual* element on your page: paragraphs, tables, layers, and so on.

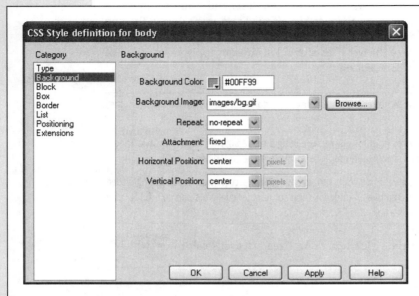

Figure 8-12:
The Background category of Cascading Style Sheet properties lets you specify a background color for a style and control the placement of background images. The Fixed option for the Attachment property is not displayed within Dreamweaver, so to get an accurate view of this property, you need to preview it in a Web browser.

Repeat

Background images—either as the background of a page or of a table—normally fill the available space by tiling (that is, repeating over and over again) across and down. A small image of a carrot added to the background of a page, for example, appears as a field of carrots—one next to each other, row after row.

But with CSS, you can control how the background image repeats. You can select from the following options:

- **repeat** tiles the image horizontally and vertically. This is the factory setting.

- **repeat-x** and **repeat-y** display a horizontal and vertical band of images, respectively. So if you'd like to have a single row of images appear at the top of a page, use the repeat-x option.

- **no-repeat** displays the image once.

Attachment

By default, the background image on a page scrolls with the rest of the page, so that as you scroll to read a long Web page, the image scrolls along with the text.

But using CSS, you can lock the image in place by choosing **fixed** from the Attachment pop-up menu. For example, say you added your company's logo to the background of a page and set the Repeat property (described on the previous page) to no-repeat. The logo now appears only once in the upper-left corner of the page. If you use the *fixed* option for this property, when a visitor scrolls the page, the logo remains fixed in the upper left corner. (Choosing **scroll** from the Attachment menu means, of course, that the background image will scroll with the page.)

Horizontal and Vertical Position

Using these controls, you can specify a position for the affected text or other Web-page element. The Horizontal position options are: **left, center, right,** and **(value)**, which requires you to type an exact number in the box and select a unit of measurement from the menu to the right. Similarly, the Vertical position options include **top, center, bottom,** and **(value)**.

These positioning options refer to the position of the styled object. For example, suppose you created a custom style that included a background image with horizontal and vertical position both set to *center*. Then you applied that custom style to a paragraph. The background image would appear in the center of that *paragraph*, not in the center of the Web page (see Figure 8-13).

Figure 8-13:
Background images aren't just for the body of a Web page. You can apply styles that include background images to any selection, even a paragraph of text. Here, a custom style with a background image is set to no-repeat (the image won't tile) and to center horizontally and vertically. The style was applied to the body of the page, resulting in the graphic appearing smack dab in the middle of the window. Meanwhile, the same style was applied to a paragraph; this time, the image floats right in the middle of the paragraph.

Likewise, if you set the horizontal position of the image to 10 pixels and the vertical position to 20 pixels, the image would start 10 pixels from the left edge of the paragraph and 20 pixels from the top edge.

If you wanted to place an image in the exact middle of the page, you'd choose *center* from both the Horizontal and Vertical Position pop-up menus, set the repeat property to no-repeat, and apply this style to the page's <body> tag (see Figure 8-13).

Block Properties

The Block Properties panel is a hodge-podge of CSS settings that affect how letters and words are displayed (see Figure 8-14).

Figure 8-14:
The Block style properties category is an eclectic mix consisting mostly of text styles. However, the Display property can be used on images, tables, and any other selection or HTML tag. Although the list is long, most of these options don't work in today's browsers.

Despite this category's name, these properties don't just apply to block-level elements (paragraphs, headlines, and so on). You can apply a style with these properties to even a single word or two. (The one exception is the Text Align property, which can apply only to paragraphs and other block-level elements.)

- **Word Spacing.** This property helps you clean up text by adding or removing space *between* words. The default value, **normal,** leaves a normal, single space between words. If you want words in a sentence to be spaced apart   like   this, then type a value of about 10 pixels. (Choose Value from the first pop-up menu, then the units you want from the second one.) The bigger the number, the larger the gap between words. You can also *remove* space between words by using a negative number—agreatchoicewhenyouwanttomakeyourpagesdifficulttoread.

Unfortunately, only a few Web browsers (Navigator 6, Opera, and the Mac version of Internet Explorer) recognize this property, so you'd be well advised to avoid it for now.

- **Letter Spacing.** This property works just like word spacing, but governs the space between *letters*. To add space l i k e t h i s, type a value of about 5 pixels. The result can make long passages of text hard to read, but a little space between letters can add a dramatic flair to short headlines and movie titles.

- **Vertical Alignment.** With this property, you can control the alignment of an object—such as an image or movie—relative to other items around it. This feature works a lot like the image-alignment options presented in Figure 5-7 on page 118.

  Two notable additions—**sub** and **super**—also let you create superscript and subscript styles when used on text. This property is a godsend when you want to properly format a trademark, copyright symbol, or footnote reference. For example, in the trademark symbol in *Cosmopolitan Farmer*™, the letters TM were selected and the super alignment applied.

Tip: The sub and super alignment options don't change the size of text. If you want to create true subscript or superscript (for chemical symbols, trademark or copyright symbols, and so on), you should also use a smaller font size in the style; 75 percent works great.

- **Text Align.** This property controls the alignment of a block-level element like a paragraph or table. You can choose from among the usual suspects—**left, center, right**—or even **justify.** (Like the text in this paragraph, justified text has both the left and right edges of the text aligned.)

  Avoid this option, however. Because Web browsers don't have the advanced controls that page-layout software does, they usually do an awful job of justifying text on a computer screen. The results are usually difficult to read and ugly.

- **Text Indent.** This useful option lets you indent the first line of a paragraph. If you enter .25 and choose *in* from the pop-up menu, you give each paragraph an attractive quarter-inch first-line indent, exactly as in a real word processor.

  You can also use a *negative* number, which makes the first line extend past the *left* margin of the paragraph, creating a hanging indent (or *outdent*)—a nice effect for bulleted lists or glossary pages. (Beware: Some browsers have trouble with negative values for this property.)

- **Whitespace.** This property controls how the browser displays extra white space (spaces, tabs, returns, and so on). Web browsers normally ignore extra spaces in the HTML of a page, reducing them to a single space character between words and other elements (see page 49). The **pre** option functions just like the HTML <pre> tag: Extra white space (like tabs, multiple spaces, and carriage returns) *in the HTML code* appear in the document window (see page 86 for more on this option). The **nowrap** option prevents lines from breaking (and wrapping to the next line) when they reach the end of the browser window.

Note: All versions of Internet Explorer ignore the Whitespace setting.

- **Display** defines how a Web browser should treat a particular block level element like a paragraph. You may be overwhelmed by the range of choices for this property—and you may be underwhelmed when you find out that most of these options aren't supported by most browsers.

  Most CSS-capable browsers understand only three of the options: none, inline, and block. The **block** option treats any item styled with this property as a block—separated from other content by space above and below it. (This is how paragraphs and headings normally appear.)

  The **inline** option treats the item like part of the current block or paragraph, so that any item styled with this property (like a picture) flows together with other items around it, as if it were part of the same paragraph.

  The **none** option is the most interesting and useful: it *turns off* the display of an item. In other words, any text or item styled with this option doesn't appear on the page. You can use JavaScript programming to switch this property on and off, making items seem to appear and disappear. (Dreamweaver doesn't provide any simple way to do this, but adventurous souls may want to check out the following tutorial, which shows how to create an expandable outline using this property: *www.webreference.com/dhtml/column12/outDisplay.html.*)

Box Properties

CSS lets you control the space that appears around any affected Web page element. You work with those properties in the Box category of the CSS Style Definition window (see Figure 8-15).

- **Width and Height.** You can specify a width and height for any styled object using these properties. Web designers use these settings most often to control layers, using Dreamweaver's Layer tools (page 369), but they can also affect other Web elements. For example, if you want a paragraph to be 100 pixels wide, create a custom style with the Width property set to 100 pixels and apply it to the paragraph.

- **Float.** If you want to move an object to the left or right of the page and have other content wrap around it, use the Float property. For example, if you want an image to sit at the right side of the page and have text flow around its left and bottom edges, choose **right** from the Float pop-up menu. The option works just like the right and left alignment options for images (page 117) and tables (page 163).

- **Clear.** Clear *prevents* an element from wrapping around any object with a right or left Float property (see above). You might want, for example, all Heading 1 paragraphs to stand out on their own lines and not wrap around an image with a right float. In that case, you'd choose the **right** option from the Clear pop-up menu when you're styling the <h1> tag.

- **Padding.** Padding is the gap that separates the content of the style—such as a paragraph of text or an image—and its border (see Figure 8-15). For example, if you put a 1-pixel border around an image and want to add 10 pixels of space between the image and the border, type *10* into the top padding box and choose *pixels* from the pop-up menu. Turn off the Same for All box if you wish to set the padding around each edge separately; then type values into each of the four boxes.

- **Margin.** The margin is the outermost space surrounding an element (Figure 8-15). It surrounds the border and padding properties of the style and lets you add space between one element and another. Use any of the values—pixels, percentages, and so on—that CSS supports.

Figure 8-15:
Top: In the CSS Box Model, every style is composed of multiple boxes, one inside the other. Each box controls certain display properties of the style. For example, the outermost box of a style is called the margin. *It controls the space between the border of the style and any other objects around the styled object such as images, paragraphs, or tables.*

Bottom: This dialog box controls the margins and padding around a styled object that uses the Box category. Its fields correspond to the measurements shown in the top diagram. For a discussion of the box model from the World Wide Web Consortium, visit: www.w3.org/TR/REC-CSS2/box.html.

Tip: You can also use the Margin properties to *eliminate* a margin entirely, if, for example, you don't like the space that browsers automatically insert between paragraphs. Type *0* in the Top margin box and *0* in the Bottom margin box to create a style with no top or bottom margins.

Border Properties

Only a few elements can have borders in HTML: tables, images, and cells. With CSS, however, you can add a border to any object from an image to a paragraph to a single exclamation point (see Figure 8-16). Even better, you can control each *side* of the border independently with its own width and color settings, or even turn *off* some parts of the border.

Figure 8-16:
Top: Add colorful and stylish borders to paragraphs, images, tables, and links with the CSS Border properties. Turning on only the bottom border for a paragraph is a great way to add a horizontal rule between paragraphs. Although HTML's Horizontal Rule object also does this, only CSS lets you control the color.

Bottom: The eight different border styles provide interesting visual diversity to the otherwise plain border.

- **Style.** This pop-up menu lets you specify the type of line used for the border. Dreamweaver gives you more options than a frame shop: **none** (the default choice),

dotted, dashed, solid, double, groove, ridge, inset, and **outset.** You can use a different style for each edge, or select a style from the top menu and turn on the Same for All box to apply the same style to all four borders. (Bear in mind that Dreamweaver itself can't display these styles. It always shows a solid border. You'll have to preview the page in a Web browser to see the effect.)

- **Border Widths.** You can set the border around each side of a styled object separately. Choose one of the preset widths—**thin, medium, thick,** or **auto**—or, if you choose (**value**) from the pop-up menu, you can type a value into the Width box and select a unit of measurement from the pop-up menu to the right. Again, you can choose from a wide range of types: **pixels, percentage, inches,** and so on. If you want to eliminate the border on one side, type *0* into the appropriate box.

- **Border Colors.** You can color each of the four borders individually using the ubiquitous Dreamweaver color box (page 34). If you don't assign any colors, but do assign border *widths*, Dreamweaver makes the borders black.

Note: You have to select a style from the pop-up menu to see the borders. If you leave this option blank or select "none," you won't see the borders even if you set the width and color.

List Properties

To exercise greater control over bulleted and numbered lists, use the CSS options on the List panel of the Style Definition window (see Figure 8-17).

- **Type.** Select the type of bullet to be used in front of a list item. Options include: **disc, circle, square, decimal** (1., 2., 3.), **lower-roman** (i, ii, iii), **upper-roman** (I, II, III), **lower-alpha** (a, b, c), **upper-alpha** (A, B, C), and **none** (no bullet at all).

- **Bullet Image.** For the ultimate control of your bullet icon, skip the boring options preprogrammed into a Web browser (like disc, circle, square, or decimal) and supply your own. Click the Browse button and select a graphics file from your site folder. Make sure the graphic is appropriate bullet material—in other words, small.

- **Position.** This property controls how the bullet is placed relative to the list item's text. The **outside** option places the bullet outside of the margin of the text, exactly the way bulleted lists normally appear on a Web page. **Inside,** on the other hand, displays the bullet within the text margin, so that the left edge of the *bullet* aligns with the left margin; Figure 8-17 should make the effect clear.

Positioning Properties

Cascading Style Sheets may be useful for formatting text and adding background colors and margins to objects, but this technology is also intended as a structural aid for laying out Web pages. Even so, Dreamweaver's own Layer tools achieve the same effects and are much easier to master (Chapter 12). You'd be well advised to skip the CSS Positioning settings and use layer tools instead.

Extensions

The final category in the Style Definition window is listed last for a good reason. Only one property in this category works in more than one Web browser, and one of them doesn't work in *any* current browser.

Figure 8-17:
Top: Take control of your bulleted and numbered lists using the CSS Style Definition window's List panel. With Cascading Style Sheets, you can even supply your own graphic bullets.

Bottom: A bullet-crazed Web page, for illustration purposes. Parading down the screen, you can see "inside" bullets, "outside" bullets, and bullets (inside and outside) made from graphics.

- **Page Break.** This property specifies, when your visitor makes a printout of your page, whether a page breaks before or after the styled object. You could apply this, for example, to the <h1> tag to make sure each printed page begins with a Heading 1 paragraph—if, that is, any browser recognized this property. None do.

- **Cursor.** Of all the Extension properties, this one holds the most promise. When a visitor moves the mouse over an object with this style applied, this property changes the cursor shape to one of fifteen different designs (a hand, an hourglass, or a crosshair, for example). Internet Explorer 4 and above, Netscape Navigator 6 and above, Mozilla, and Opera 5 and above all recognize this professional-looking property.

- **Filter.** The Filter property can apply many interesting visual effects to a page; for example, it can add a drop shadow to an image. Unfortunately, this Microsoft-only option works in the Windows version of Internet Explorer, and no other browsers.

Cascading Style Sheets Tutorial

In this tutorial, you'll create an external style sheet for a Web page on the *Cosmopolitan Farmer* Web site.

Note: As usual, this tutorial requires some half-finished starter documents from the Web. Using your Web browser, visit *www.sawmac.com/dwmx/*. Click the Tutorials link to go to the tutorials page. Then click the link CSS Tutorial–Mac files or CSS Tutorial–Win files, depending on the computer you're using.

When the files are downloaded and decompressed, you should have a folder named DWCSS on your computer, containing the Web pages and graphics for this tutorial.

Creating an External Style Sheet

Once you've downloaded the tutorial files and opened Dreamweaver, choose the DWCSS folder as your site folder, using the site-definition routine described on page 25. (For a shortcut, choose Site→New Site, click the Advanced tab, type something like *CSS Tutorial* in the Site Name field, click the folder icon next to the Local Root Folder field, navigate to and select the folder DWCSS, and then click Choose or Select. Finally, click OK.)

Now you're ready to begin defining a style sheet. In this example, you'll create a collection of styles for the Reviews section of the *Cosmopolitan Farmer* Web site.

1. **Choose File→Open; navigate to and double-click the file in the DWCSS folder called *mowers.html*.**

   The Web page contains *Cosmopolitan Farmer*'s 2002 Apartment Mower Round-up review (see Figure 8-18). The page's text is a bit boring looking, so you'll use CSS to spiff it up.

   To start, you'll create a style for the Heading 1 paragraph and create an external style sheet at the same time.

2. **If the CSS Styles panel isn't already open, choose Window→CSS Styles (or press Shift-F11).**

   The CSS Styles panel opens.

3. **On the CSS Styles panel, click the Add New Style (+) button .**

   The New CSS Style window opens (see Figure 8-19). You'll first pick the type of style you wish to create.

4. Click the Redefine HTML Tag button.

This lets you create a style for a particular HTML tag—in this case, the <h1> tag. In other words, you're going to create a formatting rule that applies automatically to every Heading 1 paragraph.

Figure 8-18:
Add style to this rather plain Web page using Cascading Style Sheets. In this tutorial, you'll improve the rather ho-hum appearance of the main section of this page—the white area in this figure.

Figure 8-19:
If you've already attached an external style sheet to a page, you can select its name from the Define In menu. That way, the new style will be added to that file. Your other option, which is what you're doing in this tutorial, is to create the new style sheet when you first create a style.

5. **Type *h1* into the Tag box, or choose "h1" from the pop-up menu.**

   In the Define In section of the New CSS Style window, the New Style Sheet File option should already be selected (see Figure 8-19).

6. **Click OK.**

   The Save Style Sheet File As dialog box appears. You're about to create the file—an external style sheet—that will store the styles for this page.

7. **Navigate to the DWCSS folder. Type *reviews.css* in the Name box, and then click Save to save the file.**

   Cascading Style Sheet files always end in .css; that's how Web servers and browsers can tell what kind of file it is.

   Having created the external style sheet, you can now create the first style, as suggested by the sudden appearance of the Style Definition window. You'll choose a font, set a size, and assign a color to the <h1> tag.

8. **Choose "Arial, Helvetica, Sans Serif" from the Font pop-up menu; type *28* in the Size box; type *#333399* in the Color field.**

   The Style Definition window should look like Figure 8-20.

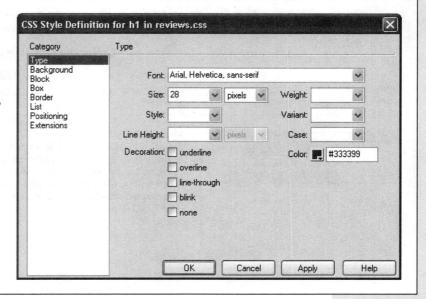

Figure 8-20:
You can set the CSS equivalents of HTML text formatting options from the Type category of the Style Definition window. (If Cadet Blue doesn't do anything for you, click the Color box and choose a color you prefer.)

9. **Click OK.**

   The Style Definition window closes and the first headline on the page is now formatted according to the style you just created. As you may have noticed, you didn't have to select the text to apply this style. Since it's an HTML tag style, it's applied *automatically* wherever the tag appears on the page.

Now, you'll create a style for the other heading on the page—an <h2> tag.

10. **On the CSS Styles panel, click the New Style button.**

The New CSS Style window opens. The Redefine HTML Tag button is already selected, and the menu in the Define In option lists the new external style sheet—*reviews.css*. In other words, Dreamweaver will add the new style to this external style sheet. All you need to do now is identify which tag you want to redefine.

11. **Type *h2* in the Tag box or choose "h2" from the pop-up menu; then click OK.**

The CSS Style Definition Window appears.

12. **Choose "Arial, Helvetica, Sans Serif" from the Font pop-up menu; type *28* in the Size box; type *#CC0000* in the Color Field; click OK.**

The window closes and the second heading on the page (the Heading 2 heading "Chinook Push-o-matic Indoor Mower") appears in its new formatting. If there had been other Heading 2 headings on this page, you'd see all of them change, too.

Editing a Style

The second heading you just redefined is the same size as the first heading. To make it smaller, to indicate it's a subhead, you'll edit the style you just created.

1. **At the top of the CSS Styles panel, click the Edit Styles radio button.**

The Edit Styles view appears (see Figure 8-21). The external style sheet—reviews.css—appears with the two new styles (h1 and h2) listed below it.

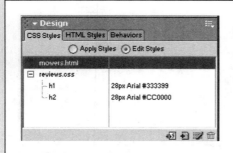

Figure 8-21:
The Edit Style view of the CSS Styles panel lists all of the styles available to the current document, including styles contained in external style sheets—in this case, reviews.css. The properties of each style appear to the right of the style name—for the h1 HTML tag style, text will appear as 28 pixel Arial in deep blue. To edit a style, double-click its name.

2. **Double-click h2.**

The CSS Style Definition window opens. (This is the same window you used when you created the style.)

3. **In the Size box, type *20* to replace the number 28, and then click OK.**

   Dreamweaver updates the style information in the external style sheet. The second headline is now a bit smaller than the first—perfect!

   If you scroll down the page a bit, you'll see the name of one of the mowers—Sampson Deluxe Apartment Mower—below the second photo. This is formatted as a paragraph, but you want it to be a second-level heading.

4. **Click anywhere in the line "Sampson Deluxe Apartment Mower."**

   You'll change this paragraph to Heading 2 using the Property inspector. (Because you've already saved CSS formatting for Heading 2, there's no need to go back to the CSS Styles panel.)

5. **From the Format pop-up menu in the Property inspector, select Heading 2.**

   If you prefer keyboard shortcuts, press Ctrl+2 (⌘-2); the heading instantly changes to match the other heading. That's the power of HTML tag styles: Once created, an HTML tag style's formatting is automatically applied wherever the tag appears.

Creating a Custom Style

Now you'll create a style to highlight the name of products that appear in the review. Notice, for example, the phrase "Chinook Push-o-matic Indoor Mower" in the first paragraph. Since the product names consist of just a couple of words *within* the paragraph, you can't redefine an HTML tag to format them globally. Instead, you'll create a custom style, which you can then apply by hand to the text.

1. **Click the New CSS Style button (+) on the CSS Styles panel.**

   The New CSS Style window opens. This time you'll create a custom style rather than an HTML tag style.

2. **Click the Make Custom Style radio button. Type *.product* in the Name box.**

   Custom styles, technically called *classes,* always begin with a period. (If you forget to start with a period, don't worry. Dreamweaver's smart enough to do it for you.)

   Because you want to add the style to the external style sheet, you don't need to do anything else in this dialog box; Dreamweaver already proposes storing it there (see Figure 8-22).

Note: Some beginners think that whenever you create a new style, you also need to create a new external style *sheet.* On the contrary, you can—and should—store more than one style in an external style sheet. In fact, if you're creating a set of styles for an entire site, put them all in the same external style sheet.

---

3. **Click OK.**

The CSS Style Definition window appears. You'll add a few new properties to make this style stand out.

Figure 8-22:
Be careful what you choose for the Define In option. If you plan to use the CSS style on other Web pages, save it in an external style sheet—reviews.css, in this case.

4. **From the Weight pop-up menu, choose** *bold*.

To make this style even more prominent, you'll add a background color to it.

5. **In the Style Definition window Category list, click Background.**

The background properties appear (see Figure 8-23).

6. **Type** *#FFCC00* **in the Background Color box.**

Or, if you don't normally dream in hexadecimal notation, you can select a color using the color box.

That's enough formatting for the .product style. Now you'll return to the document and apply it.

Figure 8-23:
Using Cascading Style Sheet properties, you can add background colors and images as well as more common properties such as text formatting.

7. **Click OK and select the Apply Styles button in the CSS Styles panel.**

   The Style Definition window closes, and the CSS Styles panel lists the new style (see Figure 8-24). This time, nothing's changed in the document window. Unlike HTML tag styles, custom styles don't show up anywhere until you apply them by hand.

Figure 8-24:
HTML tag styles, such as the redefined <h1> and <h2> tags in this tutorial, aren't listed in the Apply Styles view of the CSS Styles panel. Because this view of the panel is used for applying styles, only custom styles appear here.

8. **In the first paragraph of the review, drag to select the words "Chinook Push-o-matic Indoor Mower."**

   This is the product name you wish to format.

9. **In the CSS Styles panel, click "product."**

   Boom! Dreamweaver formats the text with the bold, colored style. Now you'll style a couple more product names.

10. **Select "Sampson Deluxe Apartment Mower" in the first paragraph and apply the "product" style to it. Do the same for the words "Anodyne 7457."**

    Your document text should look something like Figure 8-25.

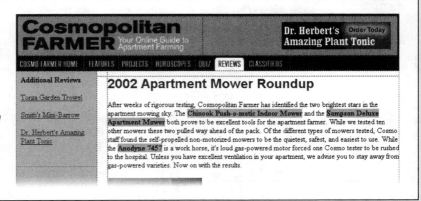

Figure 8-25:
At this point, the text in the page is coming along well. The headlines look distinctive, and you've achieved some effects (like the background color of the product names) that only CSS can accomplish. Next you'll turn your attention to making the images look great.

Formatting the Photos

CSS Styles aren't just for text. You can create styles and apply them to anything on a page—tables, images, or links, for example. In this next section, you'll improve the appearance of the product photos; specifically, you'll bless them with borders and make them hug the right side of the page.

1. **Click the New CSS Style button (+) on the CSS Styles panel.**

    The New CSS Style window opens. You could redefine the <img> (image) tag, but this would affect *every* graphic on your page. Since you want to create a style for only the two product photos, you should create a custom style that you can apply as needed.

2. **Type** *.photo* **in the Name box, make sure the Make Custom Style button is selected, and then click OK.**

    The CSS Style Definition window opens. You'll first add a border to this style.

3. **Click the Border category in the CSS Style Definition window.**

    The CSS border properties appear (see Figure 8-26). You'll add a 2-pixel, colored border.

4. **Select** *dashed* **from the first Style menu and make sure the Same for All box is turned on.**

    You'll apply the same type of border around all four edges.

Figure 8-26:
Dreamweaver has problems displaying some CSS properties. Unfortunately, the border property is one of those. To see what your creations look like, you'll have to preview them in a Web browser that understands CSS—most versions of browsers above 4.0 do.

5. In the top Width box type *2*, and make sure *pixel* is selected in the menu to the right. Also make sure the Same for All box is turned on.

If you want to set different widths for each border, uncheck the Same for All box and type different values in each of the four width boxes. Now for the color:

6. Select a color for the borders by typing *#CC0000* in the Color field for top border. (Again, make sure the Same for All box is turned on.)

That's the hex code for a fire-engine red, but you're welcome to choose any color you like (by clicking the color-picker square)—you can even choose *different* colors for the four borders.

The Style Definition window should look like Figure 8-26. Next, you'll set an alignment property that will move to the right edge of the page.

7. Click the Box category at the left side of the dialog box.

These properties affect margins, padding, and other attributes of a style (see Figure 8-27).

Figure 8-27:
Be careful not to confuse the Padding and Margin properties in the Box category. The Padding settings determine the amount of space between the styled object and its border. The Margins, by contrast, set the amount of space between the borders and other items around the object—in this case, the space between the photos and the text around them.

8. From the Float menu, select *right*.

This option works like an image's Align right property (see page 117); the graphic will snap against the right side of the browser window.

However, because text will wrap around the sides of the photos, you should add a little space between the edges of the photo borders and any text around them. The Margin properties are just the ticket.

9. **Turn off the Same for All box and type *10* in the Top, Bottom, and Left margin boxes.**

   CSS lets you set different margin sizes for each edge of an object. In this case, since the photos will already be aligned to the right edge of the page, there's no reason to add any margin to the right side.

   The Style Definition window should look like Figure 8-27. You're done with the style, now it's time to apply it.

10. **Click OK to close the CSS Style Definition window.**

    The new custom style—*photo*—appears in the CSS Styles panel. To apply it, you'll start by selecting an image.

11. **Click to select the photo—the woman in blue with a lawn mower.**

    As you can see in the tag selector at the bottom of the window, clicking the photo automatically highlights the <img> (image) tag to which you'll apply the style.

12. **In the CSS Styles panel, click *photo*.**

    The photo moves to the right edge of the page and the rest of the text flows around it. Dreamweaver can't display the CSS border properties around images, so you don't see any borders around the photo, but you will in a moment, when you preview the page.

    The small gold shield indicates where the image is in the flow of the HTML (just as when you align an image to the right).

13. **Select the second photo; apply the photo style to it, too.**

    Your photos match, as shown in Figure 8-28. Now you can preview all your hard work.

14. **Choose File→Save to save the page. Press F12 to preview the page in a Web browser.**

    Only 4.0 or later browsers display the CSS properties on this page. (And even they may have trouble, as discussed in Figure 8-28.)

Attaching an External Style Sheet

Now that you've created these styles, you may be wondering how you can use them on other pages—after all, that's the beauty of external style sheets. Once created, it's a simple process to add a style sheet to other pages in the site.

1. **Choose File→Open. Double-click the file *torga.html* in the DWCSS folder.**

   This is another review for *Cosmopolitan Farmer*. It's not yet formatted, so you'll attach the external style sheet you just created.

2. Click the Attach Style Sheet button on the CSS Styles panel (see Figure 8-1).

The Link External Style Sheet window appears.

3. Click the Browse button.

The Select Style Sheet dialog box appears. Navigate to the DWCSS folder and select the *reviews.css* file.

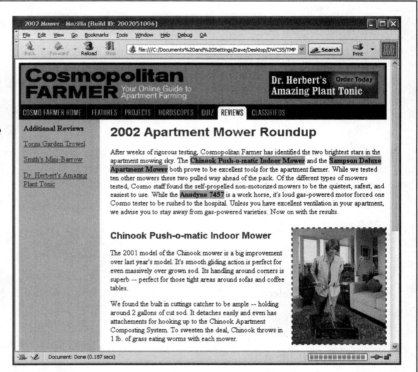

Figure 8-28:
Even browsers that understand Cascading Style Sheets can have a hard time displaying them correctly. This figure shows the completed tutorial page as viewed in Mozilla 1.0, which does a good job of displaying the styles, including the border and margins around the photo. Mercifully not shown: Netscape Navigator 4.79, which completely botches the Border property. Instead of a dashed red line around the photo, Navigator draws a solid red line around some empty space on the page and pushes the photo off the page to the far right.

4. Click OK to insert the proper path to the Link External Style Sheet window. Click OK to attach the style sheet to the page.

Notice that Dreamweaver instantly formats the top headline and two subheads using the style you created. Pretty cool—and very efficient.

5. Click the photo to select it.

You've simultaneously selected the <img> (image) tag.

6. Click *photo* in the CSS Styles panel.

Dreamweaver applies the style to the photo and aligns it with the right edge of the page.

7. **Press F12 to preview the page.**

   If you'd like to compare your finished product with the professionally completed version, visit *www.sawmac.com/dwmx/tutorials.*

Under the Hood: HTML

While Dreamweaver started life primarily as a visual Web page editor, each new version has brought enhancements to its text-editing features. Dreamweaver MX includes powerful code-editing tools that let you work on your pages' HTML, CSS, and JavaScript codes directly. In fact, in recognition of the ever-multiplying types of files used on the Web, Dreamweaver MX now lets you edit all text-based files, including XML, Java, ActionScript, and just plain text files. The code editor includes professional features such as customizable syntax highlighting, auto indenting, line numbering, and code hints. Now, Dreamweaver may be the only Web page creation program even hard-core code junkies ever need.

Roundtrip HTML

Unlike many other visual HTML editors, Dreamweaver has always graciously accepted HTML written by hand (and even by other programs). In fact, Dreamweaver has always made it easy to jump between itself and text-editing programs like HomeSite (for Windows) and BBEdit (for the Mac).

This ability, which Macromedia calls Roundtrip HTML, lets Web developers write code the way they want, without worrying that Dreamweaver will change it. For example, suppose you have a particular way of formatting your handwritten code. Maybe you insert an extra carriage return after every <td> (table cell) tag or like to use multiple tabs to indent nested tags. In such cases, Dreamweaver won't try to rewrite that to fit its own style—unless you ask it to.

Auto-Fixing Your Code

That's not to say that Dreamweaver doesn't *ever* change your code. In fact, the program can automatically fix errors when you open a page that was created in another program, including:

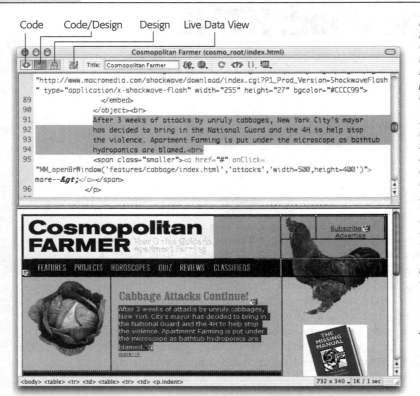

Code   Code/Design   Design   Live Data View

Figure 9-1:
In Split view (also called Code and Design view), the top half shows the inner workings of your page's HTML. The bottom half shows the "normal" Design view. Selecting an object in the visual half also selects the corresponding HTML in the code half—a great way to identify an object in your HTML. As you work in one half, Dreamweaver updates the corresponding code or design in the other. (You can switch the placement of the two halves by choosing View→Design View on Top.) Use the buttons in the document toolbar to jump between the different views. (Live Data view works with Dreamweaver's dynamic Web site tools; see page 660.)

- **Overlapping tags.** Take a look at this example:

  ```
  <p><b>Fix your tags!</p></b>
  ```

  This HTML is invalid, because the opening and closing <b> tags should appear *inside* the <p> tag. Dreamweaver rewrites this snippet correctly:

  ```
  <p><b>Fix your tags!</b></p>
  ```

- **Unclosed tags.** Tags usually come in pairs, like this:

  ```
  <i>This text is in italics</i>
  ```

  But if a page is missing the ending tag (<i>This text is in italics), Dreamweaver adds the closing tag.

- **Extra closing tags.** If a page has an *extra* closing tag (<b>bold</b></b>), Dreamweaver helpfully removes it.

Note the change from Dreamweaver 4: this feature comes turned *off* in Dreamweaver MX. If you're working on a site that was hand-coded or created by another, less capable Web-editing program, it's wise to turn this feature on, since all of those errors are improper HTML that can cause problems for browsers. (Once upon a time, for example, some Web developers deliberately omitted closing tags just to save a few kilobytes in file size. While most browsers can still interpret this kind of sloppy code, it's poor practice.)

You can turn auto-fixing on in the Preferences window (see Figure 9-2); just turn on Fix Invalidly Nested and Unclosed Tags and Remove Extra Closing Tags.

Note: The Warn when Fixing or Removing Tags option isn't really a warning as much as it is a report. By the time you see the "warning" message, Dreamweaver's already rewritten the code in your page. (You can, however, close the file without saving it to discard Dreamweaver's changes.)

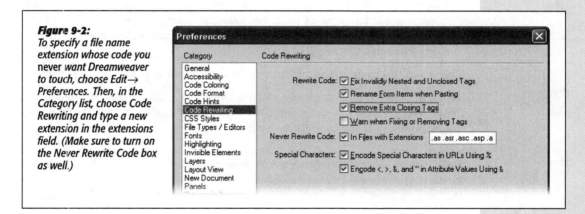

Figure 9-2:
To specify a file name extension whose code you never want Dreamweaver to touch, choose Edit→ Preferences. Then, in the Category list, choose Code Rewriting and type a new extension in the extensions field. (Make sure to turn on the Never Rewrite Code box as well.)

Dreamweaver can also change the capitalization (case) of HTML tags and properties, if you want. For example, you may prefer lowercase letters for tags and properties, like this:

```
<a href="nextpage.html">Click here</a>
```

Dreamweaver can convert uppercase tags (<A HREF="next.html">) to lowercase, or vice versa, when it finds them in pages created by other programs. (You can turn on this feature as described on page 283.)

Web Application Server Pages

Dreamweaver can leave pages with certain file name extensions untouched—pages created for *Web application servers,* for example. Web application servers process Web pages that access databases and other dynamic services like shopping cart programs and form-processing applications. Many of these systems rely on special code within the HTML of a page—code that Dreamweaver might "fix," interpreting them as HTML errors.

Unless you change its settings, Dreamweaver doesn't rewrite code in pages that are designed for the leading application server technologies: that is, files whose names end in *.asp* (Active Server Pages that run on Microsoft's IIS Web Server), *.cfm* and *.cfml* (Cold Fusion Markup Language pages that run on Macromedia's Cold Fusion Server), or *.jsp* (Java Server Pages that run on any Java Server), among others. To add an extension to this list, see Figure 9-2.

Code View

Dreamweaver provides several different ways to view a page's HTML code:

- **Code view.** In Code view, Dreamweaver simply displays your page's raw code.

- **Split view.** This shows the HTML code and the "regular" Design view simultaneously (Figure 9-1).

- **Code inspector.** Compared with Code view, this tool presents a rather cumbersome way to view a page's code. For example, it only displays the code of one document at a time. (To access the Code inspector, choose Window→Others→ Code Inspector, or press F3.)

The rest of this chapter assumes that you're using Code view for HTML editing.

To move between Dreamweaver's different views, use the document toolbar (see Figure 9-1) or choose a name from the View menu: Code, Design (the "regular" visual mode), or Design and Code (Split view).

Tip: You can quickly jump between Code and Design views by pressing Control+` (Option-`). In split view, this shortcut jumps between the two views, so you could insert an image in the design half of split view and then press Control+` to jump right into the HTML for that image in the Code half of the window.

Code view functions just like a text editor. You can click anywhere inside the window and start typing HTML, JavaScript, Cascading Style Sheet, or other programming code (such as ASP or Cold Fusion).

That doesn't mean you have to type out *everything* by hand; the Insert bar, Insert menu, and Property inspector each function while in Code view, too. Using these sources of canned HTML blobs, you can combine hands-on HTML work with the easy-to-use, rapid action of Dreamweaver's objects. This trick can be a real timesaver when you need to add a table, which would otherwise be a multiline exercise in typing accuracy. You can also select a tag (an image's <img> tag, for example) in Code view and use the Property inspector to modify it.

Tip: When you add HTML to Code view, Dreamweaver doesn't automatically update Design view, which can be disconcerting when you're working in Split view. (After all, how would Dreamweaver display a half-finished tag like this: <table border="?) Click the Refresh button in the Property inspector (see Figure 9-3), or press F5, to update the visual display.

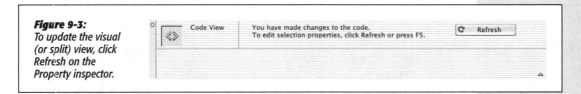

Figure 9-3:
To update the visual (or split) view, click Refresh on the Property inspector.

To help you navigate your code, Code view provides several visual cues. They include:

- **Syntax coloring.** Dreamweaver displays different elements in different colors. Comments, for example, are gray. Text is black, and HTML tags appear in blue. You can change any of these colors, and even specify unique colors for different types of tags, using the Preferences window (see Figure 9-4). Dreamweaver has separate color schemes for 23 different types of documents such as ASP, CSS, and XML files. (But do you really need different colors for HTML forms in ASP pages, HTML pages, and PHP pages? You be the judge.)

Figure 9-4:
You can control the color Dreamweaver uses to display HTML and script code in Code view. In the Preferences window, click the Code Coloring Category. Then select the type of document whose code coloring you wish to change—HTML, ASP, CSS, or whatever—and click the Edit Coloring Scheme button. In the Edit Coloring Scheme window, select an item to change—Library Item or HTML Form tag, for example—and set a text and/or background color using the color boxes. You can also make the code bold, italic, or underlined using the appropriate formatting buttons.

- **Bad code highlighted.** When you type incorrect code (an opening tag without a closing tag, say), it's highlighted in yellow (see Figure 9-5).

- **Library Items.** Library Items and uneditable regions in pages built from templates appear with a light yellow background, signifying that you can't edit them in Code view. You can change this color, too, as described on page 539. (For more on Templates and the Library, see Chapters 17 and 18.)

Figure 9-5:
Dreamweaver highlights incorrect HTML code with bright yellow highlighting in Code view (circled). If you click inside the yellow area, the Property inspector reveals the mistake. In this case, a closing tag is missing. (In Design view, on the other hand, Dreamweaver indicates mistakes by showing the HTML tag—the characters <, b, and >, for example—in front of a bright yellow background.)

You can also control Code view display using the View options menu in the toolbar (see Figure 9-6), or by using the View→Code Options submenu.

- **Word Wrap.** This option makes long lines of code wrap (at the window's edge) to the next line, so you don't have to scroll horizontally to see it all. This option affects only how Dreamweaver displays the line in the document window; it doesn't actually introduce line breaks.

- **Line Numbers.** This automatic line numbering can come in handy when debugging JavaScript code (see page 291) or when using Dreamweaver's Check Target Browser command (page 451).

- **Highlight Invalid HTML.** This is the on/off switch for Dreamweaver's friendly tendency to highlight bad HTML in Code view (see Figure 9-5).

- **Syntax Coloring.** This option turns tags, comments, and text, into colorful (and informative) text.

- **Auto Indent.** When you're working with nested HTML tags, it's often helpful to press the Tab key to indent each level of nested tags, making it easier to identify large blocks of HTML (a table and all its contents, for example). The Auto Indent option carries the same size indent onto the next line when you hit the Return or

Enter key. For example, suppose you hit the Tab key twice, type a line of code, and then hit Return. Dreamweaver would place the insertion point on the next line, indented using two tabs.

Figure 9-6:
The View Options menu on the toolbar lets you modify the display of code in Code view. The Word Wrap option, for example, forces all code to fit inside the width of the window. If a line of code extends off the page, Dreamweaver wraps it to the next line (the outlined code in this illustration). The only clue that you're looking at one long line is that the entire glob of text has only a single line number.

Code Hints

Typing code can be a chore, which is why even longtime hand-coders take advantage of anything that helps speed up the process. A perfect example is Dreamweaver MX's new Code Hints feature (shown in Figure 9-7). It lets you select tags, attributes, and even Cascading Style Sheet styles from a pop-up menu as you type.

Here's how it works. After you begin a new tag by typing an opening bracket (<), a menu pops up, listing all available HTML tags. Use your mouse or arrow keys to select a tag, or type the first few letters of the tag and let Dreamweaver select the closest matching item. When you press Enter, Dreamweaver automatically fills in the tag name. Even better, a second menu now pops up, listing all the properties of that tag.

If the feature annoys you, you can get it out of your way. You can turn off Code Hints completely, rein it in by setting a delay (so that pop-up lists don't appear immediately), or turn off Code Hints for only selected types of elements (such as tag properties). To make any of these adjustments, open the Preferences panel by pressing Ctrl+U (⌘-U) and select the Code Hints category. Make your desired changes to the Code Hints preferences, and click OK.

Tip: If you like Code Hints, you'll love the Snippets panel, which makes reusing code a snap. See page 515 for details.

Setting Code Formatting

Whenever you use the Insert bar, Dreamweaver adds a chunk of HTML that's pre-formatted for easier reading. The code for table rows, for instance, comes indented using two spaces; the code for table *cells,* meanwhile, is indented four spaces. If you're particular about how your HTML is written, Dreamweaver gives you plenty of control.

Note: If you don't work in Code view frequently, you may not care a whit how your HTML is formatted in the file—and that's fine. As long as the underlying HTML is valid (and Dreamweaver always writes valid HTML), Web browsers can display HTML formatted in many different ways. In fact, Web browsers simply ignore multiple spaces, empty lines, and other "white space" characters used to make HTML code more readable.

Figure 9-7:
The new Code Hints feature saves your tired fingers from typing tags and tag properties. Just select the appropriate item from a pop-up list and let Dreamweaver type it for you. Dreamweaver's even thoughtful enough to show you all available CSS styles when you insert a class attribute in a tag.

Dreamweaver provides several ways to control the formatting of the code it produces. Basic settings are available in the Preferences window; advanced settings for obsessive coders even let you control the formatting of individual tags (see the Power Users' Clinic box on page 285). For basic formatting settings, open the Preferences window (Edit→Preferences or Ctrl+U [⌘-U]) and click the Code Format category (see Figure 9-8). While the default settings work fine, you can still configure a number of options.

Indents

To make your code easier to read, it helps to indent nested tags and other block-level elements. But if you'd prefer that Dreamweaver quit auto-indenting such elements, turn off Use Indents. This is also your opportunity to request tabs instead of spaces for indenting lines of code; just choose Tabs from the pop-up menu.

You can also set the amount of indentation, like this:

- If Spaces is selected in the Use pop-up menu, type the number of spaces you want into the Indent Size field. The default setting is two, meaning each indent will be two spaces in the code.

- If you selected Tabs in the Use pop-up menu, the number in the Tab Size field indicates the size of each tab, measured in spaces. (The size you specify here affects only the display in Code view. In the code itself, Dreamweaver simply inserts a plain tab character.)

Text Wrapping

When a line gets long, Dreamweaver can break it into two or more lines by inserting a hard return. This can make your HTML more readable in Code view and free you from having to scroll to see all of your code. If that's the way you like it, turn on Automatic Wrapping and type a number in the After Column field. The number specifies how many characters long a line must be before Dreamweaver attempts to break it up.

This option doesn't affect how the page will look to your visitors, only how it looks in a text editor. But unlike the simulated word wrap option shown in Figure 9-6, this option adds real line-break characters to split your code into multiple, shorter lines. If you use the Code view's word wrap, you can skip this more intrusive form of text wrapping.

Note: Although Dreamweaver can shorten lines by inserting returns after a specified number of characters, it never does so if the final effect will change the appearance of the Web page. The program is smart enough not to sacrifice the quality of a page just to make the code look better in Code view. That's why some lines of HTML may be considerably longer than the limit you specify here.

Line Breaks

Windows, Mac OS, and Unix each look for a different invisible character at the end of every line of code. This expectation can cause problems when you use one kind of computer to create a page, while another OS runs the remote server that dishes out the page. Fortunately, Dreamweaver fixes the problem when it transfers a file to a Web server.

If you plan to use another text editor to edit your Dreamweaver pages, you should select your operating system from the Line Breaks pop-up menu. Doing so assures that the program on the receiving end will properly read the line breaks in Dreamweaver-produced pages.

Case for Tags and Attributes

You can write tag and property names using either uppercase letters (<B>bold</B>) or lowercase (bold); Web browsers don't care. However, *you* may care how they appear in your HTML display. If so, choose your preference from the two Case pop-up menus. Select either the lowercase or uppercase option from the two menus.

Tip: HTML may treat upper- and lowercase letters in its tags identically, but XML, an up-and-coming new language, does not. Both it and the hybrid language _XHTML_ require all lowercase tag and property names.

That's why many Web developers now use strictly lowercase characters, even in their HTML. And that's why, if you select the XHTML option when creating a new page (see Figure 1-9 on page 31), Dreamweaver will ignore an uppercase setting in the Preferences panel—even if you turn on the Override Case checkbox.

If you also turn on the Override Case checkboxes, you can make Dreamweaver scan tags and properties when opening a page created by someone else (or some other program). If their case doesn't match your preferences, Dreamweaver will rewrite them to fit the wishes of you, its master.

No Break After TD

Even though adding a line break after an opening <td> (table cell) tag may look good in Code view, in most browsers, it adds an unwanted extra space character in the table cell. Because the extra space can wreak havoc on your design, make sure this box is always turned on.

Centering

The Centering buttons let you specify which HTML tag you want Dreamweaver to use when centering block-level elements (like paragraphs) on the page. Leave Use DIV Tag turned on. The center tag won't work in future browser versions.

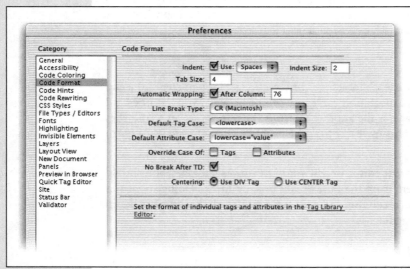

Figure 9-8:
For general control of HTML code, Dreamweaver offers the Code Format category in the Preferences window. For most people, this degree of control is overkill, but if the way HTML code appears in a page's file matters to you, go wild. (These settings don't affect how the page looks in a Web browser—only how the code appears when viewed in Dreamweaver's Code view or another text editor.)

Quick Tag Editor

Code view is great when you really need (or want) to dig into the trenches and fine-tune your HTML. But if a text editor was all you wanted, you wouldn't have bought Dreamweaver in the first place. Most of the time, you'll be working in Dreamweaver's Design view, enjoying the pleasures of its visual authoring environment.

Occasionally, however, you'll want to dip momentarily into the HTML pond, especially when you need to use some HTML that's difficult to add. You might wish you could type out a quick HTML tag on the spot, right there in Design view, without having to make the mental and visual shift required for a switch into Code view.

That's what the Quick Tag Editor is all about (see Figure 9-9).

To access the Quick Tag Editor, press Ctrl+T (⌘-T)—or, if you're feeling especially mouse-driven, click the Quick Tag editor button in the Property inspector (see Figure 9-10). Depending on what you've selected in the document window, the Quick Tag Editor opens in one of the following three modes (see Figure 9-10):

- **Insert HTML** inserts a new tag in the page. You get this mode if nothing is currently selected in your document window.

- **Edit Tag** lets you edit the tag for whatever is selected in the document window (a graphic, for example), and all its properties.

POWER USERS' CLINIC

Take Control of Code Formatting

For ultimate control over tag formatting, Dreamweaver MX introduces the Tag Library Editor. Not only does it let you control *exactly* how Dreamweaver formats every HTML tag it inserts into a page, it also lets you dictate the formatting for nine other tag libraries, such as ASP, PHP, JSP, and Cold Fusion tags.

Even if you're using some new bleeding-edge tag language unfamiliar to Dreamweaver, you're not out of luck. You can create additional tag libraries, and even import custom ASP.NET and JSP tags, as well as DTD Schemas for XML. You can also add additional tags to any library, so if the HTML standard suddenly changes, you can add new or remove obsolete tags.

To control the formatting of tags in a library, choose Edit→Tag Libraries to open the Tag Library Editor window. A list of all tag libraries appears. Click the + symbol to the left of a tag library name to see a list of tags for that library. Select a tag, and then select formatting options from the Tag Format area in the bottom half of the window.

You can control where a line breaks in relation to the tag—no line breaks after the tag; before and after the tag; or before, inside, *and* after the tag. In addition, you can choose whether any formatting rules are applied to the contents of a tag and choose the case—upper, lower, mixed—to be used when Dreamweaver adds the tags to the code.

- **Wrap Tag.** If you've selected a swath of text or other objects (two images, for example) the editor opens in this mode, which makes it easy to wrap a new tag around the current selection.

Tip: You can cycle through the modes by repeatedly pressing Ctrl+T (⌘-T).

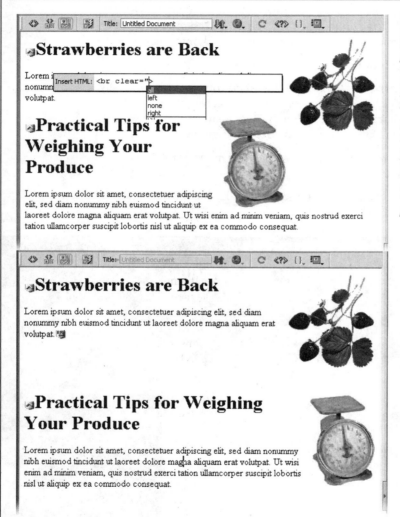

Figure 9-9:
Top: When you align an image with the right side of a page, surrounding material wraps around it—in this case, everything else (second headline, second blurb, second graphic).

Bottom: It's the Quick Tag Editor to the rescue. Now you can quickly insert the <br clear="all"> tag to the end of first blurb. This combination of tag and property means, "Turn off wrapping at this point."

Using the Quick Tag Editor

You can type tag names, properties, and property values directly into the Quick Tag Editor window. If you're editing a selected tag, you can change any of the properties listed and even add new ones. When you're done, press Enter. The Quick Tag Editor closes, and the changes take effect.

Figure 9-10:
Left: Open the Quick Tag Editor by clicking this button in the Property inspector (circled).

Right: The three modes of the Quick Tag Editor let you insert new tags, edit old tags, or wrap a new tag around a selection. The Quick Tag Editor is mobile: Drag the window by its handle (the mode name) anywhere on the screen—ideal when you want to see the part of the page you're modifying.

To make all of this even easier, the Quick Tag Editor sports a helpful list—called *tag hints*—of HTML tags and properties, for your selection pleasure. It's much like Code view's Code Hints feature: When you insert a tag, for example, a menu of available tags appears (top right in Figure 9-10). Use the up and down arrow keys or the scroll bar to move through the list. When you type the first few letters of a tag or property, Dreamweaver jumps to the nearest match in the list. (But Dreamweaver treats the two features separately, so you can set different preferences for Code Hints and the Quick Tag Editor as described in the next section.)

To choose the highlighted name, press Enter or Return. Dreamweaver adds that tag or property name to the Quick Tag Editor window. If you've selected a tag property, Dreamweaver adds the proper punctuation (href=" ", for example). The insertion point appears between the quotation marks, waiting for you to type the property's value.

Tip: When editing an existing tag in the Quick Tag Editor, press Tab to select the next property or property value. You can then type a new property or value. Shift-Tab selects the *previous* property or value.

Quick Tag Editor Preferences

If you choose Edit→Preferences and click the Quick Tag Editor category, you can adjust the Quick Tag Editor's behavior in a couple of useful ways:

- **Apply Changes Immediately While Editing.** When this option is on, you can view changes you've just made without even exiting the Quick Tag Editor; just press Tab or Shift-Tab after making the change. Dreamweaver updates your document instantly.

- **Enable Tag Hints.** *Hints* are the tag and properties that appear when using the Quick Tag editor (top right in Figure 9-10). If they get in your way, turn off this box. If you decide to leave it on, you can make the hints take longer to appear by dragging the slider to the right. In this way, the menu only appears after a certain number of seconds, so that you can type away, clutter-free. Note that the delay for Quick Tag Editor is separate from the delay for Code Hints (page 281).

Tag Inspector

The Property inspector is a handy tool. With it, you can adjust properties for all sorts of HTML tags, like a table's width or a paragraph's font. But even the Property inspector doesn't tell the whole story: some HTML tags have additional properties that don't appear there. While these are obscure and infrequently used properties for the most part, until Dreamweaver MX came along, you had to go into Code view to add them.

Dreamweaver MX introduces the *Tag inspector* (see Figure 9-11). Think of it as the über–Property inspector. For hard-core HTML fanatics, it's the best way to set properties for every HTML tag. To display it, press the F9 key, or choose Window→Tag Inspector (the same procedure also hides this panel).

The top portion of the Tag inspector displays a "tree view" of the HTML in a page. In essence, it shows the arrangement of tags as they nest within the code of a page. At the top is the opening <html> tag, followed by the <head> tag and others inside the page.

When you click a tag, *all* of its properties appear in the bottom half of the panel. You can edit any of these properties by clicking in the space to the right of the property name. You can type a new value or, for certain properties, use a pop-up menu to choose from a list of property values. For color properties, use Dreamweaver's ubiquitous color box to select just the right shade.

Unfortunately, you need to understand HTML fairly well to set the correct values. Dreamweaver doesn't make the process foolproof, leaving open the possibility that you could enter an invalid property. (To learn more about HTML tags and their properties, turn to Dreamweaver's built-in HTML reference, described next.)

Reference Panel

When it comes to building Web sites, there's a lot to know. After all, Cascading Style Sheets, HTML, and JavaScript are filled with cryptic terms and subtle nuances. Fortunately, Dreamweaver MX's Reference panel makes your search for knowledge a little bit easier. It gives you quick access to reference excerpts on eight Web topics from a variety of authoritative sources, including:

- *O'Reilly CSS Reference.* In-depth information on Cascading Style Sheets.
- *O'Reilly HTML Reference.* Complete guide to HTML tags and properties.
- *O'Reilly JavaScript Reference.* Just what it sounds like.

Figure 9-11:
Dreamweaver MX's new Tag inspector lets you edit every property of every tag on a page. What it lacks in user-friendliness (you need to know a lot about HTML to use it correctly), it makes up for in comprehensiveness.

You can even set a property value dynamically based on information retrieved from a database, using the lightning bolt button (circled). (Of course, you must first learn how to build dynamic Web sites by reading Part 6 of this book.)

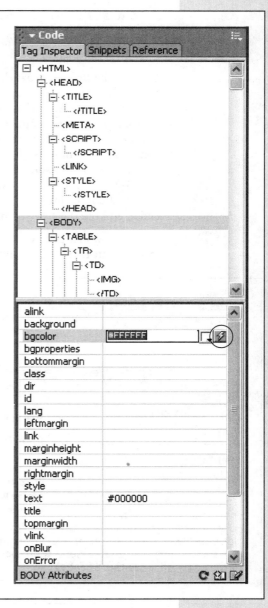

- *UsableNet Accessibility Reference.* Guidelines for making Web pages more accessible to the disabled.

- *Macromedia CFML Reference.* Complete reference to tags used in the Cold Fusion Markup Language (used with Macromedia's Cold Fusion application server).

- *Wrox ASP Reference.* More a dictionary of Active Server Page concepts than a working reference for writing ASP code.

- *Wrox JSP Reference.* Reference for Java Server Pages.

- *Sitespring Project Site Tag Reference.* Since Macromedia has stopped selling Sitespring, you'll probably find little use for this reference.

To open the Reference panel, choose Window→Reference, or press Shift-F1. The first menu at the top of the panel lets you choose the "book" you want. Once you've selected a reference, choose a particular HTML tag, CSS Style, JavaScript object, or appropriate reference topic from the menu directly below the Book menu. A description of that item appears in the main window. Depending on the reference, there may be sample usage and browser-support details. A secondary menu to the right lets you access additional information about a particular *property* or *detail* of the selected tag, style, object, or topic. For example, in Figure 9-12, to display information about the image tag's *align* property, you'd choose IMG from the Tag menu and *align* from the attribute menu.

While you won't spend every waking minute in the Reference panel, it's a good way to keep your HTML, CSS, and JavaScript chops sharp.

Figure 9-12:
Top: You can open a reference by clicking this icon on the toolbar. The reference panel opens directly to information about the currently selected tag.

Bottom: The tiny print of the default "Small font" size could make you go blind. To enlarge the font, use the panel's context menu (click the arrow in the upper-right corner of the panel), as shown here.

Inserting JavaScript

As Chapter 11 makes clear, Dreamweaver's *Behaviors* (prewritten JavaScript programs) let you add exciting interactive effects—mouse rollovers, pop-up windows, animated layers, and so on—with very little effort. But they can't do everything: When you, the native JavaScript speaker, need to wade into the depths of JavaScript programming yourself, you'll find two entrances within Dreamweaver.

The most straightforward approach, especially if you're already familiar with JavaScript programming, is to simply switch into Code view (Ctrl+` [Option-`]) and type away. Or, if you prefer, you can use Dreamweaver's Insert Script window to add your JavaScript code (see Figure 9-13).

To do so, click in either the head or body section of the page, and then choose Insert→Script Objects→Script. In the Insert Script window (Figure 9-13), choose a language from the menu: JavaScript, JavaScript1.1, JavaScript1.2, or VBScript. (The JavaScript option works with all browsers that understand JavaScript, while JavaScript 1.2 only works in 4+ version browsers. VBScript, on the other hand, works only in the Windows version of Internet Explorer.)

Just type your script into the Content section (no need to include <script> tags, as Dreamweaver handles that part), and then click OK. If you inserted the script in the body of the document, you'll see a small gold icon (indicating an invisible element on the page) to mark its location.

You can edit your script in Code view, of course. In Design view, select the script icon and then click Edit in the Property inspector.

Dreamweaver also lets you open and work on external JavaScript files (.js files) right in Code view. The program doesn't try to interpret the file as an HTML page; it won't attempt to make any of the changes described on page 276. You can just use the built-in text-editing capabilities of Code view to write your JavaScript programs.

POWER USERS' CLINIC

Dreamweaver's JavaScript Debugger

For JavaScript programmers only: The JavaScript debugger lets you debug your scripts in Netscape Navigator 4 (Mac and Windows) and Internet Explorer (Windows only) using professional techniques such as setting breakpoints, stepping over statements, and stepping into functions. To check it out, choose File→ Debug in Browser and select a browser from the submenu.

Dreamweaver checks for syntax errors in your code and alerts you if there are any problems. If everything's fine, the Dreamweaver debugger window appears and the selected browser launches.

In Code view, you can also set breakpoints for your code. Just place the insertion point inside a line of JavaScript code, and then use the toolbar as pictured here. (The toolbar also provides a quick way to jump to the various JavaScript functions in the page.)

Tip: JavaScript programming is no walk in the park. While it's certainly easier to learn than full-featured languages like Java or C++, it can still be challenging. If you want to get your feet wet, here's a great resource for basic tutorials and information on JavaScript: *www.webmonkey.com/programming /javascript/.*

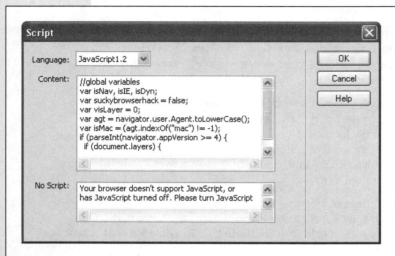

Figure 9-13:
Unlike the Code view, the Insert Script window doesn't respond to the Tab key; if you're accustomed to indenting your code, you'll need to use spaces. You can also insert noscript information—text that appears if the Web browser doesn't understand JavaScript.

EASTER EGG HUNT

Credit Where Credit's Due

Creating good software is a team effort, involving the tireless work of many dedicated individuals, most of whom never reach the celebrity status of a Bill Gates or Marc Andreesen. Yet they don't get their names on the box or the cover of the manual (even if there *were* a manual), so who's to blame them when they try to grab a little attention for their hard work?

If you'd like to meet the masterminds behind Dreamweaver's JavaScript debugger, you're in luck. This Easter Egg is, in fact, triggered by using that very same debugger. All you have to do is add a few minor modifications to any Web page.

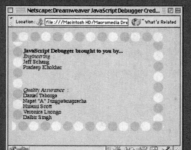

Create a new Web page and save it. Choose View→Code View to see the page's HTML source code. Click after the opening <body> tag and type:

```
<script
debuggercredits=true>
var i;
</script>
```

Next, choose File→Debug in Browser→[any browser listed]. The selected browser opens and a different page loads, displaying dancing dots and credits for the team that created Dreamweaver's JavaScript debugger.

Part Three:
Bringing Your Pages to Life

3

Forms

A Web site is a great way for you to broadcast a message, announce a new product, post late-breaking news, or just rant about the state of the world. But that's all *one-way* communication, which you may find a bit limiting. You may be curious to get some feedback from your audience. Or you may want to build your business by selling your product through the Internet as well as the traditional channels, so you need a way to gather customer information. If you want to receive information as well as give it, it's time to add *forms* to your Web design repertoire (see Figure 10-1 for a simple example). Whatever type of information you need to collect on your site, Dreamweaver's *form objects* make the task easy.

Figure 10-1:
A form can be as simple as a single empty text box (a field) and two buttons for entering a word to search a Web site, or as complex as a 100-question survey composed of fill-in-the-blank and multiple-choice questions.

Form Basics

A form begins and ends with the HTML <form> tag. The opening <form> tag indicates the beginning of the form and sets its properties; the closing </form> tag, of course, marks the form's end.

In between these tags, different objects provide the basic user interface elements—the design—of the form. Radio buttons, text fields, and pull-down menus (also called pop-up menus) are just a few of the ways you can gather input. It's perfectly OK to include other HTML elements inside a form, too. In fact, your site's visitors would be lost if you couldn't also add (and format) text that explains the purpose of each form object. And without using a table to control the layout of a form, it can quickly become an unreadable mess (see the box on page 305).

Every form element, whether it's a text field or a checkbox, has a *name* and a *value*. The name indicates what information the element is intended to collect. For example, if you want your visitors to type their email addresses into a text field, the name of that field might be *email*. The value, on the other hand, is the person's input—what your visitors type into the text field, for example, or the selections they make from a pull-down menu.

After your visitors fill out the form and click the Submit button to transmit their responses, each form element is transmitted as a name/value pair like this: *email=bob@bobville.com*. Submitting both pieces of information lets the program that processes the form figure out what the input means. After all, without a name, a value of 39 doesn't mean much (39 what? Potatoes, steps, days until Christmas?). The name/value pair (age=39) provides context for a user's input.

The Code Backstage

Creating a form is just the first step in collecting information from your Web site's visitors. You also need to connect the form to a computer program that actually *does* something with the information. The program may simply take the data from the form and email it to you. However, it could do something as complex as contacting a bank, processing a credit card payment, creating an invoice item, and notifying a shipping department to deliver the latest Stephen King novel to someone in Nova Scotia. A form is pretty useless without a program like this running on the Web server. These information-crunching programs can be written in a variety of languages—Perl, C, C#, Visual Basic, VBScript, JavaScript, Java, Cold Fusion Markup Language—and may be part of a dedicated application server like Cold Fusion Server or Microsoft's Active Server Page technology.

Writing the necessary behind-the-scenes processing software can be complex, but the concepts behind forms are straightforward:

• First, someone fills out a form on your Web page and clicks the Submit button.

• Next, the form data is transmitted over the Internet to a program on your Web server.

- The program collects the data and does something with it—whatever you and the programmer decide it should do.

- Finally, the Web server returns a page to the Web visitor. It may be a standard Web page with a message like "Thanks for the info," or a page dynamically generated by the program itself—a detailed invoice page, for example.

So how do you create the processing half of the forms equation if you're not a programmer? You can use Dreamweaver MX, of course. Part 6 of this book describes Dreamweaver's dynamic Web-building tools for creating pages that use information collected from forms in a database. If your Web server supports Active Server pages, Cold Fusion, Java Server pages, or PHP, Dreamweaver can create forms-processing programs for you.

If you're part of a Web development team in a company, you may already have in-house programmers who can help you create the processing program.

Furthermore, even if your Web-hosting company doesn't support any of the application servers that work with Dreamweaver, they probably offer free forms-processing programs as part of their services. Contact your Web host and ask about this. If it has these programs, the company will provide instructions on how to use them.

Finally, if you feel adventurous, many forms-processing programs are available for free on the Web. For a thorough sampling, see the CGI Resource Index at *http://cgi.resourceindex.com/*. Using these free programs can be tricky, however, because you need to download the appropriate program and install it on your Web server. Your Web hosting company may not even permit you to do so.

Creating a Form

In Dreamweaver, you can build forms with one-click ease using the Forms tab of the Insert bar (see Figure 10-2).

To begin, you need to insert a <form> tag to indicate the boundaries of a form.

1. **In the document window, click where you want to insert the form.**

   You might decide to place it after a regular paragraph of introductory text, for example.

2. **Click the Forms tab on the Insert bar.**

   The tab reveals fourteen form-building tool icons.

3. **Click the Form icon on the Insert bar (the far-left square).**

   Alternatively, if you're a menu-driven person, choose Insert→Form instead.

   Either way, a red, dashed-line rectangle appears in the document window, indicating the boundaries of the form. (If you don't see it, choose View→Visual Aids→Invisible Elements). The top line represents the opening <form> tag; the bottom represents the closing tag. Make sure you always insert form objects, such as buttons and menus, *inside* these lines. Otherwise, Dreamweaver will think you're trying to create a second form on the page. (It's perfectly valid to include more than one form per page, but the user can only submit one form—and its data—at a time.)

Because you can place so many other HTML elements inside a form, it's often easier to insert the form first, and add tables, graphics, text, and form objects later.

Figure 10-2:
The Forms tab on the Insert bar gives you one-click access to all of the different form elements: buttons, text fields, checkboxes, and more.

4. **If the form isn't already selected, click anywhere on the dotted red line to select it.**

   Unlike other objects, such as images, the red line of the form doesn't change its appearance when selected. The only way you know you've selected the form is by checking the Property inspector. If it displays the Form Name label at the upper-left corner, as shown in Figure 10-3, you've done it correctly.

Figure 10-3:
In most cases, you'll want to use the POST method of transmitting data to your Web server.

5. **If you like, type a name for your form in the Form Name field.**

   This step is optional. A form doesn't need a name to work, but a name is useful if you use JavaScript or a Dreamweaver Behavior (see the next chapter) to interact with the form or any of its fields.

6. **Type a URL into the Action field or select a file by clicking the tiny folder icon.**

   Your mission here is to specify the location of the program that will process the form. If someone else is responsible for the programming, ask that person what to enter here. It will be a standard Web path—either an absolute URL (one that begins with *http://*) or just the path to the server's forms-processing program. (See page 91 for more on these different kinds of links).

If you're using Dreamweaver MX's dynamic page-building tools instead, click the folder icon and select the appropriate forms-processing page (page 688) from your site folder.

Either way, the file name *doesn't* end in .html. The path might be, for example, *../cgi-bin/forms.pl*. In this case, *pl* is the extension used to indicate a program written in the Perl programming language. Other common file extensions for Web programs include *.asp* (for an Active Server Page), *.cfm* (for a Cold Fusion Markup Language page), *.jsp* (for Java Server Pages), .php (for PHP pages), or *.cgi* (for a CGI program).

7. **Using the Method pop-up menu, specify how you want the form data transmitted to the processing program (see Figure 10-3).**

   Basically, forms can transmit data to a Web server in one of two ways. The more common method, called POST, is the default method for browsers and the one you'll use most often. It sends the form data in two steps: first, the browser contacts the form program at the URL you specified in the previous step; then it sends the data to the server. This method gives a bit more security to your data, and can easily handle forms with lots of information.

   The GET method, on the other hand, transmits the form data in the URL like this: *http://search.yahoo.com/bin/search?p=dogs*. The characters following the *?* in the address represent the form data. In this instance, a single form field, named *p,* with the value *dogs,* is submitted to the server. As you can see, such a URL could get extremely long. Because some servers can't handle very long URLs, the GET method is inappropriate for forms that collect a lot of data.

8. **If you're using frames, select a target option.**

   The target option lets you specify a particular frame for displaying the results of the form submission. You can also choose the _blank option to open a new browser window to display the results. (See page 215 for more on the Target property.)

9. **Select an encoding type, if you like.**

   You usually don't have to select anything from the Enctype menu. The default value—*empty*—is almost always correct and is the same as selecting the much more longwinded "application/x-www-form-urlencoded" option.

   If you're using the File Field button (page 309) to let visitors upload files to your site, you should use the "multipart/form-data" option. In fact, Dreamweaver automatically selects this option when you add a File Field to a form. (Beware, though; this option requires special settings on your Web server and may make a form fail to function.)

You've laid the foundation for your form. Now you're ready to add the input controls to it—menus, checkboxes, and so on—as described in the next section.

Adding Form Elements

Unless you've never used a computer before, the different user-interface elements available for HTML forms should look familiar: text fields where people can type in information (their names, addresses, phone numbers, and so on); checkboxes for making multiple-choice selections that are all visible simultaneously; and menus for making selections from a list. The Forms tab of the Insert bar lets you create all of these elements and more (see Figure 10-2).

Figure 10-4:
Forms collect information using a variety of different user interface elements such as text boxes, password fields, and pop-up menus. You can even add a file field to let visitors select and upload a file to your site.

Text field (Single-line)

Text field (Password)

Text field (Multi-line)

Radio buttons

Checkboxes

File field

Pull-down menu

Buttons

What All Form Elements Have in Common

The routine for adding form elements to your document always follows the same pattern:

1. **In the document window, insert a form (see page 297).**

   Or, if the page already has a form, click inside its red border.

Tip: If the text field is the first element of the form, you can skip this step. As soon as you add a form element to a page, such as a field, checkbox, or pop-up menu, Dreamweaver automatically creates the red dotted-line form boundaries (and, behind the scenes, the corresponding <form> tags).

---

2. **Click the appropriate button on the Insert bar (see Figure 10-2).**

   Alternatively, use the Insert→Form Objects submenu. You'll soon discover that every form object on the Insert bar is also represented by a command on the Insert menu (for example, Insert→Form Objects→Text Field).

Tip: Instead of just clicking a form-element button on the Insert bar, you may prefer to drag it off the panel and into a specific position on your Web page. This trick works with any of the user controls on the Insert bar, not just text fields.

---

3. **Type a name for the freshly minted (and still highlighted) form element into the Property inspector's name box (see Figure 10-5).**

   Dreamweaver automatically names the field—for example, it might propose *textfield, textfield1,* and so on. It's a good idea, however, to give the field a new, unique name, because this name will be submitted with the user's input as a name/value pair.

4. **Set the form element's properties.**

   For example, you may be able to specify its width, height, and other variables. The following descriptions indicate which options are available.

Text Fields

When you need to collect a specific piece of information like a person's name, phone number, or address, you'll use a text field (shown in Figure 10-4). Text fields accept typed responses and are great for open-ended questions. They come in three different flavors: *single-line* fields for short responses, *password* fields to hide user input from snooping eyes, and *multi-line* fields for longer typed replies.

Once you've inserted the text field, you can adjust the following settings in the Property inspector (see Figure 10-5):

- **Char Width.** The width of a text field is measured in characters; if you type *20* for the Char Width (character width), the text field will be as wide as necessary to hold 20 typed letters. Be aware that the exact size can vary from browser to browser.

Figure 10-5:
The Property inspector looks slightly different depending on the type of text field you choose. Single-line fields let you specify the field width and the maximum number of permissible characters. Multi-line fields include height (Num Lines) and wrap settings.

- **Type.** A **single line** text field, of course, holds just one line of text. This is the most common kind of text field; use it for collecting small pieces of information, such as a last name, social security number, or credit card number.

  Multi-line fields provide a larger area for adding multiple lines of text. You'll need to use this kind of text field when offering a place to type longer comments, such as in a "Let us know what you think!" or "Nature of problem:" field.

Tip: Dreamweaver MX includes a separate button for adding a multi-line text field–called a Textarea in HTML (see Figure 10-2).

- **Password** fields hide a password being typed from the prying eyes of passing spies. Whatever your Web visitor types appears as asterisks *** (Windows) or bullets •••• (Mac) on the screen. (Of course, the information in the password field is still transmitted as plain text, just like any other form field. The masking action takes place in your visitor's browser only.)

- **Max Chars/Num Lines.** The Max Chars (maximum characters) field lets you limit the number of characters that will be accepted—a good way to help ensure that guests type the right information in the right place. For instance, if you use a field to collect the age of the visitor, odds are you won't need more than three characters to do it; very few 1,000-year-olds surf the Web these days (and those who do don't like to reveal their ages).

  When you've specified a multi-line text field, this box's label changes to Num Line; you can't limit the amount of text someone types into one of these fields. You can, however, specify the height of a multi-line text field on the screen, using the Num Lines (number of lines) field.

Note: The limit you specify here affects only how tall the field will be on the screen. Your visitors can type as many lines of information as they want. (A scroll bar will appear if the typing exceeds the size of the box you've specified with the Num Lines option.)

- **Wrap.** The often-confusing Wrap property specifies what happens when your visitor types right to the edge of the text box. (Of course, it applies to Multi-line text fields only.)

  The **Default** value varies from browser to browser; you can't rely on it to produce consistent results for all users.

  The **Off** setting prevents sentences from wrapping inside the text field. When the typed text exceeds the width of the field, a horizontal scroll bar appears at the bottom of the field, and the text scrolls to the left. The text remains on a single line until the user hits Enter or Return. You'll almost never want to use this option because it forces your visitor to scroll not only up and down, but left and right, too, to see everything she's typed.

The last two options create a text field that works like most people would expect: When the typing reaches the edge of the box, it automatically wraps to the next line. To your visitor, there's no visual difference between the Virtual and Physical options; these wrapping styles differ only in the way they format the text when it's transmitted.

The **Virtual** setting displays line breaks on the screen, in your visitor's browser only ; when the text is actually submitted, it will appear as a single line (unless the user manually inserted line breaks by pressing Enter or Return). If you create the field using the **Physical** setting, on the other hand, the browser inserts line breaks at the end of each line as it wraps. When transmitted, the text maintains these line breaks.

In general, the Virtual setting is the best approach. It doesn't insert artificial line breaks and maintains the integrity of the user's input.

• **Init Val.** Here, you can specify the Initial Value of the field—starter text that will automatically appear in the field, so that it won't be empty when the visitor begins completing the form. You can use this feature to include explanatory text inside the field itself, such as "Type your name in this box" or "Example: (212) 555-1212."

Note: If the page is one of the dynamic file types Dreamweaver works with—ASP, ASP.NET, PHP, Cold Fusion, or JSP—you'll also see a small lightning bolt to the right of this box. This button lets you add *dynamic data*—information drawn from a database—to the text field. In-depth coverage of this feature starts on page 699.)

After you're finished tweaking the text field's properties, don't forget to type a text label next to the field in your document window to let your site's visitors know what the text field is for. Short labels like "First Name," "Phone Number," or "Type your comments here" will do just fine.

FREQUENTLY ASKED QUESTION

Using the Password Field for Credit-Card Numbers

Can I use the Password field type for credit card numbers and other sensitive information?

Yes, but it won't give the information any extra security.

The Password field does one thing: It hides user input *on the screen.* Someone looking over your visitor's shoulder won't be able to read what's being typed—it'll look like a bunch of dots—but once that information is submitted over the Internet, it's just as visible as a regular text field.

To provide real security for forms information, you need an *encrypted connection* between the Web server and the user's computer. Most Web site creators use SSL (Secure Socket Layer) technology for this purpose.

Most Web browsers understand this technology, but your Web server must be specially configured to work in this mode. Contact your Web host to see if you can use SSL on your server (the answer is usually yes). If so, they'll be able to tell you how to set it up.

Checkboxes

Checkboxes (see Figure 10-4) are simple and to the point; they're either selected or not. They're great for multiple-choice questions in which your visitor is allowed to select more than one item in a group. For example, suppose you produce three different email newsletters that you send out each month. In your form, you might include some text—"Check the boxes for the newsletters you'd like to receive"—and three corresponding checkboxes, so that each visitor can sign up for only the newsletters he wants.

Once you've added a checkbox to a form, you can set up these options for it in the Property inspector (Figure 10-6):

- **Checked Value.** You're specifying here the information that, if your visitor turns on this checkbox, will be submitted when the form data is sent to your processing program. It doesn't necessarily have to match the checkbox's label (which you'll create in a subsequent step); it could, instead, transmit some special coded response to your processing application. Your visitors will never actually see this information.

- **Initial State.** If you like, your checkbox can be already checked when your Web page first appears. You may have seen this setup on sites that require you to sign up for some service. Usually there's a checkbox—already checked—down near the bottom of the form, with fine print like this: "Check here if you want to get daily, unsolicited email from our marketing department."

Note: As with many form elements, your checkbox can respond to information it retrieves from a database. The Dynamic button on the Property inspector—available only when working on a dynamic page (ASP, PHP, and so on)—lets you set the checkbox state (Checked or Unchecked) based on data in a database. (See page 701 for details.)

After adjusting the Property inspector, don't forget to return to the document window to add a text label next to the field. Let people know what the checkbox is for: "Yes, sign me up!" for example. Finally, you may want to insert another checkbox. Checkboxes don't have to come in groups, but they often do.

Figure 10-6:
All a visitor can do is turn a checkbox on or leave it blank. The actual value is defined in the box's Checked Value property.

Radio Buttons and Radio Groups

Radio buttons, like checkboxes, are very simple (see Figure 10-4); they're either selected (represented on screen as a solid circle) or not (an empty circle).

Unlike checkboxes, radio buttons restrict your visitor to making only one choice from a group, just like the radio buttons on an old-style automobile dashboard (or, if you're too young to remember those car radios, like the buttons on a blender). Radio buttons are ideal for multiple-choice questions. For example, "What is your income: A. $10–35,000, B. $35–70,000, C. $70–100,000, D. None of your business."

You can set up these options for a radio button in the Property inspector (Figure 10-7):

- **Checked Value.** This is the information that will be submitted when your visitor selects this button. Once again, it doesn't necessarily have to match the radio button's onscreen label.

- **Initial State.** Often, when a form page first loads, one radio button in each set is preselected. To do your visitors this timesaving courtesy, turn on Checked for the button that holds the default value, or the one you expect they'll choose most often.

Of course, if making a choice here is optional, then you can leave all of the buttons unselected by setting their initial states to Unchecked. However, once somebody *does* select a radio button, only the Reset button can make them *all* unselected again (see page 311 for information on creating a Reset button.)

POWER USERS' CLINIC

Giving Order to Your Forms

If you're not careful, creating forms can quickly lead to visual chaos. The different shapes and sizes of text boxes, radio buttons, and other form objects don't naturally align well with text. Use tables to get a handle on the appearance of your forms.

In the first picture at right, form elements were added next to the text on each line, forcing your eye to follow a prominent zigzag pattern created by the form's text boxes. The result is not only ugly, but also hard to read.

In the second picture, a table made of 2 columns and 13 rows (one row for each question) organizes the text and form elements into two columns. Notice that the text next to each form element aligns to the right, creating a clean edge that effectively mirrors the edge created by the form fields.

To make this work most effectively, set each text field to the same width, using the Char Width property.

When using this technique, add the <form> tag first, insert the table inside the form's dotted red boundaries, and then add form elements inside the table. If you insert a table first and then try to insert a form, Dreamweaver will only let you add it to a single cell of the table.

See Chapter 6 for more on creating tables.

Radio buttons always come in groups; only one button in the group can be selected at the same time. To achieve this effect, every button in the same group shares the same name (although they should have different Checked values). If, when testing your page, you notice that you can select more than one radio button at a time, you must have given them different names. (You can also use Dreamweaver's Radio Group object, described next. It acts as a wizard that simplifies the process of creating a group of radio buttons.) The final step in creating radio buttons is to add text labels for the entire group and each button. Simply click in the document window and type, just as you'd add any text to the page. Your whole-group-of-buttons label may take the form of a question ("How would you like to pay?"); the labels for the individual buttons might say, for example, "Visa," "MasterCard," and "I.O.U."

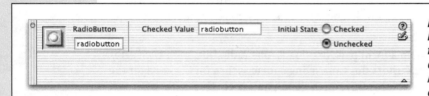

Figure 10-7:
Radio buttons are good for "Choose one:" options (e.g., "Gender: Male, Female, Undecided").

Radio Group

Although creating a group of radio buttons using the radio button object is easy, Dreamweaver MX includes the Radio Group object to make it even simpler. The Radio Group object provides a single dialog box for creating a group of radio buttons and their labels in one fell swoop. To use it:

1. **On the Insert bar, click the Radio Group button (see Figure 10-8).**

   The Radio Group window appears.

2. **Type a name in the Name field.**

   This name covers all radio buttons in the group, saving you the trouble of typing the name for each button yourself.

3. **In the Label column, click on the top Radio label. Type a label for the first button.**

   This label will appear next to the button onscreen.

4. **Hit the tab key to jump to the Value column for that button and type a value for the first button.**

   This is the "checked value" of the button. Type what you want to be passed to the Web server when somebody selects this button and submits the form.

5. **Repeat steps 3 and 4 for the second button in the group.**

   You can create additional radio buttons by clicking the + button. Follow steps 3 and 4 for each additional button you add in this way.

6. **Select a layout option for the group.**

Dreamweaver puts each radio button in the group on its own line. You can choose whether Dreamweaver uses a line break (
 tag) to separate each line or a table—one radio button per row.

Don't care for either of these options? Pick one anyway. You can always redesign the layout later.

Figure 10-8:
The Radio Group dialog box lets you quickly add multiple radio buttons to a page. The buttons form a single group that lets visitors select one of a group of options.

7. **Click OK to add the radio group to your page.**

The radio buttons and their labels are just text and buttons on the screen. You can move the buttons around, change their labels, and alter each button's properties in the Property inspector.

Pull-down Menus and Lists

Although checkboxes and radio buttons both provide ways to offer multiple choices, you should consider them only when there are relatively few choices. A form can quickly become overcrowded with buttons and boxes if there are too many options to choose from. The beauty of lists and pull-down menus (usually called *pop-up menus* on the Mac) is that they offer many choices without taking up a lot of screen space. (Figure 10-9 shows an example.)

Figure 10-9:
Top: A menu is a single compact line; a list can take up any number of lines on the page.

Bottom: The Initially Selected option lets you set up a default value.

Once you've inserted a menu or list object into your document window, here's how to adjust the Property inspector settings:

- **Type.** Menus and lists differ both in appearance (see Figure 10-9) and in function, as described in a moment. Click the one you want (Menu or List).

- **Height.** A list can be a single line tall (in which case you may as well use a menu), or many lines (allowing your visitors to see a number of choices at once). The number you type into the Height box (available for lists only) should reflect the amount of space you wish the list to take up on the page. A vertical scroll bar will appear automatically if the height you specify here is smaller than the number of items in the list.

- **Allow multiple.** Here's a key difference between menus and lists: If you turn on this option, a user can select more than one item from a list, just by pressing the Ctrl (⌘) key while clicking different options in the list.

- **List Values.** This button opens the List Values dialog box (see Figure 10-10), where you build the list of options in your list or menu. Each item is composed of two parts: a *label* (the text that actually appears in the menu or list on the Web page), and the value (the information that gets submitted with the form, which isn't necessarily the same thing as the label).

  To use this dialog box, type an item label. Press Tab (or click in the Value column) and then type the value, if you like. (See Figure 10-10 for details.)

  Including a value is optional; if you don't specify one, your form will submit the item's label *as* the value. Still, setting up a separate value is often useful. Imagine that you've designed a pull-down menu on an e-commerce site so that your visitors can choose the month in which their credit cards expire. Figure 10-10 shows what the items for such a pull-down menu might look like: The names of the months would actually appear on the menu, but when a user selects, say, April, the number 4 is what will actually be transmitted to your forms-processing program.

  Because computer programs are often more comfortable with numbers than names—and humans often the exact opposite—it makes more sense to use numbers for list values in this case.

  Another example: When offering your visitors a pop-up menu of products from which to choose, the label might be the human-friendly name of the product, such as "Blue Wool Cap." The value would be the model number that your forms-processing program can understand, such as XSD1278.

- **Dynamic values.** Dreamweaver MX can also create a *dynamic menu,* in which the labels and values of the menu are retrieved from a database. This option—available only when you insert a Menu into one of the dynamic page types described in Part 6 of this book—is great when the menu items change frequently, as it does in a list of employee names. This feature is described on page 704.

Click OK when you're finished building your menu or list. You can always return to this screen and edit the list of options. To do so, click the menu or list in the document window and then click the List Values button on the Property inspector. You return to the dialog box shown in Figure 10-10.

As with other form elements, you can, and probably should, add some explanatory text alongside the list or menu in the document window.

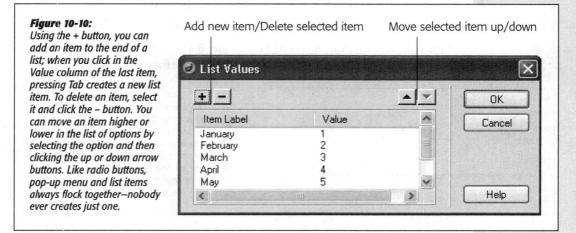

Figure 10-10:
Using the + button, you can add an item to the end of a list; when you click in the Value column of the last item, pressing Tab creates a new list item. To delete an item, select it and click the – button. You can move an item higher or lower in the list of options by selecting the option and then clicking the up or down arrow buttons. Like radio buttons, pop-up menu and list items always flock together—nobody ever creates just one.

Add new item/Delete selected item   Move selected item up/down

File Field

Receiving responses to checkboxes, radio buttons, and pull-down menus is all well and good, but what if you'd like your visitors to submit something a little more meaty—such as an entire file? Imagine a bulletin-board system, for example, that would allow users to post JPEG images of themselves or upload word processing documents to share with others. They can do just that, thanks to the *File Field* field (see Figure 10-2)—and a little magic from your Web server.

Before you get carried away with the possibilities the File Field offers, you'll need to do a little research to see if you can use it on your Web site. Although Dreamweaver makes it easy to *add* a field for uploading image files, text files, and other documents, you'll need to check with the administrator of your Web server to see if anonymous file uploads are permitted (some servers don't allow this kind of activity for fear of receiving viruses or overly large files). Then, of course, you'll have to ensure that the program that processes the form is programmed to *do* something with the incoming file—to store it somewhere on the server, for instance.

When you click the File Field button on the Insert bar (or choose Insert→Form Objects→File Field), Dreamweaver inserts a text field *and* a Browse button; together, they constitute a single File Field. When you click either one, you highlight both.

The Browse button, once it's posted on the Web and visible in somebody's browser, opens up the standard Windows or Macintosh Open File dialog box, permitting your visitor to navigate to, and select, a file for uploading.

The Property inspector offers only two settings to change (other than specifying a more creative name):

- **Char Width.** The width of a text field is measured in characters; if you type *20* for the character width, the field will be 20 characters wide.

- **Max Char.** Leave this blank, as shown in Figure 10-11.

Your File Field isn't finished until you've added a label to it in the document window, such as "Click the Browse button to select a file for uploading."

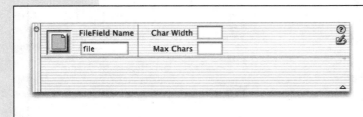

Figure 10-11:
Avoid the Max Chars Field. It's intended to limit the number of characters that the field will accept—which could pose a problem if it prevented the full path to the file from appearing in the field. In that case, the browser might not upload the file at all.

Hidden Field

Most form elements are designed to accommodate interaction from your visitors: clicking radio buttons, typing into text fields, and making choices from menus, for example. But there's one kind of field that your visitors won't even know about and will never set: the *hidden* field.

Why, you're probably asking, would you need to submit a value you already know? Hidden fields are intended to supply information to the programs that process forms—information that the program has no other way of knowing. For example, most Web hosting services offer a generic forms-processing program that collects information submitted with a form and emails it to a selected person. But how does the program know who to email the data to? After all, it's a *generic* program that's used by hundreds of other people. The solution: a hidden field. A hidden field could store the information required for the program to properly process the form—*email=me@mydomain.com,* for example.

To insert a hidden field, click the Hidden Field button on the Insert bar, or choose Insert→Form Objects→Hidden Field; a gold shield icon—Dreamweaver's symbol for HTML that won't be visible in a Web browser—appears on the page. Use the Property inspector to give the field a name and a *value*—that is, the value that will get submitted to your forms-processing program (in example above, your email address).

Buttons

No form is complete without a Submit button for your Web visitors to click as a final step (see Figure 10-2); only then do their responses set out on their way to your forms-processing application. Another button worth including is a Reset button, which your visitors can click when they've filled out a form and realize they've made an error. The Reset button clears all of the form entries and resets all of the form fields to their original values.

The Property inspector controls (Figure 10-12) for a freshly inserted button are:

- **Label field.** The label is the name that appears on the button. Dreamweaver proposes *Submit,* but you're free to substitute *Do It, Make It So,* or *Send my data on its merry way.*

  For buttons, the label *is* the value that will be submitted like other form data; that's why there's no separate Value field on the Property inspector. This quirk opens up some interesting possibilities. You could, for example, include *several* Submit buttons, each with a different label. Maybe you're creating a form for a database application; one button might say Delete, while another says Edit. Depending on which button gets clicked, the program processing the form would either delete the record from the database or modify it.

Figure 10-12:
Buttons have just three properties: Name, Label, and Action.

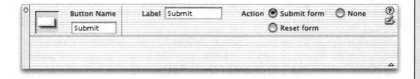

- **Action.** These three buttons govern what happens when somebody clicks your button. A **Submit** button transmits the form data over the Internet to the form-processing program. A **Reset form** button sets all the fields back to their original values. (This doesn't mean that the fields, checkboxes, or menu items are left blank, unchecked, or unselected. Instead, they return to their *initial* values, which you specified when creating these various controls. For example, if you set the Initial State property of a checkbox to Checked and your visitor unchecks the box and then clicks the Reset button, a checkmark will reappear in the box.)

  Setting the button's action to **None** means that clicking on the button has no effect on the form. "Gee, *that's* useful," you're probably thinking.

  But although the button doesn't submit the data or reset the form's fields, you'll need to choose the None option if you want to add interactivity to the button using Dreamweaver's built-in Behaviors (see the next chapter). In this way, you can use a common user-interface element—the 3D beveled look of a form button—to trigger any of many different actions, like opening a new browser window, starting or stopping a Flash movie, or popping up a message on the screen. If you're a JavaScript programmer, you can use the button to activate your own programs.

Tip: You can also use a graphic as a Submit button, thanks to something called an Image Field, thus freeing you to be more creative with the look of the button. Click the Image Field button on the Insert bar, or choose Insert→Form Objects→Image Field, to select a graphic you want to use as a button. When a Web visitor clicks the image, it submits the form and all its data. (Unfortunately, Image Fields do only one thing: submit form data. They can't be used as form Reset buttons.)

Labels and Fieldsets

Two additional form items appear on the Insert bar: Labels and Fieldsets. Unfortunately, neither are intended to work with Dreamweaver's Design view. They're essentially just shortcuts for entering code into Code view.

The Label tag

The Label tag lets you associate a label with a particular form element—a checkbox or text field, for example. Of course, you can always do that by placing plain text next to a form element on the page. But because a Label tag is "attached" to a particular form element, it's more helpful in explaining the function and layout of your form to people who use assistive technologies like screen-reading software for the blind.

To use the label tag, select a form element—check box, text field, or whatever—and click the Label button in the Forms tab of the Insert bar (see Figure 10-2). You've just wrapped the form field in a <label> tag. Now, in Code view (Chapter 9), type text within the tag on either side of the form field like this:

```
<label>Please type a password: <input name="password"
type="text" id="password"></label>
```

Tip: You can find more information on the <label> tag and how to use it with Dreamweaver's built-in HTML reference. Chose Window→Reference to open the Reference panel. Then select Label from the Tag menu to see a detailed discussion and sample usage for this tag. (If you selected a <label> tag on the page before opening the Reference panel, the panel will automatically display information on the tag.)

The Fieldset tag

The Fieldset tag is another form-organization tool, this time intended to let you group related form fields. For example, if you're creating an online ordering form, you can organize all of the "ship to" information—address, city, state, zip, and so on—into a single set. Again, this arrangement can help those using assistive technology to understand the organization and intent of a form.

In many of the latest browsers, the fieldset tag also has a visual benefit. Internet Explorer 4 and above, Navigator 6, and other newer browsers display an attractive border around fieldsets and add a useful label to identify the fields.

To use this tag, select the related form fields. They must be next to each other on screen, and can be organized within other HTML elements such as a table. Then click the Fieldset button on the Insert bar (see Figure 10-2). Type a label for the fieldset in the Label window that appears, and then click OK.

You won't see much of an effect in Dreamweaver—just the new label you typed. So preview the page (F12) in a recent version of Internet Explorer to see the both the label and a border surrounding the form elements in the set.

Validating Forms

It can be frustrating to look over feedback that's been submitted via a form on your Web page, only to notice that your visitor failed to provide a name, email address, or some other piece of critical information. That's why, depending on the type of form, you might want to make certain information *mandatory*.

For example, a form used for subscribing to an email newsletter isn't much use if the would-be reader doesn't type in an email address for receiving it. Likewise, if you need a shipping address to deliver a brochure or product, you'll want to be sure that the user included her address on the form.

Luckily, Dreamweaver provides a Behavior—a ready-made JavaScript program— that accomplishes this exact task. Called Validate Form, this Dreamweaver behavior alerts users when they haven't filled out a form properly. You can specify that a particular field can't be left blank, or that it must contain numbers only, or that it must contain a proper email address. If someone attempts to submit the form without the correct information, a small dialog box pops up identifying the mistake. You'll no longer receive blank forms.

Unfortunately there's a built-in limitation to this Dreamweaver behavior: You can only validate *text fields*. In other words, you can't check to see if a user clicked a particular checkbox or made a selection from a pull-down menu. Nor can you see if they chose a file to upload or clicked a radio button.

Nonetheless, the Validate Form behavior is a great tool for making sure you get the right information from your site's visitors. (Dreamweaver Behaviors are discussed in depth in Chapter 11.)

To validate a form:

1. **Select the form or a text field that you want to validate.**

   You can validate form fields in two ways: one field at a time or all fields at once.

   The first option involves adding the Validate Form behavior to each text field you wish to validate. The form will check to see if the field contents are valid (using one or more of the criteria you set using the steps below) after the user exits the field, either by tabbing out of the field or by clicking anywhere else on the page. This allows you to validate a particular field immediately, as soon as your visitor has finished entering information into it.

If you choose to validate the entire form, no checking takes place until your visitor clicks the Submit button. At that moment, the browser checks all the fields you specified; an error message appears if any of them don't meet the criteria you've specified. To select a form, click on its red dashed border or click <form> in the document window's tag selector.

2. **Choose Window→Behaviors.**

   The Behaviors panel appears.

3. **On the Behaviors panel, click the + button; choose Validate Form from the menu.**

   The Validate Form dialog box appears, showing the names of all text fields in the form (see Figure 10-11).

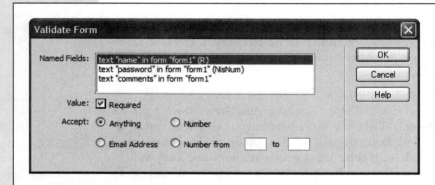

Figure 10-13:
In this example, the text field "name" must have a value in it; the field "password" is not required, but if the user does fill out this field, it must contain a number. If a form field can be left blank—the Comments field, in this example—there's no need to validate it.

4. **Select the field you wish to validate from the list.**

   You can click it with the mouse, or press the up and down arrow keys to highlight the one you want.

5. **Turn on the Required checkbox if completing a certain field is mandatory.**

6. **Using the Accept radio buttons, choose one of the four validation types.**

   Anything accepts any value—numbers, letters, or symbols.

   Number means that only numbers will be accepted in the field. You might turn this option on, for example, for text fields labeled "How old are you?" or "How much do you weigh?"

   Email Address is for fields that require an email address. Note that this feature checks for the correct email address *format,* not for a *valid* email address—it can't go out on the Internet and determine whether your visitor is trying to fool you by typing in a bogus address. In fact, this feature only checks to see if an @ symbol was used in the field.

You also can specify a range of acceptable numbers using the **Number from** option by entering starting and ending numbers. Use this for questions on your form that run along the lines of, "Rate this service from 1 to 10."

As you go, Dreamweaver helps you remember your selections by adding a letter in parentheses after each field name in the dialog box. *R* means that a value is required; *N* means that the field can be left blank; *isEmail* means that the field should contain an email address; *isNum* means that the value should be a number; and *isRange* means the value must be a number within a certain range.

If you're validating the entire form, select additional fields and add the same or different validation criteria, if you like.

7. **Click OK to apply the behavior.**

   You return to your document window, where your fields are now ready to use— and to check themselves for accurate entries. To see if it works, press F12 to preview the page in a Web browser. Try clicking the Submit button without filling out any of the text fields.

EXTENSION ALERT

Advanced Form Validation

The Validation options Dreamweaver offers are rather rudimentary. The email validation option, for example, doesn't even *really* check for a correctly formatted email address; it just looks for at least one character followed by an @ symbol followed by one more character.

Fortunately, renowned extension developer Jaro Von Flocken has written the ultimate extension for validating forms: Check Form MX. It can validate not just text fields but menus, checkboxes, and radio buttons. And unlike Dreamweaver's behavior, Flocken's extension makes sure an e-mail address is properly formatted. This extension offers many more validation options than Dreamweaver

MX's built-in behavior. Best of all, you can define your own error messages for each validation error. To get it, visit *www.yaromat.com/dw /?t=Behavior&r=validation.*

You'll also find many other form-related extensions on the Macromedia Exchange Web site (page 606). Once you're on the Dreamweaver exchange page, perform a search for the word *validate*. For example, you'll find three extensions by extension developer Massimo Foti. With these add-ons to Dreamweaver, you can check your form fields for Zip codes, phone numbers, Social Security numbers, and much more.

Forms Tutorial

In this tutorial, you'll build a simple subscription form for the *Cosmopolitan Farmer* Web site.

Note: Before you begin building the page, you'll need to download the tutorial files from this book's Web site. Using your Web browser, visit *www.sawmac.com/dwmx/.* Click the Tutorials link; then, under Forms Tutorial on the tutorials page, click <u>Mac files</u> or <u>Windows files,</u> depending on the kind of computer you're using. The files download to your computer.

When the files have downloaded and uncompressed, you should have a folder named DWForms on your hard drive, containing the Web pages and graphics needed for this tutorial. (If you're having difficulties, the Web site contains detailed instructions for downloading.)

Getting Started

You need to direct Dreamweaver's attention to the new Web site folder you've just downloaded. Full details of this process begin on page 25, but here's the *Reader's Digest* version:

1. **In Dreamweaver, choose Site→New Site.**

   The Site Definition window opens. Make sure the Advanced tab is selected.

2. **Type *Forms* in the Site Name field.**

   This is the name that Dreamweaver will use while you're working on this tutorial.

3. **Click the folder icon next to the Local Root Folder field; browse to and single-click the folder DWForms, and then click Choose. Click OK.**

   If you see a message that Dreamweaver is about to create a cache for this site, click OK.

   You've now defined the site you'll be working on in this tutorial. Defining Web sites and using Dreamweaver's site management features are discussed in depth in Part 4 of this book.

Inserting a Form and Creating a Structure

The first step to building a form requires inserting a <form> tag. This tag indicates the beginning and end of a form and encloses all of the different fields in the form. As noted earlier in this chapter, you also can insert other HTML elements, such as text and tables, within the form. In fact, you'll be using a table to make this form look better.

1. **Choose File→Open. Double-click the file called subscribe.html in the DWForms folder.**

   The page is partly designed already; it has a banner and footer.

2. **Click in the space between the banner and footer. Click the Forms tab on the Insert bar (see Figure 10-24).**

   The Insert bar now shows you the Forms icons you'll need.

3. **Click the Form button on the Insert bar (see Figure 10-2), or choose Insert→Form.**

   A red dashed rectangle appears in the document window, indicating the boundaries of the form.

4. **In the Property inspector, type** *subscribe* **in the Form Name field (see Figure 10-14).**

   You've just named your form.

5. **In the Action field, type** *http://www.sawmac.com/cosmo/response.php.*

   (Leave off the final period, as shown in Figure 10-14.)

   A form's Action property identifies the address of the program that will process the form's submitted data. In this case, you've been spared the effort of programming, or hiring a programmer to write, the required forms-processing software. Such a program already exists on the Web site whose address you've just specified, and it's waiting to process the form you're about to design.

   You may be creating your own forms processing programs if you're using Dreamweaver MX's dynamic Web-building tools described in Part 6. See the tutorial on page 708 for an example.

6. **Make sure POST is selected in the Method menu. Leave the Target and Enctype fields blank.**

   The Method indicates how the form information is sent to the forms-processing program (see step 7 on page 299).

   Now you're ready to begin building a table to design your form.

Figure 10-14:
The Action property of a form is simply the URL for the program that processes the results.

7. **Choose Insert→Table.**

   The Insert Table dialog box opens. (See Chapter 6 for the full story on tables.)

8. Use the following settings for this table: 6 rows, 2 columns, cell padding 5, cell spacing 0, width 580 pixels, border 0 (see Figure 10-15). Click OK.

Dreamweaver pops your empty table onto the screen.

Figure 10-15:
Tables are an excellent way to organize form elements of various shapes. Also see the box on page 305, which demonstrates how tables can bring order to an unruly form.

9. Click the top left cell of the table and drag down until every cell in the left column is selected.

For more on cell-selection techniques, see page 162.

Figure 10-16:
The left column of this table will hold the text that identifies the purpose of each form element. For better presentation, these labels should be aligned to the right so they appear directly across from their associated form object.

10. From the Horz (Horizontal) alignment menu in the Property inspector, choose Right (see Figure 10-16).

You want the text label for each control on this form to align at the right margin of its table column.

11. Click the top-left cell. Type *240* in the W (Width) field in the Property inspector.

You've just set the width of this cell to 240 pixels. You need to set the width of only a single cell to affect the width of all other cells in a column.

12. Click the top-right cell. Type *340* in the W field in the Property inspector.

The cells in the right-hand column all adjust to this size.

Adding Labels and Form Elements

Now that your table is in place, it's time to start adding the different parts of the form. Since text fields, radio buttons, menus, and other form elements aren't always self-explanatory, it's a good idea to add labels explaining the purpose of each element.

1. Click the top-left cell, and then type *What is your name?*

This text identifies what your visitors should type into the text field you'll add in the next step.

2. Press Tab to move the insertion point to the next cell; then click the Text Field button on the Insert bar (see Figure 10-17).

Alternatively, you can choose Insert→Form Objects→Text Field.

Figure 10-17:
Top: The Text Field button inserts, of course, a text field into your form. Bottom: The Property inspector as it looks when you've selected a text field.

3. Type *name* into the TextField box (Figure 10-17, lower left).

Every form element must have a name that describes the information it collects.

4. Type *25* into the Char Width (character width) field.

You've just specified, in characters, how wide the field will be. Setting a width does not limit the amount of text someone can type into it; it only controls the display of the field in the browser.

5. **In the left-hand column of the table, click the second cell from the top and type** *What is your email address?* **Press Tab, and then click the Text Field button on the Insert bar.**

   Alternatively, choose Insert→Form Objects→Text Field. You've just inserted another text field.

6. **In the Property inspector, type** *email* **into the TextField box. Type** *25* **in the Char Width field.**

   You've just specified the name and width of your email address field.

7. **Click the cell just below the Email question. Type** *Rate your apartment farming skills.* **Press Tab; in the Insert bar, click the Radio Button button.**

   Alternatively, choose Insert→Form Objects→Radio Button.

   In this cell, you'll be adding three grouped radio buttons. Your visitor will be able to choose only one of the three options.

8. **In the Property inspector, type** *skills* **in the RadioButton field and** *novice* **in the Checked Value field (Figure 10-18).**

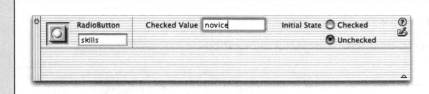

Figure 10-18:
Since grouped radio buttons share the same name, you can copy and paste the first button to add additional ones.

9. **In the document window, click to the right of the radio button and type** *Novice.*

   It's important to label each radio button, so your visitors know what they are selecting.

10. **Click the Radio Button object in the Insert bar to insert a second button. In the Property inspector, type** *skills* **in the RadioButton field, and** *intermediate* **in the Checked Value field.**

    Radio buttons in the same group share the same name; this is what prevents a user from selecting more than one button at a time.

11. **In the document window, click to the right of the radio button. Type** *Intermediate.*

    You've just labeled this button on the screen.

12. On the Insert bar, click the Radio Button button to insert the last button. In the Property inspector, type *skills* in the RadioButton field, and *advanced* in the Checked Value field. Finally, in the document window, click to the right of the radio button and type *Advanced.*

Your three radio buttons are all set.

13. Choose File→Save. Press F12 to preview your page.

Once in your browser, try out the radio buttons. Check to make sure you can select only one at a time. If you're able to select two or more buttons, you've probably typed slightly different names.

Adding a Menu and Submit Button

Only a few more elements are required to produce a fully functional form.

1. Return to Dreamweaver. Click in the left column cell just below the "Rate your skills" question. Type *Where did you hear about Cosmopolitan Farmer?*

In the next step, you'll build a pull-down menu from which users can select a response.

2. Press Tab to jump to the next cell. On the Insert bar, click the List/Menu button (or choose Insert→Form Objects→List/Menu).

Dreamweaver inserts a small box with a selection arrow—a menu—into the cell.

3. In the Property inspector, type *referral* in the name field. Click the List Values button.

The List Values dialog box appears. You'll use this box to add items to your menu.

4. Type *Select One.*

The first item on the list is actually an instruction, which lets your readers know what they need to do with the menu.

5. Press Tab.

The cursor jumps to the Value column. As noted earlier, list items *can* have separate labels and values. If you don't specify a value, your form will simply send the selected *label* to the forms-processing program. For this tutorial, you won't add a value.

6. Press Tab again to add an additional list item.

You can click the + button in the dialog box, if you prefer.

7. Type *Friend,* and then press Tab twice. Complete the list as shown in Figure 10-19.

8. Click OK.

You've just built a working menu. You'll find that it doesn't operate in Dreamweaver, however. You must preview the form in a Web browser to see the menu in action—all in good time.

Figure 10-19:
As you build your list of menu options, press Tab twice after each entry—a shortcut that saves you from having to click the + button.

9. **Click in the left table cell, below the last question you added. Type** *Add any comments here.*

    You'll add one last text field to the form so that your visitors can submit their comments and suggestions.

10. **Press Tab. Click the Textarea button on the Insert bar (see Figure 10-2).**

    Alternatively, you can choose Insert→Form Objects→Textarea. Either way, Dreamweaver inserts a text box.

11. **In the Property inspector, type** *comments* **into the TextField field. Type** *25* **in the Char Width field (Figure 10-20).**

    Doing so establishes the width of the text box in characters.

12. **Type** *4* **in the Num Lines (number of lines) field.**

    This setting controls how tall the text box appears on the Web page. It doesn't limit the amount of text that can be typed into it, however.

13. **From the Wrap menu in the Property inspector, choose Virtual (see Figure 10-20).**

Figure 10-20:
Choose Virtual in the Wrap pop-up menu to eliminate a left-to-right scroll bar in the text field..

The Wrap option determines what happens if someone types in something that's longer than the width of the box. Choosing Virtual forces extra letters to wrap to the next line of the text field, eliminating the need to have a bottom scroll bar on the field.

14. **Click in the cell directly below this new text field. On the Insert bar, click the Button button.**

    Don't confuse the Button button with a Radio Button; they're two different beasts (see Figure 10-2).

15. **In the Property inspector, change the button's Label to _Subscribe_.**

    The default label is _Submit_ (see Figure 10-21), but since this is a subscription form, you should add a more accurate label. (You _don't_ need to change what Dreamweaver here calls Button Name, which also says Submit. It doesn't show up on your Web page, and isn't used by the forms-processing program. As for the Action settings: "Submit form" transmits the form data over the Internet. "Reset form" erases any input from the user and resets the form to its original settings. "None" does nothing.)

Figure 10-21:
The Action property of a button determines what the button does with the contents of the form (see step 7 on page 299).

16. **Choose File→Save.**

    Congratulations. You've just created a fully functional Web form!

17. **Press the F12 key to preview the form.**

    Go ahead—fill it out (with bogus information, if you like). Click the Submit button when you're finished to see what happens. If you're online, your Web page sends the form information to the waiting forms-processing program specified at the beginning of the form creation process. The program sends you back a Web page reflecting your entries, exactly as though you had built a professional, working Web site.

    If nothing happens, make sure the Action property of the Form is set correctly (see page 299).

Validating the Form

Now that you have a working form, you'll add the finishing touches. Since this form will be used to subscribe to _Cosmopolitan Farmer,_ a couple of pieces of information are crucial, including the name and email address of the person who's subscribing.

Using one of Dreamweaver's Behaviors, you can make sure that no one submits a form without these two important pieces of information.

1. **Return to Dreamweaver. Click anywhere on the form's red line boundary to select it.**

   Check to make sure the Property inspector says Form Name in the upper-left corner.

2. **Choose Window→Behaviors.**

   This opens Dreamweaver's Behaviors panel, which you can use to add interactive effects to a Web page. You'll probably find it in the upper-right corner of your screen.

3. **From the + menu, choose Validate Form.**

   The Validate Form window opens, listing the three text fields in your form.

4. **Click the first item in the list ("name"). Turn on the Required checkbox (see Figure 10-22).**

Figure 10-22:
Use the Validate Form behavior to make sure your visitors don't submit empty forms. You can require them to fill out specific text fields and even check to see if the information appropriately formatted—a number or email address, for example.

Required means that the form can't be submitted unless something has been typed into this field.

5. **Click the second item in the list ("email").**

   For the email field, you'll not only specify that it's mandatory, but also that its contents must look like an email address, complete with an @ symbol.

6. **Turn on the Required checkbox. Then, from the Accept group of radio buttons, select Email Address. Click OK.**

7. **Choose File→Save. Press F12 to preview and test the page, as described in Figure 10-23.**

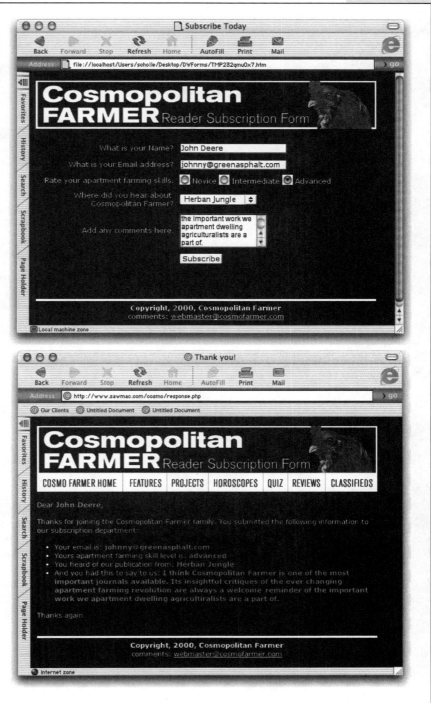

Dreamweaver Behaviors

hapter 5 makes clear how easy it is to add mouse *rollover* effects using Dreamweaver's Rollover Image object. That and other interactive features rely on *scripts* (small programs) written in the JavaScript programming language.

You *could* create the same effects without Dreamweaver, but you'd need to take a few extra steps: buy a book on JavaScript, read it from cover to cover, learn about concepts like *array, function,* and *document object model,* and spend weeks discovering the eccentric rules governing how different browsers interpret JavaScript code differently.

With Behaviors, however, Dreamweaver lets you add these dynamic JavaScript programs to your Web pages without doing a lick of programming.

Understanding Behaviors

Dreamweaver *Behaviors* are powerful prepackaged JavaScript programs that let you add interactivity to your Web pages with ease, even if you don't know the first thing about JavaScript. By adding behaviors, you can make your Web pages do things like:

- Make layers appear and disappear (see Chapter 12).

- Require visitors to fill out certain fields in a form (Chapter 10). For example, when you want to make sure an email address or name is entered before the visitor submits the form.

- Open a new browser window to a specified size, with or without scroll bars, status bar, location bar, and other Web browser "chrome."

- Let your visitors navigate a Web site using a pop-up menu.

- Give feedback to the visitor in a dialog box or in the browser's status bar.

Tip: Try it yourself. See examples of all of Dreamweaver's Behaviors on the companion Web site for this book: *www.sawmac.com/dwmx/behaviors/*

Behavior Elements

To use a behavior, you bring together three elements: an action, an event, and an HTML tag:

- The **action** is whatever the behavior is supposed to *do*—open a new browser window or display a message in the browser's status bar, for instance.

- The **event** is the *trigger* that causes the action to happen. It's usually something your visitor does, like clicking a Submit button on a form.

- Finally, you apply the event and the action to an **HTML tag** to bring interactivity to your Web page.

Let's say you want to let visitors go to different Web pages on your site by using a pop-up menu—a very common Web-page element. This pop-up menu lists the different pages of your site: *About This Company, Contact Us, See Our Products,* and so on.

When someone selects one of the options from the menu, his browser opens the Web page for that section of the site. In this case, the *HTML tag* is the pop-up menu itself (a <select> tag); the *action* is opening another Web page in the site; and the *event* brings the two together so that when your visitor makes a selection from the pop-up menu, his browser goes to the selected Web page. Voila—interactivity!

FREQUENTLY ASKED QUESTION

Behaviors and Added Code

I hear that the JavaScript that Dreamweaver produces adds excessive lines of code, unnecessarily adding to a page's file size. Is this a reason not to use Behaviors?

In some cases, it's true a JavaScript programmer could write a program that does what a Dreamweaver behavior does using less code.

However, Dreamweaver Behaviors were created to work in as many browsers as possible without producing errors in older browsers. JavaScript doesn't work the same in all browsers or in all versions of browsers; the two main brows-

ers—Netscape Navigator and Internet Explorer—understand JavaScript differently, at times so differently that programmers have to resort to elaborate workarounds, which require a lot of experience, practice, and patience.

Fortunately, the engineers at Macromedia have a vast understanding of JavaScript, HTML, and Web browsers, ensuring that Dreamweaver Behaviors work in as many browsers as possible. At times, this compatibility may lead to larger files with more lines of code, but it also gives you the assurance that your Web pages will work for the broadest audience possible.

More About Events

When people visit a Web page, they do more than just read it—they interact with it. You already know that when someone clicks a link, the browser reacts by loading a new Web page or jumping to a named anchor (page 103).

But visitors can also interact with a Web page in a variety of other ways: They may resize the browser window, move the mouse around the screen, make a selection from a pop-up menu, click an image, type inside a form field, or click a form's Reset button. Web browsers "listen to" and react to these triggering events with actions.

In JavaScript and Dreamweaver, the names of events always begin with the word "on," which essentially means "when." For example, the onLoad event refers to the moment when an object fully loads into the browser, such as when a Web page, its images, and other linked files have downloaded. Events also include the various ways someone can interact with a particular HTML tag (element). For instance, when someone moves the mouse over a link or clicks a link, the corresponding events are called onMouseOver and onClick.

GEM IN THE ROUGH

Link Events Without Loading a New Web Page

As you start to use Behaviors, you'll quickly notice that there are an awful lot of useful events associated with links. Links can respond to many user interactions, such as moving the mouse over the link, moving it away from the link, or clicking the link.

Clicking a link usually opens a different Web page. But there are times when you may want to use the onClick event to trigger an action without actually leaving the current Web page.

For instance, you might have a Web page with lots of un- usual or technical words. It would be great to program the page so that when someone clicks an unfamiliar word, a dialog box displaying its definition pops up on the screen (using the Pop-up Message action, described on page 307). Unfortunately, a Web browser doesn't know when you click on a word—there's no event associated with regular text. However, browsers *do* know when you click a link, and they can respond to this action.

But in this case, you don't want to use a real link: that would force a new page to load. You just want to use a link's onClick event.

Fortunately, you can still take advantage of all the great events links have to offer without adding links that take you away from the page. Instead of using a real URL or path for the link, you can use a "dummy" link—a link that goes nowhere.

There are two types of "dummy" (also called "null") links. The first uses the pound symbol (#). Simply select the text or graphic to which you want to add the behavior, and then, in the Property inspector, instead of adding a URL in the Link field, simply type in #. (You can also create a dummy link by typing *javascript:;* into the link field. Be sure to include both the colon and semicolon.) This dummy link doesn't load a new Web page, but gives you a link to which you can apply behaviors.

The advantage of the second method is that some brows- ers scroll to the top of the page when a visitor clicks a link that uses the # symbol, which could be disconcerting if you attached a behavior that appears far down on a page.

Note: Traditionally, JavaScript programmers have capitalized the second word in a JavaScript event (*onMouseover,* for instance). Trouble is, XHTML doesn't accept uppercase letters. So if you're creating XHTML pages, events should always be lowercased, like this: *onmouseover.*

Applying Behaviors

Dreamweaver makes adding behaviors as easy as selecting a tag and choosing an action from a pop-up menu—in the Behaviors panel.

The Behaviors Panel

The Behaviors panel is mission control for Dreamweaver's Behaviors. On it, you can see any behaviors that are applied to a tag, add more behaviors, and edit behaviors that are already applied.

You can open the Behaviors panel in any of three ways:

- Choose Window→Behaviors.

- Press Shift+F3.

- If the Design panel is open on the screen, click the Behaviors tab.

In any case, the panel appears on your screen.

Note: Dreamweaver MX includes two different types of behaviors, and it's important not to get them confused.

This chapter describes JavaScript programs that run in your audience's Web browsers. The *server behaviors* listed in the Application panel group, on the other hand, run on the Web *server* to let you access information from a database. These are described in Part 6.

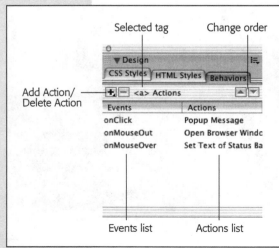

Figure 11-1:
The Behaviors panel lists all of the behaviors attached to the selected HTML tag and lets you add, edit, and delete them. Behaviors are grouped by event and listed in the order in which they occur. As you can see here, it's possible to have one event—onClick—trigger multiple actions. When one event triggers several behaviors, you can change the order in which they occur with the up and down arrows.

The currently selected tag is indicated at the top of the Behaviors panel, and a list of all of the behaviors applied to that tag, if any, appears below. Each behavior is listed in two parts: events and actions, as described earlier.

Behaviors, Step by Step

Open the Behaviors panel, and then proceed as follows:

1. **Select the object or tag.**

   You must attach a behavior to an HTML tag, such as a link (indicated by the <a> tag) or the page's body (<body> tag). Take care, however: it's easy to apply a behavior accidentally to the wrong tag. Form elements, like checkboxes and text fields, are easy—just click one to select it. For other kinds of tags, consider using the tag selector, as described on page 19, for more precision.

Tip: You can be sure which tag the behavior is applied to by looking to the right of the + and – buttons on the Behaviors panel. The tag's name is listed there as shown in Figure 11-1.

---

2. **In the Behaviors panel, add an action.**

   Click the + button in the Behaviors panel and, from the Add Action pop-up menu, select the action you wish to add (see Figure 11-3). You'll find a complete list of these behaviors and what they do beginning on page 339.

   Some actions are dimmed in the menu because your Web page doesn't have the elements necessary for the behavior to work. For instance, if you haven't included a form in your Web page, the Validate Form behavior is grayed out. Others are dimmed because they must be applied to a particular page element. For example, Jump Menu is off-limits until you've added a list/menu field to the page and selected it.

3. **In the dialog box that opens, set options for the action.**

   Each action has properties that pertain specifically to it, and you set them to your liking in the dialog box that now appears. For instance, when you choose the Open URL action, Dreamweaver asks what Web page you want to load. (Once again, the following pages describe each of these actions.)

4. **Click OK to apply the action.**

   At this point, Dreamweaver adds, to the underlying code of your page, the HTML and JavaScript required to make the behavior work. Your behavior's name appears in the Behaviors panel.

   Unlike HTML objects, behaviors usually add code to two different places in a document. For behaviors, Dreamweaver usually adds JavaScript code to the head of the document *and* to the body of the page.

---

5. Change the event, if desired.

When your newly created action shows up in the Behaviors panel, Dreamweaver displays, in the Events column of the panel, a default event (trigger) for the selected tag and action. For example, if you add a Set Text of Status Bar behavior to a link, Dreamweaver suggests the onMouseOver event. (The target browser you select—see Figure 11-2—may affect which event Dreamweaver chooses).

However, this default event may not be the only event available. Links, for instance, can handle many different events. An action could begin when your visitor's cursor moves *over* the link (the onMouseover event), *clicks* the link (the onClick event), and so on.

To change the event for a particular behavior, click the Events pop-up menu (the down-pointing arrow) next to the event name (see Figure 11-2). Select the event you want from the list of available events that appear for that particular tag. (See page 335 for a list of all available events in current versions of the most popular browsers.)

Tip: To make sure that your new behavior works on a particular browser and version, choose a browser's name from the Show Events For submenu (see Figure 11-2). Selecting older browsers from this list limits the number of events you have to choose from. Until you pick a different browser, this global, set-it-and-forget-it choice applies to all behaviors.

When you're done, you can leave the Behaviors panel open to add more behaviors to the tag, or to other tags. Select another tag, using the document window or tag selector, and repeat steps 2 through 5.

Adding multiple behaviors

You're not limited to a single behavior per HTML tag. You can, and often will, apply several behaviors to the same tag. For instance, when a page loads—the onLoad event of the <body> tag—it might preload images to be used in rollover effects,

---

FREQUENTLY ASKED QUESTION

The Vanishing Events List

I applied a behavior to a link, but the only event available is onMouseOver. What happened to all the other events?

You may have accidentally selected events for 3.0 and Later Browsers in the Events pop-up menu (see Figure 11-2). Browser versions prior to 4.0 don't work with many events.

To make sure your behavior works in as many browsers as possible, check out the Show Events For submenu (also

shown in Figure 11-2). The earlier the browser version you choose here, the fewer events you'll see listed. On the other hand, choosing an earlier browser version ensures that your behavior will work for more of your visitors. Keep in mind, however, that the vast majority of Web surfers use *at least* a version 4 browser, making the "4.0 and Later Browsers" option a safe (and rewarding) choice.

---

open a small browser window displaying a pop-up advertisement, *and* start a DHTML animation (see Chapter 12).

Nor are you limited to a single *event* per tag. For instance, you can add a number of actions to a link that are triggered by different events such as onMouseOver, onMouseOut, and onClick.

For example, if you'd set things up for a link as shown in Figure 11-1, when you click the selected link in the browser window, a Pop-up Message appears first, then a new browser window opens, and finally a message appears in the status bar.

Figure 11-2:
Dreamweaver starts out showing you a list of events available in 3.0 and Later Browsers. Since most people these days use browsers in versions 4 and higher, selecting the 4.0 and Later Browsers option is not only a safe choice, it also gives you many more events to play with.

Editing Behaviors

Once a behavior is applied, you can edit it anytime. Double-click the behavior in the Behaviors panel to reopen the Settings dialog box, as described in step 3 of the previous instructions. Make any changes you like, and then click OK.

To remove a behavior from your Web page, select it in the Behaviors panel and click the – button, or press Delete. (If you *accidentally* delete a behavior, just choose Edit→Undo Remove Behavior.)

A Quick Example

This brief example is designed to give you a clear overview of the Behavior-creation process. In it, you'll use a behavior that makes an important message appear automatically when the Web page opens.

1. **Choose File→New to create a new untitled document.**

   You'll start with a new page.

2. **Choose File→Save and save the file to your computer.**

   It doesn't matter where you save the page, since you won't be including any graphics or linking to any pages.

   You'll start the process of adding a behavior by selecting a specific tag—in this case, the page's <body> tag.

3. **In the tag selector at the lower-left corner of the document window, click <body>.**

   Once the tag is selected, you can apply one or more behaviors to it. But first, make sure the Behaviors panel is open. If you don't see it, choose Window→Behaviors. The Behaviors panel generally appears under the Design panel group on the right side of your screen..

4. **Click the + button on the Behaviors panel. From the Add Action pop-up menu, choose Popup Message (see Figure 11-3).**

   The Popup Message dialog box appears.

Figure 11-3:
Behaviors you can't currently apply are grayed out, indicating that either a necessary object is missing for your page, or you've selected an object that can't have that behavior applied to it. For example, you can't apply the Control Shockwave or Flash behavior if you don't have a Shockwave or Flash movie on the page.

5. In the message box, type *Attention! Don't miss our big sale: 2 rototillers for the price of 1!* Then click OK.

Dreamweaver adds the required JavaScript code to the page. Notice that the Behaviors panel lists the *action* called Popup Message next to the *event* called onLoad. The onLoad event triggers an action *after* a page and everything on it—graphics, and so on—have downloaded.

To see the page in action, preview it in a Web browser:

6. Press the F12 key to preview the page.

See Figure 1-17 on page 42 for more on using this preview function.

Events for 4.0 Browsers

Unfortunately, JavaScript works differently not only in different browsers, but in different *versions* of browsers. Older versions of Netscape Navigator and Internet Explorer don't recognize the same range of events as newer versions. Moreover, the latest versions of Netscape Navigator and Internet Explorer differ significantly when it comes to JavaScript (the events available in Netscape Navigator 6 are far fewer than those in Internet Explorer 6). These incompatibilities can make a chore out of developing interactive Web pages that work for the largest possible audience.

If you hope to build successful interactive Web sites, you can't get around having to learn which tag/event combinations work in which browsers. Over 95 percent of Web surfers today, however, use versions 4 or greater of Netscape Navigator or Internet Explorer, so this book concentrates on behaviors that work with those browsers. Refer to the following pages, which list and explain the most common and useful HTML tags and events that work in these browsers, whenever you apply a behavior. (Remember: The choice of events for a given tag depends on which option you've selected in the Show Event For pop-up menu [see Figure 11-2].)

Each entry shows you the name of the event as you'll see it listed in the Behaviors panel, a plain-English description of what that event really means, and the list of tags to which this event can be applied. See Figure 11-4 for the visual representations of those HTML tags. For example, you'll find out that the <select> tag represents a pop-up menu.

Mouse Events

Web designers most often use mouse *movement* events to trigger actions (like the familiar rollover image). But mouse *clicks*—on checkboxes, radio buttons, and other clickable form elements—can be mouse events, too.

***

Note: In the listing below, the many different types of *input* form elements are listed like this: <input type="button | checkbox | radio | reset | submit">. This simply means that *any* of these form elements – buttons, checkboxes, radio buttons, reset buttons or submit buttons—react to the listed event.

***

onMouseOver

Gets triggered: When the cursor moves over the tag.
Works with these tags: <a>, <area>

onMouseout

Gets triggered: When the cursor moves off of the tag.
Works with these tags: <a>, <area>

onClick

Gets triggered: When visitor clicks the tag (and releases the mouse button).
Works with these tags: <a>, <area>, <input type="button | checkbox | radio | reset | submit">

Figure 11-4:
This sample Web page illustrates HTML tags to which you can attach events. Not shown is the body of the Web page (the whole thing, in other words), whose tag is <body>, and the form portion of this page (see Chapter 10), whose tag is <form>. Whenever you set up a behavior, you must attach it to one of these tags.

onDblClick

Gets triggered: When visitor double-clicks the tag.
Works with these tags: <a>, <area>, <input type="button | checkbox | radio | reset | submit">

onMouseDown

Gets triggered: When visitor clicks the tag. The mouse button doesn't need to be released for this event to occur (note the contrast with onClick).
Works with these tags: <a>, <img>, <input type="button | checkbox | radio | reset | submit">

onMouseUp
Gets triggered: When visitor releases the mouse button while cursor is over the tag. The effect is the same as the onClick event, but this one works in far fewer browsers.
Works with these tags: <a>, <img>, <input type="button | checkbox | radio | reset | submit">

Keyboard Events

Keyboard events respond to key presses and releases. Most Web designers use them in association with form elements that accept text, such as a password or text fields. (See Chapter 10 for more on forms.)

onKeyDown
When visitor presses a key while the tag is selected. The key doesn't need to be released for this event to occur.
Works with these tags: <textarea>, <input type="file | password | text">, <a>

onKeyPress
Gets triggered: When visitor presses and releases a key while the tag is selected.
Works with these tags: <textarea>, <input type="file | password | text">, <a>

onKeyUp
Gets triggered: When visitor releases a key while the tag is selected.
Works with these tags: <textarea>, <input type="file | password | text">, <a>

Body and Frameset Events

Several events relate to actions involving an entire Web page or frameset:

onLoad
Gets triggered: When a Web page, *and* any embedded elements like images and Flash and QuickTime movies, load. Very often used for triggering actions when visitor first loads the Web page; can also be used with an image tag to signal when just that image has finished loading.
Works with these tags: <body>, <frameset>, <image>

onUnload
Gets triggered: When the Web page is about to be replaced by a new Web page (for instance, just before the Web browser loads a new Web page after visitor clicks a link).
Works with these tags: <body>, <frameset>

onResize
Gets triggered: When visitor resizes the Web browser window.
Works with these tags: <body>, <frameset>

onError
Gets triggered: When an error occurs while a Web page or an image loads.
Works with these tags: <body>, <img>

Selection and Highlighting Events

Some events occur when the visitor focuses on different parts of a Web page, selects text, or chooses from a menu.

onBlur

Gets triggered: When an element loses the focus. For instance, if the visitor is typing into a form text field and then clicks outside of that field, the onBlur event occurs. The onBlur event is also triggered when the surfer sends a window to the background. For example, suppose your visitor is reading your Web site in one window and has another open in the background. If he clicks the background window, the current page loses focus and an onBlur event occurs.

Works with these tags: <body>, <frameset>, <textarea>, <input type="button | checkbox | file | password | radio | reset | submit | text | select">

onChange

Gets triggered: When visitor changes the text in a form field.

Works with these tags: <textarea>, <input type="file | password | text | select">

onFocus

Gets triggered: When an element becomes the *focus* of the visitor's attention. For instance, clicking in a form text field gives it the focus.

Works with these tags: <body>, <frameset>, <textarea>, <input type="button | checkbox | file | password | radio | reset | submit | text | select">

onSelect

Gets triggered: When visitor selects text in a form field.

Works with these tags: <textarea>, <input type="text">

Form Events

While each element of a form—radio button, text field, checkbox—can respond to a variety of events, the whole form—the entire collection of elements—can respond to only two events:

onSubmit

Gets triggered: When visitor clicks the Submit button on a form.

Tag supported: <form>

onReset

Gets triggered: When visitor clicks the Reset button on a form.

Tag supported: <form>

Tip: You can find out exactly which browsers support which tag/event combinations. In the Macromedia Dreamweaver MX→Configuration→Behaviors→Events folder, you can find files that list the tags and events that work in different browsers, including Netscape Navigator 3.0, 4.0, 6.0 and Internet Explorer 3.0, 4.0, 5.0, 5.5 and 6.0. In addition, two files—*3.0 and Later Browsers.htm* and *4.0 and Later Browsers.htm*—contain only tag/event combinations that work in *both* Netscape Navigator and Internet Explorer of the corresponding versions.

The Actions, One by One

While events get the ball rolling, actions are, yes, where the action is. Whether it's opening a 200 x 200 pixel browser window or using HTML to control the playback of a Flash movie, you'll find an action for almost every interactivity need.

Each of the following descriptions lets you know which browsers recognize the corresponding actions. For example, "Netscape Navigator 3+" refers to Netscape Navigator 3.0 and later.

Remember that after you complete each of the sets of steps below, your new action appears in the Behaviors panel, and your Web page is ready to test. At that point, you can click the behavior's name in the Behaviors panel, where—by clicking the Events pop-up menu as shown in Figure 11-2—you can change the event that triggers it.

Navigation Actions

Many of Dreamweaver's actions are useful for adding creative navigational choices to your Web sites, giving you the opportunity to go beyond the simple click-and-load approach of a basic Web page.

Show and Hide Pop-up Menu

Windows: Netscape Navigator 4+, Internet Explorer 4+
Macintosh: Netscape Navigator 4+, Internet Explorer 4+

As the appetites of Web surfers grow, Web sites are getting bigger and more complex, sometimes making it harder to navigate the site. Instead of a handful of links, cleanly placed on the home page, you may have hundreds of links that could easily overwhelm your visitors. To maintain order, use Dreamweaver MX's new Pop-Up Menu behavior to add navigation menus that only appear when the mouse moves over related links (see Figure 11-5).

The pop-up menu is composed of invisible *layers* (see Chapter 12) that become visible when you move your mouse over a link. Aside from the wow factor of making things appear out of nowhere, the main benefit of this behavior is that you can provide lots of navigation options without squandering valuable screen space. The only drawback is that you can only use *text* in these menus, not cool graphic buttons to match your main navigation elements.

Tip: Dreamweaver's companion graphics program, Fireworks MX, lets you build the same kind of menu using graphics as well as text. Once created in Fireworks, Web pages with these menus open right up in Dreamweaver MX without a problem.

To create a pop-up menu, start by selecting a link on the page. The menu will pop up when the visitor's mouse passes over this link, so pick a link that's related to the menu you're creating. For example, if you want to create a menu that lets visitors select one of the five products you sell, using a link labeled Products would make sense.

Once you've selected this Show Pop-Up Menu from the + (Add Action) menu in the Behaviors panel, you see the dialog box shown in Figure 11-6. If you simply want to create a quick pop-up menu, you only have to use the first tab, Contents; it lets you create and arrange menu items. The other three tabs control the appearance and placement of menu items.

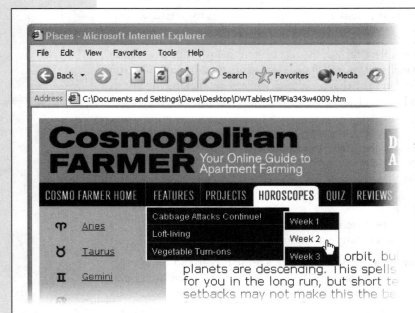

Figure 11-5:
Dreamweaver MX's new Show Pop-Up Menu behavior adds complex navigation menus to a page. You can even add nested menus, as in this example, where moving the mouse over the Features button pops up a menu with three options. Moving the mouse over the first option pops up yet another menu with three additional choices. The only limit to the number of submenus you can create is the width of your monitor: too many submenus and they'll disappear off the right edge of the screen.

- **Adding menu items.** To add a menu item, click the + button on the Contents tab. Next, in the Text field, type the words you'd like to appear for one of your menu items. You can then type a link into the Link field or click the folder icon and select a file in your site.

  If you're using frames (see Chapter 7), you can direct the link to open in a specific frame by choosing its name from the Target pop-up menu. Alternatively, to open the link in a new blank window, choose _blank. Continue, as shown in Figure 11-6, until you've covered all your menu items.

- **Deleting menu items.** To delete a menu item, select it from the list on the Contents tab and click the – button.

- **Changing the order of menu items.** To rearrange the menu you've built, select a menu command from the list on the Contents tab, and press the up or down arrow key. The order in which the items are listed in the dialog box is the order they'll take in the onscreen pop-up menu.

- **Creating a submenu.** You can also create submenus—additional menus that appear when you move your mouse over an item in the main menu. For example, in Figure 11-5, moving the mouse over the "Cabbage Attacks Continue!" link opens another menu with three additional items.

To create a submenu, select a menu item and then click the Indent button (⬛) on the Contents tab. The link becomes the first item of the submenu. As you add additional items using the + button, they become other members of the submenu. (You can't indent the top item in a menu in this way).

- **Removing an item from a submenu.** To remove an item from a submenu, select it and click the Outdent button (⬛).

Figure 11-6:
If you don't find the default color scheme, font, or layout of pop-up menus, Dreamweaver offers plenty of tools for tweaking them in the other three tabs of the Pop-Up menu dialog.

The Appearance tab offers some useful options of its own:

- **Orientation.** Select either vertical (stacked) or horizontal (side-by-side) menu items. Be careful with the horizontal option—it's easy to build a menu that extends off the right edge of the browser window, where no one can click it!

- **Font options.** Choose a font, font size, and formatting (bold or italic) for menu items. You can even set the alignment of text within each menu item—left, center, or right. These settings apply to *all* text in the pop-up menu: You can't just make one or two words bold or italic, or use different fonts for different menu choices.

- **Colors.** These menu items have two different sets of colors: one for a menu item's *up state* (its appearance when the menu appears) and one for its *over state* (its appearance when the mouse is on a menu command). These work just like rollover images, described on page 126. Use the color boxes to select the background color of the menu item and the color of the text inside the menu. Make sure you pick contrasting colors, so visitors can read the menu.

Tip: After adding this behavior to a page, Dreamweaver adds a file called *mm_menu.js* to your site's root folder. This is a JavaScript file containing most of the complex programming required to make the pop-up menu feature work. Don't delete this file! Doing so will break your pop-up menus and cause JavaScript errors in your page.

If you do accidentally delete it, just add another Pop-Up Menu behavior anywhere in your site. (If you add a submenu to a menu item, Dreamweaver also adds a graphic file called arrows.gif. Don't delete this, either.)

For more detailed design of a pop-up menu, click the Advanced tab (see Figure 11-7).

- **Cell Width.** Each item in a pop-up menu acts like a cell in a table (see page 144) with a background color, content (text of the menu item), width and height, and other properties. You can set the width to an exact pixel size by selecting Pixels from the pop-up menu and typing a number in the Width box. This is a good option if you're adding several pop-up menus to a page—one for each of the buttons of the main navigation bar, for example—and you want each menu to be the same width for visual consistency. (You can set only one pixel setting, which applies to both the menu and any submenus. Dreamweaver won't let you set this smaller than the space taken up by the text in a button.)

  If you accept the proposed setting, Automatic, Dreamweaver determines the width of the menu based on the longest menu item, and separate widths for the submenus. For example, in Figure 11-5, Dreamweaver calculated the width of the submenu with its three short items—Week 1, Week 2, Week 3—automatically.

- **Cell Height.** You can change the height of menu items in the same manner.

- **Cell Padding.** To adjust the space from the edge of a menu to the text inside the menu, type a pixel value in this box. Cell padding here works exactly like cell padding in a table, as described in Figure 6-2 on page 144.

- **Cell Spacing.** You can also adjust the space between menu items, as you would the space between cells in a table, as described in Figure 6-2.

- **Text Indent.** To add space between the left edge of the menu and text, type a pixel value in the Text Indent box. You'll probably find that the Cell padding adds enough spacing to the menu, and you won't need this option.

- **Menu Delay.** When you move your mouse off a menu, you might notice a slight delay before the menu disappears. This delay is controlled by the Menu Delay property. It's specified in milliseconds, so a delay of 1000 means the menu takes 1 second to disappear.

Of course, your first reaction might be: "I don't want no stinkin' delay! Just make the menu disappear when I move my mouse off!"

Unfortunately, if you set the delay *too* low, the pop-up menu won't appear at all. Without any delay, the menu would disappear the instant your mouse moved off the triggering link (the link you originally attached the behavior to), making the menu disappear before you could click your choice. You need some delay to allow enough time to choose from the menu; 500 ms is a good compromise.

• **Borders.** Here's where you get to decide whether any borders appear around each menu item. To turn off borders entirely, turn off the Show Borders box.

Dreamweaver even lets you specify colors for three different border elements. The border color affects the outside border (a line that encloses the entire menu). The Shadow color applies to a menu's shadow lines, which appear along the right and bottom edges of the menu, just inside of the outer border. (It's also the color of the lines that separate each menu item.) The Highlight color applies to the borders at the top and left edge of the menu. Together, these colors give a menu a 3-D appearance.

Tip: Web browsers hide any menu items that aren't visible within the available space of a frame. If your page uses frames, therefore, make sure your frame is deep enough to accommodate the expanded menu. (That's a particular concern if you create a nifty navigation bar that sits in a frame at the top of the window.)

Figure 11-7:
You can tweak the appearance of pop-up menus using the Advanced tab of the Show Pop-Up menu dialog box. Bear in mind that the preview in the bottom half of the window isn't very accurate. It doesn't show shadow and highlight colors or any text indents. To get an accurate view, you'll need to close this box and press the F12 key to preview your new menu in an actual Web browser.

By default, a pop-up menu is positioned to the right of its triggering link, and 10 pixels below. The Position tab lets you change this:

- **Positioning Options.** The Position tab offers four preset positioning options, represented by four buttons. The first button is the default position. The second button places the menu directly *below* the triggering link. The third button places the menu directly *above* the triggering link (good if you're adding the pop-up menu to a link near the bottom of a page). And the fourth button places the menu directly to the *right* of the triggering link.

- **Pixel location.** If none of those four options suits your taste, you can use these controls to pinpoint a location for the menu, expressed in pixels measured from the top left corner of the triggering link.

For example, if you enter 0 in the X box (the horizontal measurement), the menu will line up with the left edge of the triggering link. Typing 0 in the Y box (the vertical dimension) produces a menu whose top aligns with the top of the triggering link. Using 0 in *both* boxes places the menu smack-dab on top of the trigger.

Submenus are unaffected by these settings; they always overlap the right edge of the corresponding main menu item (Figure 11-5). (If you're up for it, there's an HTML workaround in the box below.)

POWER USERS' CLINIC

Taking Control of Submenus

Although Dreamweaver lets you set the position of the main pop-up menu, it doesn't offer any controls for positioning submenus. They always appear in the same place: 5 pixels in from the right edge of the menu item that triggers the submenu and 7 pixels below the top.

But you're not stuck with these settings—if you're willing to dig into the HTML of the page.

When you create a pop-up menu, Dreamweaver adds a chunk of JavaScript code to the page. You need to locate a particular line of code, located in the <head> section of the page, that looks something like this:

```
window.mm_menu_0514155110_0 =
new Menu("root",188,18,"Arial,
Helvetica, sans-serif",12,
"#FFFFFF","#000000","#000000",
"#FFFFFF","left","middle",3,0,500,
-5,7,true,true,true,0,true,true);
```

Zero in on the two numbers near the end: -5 and 7. These represent the position for any submenus added to items in the menu. However, in this case, the submenu position is relative to the upper *right* corner of the menu. So the -5 means 5 pixels in from the right edge of the menu item, and the 7 means 7 pixels down from the top edge.

Two other useful numbers appear near the beginning of line, right after 'new Menu.' In this example, they're 188 and 18, but these numbers vary from menu to menu. The 188 stands for the width of each item in the menu, and the 18 is the height. Thus, if you want submenus to appear directly below an item in this menu, replace the 5 with 188 and the 7 with 18.

If you decide to delve into the HTML code in this way, remember that every menu you add—and this includes submenus—adds a line like the one above to your Web page. So make sure you're working on the correct line.

- **Hide Menu checkbox.** Keep the Hide Menu on onMouseOut event turned on. It ensures that the menu disappears when you move your mouse off it.

Open Browser Window

Windows: Netscape Navigator 3+, Internet Explorer 3+
Macintosh: Netscape Navigator 3+, Internet Explorer 4+

No matter how carefully you design your Web page, chances are it won't look good in every size window. Depending on the resolution of your visitor's monitor and the dimensions of his browser window, your Web page may be forced to squeeze into a window that's 400 pixels wide, or it could be overwhelmed by one that's 1200 pixels wide. Designing your Web pages so they look good at a variety of different window sizes can be challenging.

It's the Open Browser Window action to the rescue. Using this behavior, you can instruct your visitor's browser to open a new window to whatever height and width *you* desire. In fact, you can even dictate what elements the browser window includes. Don't want the toolbar, location bar, or status bar visible? No problem; this action lets you include or exclude any such window chrome (see Figure 11-8).

Figure 11-8:
You, too, can annoy your friends, neighbors, and Web site customers with these unruly pop-up browser windows. Just add the Open Browser Window action to the <body> *tag of your document. Now, when that page loads, a new browser window opens with the ad, announcement, or picture you specify. Even more annoying, use the onUnload event of the* <body> *tag to open a new browser window—with the same Web page—when visitors try to exit the page. They won't be able to get to a different page, and may even encounter system crashes. Now that's annoying!*

To open a new browser window, you start, as always, by selecting the tag to which you wish to attach the behavior. You can attach it to any of the tags discussed on pages 336–338, but you'll usually want to add this action to a link with an onClick event, or to the <body> tag with the onLoad event.

Once you've selected this action's name from the + pop-up menu in the Behaviors panel, you see the dialog box shown in Figure 11-9. You have the following settings to make:

- **URL to Display.** In this box, type in the URL or path of the Web page, or click Browse and find the Web page on your computer. If you're loading a Web page on somebody else's site, don't forget to type an *absolute* URL, beginning with *http://* (see page 99).

- **Window Width, Window Height.** Next, type in the width and height of the new window. These values are measured in pixels; in most browsers, 100 x 100 pixels is the minimum size. Also, strange visual anomalies may result on your visitors' screens if the width and height you specify here are larger than the available space on their monitors.

Figure 11-9:
If you leave the window's Width and Height properties blank, the new window will be the same size as the window it opens from. (If you specify only one of the dimensions—height or width—Netscape Navigator 4 and earlier will ignore the dimension properties completely.)

- **Attributes.** Turn on the checkboxes for the window elements you want to include in the new window. Figure 11-10 shows the different pieces of a standard browser window.

- **Window Name box.** Give the new window a name here (letters and numbers only). If you include spaces or other symbols, Dreamweaver will display an error message and let you correct the mistake. This name won't actually appear on your Web page, but it's useful for targeting links or actions from the original window.

Once a new window is open, you can load Web pages into it from the original page that opened the window; simply use the name you give to the new window as the target of the link. For example, you could add this behavior to the <body> tag of a page so that when the page opens, a small new window also appears, showcasing a photo. You could add links to the main page that, when clicked, load additional photos into the small window.

If you use more than one open browser window behavior on a single page, make sure to give each new window a unique name. If you don't, you may not get a new window for each Open Browser Window action.

When you click OK, your newly created behavior appears in the Actions list in the Behaviors panel.

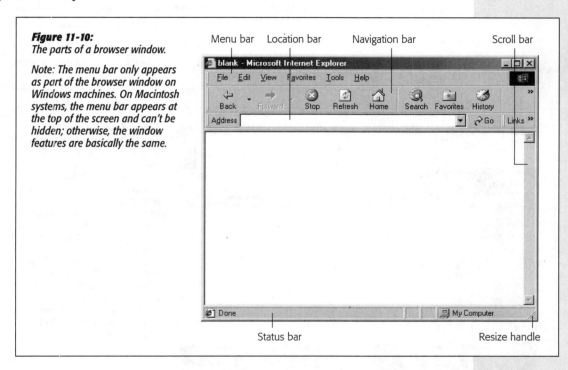

Figure 11-10:
The parts of a browser window.

Note: The menu bar only appears as part of the browser window on Windows machines. On Macintosh systems, the menu bar appears at the top of the screen and can't be hidden; otherwise, the window features are basically the same.

Menu bar   Location bar   Navigation bar   Scroll bar

Status bar   Resize handle

Go to URL

Windows: Netscape Navigator 3+, Internet Explorer 3+
Macintosh: Netscape Navigator 3+, Internet Explorer 4+

The Go to URL action works just like a link, in that it loads a new Web page. However, while links only work when you click them, this action can load a page based on an event *other than* clicking. For instance, you might want to load a Web page when your visitor's cursor merely moves over an image, or when she clicks a particular radio button.

Once you've selected a tag and chosen this action's name from the + pop-up menu in the Behaviors panel, you can make these settings in the resulting dialog box:

• **Open in.** If you aren't using frames, only Main Window is listed here. But if you're working in a frameset file (see Chapter 7) and have named each of your frames, they're listed in the "Open in" list box. Click the name of the frame where you want the new page to appear.

- **URL.** Fill in the URL of the page you wish to load. You can use any of the link-specifying tricks described on page 95: type in an absolute URL starting with *http://*, type in a path, or click the Browse button and select a page from your Web site.

Note: If you're working in frames and have the frameset file open, you can click each frame listed in the "Open in" list and assign a different URL to it. An asterisk next to the name of a frame indicates that a link points to that frame.

In other words, the same event, such as clicking a link or button, can make more than one frame change. See Figure 11-11 for an example.

Figure 11-11:
This rather complex Web page is composed of six different frames and uses the Go To URL action with flair. Clicking a single button in the navigation bar at the bottom of the page loads Web pages into four other frames. This feat is impossible using only HTML, but using Dreamweaver Behaviors, it's a snap. The Go To URL action was applied to each navigation button, with each action targeting four frames and loading a separate Web page into each.

Jump Menu and Jump Menu Go

Windows: Netscape Navigator 3+, Internet Explorer 4+
Macintosh: Netscape Navigator 3+, Internet Explorer 4+

Conserving precious visual space on a Web page is a constant challenge for a Web designer. Putting too many buttons, icons, and navigation controls on a page can quickly clutter your presentation and muddle a page's meaning. As sites get larger, so do navigation bars, which can engulf a page in a long column of buttons.

The Pop-Up Menu behavior discussed on page 339 is one solution. But it requires lengthy JavaScript code that doesn't work on all browsers. A simpler way to add detailed navigation to a site without wasting pixels is to use Dreamweaver's Jump

Menu behavior. A *jump menu* is simply a pop-up menu that lets visitors navigate by choosing from a list of links.

The Jump Menu behavior is listed in the Behaviors panel, but for a simpler, happier life, don't insert it onto your page that way. Instead, use the Insert bar or Insert menu, like this:

1. **Click where you want the jump menu to appear on your Web page.**

   It might be in a table cell at the top of the page or along the left edge.

2. **Click the Jump Menu icon (⧉). It's under the Forms tab on the Insert bar, or choose Insert→Form Objects→Jump Menu.**

   If you use the Behaviors panel instead, you first have to add a form and insert a menu into it. The Insert Jump Menu object saves you those steps.

Tip: Even though the jump menu uses a pop-up menu, which is a component of a *form,* you don't have to create a form first, as described in Chapter 10. Dreamweaver creates one automatically when you insert a jump menu.

The Jump Menu dialog box opens, as shown in Figure 11-12.

3. **Type the name of the first link in the text field.**

   You're specifying not just the first command in your pop-up menu, but also the default choice—the first one your visitor sees.

   The name you type here, by the way, doesn't have to match the page's title or anchor's name; it's whatever you want your menu to say to represent it. For instance, you can call a menu choice *Home* even if the title of your home page is *Cosmopolitan Farmer.*

4. **Enter a URL for this link in the When Selected, Go To URL field.**

   Use any of the usual methods for specifying a link (page 95).

5. **To add the next command in your pop-up menu, click the + button and repeat steps 3 and 4. Continue until you have added all of the links for this menu.**

   If you want to remove one of the links, select it from the Menu Items list and click the – button. You can also re-order the list by clicking one of the link names and then clicking the up- and down-arrow buttons.

6. **If you're using frames, use the Open URLs In pop-up menu to specify a frame in which the indicated Web page should appear.**

   Otherwise, the Main Window option loads links into the *entire* browser window.

7. In the Menu Name box, give the menu a name.

This step is optional; you can also just accept the name Dreamweaver proposes. Since Dreamweaver uses this name only for the internal purposes of the JavaScript that drives this behavior, it doesn't appear anywhere on the page.

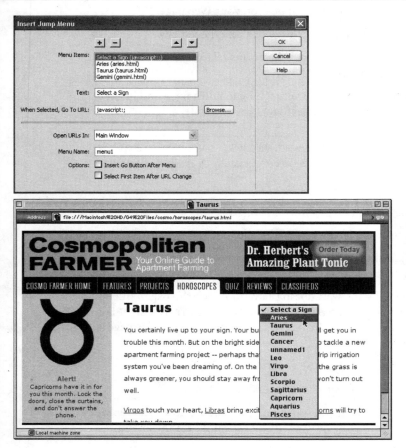

Figure 11-12:
Top: The Jump Menu dialog box shown here is set up so that the onChange event of the <select> tag triggers the Jump Menu action; that is, the Jump Menu behavior works when you select an item other than the one currently listed.

Bottom: Unless you include the Insert Go Button After Menu option, the first item of a jump menu should never be used as a link. Instead, use some descriptive text (such as "Select a Destination…") to let users know what the menu does. Then either leave the URL blank, or, if you are using frames, make the URL a JavaScript "dummy" link: javascript:; (see page 283). When placed on a page the menu is very compact, but can offer a long list of pages.

8. If you want a Go button to appear beside your jump menu, turn on "Insert Go Button After Menu."

You need to use this option only when the jump menu is in one frame, loading pages into another, or when you want to make the first item in your jump menu a link instead of an instruction (see Figure 11-12).

When you include a Go button, Dreamweaver adds a small form button next to the menu, which your visitor can click to jump to whatever link is listed in the menu. But most of the time, your visitors will never get a chance to use this Go button. Whenever they make a selection from the menu, their browsers automatically jump to the new page without waiting for a click on the Go button.

The Go button can be handy, however, when there's no selection to make. For example, if the first item in the menu is a link, your visitors won't be able to select it; it's *already* selected when the page with the menu loads. In this case, a Go button is the only way to trigger the "jump."

9. **If you want to reset the menu after each jump (so that it once again shows the first menu command), turn on Select First Item after URL Change.**

   Here's another option that's useful only when the jump menu is in one frame, loading pages into another frame. Resetting the menu so that it shows its default command makes it easy for your visitor to make another selection when ready.

10. **Click OK to apply the action and close the Jump Menu dialog box.**

    Your newly created pop-up menu appears on your Web page, and the newly created behavior appears in the Actions list in the Behaviors panel.

Tip: To edit a jump menu, click the menu in your document, and then, in the Behaviors panel, double-click the Jump Menu action in the Actions list. The settings dialog box reappears. At this point, you can change any of the options described in the previous steps, except you can't add a Go button to a jump menu that didn't have one to begin with. Click OK when you're finished.

The Jump Menu *Go* action (available on the Behaviors panel) is only useful if you didn't add a Go menu in step 8 above. In this case, if there's a jump menu on the page and you wish to add a Go button to it, click next to the menu, add a form button, and attach this behavior to it (for more on working with Forms, see Chapter 10).

Check Browser
Windows: Netscape Navigator 3+, Internet Explorer 3+
Macintosh: Netscape Navigator 3+, Internet Explorer 4+

As noted earlier, not all Web browsers work the same way. Prior to version 4, for example, Netscape Navigator and Internet Explorer couldn't handle layers or animation using Dynamic HTML. (See Chapter 12 for using Dreamweaver to create DHTML.) Cascading Style Sheets, as well, are only available for the more modern 4+ browser vintage.

Instead of confusing users of older browsers with unviewable Web pages in such cases, many Web designers build two separate Web sites: one with advanced capabilities that take advantage of all the latest bells and whistles, and another, simpler site that works with older browsers. This action, called Check Browser, automatically redirects 4.0 and greater browsers to the advanced site, and older browsers to the simpler one.

As usual, assigning this behavior begins with selecting a tag. You'll often add this action to the <body> tag of the first page of your Web site. This "gatekeeper" page determines where to send visitors when they first come to your site.

Tip: It's a good idea to make this the page viewable to older browsers—don't load it up with modern behaviors, in other words. In this way, even browsers that don't understand JavaScript can at least access the basic text of your Web site.

Then, when you choose this action's name from the + pop-up menu in the Behaviors panel, the Check Browser dialog box opens, as shown in Figure 11-13. It offers these controls:

- **Netscape Navigator.** Type the version number of Netscape Navigator you want to check for. Dreamweaver proposes 4.0, but you can change it to any number you want.

  Then, using the first pop-up menu, specify what should happen if the version of Netscape Navigator is *equal to or greater than* the number you specified. You have three choices in the pop-up menu: the browser can go to one of two new Web pages (Go to URL or Go to Alt URL, which you'll specify in step 8) or stay on the same page (Stay on This Page).

  Using the second pop-up menu, specify what to do if the version of Netscape Navigator is *less than* the number you specified.

  Once again, the browser can go to one of two new Web pages (Go to URL or Go to Alt URL) or stay on same page (Stay on This Page).

Figure 11-13:
Although the default version number is 4.0, you can enter any decimal number. So say you had a page that worked with Netscape Navigator 4.73 but not version 4.08; just type 4.73 in the Netscape Navigator text field.

Tip: If you choose the same option in both pop-up menus, you send users of *all* versions of Netscape Navigator to the same page. In other words, you can use the Check Browser behavior to separate your audience by brand of browser, rather than version. This is the way to go when you want to use behaviors that work only in one browser or another.

- **Internet Explorer.** Type the version number of Internet Explorer you want to check for. Again, Dreamweaver suggests 4.0, but you can change it to any version you wish. This number sorts and redirects Internet Explorers users by version.

  Using the third pop-up menu in the dialog box, specify what should happen if the version of Internet Explorer is *equal to or greater than* the number you specified. In the fourth pop-up menu, specify what to do if the version of Internet Explorer is *less than* the number you specified.

  As noted in the previous Tip, choosing the same option for both pop-up menus lets you screen out *all* versions of Internet Explorer (to send them to a single alternate Web site, for example).

- **Other Browsers.** If you like, choose a Web page for all *other* browsers—Opera, iCab, and so on—using this pop-up menu. Fill in the appropriate URL in the appropriate field (probably the Alt URL, described next).

- **URL, Alt URL.** These text boxes let you indicate the URLs for the redirecting commands you specified in the previous steps. For example, if you chose Go to

---

GEM IN THE ROUGH

Using Check Browser as a "Gatekeeper"

One common use of the Check Browser behavior is as a "gatekeeper" that admits only people with certain browsers into your site. For example, suppose you've jazzed up your site with all kinds of features that require a version 4-or-later browser; you want a Welcome page that lets such people proceed to the real site (and directs them there automatically after a moment), but offers everyone else only a note that they'll need a more modern browser (and tells them where they can get it).

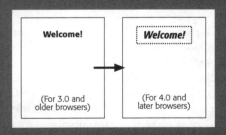

To set up this arrangement, add the Check Browser behavior to the opening page of the site (at left in the diagram shown here); in the steps on page 299, add it to the

<body> tag and use the onLoad event.

Then, in the dialog box shown in Figure 11-13, type *4* into both of the top two text boxes; choose Go to URL from the first and third pop-up menus; and type the URL for the fancy, full-fledged page (B) into the URL field.

For the other pop-up menus, labeled "otherwise" and Other Browsers, choose Stay on this Page. And *on* that page (page A), add a note like this: "Sorry, this Web site requires Netscape Navigator or Internet Explorer version 4 or higher. You can download either one for free by clicking these links," and then add links to the Netscape and Microsoft Web sites.

URL from the first pop-up menu, this is where you specify *what* URL you want those Netscape Navigator browsers redirected to. (Choose a link here using any of the techniques on page 95.)

Image Actions

Images make Web pages stand out. But adding Dreamweaver Behaviors can make those same images come to life.

Preloading Images

Windows: Netscape Navigator 3+, Internet Explorer 4+
Macintosh: Netscape Navigator 3+, Internet Explorer 4+

It takes time for images to load over the Internet. A 16 K image, for instance, takes about four seconds to download over a 56 K modem. However, once a Web browser loads an image, it stores the image in its *cache*, as described on page 476, so that it will load extremely quickly if a page requires the same graphic again. The Preload Images action takes advantage of this fact by downloading an image or images and storing them in the browser's cache, *even before* they're actually needed.

Preloading is especially important when using mouse rollover effects on a Web page (see Figure 5-13 on page 127). When a visitor moves the mouse over a particular button, it might, for example, appear to light up. If you couldn't preload the image, then the lit-up graphic for the over state wouldn't even begin to download until the cursor rolled over the button. The resulting delay makes your button feel less like a rollover than a layover.

In general, you won't need to apply this action by hand, since Dreamweaver adds it automatically when you use the Insert Rollover Image (page 126) or insert Navigation Bar (page 216) commands.

But there are exceptions, such as when you use the Preload Images action to load graphics that appear on *other* pages in your site.

For example, suppose you build a graphics-heavy Web site. People hate to wait too long for a Web page to load, but they're slightly more patient when waiting for the *first* page of a site to load. You could capitalize on that fact by adding a Preload Images action to the body of a home page (or even a page that says "Loading Web Site") that preloads most of the site's graphics. Be careful, though: If any page preloads too many images, even the most patient Web surfer may not stay around to watch the show. Remember to refer to the download stats listed in the document's status bar for the size of your Web page, as discussed on page 475.

To add the Preload Images action, select the tag to which you want to attach a behavior. Most often you'll use the <body> tag, in combination with an onLoad event.

If you've added Rollover Images or a Navigation bar to your page, this behavior may already be in the <body> of the page. In this case, just double-click the Preload Images action that's already listed in the Behaviors panel. If not, just choose this action's name from the + pop-up menu in the Behaviors panel. Either way, you're now offered the Preload Images dialog box.

Click the Browse button and navigate to the graphics file that you wish to use for preloading purposes, or type in the path or (if the graphic is on the Web already) the absolute URL of the graphic. Dreamweaver adds the image to the Preload Images list. If you want to preload another image, click the + button and repeat the previous step. Continue until you've added all the images you want to preload.

You can also remove an image from the list by selecting it and then clicking the - button. (Be careful not to delete any of the images that may be required for a rollover effect you've already created—the Undo command doesn't work here.)

When you click OK, you return to your document; your new action appears in the Behaviors panel. Here you can edit it, if you like, by changing the event that triggers it; but unless you're trying to achieve some special effect, you'll usually use the onLoad event of the <body> tag.

That's all there is to it. When your page loads in somebody's browser, the browser will continue to load and store those graphics quietly in the background. They'll appear almost instantly when they're required by a rollover or even a shift to another Web page on your site that incorporates the graphics you specified.

Swap Image

Windows: Netscape Navigator 3+, Internet Explorer 4+
Macintosh: Netscape Navigator 3+, Internet Explorer 4+

The Swap Image action exchanges one image on your page for another. (See the end of this section for detail on Swap Image's cousin behavior, Swap Image Restore.)

Simple as that process may sound, swapping images is one of the most visually exciting things you can do on a Web page. Swapping images works something like rollover images, except that a mouse click or mouse pass isn't required to trigger them. In fact, you can use *any* tag and event combination to trigger the Swap Image action. For instance, you can create a mini slide show by listing the names of pictures down the left side of a Web page and inserting an image in the middle of the page. Add a Swap Image action to each slide name, so that the appropriate picture swaps in when your visitor clicks any one of the names.

To make this behavior work, your Web page must already contain a starter image, and the images to be swapped in must be the same width and height as the original graphic. If they aren't, the browser will resize and distort the subsequent pictures to fit the "frame" dictated by the original.

To add the Swap Image behavior, start by choosing the *starter* image file that you want to include on the page. (Choose Insert→Image, or use any of the other techniques described in Chapter 5.) Give your image a name in the Property inspector, so that JavaScript will know which image to swap out. (JavaScript doesn't really care about the original graphic image itself, but rather about the space it occupies on the page.)

Tip: You can swap more than one image using a single Swap Image behavior. Using this trick, not only does a button change to another graphic when you mouse over it, but also any number of other graphics on the page can change at the same time.

An asterisk (*) next to the name of an image in the Swap Image dialog box (see Figure 11-14) indicates that the behavior will swap in a new image for that particular graphic. In the example in Figure 11-14, you can see both images that swap (marked by asterisks) with a single action.

Now select the tag to which you want the behavior attached. When you choose this action's name from the Behaviors panel, the Swap Image dialog box appears, as shown in Figure 11-14:

- **Images.** From the list, click the name of the starter image.

- **Set Source to.** Here's where you specify the image file that you want to swap in. If it's a graphics file in your site folder, click Browse to find and open it. You can also specify a path or an absolute URL to another Web site, as described on page 99.

- **Preload Images.** Preloading ensures that the swap action isn't slowed down while the graphic downloads from the Internet (see Figure 5-13 on page 127).

- **Restore Images onMouseOut.** You get this option only when you've applied this behavior to a link. When you turn it on, moving the mouse *off* the link makes the previous image reappear.

Figure 11-14:
Some actions, like the Swap Image action, can automatically add additional behaviors to a Web page. In this case, the Preload Images and Restore Images onMouseOut options actually add a Swap Image Restore action to the onMouseOut event of the currently selected tag, and a Preload Images action to the onLoad event of the <body> tag.

Swap Image Restore

The Swap Image Restore action returns the last set of swapped images to its original state. Most designers use it in conjunction with a rollover button, so that the button returns to its original appearance when the visitor rolls the cursor off the button.

You'll probably never find a need to add this behavior yourself. Dreamweaver automatically adds it when you insert a rollover image, and when you choose the Restore

Images onMouseOut option when setting up a regular Swap Image behavior (see Figure 11-14). But if you prefer, you can add the Swap Restore Image behavior to other tag and event combinations, using the general routine described on page 330. (The Swap Image Restore dialog box offers no options to set.)

Setting a Navigation Bar Image

Windows: Netscape Navigator 3+, Internet Explorer 4+
Macintosh: Netscape Navigator 3+, Internet Explorer 4+

You can easily modify a navigation bar that you've added to your Web page (see page 216) by choosing Modify→Navigation Bar. However, some advanced features of a navigation bar are only available if you use the Behaviors panel to edit the individual navigation bar images.

The Navigation Bar object specifies different graphics for each state of a navigation button: up, over, down, and over while down. But things can easily get much more complex. This behavior, for example, lets the state of a navigation bar image dictate the state of *other* images on a page, swapping images in response to a visitor's interaction with buttons on the navigation bar. Figure 11-15 shows an example of how this complex behavior might be useful.

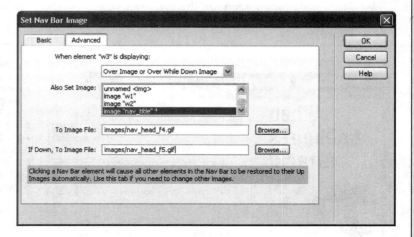

Figure 11-15:
The Advanced tab of the Set Nav Bar Image action can be used to swap other images on a Web page based on the state of a navigation button: over, over while down, or down (but not the up state). This flexibility allows for some very creative and complex interactions. When you add a swap action to an image, Dreamweaver adds an asterisk next to its name. For example, in this figure, the nav_title image has actions applied to it.

Here's how you might proceed:

1. **Place an image on your Web page. Type the name for it into the upper-left field of the Property inspector.**

   The name lets JavaScript know which image to swap out.

2. **Insert a navigation bar into the same Web page.**

   See page 216 for full instructions.

3. **Open the Behaviors panel, if it isn't already open (press Shift+F3).**

You'll notice that the Behaviors panel already lists three Set Nav Bar Image actions: one each for onClick, onMouseOut, and onMouseOver. Dreamweaver created these behaviors automatically when you inserted the navigation bar.

4. **Click one of the images in the Nav Bar.**

The image you choose will be able to control other images on the page.

5. **Double-click any of the Set Nav Bar Image actions in the Behaviors panel.**

All three actions share the same settings, so double-clicking any one of them opens the same Set Nav Bar Image dialog box—a fairly confusing system; no other Dreamweaver behavior works this way.

6. **Click the Advanced tab.**

If you've looked over page 217, then you've already encountered the Basic tab, but the advanced settings are only available from the Behaviors panel.

7. **Select the state of the navigation button from the menu.**

The behavior you're defining changes one or more images on a page depending on the *state* of the selected navigation button. You can make other images on a page respond to the over, over while down, and down states of the navigation button.

Figure 11-16:
Front: In this example, the navigation bar is composed of three graphic buttons: Week 1, Week 2, and Week 3. Back: When a visitor moves the cursor over the Week 2 button, not only does that button change to its over state, but another graphic in the lower-right corner ("The Cabbage Hunt Begins…") is swapped in.

8. From the Also Set Image list, click the name of the image you want this action to replace with another graphic.

   An asterisk to the right of a name indicates that the image already has an action applied to it.

9. Specify the image file that you wish to swap in.

   Click the Browse button and navigate to the graphic file, or type in the path or absolute URL of the graphic.

10. Repeat steps 7 and 8 until you've applied actions to all the images you wish to swap. When you're finished, click OK.

    You can't specify which events trigger this action, making it something of an oddball among the Dreamweaver Behaviors.

Message Behaviors

Communication is why we build Web sites: to tell a story, sell a product, or provide useful information that can entertain and inform our visitors. Dreamweaver can enhance this communication process with actions that provide dynamic feedback. From subtle messages in a browser's status bar to dialog boxes that command a visitor's attention, Dreamweaver offers numerous ways to respond, in words, to user interaction.

Pop-up Message

Windows: Netscape Navigator 3+, Internet Explorer 3+
Macintosh: Netscape Navigator 3+, Internet Explorer 4+

Use the Pop-up Message behavior to send important messages to your visitors, as shown in Figure 11-17. Your visitor must click OK to close the dialog box. Because a pop-up message demands immediate attention, reserve this behavior for important announcements.

To create a pop-up message, select the tag to which you want the behavior attached. For example, adding this action to the <body> tag with an onLoad event will cause a message to appear when a visitor first loads the page.

From the Add Action menu (+ button) in the Behaviors panel, choose Pop-up Message. In the Pop-up Message dialog box, type the message that you'll want to appear in the dialog box. (Check the spelling and punctuation carefully; nothing says "amateur" like poorly written error messages, and Dreamweaver's spell-checking feature isn't smart enough to check the spelling of these messages.) Then click OK.

Tip: A note to JavaScript programmers: Your message can also include any valid JavaScript expression. To embed JavaScript code into a message, place it inside braces ({ }). If you want to include the current time and date in a message, for example, add this: *{new Date()}*. If you just want to display a brace in the message, add a backslash, like this: \{ . The backslash lets Dreamweaver know that you *really do* want a { character, and not a bunch of JavaScript, to appear in the dialog box.

Set Text of Status Bar

Windows: Netscape Navigator 3+, Internet Explorer 3+
Macintosh: Netscape Navigator 3+, Internet Explorer 4+

Pop-up messages, like those described above, require your visitors to drop everything and read them. For less urgent messages, consider the Set Text of Status Bar behavior. It displays a message in the status bar of a browser window—the strip at the bottom of the window. You can add a message to a link, for example, that lets users know where the link will take them. Or you could set things up so that when a visitor moves the cursor over a photograph, copyright information appears in the window's status bar.

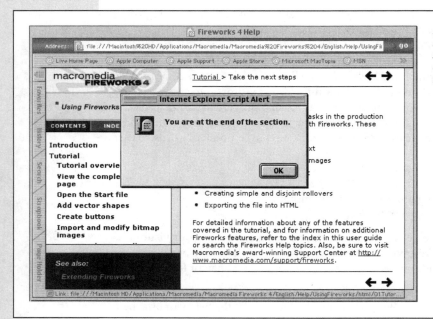

Figure 11-17:
Here a pop-up message signals the end of the online Fireworks 4 tutorial.

To apply the Set Text of Status bar action, select a tag (a very common example is a link [<a>] tag with the onMouseOver event), choose this behavior's name from the Add Action menu (+ button) in the Behaviors panel, and then, in the Set Text of Status Bar dialog box, type your message. Keep the message short: browsers cut off any words that don't fit in the status bar. Your message can also include any valid JavaScript expression, exactly as described in the previous Tip.

Set Text of Text Field

Windows: Netscape Navigator 3+, Internet Explorer 3+
Macintosh: Netscape Navigator 3+, Internet Explorer 4+

Normally, a text field in a form (page 301) is blank. It sits on the page and waits for someone to type into it. This behavior, by contrast, can save your visitors time by filling in form fields automatically with answers that have become obvious.

For instance, imagine you've created a Web survey that has a series of questions. The first question might require a yes or no answer, along the lines of: "Do you own a computer?" And you've provided radio buttons for Yes or No. The second question might be, "What brand is it?" followed by a text field where your visitors can type in the computer brand.

But if someone answers "No" to question 1, there's no point in her typing a response to the second question. To help keep things moving along, you can set the second question's text field so that it says: "Please skip to Question 3." To do so, simply add the Set Text of Text Field action to the onClick event of the No radio button of Question 1.

To apply the Set Text of Text Field action, make sure your page includes a form and at least one text field. Because this behavior changes the text in a form text field, you won't get very far without the proper HTML on the page.

Select the tag to which you want the behavior attached. In the example above, you'd attach the behavior to the form's No radio button with an onClick event. However, you aren't limited to just form elements. Any of the tags discussed on pages 336–338 will work.

When you choose Set Text of Text Field from the + pop-up menu in the Behaviors panel, the Set Text of Text Field dialog box opens. Make the following changes:

- **Text Field.** The menu lists the names of every text field in the form; choose the name of the text field whose default text you'll want to change. (See Chapter 10 for the full story on building online forms in Dreamweaver.)

- **New Text.** Type the text you'll want that field to display. Take care not to make the message longer than the space available in the field.

   (Once again, your message can include a JavaScript expression, as described in the Tip on page 359.)

Tip: Only one action that ships with Dreamweaver MX works with forms: the Validate Form action. It can prevent visitors from submitting forms that are missing information or that contain improperly formatted information. For instance, if somebody leaves the Your Name text field blank, this action opens an error box and asks her to enter her name. This action is described on page 313.

Set Text of Layer
Windows: Netscape Navigator 4+, Internet Explorer 4+
Macintosh: Netscape Navigator 4+, Internet Explorer 4+

Another way to get your message across is to change the text that appears in a layer (see Chapter 12). This action has an added benefit: it lets you use HTML code to *format* the message that appears in the layer. (Actually, the "Set Text" part of this action's name is a bit misleading, since this action also lets you include HTML code, images, forms, and other objects in the layer—not just text.)

As always, you start by selecting a tag. In this case, you might select a link, for example, so that moving the mouse over the link changes the text in the layer: "Click here to see our choice of the best tomatoes of the season."

When you choose this action's name from the + pop-up menu in the Behaviors panel, you get these controls in a dialog box:

- **Layer.** The menu lists the names of every layer on the Web page (Chapter 12); choose the name of the layer whose text you want to set.

- **New HTML.** In this field, type the text you wish to add to the layer. You can type in a plain text message, for example, or use HTML source code to control the content's formatting.

  For instance, if you want a word to appear bold in the layer, place the word inside a pair of bold tags like this: *important*. Or if you'd rather not mess around with HTML codes, you can also design the content using Dreamweaver's visual design view—that is, right out there in your document window. Copy the HTML source from the code view (Chapter 9), and then paste it into this action's New HTML field. You can also include a JavaScript expression, if you know JavaScript, as described in the Tip on page 359.

Tip: Dreamweaver provides many prewritten JavaScript programs that let you manipulate layers (animate, drag, hide, or show them, for example). These behaviors are described in Chapter 12.

Set Text of Frame

Windows: Netscape Navigator 3+, Internet Explorer 3+
Macintosh: Netscape Navigator 3+, Internet Explorer 4+

Like the Set Text of Layer action, the Set Text of Frame action replaces the content of a specified frame with HTML you specify. It's like loading a new Web page into a frame, only faster. Since the HTML is already part of the page that contains this action, your visitors don't have to wait for the code to arrive from the Internet.

To apply the Set Text of Frame action, create frameset and frame pages (see Chapter 7). When you select a tag in any of the frames—even the one whose content you intend to replace—and then choose this action from the + pop-up menu in the Behaviors panel, the Set Text of Frame dialog box opens:

- **Frame.** The menu lists the names of every available frame. Choose the name of the frame where you'll want the text to appear. (See page 212 for detail on naming frames.)

- **New HTML.** Type the text you want the frame to show. You can type in a plain text message, or use HTML source code to control the content's formatting: *<b> like this </b>* for bold, for example.

  You can also copy the HTML currently in the frame by clicking the Get Current HTML button, which copies the HTML source into the New HTML Field. Once it's there, you can then modify it as you see fit. You'd use this technique if, for example, you wanted to keep much of the formatting and HTML of the original page. Be careful, however. This action can only update the *body* of the frame; any code in the <head> of the frame will be lost. You can't add behaviors, meta tags, or other <head> content to the frame.

  Finally, as in most of these message actions, you can include a JavaScript expression as part of the text; see the Tip on page 359.

- **Preserve Background Color.** This option ensures that the background color of the frame won't change when the new text appears.

Multimedia Actions

Multimedia, from background sounds to fully interactive Flash movies, can add a depth of experience that goes well beyond basic HTML. Several Dreamweaver actions let you play sounds, Flash movies, and Shockwave movies. (For more information on incorporating multimedia elements into your Web pages, see Chapter 13.)

Control Shockwave or Flash

Windows: Netscape Navigator 3+, Internet Explorer 4+
Macintosh: Netscape Navigator 3+, Internet Explorer 4+

Flash and Shockwave have become standard elements of many Web sites, and as more and more sites combine Flash and Shockwave movies with regular HTML, it becomes increasingly useful to be able to control how those movies play. With the Control Shockwave or Flash action, regular HTML objects can control the playback of a movie. For example, you could add a set of small VCR-like control buttons—Play, Stop, Rewind—to a page. These graphics—regular HTML on the page—could control the playback of a Flash or Shockwave movie.

1. **Add a Flash or Shockwave movie to the page.**

   See Chapter 13 for details.

2. **Select the movie and name it in the Property inspector (page 406).**

   Dreamweaver uses this name to identify the movie in the JavaScript that runs the behavior.

3. **Select the tag to which you want the behavior attached.**

   This might be a dummy link (see page 329) attached to a button graphic. Using the onClick event would help simulate the function of a button.

4. **From the + pop-up menu in the Behaviors panel, choose Control Shockwave or Flash.**

The Control Shockwave or Flash dialog box opens, as shown in Figure 11-18.

Figure 11-18:
The Control Shockwave or Flash action lets you control the playback of a movie. You can only choose one type of control per action, however. So if you wanted to play a movie from a particular frame, you would need to add two actions: the first would use the Go To Frame option, and the second would use the Play option to start the movie.

5. **Choose how you want this action to control the movie.**

You have four options for controlling a movie: Play (starts the movie from the current frame), Stop, Rewind (to the first frame), or Go To Frame (jumps to a frame you specify by typing its number into the Go To Frame field).

6. **Click OK.**

Play Sound

Windows: Netscape Navigator 3+, Internet Explorer 4+
Macintosh: Netscape Navigator 3+, Internet Explorer 4+

The Play Sound action lets you embed a sound file in a Web page and trigger its playback using any available event.

That's the theory, anyway. In practice, this action meets with mixed success, because browsers don't have a built-in sound feature. Instead, they rely on plug-ins to play sound files. But JavaScript (that is, Dreamweaver Behaviors) can't control some plug-ins, and some plug-ins can handle only certain types of sound files; the bottom line is that you may wind up with a silent Web page. Therefore, you shouldn't use the play sound action for mission-critical Web pages.

If sound is absolutely essential for your Web page, you're better off using a Flash or Shockwave movie (see Chapter 13) and including a Control Shockwave or Flash Movie behavior (see above).

If, after all of those disclaimers, you still want to try this behavior, follow the usual steps. Select the tag to which you want the behavior attached. (The <body> tag would be the most likely candidate. Using the onLoad event, you could make the sound begin after the page has loaded.)

Then, from the + pop-up menu in the Behaviors panel, choose Play Sound. In the resulting dialog box, click the Browse button; navigate to, and double-click, the sound file you want to play. The most common sound formats include WAV (.wav), midi

(.mid), AU (.au), and AIFF (.aiff). (If the file isn't already in your Web site folder, Dreamweaver offers to save a copy there.) Finally, click OK.

Check Plug-in

Windows: Netscape Navigator 3+, Internet Explorer 4+ (for Flash and Shockwave plug-ins only)
Macintosh: Netscape Navigator 3+

Flash animations, QuickTime movies, and Shockwave games can add a lot of excitement to any Web site. Unfortunately, they don't work unless your visitors have downloaded and installed the corresponding browser plug-ins (see page 129 for more on this topic).

The Check Plug-in behavior can detect whether or not your visitor's browser has the required plug-in installed (Flash, Shockwave, LiveAudio, Netscape Media Player, or QuickTime), and if not, to redirect your visitor to a special page for such less-fortunate Web surfers. It has one serious drawback, however, which is described in the Workaround Workshop sidebar below.

Because this action loads a new Web page, starting by selecting a link (<a> tag) with an onClick event is a good idea. This way, when your visitors click the link, they see one page if they have the plug-in, and another if they don't.

Then, when you choose Check Plug-in from the + pop-up menu in the Behaviors panel, a dialog box (Figure 11-19) lets you make the following settings:

- **Plugin.** From the pop-up menu, choose the plug-in's name, or type its name in the Enter field.

  The plug-in options available in the menu are Flash, Shockwave, LiveAudio, Netscape Media Player, and QuickTime. Only the Flash and Shockwave options work with Internet Explorer (see the box below).

WORKAROUND WORKSHOP

When Checking Doesn't Check Out

The Check Plug-in action is a great idea, but it doesn't work for everyone.

It works fine in Netscape Navigator. But Internet Explorer can't detect plug-ins using JavaScript; therefore, this action can't detect most plug-ins for Internet Explorer.

If you need to check only for the Flash or Shockwave players, Dreamweaver solves part of the problem by adding some computer instructions in a language that Internet Explorer can understand: VBScript. These instructions let Internet Explorer check for the Flash or Director players in

Internet Explorer *for Windows.*

Unfortunately, those special codes don't work on Internet Explorer prior to version 5 on the Mac. These older versions of Internet Explorer for the Mac are therefore left without any way of detecting whether or not the appropriate plug-ins are installed.

This technical snafu explains why this Dreamweaver behavior isn't actually very useful except to people who care only about Netscape Navigator users.

• **If Found, Go To URL/Otherwise, Go To URL.** Using these text fields, specify the Web pages to which your visitor will be directed if the plug-in is, or isn't, installed.

You can indicate these pages just as you would any link (see page 95). For example, if the Web page is part of the site you're working on, click Browse to locate and open the Web page document.

Tip: If you leave the If Found, Go To URL field empty, the visitor who has the correct plug-in installed will stay right there on the same page. Use this arrangement when you apply the action to a <body> tag with an onLoad event, and the page *contains* the plug-in object.

Figure 11-19:
If it isn't listed in the pop-up menu, you can type in the name of the plug-in you wish to check. If you have the plug-in installed in Netscape Navigator, you can find its name by choosing Help→About Plug-ins in Netscape Navigator, which produces a list of currently installed plug-ins and their names.

The Otherwise, Go To URL page could let users know that they need a plug-in to view the site. Furthermore, it should offer a link to the site where the plug-in can be found.

• **Always go to first URL if detection is not possible.** Remember that Internet Explorer can't detect all plug-ins. It wouldn't make sense to send Internet Explorer users to a "You don't have the correct plug-in" page when they might very well have it installed. If you turn on this box, your Web page will assume that the plug-in *is* installed if it can't determine otherwise.

Tip: However you plan to use this action, always make sure that you give users who don't have the plug-in a way to quickly and easily download and install it, so that they can return to your site to bask in the glorious multimedia experience you've created for them.

Advanced Actions

Dreamweaver has two advanced behaviors that let you call custom JavaScript functions and change the properties of various HTML elements. Both of these actions require familiarity with JavaScript and HTML (Chapter 9). Unlike the other Dreamweaver behaviors, these two can easily generate browser errors if used incorrectly.

Call JavaScript

Windows: Netscape Navigator 3+, Internet Explorer 3+
Macintosh: Netscape Navigator 3+, Internet Explorer 4+

You can use the Call JavaScript behavior to execute a single line of JavaScript code, or to call a JavaScript function that you've added to the <head> section of your Web page.

When you select a tag and choose this behavior's name from the Behaviors panel, the Call JavaScript dialog box opens. If you want to execute a single line of JavaScript code, simply type it in. For instance, if you wanted to make the browser window close, you would type *window.close()*. If you want to call a JavaScript function, type the function name, like this: *myFunction()*.

Change Property

Windows: Netscape Navigator 3+, Internet Explorer 3+
Macintosh: Netscape Navigator 3+, Internet Explorer 4+

The Change Property action can dynamically alter the value of a property of any of the following HTML tags: <layer>, <div>, <span>, <img>, <form>, <textarea>, or <select>. It can also change properties for radio buttons, checkboxes, text fields, and password fields on forms (see Chapter 10). As with the previous behavior, this one requires a good knowledge of HTML and JavaScript. Dreamweaver's built-in HTML and JavaScript references (page 288) can help you get up to speed.

Select a tag, choose this behavior's name from the + pop-up menu in the Behaviors panel, and then fill in the dialog box like this (see Figure 11-20):

* **Type of Object.** The pop-up menu lists the eleven HTML tags that this behavior can control. Choose the type of object whose property you wish to change.

POWER USERS' CLINIC

Closing Browser Windows with the Call JavaScript Behavior

Suppose you've added an Open Browser Window behavior to your home page, so that when visitors come to your site, a small window opens, displaying a Web page that advertises some new feature of your site.

Well, after they've read the ad, your visitors will want to close the window and continue visiting your site. Why not make it easy for them by adding a "Close this Window" button?

To do so, simply add a graphic button (text works fine too)

and add a dummy (null) link to it (that is, in the Property inspector, type *javascript:;* into the Link field). Next, add the Call JavaScript behavior; in step 3 of the instructions on the facing page, type the following line of JavaScript code: *window.close()*.

Finally, after you click OK, make sure that the event is set to onClick in the Behaviors panel.

That's all there is to it; the link you've added to the pop-up window offers a working Close button.

- **Named Object.** From this pop-up menu, choose the name of the object you want to modify. (This step shows you how important it is to name HTML objects in advance.)

- **Property.** Choose the property you want to change (or, if you know enough about JavaScript, just type the property's name in the Enter field).

Because Netscape Navigator and Internet Explorer recognize different properties for many HTML elements, you can use the pop-up menu to the right of the Property menu to specify the browser type and version you're targeting. Unfortunately, you can only select one browser for each Change Property action you apply. If you want to use this action for both browser brands, you'll need to apply it twice: once for each browser.

- **New Value.** Type the new value you wish to set for this property. This value should be appropriate to the type of property you'll be changing. For example, if you're changing a background color, the value should be a color—*#FF0066*, for example.

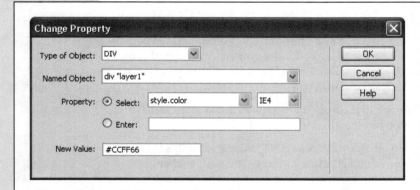

Figure 11-20:
Not only does the Change Property behavior require a good bit of knowledge about HTML, browsers, and JavaScript, but its effectiveness is limited to specific browsers. You may have to apply this action multiple times to target multiple browsers, since Netscape and Internet Explorer are so dissimilar.

Adding More Behaviors

Dreamweaver comes with the 27 preprogrammed behaviors described in this chapter, but you can download many additional behaviors from various Web sites, including Macromedia's Exchange Web site. Once you've downloaded them, you can easily add them to Dreamweaver, as described in Chapter 19.

Dreamweaver's Behaviors can open a new world of interaction for your Web pages. Without having to understand the complexities of JavaScript and cross-browser programming, you can easily add powerful and interesting effects that spice up any Web visitor's experience.

Layers: Interactivity and Animation

The first MTV generation has grown up—and discovered the Web. Unfortunately, putting the average home page next to the average music video is like pitting a minivan against a Maserati. If you want to keep restless eyes glued to your site, adding attention-grabbing animation and interactivity may do the trick.

Using Behaviors (Chapter 11) and a clever design tool called *layers,* you can make pictures dance across the screen, add pop-up tooltips to your links, and even create Web page sticky notes that visitors can drag around the window. Without Dreamweaver, such animation would require a complex mixture of HTML, programming, and Cascading Style Sheets (Chapter 8) that could leave you crying into your keyboard. You, however, as a Dreamweaver owner, can create these effects without any assistance from therapy or antidepressants.

Tip: As when using any cool new technology, have mercy on your audience when adding interactive effects. Make sure any animations you use contribute to the message of your site and don't become distracting gimmicks whose novelty wears off after the first viewing. Making a news bulletin wiggle across the screen might look neat, but it's pretty hard to read.

Creating Layers

A layer is a rectangular container that holds other page material—images, text, form elements, and even other layers. In this regard, it acts like a table cell (page 144). And as with a cell, you can define a layer's width and height and give it a background color or image.

But that's where the similarities end. What really sets a layer apart from other page elements is the way you can give it an exact position on a page. Want an image to appear exactly 100 pixels from the top edge of the browser window and 200 pixels from the left? Add a layer at that spot and insert an image in the layer—no jury-rigged table scaffolding required.

Figure 12-1:
Dreamweaver makes it easy to add simple animations to a Web page. Using the program's animation tools, you can make items fly—or fall, like this leaf on the www.safetreekids.net Web page—across your pages.

Furthermore, because a layer uses *both* HTML and Cascading Style Sheets, it offers you a much wider range of control and flexibility, from exact screen placement to animation. For example, you can hide or show layers on the screen, nest them, and stack or overlap them. And you can control layers with JavaScript, effortlessly adding live interactive effects like animation.

As you probably know by now, any Web technology this powerful must come at a price: Since layers rely on Cascading Style Sheets, only version 4.0-and-later Web browsers can display them. Older browsers just ignore layer information and display their contents in the normal flow of the page—no exact positioning, no cool animation. To make matters worse, Netscape Navigator 4 has a notoriously hard time with layers, and often displays them incorrectly (see page 378).

Tip: The members of the W3C, the body that approves Web technology standards, originally envisioned layers as a tool for laying out pages. They hoped that layers, with their exact positioning properties, would let Web designers achieve the level of control found in print design.

But don't rely on layers for layout. Most new browsers can position layers accurately on the screen, but the complexities of complete page designs frequently overwhelm the current browser crop. Use tables (Chapter 6) to lay out your pages instead. (If you're a courageous and forward-looking Web designer, see the box on page 145 for layer-based design resources.)

Drawing with the Layer Tool

Dreamweaver wouldn't be Dreamweaver if it didn't give you several ways to perform a certain task, such as creating a layer. You can drag to create one freehand or use a menu command to insert a full-blown, complete layer. Your choices are:

- **Use the Layer tool.** The Layer tool is in the Insert bar, under both the Common Layout tabs (see Figure 12-2). Click the Layer button and then drag the + cursor diagonally in the document window to create a box—the outline of the layer.

- **Use a menu command.** To insert a layer at the insertion point, choose Insert→Layer.

If you don't like the looks of the default layer that Dreamweaver inserts, choose Edit→Preferences, select the Layers category, and adjust the default layer's properties there. Add a background color, for example, or increase the layer's size. From then on, you can instantly create your favorite kind of layer using the Insert→Layer command.

Note: The Insert→Layer command makes it easy to place a layer inside of a table cell or another layer; however, this is not always a good idea. Layers inside table cells cause serious display problems in some browsers; furthermore, *nested* layers don't work well in Netscape Navigator 4 (see page 373 for more on nesting).

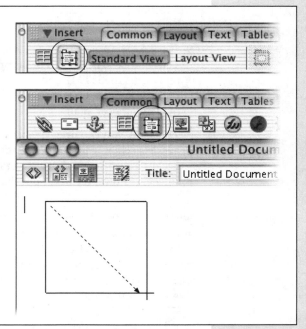

Figure 12-2:
The Layer tool on the Insert bar lets you add layers to your pages simply by drawing them in the document window. If you're creating multiple layers, hold down the Ctrl (⌘) key while drawing a layer. When you release the mouse, the Layer tool will remain selected, ready to draw the next layer.

However you create the layer, its outline appears in the document window with a blinking insertion point inside. As with table cells, you can type text into the layer or insert other objects—such as images or movies—into it.

Tip: The Layer tool doesn't work in Layout view or Code view. If the tool is grayed out in the Insert bar, make sure to switch back to Standard view (see Figure 6-3 on page 145).

Unless you fill it up or add a background color to it, a layer is invisible, like an empty, borderless table. Since it's difficult to identify, select, and modify something that's invisible, Dreamweaver adds visual cues to make working with layers easier (see Figure 12-3):

- **Layer marker.** The gold shield with the letter C represents the spot within the HTML of the page where the code for the layer actually appears.

  While HTML objects generally appear in the document window in a top-to-bottom sequence that mirrors their order in the HTML source code, the position of layers themselves doesn't depend on where the layer-creating code appears in the page's HTML. In other words, it's possible to have a layer appear near the bottom of the page, whose actual code may be the first line inside the body of the page (see Figure 12-3).

  Click the shield icon to select the layer. Note, however, the difference from the selection handle (described next): When you drag a layer marker, you don't move the layer in the page layout. Instead, you reposition the layer's code in the HTML of the page.

  That quirk can be tricky. For instance, be careful not to drag a layer marker (which represents the HTML code) into a table. Putting a layer inside a table can cause major display problems in some browsers. In Netscape 4, the layer's contents may not appear at all.

  That said, you *can* draw a layer so that it *overlaps* a table, or even appears to be inside a cell; just make sure the gold layer marker itself is not inside a cell. If you use the Layer tool to draw a layer (page 371), you avoid this problem completely, since Dreamweaver won't put the code in a cell.

Tip: The layer marker takes up room on the screen and can push text, graphics, and other items next to it out of the way. In fact, even the thin borders Dreamweaver adds to tables and layers take up space in the document window, and the space they occupy may make it difficult to place layers precisely. The keyboard shortcut Shift+Ctrl+I (Shift-⌘-I) hides or shows invisible items like layer markers. The Hide All Visual Aids option from the Document toolbar does the same thing (see page 18). It's a good idea to hide visual aids while you're drawing layers.

- **Selection handle.** The selection handle provides a convenient handle to grab and move a layer around the page. The handle appears when you select the layer or when you click inside the layer to add material to it.

- **Layer outline.** A thin, gray, 3-D border outlines each layer. Like the layer marker and selection handle, it's only there to help you see the boundaries of the layer and doesn't appear when the page is viewed in a Web browser. You can turn it on and off by choosing View→Visual Aids→Layer Borders. (When you hide the borders, layer markers remain, but at least hiding borders gives you a quick preview without opening your Web browser.)

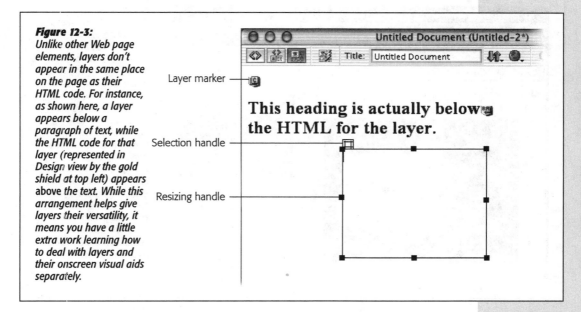

Figure 12-3:
Unlike other Web page elements, layers don't appear in the same place on the page as their HTML code. For instance, as shown here, a layer appears below a paragraph of text, while the HTML code for that layer (represented in Design view by the gold shield at top left) appears above the text. While this arrangement helps give layers their versatility, it means you have a little extra work learning how to deal with layers and their onscreen visual aids separately.

Layer marker

This heading is actually below the HTML for the layer.

Selection handle

Resizing handle

Nesting Layers

Later in this chapter, you can read how to animate a layer so that it moves across the screen. But suppose you want a more advanced effect, like a group of layers that move in a synchronized choreography. You could animate each layer independently, of course, or you could harness the power of *nested* layers.

Nesting doesn't necessarily mean that one layer appears inside another layer; rather, it means that the HTML for one layer is written inside the code for another layer. The nested layer itself can appear anywhere on the page (see Figure 12-4). The main benefit of nested layers is that the *parent* layer—the layer containing the HTML of one or more other layers—can control the behavior of its *child* layers.

For example, suppose you create one layer and nest two layers inside it. If you move the parent layer on the screen, the two child layers follow it, which gives you an easy way to move several layers in unison. Furthermore, the parent layer can control the visibility of its children. When you hide the parent layer (see page 384), the nested layers also disappear.

Note: Netscape 4 has big problems displaying nested layers. For example, it often ignores the positioning and visibility you specify. If you need to make your pages compatible with Netscape 4 browsers, it's best to avoid nesting layers or, at the very least, use Dreamweaver's built-in Netscape fix, which is described in the box on page 378.

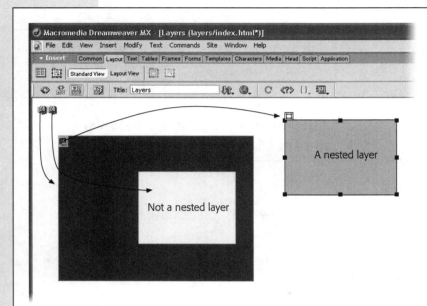

Figure 12-4:
An inner nested layer doesn't necessarily appear inside the outer one. The HTML code for the layer at right is nested inside the large gray box layer. On the other hand, one layer that appears inside another isn't necessarily a nested layer, either; the lightest gray box here, for example, isn't nested at all. One sure-fire way to identify a nested layer is to click a layer marker (the gold shield) within a layer; the nested layer's selection handle appears, as shown here.

Here's how to create a nested layer:

- Click inside a layer, and then choose Insert→Layer. You get a new, nested layer inside it.

- Drag the Layer tool from the Insert bar and drop it inside a layer on the page. (Note that this isn't the same procedure described on page 371, in which you click the Layer button and then drag in the document window.)

- While pressing the Ctrl (⌘) key, drag one layer in the *Layers panel* (see Figure 12-5) onto another layer. The layer you drag becomes the child of the layer you drop it on. The nested layer appears indented in the Layers panel, also shown in Figure 12-5. To un-nest a layer, drag it above or below the parent layer in the Layers panel.

The layer marker for a nested layer appears inside the border of the outer layer.

Tip: You can also set Dreamweaver's preferences so that any layer you draw on top of another layer in the document window is automatically nested. Choose Edit→Preferences, click the Layers category, and turn on Nest when Created Within a Layer.

Undoing nested layers

If you later want to un-nest a nested layer, just drag its layer marker to a new spot in the document window—outside of any other layers.

The Layers Panel

The Layers panel helps you manage the layers in a document (see Figure 12-5). To open it, choose Window→Others→Layers, or press F2.

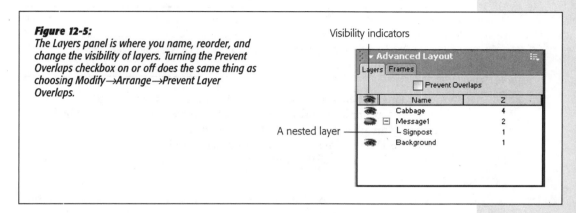

Figure 12-5:
The Layers panel is where you name, reorder, and change the visibility of layers. Turning the Prevent Overlaps checkbox on or off does the same thing as choosing Modify→Arrange→Prevent Layer Overlaps.

Visibility indicators

A nested layer

The panel lists all layers in the document, and the three columns provide information on each layer:

- **Visibility.** If left to its own devices, Dreamweaver makes the contents of all layers visible on the page. But there are situations where you may want to make a certain layer (and its contents) invisible in your visitors' Web browsers.

  The power of the Visibility property is that, using Dreamweaver Behaviors, you can later make the layer visible again, on cue. Imagine a Web page where you've superimposed many hidden layers on a diagram of a car engine. You could set

---

WORKAROUND WORKSHOP

Converting a Layer Grid to a Table

If the Prevent Overlaps box in the Layers panel is turned on, you won't be able to draw one layer on top of another. Nor will you be able to drag a layer onto or over another layer. Dreamweaver 3 aficionados once exploited this feature to create a layer-based design, assembling various rectangles on the screen to hold the different pieces of the Web page, and then converted the finished result into a table. These Dreamweaver veterans took advantage of the fact that the program can convert each layer into a table cell—but only if the layers don't overlap.

Layout view (introduced in Dreamweaver 4) renders this workaround obsolete (see Chapter 6). But if you're still in the habit of using layers as though they're design tables, turn on the Prevent Overlaps box, draw your page design using the Layer tool, and then choose Modify→Convert→ Layers to Tables. Be prepared for some additional labor, however. Tables created this way don't always hold up well after you start adding text and graphics to them; the cells typically expand in ways that ruin the design.

---

this up so that moving the mouse over a part of the image reveals a layer, complete with text that describes the corresponding engine part. (Page 384 shows you how to create this effect.)

To change a layer's visibility, click in the Eye column next to the layer's name. An open eye indicates a layer is visible; a closed eye, hidden. No eye icon at all represents the factory setting (that is, visible).

Tip: The Property inspector can set a layer's invisibility, too. In fact, one option, Inherit, is available *only* from the Property inspector. If you set the visibility property of a child layer (one that's nested inside another layer) to inherit, it will adopt the visibility settings of its parent. If the parent layer is invisible, the child layer is, too.

• **Layer name.** When you create a layer, Dreamweaver gives it a generic name—Layer1, for example. To provide a more descriptive name, one that will make it easier to remember which layer is which, double-click the layer name and type a new name. (Layer names must start with a letter and can only contain letters and numbers. As Dreamweaver is quick to remind you, spaces and other punctuation aren't allowed.)

Clicking a layer name is another way to select a layer in the document window.

Note: Don't rename a layer if you've already used it in a Dreamweaver behavior such as the Show/Hide Layers action (see page 384). JavaScript uses your layer names to "talk to" the layers. If you change a layer's name in the Layers panel, Dreamweaver doesn't automatically update the name in the JavaScript code in your page. The behavior, therefore, will no longer work. In that case, you'll need to edit the behavior using the new layer name (see page 333).

• **Z-Index.** Welcome to the third dimension. Layers are unique in the world of Web elements, because they "float" above (or even behind) a Web page and can overlap each other, completely or partially.

EASTER EGG HUNT

Franchises Still Available. Call Today.

You'll find a surprise hidden in Dreamweaver's Layers panel. Draw a layer on a page, and open the Layers panel (press F2). Double-click the layer's name, and then type *ToastYourOwn*. The dialog box shown here appears.

If you click Yes (and you're online), you'll be taken straightaway to the home page for Toast Your Own, a prom-

ising chain of coffee shops. (The twist to this coffee-shop chain: Instead of having the bozos behind the counter serve you burnt, or, even worse, undercooked toast, you take your coffee and fresh-baked bread, sit down at one of the well-lit tables, and pop the bread into one of the many conveniently situated toasters.) Have it your way, indeed!

So, I see you want to toast your own...

No   Yes

If you were awake in high school Algebra, you may remember the graphing system in which the X axis (a line pointing to the right) specified where a point was in space left-to-right, and the Y axis specified where the point was vertically. And if you were awake *and* paying attention, you may remember that the Z axis denotes a point's position in *front-to-back* space. When you draw a three-dimensional object on this type of graph, you need to use all three axes: X, Y, and Z.

The Z-Index of layers doesn't make your Web page *appear* three-dimensional; it simply specifies the "front-to-backness" of overlapping layers. The Z-Index, in other words, controls the stacking order of layers on a page, and is represented by the number in the Z column of the Layers panel (see Figure 12-5).

In most cases, the page itself lies behind all layers, and the layers stack up from there. In other words, the higher the layer number, the higher the layer, so that a layer with a Z-Index of 4 appears *behind* an overlapping layer with a Z-Index of, say, 7. However, you can also use a negative Z-Index—for example, -1—to place a layer behind the plane of the Web page. (These numbers have no relation to the actual number of layers on a page. You could have three layers with Z-Indexes of 2, 499, and 2000, if you chose. You'd still just have three layers, one on top of the other in ascending order.)

To change the Z-Index of a layer, click the number in the Z column and type another number. Software veterans will find that Dreamweaver's Layers panel works just as it does in Photoshop or Fireworks: you can drag a layer's name up or down the list to the desired position. The layer at the top of the list (highest number) is in front of all other layers, while the layer at the bottom of the list (lowest number) appears behind all other layers.

Modifying Layer Properties

Once you've drawn a layer, it isn't locked down on the page. Using the Property inspector, you can rename it, resize it, move it, align it with other layers, and set many other properties.

But first, you need to select the layer using one of these methods:

- Click the layer's name in the Layers panel (see page 375).
- Click the layer's selection handle (see Figure 12-4).
- Click the layer's border.
- Click the marker that indicates the HTML code for the layer (see Figure 12-4).

And if that isn't enough ways to select a layer—Macromedia's programmers never sleep—you can also Shift-click a layer. This technique also lets you select multiple layers, so that you can set the properties of (or align) many layers at once. If you're working in a layer or have a layer selected, Shift-clicking another layer selects them both. You can continue to Shift-click to select additional layers. (Shift-click a second time to deselect a selected layer.)

Resizing Layers

When you select a layer, eight handles appear around the edges of the layer (see Figure 12-4). You can drag any of these handles to change the layer's dimensions. The corner handles resize both the width and height simultaneously.

You can also use the keyboard to resize a layer. First select the layer, and then do one of the following:

• Press the Ctrl (⌘) key and press the arrow keys to change the layer's size by one pixel. The up and down arrow keys adjust the layer's height; the left and right arrows affect its width.

• To change the size *ten* pixels at a time, press Shift+Ctrl (Shift-⌘) and press the arrow keys.

For better precision, use the Property inspector to set an exact width and height for the layer (see Figure 12-6). Type a value in the W and H boxes to change the width and height of the layer, respectively. You can specify any unit of measurement that Cascading Style Sheets understands: px (pixels), pc (picas), pt (points), in (inches), mm (millimeters), cm (centimeters), em (height of the current font), ex (height of current font's x character), or % (percentage). To do this, type a number *immediately* followed by the abbreviation for the unit. For example, type *2in* into the W box to make the layer 2 inches wide.

Another benefit of using the Property inspector is that Dreamweaver lets you resize multiple layers at once. Shift-click two or more layers to select them, and then type new widths and heights. Dreamweaver sets all selected layers to these same dimensions.

Note: If the Prevent Overlaps feature is enabled (see Figure 12-5), you can't drag any of a layer's resize handles over another layer. In other words, layers can't be resized to overlap other layers *when dragging*. But if you use the Property inspector to change the dimensions of a layer, Dreamweaver *always* allows overlaps.

Moving Layers

Moving a layer is just as simple as resizing. Drag any border or the layer's selection handle (shown in Figure 12-4). (Avoid the eight resize handles, which change the size of the layer when dragged.)

For less speed but greater precision, you can move a layer using the keyboard. First select the layer and then do one of the following:

- To move a layer one pixel at a time up, down, left, or right, press the corresponding keyboard arrow key.
- Press Shift while using an arrow key to move a layer ten pixels at a time.

As you'd guess, you can also control a layer's placement using the Property inspector (see Figure 12-6). Dreamweaver measures a layer's position relative to the left and top edges of the page (or, for nested layers, from the left and top edges of the parent layer). The Property inspector provides two boxes for these values: L specifies the distance from the left edge of the page to the left edge of the selected layer; T specifies the distance from the top edge of the page to the top of the selected layer.

To position a layer using the Property inspector, select the layer, using any of the methods described on page 377, and type distances in the L and T boxes. You can use any of the units of measurement mentioned previously. You can even use negative values to move part or all of a layer off the page entirely (offstage, you might say), which is something you'd do if you intended a subsequent animation to bring it *onstage*, into the document window (see page 390).

For example, if you drew a 100-pixel-tall and 50-pixel-wide layer, you could move it to the very top-left corner of the page by selecting it and typing *0* in both the L and T boxes. To position that same layer so that it's just off the left edge of the page, type *-50px* in the L box.

Tip: You can't move a layer completely off the screen by dragging it. If you try, Dreamweaver rudely snaps the layer back to its previous position when you release the mouse. To completely move a layer out of sight, you must use the keyboard or Property inspector.

Aligning Layers

At times you may want to align several layers so that their left, top, bottom, or right edges line up with each other. Dreamweaver's Align command will do just that; it can even make the width and height of selected layers the same.

The layer you select *last* dictates how Dreamweaver aligns the layers. For example, say you have three layers—A, B, and C, and select them in order from A to C. You then align them to Left. Dreamweaver uses the left edge of layer C (the last one you selected) as the value for the other layers.

To use this feature, select two or more layers (by Shift-clicking them), choose Modify→Align, and then select one of the following options from the submenu:

- **Left** aligns the left edges of all selected layers. In other words, it gives each layer the same L property.

- **Right** aligns the right edges.

- **Top** aligns the top edges, so that the T properties are all set the same.

- **Bottom** aligns the bottom edges of the layers.

- **Make Same Width** sets the width of all selected layers (the W box in the Property inspector) the same. **Make Same Height** does the same for the height of the layers.

Layer Properties

Dimensions, Z-Index, and positioning aren't the only aspects of layers you can adjust using the Property inspector. To see the other options, first select a layer using any of the techniques described on page 377—click its name in the Layers panel, for example—and then inspect the Property inspector (Figure 12-6)

FREQUENTLY ASKED QUESTION

Decoding DHTML

I've heard people talk about DHTML. What is it, and how is it different from HTML?

DHTML, or Dynamic HTML, is a combination of Web technologies that, among other things, let you animate elements on a page. You can hide (and then show) text, graphics, and other objects, and even make an object draggable within your browser window (imagine a Web page that's a functional jigsaw puzzle). HTML, JavaScript, and Cascading Style Sheets make these kinds of effects possible.

HTML, of course, provides the framework and content for any Web page. It includes the tags that let you insert tables, graphics, and text. Cascading Style Sheets provides exact pixel-level positioning of content on a page (it's what makes Layers possible). Finally, JavaScript (the programming language behind Dreamweaver Behaviors) brings the D to DHTML by providing interactive controls for the page's elements, including layers' properties. In short, DHTML is nothing more than the use of these three Web technologies to produce interactive and dynamic Web pages.

Background image and color

You can set a layer's background in the same way you would for a table or table cell. To add a background image to the layer, click the folder icon next to the Bg Image field, and then select an image from your site folder. As usual, Dreamweaver tiles the image, if necessary, until the entire layer is filled with repeating copies of the graphic.

Setting a background color is even easier. Just use the Bg Color box (see page 34) to select a color or sample a color off the screen.

Figure 12-6:
You can set most layer properties in the Layers panel—but the Overflow and Clipping properties are available only here.

Tag

Information about the size, position, visibility, and other properties of a layer is, behind the scenes, described using Cascading Style Sheets, but it's actually stored in an HTML tag within the page. The Tag pop-up menu lets you choose which kind of tag you'll want to store your layer's properties. (Here's another example of Dreamweaver's over-achieving excess: two of the tags work only in a single browser version. In real life, you'll only use one of these options: the DIV tag.)

- **DIV** is the best choice. A <div> tag indicates a block-level element, like a paragraph or header. But unlike other block-level elements, the <div> tag has no intrinsic formatting—it's an empty vessel waiting to be filled with formatting information (in this case, layer properties).

- **SPAN** is used for formatting chunks of text *within* a paragraph—a few words on a line, for example. Although using the <span> tag works with layers, the block-level <div> tag is a more logical choice, since a layer really is like a block, sitting on the page in all its square glory.

- The **LAYER** and **ILAYER** options work only in Netscape Navigator 4. Navigator 6 doesn't even recognize them. Consider these tags refugees of the browser war—gone and soon to be forgotten.

Overflow

Suppose you draw a square layer, 100 x 100 pixels. You fill it with a graphic that's 150 x 162 pixels—that is, larger than the layer itself.

You've already seen how a table cell reacts to this situation: it simply grows to fit the content inside it. Layers, however, are more (or less) flexible, depending on your choice of Overflow option in the Property inspector. These choices let you decide how browsers handle the excess part of the image:

- **Visible** makes the layer grow to accommodate its contents. This is the default setting.

- **Hidden** chops off the excess. In the example, only the top-left 100 x 100 pixels of the image are visible.

- **Scroll** adds scroll bars to the layer, so that a visitor can scroll to see all of the layer's contents. This feature offers an interesting way to add a small, scrollable window within a Web page; it's like a frame, but without requiring a frameset. Imagine letting visitors scroll and read through a small "Latest Company News" box, without disturbing anything else on the page. Unfortunately, this option doesn't work in Netscape 4, OmniWeb, or Opera.

- **Auto** adds scroll bars to a layer *only* if necessary to accommodate its oversize contents. This feature doesn't work in Netscape 4, OmniWeb, or Opera, either.

Dreamweaver can display only the Visible option. If you want to see the effect of any other Overflow setting, you must test the effect in a Web browser (see Figure 1-17).

Note: Various Web browsers handle the Overflow property differently. For example, Netscape Navigator 4.73 for Windows can't display scroll bars; the Mac version of Internet Explorer 5 often doesn't display the contents of a layer at all when the Overflow option is set to scroll. Test your design thoroughly if you use the Overflow setting.

Clip

The Clip property can hide all but a rectangular piece of a layer (see Figure 12-7). In most cases, you should avoid this property; not only is it rarely useful, but it's also a waste of precious bandwidth.

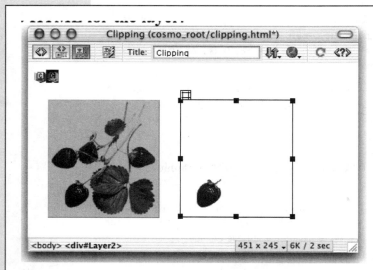

Figure 12-7:
A layer's Clip property lets you display only a selected section of the layer. In this example, the layer to the left has no clipping set, while the layer to the right has a clipping box that hides all but a single strawberry from sight. Notice that the layer itself remains the same size—as indicated by the gray outline. Only the visible portion of that layer is changed.

For example, say you put a large graphic into a layer, but only wanted to display one small area—like the single strawberry shown in Figure 12-7. You could use the Clip property, but the Web browser still has to download the *entire* graphic—not just the clipped area. You're much better off just preparing the smaller graphic at the right size to begin with (see Chapter 5). The kilobytes you save may be your own.

(In theory, you could use JavaScript to *move* the clipping area, creating an effect like a spotlight traveling across the layer. Although that might be a more useful purpose for the Clip property, Dreamweaver unfortunately offers no tools for doing it.)

If you're not convinced, and you still want to clip a layer in Dreamweaver, here's a sure-fire technique:

1. **Click inside a layer whose contents you wish to clip.**

   The layer should already contain an image.

2. **Choose Insert→Layer.**

   Dreamweaver adds a nested layer. You'll use this layer to determine the coordinates of the clipping box.

3. **Drag and resize the nested layer until it exactly covers the part of the layer you wish to show.**

   This is easy to do, because Dreamweaver lets you see the contents of the underlying layer. In Figure 12-7, a nested layer was positioned and sized so it precisely covered the strawberry. For better precision, hide all invisible elements in the page (View→Visual Aids→Hide All).

4. **Select the nested layer and note its L, T, W, and H properties, which you can read in the Property inspector.**

   You can write them on scrap paper, for example. These numbers will let you calculate the exact dimensions of the clipping box.

5. **Delete the nested layer.**

   You needed it only to get the measurements in step 4.

6. **Select the first layer and fill in the Clip boxes in the Property inspector, using the numbers from the nested layer as a guide.**

   In the Clip's L box, enter the nested layer's L value; in the T box type the T value you wrote down in step 4. Add the nested layer's L and W values and type the result in the R box. Finally, in the B box, type the total of the T and H values you wrote down in step 4.

Only the area covered by the nested layer now appears.

Hiding and Showing Layers

Do you ever stare in awe when a magician makes a handkerchief disappear into thin air? Now you, too can perform sleight of hand, right on your very own Web pages, making layers disappear and reappear with ease. Although it's not magic, Dreamweaver's Show-Hide Layers behavior is undoubtedly a nifty piece of JavaScript programming.

Show-Hide Layers takes advantage of the Visibility property of layers on your page. You can use it for things like adding pop-up tooltips to your Web page, so that when a visitor's mouse moves over a link, a layer appears with a more detailed explanation of where the link goes (see Figure 12-8).

Figure 12-8:
Using Dreamweaver's Show-Hide Layers behavior, you can make layers appear and disappear. In this example at http://www.safetreekids.net/awesome/parts.html, several layers lie hidden on the page. When a visitor moves the mouse over different parts of the tree cross-section, informative graphics, each placed in a hidden layer, suddenly appear. Moving the mouse away returns the layer to its hidden state. Notice how the information bubble overlaps the tree image and the text above it—a dead giveaway that this page uses layers.

The following steps show you how to create this remarkable special effect. Note, however, that the process requires some familiarity with Dreamweaver Behaviors, which are described in Chapter 11. For example, there you'll find out that behaviors are special effects that require you to specify an *event* (something your visitor does that triggers the effect) and an *action* (the effect itself), and that you must attach a behavior to a specific *tag*.

1. **Add layers to your Web page using the techniques described on page 371. Use the Visibility setting (page 375) to specify how you want each layer to look when the page loads.**

   If you want a layer to be visible at first, and then to disappear when your visitor does something specific, set the layer to Visible. If you want it to appear only after some specific event, set it to Hidden.

2. **In the tag selector, click the tag to which you want the behavior attached.**

   Web designers often attach behaviors to link (<a>) tags. But you can also attach
   them to images or, as in Figure 12-8, to an image map (see page 124), which
   defines hotspots on a single graphic. To create this effect, you'd attach two behaviors to each hotspot in the document window (that is, to each <area> tag in
   HTML): one to show the layer, using the onMouseOver event, and one to hide
   the layer, using the onMouseOut event.

Note: If this is all Greek to you, see page 124 for more on image maps and hotspots, page 330 for more
on attaching behaviors to tags, and page 335 for details on event types.

---

3. **If it isn't already open, choose Window→Behaviors to open the Behaviors panel.**

   The Behaviors panel (as pictured in Figure 11-1) appears. It lets you add, remove and modify behaviors.

4. **Click the + button on the panel. Select Show-Hide Layers from the menu.**

   The Show-Hide Layers dialog box appears (see Figure 12-9). You'll use this box
   to tell Dreamweaver what layer you intend to work with first.

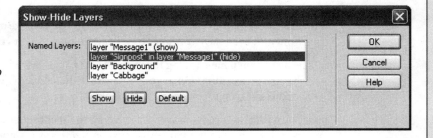

Figure 12-9:
*The Show-Hide Layers
box lets you control
multiple layers at once.
In this example, the
Message1 layer is set to
appear; the Signpost
layer Signpost will
vanish when the
behavior is triggered.*

5. **Click a layer in the list of named layers.**

   Here's an example of why it's useful to give your layers descriptive names. It's
   difficult to remember which layer is which when all have the Dreamweaver default names (Layer1, Layer2, and so on).

6. **Choose a Visibility setting for the layer by clicking one of the three buttons,
   Show, Hide, or Default.**

   You're now determining what will happen to the layer when someone interacts
   with the tag you selected in step 2. Show makes the layer visible, Hide hides the
   layer, and Default sets the layer's Visibility property to the browser's default value
   (which is usually the same as the Inherit value described on page 376).

   The choice you selected appears in parentheses next to the layer's name, as shown
   in Figure 12-9.

---

7. **If you like, select another layer and apply another visibility option.**

   A single Show-Hide Layers action can affect several layers at once. A single action can even make some visible and others invisible. (If you apply an action to a layer by mistake, select the same option again to remove it from the layer.)

8. **Click OK to apply the behavior.**

   The Show-Hide Layers action is now listed in the Behaviors panel, as is the event that triggers it. For more information on using and setting events, see page 335.

Once you've added Show-Hide Layers, you can preview the behavior in a Web browser (Dreamweaver can't display behaviors by itself). As with other Dreamweaver Behaviors, you can edit or delete this action; see page 333.

Creating Draggable Layers

For a truly interactive Web experience, you can create *draggable* layers that let your visitors rearrange Web page elements themselves. Imagine taking last year's Christmas photo and turning it into a Web-based picture puzzle, which your kids and friends can try to piece together. You could even create a magnetic poetry page, where visitors can drag words around the screen to create their own stream-of-consciousness rants.

Dreamweaver's Drag Layer behavior lets you free a layer from its normally sedentary existence. You can control how the layer is dragged, make it snap into a predefined position, and even have it trigger other exciting JavaScript commands.

Once again, you'll have to slog through Chapter 11 to learn something about Behaviors before proceeding. Once you've grasped the concepts of events, actions, and attached HTML tags, you're ready to begin.

Start by adding a layer to a Web page, using the techniques described on page 371. You may want to give it a name that fits—*puzzle1,* for instance.

You must now attach a behavior to an HTML tag (see page 331). Very often, you'll add this behavior to the <body> of the page, so that the Drag Layer behavior makes the layer draggable right when the page loads.

If the Behaviors panel isn't on the screen, choose Window→Behaviors. From the + menu on the panel, choose Drag Layer to make the Drag Layer dialog box appear (see Figure 12-10). Fill it out like this:

- **Layer.** Select the layer you want to manipulate. You can only select one layer per Drag Layer action. If you want to make several layers draggable, you'll have to apply this behavior once for each layer. (The exception is nested layers, in which case you add the Drag Layer behavior to the parent layer. When your visitor drags that layer, the nested layers follow along.)

- **Movement.** You can control where the layer can be dragged by selecting one of two options from the Movement menu:

Unconstrained puts no limits on the layer. Visitors can freely drag the layer anywhere on the page; they can even drag most of the layer past the edges of the browser window. **Constrained** lets you limit the area the layer can move in. Four fields—Up, Down, Left, and Right—define the limits of the drag area. Each field accepts a pixel value that indicates how far in a particular direction the layer can move.

Figure 12-10:
The Drag Layer dialog box lets you set many different properties for a draggable layer, including setting a Drop Target—a location on the page where the layer is supposed to end up.

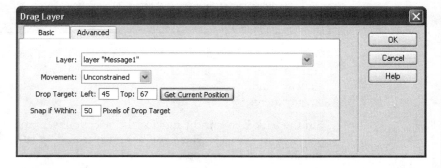

For example, suppose you've put a layer smack-dab in the middle of the window. If you type *50, 20, 100,* and *150* in the Up, Down, Left, and Right boxes, visitors will be able to drag the layer no more than 50 pixels up, 20 pixels down, 100 pixels to the left, and 150 pixels to the right. Leaving a field blank means there's no constraint in that direction. For example, if you leave the Up field empty, visitors will be able to drag the layer all the way to the top (and almost out) of the browser window.

Tip: If you want to limit a layer's movement so it can only move left and right (like a slider on a control panel), choose Constrained from the Drag Layer dialog and type *0* in both the Up and Down boxes. To limit its movement to up and down—like an elevator—type *0* in both the Left and Right boxes.

• **Drop Target.** Setting a Drop Target is optional. But it can be useful when your goal is to have visitors drag the layer to a *specific place* on the page. For example, you could create a jigsaw-puzzle Web page where each piece of the puzzle is placed in its own layer. When the page loads, all of the pieces are spread around the page, and your visitor's challenge is to put the pieces together. Each puzzle piece must go in a specific place, so each layer gets its own drop target. (This option works well with the Snap option described next. It can also trigger *another* JavaScript program, as described below.)

The value in the Left field represents the distance, in pixels, from the left edge of the browser window to the top-left corner of the layer. The value in the Top field is the distance from the top of the browser window to the top-left corner of the layer. For example, say you want the top-left corner of the layer to end up 50 pixels from the left of the browser edge and 100 pixels down from the top; in this case, you'd type *50* and *100* in the Left and Top boxes, respectively.

Note: When you're using nested layers, the Top and Left values refer to distances relative to the Top and Left positions of the parent layer. For example, say you've nested a layer inside of another layer whose top margin is 50 pixels from the top of the page and whose left margin is 100 pixels from the left edge of the page. If you add a drop target to a nested layer, and set the Top and Left values to 20 and 30, the *actual* location of the drop target on the page will begin at 70 pixels from the top of the page and 130 pixels from the left edge of the page.

To help you figure all this out, the Get Current Position button calculates the current coordinates of the layer on the page. This may not seem so useful: After all, why would you want to create a drop target in the first place, if the layer is already there?

But the trick is to start by moving the layer you want to make draggable to the position on the page where you'll want it to *end up* (that is, where the visitor should drag it). Then apply the Drag Layer behavior and *then* click the Get Current Position button. Later, after you've finished setting the other properties and clicked OK, you can move the layer to its *starting* position (where it will appear before the visitor drags it).

- **Snap if Within.** One problem with the Drop Target feature is that the drop area is marked by a *single pixel* on the page. Dragging a layer *exactly* to that spot would require that your audience have the patience of Job and the hand of a neurosurgeon.

  Fortunately, you can bend your visitors in the right direction with the help of the Snap if Within option. When a visitor drags the layer within a certain distance of the drop target, this option makes the layer snap right into place. If you type *100*, for example, when a visitor drags the layer and releases the mouse button when the layer's upper-left corner is within 100 pixels of the drop target, that's close enough for government work; it will immediately pop into place.

The previous settings are all you need to create a basic draggable layer. You can click OK at this point to close the dialog box and apply the action. But if you want to give your draggable layer even more sophisticated and professional features, click the Advanced tab to set additional properties (see Figure 12-11).

- **Drag Handle.** By default, Entire Layer is selected, meaning that a visitor can click *anywhere* on the layer to drag it. But in some cases, you may want to require visitors to click a specific portion of the layer—a handle—in order to drag the layer. For example, perhaps your layer contains a picture of a tool box. You could define the part of the picture with the tool box's handle as the layer's drag handle.

  Choose Area Within Layer from the Drag Handle menu to define the handle area. Four fields (L, T, W, and H) appear on the Advanced tab. You specify the draggable area relative to the layer itself. L represents the distance from the left edge of the layer, T the distance from the top of the layer, and W and H represent the width and height of the handle.

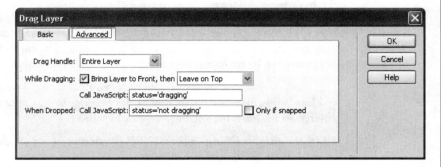

Figure 12-11:
Here, a JavaScript statement (status= 'dragging') shows the word dragging *in the browser's status bar when someone drags the layer—and the words* not dragging *when the layer is released.*

- **While Dragging.** As discussed on page 376, layers can overlap each other in a stack. A layer's Z-Index determines where it belongs in the stacking order of the page. By default, the Bring Layer to Front option is turned on, so that the layer doesn't get hidden behind other layers as someone drags it around the page. If you want to leave the layer behind other layers as it's dragged, turn off this option.

  Also, you can control whether the layer stays on top or returns to its place in the stacking order when it's dropped after dragging. The Leave on Top option is selected by default, meaning that when the visitor drops the layer, it stays on top. In fact, it jumps to the very top Z-Index level of the page, above even the layers it *doesn't* actually overlap. (If you turned off Bring Layer to Front, this option has no effect.)

  If you want to return the layer to its original level in the stacking order, choose "Restore z-index." Now the layer can appear on top while it's being dragged, but once released, it returns to its original order.

- **Call JavaScript.** These final settings are fun and powerful, but require solid knowledge of JavaScript. The first Call JavaScript box is where you type a JavaScript command or *function call* that you want to run while the layer is dragged. The second box lets you specify a command or function that's called when the layer is dropped.

  Turn on "Only if snapped" if you want the command to run only if the layer is dropped on a target. For example, you could make a dialog box that says "Bullseye!" appear when your visitor drops a layer directly over a target on the page. For another example of these options, see Figure 12-11.

Once you've added your fancy new behavior, you can test it by pressing F12 and previewing it in a Web browser. As with any other behavior, you can edit the Drag Layer behavior using the instructions on page 333.

Animating Layers

Nobody looks at banner ads anymore, but how about a banner ad that flies across the top of the page—towed by a tiny airplane graphic? The latest crop of Web browsers lets you move layers around the screen to produce exciting animated designs.

This kind of dynamic behavior generally requires a deep knowledge of JavaScript and Cascading Style Sheets, as well as the experience and patience to deal with the differences between the various browser brands.

All of the programming skill and Web development experience needed to create animations is built right into Dreamweaver. With Dreamweaver's Timeline tools, you can create elaborate and complex animations, and even time-based actions like automated slide shows.

Tip: If you've used Macromedia's animation-driven programs, Flash and Director, picking up Dreamweaver's tools is a snap. Dreamweaver uses an animation interface very similar to those programs'.

Understanding Animation

Programming animation requires that you specify two things: *movement* and *time*. Imagine a ball moving across the screen; it takes the ball two seconds to travel from the left side to the right. A Web browser creates animation by drawing the ball in several different positions over several fractions of a second, so that you see the effect of smooth motion across the screen.

Each of these drawings occurs in a moment of time, referred to as a *frame*—the fundamental building block of computer (or Disney) animation. A collection of frames makes up a *timeline*. Think of a timeline as a strip of movie film where each frame in the filmstrip contains one picture. When the strip is played back from beginning to end, you have a movie.

A Dreamweaver timeline can play back either when the page first loads or when your visitor does something that you specify. For instance, you can add a button to a page that, when clicked, plays an animation on the screen.

Animation The Easy Way

To create an animation, you'll place a graphic into a layer, and then direct that layer to move around the Web page, carrying the image on its back. Animating a layer involves some very sophisticated JavaScript programming code. In fact, the code required to animate a layer can take up more lines of code than the actual HTML of the page. Trying to create such a program yourself could take weeks. But Dreamweaver can do it in seconds by recording the movement of your mouse as you drag a layer around the document window.

To draw an animation on the screen, select a layer to animate, using one of the techniques described on page 371. Now choose Modify→Timeline→Record Path of Layer. The Timelines panel appears, and Dreamweaver is ready to record your animation. (The Timeline feature is described in detail on page 392.)

Grab the layer by its selection handle or border and drag around the page. A trail of gray dots follows your cursor, indicating the path your animation will follow. Dreamweaver doesn't record the timing of your drag, just the path, so take your time to make sure that the motion is exactly what you want. You'll specify the speed of the animation later, as described in Figure 12-12.

Figure 12-12:
The easiest method of creating an animation simply requires you to drag a layer along the route you want the animation to take. Dreamweaver can record this path and save it as an animation.

When you release the mouse, a particularly chatty dialog box appears. It tells you that you can animate the following layer properties: Left, Top, Width, Height, Z-Index, and Visibility. You'll learn how to do all of this shortly. (By the way, the window also informs you that Netscape Navigator 4—that infernal bottleneck to innovation—*can't* animate the widths and heights of layers.)

Click OK (and, while you're at it, turn on the "Don't show me this message again" box). A gray line appears across the document window, winding its way along the path you just created. Meanwhile, a line with a series of hollow dots appears in the now-open Timelines panel, as shown in Figure 12-12.

If you turn on the Autoplay box (shown in Figure 12-12), your animation will play as soon as the page loads. This is a common choice, since it plays your breathtaking animation immediately upon your visitor's arrival. You can, though, start the animation by other means using the Play Timeline behavior, described on page 400.

Also, if you want to repeat your animation over and over again—perhaps making an animated bee fly incessantly around your page, in hopes of distracting your visitor from studying your site's privacy policy—turn on the Loop box.

Tip: Because looping immediately jumps from the end of the animation to the beginning, make sure whatever you're animating starts and ends at roughly the same place on the page. Otherwise, it will look as if the layer suddenly disappeared from one area of the page and then reappeared somewhere else.

At this point, you can press F12 to preview your animation in a browser (make sure you selected the Autoplay option). You can also preview it right in the document window using the Timelines panel (see Figure 12-13). Click the Rewind button, and then click and hold the Forward button; Dreamweaver plays each frame of the animation. Or grab the playback head and drag it back and forth to move backward and forward through the animation.

Once you've added an animation to the timeline, you can edit many of the animation's properties, such as its speed or movement. (See "Animating with key frames" on page 394.)

Figure 12-13:
The Timelines panel lets you modify animations, view different timelines, and control how animations play back in a Web browser. In addition, in Dreamweaver, you can view different frames of any timeline by using the playback head and the various arrow buttons. You can go directly to any point in the animation by dragging the playback head left or right. The number in the Current Frame box indicates which frame you're currently viewing. You can move forward or backward one frame by clicking the right or left arrows. Holding down either button plays the animation (either forward or in reverse). Click Rewind to jump to the first frame in the timeline.

Understanding Timelines

The Timelines panel is the control center for your Dreamweaver animations (see Figure 12-13). Choose Window→Timelines to open it, or press Alt-F9 (Option-F9).

Note: Timelines, frames, key frames, and other terms associated with Dreamweaver's animation tools are not a part of HTML, JavaScript, or CSS. There's no tag called *key frame* and no JavaScript command called *play.* Dreamweaver's Timelines panel and animation capabilities are the result of sophisticated programming on the part of the program's engineers, and as such, are specific to Dreamweaver.

The bottom half of the panel displays numbered rows called *channels,* which denote individual layer animations. For example, in Figure 12-14, a single animation sits in channel 1, represented by the solid color bar with a line running through it (called the *animation bar*). The numbers along the top of those rows indicate the frames, showing that the animation bar pictured here is 40 frames long. Since a frame is an individual drawing of a layer at a specific time and position, a Web browser would move the layer 40 times to complete this animation.

You can add multiple animations to a timeline, too, so that two or more layers move simultaneously across the screen. Each of those animations would appear in its own channel in the Timelines panel.

While the number of frames in a channel determines the number of times the Web browser will move the layer, it doesn't directly dictate the *speed* at which the animation plays. The speed is determined by the *frame rate* shown in the Fps (frames per second) box. By default, the timeline's frame rate is 15 fps. In other words, it takes one second to play 15 frames. The sample 40-frame animation in Figure 12-13 would thus take about 3 seconds to play back. If you decreased the speed to 8 fps, the same animation would take longer to play (around 5 seconds).

The lower the frame rate, the more the animation stutters; the higher the rate, the smoother the animation. Compared to a feature film's rate of 24 fps, the default rate Dreamweaver supplies may appear low. However, it's wise to stick with the supplied 15 fps, since redrawing layers is a complex process that requires a lot of power from the Web browser (and the computer it's running on). You can specify a higher frame rate, but a Web browser may not be able to obey. In order to draw each frame, it may need to slow the animation down.

Tip: Although it's possible to tell Dreamweaver to animate, say, 17 different layers at a frame rate of 36 frames per second, you probably won't see the effect you want. In fact, most likely, the Web browser will slow to a crawl and your animation will look like it's moving in slow motion as the Web browser dutifully draws every frame in the timeline, regardless of how long it takes and no matter what speed you specified.

Be careful when creating complex animations. Test them in a variety of browsers, and, if possible, on slower computers. That's the only way to make sure that your stunning animations don't wind up resembling paint-drying contests.

Adding a timeline

Dreamweaver automatically creates a timeline when you animate a layer by recording its path. But you can also add a timeline manually by choosing

Modify→Timeline→Add Timeline in the Timelines panel. A new, empty timeline appears, to which you can add layers and create animations.

Adding layers to the timeline

As noted earlier in this chapter, there's an Easy Way to animate a layer—just by dragging it. Unfortunately, at times, you'll find the Easy Way to be less than accurate; as has been noted many times before, drawing with a mouse is like using a bar of soap to paint the Sistine Chapel. Furthermore, you can't create a straight line using this method.

To get around these drawbacks, you can use the Harder But More Precise way: selecting a layer (or several) and choosing Modify→Timeline→Add Object to Timeline.

Tip: A quick way to add a layer to the timeline is to drag it from the document window into one of the Layer channels on the Timelines panel.

When you add a layer, a new animation bar appears in one of the channels of the Timelines panel. The animation bar starts out as a solid blue span of 15 frames (one second) that contains the layer's name and begins and ends with a white dot. To extend the animation's length, drag the white dot in frame 15 to the right. For example, if you wanted to make a 10-second-long animation, you'd drag the dot out to frame 150.

You can also move the entire animation bar by dragging the bar along the timeline—a useful tactic when you want to add a slight delay to an animation, or stagger several different animations in the same timeline. For example, imagine you wanted to make two snowflakes (two layers, each with an image of a snowflake) appear at the top of the browser window and float down the page; but you also want the second snowflake to enter the scene about one second after the other. Drag the animation bar with the second snowflake animation so it begins on frame 16, one second after the first snowflake falls.

Animating with key frames

The white dots in the animation bar, called *key frames,* are your main tool for controlling an animation. In fact, when you add a layer to the timeline by using the Modify→Timeline→Add Object to Timeline command (or by dragging the layer onto a channel), key frames are the *only* way to give the frame a movement path.

Each animation begins life with two key frames, one each for the animation's beginning and ending positions. So far, the layer is in the same position in both key frames. In other words, it doesn't go anywhere when the animation plays.

By adding and manipulating key frames, you can tell Dreamweaver where you want your layer to wind up at certain points in its motion. The program automatically calculates the layer's position in all of the intermediate frames, saving you endless tedium and grief.

For example, on a brand-new animation with only two key frames (beginning and ending positions), click the second key frame, which selects the corresponding layer in the document window. Drag the layer to the spot on the page where you wish the animation to *end* and let go. Now when you play the animation, the layer travels from its starting position to the *new* ending location. Similarly, you can change the beginning position of the layer by selecting the first key frame and dragging the layer.

Tip: For compulsive precision, you can also specify a new position for a layer by clicking the key frame in the timeline and setting the layer's L and T properties in the Property inspector (see page 379).

Adding key frames to a timeline

Of course, you won't get far in life just making your layers fly from point A to point B. If you add more key frames between the starting and ending ones, you can define new spots for your layer-in-motion to hit at certain times as it putters on its way to the ending spot. (In fact, when you create an animation the Easy Way, by dragging a layer around the screen, Dreamweaver automatically generates dozens of key frames, as shown in Figure 12-12.)

To manually add a key frame, click a frame inside the animation (one of the blue frames) in the Timelines panel animation bar—one that's not already a key frame. When you click, the playback head (the red box that appears among the frame numbers) moves to the frame.

Now choose Modify→Timeline→Add Keyframe. A hollow circle appears in the animation bar at the frame you selected. You can also press F6 to add a new key frame at the selected point in the animation bar.

Tip: You can conserve a few precious calories by Ctrl-clicking (⌘-clicking) the frame you wish to turn into a key frame. The cursor turns into a tiny hollow circle and instantly creates a new key frame.

Having created a new key frame, you're ready to specify the layer's new position at this point, confident that Dreamweaver will automatically regenerate its movement from the key frames before and after the one you just added.

Tip: To delete a key frame, select it in the timeline and press Shift-F6, or choose Modify→Timeline→Remove Keyframe.

Modifying layers at key frames

Key frames define the position of a layer at a particular moment in the animation. Once you've created a new key frame, the corresponding layer is selected in the document window; you can then drag it to a new location. When you release the mouse, Dreamweaver redraws the gray path line to indicate the new path the animation follows, leading up to, and away from, your new key frame.

Similarly, you can adjust your moving layer's position at any *existing* key frame just by clicking the corresponding spot in the timeline and then dragging the layer on your screen.

But you can do more than change a layer's *position* at each key frame. You can also change other properties at each spot, like this:

- **Visibility.** Use the Property inspector to set the Visibility property of a layer at a particular key frame (see page 375 for information on setting the Visibility property). You'll therefore make the layer disappear (or reappear) on cue. There's no way to fade the layer out gradually; it's either visible or hidden.

  To make a layer disappear and reappear later in the animation, click a key frame and set Visibility to Hidden. Ctrl-click (⌘-click) consecutive frames to create a series of hidden key frames. Change the last key frame to Visible at the point when you want the frame to reappear.

- **Z-Index.** You can also change the stacking order of the layer at a particular key frame. Click the key frame and use either the Property inspector or Layers panel to set the layer's Z-Index (page 376).

  Imagine a moon, for instance, flying around a planet. It moves from behind the planet at first, orbits around the front of the planet, and then eventually disappears back behind it. In this example, the planet would be in one layer, the moon in another.

  At first, the Z-Index of the planet would be greater than that of the moon. After the moon moves from behind the planet, you would add a key frame, and increase the moon's Z-Index so that it's larger than the planet's, putting the moon layer in front of the planet.

WORKAROUND WORKSHOP

Straight-Line Animation

When an animation has more than one key frame, Dreamweaver always creates a curved path from one key frame position to the next—a real problem if you want to create a straight zigzag motion. There's only one way to create a sure-fire, straight-line path: Create an animation with only two key frames. If you try to introduce a third point between them, Dreamweaver goes right back to curving your path.

The workaround, therefore, involves creating a new animation bar for *each* straight-line motion segment. After adding the layer to the timeline, in other words, define its starting position on the screen using the first key frame. Now click the ending-point key frame, and then define the

ending position of the first straight line (the end of the "zig").

Now you're ready to create another animation bar, which will create the "zag." Click the frame just after the last key frame, select the layer on the screen, and choose Modify→Timeline→Add Object to Timeline. Now that the second animation bar has appeared, you can click *its* first and last key frames, positioning the layer on each.

To create a third straight-line movement, choose Modify→Timeline→Add Object to Timeline *again,* and set the starting and ending positions for *its* key frames. Continue this process until you've added animation bars for each stroke in the zigzag path.

After the moon crosses the face of the planet, you would add another key frame and set its Z-Index back to its original setting—lower than, and behind, the planet.

- **Width and Height.** You can also change the dimensions of a layer at a key frame by changing the W and H fields in the Property inspector (see page 378). The effect is very interesting: Not only does the layer change size when it reaches that key frame, but it automatically and gradually changes size in each frame in between. (Unfortunately, this feature doesn't work in Netscape Navigator 4.)

Controlling animation speed using key frames

Once you create a key frame, you can move it in the timeline by dragging it (see Figure 12-14). This is how you control the *pace* of movement between key frames. The more frames between key frames, the slower the movement; fewer frames means faster movement.

For example, in Figure 12-14, a 25-frame animation of a leaf moving along a path has three key frames. The second key frame is selected, showing that the leaf is only about halfway along the path (the gray line). As you can see in the timeline, there are 19 frames from the first key frame to the midpoint. There are only 3 frames, however, from the second key frame until the final one. In other words, it takes about 20 frames (a little over a second) for the leaf to travel halfway along the path. The last half goes much faster—only about 4 frames, or less than 1/4 second.

In this example, the leaf will travel leisurely along the screen, until it reaches the midway mark in its path, and will then scream quickly to its destination. If you drag the middle key frame to the center of the animation bar, the leaf will travel at the same speed throughout the animation.

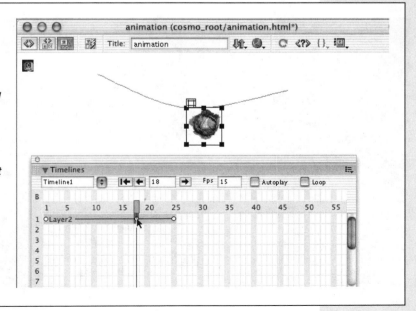

Figure 12-14:
You can move any key frame by dragging it in the timeline. To make an animation run longer, drag the last key frame to the right. This increases the total number of frames in the animation. It also spreads out any key frames within the animation bar, making the overall animation slower. To only move the last key frame, and prevent Dreamweaver from redistributing other key frames, press Ctrl (⌘) while dragging the end frame.

The Behaviors channel

Directly above the frame numbers that appear in the Timelines panel, you'll find another row of frames labeled B. It's the Behaviors channel. You can use this channel to trigger a Dreamweaver behavior at a particular frame in the timeline. (See Chapter 11 for the exhaustive, and exhausting, story on Behaviors.)

In fact, you may have already used the B channel without even knowing it. When you turn on the Loop box in the Timelines panel, Dreamweaver inserts a Go To Timeline Frame behavior into the Behaviors channel in the last frame of your animation (see Figure 12-15). This behavior (see page 401) causes the animation to return to the first frame in the timeline and play again.

Suppose you want an alert box with the word "Boom!" to appear at the instant when one animated layer touches another. All you'd have to do is select the frame where the two layers meet, and then add a Pop-up Message action to the Behaviors channel.

Tip: You don't actually have to have *any* animation on the page to take advantage of the Behaviors channel. Say, for example, you want a new browser window to appear exactly four seconds after a Web page loads—a delayed pop-up ad, perhaps. You'd just add an Open Browser Window action to frame 60 in the Behaviors channel, and then turn on the Autoplay checkbox in the Timelines panel.

To add a behavior to the timeline, just click the relevant frame in the Behaviors channel of the Timelines panel—for example, the frame where two layers collide. (Click key frames in the animation bars below to see where the action is at any given frame, and *then* click in the Behaviors channel. The Behaviors channel doesn't have key frames.) The frame in the Behaviors channel turns black to show it's selected.

GEM IN THE ROUGH

Create an Automated Slide Show

Most people think of Dreamweaver's Timeline feature in terms of *moving layers* around the screen. If you drag something else into the Timelines panel, like a graphic, you'll find that you can't make it fly around. You can, however, make its *properties* change over time. And that's just the feature you need if you want to create an automated presentation of your photos.

Here's how to do it. Add an image to the timeline, either by dragging it to the timeline or by selecting the image in the document window, and choose Modify→Timeline→Add Object to Timeline.

Then decide how frequently you want the image to change.

For example, maybe you want a new image to appear every two seconds. If the timeline's frame rate is 15 fps, you'll want to change the image every 30 frames. Create as many key frames as you have images, spaced 30 frames apart.

Then select each key frame and use the Property inspector to change the Src property for each. The Src property, of course, identifies the graphics file in your site folder. In other words, you can swap one image in for another at a specified time. (For best results, make sure all the images you use are the same size.)

When you play the timeline, a new image appears every other second.

Now open the Behaviors panel (Windows→Behaviors), click the + button, and choose a behavior from the menu. For example, you could make a new browser window pop up by selecting the Open Browser Window behavior. (See Chapter 11 for a complete list of Behaviors.)

Figure 12-15:
The Behaviors channel lets you add time-based behaviors to your page. Change the text in a layer every 10 seconds, for example, or write a new message to the Web browser's status bar when an animation reaches its last frame.

After you've added a behavior to the channel, a dash appears in the frame, and the Behaviors panel lists the event (it should look something like this: *onFrame36*). Unlike with a regular behavior, you can't select an event (see step 5 on page 332). The frame itself acts as the event by triggering the action when the timeline reaches the specified frame.

You can move your newly created Frame behavior by dragging it left or right in the Behaviors channel, or remove it altogether by clicking its frame, clicking its name in the Behaviors panel, and then clicking the – button in the Behaviors panel.

Tip: Once you click inside the Behaviors channel, Dreamweaver will only let you *add* behaviors to that channel. If you try to add a behavior to another object in the page (by selecting a link or the body tag, for instance, and adding a behavior), Dreamweaver insists on adding it to the Timeline instead. To get past this little bug, click one of the animation layers inside the Timelines panel to deselect the Behaviors channel.

Adding and deleting timelines

You can create several different animations on one page, each on its own timeline, and control them using the behaviors described in the following pages. For example, you might want to have a layer fly onto the page when your visitor's mouse moves over a navigational button, and off screen when the mouse moves off the button. The fly-on, fly-off layer might supply information about where the button leads, or even contain a submenu of additional buttons.

To add an additional timeline, open the Timelines panel, perhaps by pressing Alt-F9 (Option-F9); then choose Modify→Timeline→Add Timeline. A new timeline appears in the Timeline field in the upper left of the panel.

Dreamweaver proposes generic names like Timeline1 and Timeline2, and so on; to provide a more recognizable name—*fly* or *submenu1*, for example—select the name of the timeline from the menu in the Timelines panel. Choose Modify→Timeline→ Rename Timeline. In the dialog box that appears, type the new name and click OK.

It's a good idea to name a timeline immediately after creating it. If you change its name after applying behaviors that control the timeline, they won't work. You'll then need to edit each behavior to give it the timeline's new name.

If you decide you don't want a timeline any longer, you can delete it. Select a timeline from the Timelines panel, and choose Modify→Timeline→Remove Timeline. (Doing so removes all animations and actions in that timeline, but doesn't delete the layers themselves.)

Controlling Playback

Suppose you've created an automated slide show (see page 398). The page loads, and every few seconds a new slide appears. But what if you wanted to let the viewer control the slide show—pausing it, for example, when a particularly interesting image appears, and then restarting it when ready? Or what if you wanted to give your audience the option to rewind back to the beginning or jump to a particular slide?

Special Dreamweaver Behaviors give you this kind of playback flexibility.

Note: If you haven't created at least one timeline, these behaviors are grayed out in the Behaviors panel.

Starting and Stopping Timelines

As mentioned earlier in this chapter, the Autoplay box in the Timelines panel makes a timeline play automatically when the page loads. You might, however, want to start a timeline based on some other action, such as when your viewer clicks a Play button.

Tip: When using behaviors to *control* a layer, don't apply the behavior *to* the layer. In fact, if you select a layer, these behaviors are grayed out in the Behaviors panel. Behaviors are attached to items that *cause* something to change—for example, a link, that when clicked, starts an animation on the page—and not the thing you wish to change (in this case, a layer).

To give your visitors this push-button control, use the Play Timeline behavior, which you might attach to a Play-button graphic. (For best effect, add a dead link to an image on the page [as described on page 329] and then attach the behavior to that link.) Select a tag, click the + button on the Behaviors panel, and choose Timeline→

Play Timeline. The Play Timeline window appears (see Figure 12-16). There's only one option: select a timeline to play from the menu. Click OK, and then change the triggering event from the Behaviors panel.

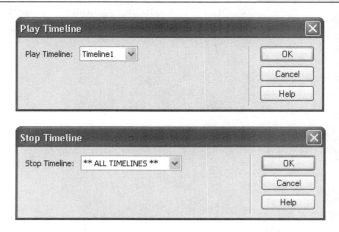

Figure 12-16:
Top: Start any timeline on the page with the Play Timeline behavior. This behavior plays a timeline from its current frame—not necessarily its beginning. So, if you applied a Stop Timeline action, and later used a Play Timeline, the specified timeline would begin playback from the point it was last stopped. Bottom: Stop any or all timelines dead in their tracks with the Stop Timeline behavior. Use it to add a Pause button to an animated page.

If you let someone start an animation on the page, it's only courteous to let him stop it, too. You apply the Stop Timeline behavior just like the Play Timeline action. The dialog box looks similar, too (see Figure 12-16). The one difference: In addition to selecting any one timeline to stop, the Stop Timeline menu also includes the ** ALL TIMELINES ** option, which stops playback of all timelines at once.

Again, this action works well when attached to a Pause-button graphic. Add the button to the page, wrap it in a dead link (see page 329), and then attach this behavior to that link, using the onClick event.

Go To Timeline Frame

You can also jump to a specific point in a timeline with the Go To Timeline Frame behavior. You could use this, for example, to jump to the end of an animation (Fast Forward), or jump back to the beginning (Rewind).

Figure 12-17:
The Loop box in the Go To Timeline Frame dialog box lets you specify the number of times you wish to play a timeline. This option only works when the behavior is attached to a frame in a timeline's Behaviors channel (see page 398).

Apply it as you would any Dreamweaver behavior (for detailed directions, see page 330): Select a tag, click the + button in the Behaviors panel, and choose Timeline→Go To Timeline Frame. A dialog box appears (see Figure 12-17). Choose a timeline from the menu, and then type a frame number in the Go to Frame box. For example, to rewind to the beginning of a timeline, select the timeline and type *1* in the box.

Flash, Shockwave, and Other Multimedia

With Cascading Style Sheets (Chapter 8), Dreamweaver Behaviors (Chapter 11), and Images (Chapter 5), you can bring your Web pages to life with interactivity and animation. But as you may have noticed, more and more Web pages these days blink, sing, and dance with sound, video, and advanced animation.

You can create these effects too, but you'll need outside help from programs like Flash, Director, or Java, all of which are designed to create complex multimedia presentations. Dreamweaver provides powerful tools for adding these external media files and embedding them within your Web pages.

Four warnings, however. First, while all of the technologies discussed in this chapter let you expand your Web pages into new and exciting territory, they also require external applications (not just a Web browser). These programs, usually called *plug-ins,* are controversial in the Web development community, mainly because they limit your audience. Not all Web site visitors have the necessary plug-ins installed on their computers. Those guests must choose from three equally unpalatable options: go to a different Web site to download the plug-in; skip the multimedia show (if you've built a second, plug-in-free version of your site); or skip your Web site entirely. All media types in this chapter require a plug-in of some kind; see each section for more detail.

Second, it's worth noting that these effects can bulk up your Web site considerably, making it slower to load—and making it still more likely that some of your visitors (especially those using dial-up modems) won't bother sticking around.

Third, these flashy multimedia effects are easy to overuse. Blink and flash too much, and you'll find your audience beating a hasty retreat for the cyber-exits.

Finally, creating external movies, animations, or applications is an art (and a book or two) unto itself. This chapter is a guide to *inserting* such add-on goodies into your Web page and assumes that a cheerful programmer near you has already *created* them.

Figure 13-1:
External multimedia files like this Flash movie can add a dimension of sound, animation, and interactivity that brings new life to a site, and makes possible a complexity that's difficult to emulate using HTML alone. In this case, clicking the man on the pole adjusts your score and lets you play for bonus points.

Flash

Flash is quickly becoming the standard for Web animation, and with good reason: Macromedia's Flash technology produces high-quality, animated images—known as Flash movies—at a relatively small file size. Its drawings and animations are *vector graphics,* which means that they use mathematical formulas to describe objects on the screen. By contrast, bitmap technology like GIF and JPEG graphics include data for every pixel of an image, gobbling up precious bytes and adding download time. Flash's vector graphics save file size with their compact mathematical expressions.

Flash can also handle MP3 audio and advanced programming features, providing an added dimension of sound and interactivity that can make a plain HTML page look dull by comparison. For example, advanced Flash gurus can build automatic score tracking into an online game or add a cannon-firing animation each time the player clicks the mouse. While Dynamic HTML (see Chapter 12) can do some of these things, Flash movies are easier to create. An intriguing advantage of Flash movies is that they look and work exactly the same on every browser, whether on Windows or Mac. (Don't try *that* with HTML.)

Of course, all of this power comes at a price. Although Dreamweaver has some limited Flash-creation abilities (such as Flash buttons, as discussed on page 128), you need another program, such as Macromedia Flash or Adobe Live Motion, to produce full-fledged movies. These programs aren't difficult to learn, but they're more programs to buy and more technologies to get under your belt.

Furthermore, your visitors can't play Flash movies without the Flash Player plug-in (page 129). If they don't have it, they'll have to download and install it—a sure spontaneity-killer. Fortunately, chances are your visitors already have it—all major browsers (even Opera) now come with the Flash plug-in installed. In fact, Macromedia says that (insert grain of salt here) over 98 percent of Web browsers in use now have some version of the player (a much smaller percentage has the *latest* version of Flash).

Inserting a Flash Movie

To insert a Flash movie into a Web page, click where you want to insert the movie; then choose Insert→Media→Flash (or click the Flash button ⬤ on either the Common or Media tab of the Insert bar). Either way, a Select File dialog box appears. Navigate to the Flash movie file (look for a .swf extension) and double-click it. Dreamweaver automatically determines the width and height of the movie and generates the appropriate HTML to embed it into the page. The movie appears as a gray rectangle with the Flash logo in the center; you can adjust its settings as described in the next section.

Note: As with other files you include in a Web page, such as graphics or external Cascading Style Sheets, you can keep Flash movies anywhere inside your site. However, if your Flash movie contains links—for instance, if it's an animated navigation bar—keep the Flash movie file in the same folder as the Web page itself. Otherwise, links in the movie may not work. For a workaround to this problem, see the box on page 407.

To preview Flash files directly in Dreamweaver, just select the movie and then click the Play button on the Property inspector (see Figure 13-2). To stop the movie, click the same button, which has become a Stop button.

POWER USERS' CLINIC

The <object> and <embed> Tags

If you choose View→Code after inserting a Flash movie, you may be surprised by the amount of HTML Dreamweaver deposits in your page. You may also encounter some HTML tags you've never heard of, including <object>, <embed>, and <param>. These tags provide browsers with the information they need to launch the Flash Player and play a Flash movie. These tags are also used for other embedded media (Shockwave, for example).

The <object> and <embed> tags do the same thing in different browsers. Netscape uses <embed> to insert movies and other plug-in media, while Internet Explorer uses the <object> tag to insert ActiveX controls. For maximum browser compatibility, Dreamweaver adds *both* tags. Browsers ignore HTML tags that they don't understand, so this method doesn't cause problems.

If your page has lots of Flash movies—numerous animated buttons, perhaps—you can play all of them at once by pressing Shft+Ctrl+Alt+P (Shift-Option-⌘-P). Sit back and watch the show. To stop all running movies, press Shift+ Ctrl+Alt+X (Shift-Option-⌘-X). (You can also preview Shockwave movies [see page 411] in Dreamweaver. And no wonder: Macromedia makes Shockwave, too.)

Flash Movie Properties

You'll rarely have to change the default properties created by Dreamweaver. But if you ever want to change the margin of space around a movie, restore it to original size after resizing it, or swap in a different movie, the Property inspector is the place to do it.

Naming a Flash Movie

As with images and navigation buttons, you can use JavaScript to control Flash movies. For example, Dreamweaver's built-in Control Shockwave or Flash behavior lets you start, stop, or jump to a specific frame in a Flash movie (see page 363).

As noted on page 363, however, if you plan to use JavaScript with your Flash movie, you need to give the Flash element a name. To do that, type the name you wish to use in the Name field (the box directly below "Flash" in the Property inspector). JavaScript uses this name to identify the movie in its code.

Note: As shown in Figure 13-2, all of the plug-in technologies described in this chapter let you set additional parameters governing the embedded media's behavior. You can find out about additional HTML properties for Flash in the Flash manual. See the box on the facing page for an example.

Figure 13-2:
Dreamweaver MX is now integrated with the Flash authoring program. When you insert a Flash movie into a page, Dreamweaver can keep track of the original Flash file. Click the Edit button; Flash starts up and opens the Flash file for you to edit.

The Movie File

The File field specifies the path to the Flash movie file on your hard drive. To select a different file, type a new path into the File field, or click the folder icon to access your site folder's contents.

Src Property

As with Fireworks files (page 123), Dreamweaver can keep track of the original Flash file you used when creating a Flash movie. That's fortunate because, once again, Flash movies start off in the program's native format (as *.fla* files) and then must be exported as *.swf* (Flash movie) files, which are viewable on the Web.

POWER USERS' CLINIC

Overcoming the Limits of Links in Flash Movies

When you create Flash movies in Macromedia Flash or Adobe LiveMotion, you can embed links in the movie itself. You can create navigation bars, for instance, or animated pushbuttons that open Web pages.

But links in a Flash movie add a great deal of complexity to your site. When you link from a Flash movie to a Web page, the link is stored in the movie itself, not in the Web page that *contains* the movie. So if the Flash file isn't in the same directory (folder) as the Web page containing it, a browser may get confused: should it follow a path relative to the *Web page* or relative to the *Flash file?* In fact, different browsers handle this differently. (It's similar to the problem introduced by document-relative links in a Web site, as described on page 92.)

You could avoid the problem by simply storing the Flash movie in the same folder as the Web page. However, this is an imperfect solution because, for example, you won't be able to use a single animated Flash navigation bar on the different pages of your site, filed in different folders.

Instead, you can use a little trick to make your document-relative links work no matter where you file your Flash movies. First, when creating your Flash movie, make sure that any document-relative links in it are spelled out relative to the Flash movie's folder location. For instance, if you save your movie in a folder called *flash,* and you wish it to link to a page called *welcome.html* located one level up from the flash folder, the correct link, relative to the movie, would be *../welcome.html.*

Next, after you insert the Flash file into your Web page, click Parameters on the Property inspector. The Parameters window opens, as shown here. Now you can add additional properties for plug-in media. In this case, you'll use the Base property to instruct the Flash Player to use a different URL as the starting location for any links in the Flash movie. In other words, instead of following the link in the movie, the player first appends the path specified by the Base property's value.

Here's an example: Suppose the Flash movie mentioned above—the one that links to the *welcome.html* page—is on a page in the same folder as welcome.html. The document-relative path from that page to the welcome page is *welcome.html*—but *../welcome.html* relative to the Flash movie. Since the link is in the Flash movie, the path relative to it should work. But some browsers try to follow the path relative to the *Web page,* leading to broken links.

Using the BASE parameter, you can specify that *all* links in the movie should be followed relative to the movie. Here's one instance where a root-relative path comes in handy. Since document-relative links in Flash movies can confuse browsers, a root-relative path is the only way to indicate the exact location of a file within a site. In this case, suppose the *flash* folder is stored in the site's root folder; a root-relative path to the folder with the Flash movie would be /flash/. (For more detail on document- and root-relative links, see page 92; also see Chapter 14.)

The Src (source) property field indicates where the original Flash file is stored. Clicking the Property inspector's Edit button launches Flash and opens the original Flash file. You can then make any changes you wish to the movie and, in Flash, click Done. Flash exports the updated .swf file into your site, replacing the previous version of the file.

Note: In Windows, this feature has a bug. If the original Flash file is already open in Flash and you click Edit in Dreamweaver, the Flash program launches *again,* opening the Flash file a second time. This duplication can lead to editing errors and devours valuable computer resources. Before you click Edit in the Property inspector, make sure the file isn't already open in Flash.

Movie Size

Although dragging to enlarge a GIF or JPEG image can turn it into a pixellated mess, you can usually resize Flash movies without problems, since their vector-based images are based on mathematical formulas that scale nicely. (The exception is when you've included bitmap images, such as GIFs or JPEGs, in your Flash movie. Then, as when resizing an image in a Web page, you'll see distortion and pixellation in the movie.)

To resize a movie, do one of the following:

- Select the movie in the document window; drag one of the three resizing handles that appear at the edges of the movie. To avoid changing the movie's proportions in the process, press Shift as you drag the lower-right corner handle.

- Select the movie in the document window; type new width and height values into the W and H boxes in the Property inspector. You can also use percentage values, in which case Web browsers scale your movie to fit the window.

If you make a complete mess of your page by resizing the movie beyond recognition, just click Reset Size in the Property inspector.

Play Options

The Loop and Autoplay checkboxes control how the Flash movie plays back. When you turn Loop on, the Flash movie plays over and over again through an endless loop, an approach advertisers often choose for use in animated banner ads.

The Autoplay checkbox instructs the Flash movie to start playing when the page loads.

Note that neither of these options overrides specific programming instructions in the Flash movie. For instance, if you've added a Stop action to the final frame of a movie—an action that stops the movie at that frame—then the Loop option will have no effect.

Margins

Flash-movie *margins* are especially useful if you've wrapped text around the movie on the page; they determine how much buffer space falls between the movie and the text.

To add space above and below a selected movie, type a number of pixels into the V space field in the Property inspector (you only need to type a number; don't add *px* to specify pixels). Press Enter to see the results of your change. To add space to the left and right, type a pixel measurement in the H space field. Ten or twenty pixels usually provide an attractive amount of space. Unfortunately, you can't specify independent values for each of the four margins—only top/bottom and side/side.

Quality Settings

If your Flash movie's heavy data requirements overwhelm a visitor's computer, it may run slowly and appear choppy, especially if the animation is action-packed and complex. Until the day when everyone has a one-gigahertz computer with two gigabytes of RAM, you may need to adjust the quality settings of your Flash movies to help them look better on all computers, from the sluggish to the speedy.

By default, Dreamweaver sets the quality to High, but you can choose any of the following four settings from the Quality menu in the Property inspector:

- **High** provides the greatest quality, but the movie may run slowly on older computers.

- **Low** looks terrible. This setting sacrifices quality by eliminating all *antialiasing* (edge smoothing) in the movie, leaving harsh jaggy lines on the edges of every image. Movies set to Low quality look bad on *all* computers; to accommodate both the fast and the slow, use Auto High or Auto Low.

- **Auto Low** forces the movie to start in Low quality mode, but to switch automatically to High if the user's computer is fast enough.

- **Auto High** makes the movie switch to low quality mode only if the user's computer requires it. In this way, you can deliver a high-quality image to most users, while still letting those with slow computers view the movie. This is the best choice if you want to provide a high-quality image, but still make your movie accessible to those with older computers.

Scaling

When you resize a Flash movie, changing its original proportions, your visitors' Web browsers will scale or distort the movie to fit the newly specified dimensions. Scaling becomes an issue particularly when, for example, you give a Flash movie *relative* dimensions (setting it to, say, 90 percent of the browser window's width), so that it grows or shrinks as your visitor's browser window grows or shrinks.

The Scale property lets you determine *how* the Flash Player plug-in scales your movie. For example, in Figure 13-3, the top movie's original size is 200 pixels wide and 50 pixels tall. But if you resize the movie so that it's *300* x 50 pixels, one of three things may happen, depending on the choice of Scale setting you make:

- **Show All.** This setting, the default, maintains the original aspect ratio of the movie (second from top in Figure 13-3). In other words, although the overall size of the movie may go up or down, the movie's width-to-height proportion remains the same. This keeps the movie from distorting, but it may also cause borders to appear on the top, bottom, or either side of the movie. (To hide the borders, match the movie's background color to the color on the page, as described on the preceding page.)

- **No Border.** This setting resizes the movie according to your specifications *and* maintains its aspect ratio, but may also crop the sides of the movie. Notice how the top and bottom of "Cosmopolitan Farmer" are chopped off (third from top in Figure 13-3).

- **Exact Fit.** This option may stretch your movie's picture either horizontally or vertically. In Figure 13-3 (bottom), "Cosmopolitan Farmer" is stretched wider.

Figure 13-3:
A Flash movie's Scale property specifies how a movie should be scaled when its Width and Height properties are set differently than in the original movie. If you've resized a movie, press F12 to see how it looks in a Web browser; then, if necessary, choose a different setting from the Scale pop-up menu in the Property inspector.

Alignment

You can align Flash movies relative to the paragraphs around them, just as you do with images. In fact, the alignment options in the Property inspector work exactly the same as image-alignment properties discussed on page 117. For example, choosing Right from the Align menu positions the movie at the right of the screen and wraps text around its left side. (If the movie is inside a cell, Align Right moves it all the way to the right of the cell.)

Background Color

To set a background color for a Flash movie, use the Bg color box in the Property inspector. This color overrides any background color set in the movie itself; it fills the space where the movie appears when the page first loads (and the movie hasn't).

Shockwave

As the Internet-ready form of movies created with Macromedia's Director, Shockwave is an older brother to Flash. Director began life as a program for creating CD-ROMs, so it has a history as a tool for developing complex interactive presentations. When the Web exploded onto the scene, Director quickly morphed into a Web-authoring tool. Because of its CD background, Shockwave offers far more complex programming possibilities, and it's ideal for detailed interactive presentations.

Figure 13-4:
At times, it can be hard to tell the difference between the various external media types. This Shockwave game offers animation and interactivity just like a Flash movie. However, for highly interactive games that require precise timing and action, Shockwave is usually a better choice, thanks to its advanced 3-D features and built-in physics principles (like gravity and collision detection). To sample this technology, go to www.shockwave.com. There you'll find a mixture of Flash and Shockwave movies. (In this figure, only the rectangular area representing the basketball court is the Shockwave movie.)

Like Flash, Shockwave requires a plug-in; the difference is that the Shockwave plug-in doesn't generally come preinstalled with Web browsers. If you include Shockwave animations in your Web site, many of your visitors will need to download the Shockwave player—a 3.5-megabyte download!

That annoying requirement is a good argument against using Shockwave for general-audience Web sites. Some of your visitors—especially the ones that don't have cable modems or DSL—may not put in the time and effort required to enable their browsers to view your masterpiece.

But if you just can't do without Shockwave, you insert a Shockwave movie into a Web page just as you would any multimedia format. Click where you want to insert the movie; then choose Insert→Media→Shockwave (or click the Shockwave button on the Insert bar). Either way, a Select File dialog box appears. Find and double-click the Shockwave movie file (look for the .dcr extension).

The Shockwave movie appears as a gray rectangle with the Shockwave logo in the center. But Dreamweaver can't automatically calculate the dimensions of Shockwave movies, so you need to type the width and height of the movie in the W and H fields of the Property inspector. Use the same dimensions you specified when creating the file in Director.

You can preview Shockwave files directly in Dreamweaver by selecting the movie and clicking Play on the Property inspector. To stop the movie, click the same button (which is now a Stop button).

You resize a Shockwave movie just as you would a Flash movie, as described on page 408.

Shockwave Movie Properties

The only Shockwave movie property you have to set by hand is the width and height of the movie. Most of the time, you won't need to bother changing the default properties. The Property inspector does, however, let you change the movie's name (a requirement for using JavaScript to control its playback), substitute a different movie, choose the movie's alignment relative to the text around it, specify a background color, select an ActiveX ID, or specify top/bottom or side/side margins. All of these options work just as they do for Flash movies (see page 406).

Java Applets

A few years ago, it seemed that the whole world was going Java crazy. Created by Sun Microsytems, this powerful programming language seemed to offer an end to cross-platform problems. Programs written in Java can run on any operating system: Mac, Unix, Windows, whatever. Java also offered programmers the opportunity to write sophisticated applications that could run in the form of a compact file, called an *applet,* within any browser. Java applets can provide sophisticated graphics and user interface elements that go well beyond what HTML can do. In fact, Java can be used not only for graphics and multimedia, but to build complete applications like word processors, spreadsheets, or mortgage calculators that can live right in a Web page. For loads of sample applets, visit *www.javaboutique.com.*

In the end, Applets didn't make as big a splash on Web pages as industry forecasters originally thought. One of Java's limitations is that its applets don't work unless a Web-page visitor has a special software program called a Java Virtual Machine. This program translates the Java code into instructions appropriate for the visitor's particular operating system. As with plug-ins, virtual machines require lengthy downloads and installations that scare off many potential users. In addition, unlike JavaScript, which is fairly easy to learn, Java is not for the faint of heart. It's a complex language that requires a lot of skill and practice to do well.

But when the time comes that you've been handed a Java applet for insertion onto, say, a client's page, here's how to do it.

To insert a Java applet, choose Insert→Media→Applet, or click the Applet button on the Media tab of the Insert bar. When the Select File dialog box appears, find and double-click the Java applet file you want to insert. (Java applets have a .class or .jar extension.)

Figure 13-5:
In this example, a Java applet lets you interactively determine whether your body mass is appropriate for your age and height. Through the use of custom interface elements (such as the sliders under the height and weight columns), you control the size of the "man" and receive instant feedback in various form fields. (In this example, only the area between the two horizontal rules is the actual applet. Everything else is HTML.)

After you insert it, the applet appears on your Web page as a gray box with a coffee cup logo in the middle. Unfortunately, you can't preview it within Dreamweaver; press the F12 key to see it run in your Web browser.

Applet Properties

You set properties for applets using the Property inspector (see Figure 13-6), just as for any HTML object. The name, margins, alignment, and width/height controls work just as they do for Flash movies (see page 406). Java applets, however, offer a few specialized controls:

- **Code.** The name of the applet file appears in the Code field. If you wish to use a different file, click the folder icon and select another applet.

- **Base.** The Base field lists the folder that contains the applet file. When you insert an applet, Dreamweaver automatically fills in this field.

- **Alt.** For the benefit of visitors whose browsers don't support Java (or who have turned Java off), you can provide an alternative image or text description. Type the text in the Alt field, or click the little folder icon and select a GIF or JPEG file that will appear in place of the Java applet. The image will appear automatically if the Java Virtual Machine isn't installed.

Some applets may have properties in addition to the ones listed in the Property inspector. To add these properties, click the Parameters button. For example, the applet ticker.class shown in Figure 13-6 produces a ticker-tape display on a Web page. In order to let the applet know what message it needs to present, you add a parameter called *message*. The value of that parameter would be the message: "Welcome to my home page. This ticker-tape display is truly annoying, isn't it?"

Figure 13-6:
You set up the options for a Java applet just as you would any other object— using the Property inspector.

ActiveX Controls

ActiveX controls are miniature applications that work like plug-ins in Web browsers. In fact, the Flash Player for the Windows version of Internet Explorer *is* an ActiveX control.

However, this powerful technology can handle much more than multimedia; it can plug right into your computer, accessing files and other programs, or enabling spreadsheets and other productivity programs, right in a Web page.

Unfortunately, this Microsoft technology only works on Windows machines *and* only in Internet Explorer. As a result, it has yet to gain a foothold on the Web—and it may never. But if you're required to incorporate an ActiveX control into your site (perhaps because Microsoft is your client), then here's how to do it.

To insert ActiveX controls that you've programmed in Visual Basic or found on the Web, just choose Insert→Media→ActiveX. An ActiveX icon appears on the Web page, selected so that you can now change its options using the Property inspector.

ActiveX Properties

Some of the settings you can change for ActiveX controls (see Figure 13-7) are the same as you'd find for the other technologies described in this chapter (page 406): name, width/height, alignment, and margins, for example. A few others are unique to this technology:

ClassID

The ClassID identifies the ActiveX control for the browser. Dreamweaver includes three ClassIDs in the pop-up menu: Real Player, Shockwave, and Flash. (Selecting either of the last two simply changes the ActiveX icon on the page to either Shockwave or Flash.) The Real Player option lets you insert a control for including Real Video or Audio files on a page.

Figure 13-7:
ActiveX controls can vary widely in what functions they perform, so there is no standard set of properties for all controls.

Embed and Src

If there is a comparable Netscape plug-in for the ActiveX control you're adding to the page, you can turn on the Embed checkbox to add the <embed> tag. This way, Netscape and Mac users can also enjoy the benefits provided by the ActiveX control.

The HTML <object> tag specifies the ActiveX control and its properties. Netscape Navigator, on the other hand, uses the <embed> tag for adding plug-ins. Some external multimedia files, such as Flash, Shockwave, and Real Video, can use either an ActiveX control or a plug-in. In order to make both the ActiveX control and the Netscape plug-in available, you need to have both <object> and <embed> tags in the HTML code for your page (see the box on page 405).

If you turn on the Embed checkbox, you'll need to specify a file for the plug-in to use in Netscape. For example, a .swf (Flash movie) file would be used as a Src file for the Flash Player plug-in. To choose a file, click the folder icon and select it from your site folder (if it's not already there, Dreamweaver offers to copy it there for you).

- **Base.** The Base field indicates the URL for the ActiveX control. If the visitor doesn't already have the ActiveX control on her PC, Internet Explorer will go to this URL, download the control, and install it.

- **ID.** An ActiveX control's ID is used to pass information to other ActiveX controls.

- **Data.** Some ActiveX controls require an additional data file. Enter the name of that file in this field. Consult the instructions for your particular ActiveX control to find out if an additional file is necessary.

- **Alt.** For browsers that don't support the <object> tag, you can provide an alternative image. Click the folder icon and select a GIF or JPEG file from your Web site. Because ActiveX only works in one browser and one platform, give strong consideration to providing an Alt image: "Sorry, you're out of luck! Buy a Windows PC and use Internet Explorer next time!" (This option doesn't work if you've turned on the Embed checkbox in the Property inspector.)

Plug-ins

Flash and Shockwave may be among the most popular plug-ins, but they're by no means the only ones (see Figure 13-8). The Web teems with other plug-ins that add new features to a Web browser. The Adobe Acrobat plug-in, for example, lets you view PDF files directly inside a Web browser window; the Real Video lets you watch video in a tiny window.

Figure 13-8:
With the QuickTime plug-in for Mac or Windows, your visitors can view and listen to QuickTime movies embedded directly in a Web page.

Dreamweaver's Plug-In object offers a generic method of inserting media that require a plug-in. It doesn't address any of the specific needs of any one plug-in technology like, say, Real Video (see the box on the facing page). As a result, just adding

Dreamweaver's Plug-in object to your Web page is no guarantee that the plug-in will work. You may need to set additional properties or information; the software company responsible for the plug-in can provide details.

Then, of course, including any plug-in-dependent media in a Web page is always a risky proposition. If your visitors don't have the plug-in, they may be unwilling to go through the process required for downloading and installing the appropriate software. Before including any media that might discourage visitors, make sure it's absolutely necessary for your site.

To insert a plug-in file, choose Insert→Media→Plug-in, or click the Plugin button on the Media tab of the Insert bar. Either way, the Select File dialog box appears. Find and double-click the media file for the particular plug-in. For example, if you're embedding a QuickTime movie into a Web page, you'd locate a file ending in .mov.

Dreamweaver inserts the media file into your Web page. It looks like a light gray square with a jigsaw-puzzle piece on it; you can preview it using the Play button.

Plug-in Properties

When you select a plug-in object in your Web page, the Property inspector displays some basic properties (see Figure 13-9). Since each plug-in is unique, you may need to set additional properties in order to make it work properly. To view these specialized options, click the Parameters button on the inspector. For example, when inserting a QuickTime movie, you can add the parameter *autostart* with a value of *true* to make the movie automatically begin playback when the page loads.

As usual, some of the Property inspector options are fairly standard: name, height/width of the movie, alignment, and margins. The other settings include:

- **Src.** The Src property indicates the path to the media file in your Web site folder; Dreamweaver fills this in automatically when you select a file. The plug-in relies on this path to locate the media file. To swap in a different media file, you can click the folder icon.

EXTENSION ALERT

Plug-in Support at Macromedia Exchange

The Plug-in object is a simple way to embed code for plug-in files. Unfortunately, because it's designed as a generic method of adding files for any and all plug-ins, it's not pre-tailored for any one plug-in, such as the Real Media Player.

That's not to say that you can't add ready-to-use plug-in objects to your Web pages in software—you can. If you visit the Macromedia Exchange (*www.macromedia.com /exchange/dreamweaver/*), you can find *extensions* (see page 606) that help you insert media in a variety of different plug-in formats. These extensions help you put the proper code in your page to make the plug-in work.

Once on the Exchange Web site, choose Rich Media from the Browse Extensions menu. You'll find extensions that help you add QuickTime, Real Video and Audio, and other plug-in-dependent media. For more on using the Macromedia Exchange, see Appendix A.

- **Plg URL.** If you know the URL of the Web page from which the user can download the necessary plug-in, enter it in this field. If your visitor's browser doesn't have the plug-in, it will automatically attempt to download it from this URL.

- **Border.** To insert a border around the plug-in file, type a line-thickness pixel value in the Border field. (Unfortunately, not all browsers recognize this property.)

Figure 13-9:
Clicking Play plays the file indicated in the Src field— if you have the plug-in installed in the proper browser folders.

Part Four:
Building a Web Site

4

Introducing Site Management

As the dull-sounding name *site management* implies, organizing and tracking your Web site's files is one of the least glamorous, most time-consuming and error-prone aspects of being a Web designer. On the Web, your site may look beautiful, run smoothly, and appear to be a gloriously unified whole, but behind the scenes it's nothing more than a collection of varied files—HTML, images, Cascading Style Sheets, Flash movies, and so on—that must all work together. The more files you have to keep track of, the more apt you'll be to misplace one. A single broken link or missing graphic can interfere with the operation of your entire site, causing personal—even professional—embarrassment.

Fortunately, computers excel at tedious organizational tasks. Dreamweaver's site management features take care of the complexities of dealing with a Web site's many files, freeing you to concentrate on the creative aspects of design. In fact, even if you're a hand-coding HTML junkie and you turn your nose up at all visual Web page editors, you may find Dreamweaver worth its weight in gold just for the features described in this and the next two chapters.

Where the first three parts of this book describe how to create, lay out, and embellish a Web site, this part offers a bird's-eye view of the Web production process as you see your site through to completion and, ultimately, upload it to the Internet.

To get the most out of Dreamweaver's site management features, you need to be familiar with some basic principles for organizing Web files, as discussed in the next section.

Structuring a Web Site

When you build a Web site, you probably spend hours providing your visitors with carefully planned links, helpful labels, and clear, informative navigation tools. You want your *site architecture* to make it easy for them to understand where they are, where they can go, and how to return to where they came from (see Figure 14-1). Behind the scenes, it's equally important to organize your site's files with just as much clarity and care, so that you can find *your* way around when updating or modifying the site later. And, as on your home computer, a Web site's main organizational tool is the humble folder.

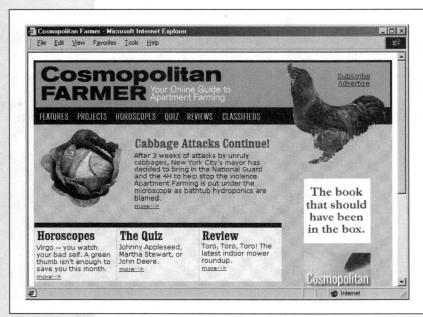

Figure 14-1:
A good site has an easy-to-understand structure. Content is divided into logical sections, and a prominent navigation bar (the row of black buttons in this image) gives visitors quick access to information. When building a site, this "information architecture" provides a useful model for naming and creating the folders that will hold the site's files.

You organize files on your computer every day, creating, say, a folder called Personal, within which are folders called Financial Planning and Vacation Pictures. Inside the Vacation Pictures folder, you have separate folders for your memories of Maui, Yosemite, and the Mall of America.

The same principle applies to the folders that make up a Web site. All Web sites have one primary folder—the *root folder*—that holds all of the site's Web pages, graphics, and other files used in the site. The root folder usually contains additional folders for further subdividing and organizing the site's files.

A good structure (see Figure 14-2) speeds up the production and maintenance of your site by giving you quick access to whatever graphic, style sheet, or Flash movie you're looking for. But don't fall into the trap of becoming so obsessed that you put every graphic or Web page you create in its own separate folder; creating a structure for the files in a site should make your job easier, not harder.

Tip: If you already have a Web site that suffers from lack of organization, it's not too late. Dreamweaver can help you reorganize your files quickly and accurately. Take the following rules to heart and then turn to "Organizing Site Files" on page 431, to learn how you can use Dreamweaver to knock your current site into shape.

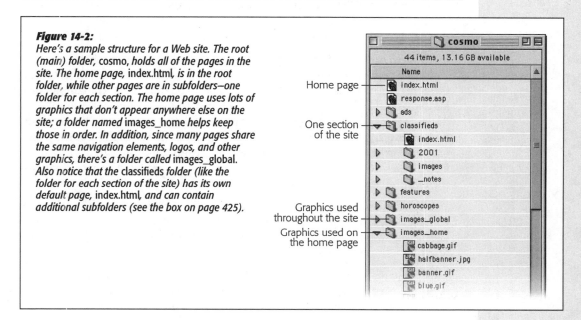

Figure 14-2:
Here's a sample structure for a Web site. The root (main) folder, cosmo, holds all of the pages in the site. The home page, index.html, is in the root folder, while other pages are in subfolders—one folder for each section. The home page uses lots of graphics that don't appear anywhere else on the site; a folder named images_home *helps keep those in order. In addition, since many pages share the same navigation elements, logos, and other graphics, there's a folder called* images_global. *Also notice that the* classifieds *folder (like the folder for each section of the site) has its own default page,* index.html, *and can contain additional subfolders (see the box on page 425).*

Here, then, are some guidelines for effective site organization:

- **Plan for future growth.** Like ever-spreading grapevines, Web sites grow. Today you may only have enough words and pictures for ten Web pages, but tomorrow you'll put the finishing touches on your new thousand-page online catalog. It may seem like overkill to create a lot of folders for a small site, but better to start with a solid structure today than find yourself knee-deep in files tomorrow.

  For instance, it's useful to create additional folders for graphics files that appear within each section of the site. If a section of your site is dedicated to promoting your company's products, create a folder called Products for storing product Web pages. Create an additional folder called Images to store the pictures of those products. Then, when you add more products or images, you know right where to put them.

- **Follow the site's architecture.** Take advantage of the work you've already done in organizing the content on your site. For instance, *Cosmopolitan Farmer*'s content is divided into six main sections: Features, Projects, Horoscopes, Quiz, Reviews, and Classified Ads, as shown in Figure 14-1. Following this architecture, it makes sense to create folders—features, projects, and so on—in the site's root folder for each section's respective Web pages. If one section is particularly large, add additional subfolders.

• **Organize files by type.** After you create folders for each section of your site, you'll probably need to add folders for storing other types of files like GIFs, JPEGs, Cascading Style Sheets, external JavaScript files, and PDF files. Most sites, for instance, make extensive use of graphics, with several graphics on each page. If that's the case for you, you need to file those images neatly and efficiently.

One way to organize your graphics is to create a folder for images that appear on your home page and another for images that appear elsewhere in the site. Often, the home page is visually distinct from other pages on the site and contains graphics that are unique to it. You can create a folder (*images_home*, for example) in the root folder for images that only appear on the home page. Create another folder (*images_global*, for example) to store graphics that all or most of the pages use, such as the company logo, navigation buttons, and other frequently used icons. When you add images to other pages of your site, you'll know to look for them in this folder.

• **Use Understandable Names.** While file names like *1a.gif*, *zDS.html*, and *f.css* are compact, they aren't very explanatory. Make sure file names mean something. Clear, descriptive names like *site_logo.gif* or *directions.html* will make it a lot easier for you to locate files and update pages.

This principle is especially important if you work as part of a team. If you're constantly explaining to your coworkers that *345g.gif* is the banner for the home page, changing the file name to *home_banner.gif* could save you some aggravation. There's a tradeoff here, however, as long file names can waste precious bytes: a name like *this_is_the_image_that_goes_in_the_upper_right_corner_of_the_home_page.gif* is probably not a good idea.

It's also helpful to add a prefix to related files. For example, use *nav_* at the beginning of a graphic name to indicate that it's a navigation button. In this way, you can quickly identify *nav_projects.gif*, *nav_quiz.gif*, and *nav_horoscopes.gif* as graph-

---

UP TO SPEED

Naming Your Files

The rules for naming files in Windows and Macintosh are fairly flexible. You can use letters, numbers, spaces, and even symbols like $, #, and ! when naming folders and files on these operating systems.

Web servers, on the other hand, are far less accommodating. Because many symbols—such as &, @, and ?—have special significance on the Web, using them in file names can confuse Web servers and cause errors.

The precise list of no-nos varies from Web server to Web server, but you'll be safe if you stick to letters, numbers, the hyphen (-), and the underscore (_) character when naming files and folders. Stay away from spaces. File names like *company logo.gif* or *This company's president.html* probably won't work on most Web servers. Replace spaces with underscores or inner caps—*company_logo.gif* or *companyLogo.gif*—and remove all punctuation marks.

---

ics used in a page's navigation bar. As a bonus, when you view the files on your computer or in Dreamweaver's Site panel (see Figure 14-5), they'll appear neatly sorted by name; in other words, all the *nav_* files will cluster together in the file list.

Tip: If you use a Mac, you might not be familiar with the three or four letters that follow Web file names. These letters, or *file name extensions,* tell Windows computers what program should open the file; they're used universally as part of all Web files' names.

The trick is that Windows and Macintosh computers use slightly different extensions. For example, in Windows, Web page names are often followed by *.htm,* whereas the Mac uses *.html.* In most cases, the Windows and Macintosh extension versions are interchangeable. The one exception is JPEG files: some Windows computers don't understand the Mac extension *.jpeg.* It's best to stick to the Windows extension, *.jpg.*

To specify the extension Dreamweaver uses when saving Web pages, choose Dreamweaver→Preferences to open the Preferences window. Click the General category, turn on Add Extension When Saving, and type the extension in the box. You can type *.html, .htm,* or any other extension you wish.

- **Be consistent.** Once you've come up with a system that works for you, follow it. Always. If you name one folder *images,* for instance, don't name another *graphics* and a third *pretty_pictures.* And certainly don't put Web pages in a folder named *images,* or Flash movies in a folder named *style_sheets.*

In fact, if you work on more than one Web site, you may want to use a single naming convention and folder structure for all of your sites, so that switching between them will go more smoothly. If you name all your graphics folders *im-*

FREQUENTLY ASKED QUESTION

All Those Index Pages

Why are so many Web pages named index.html*?*

If you type *www.cosmofarmer.com/* into a Web browser, the *Cosmopolitan Farmer* home page opens on your screen. But how did the Web server know *which* page from the site to send to your browser? After all, you didn't ask for a particular Web page, like *www.cosmofarmer.com/about.html.*

When a Web server gets a request that doesn't specify a particular Web page, it looks for a default Web page—usually named *index.html* or *index.htm.* It does the same thing even when the URL you've typed specifies (with a slash) a folder inside the site root, like this: *www.cosmofarmer.com/horoscopes/.* In this case, the Web server looks for a file

called index.html inside the *horoscopes* folder, and—if it finds the file—sends it to your Web browser.

If the Web server doesn't find an index.html file, two things can happen, both undesirable: The Web browser may display either an ugly error message or a listing of all the files inside the folder. Neither result is user-friendly.

While your site will still function without this step, it's good form to give the main Web page inside each folder in your site the proper default page name. Web servers use different names for these default pages—*index.html* or *default.html,* for example—so check with your Web server's administrator or help desk.

---

ages, then no matter what site you're working on, you already know where to look for GIFs and JPEGs.

Tip: Put only files that will go on your Web site in the root folder and its subfolders. Keep your source files—the original Photoshop, Fireworks, Flash, or Word documents where you created your content—stored elsewhere on your computer. This way, you're much less likely to accidentally transfer a 14.5 MB Photoshop file to your Web server (a move that would *not* gain you friends in the IT department). But if you insist on keeping all those files together with your Web site files, check out Dreamweaver MX's new *cloaking* feature. Using it, you can prevent certain file types from being transferred to your Web server when using Dreamweaver's FTP feature.

Defining a Site

Organizing and maintaining a Web site—creating new folders and Web pages; moving, renaming, and deleting files and folders; and transferring pages to a Web server—used to require going back and forth between a couple of different programs. With Dreamweaver's site management features, however, you can do it all from within the program. But in order to take advantage of these features, you must first *define* the site; in other words, give Dreamweaver some basic information about it.

Defining the site involves showing Dreamweaver which folder contains your Web site files (the root folder) and setting up a few other options. You've already learned how to do this site-building using Dreamweaver MX's new Site Definition Wizard (page 25). But for fine-tuning your settings, it's time to get to know the advanced Site Definition window.

Start by choosing Site→New site to open the Site Definition window (Figure 14-3); then click the Advanced tab to access Dreamweaver's advanced settings. There are seven categories of information for your site, but to get up and running, you need to provide information only for the first category: Local Info. (The remaining six categories are discussed in Chapters 15 and 16.)

The following are the options on the Local Info tab.

FREQUENTLY ASKED QUESTION

Bringing Your Own Web Site

I already have a Web site. Will Dreamweaver work with it?

Yes. In fact, Dreamweaver's site management features are an invaluable aid in organizing the files of an existing site. As you can read in "Organizing Site Files" on page 431, you can use Dreamweaver to rearrange, rename, and re-organize files—tasks that are extremely difficult and time-consuming to do by hand. Furthermore, Dreamweaver lets you clean up and reorganize a site without breaking links. So Dreamweaver can be just as useful for working with a completed site as it is for creating one from scratch.

To work on an existing site, first save a copy of all site files on your computer, all in one folder. When defining the site (see page 25), choose this folder for the local root folder.

Site Name

Into the Site Name field, type a name that briefly identifies the site for you—and Dreamweaver. This is the name that appears, among other places, on the Site pop-up menu on the Site panel (Figures 14-5 and 14-6), so that you can tell what site you're working on.

Figure 14-3:
The Basic tab of the Site Definition window provides a simple method for new users to set up a Web site. But experienced users can take advantage of the greater options available under the Advanced tab shown here. The seven categories listed on the left side of the window are discussed in this and the next two chapters.

Site Definition for Cosmoplitan Farmer

Basic | Advanced

Category
- Local Info
- Remote Info
- Testing Server
- Cloaking
- Design Notes
- Site Map Layout
- File View Columns

Local Info

Site Name: Cosmoplitan Farmer

Local Root Folder: E:\money losing proposition\

☑ Refresh Local File List Automatically

Default Images Folder: E:\money losing proposition\cosmo_root\i

HTTP Address: http://www.cosmofarmer.com

This address enables the Link Checker to detect HTTP links that refer to your own site.

Cache: ☑ Enable Cache

The cache maintains file and asset information in the site. This speeds up the Asset panel, link management, and Site Map features.

OK | Cancel | Help

Local Root Folder

Identify your site's local root folder—the folder that contains all files belonging to your site—by clicking the folder icon to the right of the Local Root Folder field. The procedure is described in Figure 1-7 on page 28. (Also see the box on page 26 for more information on local root folders.)

All of Dreamweaver's tools for managing your sites' files rely on the local root folder. Once you've defined a site, you see all of its files listed in the Site panel. Make sure to turn on the Refresh Local File List Automatically checkbox so that new files—graphics, Web pages, and so on—automatically appear in the Site panel as you add them. Alternatively, click the Refresh button (Figure 14-5) each time you want to see your recent changes in the site files list.

Default Images Folder

For a graphic image to work properly on the Web, you can't just add it to a Web page (Chapter 5); you also have to store a copy of the graphics file in the local root folder or one of its subfolders. In other words, if you link to a graphic that's sitting on your computer's hard drive *outside* of the root folder, the Web browser will never find it.

Dreamweaver MX offers a new feature that puts images in the right place even if you forget. When you add a stray graphics file to a page in your site, the program automatically copies the file into your Default Images folder. In fact, even if you drag a graphic from your desktop onto a Web page in progress, Dreamweaver copies the file to the Default Images folder without missing a beat.

The process of choosing the Default Images folder is the same as selecting a local root folder. Click the folder icon and select the proper folder, which can be an existing folder in your local root or a new one you create on the spot. (If you're following the process described on page 426, select the images_global folder here.)

HTTP Address

If you use absolute URLs to link to pages within your site (page 92), you must fill out the HTTP Address field in order for Dreamweaver's link management features to work properly. Type your site's full URL beginning with *http://*. Dreamweaver uses this address to check for broken links within your site and to correctly rewrite links if you move pages around.

Note: This step is necessary *only* if you use absolute URLs to link to pages, graphics, or other supplemental files *within* your site. For example, maybe your Web master directs you to link a form to *http://www.yourdomain.com/cgi/formscript.php* instead of using a document relative link. In most cases, if you're doing all the development with Dreamweaver, you won't run into this situation, and you can leave the HTTP address field empty.

Cache

The cache is a small database of information about the files in your site. It helps Dreamweaver's site management features work more efficiently. Leave this checkbox turned on.

Once you've provided the local information for your site, click OK to close the Site Definition window and begin working.

Editing or Removing Defined Sites

Sometimes you need to edit the information associated with a site. Perhaps you want to rename the site, or you've reorganized your hard drive and moved the local root folder to a different location, and you need to let Dreamweaver know what you've done.

To edit a site, open the Edit Sites dialog box (choose Site→Edit Sites or, in the Site panel, choose Edit Sites from the Site pop-up menu) and double-click the name of the site you want to edit. The Site Definition window opens (see Figure 14-3). Now you can type a new name in the Site Name box, choose a new local root folder, or make any other changes. Click OK to close the dialog box when you're done.

Once you've finished a site and are no longer working on it, you may wish to remove it from Dreamweaver's list of sites. To delete a site from the list, open the Define Sites dialog box as described above, click to select the site you wish to delete, and click Remove.

A warning appears telling you that this action can't be undone. Don't worry; deleting the site here doesn't actually *delete* the site's images, Web pages, and other files from your computer. It merely removes the site from Dreamweaver's list of defined sites. (You can always go back and define the site again, if you need to, by following the steps on page 25.) Click Done to close the Edit Sites window.

Tip: If you do, in fact, want to delete the actual Web pages, graphics, and other site components, you can either switch to the desktop (the Finder or Windows Explorer, for example) and delete them manually, or delete them from within Dreamweaver's Site panel, described in this chapter.

Exporting and Importing Sites

When you define a site, Dreamweaver stores that site's information in its own, private files. If you want to work on your site using a different computer, therefore, you must define the site again for *that* copy of Dreamweaver. In a design firm where several people might be working together on many different sites, that's a lot of extra setup. In fact, even if there's just one of you working on two computers, duplicating your efforts is a pain.

So that you can put your time to better use, a new feature in Dreamweaver MX lets you import and export site definitions. For example, you can back up your site definition files—in case you have to reinstall Dreamweaver—or export a site definition for others to use.

To export a site definition:

1. **Choose Site→Edit Sites.**

   The Edit Sites window appears, listing all sites you've defined.

2. **Select a site from the list, and then click Export.**

   If the site definition includes remote site information (page 477), you'll see a panel called Export Site (Figure 14-4). If you're simply making a backup of your site definition because you need to reinstall Dreamweaver, select "Back up my settings." The other option, "Share settings," is useful when you don't want to give someone else your user name and password to the Web server.

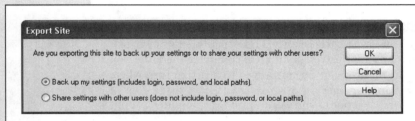

Figure 14-4:
Maybe your local root folder is on the C: drive, but it's on the E: drive on someone else's computer. In that case, click "Share settings with others."

3. **Click OK.**

   The Export Site panel appears.

4. **In the Export Site panel, specify where you want to save the file and give it a name.**

   If you're merely making a backup, saving the file to that site's local root folder is a good choice.

Note: Mac users can also access the site import and export features directly from the Site menu. Choose Site→Export or Site→Import.

In Windows, you don't have these options on the main Site menu, but you can access them from the Site panel. Press F8 to open the Site panel and choose either Import or Export from its Site menu.

Once you have a site definition file, you can import it into any version of Dreamweaver MX as follows:

1. **Choose Site→Edit Sites.**

   The Edit Site panel appears.

2. **Click Import.**

The Import Site panel appears. Navigate to a site definition file—look for a file ending in .ste. Select it, and then click OK.

If you're importing the site definition to a computer other than the one you used to export the site, you may need to perform a few more steps. If Dreamweaver can't locate the local root folder in the site definition file, it will ask you to select a local root folder on the new computer, as well as a new default images folder.

Organizing Site Files

Once you've defined your local site, Dreamweaver helps you organize your files, create folders, and add new Web pages to your site using the Site panel as your command center. To open the Site panel, choose Site→Site Files, or just press F8.

The Site panel isn't identical on Windows and Macintosh (see Figures 14-5 and 14-6). For example, the Windows version offers an unlabeled View pop-up menu (shown in Figure 14-5) with these options:

- **Local View** shows the files in your local root folder.

- **Map View** shows a map of your site (see page 437).

- **Remote View** shows files on the Web server in the remote root folder (page 477).

- **Testing Server** view is useful only when you're creating the dynamic database-driven sites discussed in Part 6 of this book.

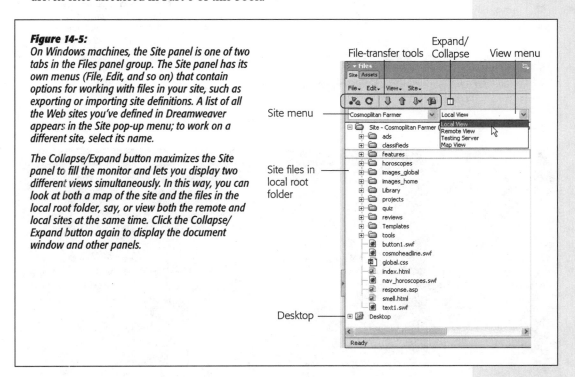

Figure 14-5:
On Windows machines, the Site panel is one of two tabs in the Files panel group. The Site panel has its own menus (File, Edit, and so on) that contain options for working with files in your site, such as exporting or importing site definitions. A list of all the Web sites you've defined in Dreamweaver appears in the Site pop-up menu; to work on a different site, select its name.

The Collapse/Expand button maximizes the Site panel to fill the monitor and lets you display two different views simultaneously. In this way, you can look at both a map of the site and the files in the local root folder, say, or view both the remote and local sites at the same time. Click the Collapse/Expand button again to display the document window and other panels.

Expand/
File-transfer tools   Collapse   View menu

Site menu

Site files in
local root
folder

Desktop

Still, in its most basic incarnation, the Site panel displays the files in the current site's local root folder. This list looks and acts just like Windows Explorer or the Macintosh Finder: you see names, file sizes, and folders. You can view the files inside a folder by clicking the + (▶) symbol next to the folder (or simply by double-clicking the folder). Double-click a Web page to open it in Dreamweaver.

Tip: Windows users can quickly hide and show the panel groups by clicking the Show/Hide Panels button at the left edge of the panel groups (see Figure 14-5). On small monitors, this can give you the breathing room you need to work efficiently on your Web pages. You can also resize the panel groups by dragging this button left or right. And pressing F4 hides (or shows) all of the panels, including the Property inspector and Insert bar.

Site Files view   Site Map view   File-transfer tools

Sites menu

Testing Server

Hide/Show remote files   Remote site   Local site

Figure 14-6:
In the Mac version of Dreamweaver, the Site panel is a floating window (just as in Dreamweaver 4). A list of all the Web sites you've defined in Dreamweaver appears in the Site pop-up menu; to work on a different site, select its name. The Site panel also includes tools for creating a Site Map and for transferring files between the local and remote sites (see Chapter 16). The computer icon at the bottom of the Site panel, new in MX, lets you browse your computer's entire file system—not just the local root folder— which comes in handy when you want to locate a page or graphic that's not part of your site.

FOR WINDOWS USERS

The Windows Site Panel

In the Windows version of Dreamweaver, the Site panel is docked on the edge of the screen with other panels.

If you're used to Dreamweaver 4, this is a bit of a change. To see a side-by-side view of both the remote site files and local site files, click the Expand/Collapse button (identified in Figure 14-5). The Site panel fills the screen and looks just like the Macintosh Site panel (shown in Figure 14-6). The obvious drawback is that you can't work on a Web page while the Site window is maximized, because you can't even see it. Click the Expand/Collapse button again

to minimize the Site panel and gain access to your document window.

To get around this limitation, you can undock the Site panel: grab the Files panel group by its grip—the column of dots to the left of the word Files—and drag it toward the middle of the screen. (Stay away from the edges of the screen. This may simply redock the panel group.) The panel group then becomes a floating panel. You're now free to resize the Site panel even after expanding it.

The panel can also display a list of files on the Remote site—that is, on the Web server—or a map of your site. Of course, before you've posted your site on the Web, this list is empty; information appears here only after you connect to your Web server. When building database-driven sites, you can also display files on a *testing server* (page 623).

Tip: You can even open certain types of files in an outside program of your choice by defining an external editor for the file type. For example, you can tell Dreamweaver to open GIF files in Fireworks, Photoshop, or other image editor. (See "Setting Up an External Editor" on page 121 for more on this feature.)

Adding New Folders and Files

The Site panel provides a fast way of adding blank Web pages to your site. With one click, you can create a new page in any folder you like, saving several steps you'd otherwise have to perform using the File menu.

Adding files

To create a new, blank Web page, open the Site panel using one of the methods described on page 431, then right-click (Control-click) a file or folder in the Site panel.

In the contextual menu that appears, choose New File. Dreamweaver creates a new, empty Web page. (Actually, the page doesn't have to be empty; you can edit the file Dreamweaver uses as its default new page, as described in the box below.)

The new file appears in the Site panel with a highlighted naming rectangle next to it; type a name for the page here. Don't forget to add the appropriate extension—.htm or .html—to the end of its name.

POWER USERS' CLINIC

Changing the Default New Page

Whenever you make a new Web page—for example, by choosing File→New or by right-clicking (Control-clicking) an existing file in the Site panel—Dreamweaver gives you a blank, white document window. But what if you always want your pages to have gray backgrounds—or mauve?

Every new Web page you create is actually an untitled *copy* of a default template document called Default.html. (You'll find it in the Macromedia Dreamweaver MX→ Configuration→DocumentTypes→NewDocuments folder.) You can open this file within Dreamweaver and edit it however you like: change its background color, margins or text color, or whatever, so that all subsequent new

pages you create inherit its settings. Consider making a backup of this file before editing it, however, so that you can return to the factory settings if you accidentally make a mess of it.

You'll also notice lots of other files in this folder. Since Dreamweaver MX can create lots of different file types— Cascading Style Sheets, Active Server pages, and so on— you'll find a default blank file for each. You can edit any of these—but don't, unless you're sure of what you're doing. You can easily mess up some of the more complex file types, especially those that involve dynamic Web sites.

Adding folders

You can add folders to your site directly in Dreamweaver using the Site panel. Just right-click (Control-click) a file or folder in the local files list. If you click a file, Dreamweaver creates the new folder in the same folder as that file; if you click a folder, you get a new folder inside it.

From the contextual menu, choose New Folder.

If you crave variety, you can add a folder another way. Select a file or folder in the Site panel and then:

- *Windows:* In the Site panel, choose File→New Folder.
- *Macintosh:* Choose Site→Site Files View→New Folder.

Finally, in the naming rectangle that appears in the Site panel, type a name for the new folder.

Moving files and folders

Because the Dreamweaver Site panel looks and acts so much like the Windows Explorer and Macintosh Finder, you may think it does nothing more than let you move and rename files and folders on your computer. You may even be tempted to work with your site files directly on the Mac or Windows desktop, thinking that you're saving time. However, when it comes to moving the files and folders in your site, Dreamweaver does more than your computer's desktop ever could.

In your Web travels, you've probably encountered the dreaded "404: file not found" error. This "broken link" message doesn't necessarily mean that the page doesn't exist, just that your Web browser didn't find the page at the location (URL) specified by the link you just clicked. In short, someone working on that Web site probably moved or renamed a file without updating the link. Because Web site files are interrelated in such complex ways—pages link to other pages, which include paths to graphics, which in turn appear on other pages—an action as simple as moving one file can wreak havoc on an entire Web site. That's why you shouldn't drag Web site files around on your desktop or rename them in Windows Explorer or the Macintosh Finder.

In fact, moving and reorganizing Web site files is so headache-ridden and error-prone that some Web designers avoid it altogether, leaving their sites straining under the weight of thousands of poorly organized files. But you don't have to be one of them: Dreamweaver makes reorganizing a site easy and error-free. When you use the Site panel to move files, Dreamweaver looks for actions that might break your site's links and automatically rewrites paths of links, images, and other media.

Note to programmers: If your custom JavaScript programs include paths to images, Web pages, or other files in your site, Dreamweaver can't help you. The program updates *links* it created, but not *paths*, when you reorganize your site with the Site panel.

Just be sure to do your moving from within Dreamweaver, like this: In the Site panel, drag the folder or file into its new folder (see Figure 14-7). To move multiple files, Ctrl-click (⌘-click) each of the ones you want to move, then drag them as a group; to deselect a selected file, Ctrl-click or ⌘-click it again. You can also select one folder or file and Shift-click another to select all files and folders in the list between the two.

When you release the mouse button, the Update Files dialog box appears (Figure 14-7); just click Update. Dreamweaver updates all the links for you.

Tip: If you accidentally dragged the file or folder to the wrong location, click Don't Update. Then drag the file back to its original location and, if Dreamweaver asks you, click Don't Update once again.

Figure 14-7:
Top left: You can move files and folders within the Site panel just as you would in Windows Explorer or the Macintosh Finder. Simply drag the file into (or out of) a folder. But unlike your computer's file system, Dreamweaver constantly monitors the links between Web pages, graphics, and other files.

Bottom right: If you move a file using Windows Explorer or the Finder, you'll most likely end up breaking links to that file or, if it's a Web page, links in that file. By contrast, Dreamweaver is smart enough to know when moving files will cause problems. The Update Files dialog box lets you update links to and from the file you're moving, so that your site keeps working.

Renaming files and folders

Renaming files and folders poses the same problems as moving them. Because links include file and folder names, altering a file or folder name can break a link just as easily as moving or deleting the file or folder.

Say you've created a new site with a home page named *home.html*. You cheerfully continued building the other pages of your site, linking them to *home.html* as you went along. But after reading this chapter and checking to find out what default file name your Web server requires (see page 425), you found that you need to rename your home page file *index.html*. If you were to rename the file *index.html* using Windows Explorer or the Macintosh Finder, every link to *home.html* would result in a "file not found" error.

Dreamweaver, on the other hand, handles this potential disaster effortlessly, as long as you rename the file in the Site panel instead. To do so, just click the file or folder in the Site panel. Pause a moment, and click the *name* of the file or folder. (The pause ensures that Dreamweaver won't think you just double-clicked the file for editing.)

A renaming rectangle appears; type the new name. Be sure to include the proper extension for the type of file you're renaming. For example, GIFs end with .gif, Cascading Style Sheets end with .css. Although Dreamweaver lets you name files without using an extension, the extensionless files won't work when you move them to a Web server.

Finally, in the Update Files dialog box (see Figure 14-7), click Update. Dreamweaver updates all the links to this file or folder to reflect the new name.

Caution: It bears repeating: never rename or move files and folders *outside* of Dreamweaver. If you use Windows Explorer or the Macintosh Finder to reorganize the files in your site, links will break, images will disappear from your pages, and the earth will open underneath your feet. (Well, actually, that last thing won't happen, but it might *feel* that way when your boss comes in and says "What's happened to our Web site? Nothing works!")

If you've edited files outside of Dreamweaver by accident, see page 458 to learn how to find and fix broken links.

Deleting files and folders

It's a good idea to clean up your site from time to time by deleting old and unused files. Just as with moving and renaming files, you delete files from the Site panel.

To delete a file or folder, just click to select it in the Site panel and press Backspace or Delete. (To select multiple files or folders, Ctrl-click [⌘-click] them as described on page 460.) If the doomed file or folder isn't referenced by any other page on the site, a simple "Are you sure you want to delete this file?" warning appears; click Yes.

Figure 14-8:
When you delete files in the Site panel, Dreamweaver warns you if other pages reference (link to) the file. If you click Yes, you'll have to go back and repair the links. Dreamweaver gives you a convenient way to do it—the Change Links Sitewide command—and reminds you of it in this dialog box.

However, if other files link to the file—or to files within the folder—that you're deleting, then a warning dialog box (Figure 14-8) appears, informing you that you're about to break links on one or more pages in your site. The message even lists the first few pages that use the file. If you've made a mistake, click No to leave your site untouched.

If you're sure you wish to delete the file, click Yes. And yes, this move does *break links* in all the pages listed. Repairing those links, which usually means linking them to a new page, requires a separate step: using the Site→Change Links Sitewide command, as described on page 464.

Viewing a Site Map

While the Site panel's list of files and folders is a great aid in managing those files, it doesn't give you a picture of how your site's Web pages are linked together. You can see that the *index.html* file in the root folder is the site's home page, for instance, but you can't see how it relates to the other pages in the site. In other words, you can't tell which pages link to or from it. To see those relationships, you need Dreamweaver's Site→Site Map view.

The Site Map is a visual guide to the links in a site (see Figure 14-9). An icon representing the home page appears at the top of the map, and arrows connect the home

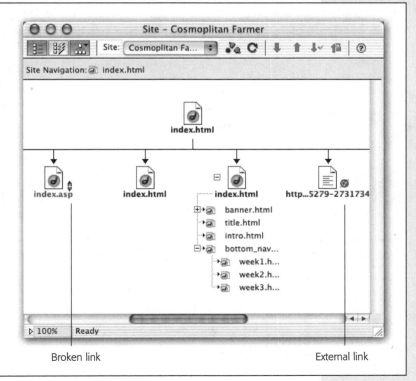

Figure 14-9:
The Site Map displays icons for each link in a Web site. Symbols provide added information about the pages. The globe icon ( ) indicates an external link such as www.yahoo.com. The broken link icon ( ) indicates that the file either doesn't exist or has been misfiled, so that the link won't work. Dreamweaver also highlights the name of the missing file in red. For more on finding and fixing broken links, see page 458.

Broken link   External link

page to icons representing each of the links it contains. As shown in Figure 14-9, special icons clearly mark external, broken, and email links. Furthermore, the Site Map does more than just provide a visual overview; it also gives you an easy way to rename files and even retitle Web pages.

Setting Up Site Map View

To view a Site Map, you'll first need to do a little preparation:

1. **Choose Site→Edit Sites (or choose Edit Sites from the Site menu in the Site panel).**

    The Edit Sites window appears, listing all of your sites.

2. **In the Edit Sites dialog box, click a site name and click Edit (or just double-click the site name).**

    The Site Definition window opens.

    If you're defining this site for the first time, you can also follow the instructions on page 426 now.

3. **In the Category list, choose Site Map Layout.**

    You see the dialog box shown in Figure 14-10.

Figure 14-10:
This box lets you define the site's home page and set preferences for using Site Map view. In general, the values Dreamweaver proposes are fine. In fact, if your home page file is named index.html *or* index.htm, *you don't have to do anything, because Dreamweaver automatically sets it as the home page. But if you use a different file name, like default.html, you must specify it in the Home Page field.*

4. **Click the folder icon next to the Home Page field and navigate to the home page file in the site's root folder.**

    Click Select (Windows) or Open (Mac) to set this page as the home page.

    Remember that your home page must be in the root folder. Technically, you *can* choose a file that's buried several folders deep in your site folder, but don't do it——unless, of course, you really want to tell people to visit your company's home page at *www.mycompany.com/about_us/about_me/my_dog/ralphie.html*. By specifying a home page in the outer level of your root folder, you can assure that the home page will be at *www.mycompany.com*.

5. **Set any other Site Map preferences you wish.**

The **Number of Columns** field determines how many links can be displayed in a single row of the Site Map (see Figure 14-9). For instance, if you set the number of columns to five, but the home page has ten links on it, the Site Map only has enough columns for the first five links; the remaining five icons get bumped down to a second row directly below the first. Displaying more than one row of links from the home page can be confusing, so it's best to use a number of columns that's at least equal to the number of links on the home page. Dreamweaver's default value of 200 is just fine.

The **Column Width** represents the width, in pixels, of each column. As you can see in the box on page 437, file names and page titles may not fully appear if the column width is too small. Again, stick with Dreamweaver's default value of 125.

Using the **Icon Labels** buttons, choose whether you'll want the Site Map to display the file name *(index.html)* or page title ("Welcome to *Cosmopolitan Farmer*") next to each page's icon. Shift+ Ctrl+T (Shift-⌘-T) toggles between the two views when viewing the Site Map.

Once you've got your Site Map on display, you can hide certain files for the sake of clutter reduction by marking them as hidden. To make sure they stay hidden, leave **Display files marked as hidden** turned off. You can always make the hidden files reappear using the steps described on page 441.

The **Display dependent files** option will make GIF, JPEG, CSS, Flash, and all other non-HTML files show up in the Site Map. Since this can make the site map a confusing jumble of files, it's best to leave this option turned off.

6. **Click OK.**

You return to the Site panel.

Viewing and Customizing Site Map View

Once you've set up Site Map view as described above, do one of the following to see the results:

- **Windows.** Choose Map View from the Site panel's unlabeled View menu (identified in Figure 14-5). Because the Site panel is very narrow, you can click the Split View button (also shown in Figure 14-5) to maximize the map.

- **Macintosh.** Click the Site Map button/pop-up menu in the Site panel (shown in Figure 14-11). The pop-up menu offers you two options: Map and Files, which displays the site's local files in the right pane of the Site panel and the Site Map in the left pane, and Map Only, which fills the Site panel with the map (Figure 14-9). Unfortunately, if you resize the Site panel, the Site Files list frequently reappears. The only way to overcome this bug is to choose Map Only again.

Figure 14-11:
On Macs, the Site Map button in the Site panel lets you see either a single-pane window (Map Only) or a double-pane window (Map and Files). If you're on Windows, you can also see this view if you tell Dreamweaver to use the Dreamweaver 4 workspace (see page 17).

When you first view the Site Map, only the first two levels—the home page and all of the pages linked from it—appear. A + symbol next to a page indicates that there are additional links on that page; clicking the + expands the list of links on that page. If those pages, in turn, have links, additional + symbols appear. You can continue to follow the links by expanding each page, but viewing too many levels at once can bring a confusing complication; see the box below for advice.

As in the Site file list, you can open a page by double-clicking its icon in the Site Map. In fact, selecting a page in the Site Map highlights the corresponding page in the File list, and vice versa.

GEM IN THE ROUGH

Don't Get Lost in the Site Map

The Site Map clearly displays links between pages, but if you're not careful, you may end up chasing your tail. Very often, Web pages link back and forth to each other. For example, the home page may link to a page in the site that, in turn, links back to the home page.

In the example illustrated here, the advertising page ("Advertise with *Cosmopolitan Farmer*") has a link to the home page (*"Cosmopolitan Farmer"*), which links to the advertising page, which links back to the home page, which links to the advertising page…and so on. All four of the pages

indicated by arrows are, in fact, the same page!

As shown in this Site Map, the advertising page is a link from the home page. When you then click the + to expand the advertising page, you see a duplicate icon for the home page (whose original icon appears at the top of the Site Map). When you click the + sign next to the home page icon under the advertising page, you don't get a new level of site links, even though the Site Map displays it that way. What you've done is "re-expand" the home page and display more duplicate icons.

Identifying pages in the Site Map

The Site Map view starts out showing the file name of each Web page, which can be less than informative. If you've structured your site (as recommended on page 422) so that the main page for each section of the site is stored in a different folder and is named *index.html,* the Site Map will be an unhelpful sea of *index.html* labels (see Figure 14-9).

A better approach: use each page's *title* as the icon label. You can do this when you first set up the site, as described on page 438, or else choose View→Show Page Titles (Windows) or Site→Site Map View→Show Page Titles (Mac). Repeat the same command to see the file names again. The keyboard shortcut is a fast way to toggle between the two views: Shift+ Ctrl+T (Shift-⌘-T).

Viewing just part of a Web site

When viewing large Web sites, you might find the Site Map awkward. Perhaps you're working on just a single section and don't want to be bothered with the extraneous details of the rest of the site. No problem: you can isolate a particular page when viewing the Site Map. Click a page in the Site Map and choose View→View as Root (Windows) or Site→Site Map View→View as Root (Mac). The page you selected appears as the top-level page in the Site Map (see Figure 14-12).

Figure 14-12:
This Site Map is zoomed in on a single page (Hydroponic Strawberry Kit), which appears at the top level of the Site Map where the home page normally would be. The path from the home page to this file appears above the map in the Site Navigation bar. The home page is titled Cosmopolitan Farmer. A link from the home page leads to a page titled Cosmo Farmer Classifieds, which in turn links to the Hydroponic Strawberry Kit page. To once again view the home page as the top level of the Site Map, click its name in the Site Navigation bar.

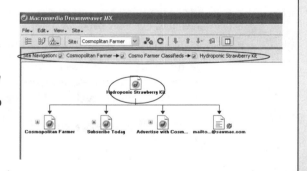

Hiding extraneous links

Like some people you may know, the Site Map loves detail: it includes *all* links from your pages, including external links and email links. At times, this may be a bit more information than you need. Suppose you provide 200 email addresses on a single page; you probably don't need to see all of those listed in the Site Map.

Fortunately, Dreamweaver lets you hide any links you wish. All you have to do is select the files you want to hide (Shift-click them, or drag across a group of them) and then choose View→Show/Hide Link (Windows) or Site→Site Map View→Show/ Hide Link (Macintosh); Dreamweaver makes them disappear.

To show hidden files again, choose View→Show Files Marked as Hidden (Windows) or Site→Site Map View→Show Files Marked as Hidden (Mac). Dreamweaver makes all hidden files appear with their names italicized, indicating that you've marked them as hidden. You can turn off a file's "hidden" status by selecting it and choosing View→Show/Hide Link (Windows) or Site→Site Map View→Show/Hide Link (Mac).

Renaming Pages in the Site Map

You can rename files in Site Map view, which works similarly to renaming them in the File List view. However, only the Site Map lets you easily change the *titles* of your site's Web pages. In fact, this is one of the best features of the Site Map. While displaying the page titles, you can quickly scan your site for missing or incorrect page titles and fix them in just a few steps.

You rename a file in the Site Map just as you do in the Site panel; the steps appear on page 460. In this case, just be sure you're looking at the right kind of data—either page titles or file names—before you begin. Press Shift+ Ctrl+T (Shift-⌘-T) to switch back and forth when viewing the Site Map.

When you're finished, Dreamweaver rewrites the title in the HTML of the page. The new title also appears next to the page icon.

Site Assets

Web pages integrate lots of different elements: GIFs, JPEGs, links, colors, and Flash and Shockwave movies, to name just a few. In a large site with lots of files, it can be a challenge to locate a particular image or remember an exact color.

To make the process easier, Dreamweaver provides the Assets panel. For want of a better generic term, Macromedia defines the term *asset* to mean any element you use on a Web page, such as a GIF file, a link, or even an individual color.

Viewing the Assets Panel

Dreamweaver lists your site's assets on the nine category "pages" of the Assets panel (Figure 14-13). To open the panel, choose Window→Assets, or press F11.

WORKAROUND WORKSHOP

Printing Your Site Map

After perfecting your site map, you may want to make a hard copy of it. While Dreamweaver won't print the Site Map (why, Macromedia, why?), you can save it as a graphic and then print it. In Site Map view, do one of the following:

Windows: Choose File→Save Site Map. Choose a file format—PNG or BMP—for the graphic, name it, and save it to your computer.

Macintosh: Choose Site→Site Map View→Save Site Map→Save Site Map as JPEG or Save Site Map as PICT. Name the file and save it to your computer.

To print the resulting graphics file, double-click it to open it into, say, Image Viewer (Windows) or Preview (Macintosh). You can print it from there.

You select an asset in the list by clicking its name; a miniature preview appears above the Assets list. To preview a movie, click the green arrow that appears in the preview window.

Figure 14-13:
Most of the commands in the Context menu are duplicated in the panel itself, but three options appear only on this menu. Recreate Site List comes in handy if you've added or deleted files outside Dreamweaver; it rebuilds the site cache and updates the list of assets. Copy to Site copies the selected asset to another site. Locate in Site opens the Site panel and highlights the file of the asset you selected in the Assets panel. You can also open a contextual menu by right-clicking (Control-clicking) any asset in the list.

The assets panel highlights nine different categories of site elements. To view the assets in a particular category, click its icon at the left of the Assets panel.

- The **Images** category lists all of the GIF, JPEG, and PNG files in your site.

- The **Colors** category shows all of the colors specified in the Web pages and embedded style sheets of your site. These include link colors, background colors, and text colors. Unfortunately, it doesn't include colors you've specified in linked style sheets. (For more detail on linked style sheets, see page 238.)

- The **URLs** category lists all external links—not just standard *http://* links, but also email links, FTP addresses, and JavaScript links. (For an example of a JavaScript link, see the box on page 367.)

- The **multimedia** categories—Flash, Shockwave, and Movies— are roughly equivalent. They each display movie files with their corresponding extensions: .swf (Flash), .dcr (Shockwave), and .mov or .mpg (QuickTime and MPEG).

- The **Scripts** category lists JavaScript or VBScript files. This category only includes external script files that Web pages link to. Scripts that are embedded into a Web page—like those created using Dreamweaver Behaviors—are not listed.

• 📄 📖 The last two categories—**Templates** and **Library**—are advanced assets that streamline Web site production. They're discussed in depth in Chapters 17 and 18.

You can switch between two different views for each asset category—Site and Favorites—by clicking the radio buttons near the top of the Assets panel. The Site option lists all the assets that appear in the Site for the chosen category. Favorites lets you create a select list of your most important and frequently used assets (facing page).

Note: Dreamweaver MX's new cloaking feature lets you hide files from many sitewide tasks including the Assets panel. So, if you have a folder with thousands of image files that you'd rather not appear on the Assets panel, you can hide that folder and its files. See page 492 for more on this new feature.

If, as you are working on a site, you add additional assets—for example, you create a new GIF image in Fireworks and import it to the site—you'll need to update the Assets panel. Click the Refresh List button (🔄) to update the list of assets.

Inserting Assets

The Assets panel's prime mission is to make using assets easier. From the Assets list, you can add graphics, colors, and links to your pages with a click of the mouse. Most of the categories on the panel refer to external files that you can include on a Web page: images, Flash, Shockwave, movies, and scripts.

The easiest way to insert an asset file is to drag it from the Assets panel into the document window. You can drag the asset anywhere on the page you'd normally insert an object: in a table cell, at the beginning or end of a page, or within a paragraph. Script assets can go in the head of a Web page (see Figure 14-14).

POWER USERS' CLINIC

The Return of Root-Relative Paths

Chapter 4 explains the different types of link paths—absolute, document-relative, and root-relative—that Dreamweaver understands (see page 91). While it's best to use document-relative paths for linking to pages within your own site, or for adding images and other media to a page, you may notice that Dreamweaver frequently displays root-relative paths in its site-management tools.

For instance, the list in the Assets panel includes the full root-relative path of each asset: */images_home/banner.gif*, for example. The initial / indicates the root folder of the site, and the information that follows indicates the rest of the path to that asset. In this example, the graphic asset *banner.gif* is in a folder called *images_home*, which is itself in the site's root folder. Dreamweaver needs to look no further than the root folder to find the asset in question.

Root-relative paths indicate a precise location within a site and let Dreamweaver know where to find a file. This doesn't mean, however, that *you* should use root-relative paths in your Web sites. Use document-relative paths; let Dreamweaver do its own thing.

(If you're billing by the hour, you may prefer the long way: click in the document window to plant the insertion point, click the asset's name, and then click Insert at the bottom of the Assets panel.)

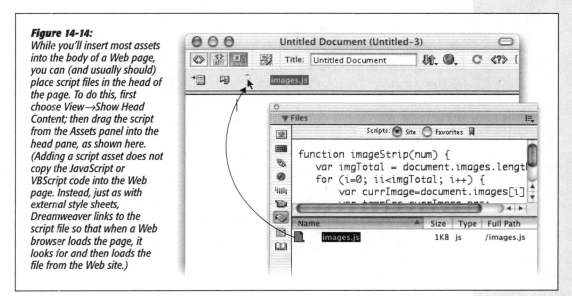

Figure 14-14:
While you'll insert most assets into the body of a Web page, you can (and usually should) place script files in the head of the page. To do this, first choose View→Show Head Content; then drag the script from the Assets panel into the head pane, as shown here. (Adding a script asset does not copy the JavaScript or VBScript code into the Web page. Instead, just as with external style sheets, Dreamweaver links to the script file so that when a Web browser loads the page, it looks for and then loads the file from the Web site.)

Adding color and link assets

Color and link assets work a bit differently than other asset files. Instead of standing on their own, they *add* color or a link to images or text you've selected in the document window. (You can add colors to any text selection, or add links to images and text.) In this way, you can quickly add a frequently used link—the URL to download the Flash player or Adobe Acrobat reader, for example.

To do so, start by highlighting the text (to change its color or turn it into a link) or image (to turn it into a link). In the Assets panel, click the appropriate category button—Colors or Links. Click the color or link you want, and then click Apply. (Alternatively, you can drag the color or link asset from the panel to the selection.)

Note: Applying color to text using the Assets panel simply wraps the selected text in a <font> tag. If you're using style sheets to format your pages, see the box below for another method of using color assets.

Favorite Assets

On a large site, you may have thousands of image files, movie files, colors, and external links. Because scrolling through long lists of assets can be a chore, Dreamweaver lets you create a compact list of your favorite, frequently used assets.

For example, you might come up with five main colors that define your site's color scheme, which you'll use much more often than the other miscellaneous colors on the Assets list. Add them to your list of favorite colors. Likewise, adding graphics files you use over and over—logos, for example—to a list of favorites makes it easy to locate and insert those files into your pages. (Don't forget that you can also use Dreamweaver's Library and Template features for this function. They're similar but more powerful tools for keeping frequently used items at the ready. Turn to Chapter 18 for the details.)

Identifying your Favorites

If the color, graphic, or other element to be added to your Favorites list already appears on your Assets panel, highlight it in the list and then click the Add to Favorites button (**■**).

Even quicker, you can also add favorites as you go, snagging them right from your Web page in progress. If you're working on your site's home page and you insert a company logo, for example, that's a perfect time to make the logo a favorite asset.

Simply right-click (Control-click) the image. From the contextual menu, choose Add to Favorites. Dreamweaver instantly adds the graphic to your list of favorites. You can do the same with Flash, Shockwave, and QuickTime files, as well as with links. (Unfortunately, this shortcut doesn't work for colors and script files.)

When it comes to colors and links, there's another way to turn them into Favorites. In the Assets panel, select the Color or URLs category, click the Favorites radio button, and then click the New Asset button (**■**). Then:

- If you're adding a favorite color, the Dreamweaver color box appears. Select a color using the eyedropper (see page 34).

- If you're adding a favorite link, the Add URL window opens. Type an absolute URL in the first field, either a Web address starting with *http://* or an *email* link

---

GEM IN THE ROUGH

Better Use of Color Assets

Although color assets are only meant for coloring text, you can use them any time Dreamweaver's eyedropper tool appears, such as when you're about to apply color to tables, table cells, links, pages, and other elements. In other words, anytime you need a frequently used color, you can hop right to the assets panel rather than pecking around on the color palette or trying to find another occurrence of the color on your screen.

Whenever you click a color box—in the Page Properties window,

Property inspector, or Style Definition window, for example—a color palette appears, and the cursor changes to an eyedropper. You could, of course, use this eyedropper to pick a color from the palette or to sample a color from the screen. But if you've already used the color in your site—or saved it in the Favorites list (see above)—just grab it from the Assets panel. To do so, move the eyedropper to the colored swatch in the Assets list and click.

(*mailto:subscriptions@cosmofarmer.com*). Next, type a name for the link in the Nickname field—Netscape Download or Subscription Email, for instance—and then click OK.

Your new color or link appears in the Favorites list.

Using your Favorites

You insert assets from the Favorites list into your Web pages just as you would any assets; see page 444.

Removing Favorites

Removing assets from the Favorites list is as straightforward as adding them: just select one in the Favorites list of your Assets panel and then press Delete. The Remove from Favorites button ( ) on the Assets panel does the same thing; yet another approach is to use the Context menu (see Figure 14-13).

Don't worry; removing an asset from the Favorites list *doesn't* delete that asset from the Assets panel—only from the Favorites list. You can still find it listed if you click the Site radio button.

Organizing Favorite assets

On a large site with lots of important assets, even a Favorites list can get unwieldy. That's why you can set up folders within the Assets panel to organize your assets. For example, if you use lots of ads on a site, create a folder in the Image assets Favorites called Ads or, for even greater precision, create multiple folders for different types of ads: Banner Ads, Half Banner Ads, and so on.

You can then drag assets into the appropriate folders, and you can expand or contract each folder to show or hide the assets inside (see Figure 14-15). (These folders simply help you organize your Assets panel; they don't actually appear anywhere

Figure 14-15:
In addition to using folders to organize your favorites, you can also give a favorite asset an easily identifiable nickname. Instead of listing a favorite image using its file name—148593.gif—use an easily understood name like New Product. Naming favorite colors can be particularly helpful—a nickname like Page Background is more descriptive than #FF6633. To name a favorite asset, click to select it, pause a moment, and click again to edit its name. (These nicknames only apply in the Assets panel; they don't rename or retitle your files.)

within the structure of your site. Moving a favorite asset into a folder in the Assets panel doesn't change the location of files within your site.)

To create a Favorites folder, click the appropriate category button at the left edge of the Assets panel (any except the bottom two; you can't create folders for Templates and Library items). Click Favorites at the top of the Assets panel (you can't create folders in Site view). Finally, click the folder button () at the bottom of the Assets panel. When the new folder appears with its naming rectangle highlighted, type a new name for the folder and then press Enter. (Don't use the same name for more than one folder.)

To put an asset into a folder, just drag it there from the list. And if you're really obsessive, you can even create subfolders by dragging one folder onto another.

Testing Your Site

A s you've no doubt realized by now, there are quite a few steps involved in building a Web site. At any point in the process, it's easy to introduce errors that affect the performance of your pages. Both small mistakes, like typos, and site-shattering errors, like broken links, occur frequently in the Web development cycle.

Unfortunately, Web designers often don't develop a good procedure for testing their sites. This chapter offers some helpful techniques for testing your site, including using Dreamweaver's wide array of site testing tools.

Site Launch Checklist

Don't wait until you've finished your site before embarking on a thorough strategy of testing. By that time, serious design errors may have so completely infested the pages of your site that you may have to start over, or at least spend many hours fixing problems that could have been prevented early on.

- **Preview early and often.** The single best way to make sure a page will look and function the way you want it to is to preview it in as many Web browsers as possible. Use Dreamweaver's Preview command (see Chapter 1) to preview your page in every browser you can get your hands on. Make sure the graphics look right, that your layout remains the same, and that advanced technologies like Cascading Style Sheets, Dreamweaver Behaviors, and layers work as intended.

  For a thorough evaluation, however, you should preview your pages using every combination of browser *and* operating system you think your site's visitors might use. Enroll co-workers, family members, and household pets, if necessary, in this effort. At the very least, test your pages using Internet Explorer 5 and 6, and (to a lesser extent) Netscape 4, on *both* Mac and Windows. If you have access to an AOL account—like 34 million other people around the world—use it. And as the population of Netscape 7, Mozilla, and Opera users grows, add these to your test schedule, too.

Unfortunately, you'll discover that what works on one browser/operating system combination may not work on another. That's why you should preview your designs *early* in the process of constructing your site. If you design a page that doesn't work well in Netscape 4 on the Mac, for example, it's better to catch and fix that problem immediately than discover it after you've built 100 pages based on that design.

- **Check pages in target browsers.** Dreamweaver's Check Target Browsers command (see the facing page) is a helpful diagnostic tool; it analyzes the code of your Web pages and checks for compatibility with various versions of Netscape Navigator and Internet Explorer.

  Once again, take this step early in the process of building your site. After completing a preliminary design for your home page, for example, use this tool to see if the code will work in the browsers you're aiming for.

- **Validate your pages.** Dreamweaver MX includes a new tool that lets you compare your Web pages against agreed-upon standards for HTML and other Web languages. It checks to make sure your pages are *valid* (that they conform to these standards).

  Valid pages are more likely to work on all Web browsers—not just Internet Explorer. And if you envision your site on mobile devices such as cell phones and palmtops, valid pages are again a better bet. In fact, you can even validate your Web pages to see if they conform to Wireless Markup Language (WML).

- **Check for accessibility.** Not everyone experiences the Web in the same way. People with poor vision, for example, will miss out on the beautiful, full-color banner and navigation buttons you've created. To help you build Web sites that don't shut out people with disabilities, Dreamweaver MX can check your Web site to make sure it conforms to Section 508 (a regulation mandating that Web sites built by or for the Federal Government are accessible to those with disabilities).

Some troubleshooting steps should come at the end of the process, when a page (or entire site) is ready to be moved to a Web server:

- **Check spelling on your pages.** Amazingly, this simple step is often overlooked. As a result, it's easy to find otherwise professional-looking Web pages on the Internet that are undermined by sloppy spelling. To learn how to use Dreamweaver's built-in spell checker, see page 57.

- **Check your links.** As the name indicates, a Web site can be a complex and twisted collection of interconnected files. Web pages, graphics, Flash movies, and other types of files all work together. Unfortunately, if one file is moved or deleted, problems can ripple through the entire site. Use Dreamweaver's Check Links command to identify and fix broken links (see page 458).

- **Run site reports.** It's always the little things. When building a Web site, small errors inevitably creep into your pages. While not necessarily life-threatening, forgetting to title a Web page or to add an Alt property to an image does diminish the quality and professionalism of a site. Use Dreamweaver's site-reporting feature to quickly identify these problems (see page 468).

Check Target Browsers

As noted earlier in this book, different browsers don't always display HTML in the same way. What's worse, older browsers don't even *understand* a lot of the code that Dreamweaver can produce, because it may conform to HTML standards that were developed only in recent years.

The best way to ensure that visitors see your site the way you intend it is to frequently preview your pages in as many browsers on as many computers as possible. In this way, you can identify and fix problems early.

But if you don't happen to have old computers with old browsers lying around your basement, Dreamweaver can identify elements of a page that won't work in older browsers, or that might be supported by only a single browser. For example, the <layer> tag (see page 381) works *only* in Netscape 4, while the <marquee> tag is specific to Internet Explorer.

The File→Check Target Browsers command checks the HTML of pages you've selected and generates a report that tells you if you've used code that doesn't work in various versions of Internet Explorer or Netscape Navigator. You can choose which versions of the browsers you'd like to test, all the way back to the 2.0 version, which is still being used by Jason P. O'Gillicuddy of Muddy Ditch, Kansas.

Dreamweaver then creates a Web page listing any errors it's found (see Figure 15-1). The most common culprits are Cascading Style Sheets, layers, and JavaScript created by Dreamweaver's Behaviors. These relatively new Web technologies work only in the more recent browsers—versions 4 and later.

Keep in mind that Dreamweaver doesn't actually *test* your pages in these different browsers. It merely compares the HTML in your page against a series of files—called browser profiles—that identifies which HTML tags the various browsers understand. In other words, don't count on this feature to help you with the subtle differences between browsers—such as Navigator 4's troubles with layers (documented in Chapter 12). Just because a browser is programmed to understand a particular piece of HTML doesn't mean it always does the job correctly. Throughout this book, you'll find information on these kinds of problems, but there's no substitute for thoroughly testing your pages in as many browsers as you can find.

Once you've identified any errors, you can either choose to remove the offending code—perhaps by getting rid of a rollover effect or abandoning layers—or live with the fact that not everyone on earth will be able to view your site.

Tip: One effective strategy in solving such problems involves Dreamweaver's Check Browser behavior, which is described on page 351. You can use this feature to direct visitors to pages that you've built specifically for their browser version.

If your Web site absolutely must work with older versions of browsers, you'll need to steer clear of layers and other new technologies, and use the Check Target Browsers command. But before abandoning such useful and advanced features, keep in mind that well over 90 percent of the Web-surfing public uses version 4 or later of Internet Explorer or Netscape Navigator.

Select files
Stop checking
More information
Save results
View results as
Web page

Figure 15-1:
If the description of the error doesn't completely fit inside the results window, click More Information to open a new window with a complete description.

You can check either an open page or any or all pages in a site by following these steps.

1. **Choose Window→Results→Target Browser Check.**

   The keyboard shortcut is Shift+Ctrl+F8 (Shift-Control-F8). Either way, you open the Results panel to the Target Browser Check tab (see Figure 15-1).

Tip: If you want to check just the page you're working on, then save it (the command works on the last *saved* version of the file) and choose File→Check Page→Check Target Browsers.

---

2. **Using the green arrow in the Target Browser Check panel, select which files to check.**

   The green arrow provides a menu with three options. The first checks the page you're currently working on. The second option checks all pages in your site, and the final option checks only files (or folders of files) you've selected in the Site panel. (For tips on selecting files in the Site panel, see the box on page 460).

   Dreamweaver opens the Check Target Browsers dialog box (see Figure 15-2.)

3. **Select one or more browsers from the list.**

   To select more than one browser, Ctrl-click (⌘-click) their names. (Similarly, Ctrl-click or ⌘-click a browser name to remove it from a selection you've built up.)

4. **Click Check.**

   Dreamweaver checks each page and generates a list of any errors it finds (see Figure 15-2).

Tip: Dreamweaver 4 used to produce a Web page, rather than a dialog box, listing the errors. If you prefer that view, click the globe icon in the Check Target Browser panel (see Figure 15-1). To save a file with the results, click the floppy disk icon. You could, for example, consult the saved file as a checklist for fine-tuning each page and removing any egregious errors.

Figure 15-2:
You can check the HTML of your pages against the capabilities of any or all of the browsers listed, but limit your choices to the browsers your visitors will be using. If you choose an old browser like Netscape Navigator 2.0, Dreamweaver will generate a long list of errors, since most of the HTML code Dreamweaver generates weren't even around back when Navigator 2.0 was in circulation.

5. **Review the results.**

   The results list displays three columns of information: the name of the file with errors; the line number the error occurs on; and a description of the error, including which browser won't work with the code. (The line numbers refer to lines in the HTML code of your page. See Chapter 9 for details on Code view.)

   An error appears when a browser doesn't understand a particular HTML tag or property. For example, Internet Explorer 3 has a very limited understanding of JavaScript; therefore, you'll see an error listed for every page where you used an *image rollover* effect (page 126). The error indicates that IE 3 doesn't understand the JavaScript code, and the rollover won't work.

   Don't panic if you run this command on your site and see lots of errors. The errors don't mean that *you* made mistakes. They simply indicate that one of the browsers you selected doesn't understand some of the tags Dreamweaver inserted.

   Furthermore, Dreamweaver is often smart enough to use *two* tags—one each for Navigator and Internet Explorer—to get the job done. For example, to eliminate the margin that appears at the left edge of a page, you have to set the Left Margin *and* Margin Width properties of the page (see step 10 on page 33). But because Navigator doesn't understand the Left Margin property (it only works in Internet Explorer), you'll still get an error if you check your page against Navigator browsers. In other words, an error reported by Dreamweaver doesn't necessarily mean that your page won't work in a specified browser.

This command is a good way to quickly learn about the different HTML tags each browser recognizes. In time, you'll probably know enough to avoid using elements that don't work for the browsers your visitors use, and you'll find this command unnecessary.

Validating Web Pages

The Web is a far-flung collection of technologies, programming languages, and people all working together. When you think about it, it's pretty amazing that an 11-year-old in Fargo, North Dakota can create a Web site viewable by millions of people around the world, or even that hundreds of different browsers, from Internet Explorer to cell phones, can browse the same Web site. This kind of global communication owes its success in large part to the World Wide Web Consortium (the W3C), an organization composed of representatives from universities, research institutions, corporations, and government agencies dedicated to creating standards for different Internet-related technologies.

The W3C developed standards for HTML, XHTML, CSS, XML, and other Web languages, and continues to create new standards as technologies evolve. Thanks to these standards, companies have a guide to follow when creating new Web browsers.

It sure would be great if all companies followed the standards when building Web browsers, and all Web designers followed the standards when building Web pages. Then anyone with any Web browser could view any Web page. What a wonderful world *that* would be—you'd never have to test your Web pages in different browsers.

Of course, this kind of utopian thinking hasn't always been applied by the major browser makers, Netscape and Microsoft. As a result, Web developers have been forced to come up with techniques to deal with the way different browsers display HTML.

Fortunately, the situation is improving; browser makers are making more of an effort these days to stick to the W3C's recommended standards. And you can, too: Dreamweaver MX includes a new tool for making sure your pages meet the standards set by the W3C.

Setting Validation Preferences

There are different standards for different versions of HTML. In fact, there are different standards for many other languages you could potentially use on the Web, including XHTML (page 5) and Cold Fusion Markup Language (Macromedia's server-side programming language). Before you get started, you need tell Dreamweaver which of these standards it should validate your Web pages against.

To set validation preferences, choose Edit→Preferences. In the Preferences window, select the Validator category (see Figure 15-3) and turn on the languages you want Dreamweaver to validate against.

You'll notice that sometimes you can select more than one option, and sometimes you can't. That's because the HTML 2.0 standard is part of the HTML 4.0 standard. So if you select HTML 4.0, there's no need to also select HTML 2.0.

Tip: There are many options, so here are some tips for getting started: If you're creating regular HTML pages, choose HTML 4.0, since most browsers understand this version. If you've decided to upgrade to XHTML, turn on XHTML 1.0 Transitional, which is the kind of XHTML that Dreamweaver generates. (If you're using frames, however, select XHTML 1.0 Frameset. Dreamweaver doesn't follow the XHTML 1.0 Strict standard in its own code, so you'll run into constant errors if you validate a Dreamweaver-generated page using this option.)

You're now ready to validate, as described in the next section.

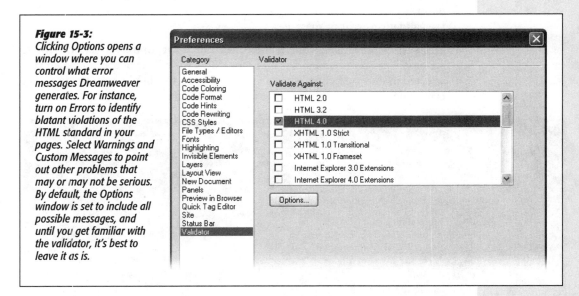

Figure 15-3:
Clicking Options opens a window where you can control what error messages Dreamweaver generates. For instance, turn on Errors to identify blatant violations of the HTML standard in your pages. Select Warnings and Custom Messages to point out other problems that may or may not be serious. By default, the Options window is set to include all possible messages, and until you get familiar with the validator, it's best to leave it as is.

Validating Web Pages

Once you've set up the validator preferences, you can check either an open page or any pages selected in the Site panel (page 460) by following these steps:

1. **Choose Window→Results→Validation.**

   The keyboard shortcut is Shift+Ctrl+F7 (Shift-Control-F7). Either way, the Results panel opens, showing the Validation tab (Figure 15-4).

---

2. **In the Validation panel, click the green arrow and select which files to check.**

   The green arrow reveals a menu with five options. The first checks the page you're currently working on. The third option checks all pages in your site, and the fourth option checks just those files which are selected in the Site panel.

   Selecting Settings from this menu opens the Validator Preferences window shown in Figure 15-3.

Note: You can also validate the file as an XML file by choosing Validate as XML. (Note to the technical: This option merely makes sure the XML is "well-formed." It doesn't check it against a Document Type Definition [DTD].)

3. **Review the results.**

   Dreamweaver displays the results in the Validation panel (Figure 15-4). Each validation message is divided into three columns: the first lists the file, the second lists which line in the code the message applies to, and the third describes the validation error or message.

   Messages begin with an icon that indicates the severity of the validation error. A red stop sign identifies a violation of the standards of one of the languages you selected in the Preferences window. In some cases, this might indicate that a tag is missing or incorrectly closed—a serious problem.

GEM IN THE ROUGH

Is the Validator Valid?

The intentions behind Dreamweaver's Validation tool are commendable: to help you make pages that work on more browsers for more people. However, if you don't have a fundamental understanding of the validation process, you may come to the incorrect conclusion that your Web site is a rotten mess of invalid code.

Say you've built a dynamic, database-driven Web site like those described in Part 6. Dynamic Web pages contain *server-side* programs that include lots of programming code. That code is processed on the Web server's side of the Internet, on what's called an *application server.* Once the application server does its business by accessing a database, retrieving information and incorporating it into a

final Web page, the end result is a Web page like any other: HTML code without the programming.

The problem is, Dreamweaver's validator doesn't validate the final product—just the complete document with all its Visual Basic, Java, Cold Fusion Markup, or PHP programming code. Since Dreamweaver can't distinguish that code from the HTML, you'll see all sorts of validation errors. In all likelihood, these errors *won't* be in the Web page your site's visitors see.

The best way to validate this type of page is to do it online: Put your finished dynamic page on a publicly accessible Web server and use the W3C's online validation tool located at *http://validator.w3.org/.*

Other stop-sign errors aren't necessarily fatal. For example, when you insert a Flash movie, Dreamweaver uses the <embed> tag to insert information needed by Netscape to play the movie—a tag that's deprecated in the HTML standards. You'll get all manner of errors if you validate a page containing this tag, even though it's necessary for viewing the Flash movie in Netscape.

Less serious problems are flagged with little message balloons. These may inform you that the page has *no* problems, or point out optional fixes. (See the next page for a list of common errors and messages.)

You may also encounter yellow "yield sign" icons. These indicate a potential problem that Dreamweaver couldn't completely evaluate. These usually occur when you validate against any of the HTML standards that have an unclosed <p> tag. Since the official HTML standard lets you get away with using a <p> tag without the closing </p>, Dreamweaver can't determine if this is a mistake or not.

Note: Dreamweaver MX can't validate CSS code. If you want to make sure your Cascading Style Sheets are valid, use the free online validation service from the W3C at *http://jigsaw.w3.org/css-validator/*.

The site provides several techniques for validating CSS. You can provide a URL to an external CSS file, copy and paste CSS code into a Web form, or upload a CSS file. Using any of these methods, you'll receive an online evaluation of your CSS code.

---

4. **Fix the errors.**

   Alas, Dreamweaver doesn't provide any tools for *fixing* validation errors. It's up to you and your knowledge of HTML to go into the code and fix any problems. For assistance, check out the online HTML reference (see page 288).

   To get started, double-click an error in the Validation results panel. The Web page opens in split view, with the invalid HTML code selected. You can then delete or modify the offending code. Keep in mind, though, that the code Dreamweaver produces is the result of many thousands of hours of engineering and testing. Unless you're sure you know how to fix a problem, you might just want to trust the code Dreamweaver produces.

Figure 15-4:
In addition to viewing coding errors here, you can save them errors as an XML file by clicking the disk icon (to preserve for future generations) or view them in a Web browser by clicking the globe icon.

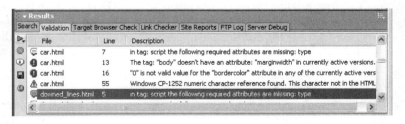

Common Validation Errors

Although a complete reference for creating valid Web sites would fill a book of its own, here are some errors you'll encounter frequently when using Dreamweaver's validator:

- **In HTML 4.0, FONT is deprecated.** You'll encounter this message whenever you've used the text formatting tools on the Property inspector. It indicates that the <font> tag is on its way out. The W3C is now recommending the use of Cascading Style Sheets (Chapter 8) for formatting text.

- **The tag: "embed" is not allowed within: "object." It is only allowed within: .** This cryptic, and incomplete, error appears when you insert Flash movies (including Flash Buttons and Flash Text, as described on page 128). Other errors related to the <embed> tag may also appear, including "The tag: 'embed' doesn't have an attribute: 'quality' in currently active versions." Ignore them.

- **In tag: script the following required attributes are missing: type.** This message indicates that the <script> tag used to insert JavaScript programs is missing the following Type property. Dreamweaver MX inserts this property correctly, but Dreamweaver 4 didn't. If you used Dreamweaver 4 to build your site, you'll get this error message for any page that uses a Dreamweaver behavior. To fix it, add *type="text/JavaScript"* to the <script> tag.

- **The tag: 'body' doesn't have an attribute: 'marginwidth' in currently active versions.** (Similar messages for "marginheight" may also appear.)

  If you set the left and top margin of a page using the Page Properties window (see step 10 on page 33), you'll encounter this message. This is a Netscape-specific property and not part of any HTML standard. Internet Explorer's Leftmargin and Topmargin properties are similarly browser-specific. Although this poses no real problems—other browsers ignore this property—the recommended solution is to use Cascading Style Sheets to set the margins of a page.

Find and Fix Broken Links

Broken links are inevitable. If you delete a file from your site, move a page or graphic outside of Dreamweaver, or simply type an incorrect path to a file, broken links and missing graphics may result. In the B.D. era (before Dreamweaver), the only way to fix such problems was to methodically examine every page and every link on every page in your site. Fortunately, Dreamweaver's link-checking features can automate the process of tracking down broken-link problems.

Note: In this context, a *link* doesn't only mean a hyperlink connecting one page to another. Dreamweaver also uses the term to include the paths that identify external files incorporated in your Web page, such as GIFs, JPEGs, external CSS style sheets, and Flash movies. For example, if a graphic is missing or isn't in the place specified by the Web page, Dreamweaver will report a broken *link*.

Finding Broken Links

The Check Links Sitewide command scans an entire site's worth of files and reports all links and paths that don't lead to a file. (It's one of Dreamweaver's site management features, meaning that you have to define a local site before using this command; see page 25.) Note that Dreamweaver only checks links and paths *within* the local site folder; it doesn't check links that lead to other people's Web sites.

Note: If your local site contains a lot of pages, you may want to not check the links in one or more folders whose pages *you know* have no broken links. You can exclude files from the Check Links Sitewide operation using the new Cloaking feature described on page 492. Doing so also makes the link-checking operation go faster.

Checking just one page

To check links on an open page, save it in your local site folder. Then choose File→Check Page→Check Links (or press Shift-F8). Dreamweaver scans the page and opens the Link Checker window, which lists files containing broken links (see Figure 15-5). If Dreamweaver doesn't find any broken links—you HTML god, you—the window comes up empty.

Checking specific pages

You can also check links just on specific pages of your site from the Link Checker panel:

1. **Choose Window→Results→Link checker.**

   The Link Checker panel opens.

2. **Use the Site panel to select the site you wish to check (see Figures 14-5 and 14-6 on pages 431 and 432).**

   If you're already working on the site you want to check, you can skip this step.

3. **In the Site panel, select the files you'd like to check.**

   For techniques on selecting files and folders in the Site panel, see the box on page 460.

Tip: Selecting a folder will make Dreamweaver scan all files in that folder.

---

4. **Click the green arrow icon in the Link Checker panel. From the menu that appears, choose Check Links for Selected Files/Folders in Site.**

   Alternatively, you can right-click (Control-click) the selected files, and then choose Check Links→Selected Files/Folders from the contextual menu.

   Either way, Dreamweaver scans the pages and opens the Link Checker panel (Figure 15-5).

Checking the entire Web site

You can check all the links on all pages of your Web site in either of two ways:

- Open the Web site you want to check (press F8 to open the Site panel and use the panel's menu to select the site), and then choose Site→Check Links Sitewide. (In the Windows version of Dreamweaver, this option only appears in the Site menu on the Site panel.) Or use the keyboard shortcut, Ctrl+F8 (⌘-F8).

- Open the Link Checker panel (Window→Results→Link Checker), click the green arrow icon and, from its menu, choose Check Links for Entire Site.

Once again, Dreamweaver scans your site and opens the Link Checker panel, which lists files containing broken links (Figure 15-5).

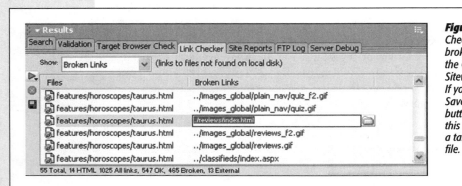

Figure 15-5:
Check your site for broken links using the Check Links Sitewide command. If you wish, click the Save (floppy disk) button to save all of this information into a tab-delimited text file.

Fixing Broken Links

Of course, simply finding broken links is only half the battle. You also need to *fix* them. The Link Checker panel provides a quick and easy way to do this:

1. **In the Link Checker panel, click a path in the Broken Links column (see Figure 15-5).**

   The path is highlighted, and a tiny folder icon appears to the right.

UP TO SPEED

Selection Shortcuts for the Site Panel

You'll often want to use the tools in the Results panel on more than one page in your Web site. Fortunately, most of these tools can work on multiple pages in the Site panel.

You probably can figure out that you should click a file to select it. But you can also select *several* files that are listed consecutively: Click the first one, scroll if necessary, and then, while pressing Shift, click the last one. Dreamweaver

highlights all the files between your first and final clicks.

If you want to select several files that aren't consecutive in the list, the trick is to click each one while pressing the Ctrl (⌘) key.

Once you've selected one or more files, you can *deselect* one by Ctrl-clicking (⌘-clicking) it once again.

Tip: The Link Checker panel shows you which pages *contain* broken links, but doesn't show you the text or images of the broken links themselves, which can make it difficult to figure out how you're supposed to fix them ("Was that a button that links to the home page?"). In such a case, *double-click* the file name in the Link Checker panel. Dreamweaver opens the Web page, and, even better, highlights the link on the page.

Once you've determined where the link should lead ("Oh yeah. That's the button to the haggis buffet menu"), you can fix the link on the page (see page 106) or go back to the Link Checker panel and make the change as described in the next step.

2. **Click the tiny folder icon.**

   The Select File dialog box opens. From here, you can navigate to and (in the next step) select the correct page—the one the broken link *should* open.

   If you prefer, you can type a path directly in the Link Checker panel. Doing so usually isn't a good idea, however, since it's difficult to understand the path from one page to another by just looking at the Link Checker panel. Searching for the proper page using the Select File dialog box is a much more accurate method.

3. **Double-click a Web page.**

   The dialog box disappears, and Dreamweaver fixes the link.

   If your Web site contains other links pointing to the same missing file, Dreamweaver asks if you'd like to update those pages, too—an amazing time saver that can quickly repair broken links on dozens of pages.

Note: Dreamweaver's behavior is a bit odd in this regard, however. Once you fix one link, it remains selected in the Link Checker panel. You must click another broken link, or one of the buttons in the window, before Dreamweaver asks if you'd like to fix that same broken link on other pages.

4. **Continue to fix broken links, following steps 1 through 3.**

   When you've repaired all the broken links, click the close button.

Listing External Links

Although Dreamweaver doesn't verify links to other Web sites on your pages, it does show you a list of such *external links* when you run the link checker. To see this list, choose External Links from the Show menu of the Link Checker panel (see Figure 15-6). The list includes absolute URLs leading to other sites (like *www.yahoo.com*) as well as email links (like *mailto:Webmaster@cosmofarmer.com*).

This window can be especially useful if, for example, you've created a link to a certain external Web site several times throughout your Web site:

1. **Choose Site→Check Links Sitewide (or press Ctrl+F8 [⌘-F8]).**

   (Windows users must use the Site menu on the Site panel.) Dreamweaver scans your site and opens the Link Checker panel.

2. **From the Show pop-up menu, choose External Links.**

The window lists links you've created to sites outside your own.

3. **Click the external link you want to change.**

Dreamweaver highlights the link, indicating that you can now edit it.

4. **Type the new URL; press Enter.**

If other pages contain the old URL, Dreamweaver asks if you would like to up-date them as well. If so, click Update; the deed is done.

Figure 15-6:
Although Dreamweaver can't check external links, you can use this window to change the URL of an external link. You can save the list of external links in a tab-delimited text file; click the Save (floppy disk) button to do so (this saves information on all broken links and orphaned files as well). You could use this as a checklist for manually verifying that the external links work.

Orphaned Files

The Link Checker panel also provides a list of files that aren't used by any Web page in the site—*orphaned* files, as they're called. You wind up with an orphaned graphic file when, for example, you save a GIF into your site folder, but then never use it on a Web page. Or suppose you eliminate the only link to an old page that you don't need any more, making it an orphaned file. Unless you think you might link to it in the future, you can delete it to clean up unnecessary clutter in your site.

In fact, that's the primary purpose of this feature: to locate old and unused files and delete them. Here's how it works:

1. **Choose Site→Check Links Sitewide, or press Ctrl+F8 (⌘-F8).**

Dreamweaver opens the Link Checker panel.

2. **From the Show menu, choose Orphaned Files.**

The list of orphaned files appears (see Figure 15-7).

3. **Select the files you want to delete.**

You can use any of the selection methods described on page 460.

4. Press Delete.

Dreamweaver asks if you really want to delete the files. Click OK if you do, or Cancel if you suddenly get cold feet.

Figure 15-7:
Identify (and delete) unused files using Dreamweaver's Link Checker. Because the Link Checker can find external links and orphaned files as well as broken links, you'll probably use this box a few times, using the Show menu to isolate the different types of link.

5. Click the close button when you're finished.

Before you get spring-cleaning fever and delete all orphaned files in your site, however, keep a few pointers in mind:

- Just because a file isn't *currently* being used doesn't mean you may not want it later. For example, say you have an employee of the month page. In March, you included a photo of Robin Albert, your best salesperson. In April, someone else got the award, so you removed Robin's photo. Just because you're not using that photo now—rendering it an orphaned file—doesn't mean that next month you won't need it again, when Robin develops a spurt of motivation. Make sure a file is really useless before deleting it.

- More important, Dreamweaver may flag orphaned files your site actually needs. For example, some sites include what's called a *splash page:* an introductory page that first appears when someone comes to the site. It might be a page with a bold graphic and the text "Click here to enter the site." Or it might be a fancy Flash movie intended to make a big impact on your visitors. Usually, this page is nothing more than a welcome mat that leads to the *real* home page. Since it's simply an introductory page, no other page in the site links to it. Unfortunately, that's precisely what Dreamweaver considers an orphaned file.

- If you write your own JavaScript code, you may reference graphic files and Web pages. Dreamweaver doesn't keep track of these references, and will identify those files as orphans (unless they're inserted or linked to elsewhere in the page or site).

On the other hand, Dreamweaver is somewhat smarter when it comes to Behaviors. It can track files referenced as part of its own JavaScript programs—for example, graphic files you use in a rollover effect—and doesn't list them as orphaned files.

The bottom line is that while this report is useful, use it cautiously when deleting files.

Changing a Link Throughout a Site

Suppose you've created a page on your site to teach your visitors about the basics of the HTML language. You think this would be really, really helpful to your visitors, so you create links to it from every page on your site. After a while, you realize you just don't have the time to keep this page up-to-date, but you still want to help your visitors get this information. Why not change the link so it points to a more current and informative source? Using Dreamweaver's Change Link Sitewide command, you can do just that.

1. **Choose Site→Change Link Sitewide.**

   The Change Link Sitewide dialog box opens (see Figure 15-8).

Note for Windows Users: The Site menu appears on the Site panel *and* on Dreamweaver's main menu. However, only the menu on the Site panel offers the Change Link Sitewide command. (If the Site panel is closed, press F8 to open it.)

This dialog box offers two different fields: Change All Links To and Into Links To. Understanding what you're supposed to do at this point is easier if you imagine that the first label is actually "Change All Links That *Currently* Point To." In other words, first you'll indicate where those links point now; then you'll indicate where you'd like them to go instead.

At this point, you can type the new Web address into the Change All Links To field. For example, if your aim is to round up every link that now points to Yahoo and redirect them to Google, you could start by typing *www.yahoo.com* here.

If the links you're trying to change refer to a page in your own site, however, proceed like this:

2. **Click the folder icon to the right of the Change All Links To field.**

   The Select Link to Change dialog box opens. You're about to specify the file that the links point to *now*.

Figure 15-8:
Dreamweaver uses a root-relative link to specify the page, as indicated by the slash (/). Don't worry: this doesn't mean Dreamweaver will make the link root-relative. It's just how Dreamweaver identifies the location of the page in the site. See page 92 for more on root-relative links.

3. **Select a file in the local site folder; click Select (Windows) or Save (Mac).**

In the following steps, Dreamweaver will change every link that leads to *this file*, whether it's a graphic, cascading style sheet file, or any other external file that can be part of a Web page.

Tip: As a shortcut to following steps 1, 2, and 3, you can select a file in the Site panel, *then* choose Site→Change Link Sitewide. Dreamweaver automatically adds the selected file's path to the Change All Links To field.

Now it's time to substitute the new URL or file—the one to which all of those links will be redirected. If you're reassigning them to a different Web site, you can type its URL directly into the Change All Links To field. For instance, in the previous example, you can type *www.google.com*.

Tip: For a quicker way to change one external link into another, see Figure 15-6.

If you'd like the changed links to point to a file on your own Web site instead, proceed like this:

4. **Click the folder icon to the right of the Into Links To field.**

The Select Link to Change dialog box opens.

5. **Select a file in the local site, and then click Select (Windows) or Save (Mac).**

You've just selected the new file you wish to link to. In other words, every link that once led to the file you selected in step 3 will now link to this file. You can select graphics, cascading style sheet files, and any other external files you can include in a Web page.

You'll get unpredictable results, however, if you change a link that points to a graphic file into, say, a link that points to a Web page, or vice versa. Make sure the "before" and "after" links share the same file type: Web page, style sheet, or graphic.

6. **Click OK to make the change.**

The same Update Files dialog box you encountered in the last chapter appears, listing every page that will be affected.

7. **Click Update to update the pages.**

Dreamweaver scans your site and updates the pages.

Cleaning Up HTML

You've been reading about what great HTML code Dreamweaver writes, and how all you hand-coders need to get on the WYSIWYG bandwagon. But there are exceptions to every rule. In the process of formatting text, deleting elements, and—in general—building a Web page, it's quite possible to end up with less-than-optimal HTML coding. While Dreamweaver usually catches potentially sloppy HTML, you may nonetheless run across instances of empty tags, redundant tags, and nested <font> tags in your Dreamweaver pages.

For example, if you attach a link to some picture and text, and later delete the linked item, Dreamweaver may leave the leftover code for the link in place like this:

```
<a href="index.html"> </a>
```

This empty tag doesn't serve any purpose and only adds unnecessary code to your page. Remember, the less code your page uses, the faster it loads. Therefore, eliminating redundant tags can improve the download speed of your site.

Another possible source of errors is you. When you type HTML in Code view or open pages created by another program, you may introduce errors that you'll need to clean up later.

Note: Dreamweaver MX is much better at housecleaning than Dreamweaver 4. You'll have less clean up to do, because MX is far less likely to cause most of these problems in the first place.

Aware of its own limitations (and yours), Dreamweaver comes with a command that's designed to streamline the code in your pages: Clean Up HTML. This command not only improves the HTML in your page, it can also strip out other nonessential code such as comments and special Dreamweaver markup code, and eliminate a specific tag or tags.

Tip: The Clean Up HTML command is extremely useful. Once you've tried it a few times, you'll probably want to use it on all your pages. Unfortunately, it doesn't come with a keyboard shortcut. This is a classic case when Dreamweaver's *keyboard shortcuts editor* is just the white knight you need; using it, you can add a key combination to trigger this command from the keyboard. See page 601 for details.

To use this command:

1. **Open a Web page to clean up.**

   Unfortunately, this great feature only works on one page at a time. No cleaning up a site's worth of pages in one fell swoop! Accordingly, it's best to first use the Site Reports feature (see page 468) to identify problem pages. *Then* open them in Dreamweaver and run this command.

2. **Choose Commands→Clean Up HTML.**

   The Clean Up HTML window appears (see Figure 15-9).

3. **Turn on the checkboxes for the options you want.**

   Here's a rundown:

Empty Tags deletes any tags that don't actually modify anything. For example, you might delete some text that had been set in boldface, leaving behind opening and closing bold tags without any text in between: <b></b>. Or you might delete an image within a link, leaving behind a useless pair of <a> tags. It's always a good idea to check this option.

Figure 15-9:
The Clean Up HTML command improves the speed of a Web page by stripping out redundant, useless code. The Specific Tags option can even strip out useful tags, although the Find and Replace command provides a much more powerful method; see page 585).

Redundant Nested Tags deletes tags that appear within other tags of the same type, like this: <b>You can't get any <b>bolder</b> than bold</b>. The second set of bold tags does no good, so choosing this option would produce this: <b>You can't get any bolder than bold</b>—an extremely useful option.

Non-Dreamweaver HTML Comments deletes any comments *not* inserted by someone using Dreamweaver. Web designers place notes within code to give directions or explain parts of the code. (These comments are invisible in a Web browser. They appear only in the Code view, or as a gold comment icon in the document window.) Since comments are often added as an aid for maintaining a Web page, you may not want to choose this option. However, if the page is finished, and you doubt you'll need the information the comments contain, you can decrease the file size of a page by using this option.

Dreamweaver Special Markup deletes any special code Dreamweaver inserts. Dreamweaver relies on certain code in some of its features, including tracing images (Chapter 6), Templates (Chapter 18), and Libraries (Chapter 17). Choosing this option also eliminates the special code that enables those features, so use this option with care. (Since the Template feature adds a great deal of this specialized code, Dreamweaver MX includes a Template Export command that lets you export an entire site with all Template code removed. See page 565.)

Specific Tag(s) deletes HTML tags you specify. Type the name of the tag (without brackets) in the field like this: *font.* To remove multiple tags at once, separate each tag name by a comma like this: *font, blink.*

Be careful with this option. Since it lets you remove *any* tag from a page, it's easy to delete an important and necessary tag (like the <body> tag) from your page by accident. Furthermore, Dreamweaver's Find and Replace command provides much more powerful tools for performing this kind of surgery (see Chapter 19).

Combine Nested <font> Tags when Possible combines multiple font properties into a single tag, as in the example above. This, too, is a useful option to turn on.

If you want to see a report of all the changes Dreamweaver makes to a page, turn on **Show Log on Completion**.

4. **Click OK to clean up the page.**

   If you selected Show Log on Completion, a dialog box then appears, listing the types and number of changes that Dreamweaver made to the page.

As long as you keep the page open, you can undo changes Dreamweaver made. Suppose you asked Dreamweaver to remove any comments, then suddenly realized you really did need them. Ctrl+Z (⌘-Z) will do the trick. You can also use the History panel, which lists this step as Clean Up HTML in (page 60).

Site Reporting

The Clean Up HTML command is a great way to make sure your code is well-written. But what if you forget about it until after you've built all 500 pages of your site? Do you have to open each page and run the command—whether there's a problem or not?

Fortunately, no. Dreamweaver's Site Reports feature makes identifying problems throughout a site a snap. As well as locating the problems fixed by the Clean Up HTML command, it makes Dreamweaver check your pages for other problems, such as missing titles, empty Alt properties for images, and other problems that might make your Web site less accessible to disabled Web surfers.

Tip: To save time when running a report, you can exclude select folders from a Site Report operation using the new Cloaking feature described on page 492.

After running a report, Dreamweaver displays a list of pages with problems. Unfortunately, the Site Reports feature only finds problems; it doesn't fix them. You have to open and fix each page individually.

To run a report on one or more Web pages, proceed like this:

1. **Choose Site→Reports.**

   The Reports window opens (see Figure 15-10).

2. **From the Report On menu, select the files to analyze.**

   Dreamweaver can report on a single Web page, multiple pages, or even an entire site. Choose **Current Document** to check the Web page that's open at the moment. **Entire Current Local Site** checks every Web page in the local site folder, including folders inside it. This option is great when you want to check your entire site prior to uploading it to a Web server and making it "live" (more on that in Chapter 16).

Selected Files in Site checks only the files you choose in the Site panel. You need to open the Site panel and select files in the local file list for this to work. (See the box on page 460 for methods on selecting files in the Site panel.) Choose this option when you've modified or added pages to a site, and are ready to move them to the Web server.

Folder checks all Web pages in a selected folder. After you choose this option, an empty field and a folder icon appear. Click the folder icon; a dialog box gives you the opportunity to locate and select the folder you wish to check, including any folders inside it. You can also use this option when you wish to check pages that aren't actually part of the current site.

Figure 15-10:
Dreamweaver's Site Reports feature makes quick work of finding common page errors. It's also one of Dreamweaver's many customizable features. You can download additional types of reports from the Macromedia Exchange Web site or even program your own. For more information on customizing Dreamweaver and using Macromedia Exchange, see page 606.

3. **Select the types of reports you want Dreamweaver to generate.**

The Reports window is divided into two types of reports. The first set, Workflow reports, deal with features that facilitate working with others as part of a production team (see the following chapter). The second type, HTML reports, are useful for locating common errors, such as forgetting to title a Web page or forgetting to add an Alt property to an image.

Three of the HTML report options—**Combinable Nested Font Tags**, **Redundant Nested Tags**, and **Removable Empty Tags**—search for pages with common code mistakes. These are the same problems fixed by the Clean Up HTML command (page 465).

The **Accessibility** report—new in Dreamweaver MX—lets you see how usable your site is to people with disabilities. This sophisticated command checks to see how well your pages conform to Web accessibility guidelines mandated by the U.S. Government and recommended by the W3C (page 114). This option produces detailed reports, so it's usually best to run it separately.

Turn on **Missing Alt Text** to search for pages with images that are missing an alternate text description (page 114). If you select the Accessibility option, you can leave this turned off; the Accessibility analyzer already includes missing Alt text.

Finally, turn on **Untitled Documents** to identify pages that are either missing a title or still have Dreamweaver's default title ("Untitled Document").

4. **Click Run.**

   Dreamweaver analyzes the pages you specified. It then produces a report that lists pages that match your report settings (see Figure 15-11). Each line in the Results window displays the name of the file, the line number where the error occurs, and a description of the error.

Note: Depending on the size of your site and the number of reports you choose to run, this feature can take a while to process. If you decide that the report is taking too long, you can always stop it by clicking the icon in the lower-right corner of the Results panel. It looks like a red stop sign with an X through it, and only appears while a report is running.

Figure 15-11:
Unfortunately, as part of the reporting process, Dreamweaver also searches files that aren't Web pages, such as the XML files that Dreamweaver produces behind the scene, as part of its normal routine. You can safely ignore files in your reports that end in .xml.

5. **In the results panel, double-click the file to open it.**

   Dreamweaver opens the file and automatically highlights the offending code.

6. **Fix the problem according to its type.**

For a page containing **Combinable Nested Font Tags**, **Redundant Nested Tags**, or **Removable Empty Tags** errors, use the Clean Up HTML command as described on page 465.

Figure 15-12:
The life cycle of a typical HTML error.

Top: After running a report, you might find a common HTML error like an empty link tag (top). Select the page in the Results window and click Open.

Second from top: The page opens with the offending code selected in split Code View. Since you can fix this particular error—and more—with the Clean Up HTML command, choose Commands→Clean Up HTML.

Middle: The Clean Up HTML window opens. Even though you can just clean up the error you identified earlier, it won't hurt to clean up other possible problems that might appear in your code (and somewhere else in the site report Results window). Click OK to clean up the HTML.

Bottom: Dreamweaver does its magic and reports back to you. Mission accomplished—code cleaned.

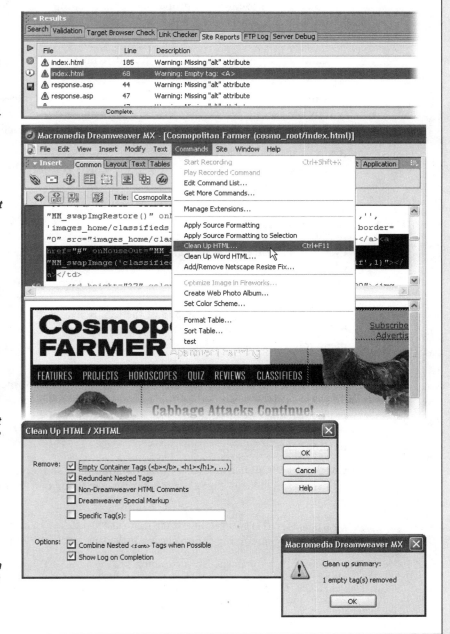

For pages missing a title, add one using the technique described in step 5 on page 32.

For Accessibility problems, read the detailed discussion below.

You can add **Missing Alt** properties using the Property inspector, as described on page 114, but you may find it faster to use Dreamweaver's powerful Find and Replace command (page 596).

7. **Continue opening files from the Results window and fixing them until you've corrected each mistake.**

Unfortunately, Dreamweaver doesn't provide a quick, one-step method to fix any of these problems. Except when using the Find and Replace tip for adding missing Alt text, you must open and fix each page individually.

If you want to save the results of your report, click the Save Report button. Dreamweaver opens a Save As dialog box, and lets you save the report as an XML file.

Accessibility

Even the clearest, most well-planned Web sites can pose a real challenge to people with vision problems. To make Web sites more accessible to them, the Web Accessibility Initiative (WAI)—a part of the World Wide Web Consortium—has proposed guidelines for the design of Web sites. In fact, the U.S. government has mandated its own set of guidelines (Section 508 of the U.S. Rehabilitation Act) for all Web sites built by and for the government. (And even if you're not working for the government, following these guidelines will improve your site by making it accessible to a larger audience.)

Dreamweaver MX provides several newly enhanced tools for meeting these guidelines and helping Web designers build more accessible sites (page 114). But for comprehensive analysis of your site, use the Accessibility site report. With it, you can evaluate your Web pages to make sure they comply with W3C guidelines and the requirements of Section 508.

Checking your site against accessibility standards is similar to running any other report. Follow steps 1–4 on page 468, taking care to turn on the Accessibility checkbox.

Once the report is complete—which may take awhile for an entire site—the process of identifying and fixing the errors is a little different than with other reports.

1. **Select an error in the Results panel (see Figure 15-3).**

Accessibility errors come with one of two designations: *Failed* and *Manual*. A failure (marked by a red X in the Results panel) indicates that some item on the page fails to meet one of the prescribed guidelines. The most common failure is missing Alt text for graphics.

"Manual" errors are those that Dreamweaver's not sure about. Check them manually and make corrections, if you deem them necessary.

In both cases, fixing the problems is up to you; Dreamweaver doesn't do any auto-fixing here.

Tip: You can set up the Insert Image command to help you with missing Alt tags; see page 114. In addition, you'll find some guidance in the new accessibility guide built into the Reference panel (page 288).

---

2. **Click the More Information (i) button in the Results panel.**

The Reference panel shows a description of the problem and techniques for fixing it (see Figure 15-13).

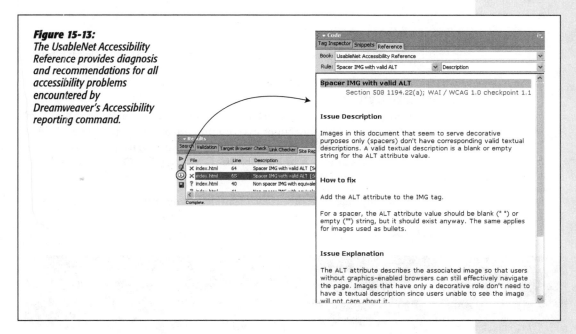

Figure 15-13:
The UsableNet Accessibility Reference provides diagnosis and recommendations for all accessibility problems encountered by Dreamweaver's Accessibility reporting command.

3. **Double-click the name of the file in the Results panel.**

As with other reports, Dreamweaver opens the file and automatically highlights the offending code. You can then make the recommended changes and save the page.

Accessibility Priorities

As you'll quickly learn, there are a *lot* of different guidelines for creating accessible sites. The whole issue can be confusing (some helpful resources are listed on the next page).

To get started, here are a few of the priority items recommended by the WAI:

- **Images, animations.** Use the Alt property to describe the function of each visual element on a page (page 114).

- **Image maps.** Make sure to provide Alt descriptions for each link in an image map (page 124).

- **Hypertext links.** Use understandable text for all links. Try reading it aloud to make sure the text clearly indicates where the link goes. Avoid "click here" links.

- **Organizing page content.** Use headings, lists, and consistent structure. Avoid the <font> tag; instead use Cascading Style Sheets for text styling.

- **Graphs, charts.** Summarize information contained in informational graphics.

- **Scripts, applets, plug-ins.** Provide alternative content in case active features are inaccessible or unsupported.

- **Frames.** Use the noframes element (see the box on page 205) and title each frame page.

Accessibility Options

Dreamweaver's accessibility report covers all the WAI recommendations and Section 508 requirements. This thoroughness is commendable, but it may be more than you need. To pare down the report to just the guidelines that apply to your site, choose Site→Reports and turn on the Accessibility box. Click Options to open the window shown in Figure 15-14.

You can disable any rules Dreamweaver uses to evaluate your pages. To turn off an entire category—forms, frames, or tables, for example—click the name and click Disable. If you'd like to get more specific, click the + button next to a category name

---

UP TO SPEED

Making Accessible Web Sites

Building Web sites that meet everyone's requirements can be daunting. Unless you have screen-reader software to simulate the experience of a visually impaired visitor, or a crew of people with a variety of impairments (from color-blindness to repetitive stress injury), to test your site, how do you know what it takes to build a fully accessible Web site?

Fortunately, there are plenty of resources to get you started. The best place to start is at the Web Accessibility Initiative's Web site, especially their accessibility resources page: *www.w3.org/WAI/Resources/*.

Here you'll find lots of information, including examples of different disabilities some Web surfers face, plus tips, checklists and techniques for making sites accessible. And if you do want to see how screen readers work with your site, you can download a demo of JAWS, one of the most popular screen readers, at *www.freedomscientific.com/fs_downloads/jaws.asp*.

Finally, Macromedia dedicates an entire section of its site to accessibility issues: *www.macromedia.com/macromedia/accessibility/*. Here, you'll find explanations of the issues, tips for using Macromedia products, and a showcase of accessible Web sites.

---

to expand a list of individual rules for that category. You can select and disable one or more rules. For example, if your site doesn't use frames (Chapter 7), you'll save time and Dreamweaver's energy by turning off the frames category.

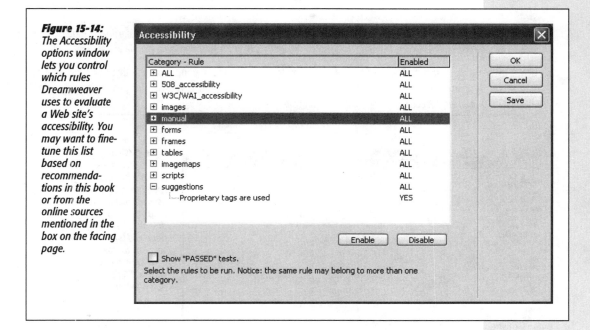

Figure 15-14:
The Accessibility options window lets you control which rules Dreamweaver uses to evaluate a Web site's accessibility. You may want to fine-tune this list based on recommendations in this book or from the online sources mentioned in the box on the facing page.

Download Statistics

Remember the joke that WWW really stands for "World Wide Wait"? Even as more and more people upgrade to speedy DSL and cable modems, file size is the constant foe of the Web designer. What takes only a moment to load from your computer's hard drive could take minutes to travel across the Internet. The more information you put into a Web page, the more time it will take to load.

You can judge how big your page is, and therefore how long it will take to download, by looking at the download stats in the status bar at the bottom of the Document window. You'll see something like this: *5k/2 sec.*

The first bit of information tells you the total size of your Web page and any files included in the page. That's an extremely helpful statistic, because even though a Web page document itself may only be 1 K in size, a 20 K GIF image actually blows it up to 21 K.

Next to the file size, you see how long, in seconds, it will take to download the Web page and all its graphics and other elements. Of course, each visitor's connection speed may be different, depending on whether she's using a cable modem, gas-powered 14.4 Kbps dial-up modem, or whatever. By default, Dreamweaver calculates this figure based on the time it would take a 28.8 Kbps modem to download the page.

You can change this setting easily enough, however; open the Status Bar Preferences window by choosing Edit Sizes from the status bar's window-size pop-up menu. Alternatively, choose Edit→Preferences and click the Status Bar category of the Preferences window; either way, proceed as described in Figure 15-15.

Caution: People hate to wait. You may think that the graphic design of your Web site is so compelling that even if it takes a full minute to download that zippy new Flash home page, people will stick around.

Think again. Research shows that 10 seconds is the maximum amount of time that someone will stay focused on a task while waiting. That means if you're designing a Web site for people with 28.8 Kbps modems, keep your pages below 34 K in size.

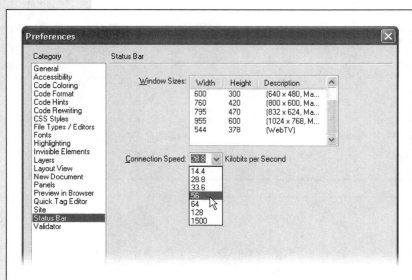

Figure 15-15:
In this dialog box, you can change the connection speed that Dreamweaver uses in calculating how long your page will download. A 34 K Web page will take about 10 seconds to download with a 28.8 Kbps modem; if you choose 56 Kpbs from the pull-down menu, the status bar will list the download time as 5 seconds. Choose the connection speed that you think most visitors to your site will be using. When you aren't sure, err on the side of caution by using a lower speed.

GEM IN THE ROUGH

Caching In

Behind the scenes, Web browsers store the graphics they download onto the computer's hard drive. This is a speed trick. If you click your Back button to return to a Web page whose graphics files the browser has already downloaded, the browser simply pulls them out of the *cache*—off the hard drive, in other words—instead of re-downloading them. This arrangement makes the page load more quickly, since the hard drive is generally much faster than the modem.

As a Web designer, you can capitalize on this standard Web-

browser feature by reusing the same graphics files on more than one page of your site. For instance, you might create a navigation bar composed of small graphic buttons (Home, Contact Us, Products, and so on). If you reuse those buttons on other pages of the site, those pages will appear to download more quickly.

If you do capitalize on this trick, be aware that the download stats in Dreamweaver's status bar may not reflect the added speed boost that's provided by cached graphics.

Moving Your Site to the Internet

Building Web pages on your computer is a big accomplishment, but it's not the whole job. Your beautifully designed and informative Web site will simply languish in obscurity on your hard drive unless you move it to a Web server.

Fortunately, once your Web site is ready for prime time, you can put it on a server without ever leaving the comfort of Dreamweaver. The program includes simple commands for transferring files back and forth between the Web server and your desktop.

Depending on how you operate, choose one of these two methods for transferring your files:

- If you're the sole Web developer for a site, Dreamweaver's Get and Put commands are the easiest way to go.

- If, on the other hand, there's a group of people working on your site, Dreamweaver's Check Out and Check In tools let you move files at will without wiping out others' hard work. In addition, this group feature integrates seamlessly with two other industrial-strength Web-collaboration tools: Microsoft's Visual SourceSafe and WebDAV, an open-source file management tool.

Either way, you begin by defining a remote site.

Defining a Remote Site

As you create your Web site on your computer, you keep it in a *local site folder* (page 26), often called a *local site* for short. You can think of a local site as a work-in-progress. As your site is under construction—whether you're building it from scratch or adding and modifying pages—you'll routinely have partially finished documents sitting on your computer.

Then, when you've perfected and tested your pages using the techniques described in Chapter 15, you're ready to transfer them to a Web server that's connected to the Internet. Dreamweaver refers to the Web-server copy of your files as the *remote site*, and the program provides five methods for transferring files between it and your local site:

- **FTP.** By far the most common method is *FTP*, or File Transfer Protocol. Just as HTTP is the process by which Web pages are transferred from servers to Web browsers, FTP is the traditional method of transferring files over the Internet, and it's the one to use if a Web-hosting company or Internet Service Provider (ISP) provides the home for your Web pages.

- **Over the local area network.** If you're working on an intranet, or if your company's Web server is connected to the company network, you may also be able to transfer files just as you would any files on your office network (using the Network Neighborhood, My Network Places, Chooser, or Connect to Server command, depending on your operating system), without even connecting to the Internet.

- The last three options—**RDS, SourceSafe, and WebDAV**—are advanced file management systems used for collaborative Web development; they're discussed on page 484.

Setting Up a Remote Site with FTP

You can set up a remote site only if you've first set up a *local* site on your computer. Even if you're just putting up a temporary site while working on your *real* Web site, you must at least have the temporary site constructed and defined in Dreamweaver (see page 426).

Once that's done, here's how you go about creating an Internet-based mirror of your local site folder:

FREQUENTLY ASKED QUESTION

Beyond Dreamweaver

Do I have to use Dreamweaver to move my files to the Web server?

No. If you're used to using another program for this purpose, such as CuteFTP (Windows) or Fetch (Mac), you can continue to use it and ignore Dreamweaver's Remote Site feature.

However, if you've never before used Dreamweaver to move files to a server, you may want to at least try it; you'll find that Dreamweaver simplifies much of the process. For example, when you want to move a file from your computer to the Web server using a regular FTP program, you must first locate the file on your local machine and then navigate to the proper folder on the Web server. Dreamweaver saves you both steps; when you select the file in the Site panel and click the Put button, Dreamweaver automatically locates the file on your computer and transfers it to the correct folder on the Web server.

---

1. **Choose Site→Edit Sites.**

   You can also choose Edit Sites from the Site panel's Site menu.

   The Edit Sites dialog box opens, listing all sites that you've defined so far. You're about to create a living, Internet-based *copy* of one of these hard drive–based local sites.

2. **Click the name of the site you want to post on the Internet, and then click Edit.**

   Alternatively, just double-click the site name in the list. The Site Definition window appears for the selected site, as shown in Figure 16-1.

Tip: You can also define the remote site and the local site simultaneously, when you first begin creating a Web site (as described on page 25). Even then, however, Dreamweaver requires that you first give the site a name and choose a local root folder. At that point, you rejoin the steps described here.

---

3. **Click the Advanced tab.**

   You can also use the Site Definition Wizard (Basic tab) to set up a remote site. However, since the wizard requires you to step through screen after screen of setup information—even after you've already supplied most of it—the Advanced tab is faster.

4. **In the Category panel, click Remote Info. From the Access pop-up menu, choose FTP.**

   The Site Definition window now shows menus and fields for collecting your connection information (see Figure 16-1).

5. **Fill in the FTP Host field.**

   Your *FTP host name* may be a name like *www.cosmofarmer.com* or *ftp.cosmofarmer.com*. It never includes directories, folders, or slashes (like *www.cosmofarmer.com/home*), never includes codes for the FTP protocol (*ftp:// ftp.cosmofarmer.com*), and is never only a domain name, such as *cosmofarmer.com*. It might also be an IP address, like 64.226.76.52.

   If you don't know the host name, there's only one way to find out: Call your Web-hosting company or ISP or check its Web site.

6. **In the Host Directory field, type the path to the *root directory*.**

   You're specifying which *folder* within your Web hosting account will contain your Web page files and serve as the root folder for your site.

   Just as on your own hard drive, all the files of your Web site on the Web will be completely contained inside a master folder referred to as the *root folder*. But when you connect to your Web server using FTP, you're rarely connected to the root folder itself. Instead, you usually connect to a folder that isn't accessible over the Web—some administrative folder for your Web account, often filled with folders for log reports of your site's Web traffic, databases, and other files not visible over the Web.

Your hosting account's root directory folder (or even a folder within it) is where you place your *site's* root folder; that's why you're typing its name here. Common names for the root folder at ISPs or Web-hosting companies are *docs, www, htdocs, public_html,* or *virtual_html.* (Call your Web hosting company or ISP to find out.)

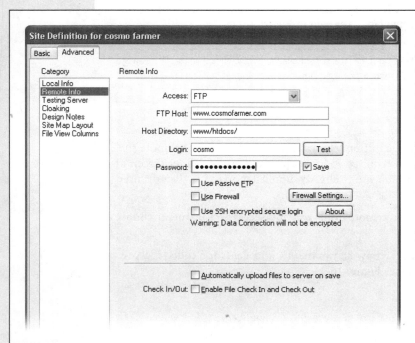

Figure 16-1:
If a Web hosting company or ISP will host your Web site, you'll use FTP to put your site on the Web. To make sure you have all the information you need to connect to the Web server, ask your ISP for these four pieces of information: (1) the FTP host name of the server, (2) the path to the root directory for your site (3) your login name and (4) your password. (If the Web server comes with your email account, your login and password may be the same for both.)

The information you give Dreamweaver here represents the path from the FTP folder to the root folder. It may look like this: *www/htdocs.* In effect, you're telling Dreamweaver: "After connecting to the Web server, you'll find a folder named www. Inside *this* folder is another folder, htdocs. Put my site files in there." In other words, htdocs is the Web site's root folder on the remote hosting account.

7. **In the Login field, type your user name; type your password in the Password field.**

Dreamweaver uses bullets (•••) to display your password so that passing evildoers in your office can't see what you're typing.

If you want Dreamweaver to remember your password each time you use the program, turn on the Save checkbox. This way, you won't have to type your password each time you connect to the Web server.

Note: For security reasons, don't turn on the Save box if you access the Web using computers at, say, your local library, or anywhere else where people you don't trust may use the machine. Otherwise, you might just awake one morning to find the following splattered across your home page: "Hi there! Welcome to Jack's house of illegally acquired and unlawfully distributed music, featuring Metallica's greatest hits."

8. **Turn on the Use Passive FTP or Use Firewall boxes, if necessary.**

    If you're building sites from your home, home office, or small company, you may never need to use these technical options.

    Many corporations, however, use *firewalls*: hardware- or software-based gateways that control incoming and outgoing traffic through a network. Firewalls protect the company network from outside hackers; unfortunately, they also limit how computers inside the network—*behind the firewall*—can connect to the outside world.

    (If your company's system administrator confirms that you have a firewall, you'll need to also get the name of the firewall host computer and its port number. Click the Firewall Settings button, which opens the Site Preferences dialog box). Your firewall configuration may also require *passive FTP*—a method of connecting using your local software, rather than the firewall server. Check with your administrator to see if this is the case, and, if so, turn on the Use Passive FTP checkbox.

9. **If your Web server recognizes *SSH* (secure shell), you may want to connect to it using an encrypted connection.**

    Dreamweaver's SSH feature lets you send your user name and password in an encrypted form to the Web server. That way, anyone who happens to be "listen-

Make the Wizard Disappear with One Click

Dreamweaver's Site Definition Wizard makes the process of defining a new site easy. It guides you through the process of filling in the parameters Dreamweaver needs to know. (You encountered it in Chapter 1; see page 25.)

If you're defining a new site *and* you already have a remote site set up on a Web server, you can go ahead and use the wizard to add all of your remote login information. Once the site

definition is done, you can immediately start transferring files to the server. The information requested by the wizard is exactly the same as described in the instructions on these pages.

However, if you've already defined a Web site, it's a lot easier to click the Advanced tab. This way, you can skip all of the information you've already supplied and jump immediately to the Remote Information category.

ing" to your Internet transmissions won't be able to intercept your login information and take control of your site.

You can take advantage of encryption only if your Web server recognizes SSH. You also have to download and install the necessary software. The setup is rather elaborate, but you'll find specific instructions on Macromedia's Web site, whether you're using a Mac (*www.macromedia.com/support/dreamweaver/ts/documents/mac_ssh.htm*) or Windows (*www.macromedia.com/support/dreamweaver/ts/documents/ssh.htm*).

10. **Turn on the "Automatically upload files to server on save," if you wish.**

    Use this option with care. Because it makes Dreamweaver upload the file over the Internet each time you save, it slows you down and runs the risk of putting incomplete Web pages on your server.

    For example, suppose you're working on your site's home page. After adding a new table to the page, you instinctively save it. If "Automatically upload" is turned on, Dreamweaver uploads the page to your server so that everyone can see the home page with the new (and embarrassingly empty) table. It's better to just upload the page after you're totally finished with it.

11. **If you and your team of Web developers all use Dreamweaver, turn on Enable File Check In and Check Out and fill in the corresponding options (see Figure 16-2).**

    If you do wind up using the checking out feature (page 494), you can save yourself some clicks by turning on Check Out File when Opening. (Fill in your name and email address, too, as shown in Figure 16-2.) Now you can check out a file from the remote server just by double-clicking its name in the Site Files list.

12. **Click OK to return to the Edit Sites dialog box; click Done.**

    The Edit Sites dialog box closes, and the Site panel opens.

At this point, you're ready to connect to the Web server and transfer files. If you're the only person working on the site, Dreamweaver's Get and Put commands will do the trick (page 486). If, however, you're part of a development team, use Dreamweaver's Check In and Check Out feature, described on page 494, instead.

Figure 16-2:
If you work on the site in several different locations (for example, from home and your office), use a different name for each location—BobAtHome and BobAtWork, for example. In this way, you can identify which files you've checked out to your home computer and which to your computer at work.

Setting Up a Remote Site over a Local Network

If you're working on an intranet, or if your company's Web server is connected to the company network, you may also be able to transfer your Web files just as you'd move any files from machine to machine. Dreamweaver provides the same file transfer functions as with FTP, but setup is simpler.

Follow steps 1 and 2 of the previous instructions; but in step 3, click the Remote Info category, and then choose Local/Network from the Access pop-up menu. Menus and fields for collecting your connection information appear in the Site Definition box (see Figure 16-3).

Now click the folder icon next to the Remote Folder field. In the resulting dialog box, navigate to and select your site's remote root folder. On a local network, this folder functions as the root folder on your company's Web server (see page 26), even though it's actually still within the walls of your building. (For differences on selecting root folders on Windows and Macs, see Figure 14-3.)

Wrap up with steps 10 and 11 of the previous instructions. At this point, you're ready to connect to the Web server and transfer files.

Figure 16-3:
The Refresh Remote File List Automatically box updates the list of files in the Site panel. But automatic updating slows down the process of moving files to the remote site, so you may want to avoid this option when you begin a session of moving many files. You can always refresh the list by clicking the Refresh button on the Site panel (page 487).

Figure 16-4:
RDS, Remote Development Service, is a feature of the Cold Fusion application server. However, even if you use Cold Fusion, you may not be able to use RDS. Most Web hosting companies that offer Cold Fusion server turn off RDS as it can create potential security problems.

Setting Up a Remote Site with RDS

RDS—Remote Development Service—is a feature of Macromedia's Cold Fusion Server. It lets designers work on Web files and databases in conjunction with a Cold Fusion application server. If you aren't using Cold Fusion, then this option isn't for you.

To create a remote site in Dreamweaver that will work with RDS, follow steps 1 and 2 on page 479. In step 3, click the Remote Info category, and then choose RDS from the Access pop-up menu (see Figure 16-1).

The Site Definition window displays a version number, a short description, and a Settings button. Click Settings to open the Configure RDS Server window, shown in Figure 16-4. Fill in the dialog box as directed by your server administrator or help desk.

Setting Up a Remote Site with WebDAV

Dreamweaver includes two other methods of accessing a remote site: WebDAV (an *open-source* program, meaning a collaborative effort by volunteer programmers all over the world) and Microsoft's Visual SourceSafe. Both technologies are designed to address one of the biggest problems when collaborating on a Web site: file management and version control.

For instance, all kinds of havoc can result if two people edit a page simultaneously; whoever uploads the page to the Web server *second* winds up wiping out the changes made by the first person.

What you need is a way to prevent more than one person from working on the same file at the same time. WebDAV, short for Web-based Distributed Authoring and Versioning, provides one such solution. It integrates seamlessly with Dreamweaver's Check In and Check Out feature, described on page 494.

Note: Both WebDAV and SourceSafe are advanced options used by corporations that require a good deal of technical expertise; consider using them only if you have someone on staff who can guide you in setting them.

Both Microsoft Internet Information Server (IIS) and Apache Web Server can work with WebDAV. To find out if your Web server can handle WebDAV (and to find out the necessary connection information), consult your Web server's administrator.

To create a remote site in Dreamweaver that will work with WebDAV, follow steps 1 and 2 on page 479. In step 3, click the Remote Info category, and then choose WebDAV from the Access pop-up menu.

The Site Definition window displays a version number, a short description, and a button labeled Settings. Click Settings to open the WebDAV Connection window, shown in Figure 16-5. In this dialog box, type the URL of the root directory on the WebDAV server (beginning with *http://*), your user name, email address, and password. (If you don't know these three bits of information, ask the server administrator or help desk.) Click OK.

As a final step, turn on the Check Out Files when Opening checkbox in the Site Definition dialog box. Click OK, then Done. You're ready to connect to the Web server and transfer files, as described on page 491.

Figure 16-5:
WebDAV is a powerful tool for working on a large site with other people. It's built into server packages like Microsoft Internet Information Server and Apache.

Setting Up a Remote Site with SourceSafe

Microsoft originally created Visual SourceSafe for managing team software development. Like WebDAV, SourceSafe makes sure you don't accidentally stomp on someone else's hard work by overwriting a Web page they just modified. In addition, this sophisticated program tracks different versions of files and lets an administrator "roll back" to previous versions of a Web page, or even an entire site; it's the granddaddy of Undos.

To take advantage of this power, however, you need a Visual SourceSafe (VSS) server and VSS database already set up. In addition, Windows users need to install Microsoft Visual SourceSafe Client version 6 on their PCs.

***

Note: The Visual SourceSafe option is not available to Mac users of Dreamweaver MX.

***

Once you've installed the VSS Client software, and you've created and defined a local site (see page 426), you're ready to configure Dreamweaver for SourceSafe using the Site Definition window. Basically, you tell Dreamweaver where to find the SourceSafe database and how to sign on to the server.

Once again, follow steps 1 and 2 on page 479. But in step 3, click the Remote Info category, and then choose SourceSafe from the Access pop-up menu. In the resulting dialog box, click Settings to reveal the Open SourceSafe Database dialog box, shown in Figure 16-6.

Click Browse to select the Visual SourceSafe (VSS) database file on your computer (or type in the file path, if you know it, into the Database Path field)—the *srcsafe.ini* file that Dreamweaver uses to initialize SourceSafe.

Then, in the Project field, fill in the name of the *project* within the VSS database that you wish to use as the remote root folder. (A VSS database can have many projects and Web sites listed in it. Make sure you enter the right project name for this site. If in doubt, contact the administrator of the Visual SourceSafe database.) Type your user name and password into the appropriate fields; again, ask the administrator for guidance.

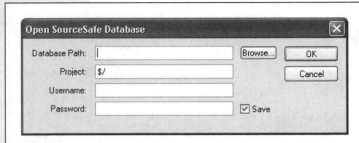

Figure 16-6:
Dreamweaver supports Microsoft's Visual SourceSafe system. Many corporations use this powerful file-control system to control access to files in large projects involving many people.

Click OK. But before dismissing the Site Definition dialog box, turn on Check Out Files when Opening, so that Dreamweaver's Check In and Check Out feature (see page 494) will work with the VSS system. Click OK, then Done. You're ready to connect to the Web server and transfer files. Both WebDAV and SourceSafe use Dreamweaver's Check In and Check Out process, described on page 495, for transferring files.

Transferring Files

Once you've told Dreamweaver *how* you plan to ship off your Web page files to the Net, you can set about *doing* it. Thanks to Dreamweaver's Site panel, the whole process takes only a few steps.

Note: If you're using WebDav, SourceSafe, or Dreamweaver's Check In/Check Out process, use the steps describe on page 494 for transferring files.

Moving Files to the Web Server

To transfer files to your Web server:

1. **Open the Site panel (Figure 16-7).**

   Choose Site→Site Files (or press F8).

2. **From the Site menu, choose the name of the site whose files you wish to move (if it isn't already selected).**

   The Site panel displays files for the selected site. (See Figure 16-7.)

3. **From the file list in the Site panel, select the files to upload to the Web server.**

To move a folder and every file inside it, just select the folder. (In other words, you can transfer your *entire* Web site to the server by simply selecting the local root folder—the folder listed at the very top of the Local Folder file list.) When only a few files have changed, you can also select only certain files or folders for uploading, using any of the techniques described on page 460.

Note to Windows users: if you don't see the files you wish to upload in the Site files list, you may have Remote View selected. Select Local View to see only those site files on your computer.

Figure 16-7:
The Site panel in Windows (top) and on the Mac (bottom) looks slightly different. Both, however, offer toolbar buttons for uploading and downloading your Web files to the actual Web server that will dish them out to the adoring public. (See Chapter 14 for much more on this important window.)

When you use do-it-yourself FTP programs like WSFTP or Fetch, you have to specify a folder location for every file you transfer to the Web server. But here's one of the great advantages of letting Dreamweaver do your file-shuffling; it already knows where the files should go on the remote site. The local and remote sites are, after all, mirror images, so Dreamweaver simply puts files in the corresponding folders on the remote site.

For example, suppose you select the file mayo.html, which is in a folder called Condiments, which is itself stored in the local root folder. When you transfer the file, Dreamweaver knows to put this file in the Condiments folder in the root folder on the remote site.

A hush falls over the audience; you're ready to go live with your Web page.

4. **Click the Put files button—the up arrow—on the Site panel (identified in Figure 16-7).**

Alternatively, you can choose Site→Put, or use the keyboard shortcut Shift+Ctrl+U (Shift-⌘-U).

Several things happen when you do this: First, if you're using an FTP connection, Dreamweaver attempts to connect to your Web server, dialing your modem if necessary. It may take a minute or so to establish a connection; the Connect button (see Figure 16-7) displays a bright green light when Dreamweaver is connected.

Next, if any of the files you're transferring are currently open and have unsaved changes, Dreamweaver asks if you want to save the files before transferring them to the server. Click Yes to save the file, or, if there are multiple unsaved files, click the Yes To All button to save all of them before posting them online.

In addition, Dreamweaver asks if you wish to also transfer any *dependent files* (see Figure 16-8). Dependent files are graphics, frame pages in a frameset, or external Cascading Style Sheets files that you've placed onto a page.

This feature can save you considerable time and hassle; no need to hunt for and upload each graphic file yourself. On the other hand, if all the dependent files are *already* on the server, having Dreamweaver transfer the same files again is a waste of time.

For example, suppose you've simply changed some words on a Web page that you'd previously put on the server. The graphics were transferred when you originally uploaded the page, and you haven't added any additional graphics to the page. Since all the dependent files are already on the server, you only need to transfer the Web page file itself. Dreamweaver lets you make the choice.

Tip: If you turn on the Don't Ask Me Again box and then click Yes, Dreamweaver will *always* copy dependent files without asking. On the other hand, if you turn on the Don't Ask Me Again box and click No, Dreamweaver will *never* copy dependent files.

If you want the Dependent Files dialog box to appear again after you've turned it off, hold down the Alt (Option) key when you transfer a file (using any method *except* a keyboard shortcut). Or choose Edit→Preferences→Site Category to turn this feature on or off.

---

5. **Click Yes to transfer dependent files, or No to only transfer the files you selected.**

Dreamweaver copies the files to the Web server. If you're copying a file that's inside a folder that isn't already on the remote site, Dreamweaver creates the folder as well. In fact, Dreamweaver will create as many subfolders as necessary to make sure every file is transferred to the same folder location on the remote site as it is in the local site. (Try doing *that* with a regular FTP program.)

6. **Continue using the Put button to transfer all files in your Web site to the remote site.**

Depending on the number of files transferred, this operation can take some time. Transferring files over the Internet using FTP isn't nearly as fast as copying files from one hard drive to another (see the box on page 492).

Figure 16-8:
The Dependent Files feature of Dreamweaver's File Transfer command makes sure all necessary files—graphics, Flash movies, and so on—are copied to the Web server along with your Web pages.

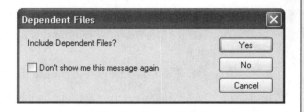

Other ways to move files to the Web server

In the Site panel, you can also *drag* a file from the Local Folder list into the Remote Site list. (In Windows, expand the Site panel first, as described in the box on page 432.) But don't do it: it's too easy to drag a file into the wrong place. If you drag a file to the wrong folder on the remote site, for example, you'll probably break all the links on the page. It's much better to let Dreamweaver keep track of where files should go in the organization of your site. (However, if you're already in this mess, see "Find and Fix Broken Links" on page 458.)

You can also copy your current document to the Web server without using the Site panel at all. You can go directly to the Put command when, say, you finish building or modifying a Web page and want to immediately move it to the Web server. Just choose Site→Put or press Shift+Ctrl+U (Shift-⌘-U); Dreamweaver automatically copies the fresh page to the proper folder online.

The toolbar also provides a quick menu shortcut for this operation, as shown in Figure 16-9.

Figure 16-9:
To transfer the current document to a Web server, click the File Status button (circled) and choose Put. You can also use this menu to retrieve a copy of this file from the server (Get), use Dreamweaver's Check In and Out features (see page 494), or review Design Notes (page 503) for the page.

Getting Files from the Web Server

So far, this chapter has described getting your hard drive–based Web pages *to* the Internet. Sometimes, however, you'll want to download one or more files *from* the Web server. Perhaps you've made a horrible (and irreversible) mistake on the local copy of a file, and you want to retrieve the last version from the Web server, using the remote site as a last-ditch backup system. Or perhaps someone else uploaded some files to the site, and you want to download a copy to your own computer (although the Synchronize feature described on page 500 would also work).

To get files from the remote site, open the Site panel (press F8) and proceed as follows:

1. **From the Site menu, choose the site whose files you wish to retrieve.**

   Windows: From the Site panel's View menu (see the box on page 431), choose Select Remote View.

   Macintosh: If only the Local Folder files are visible, click the tiny white triangle in the lower-left corner and make sure that the Site File view button is selected (see the box on page 432).

2. **Click the Connect Button.**

   Dreamweaver tells you that it's attempting to connect to the Web server. Once the connection has been made, a list of files and folders appears in the Remote Site list, and the Connect button displays a bright green dot. (Dreamweaver automatically disconnects you after 30 minutes of inactivity, and the green dot turns black. It's usually a good idea not to stay connected to a server indefinitely, since doing so takes processing power away from the server and poses a security risk.)

WORKAROUND WORKSHOP

Don't Replace the Wrong File

One strange feature of the Site panel's Get and Put commands may get you in trouble. Suppose, having just added new information to the home page (index. html), you want to transfer it to the Web server. You select it in the Local Folder list—but then you accidentally click Get instead of Put.

Macromedia Dreamweaver MX

? Do you wish to overwrite your local copy of C:\Inetpub\wwwroot\aspNet_cosmo_root\index.asp?

Yes   No

Not knowing your true intention, Dreamweaver dutifully retrieves the index.html file *from* the Web server and prepares to replace (wipe out) the newly updated home page on your computer.

Fortunately, Dreamweaver also opens a warning message asking if you really want to overwrite the local file. Click No. This may result in an "Transfer failed" error box, but that's a small price to pay for saving your hard work.

The opposite happens if you select a file in the Remote Site list and click the Put button: Dreamweaver tries to replace the remote file with the local version. If that's not what you meant to do, be sure to click No. Remember that the warning message is your last chance to avoid a potentially disastrous mistake.

Tip: Dreamweaver disconnects from the Remote site after 30 minutes of inactivity. If you'd like to change this setting, press Ctrl+U (⌘-U) to open the Preferences window. Click the Site category and change the number listed in the Minutes Idle box. Be aware, however, that some Web servers have their own settings and may disconnect you sooner than you've specified.

If you're connected to the Web server over a local network as described on page 483, the Connect button is dimmed, and you can skip this step. You only use the Connect button when connecting to the Web server via FTP, RDS, Visual SourceSafe, or WebDAV.

3. **From the Remote Site file list, select the files you wish to download from the Web server.**

   For techniques on selecting files in the Site panel, see page 460. To download a folder and every file inside it, just click the folder. This technique also lets you get your *entire* Web site from the server; just click the remote root folder, which appears at the very top of the Remote Site file list.

4. **Click the Get files button—the down arrow.**

   Alternatively, you can choose Site→Get, or use the keyboard shortcut Shift+Ctrl+D (Shift-⌘-D).

   If the *local* version of any file you are getting from the remote site is currently opened and has unsaved changes, Dreamweaver warns you that those changes will be lost. (No surprise there; copying a file from the remote site automatically replaces the same file in the local site, whether it's open or not.) Dreamweaver also warns you if you're about to replace a local file that's *newer* than the remote one.

   In addition, Dreamweaver offers to transfer any dependent files, as described in Figure 16-8.

POWER USERS' CLINIC

Troubleshoot with the FTP Log

If you're having problems moving files using Dreamweaver's FTP command, you may be able to find some clues in the records Dreamweaver keeps when transferring files. If you've used other FTP programs, you may have seen little messages that are sent back and forth between the Web server and the FTP program like this:

200 PORT command successful.
LIST
150 Opening ASCII mode data connection for /bin/ls.

Dreamweaver also sends and receives this information, but keeps it hidden. To see the FTP log, choose Window→ Results→FTP Log (you'll also find an FTP button on the Mac's Site panel and, when it's expanded, the Window's Site panel). The FTP log panel opens at the bottom of the screen in the Results panel group. Any errors appear in this log.

For example, if you encounter a "cannot put file" error, it may mean that you're out of space on your Web server. Contact your ISP or the administrator of your Web server for help.

---

5. **Click Yes to transfer dependent files, or No to only transfer the files you se-lected.**

    Dreamweaver copies the files to the local site folder, creating any folders necessary to replicate the structure of the remote site.

Cloaking Files

You may not want *all* files transferred to and from the Remote site. For example, as part of its Library and Template tools, Dreamweaver creates folders inside your local root folder. The Library and Templates folders don't do you any good on the Web server; their sole purpose is to help you build the site on your computer. Likewise, you may have Photoshop (.psd), Flash (.fla), or Fireworks (.png) files in your local root folder. They're inaccessible from a Web browser and take up a lot of disk space, so they shouldn't be transferred to the Web server when you move your site online.

To meet such challenges, Dreamweaver MX includes a new feature called *Cloaking*. It lets you hide folders and specific file types from many file transfer operations, including get/put files, the check in/check out feature (page 494), and site synchronization (page 500). In fact, you can even hide files from many sitewide Dreamweaver lists, including reports (page 468), search and replace (page 442), check and change links sitewide (page 464), and the Assets panel (page 442).

Dreamweaver lets you cloak specific folders in your site or particular file types (those that end with a specific extension such as .fla or .png). Each type of cloak requires a different technique.

To hide specific types of files:

1. **Choose Site→Edit Sites.**

    The Edit Sites window opens, listing all sites you've defined in Dreamweaver.

2. **Select the Site you wish to use cloaking on and click Edit.**

    That site's Site Definition window opens.

FREQUENTLY ASKED QUESTION

Abort! Abort!

I accidentally started uploading my entire site to the Web server, and it's taking forever. How do I stop this crazy thing?

In addition to taking a fair amount of time, FTP transfers tie up Dreamweaver, preventing you from doing anything until the transfers are complete.

However, you're not stuck waiting, and even if you make a mistake in uploading (or downloading) your files, there's a way out.

Just click the Cancel button on the Status window to stop the transfer and return Dreamweaver to your control.

3. **Click the Cloaking category.**

   The cloaking settings appear (see Figure 16-10). The factory setting is On for every site you define. (If you want to turn it off, just click to uncheck the Enable Cloaking box.)

Tip: You can quickly turn cloaking on and off by right-clicking (Control-clicking) any file or folder in the Site panel and selecting Cloaking→Enable Cloaking from the context menu. A checkmark next to Enable Cloaking means cloaking is turned on.

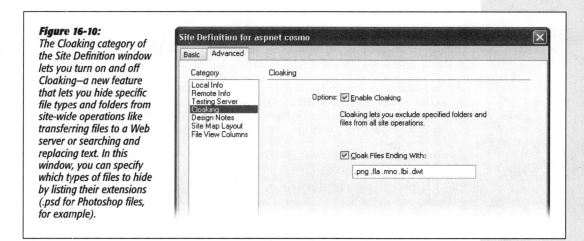

Figure 16-10:
The Cloaking category of the Site Definition window lets you turn on and off Cloaking—a new feature that lets you hide specific file types and folders from site-wide operations like transferring files to a Web server or searching and replacing text. In this window, you can specify which types of files to hide by listing their extensions (.psd for Photoshop files, for example).

4. **Turn on Cloak Files Ending With.**

   Dreamweaver identifies file types by their extensions (.png for Fireworks files, for example).

Note: Mac programs don't always add these filename suffixes, but without them, Dreamweaver can't cloak.

---

5. **In the text box, type the extensions you wish to cloak.**

   Each extension should start with a period followed by three or four letters. To type multiple extensions in the box, separate them with a space.

6. **Click OK twice to close this window and the Edit Sites window.**

   All cloaked files have a red slash through them in the Site panel.

You can also cloak a folder using the Site panel like this:

1. **Open the Site panel by pressing F8.**

   Alternatively choose Site→Site Files.

---

2. **Right-click (⌘-click) a folder in Local Files view.**

   A contextual menu appears with many site-related options.

3. **Select Cloaking→Cloak.**

   Dreamweaver adds a red slash through the folder's icon in the Site panel. All files and folders inside the cloaked folder are hidden as well, as indicated by the red slashes through their icons.

Note: You can't hide individual files in the Site panel—only *folders* and *file types*.

Once you've cloaked a folder, it and any folders inside it disappear from Dreamweaver's file transfer functions. Files with specific extensions that you specified in the Preferences window are also hidden.

However, there are exceptions. You can override the cloaking, for example, by selecting a cloaked folder or file and then using the Get or Put file buttons as described on page 486. Dreamweaver assumes that since you specifically selected that file or folder, you intend to override the cloaking feature.

Dreamweaver also ignores cloaking if you answer Yes in the Include Dependent Files message box (Figure 16-8) when you put or get files. In that case, Dreamweaver transfers all dependent files, even if they're cloaked (this applies to Library and Template files as well).

Check In and Check Out

If you're the sole developer for a Web site, the Site panel's Get and Put buttons are fine for transferring your files. But if you're on a team of developers, these simple tools can get you in trouble.

For example, suppose your boss emails you an important announcement that he wants posted on the home page immediately. So you download the home page from the Web server and start to edit it. At the same time, your co-worker Bob notices a typo on the home page. He downloads it, too.

You're a much faster worker than Bob, so you've added the critical news to the home page and moved it back to the Web server. But now Bob transfers his corrected home page to the Web server, *overwriting* your edits and eliminating that urgent notice you just uploaded. (An hour later, your phone rings. It's the boss.)

Without some kind of system to monitor who has what file, and to prevent people from overwriting each other's work, collaborative Web development can be a chaotic mess. Fortunately, Dreamweaver's Check In and Check Out system provides a civilized answer to this problem. It works like your local public library: When you check a file out, no one else can have it. When you're finished, you check the file back in, releasing control of it, and allowing someone else on the team to check it out and work on it.

To use the Check In/Check Out feature effectively, it helps to keep a few things in mind:

- When you're developing a Web site solo, your local site usually contains the most recent versions of your files. You make any modifications or additions to the pages on your computer first and *then* transfer them to the Web server.

  But in a collaborative environment where many people are working on the site at once, the files on your hard drive may not be the latest ones. After all, your co-workers, like you, have been updating pages and transferring them to the Web server. The home-page file sitting in the local site folder on your computer might be several days older than the file on the remote site. This is why checking out a file from the *remote* site, rather than editing from the copy on your computer, is so important. It guarantees that you have the latest version of the file.

- In a collaborative environment, nobody should post files to the Web server using any method except Dreamweaver's Check In and Check Out system.

  The reason is technical, but worth slogging through: When Dreamweaver checks out a file, it doesn't actually *lock* the file. Instead, it places a small, invisible text file (with the three-letter suffix *.lck*) on both the remote server and in your local site folder. This text file indicates who has checked out the file. When Dreamweaver connects to a remote site, it uses these files to know which Web files are in use by others.

  But only Dreamweaver understands these .lck files. Other FTP programs, like WSFTP (Windows) or Fetch (Mac), gladly ignore them and can easily overwrite any checked-out files. This risk also applies when you simply copy files back and forth over the office network.

- All Dreamweaver users must configure their remote site to use Check In and Check Out (see page 482). If just one person doesn't do it, you risk overwritten files.

Note: Visual SourceSafe and WebDAV users are free of these last two constraints. As long as everyone working on the site uses programs that support the Visual SourceSafe client or the WebDAV protocol, they can work seamlessly with Dreamweaver users. And vice versa.

Checking Files Out

When you want to work on a file in a collaborative site, you check it out from the Web server. Doing so makes sure that *you* have the latest version of the file, and that nobody else can make changes to the file.

Note: There's nothing to check out when you're creating a *new* page for the site. Since the only version of the file in the universe is on your computer, there's no fear that someone else might work on it at the same time as you. In this case, you only need to check the file into the site when you're done (see page 498).

You check out a file using the Site panel; if it's not open, press F8 or choose Site→Site Files. Then choose the remote site you wish to work on from the Site menu (shown at top in Figure 16-11).

Now you're ready to begin. From the Local Folder file list in the Site panel, click to select the files you wish to check out from the Web server—or, to check out an entire folder and every file inside it, just select the folder.

You may in some instances want to select a file from the Remote Site list as well. For example, maybe you need to modify a page that you didn't create, and which you've never before checked out. In this case, the file isn't *in* your local folder, so you must select it from the Remote Site list. First, connect to the Web server by clicking the Connect button (see Figure 16-7). After Dreamweaver connects to the server, the remote files appear in the Remote Site list. Select the ones you wish to check out.

Tip: If, when you define the remote site (page 482), you select the Check Out File when Opening option, you can also check out (and open) a file by double-clicking it in the Site panel. This is a quick way to open a page for editing while still using Dreamweaver's Check Out feature.

In any case, now just click the Check Out files button on the Site panel (see Figure 16-11), or choose Site→Check Out, or use the keyboard shortcut Shift+Ctrl+Alt+D (Shift-Option-⌘-D). (Not enough fingers? See page 601 to learn how to change Dreamweaver's shortcuts.)

Windows note: You must use the Site menu on the Site panel for these operations. In fact, many of the actions you can take on files selected in the Site panel are accessed through the menus that appear on that panel (see the box on page 431).

Dreamweaver asks if you wish to also check out any dependent files (see Figure 16-8). Be careful checking out dependent files; clicking Yes here *locks* all of those files so that nobody else can modify them. If you check out both a page and its linked exter-

---

WORKAROUND WORKSHOP

Manual Checkout Override

Occasionally you may wish to erase the checked-out status of a file. Suppose, for example, someone who's checked out a lot of files suddenly catches the plague and can't continue working on the site. In order to free those files so others can work on them, you should undo his checkout (and quarantine his cubicle).

To do this, select the checked-out file in the Site panel. Choose Site→Undo Check Out. (Windows users must use

the Site menu on the Site panel.) As Dreamweaver warns you, doing this also copies the remote site version of the file to your local site; you can stop the process, if necessary, by clicking Cancel. When complete, a padlock icon appears next to the file.

You can also use this technique if, after checking out a file, you've made a horrible mistake on the page and wish to revert to the copy on the Web server.

nal style sheet, for example, whoever's responsible for maintaining your site's styles won't have access to the sheet. When she needs to add a new style, she'll be stuck until you check the style sheet back in.

When you check files out, Dreamweaver copies them to your computer and marks them as checked out so others can't change them. As when uploading and downloading files, checking out files can take time, depending upon how fast your computer can communicate with the Internet.

After you've checked out a file, a green "checked-out" checkmark appears next to its name in the Site panel (see Figure 16-11). You can now open and edit it, and (when you're done) check the file back in.

If you attempt to check out a file someone else has already checked out, Dreamweaver tells you as much. It also gives you the option to override their checkout; but unless you're the boss, resist the temptation, for two reasons. First, your colleagues may have made some important changes to the page, which will be wiped out by your shenanigans. Second, because you so rudely stole the file, they may decide to stop talking to you.

A better way to work with someone who's checked out a file you need is to use Dreamweaver's email feature. You can see who checked out a file by consulting the Checked Out By column (Figure 16-11). Even better, if you click the name, Dreamweaver opens your email program and addresses an email to that person, so you can say: "Hey Bob, you've had the home page checked out for two days! I need to work on it, so check it back in!"

The name and email address Dreamweaver uses depends on the information they provided, just as you did when you configured your computer for remote site use (see page 482).

Figure 16-11:
A padlock icon denotes files you've checked into the remote site, a reminder that you must check the file out before working on it. A green checkmark indicates that you've checked out the file; a red check means someone else has checked it out.

Checking Files In

When you're ready to move a page you've edited back onto the server, you check it in. (You also check in *new* files you've created.)

To check in files, open the Site panel (press F8), choose the site you're checking into from the Site pop-up menu, and (using the Local Folder file list in the Site panel) select the files you wish to check in to the Web server. As always, you can click a folder to check it out, along with every file inside it.

The files you select should be files you've checked out, or brand-new files that have never been on the Web server. If you attempt to check in a file that someone else has checked out, Dreamweaver warns you with a message box. Click Cancel to stop the check-in procedure, so that you won't overwrite the checked-out file on the server.

Dreamweaver also warns you if you try to check in a file that's older than the server copy. Again, unless you're sure this is what you want to do, click Cancel.

Tip: If you want to check the page you're currently working on into the remote site, use the toolbar in the document window (see Figure 16-9).

You can check in the selected files in any of the usual ways:

- Click the Check In files button (see Figure 16-11).

- Choose Site→Check In. (Windows users must use the Site menu on the Site panel.)

FREQUENTLY ASKED QUESTION

Get and Put, In and Out

I'm using Dreamweaver's Check In and Check Out buttons to transfer my files. What do the Get and Put buttons do when the Check In/Out feature is enabled?

If you're using Check In and Out, the Get and Put commands don't function exactly as described on page 486. *Get* copies the selected file or files to your local site. However, Dreamweaver draws a small lock icon next to each of these "gotten" files in your Local Folder list. The files are locked, and you shouldn't edit them. Remember, checking out a file is the only way to prevent others from working on it. If you edit a locked file on your computer, nothing is stopping someone else from checking the page out from the Remote site, editing it, and checking it back in.

But using the Get command in such a situation can still be useful. For example, suppose someone just updated the

site's external style sheet. Pages you're editing use this style sheet, so you'd like to get the latest version. You don't want to *edit* the style sheet itself, so you don't need to check it out. By using Get instead of checking out the pages, you can keep a reference copy on your computer without locking it for anyone else and without having to check it back in later.

Put, on the other hand, simply transfers the file on your local site to the remote site. This is usually a bad idea when you're also using the Check In/Check Out feature. The remote site should be your reference copy; several rounds of revisions may have been made to a file since you last checked it out. Your local copy will be hopelessly out of date, and moving it the server using Put will destroy the most recent version of the file.

- Use the keyboard shortcut Shift+Ctrl+Alt+U (Shift-Option-⌘-U). (See page 601 to learn how to change the Dreamweaver shortcut to something less cumbersome.)

Dreamweaver asks if you wish to also check in any dependent files (see Figure 16-8). You should transfer dependent files only if you first checked them out, or if the dependent files are new and have never been uploaded to the server. If you attempt to check in a dependent file that someone else has checked out, Dreamweaver warns you with a message box.

After you've clicked through all message boxes, Dreamweaver copies the files to the Remote site. Once you've checked in a file, a padlock icon appears next to its name in the Site panel (see Figure 16-11); checking in locks the file so that you don't accidentally change the local copy. If you wish to modify the file in some way, check it out again (see page 495).

Generating a Report on Checked-Out Files

As described in Chapter 15, Dreamweaver can generate a series of reports on the files in your site. One of those reports lets you see which files a specific person has checked out. In this way, for instance, you can identify all the files you've checked out, or all the files that have been checked out by your co-worker Bob (who has since left the company).

To generate a report, follow the steps described on page 468. Turn on the Checked Out By option when specifying the type of report to run. Then click Report Settings. In the dialog box that appears, type the person's name as it appears in the Checked Out By column (Figure 16-11). (To find *all* checked-out files, leave the box blank.) Click OK, and then click Run to generate the report.

Unfortunately, a couple of issues undermine the usefulness of the "Checked Out By" report. First, if you're connected to the Remote server using FTP, you'll wait quite a while; Dreamweaver needs to download a lot of information, which, even on a small site, can take a long time.

Note: If you find the report is taking too long, you can stop it in its tracks by clicking the Stop button (the red stop sign icon) in the Site Reports panel (see Figure 16-12).

Figure 16-12:
Running a report to see who has checked out which file is a great idea. Unfortunately, this feature may not produce very useful results.

Second, the report you finally get isn't very useful (see Figure 16-12). The operations you're most likely to perform on checked-out files—checking them back in, undoing their checkout status, or contacting the person who checked them—require you to switch to the Site panel. Because there's no link between the report and the Site panel, you can't, for example, make Dreamweaver highlight the reported files in the Site panel.

Synchronizing Site Files

As you might suspect when you keep two sets of files—Local Folder and Remote Site—it's easy to lose track of which files are the most recent. For example, say you finish your Web site and move all the files to the Web server. The next day, you notice mistakes on a bunch of Web pages, so you make corrections on the copies in your local site. But in your rush to fix the pages, you didn't keep track of which ones you corrected. So although you're ready to move the corrected pages to the Web Server, you're not sure *which* ones you need to transfer.

When you use the Check In/Check Out feature described on page 494, you avoid this problem altogether. Using that system, the version on the Web server is *always* the latest and most definitive copy—*unless* you or someone else has checked that file out. In that case, whoever checked the file has the most recent version.

But if you're operating solo, for example, and don't use the Check In/Check Out feature, you may get good mileage from the Synchronize command, which lets you compare the remote and local sites and transfer only the newer files in either direction. (In fact, since the Synchronize command uses the Get and Put methods of transferring files, *don't* use it if you're also using Check In and Check Out [see the box on page 498.])

To synchronize your sites:

1. **Choose Site→Synchronize.**

   Windows users should use the Site menu on the Site panel; Mac users should choose from the menu bar (with the Site panel open and in front of any open documents).

   The Synchronize Files dialog box appears (see Figure 16-13).

Figure 16-13:
Dreamweaver lets you make sure your files on your remote and local sites match. Using its Synchronization command, you can copy newer files from your computer to the Web server, or get newer files from the remote site. (The Synchronization command is not available if you're using Visual SourceSafe.)

2. **Using the Synchronize pop-up menu, specify the files to update.**

   You can either synchronize all files in the current Web site, or just files you've selected in the Local Folder list. This last option is good when you have a really big site and you want to limit this operation to just a single section of the site—one folder, for example. For site file selection techniques, see page 460.

3. **Using the Direction pop-up menu, choose where you'd like to copy newer files.**

   You have three choices. **Put newer files to remote** updates the Web server with any newer files from your local site folder. It also copies any *new* files on the local site to the remote site. Use this option when you've done heavy editing to the local site and you want to move all new or modified pages to the Web server.

   Get newer files from remote does just the reverse: it updates your local site folder with any newer (or new) files from the remote site. Here's one instance where the synchronize feature comes in handy in team-design situations. If you've been out of the office for a while, click this option to download copies of the latest site files. (Note that this doesn't check any files out; it merely makes sure you have the latest files for your own reference.)

   Get and put newer files is a two-way synchronization. Any new files on the local site are transferred to the remote site and vice versa. The result is that both "sides" contain the latest files.

4. **Turn on the Delete checkbox, if desired.**

   The wording of this option reflects the option you selected in the previous step. If you're moving newer files *to* the remote site, it says "Delete remote files not on local drive." It's a useful option when, for example, you've spent the afternoon cleaning up the local copy of your site, deleting old, orphaned graphics files and Web pages, for example, and you want Dreamweaver to update the Web server to match.

   If you chose to transfer newer files *from* the remote site, Dreamweaver lets you "Delete local files not on remote server." Use this feature when your local site is hopelessly out of date with the remote site. Perhaps you're working on the site with a team, but you've been on vacation for two months (this is, of course, a hypothetical example). The site may have changed so significantly that you want to get your local copy in line with the Web site.

Note: Of course, you should proceed with caution when using *any* command that automatically deletes files. There's no Undo for these delete operations, and you don't want to accidentally delete the only copy of a particular page, graphic, or external Cascading Style Sheet.

If you chose the "Get and put newer files" option in step 3, the Delete checkbox is dimmed and unavailable. This option truly synchronizes the two; Dreamweaver copies newer files on the remote site (including files that exist on the Web server but not on your computer) to your local site, and vice-versa.

5. **Click Preview to begin the synchronization process.**

Dreamweaver connects to the remote site and compares the two sets of files—if your site is large, a time-consuming process. When it finishes, the Synchronize preview window appears (see Figure 16-14), listing which files Dreamweaver will delete and which it will transfer.

6. **Turn off the Action boxes next to any files you don't want Dreamweaver to touch.**

For example, if you realize that Dreamweaver is going to delete a file that you *know* you need, uncheck the box next to that file. When you do this, "skip" appears next to the file in the Status column (see Figure 16-14). This is your last chance to determine which files you want to transfer and delete, and which you want to leave untouched.

7. **Click OK to proceed, or Cancel to stop the synchronization.**

If you click OK, Dreamweaver commences copying and deleting the chosen files. If you want to stop this process, click the red Stop icon in the Synchronize window (see the box on page 492).

8. **Click Close.**

Tip: If you just want to *identify* newer files on the local site without synchronizing them (to run a report on them, for example), choose Edit→Select Newer Local in the Site panel menu bar (Windows) or choose Site→Site Files View→Select Newer Local (Mac). Dreamweaver connects to the remote site and compares the files, then, in the Site panel's Local Folder list, highlights files on the Local site that are newer than their remote counterparts.

You can also identify newer files on the remote site: Choose Edit→Select Newer Remote from the Site panel menu bar (Windows) or choose Site→Site Files View→Select Newer Remote (Mac). As with the Synchronization command, these options are unavailable if you're using Visual SourceSafe (page 485).

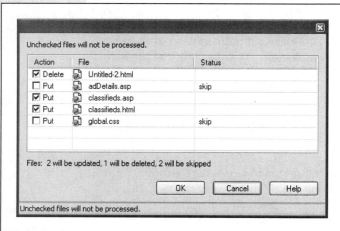

Figure 16-14:
The Synchronize window lets you preview any actions Dreamweaver intends to take to synchronize the files on your local and remote sites. You can deselect any actions you don't want, or simply back out of the whole process without making any changes by clicking Cancel.

Communicating with Design Notes

Lots of questions arise when a team works on a Web site: Has this page been proof-read? Who is the author of the page? Where did this graphic come from? Usually, you must rely on a flurry of emails to ferret out the answers.

But Dreamweaver's Design Notes dialog box (Figure 16-15) eliminates much of that hassle by letting you attach information, such as a Web page's status or author, to a file. You can open these notes (from the Site panel or from a currently open document), edit them, and even share them with others. In this way, it's easy to leave notes for other people—such as, "Hey Bob, can you make sure that this is the most recent photo of the Anodyne 1000?" You can even add notes to files other than Web pages including folders, images, Flash movies, and external Cascading Style Sheets—anything, in fact, that appears in the Site panel.

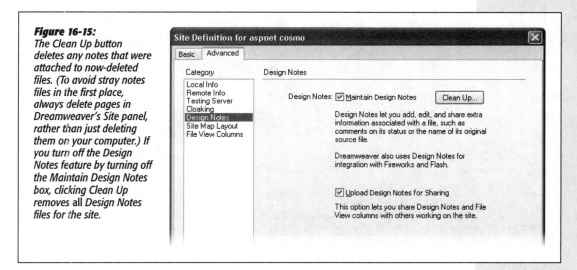

Figure 16-15:
The Clean Up button deletes any notes that were attached to now-deleted files. (To avoid stray notes files in the first place, always delete pages in Dreamweaver's Site panel, rather than just deleting them on your computer.) If you turn off the Design Notes feature by turning off the Maintain Design Notes box, clicking Clean Up removes all Design Notes files for the site.

Setting Up Design Notes

You can't use Design Notes unless the feature itself is turned on. To find out, open the Site Definition dialog box by double-clicking the site's name in the Edit Sites dialog box (choose Edit Sites from the Site menu or the pop-up menu in the Site panel). In the Category list, click Design Notes; as shown in Figure 16-15, two check-boxes pertain to the notes feature:

- **Maintain Design Notes.** This checkbox lets you create and read notes using Dreamweaver's File→Design Notes command (see the next section).

- **Upload Design Notes for Sharing.** If you're using Design Notes as part of a team, turn on this checkbox, which makes Dreamweaver upload design notes to the remote site, so that your fellow team members can read them.

Note: Design Notes are especially useful for keeping track of pages that are built and maintained by a team of developers. But if you're a solo operator and still want to use them—maybe you're the type with a hundred Post-it notes taped to the edges of your monitor—then turn off Upload Design Notes for Sharing. You'll save time and server space by preventing Dreamweaver from transferring note files to the Web server.

Click OK to close the Site Definition dialog box. You can double-click another site in the Edit Sites dialog box to turn on its Design Notes feature, or click Done.

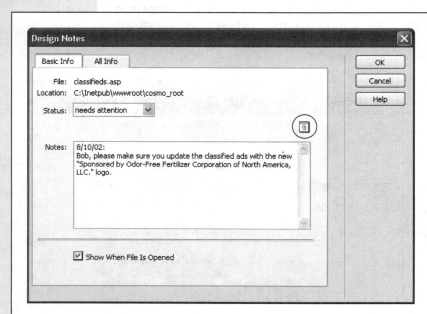

Figure 16-16:

If you want the Design Notes window to open whenever someone opens the page, turn on Show When File is Opened. This option makes sure no one misses an important note attached to a Web page. When the page is opened in Dream-weaver, the Design Notes window appears automatically. (This option has no effect when adding notes to GIFs, JPEGs, Flash movies, or anything other than a Web page.)

Adding Design Notes to a File

To add a design note to a document you're working on, choose your favorite method:

- Choose File→Design Notes.

- Choose Design Notes from the File Status menu in the toolbar (see Figure 16-9).

- Right-click (Control-click) a file in the Site panel (or an external object, such as a graphic or Flash movie, in the document window), and choose Design Notes from the contextual menu.

In any case, the Design Notes window now opens (Figure 16-16). If you like, you can use the Status pop-up menu to let your team members know where the file stands. For example, is it ready to move to the Web server? Is it just a draft version? Or is there something wrong with it that requires specific attention? Dreamweaver pro-vides eight different options: draft, revision1, revision2, revision3, alpha, beta, final, and needs attention. If these categories don't match your workflow—for example, you want a "needs proofing" flag—you can change them; see the box on page 506.

The note itself, which you type into the Note box, could be a simple question you have for the author of the page ("Are you sure '*Nsync: Defining a New Musical Language for the Modern Age' is an appropriate title for this article?") or more information about the status of the page ("Still need shot of apartment sod kit").

Tip: Click the calendar icon (circled in Figure 16-16) to pop the date into your note—a great way to keep a running tally of notes and the dates they were made.

When you click OK, Dreamweaver creates a file with all note information in it. This file ends with the extension .mno and begins with the name of the file; for the file index.html, for example, the note would be called *index.html.mno*.

Dreamweaver stores notes in a folder called *_notes* that it keeps in the same folder as the page or file. For example, if you add notes to the home page, Dreamweaver stores the notes file in the *_notes* folder inside the root folder.

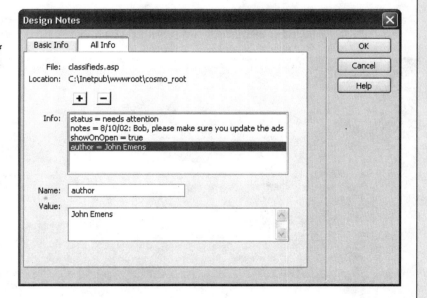

Figure 16-17:
Dreamweaver lets you create your own types of notes in the All Info tab of the Design Notes window. This lets you add more information to a page such as its author or designer. If you want to delete a note you've added, it's a simple matter of clicking on the note in the Info box and clicking the – (minus) button.

Viewing Design Notes

You can view design notes in a number of ways. If the note's author turned on Show When File Is Opened (Figure 16-16), of course, the Design Notes window opens automatically when you open that page.

Otherwise, to look at a note, you have any number of options:

- Choose File→Design Notes.

- Choose Design Notes from the document window's toolbar (see Figure 16-9).

- Double-click the small yellow balloon icon in the Notes column of the Site panel (see Figure 16-18). (This column is available in Windows only when the Site panel is expanded. See the box on page 432.)

- Right-click (Control-click) an embedded object like a graphic or Flash Movie, right there in the document window, and choose Design Notes from the contextual menu.

Organizing the Columns in the Site Panel

The Site panel's columns identify a file's name, file size, modification date, type, and so on.

Windows note: The Site panel doesn't display columns when it's docked with the other panels. You must click the Expand button (see the box on page 432) to maximize the Site panel.

This may be more information than you're interested in—or it might not be enough. So remember that Dreamweaver lets you show or hide these various columns, change

---

POWER USERS' CLINIC

Create Your Own Status Menu

The Status pop-up menu in Design Notes is a great feature. With a flick of the mouse, you can assign a status to a page or file, letting others know if a page is finished or just a rough draft. But the preset status options may not exactly fit your process. Your team may not use the terms "alpha" or "beta." Instead, you may have other stages you'd like to add, such as "copy edit," to signify that a page is ready to be proofread and tested.

With a little sly hacking, you can change the status categories to suit your needs. The file Design Notes.htm, in the Dreamweaver MX→Configuration→Commands folder, holds the key to this puzzle. Start by making a safety copy of the file; you can always return to it if something goes wrong.

Then open this file in a text editor like NotePad or SimpleText, or even within Dreamweaver's Code view (page 278). Find line 28 in the file, which looks like this:

```
var STATUS_ITEMS = new
Array("","draft","revision1",
"revision2","revision3",
"alpha","beta","final","needs
attention");
```

The words between the double-quotes are the choices that appear in the Status menu. You can change or delete them as you see fit (if you delete one, be sure to delete the word, both sets of quotation marks, and the following comma). Then, after saving changes to the file, quit and restart Dreamweaver, where you'll see your new, improved Status pop-up menu ready for action.

To make sure you and your co-workers see the same choices, give each of them the modified Design Notes.htm file, and advise them to put it in their own Dreamweaver MX→Configuration→Commands folders.

---

their order, or even create new columns with information retrieved from a file's Design Notes (page 508).

Tip: You can adjust the relative widths of these columns by dragging the dividing line between the column names. You can also sort all the pages listed in this window by clicking the relevant column's name. Clicking Modified, for example, sorts the files so that the newest appear first. Click a second time to reverse the sort, placing oldest files first.

Figure 16-18:
A yellow speech bubble in the Notes column of the Site panel indicates a Design Notes file.

When you're setting up a Web site in the Site Definition window (see page 426), you can view the column setup by clicking the File View columns category (Figure 16-19). If you're already working on a Web site, you may find it faster to choose View→File View Columns in the Site panel (Windows) or Site→Site Files View→File Views Column (Mac).

Once you're looking at the display shown in Figure 16-19, you can perform any of these stunts:

- **Reorder columns.** Click a column name in the Site Definition window to select it. Then click the up and down arrow buttons to move the column one spot to the left or right, respectively, in the Site panel.

- **Hide columns.** You may not care what date a file was last modified or whether it's a folder or Web page. If that's the case, hide the column by clicking its name in the Site Definition window and then turning off the Show checkbox (see Figure 16-19). (You can always return to the Site Definition window and turn the column back on.)

- **Share a column.** If you work with a team of designers, you might want to make newly added columns (see the next section) visible to them, too. (See Figure 16-19 for details.)

- **Adding Columns.** You can add informational columns of your own, as described next.

• **Deleting columns.** Click the column name, and then click the minus (–) button to delete the column. (Dreamweaver doesn't let you delete the built-in columns: Name, Notes, Type, Modified, and so on.)

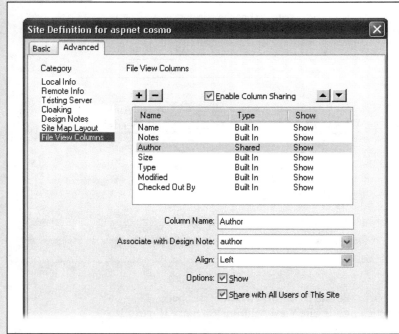

Figure 16-19:
If you're working with others, you'll probably want to share any columns you add. Click the Enable Column Sharing box; then, you'll be able to see columns that others on your team have added, and they'll be able to see columns you've added (if you've turned on Share with All Users of the Site for each column, of course).

"All Info" Design Notes in Column Views

Your Site panel offers columns for all the usual information bits: Name, Checked Out, and so on. But you may someday wish there were a column that showed each page's status, so that your Site panel could show you which files need proofreading, or who wrote each article, or which pages are being held until a certain blackout date.

You can indeed add columns of your own design, although the process isn't streamlined by any means. It involves two broad efforts: First, using an offshoot of the Design Notes feature described earlier, you set up the new columns you'll want displayed. Then, using the column-manipulation dialog box shown in Figure 16-19, you make them visible in the Site panel.

Phase 1: Defining the new information types

You create new kinds of informational flags—primarily for use as new columns in the Site panel—using the Design Notes dialog box described above.

Here's the rundown:

1. **Choose File→Design Notes.**

   The Design Notes window appears. (You can summon it in various other ways, too, as described on page 505.)

2. **Click the All Info tab.**

   This peculiar window shows the programmery underbelly of the Dreamweaver Notes feature. It turns out that it stores every kind of note as a name/value pair. If you used the main Notes screen (Figure 16-15) to choose Beta from the Status pop-up menu, for example, you'll see a notation here that says "status=beta." (*Status* is the name of the info nugget; *beta* is the value.) If you turned on the option called Show When File is Opened, you'll see "showOnOpen=true." And if you typed *Badly needs updating* as the note itself, you'll see "notes=Badly needs updating" on this screen.

   But those are just the built-in info types; you're free to create your own.

3. **Click the + button.**

   You may wonder why you'd do this; after all, you can type a lot of information in the Notes box under the Basic Info tab. The primary benefit of creating new types of notes is that you can display that information in the Site panel.

4. **Type the name of the new note in the Name field.**

   It might be Author, for example, so that you can note who wrote the text of each page. Or it could be Artist, if you wish to add a note to each image specifying who created it. Maybe you need a column called Hold Until, which lets you know when certain information is OK to publish online.

5. **Press Tab (to jump to the Value field); type the contents of the note.**

   This might be the actual name of the author or artist—Jane Stevens, for example—or the actual "Hold Until" date.

Tip: Keep the value short—one or two words. Otherwise, the narrow Site panel column will chop off the latter part of it. If you've got enough screen real estate, you can resize the columns by dragging the divider bars between column names.

   Repeat steps 3–5 if you want to add more notes to the page or file.

6. **Click OK.**

   The dialog box closes.

Phase 2: Adding the column

Just creating a new note type gets you only halfway home; now you have to tell Dreamweaver that you want to *see* that information in the Site panel, like this:

To add a column:

1. **Choose View→File View Columns in the Site panel (Windows) or Site→Site Files View→File Views Column (Mac).**

   The File Views dialog box appears.

2. **Click the + button (Figure 16-19).**

   A new, untitled column is added to the list, complete with three fields that need filling in (they now say "untitled").

3. **In the Column Name box, type the column-heading name you want to appear in the Site panel.**

   Make it short and descriptive. If possible, it should match the note type (Author, Artist, Hold Until, or whatever).

4. **Press Tab. Type the name of the Design Note you wish to use for this column.**

   This is the name part of the name/value pair described in step 4 of the previous instructions. For example, if you added a note named Author to a file, you would type *author* here. Capitalization doesn't matter.

   There's a pop-up menu here, too, but it always lists the same four options: Status, Assigned, Due, and Priority. If you choose Status, you'll get a column that reflects your choice from the Status pop-up menu shown in Figure 16-16. The other three options do nothing *unless* you created a matching note type in step 4 of the previous instructions. (It would be nice if this pop-up menu listed *all* of the note names you've created, so that you didn't have to remember them. Maybe in Dreamweaver MX: The Sequel.)

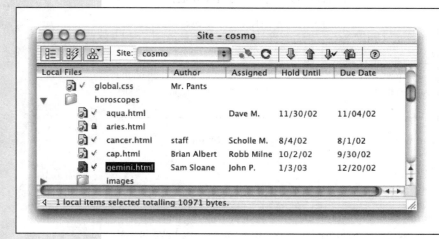

Figure 16-20:
The Site panel can show newly created kinds of status information. Each is actually a Design Note you've invented. To sort the list, click the gray column heading.

Before you wrap up the column-adding procedure, you can, if you wish, choose an alignment option for the text in the Site column (left, right, or center). Check to make sure that the Show checkbox is turned on (otherwise, your new column won't appear, and you've just defeated the purpose of this whole exercise). Finally, turn on Share with All Users of the Site, if you like.

The Share feature works like this. The next time you connect to the remote site, Dreamweaver uploads a file containing your newly defined column information. The next time another member of the team connects to the remote site, *his* copy of Dreamweaver downloads this file, so that his Site panel shows the same columns yours does.

Note: The column-sharing feature is very handy; it lets everyone working on a site share the same note information. But it works properly only if everyone on the team has the Enable Column Sharing box turned on (see Figure 16-19).

---

5. **Click OK.**

   You should now see the new information column in your Site panel, as shown in Figure 16-20. (If not, you may need to widen the window to reveal the additional column.)

DREAMWEAVER MX: THE MISSING MANUAL

Part Five:
Dreamweaver MX Power

5

Chapter 17: Snippets and Libraries

Chapter 18: Templates

Chapter 19: Automating Dreamweaver

Snippets and Libraries

Y
ou've finished the design for your company's new Web site. It looks great and
your boss is ecstatic. But you've only just begun. There are hundreds of pages
to build before you launch. And once the site's online, you'll need to make
endless updates to keep it fresh and inviting.

This is where Dreamweaver's Snippet and Library features come in, streamlining
the sometimes tedious work of building and updating Web pages.

As you build more and more Web pages (and more and more Web sites), you may
find yourself creating the same Web page elements over and over again. Many pages
of a site may share certain common elements that are always the same: a copyright
notice, a navigation bar, or a logo, for example. And you may find yourself frequently
using more complex items, such as a pop-up menu listing the twelve months of the
year, or a particular table design you use for photos and their captions.

Re-creating the same page elements time after time is tiresome and—thanks to
Dreamweaver—unnecessary. Dreamweaver provides two subtly different tools for
reusing common page elements: *Snippets* and *Library Items*.

Snippets Basics

Snippets aren't fancy or complex, but they sure save time. A snippet—new in
Dreamweaver MX—is simply a chunk of code that you store away and then plunk
into other Web pages. It could be HTML, JavaScript, or any of the other programming languages you might encounter. Dreamweaver comes with hundreds of snippets organized into different folders, like Comments (for creating HTML comments),

Footers (canned footer designs), and Form Elements (useful form parts like pop-up menus).

For example, say you always use the same table design to create a sidebar on a page (see the example on page 518). Each time you want to create a similar table, you could go through all the same steps to build it—or you could turn that table into a snippet, and then, with a simple double-click, add it to page after page of your site.

You keep these code chunks in the Snippets tab of the Code panel (see Figure 17-1). You access them in any of several ways:

- Choose Window→Snippets.
- Press Shift-F9.
- Click the Snippets tab on the Code panel.

Above and beyond Dreamweaver's preinstalled snippets, you can quickly build a collection of your own.

Using Snippets

Snippets come in two varieties: those that are a simple block of code and those that wrap around the current selection in the document. For example, in the Text folder of the Snippets tab, you'll find a snippet called Service Mark. Adding this snippet to a page inserts the code *^{sm}*, creating a superscripted service mark (sm) symbol.

But on occasion, you may want to wrap code around something you've selected on the page. You may want to add an HTML comment to your page (a message that won't appear in a Web browser, but that you can use for helpful notes to yourself or other Web designers). The "Comment, multi-line" snippet (in the Comments folder) can help you add such comments quickly. It wraps whatever you've selected within opening (<!--) and closing HTML comments (-->). Adding an HTML comment is as easy as typing the comment, selecting it, and then inserting this snippet.

Note: Unfortunately, unless the snippet's description (visible in the Snippet Panel's *Description* column) specifies that the snippet wraps, there's no way to tell whether a snippet is intended to wrap around a selection. You either have to try the snippet, or open the snippet in editing mode (see page 519) to find out. (While you've got the snippet open, you can add a note to its description indicating its ability, or inability, to wrap.)

To add a snippet to a Web page, click in the document where you want the item to go, or select the object you wish to wrap with a snippet. Then:

- Double-click the name of the snippet on the Snippets tab of the Code panel.
- Select the snippet on the Snippets tab and click Insert.

You can also drag the snippet from the panel into the document window. If the snippet is supposed to wrap a selection, drag the snippet onto the selected object.

Snippets can be used in either Design or Code view (see page 278), but some snippets make sense only in Code view. For example, the JavaScript snippets that come with Dreamweaver typically have to be inserted in the <head> of a page, inside of <script> tags. To use them, you must switch to Code view, insert the script tags, and then put the snippets inside.

Snippets simply dump their contents into a document; Dreamweaver doesn't step in to make sure that you're adding the code correctly. Unless you're careful—and have some knowledge of HTML—you might end up adding snippets that make your Web page unviewable. (For advice on how to avoid such pitfalls, see the box on page 520.)

Figure 17-1:
The Snippets tab on the Code panel contains reusable chunks of code—snippets—which you can organize in folders. After selecting a snippet from the list, a preview appears in the preview pane. In this example, you can see a preview of the snippet: a simple table with a colored background and dummy text. Snippets can have either a graphic preview (as in this example) called design preview, *or a* code preview, *which is the raw code. Code previews are useful for snippets that aren't visible in Design view, such as JavaScript code. You assign the preview type when you create a snippet.*

Snippets   Preview

Insert selected snippet

New folder

Delete
Edit
New snippet

Creating Snippets

Dreamweaver comes with a lot of snippets, many of which you may have no use for. No problem—it's simple to create snippets of your own. Here's how:

1. **Create and select the code you wish to turn into a snippet.**

   You could, for instance, select table in Design view, or select the opening and closing <table> tags (as well all code between them) in Code view.

   If you make a snippet out of code that isn't visible in Design view, such as a JavaScript program or content that appears in the <head> of the page, you'll need to switch into Code view first and then select the code.

2. **Click the New Snippet button on the Snippets tab (Figure 17-1).**

   The Snippet window appears (Figure 17-2), displaying the code you selected in the Insert field.

Tip: If you skip step 1, and just click the New Snippet button, you can either type the code or paste a previously copied selection into the Insert box (see step 6).

---

3. **Title the snippet.**

   The name you type in the Name field appears in the Snippet tab. Make sure to give it an easily understood name.

4. **In the Description field, type identifying details.**

   This step is optional, but useful. Use this field to provide a description of when and how to use the snippet and whether the snippet wraps a selection or not.

5. **Select a Snippet type.**

   Wrap Selection makes the code wrap code around a selection (Figure 17-2) when you use the snippet in your Web pages. The Insert Block option is for a snippet that is a single block of code inserted into the document—for example, a basic table design.

6. **If necessary, add the code for the snippet.**

   If you initially selected code in the document window, it already appears in the Insert Before or Insert Code field. If you're creating a wrapping Snippet, then some code will go in the Before field and some in the After field.

   For example, say you wanted to create a snippet that would let you set off a paragraph of text by adding a horizontal rule at the beginning of the paragraph and one at the end. In both the Insert Before and Insert After fields, you'd type <hr>—the HTML code for a horizontal rule.

7. **Select a Preview Type.**

The preview type determines how the snippet will appear in the Preview pane of the Snippets tab (see Figure 17-1). *Design* means the snippet will look as it would in Design view—a snippet of a table will appear as a table. *Code view* means the code itself will appear in the Preview pane (in that case, a snippet for a horizontal rule would preview like this: <hr>). Use Code preview for snippets that aren't visible in Design view, such as JavaScript code.

8. **Click OK.**

The snippet is added to the Snippets tab, and you can then drop it in your Web pages using any of the techniques described on page 516.

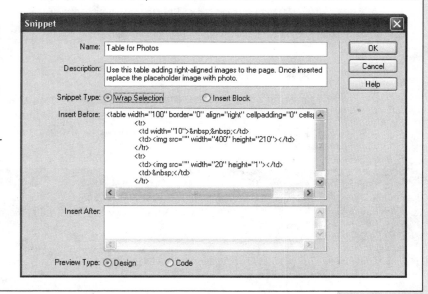

Figure 17-2:
The Snippet window lets you create reusable chunks of HTML called snippets. For snippets that wrap around a currently selected object on the page—for example, a snippet that adds a link to any selected text or graphic—you put code in the two insert boxes. The code that appears before the selected object goes in the top box, and code after the object appears in the bottom box.

If you need to go back and edit a snippet—change the code, type, description, or name—select the snippet in the Snippets tab and click Edit Snippet (Figure 17-1). You can also right-click (Control-click) on the snippet name and select Edit from the contextual menu. Whichever method you chose, the Snippet window (Figure 17-2) appears. Make your changes and click OK.

Organizing Snippets

To keep snippets organized, you can create new folders to store them by category. To add a folder to the Snippets tab, click the New Folder button (see Figure 17-1). An untitled folder appears; type a name for it. If you select a folder before clicking New Folder, Dreamweaver creates the new folder *inside* that folder. You can move folders around by dragging them into other folders.

Tip: To drag a folder to the top level of the Snippets list, you have to drag it all the way to the *bottom* of the tab, below any other folders. If you try to drag it to the top, Dreamweaver puts the folder inside the top folder in the list.

To move a snippet into or out of its folder, simply drag it. If you drag a snippet over a closed folder without releasing the mouse, that folder expands to reveal the folders inside, if any.

To delete a snippet, select it from the Snippets tab and click the Delete Snippet (trash can) button (see Figure 17-1). Quicker yet, press the Delete key.

Tip: Instead of deleting some of the less-than-useful snippets that ship with Dreamweaver, consider creating a folder to contain them. You may find a use for them some day.

Built-in Snippets

Many of the snippets that come with Dreamweaver offer solutions to specific problems you may never encounter, like a page footer containing two lists of links and a copyright notice. However, some of them are useful for most Web developers. Here are some examples:

UP TO SPEED

A Snippet of Caution

Snippets aren't as smart as other Dreamweaver features. Dreamweaver's usually good about warning you before you make a mistake, but it doesn't make a peep if you're adding a snippet incorrectly.

For instance, when you use one of the program's form snippets to add, say, a text field to a page, Dreamweaver doesn't check to see whether you're really putting the snippet into a form. Dreamweaver doesn't let you know whether the required <form> tag is missing, and certainly won't add it itself. Furthermore, if you're working in Code View, Dreamweaver lets you add snippets to the <head> or even outside the <html> tags altogether, which is useful when creating dynamic Web pages that include server-side programming code, but just creates messy and invalid HTML on normal Web pages.

Furthermore, snippets don't take advantage of Dreamweaver's site management features to keep track of links or paths to images. Suppose you create a snippet that includes an image. If you insert that snippet into another page, the image may or may not display correctly. If you create a snippet that includes a link from one page to another on your site, that link is also unlikely to work in another page.

So it's best to create snippets without images or links—but there are workarounds. For instance, you can create snippets with fake links—use nothing but the # symbol for the link, for example—and update the link later. For images, you can use Dreamweaver's Image Placeholder object to simulate a graphic in a snippet (choose Insert→Image Placeholder). After adding the snippet to the page, update the placeholder with your real image file.

If you want to create reusable content that can keep track of links and images, see Dreamweaver's Library feature, as described on the next page.

- **Comments Snippets.** The snippets in the Comments folder are great for turning any selection into a comment. For example, suppose you want to leave a message to other developers working on a page. Just type the message into the document window, select it, and insert the "Comments, multi-line" snippet. It's faster than using the Comments object in the Insert bar.

- **Close Window Button.** When you create a pop-up window (page 345), this snippet lets you add a close button to let people dismiss the window. The Close Window Button snippet (in the Form Elements folder) places a form button with the words Close Window on the window page, complete with the JavaScript necessary to close the window when your visitor clicks the button.

- **Dropdown Menus.** If you create a lot of forms for your sites (see Chapter 10) you'll find some useful snippets in the Form Elements folder, especially in the Dropdown Menus subfolder. For example, the "Numbers 1–12" snippet inserts a menu with the numbers 1–12 already coded into it—great for capturing those credit card expiration dates on an e-commerce site.

Library Basics

Imagine this situation: You manage a relatively large Web site consisting of thousands of Web pages. At the bottom of each page is a simple copyright notice: "Copyright MyBigCompany. We reserve all rights—national, international, commercial, noncommercial, and mineral—to the content contained on these pages."

Each time you add another page to the site, you *could* retype the copyright message, but this approach invites both typographic errors and carpal tunnel syndrome. And if you must *format* this text too, then you're in for quite a bit of work.

Fortunately, Dreamweaver's Library can turn any selection in the document window (a paragraph, an image, a table) into a reusable chunk of HTML that, later, you can easily drop into any Dreamweaver document. The Library, in other words, is a great place to store copyright notices, navigation bars, or any other chunk of HTML you use frequently.

But this is only half of the Library's power. Each Library item that you add to a Web page is actually only a copy, which remains linked to the original. Thanks to this link, whenever you update the original Library item, you get a chance to update every page that uses that item.

Suppose your company is bought, for example, and the legal department orders you to change the copyright notice to "Copyright MyBigCompany, a subsidiary of aMuchBiggerCompany" on each of the Web site's *10,000 pages.* If you had cleverly inserted the original copyright notice as a Library item, you could take care of this task in the blink of an eye. Just open the item in the Library, make the required changes, save it, and let Dreamweaver update all the pages for you (Figure 17-3).

Compared to Snippets, Library items are much smarter. They possess the unique ability to update the same material on an entire Web site in seconds and can successfully deal with links and images. Unlike Snippets, however, Dreamweaver's Library feature is site-specific. In other words, each site that you've defined in Dreamweaver (page 426) has its own Library; you can't use a Library item from one site on a page from a different site.

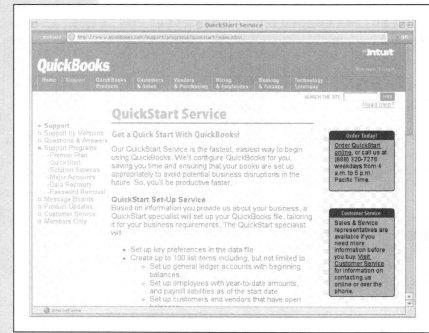

Figure 17-3:
This Dreamweaver-created site takes advantage of Library elements. The "Order Today" and "Customer Service" boxes use some fancy table work and would be a pain to re-create on every page. Even copying and pasting the HTML would be error-prone and potentially laborious. If they're Library elements, however, you can add them to pages with a simple drag and drop. And if any of the information in the sidebars changes, all you have to do is edit a single Library file to update the site.

Create and Use Library Items

To create a Library item, start by opening the Library window. Choose Window→Assets, and click the Library items button (it looks like an open book, as shown in Figure 17-4) to reveal the Library category.

Now select the part of your document that you wish to save as a Library item: a blob of text, a graphic, or whatever.

Note, however, that Library items can only contain page elements that appear in the document window—in other words, only HTML from the <body> of a Web page. You can't include anything that appears in the *head* of a page, like timelines (see page 392), Cascading Style Sheets, Dreamweaver Behaviors (Chapter 11), or meta tags. Furthermore, Library items must include a complete set of HTML tags—both an opening and closing tag—as well as all tags necessary to complete the original object. For example, Dreamweaver won't let you turn just a single cell, row, or column in a table into a Library item. If you try, Dreamweaver will add the *entire* table to the Library.

Tip: Use the tag selector (see page 19) to make sure you select the precise tag information you want.

Next, add the selection to the Library. As you may expect, Dreamweaver provides several ways to do this:

- Drag the highlighted selection into the list of Library items.
- Click the New Library Item button (Figure 17-4).
- Choose Modify→Library→Add Object to Library.
- Press Shift+Ctrl+B (Shift-⌘-B).

The new item appears in the Assets panel, bearing the jaunty name "Untitled." Just type to replace that proposal with a more useful name, such as *Copyright notice* or *Logo*. Your new Library element is ready to use.

Figure 17-4:
The Asset panel's Library category lists the name, file size, and location of each Library item in the current local site. When you select a Library item from the list, you see a small preview. In this example, the Library item "footer" is a black line, a copyright notice, and an email link.

Add Library Items to a Page

To add a Library item to a Web page, just drag it directly out of the Assets panel onto your page. (The long way: Click to plant your insertion point in the Web page, click the Library item you want in the Assets panel, and click the Insert button on the Assets panel, shown in Figure 17-4.)

When you insert a Library item into a Web page (or turn a selected item *into* a Library item), it sprouts a light yellow background color—or, in the case of nontransparent graphics, it takes on a gray, darkened look. The highlighting indicates that Dreamweaver intends to treat the Library item as a single object, even though it may be made of many different HTML elements. You can select it or drag it around, but you can't change it.

Remember, too, that the placed Library item is linked to the original copy in the Library. The copy in your document will change automatically to reflect any changes you make to the copy in the Library, using the technique described next.

Tip: You can break the link between the Library and a Library item you've *already* placed onto a Web page. Select the item on the page and then click Detach from Original in the Property inspector (Figure 17-5). Dreamweaver removes the comment tags (see the box below), thus breaking the link to the Library.

You can also insert the HTML of a Library item *without* maintaining a link to the Library by pressing the Ctrl (⌘) key when adding it to your document. Now the HTML on this page won't be updated when you change the original Library file.

Don't use this method if the Library item contains images or document-relative links, however. Dreamweaver doesn't update the links with paths appropriate to the document's location when you insert the Library item. In this case, to unlink a Library item, use the method described in the first paragraph of this tip.

Edit Library Items

You'll appreciate the real power of Library items when it's time to make a change. When you update the file in the Library, all the pages that you've graced with that item update themselves, too.

Start by opening the Library, as described on page 522. Then:

1. **Open the Library item that you want to edit.**

   You can do this by double-clicking the Library item in the Assets panel, by highlighting it and then clicking the Edit button Figure 17-4), or by highlighting a Library item on a Web page and then clicking the Open button on the Property inspector (Figure 17-5). (You can also open the library item file—.lbi file—in the Library folder of your site's root directly from the Site window.)

POWER USERS' CLINIC

Under the Hood of Library Items

Behind the scenes, Dreamweaver stores the HTML for Library items in basic text files. Those files' names end with the extension *.lbi,* and they stay in the Library folder inside your local site folder (page 429).

When you insert a Library item into a Web page, Dreamweaver inserts the item's HTML and adds a set of *comment* tags. These tags refer to the original Library file and help Dreamweaver remember where the Library item be-

gins and ends. For instance, if you turned the text "Copyright 2001" into a Library item called *copyright* and inserted it into a Web page, Dreamweaver would add the following HTML to the page:

```
<!--
#BeginLibraryItem "/Library/
copyright.lbi"-->Copyright
2001<!--#EndLibraryItem-->
```

Dreamweaver opens what looks like a miniature Web page document, containing nothing but the text, graphics, or other elements of the Library file.

2. Edit away.

A Library item is only a selection of HTML—it's not a complete Web page—so you can't edit page properties like the title or background color. Also, Library items can only be inserted in the body of a Web page, so stick with objects that would normally appear in the document window, such as links, images, tables, and text. Don't add any code that appears in the head of a Web page, such as Cascading Style Sheets, meta tags, behaviors, or timelines.

Tip: Library items can't contain CSS Style Sheets, but pages that include Library items might use style sheets to affect the formatting and display of the Library item. Trouble is, you won't see any CSS formatting when you're editing the Library item. The solution: Use Design Time style sheets, which let you temporarily attach an external style sheet to the Library item during editing (see page 243).

Figure 17-5:
The path of the selected Library item appears after the word Src.

3. Choose File→Save.

If there are any pages that use the Library item, Dreamweaver opens the Update Library Items window. You see a list of all pages that use the Library item.

4. Click Update.

Dreamweaver opens the Update Pages window, updates the HTML in all the pages that use the Library item, and then lists all of the files that it changed.

On the other hand, you don't necessarily have to click Update. Perhaps you have a lot of changes to make to the Library item, and you just want to save the work you've done so far. You're not done editing it yet, so you don't want to waste time updating pages you'll just have to update again. You can always update later (see the box on page 564); in that case, click Don't Update.

5. Click Done.

Renaming Library Elements

To rename something in your Library, click its name on the Assets panel (Figure 17-4). On the Mac, the name immediately becomes highlighted for editing; on Windows, you must pause briefly, click again, and *then* type the new name.

If you've already added the item to your Web pages, Dreamweaver prompts you to update those pages. Click Update; otherwise, the link will break between those pages and the Library.

Tip: If you accidentally click Don't Update, don't panic. Simply change the Library item back to its original name, and then *re*-rename it. Don't forget to click Update this time!

Deleting Library Elements

You can delete unnecessary elements from your Library at any time, but do so with caution. When you delete something from the Library, Dreamweaver leaves behind every copy of it that you've already placed onto your Web pages—complete with links to the now-deleted Library item.

In other words, you won't be able to edit the copies on your Web pages until you break those links. If you do indeed want to edit them, you'll have to do that manually on each page where the Library item appears, selecting the item and then clicking the Detach from File button (see Figure 17-5).

You've been warned; now here are the instructions. To get rid of a Library item, click it in the Assets panel, and then do one of the following:

• Click the Trash can icon in the Assets panel.

• Press the Delete key.

• Right-click (Control-click) the item's name and choose Delete from the contextual menu.

Tip: If you ever delete an item from the Library accidentally, you can re-create it, provided you've used it somewhere on one of the Web pages in the site.

Open the page containing the Library item; click the Library item to select it. Click Recreate on the Property inspector (Figure 17-5) to make it anew. (It means "re-create"; it has nothing to do with recreation at, say, the local community center.) A new Library item appears in the Library, using the name and HTML from the item you selected.

Library Tutorial

In this tutorial, you'll turn the *Cosmopolitan Farmer* copyright notice into a reusable Library item and add it to several pages in the site.

Note: The tutorial in this chapter requires the example files from this book's Web site, *www.sawmac.com/ dwmx*. Click the Tutorials link to go to the tutorials page. Click to download <u>Library Tutorial–Mac Files</u> or <u>Library Tutorial–Windows Files,</u> depending on the kind of machine you're using.

After your browser downloads and decompresses the files, you should have a DWLib (short for Dreamweaver Libraries) folder on your computer, containing the Web pages and graphics needed for this tutorial. If you're having difficulties, the Web site contains detailed instructions for downloading the files you'll be using with this book.

Creating a Library Item

Keep track of the location of the DWLib folder; you'll need it in the next step.

1. **Following the instructions on page 25, create a local site in Dreamweaver, choosing the DWLib folder as the root folder.**

   Name the site and set the root folder in the Local Info category of the Site Definition window. (Don't worry about the Remote Info, Design Notes, or any of the other categories.)

2. **In the Site window, double-click the file *index.html*.**

   The home page opens.

3. **Scroll to the bottom of the page and select the copyright.**

   Copyright information should be on every page of the site, so it makes a perfect candidate for a Library item. Notice that the copyright information is more than just text; it's actually a small table. The best way to select it is to click inside the text, and then click the <table> tag in the status bar of the document window.

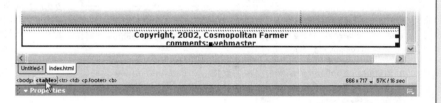

Figure 17-6:
Here, clicking <table> in the tag inspector selects the table containing the site's copyright notice.

4. **Choose Window→Assets and click the Library button.**

   The Assets panel opens and displays the Library category.

5. **Click the New Library Item button on the Assets panel.**

   A warning message appears, saying that the Library item may not look the same in other pages. Dreamweaver is trying to tell you that Library items can only contain HTML from the body of a Web page—not Cascading Style Sheets. (You can still include HTML, such as this table, that's had a style applied to it; just make sure that any *pages* to which you add the Library item have the appropriate style sheets.)

   The text in this example *is* formatted using a style sheet, so sure enough, it won't look the same in pages that don't have the same style sheet. In this exercise, however, that won't be a problem, since all the pages in the site share the same linked external style sheet (see page 234).

   Click OK to dismiss the warning. The copyright-notice item appears in the Library list, with an "Untitled" naming rectangle next to it.

6. Type *footer* next to the new item on the Assets panel.

You've just checked this standard blob of text into your Library. It's ready to use anywhere else on your site.

7. In your Site window, double-click the file in the *horoscopes* folder called pisces.html.

Notice that this page is missing a copyright notice at the bottom of the page.

8. Drag the *footer* Library item from the Assets panel to the bottom of the Pisces page, as shown in Figure 17-7.

You can recognize the newly inserted Library item by its yellow background. Click the text in the item and notice that you can't edit it; Dreamweaver treats it like a single object.

Figure 17-7:
In addition to dragging a Library item into the document window, you can also insert the item, by placing the insertion point in the document window and clicking the Insert button on the Assets panel.

9. Add the footer Library item to the other pages in the *horoscopes* folder.

There are eleven other pages in this folder. Open each page (by double-clicking its name in the Site window) and repeat step 8. All right, you don't have to do *all* of the pages, but at least do three or four to experience the full impact of what's next.

(You can close and save the pages as you go, or leave them open. Leave at least one open at the end and go on to step 10.)

10. Notice the mistake!

The copyright notice has the wrong date. The year 2000 is long gone! Oh, great—you'll have to change the date on every page. Fortunately, you've used a Library item; making the change will be a breeze.

11. **Double-click the footer item's icon (not its name) in the Assets panel.**

    The Library item opens up, ready for editing.

12. **Change *2000* to the current year. Choose File→Save.**

    The Update Library Items dialog box appears, listing all of the pages in the site that use the footer item.

13. **Click Update.**

    Dreamweaver opens the Update Pages dialog box and updates all the Web pages that use the footer item.

14. **Click Close to close the Update Pages dialog box.**

    And *now* if you open a file in the *horoscopes* folder, you'll find that the copyright date is correct.

    Now imagine that you just used this auto-update feature on a 10,000-page site. Sit back and smile.

Templates

Some Web designers handcraft sites with loving care, changing layouts, colors, fonts, banners, and navigation from page to page. But that approach isn't always practical—or desirable. Consistency is a good thing. Web pages that look and act similarly reassure visitors; when only important material changes from page to page, readers can concentrate on finding the information they want. Even more important, a handcrafted approach is often unrealistic when you're designing on a deadline.

This is where *templates* come in. Frequently, the underlying design of many pages on many Web sites is identical (see Figure 18-1). For instance, a company Web site with an employee directory may dedicate a single Web page to each employee. Each employee page probably has the same navigation bar, banner, footer, and layout. Only a few particulars differ, such as the employee name, photo, and contact information.

Template Basics

Templates let you build pages that share a similar structure and graphic identity, quickly and without having to worry about accidentally deleting or changing elements. They come in very handy when you're designing a site for which other, less Dreamweaver-savvy individuals are responsible for adding new pages. If you use a template, these underlings will be able to modify only the areas of a page that you, the godlike Dreamweaver guru, define.

A new page based on a template—also called a template *instance*—looks just like the template, except that you can only edit certain areas of the page, called, logically enough, *editable regions*. In the example shown in Figure 18-1, one editable region includes the question-and-answer text area; the rest of the page remains untouched and is, in fact, locked.

Prior to MX, Dreamweaver Templates were very basic: A portion of a page built from a template was either *locked* or *editable*. But in Dreamweaver MX, you can add subtle controls to template instances. Here's an overview of the features you'll encounter when creating and using templates:

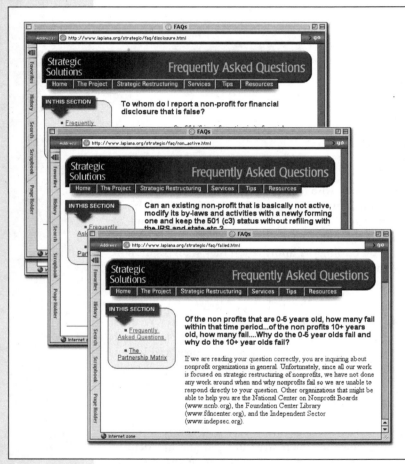

Figure 18-1:
These three Web pages are part of a section of a Web site dedicated to answering frequently asked questions. The pages each provide the answer to a different question, but are otherwise identical, sharing the same banner, navigation buttons, sidebar, and footer. This is a common scenario for most Web sites that include news stories, employee profiles, product pages, or press releases. In fact, it's so common that Dreamweaver has a special feature—Templates—to help you build such pages.

- **Editable Regions.** These are the basic building blocks of a template. (They work the same as they did in earlier versions of Dreamweaver.)

  An editable region is a part of a page—a paragraph, table cell, or headline, for example—that people can change on pages created from a template. A template page can have multiple editable regions—for example, one in a sidebar area and another in the main content section of a page.

- **Editable Tag Attributes.** There may be times when you want to make a particular tag *property* editable. For instance, if you'll want to specify a different background color for each page, you'll want to permit changes to the <body> tag's Bgcolor property.

  Or perhaps you've built a template that includes a photo with some complex formatting (left aligned and a Cascading Style Sheet applied, for example). Turning the entire image into an editable region could pose problems: When someone creates a new page from the template and then inserts a new photo, all of the formatting information can get lost. Instead, you could make just the image's *Src* property editable. People would then be able to insert new images for each page without inadvertently ruining the photo's formatting. (If the Width and Height properties varied from image to image, you could also make those attributes editable.)

- **Repeating Regions and Repeating Tables.** Some Web pages include *lists* of items: catalogs of products, lists of news articles, albums of photos, and so on. Dreamweaver MX lets you define *repeatable* regions for pages like this.

  For example, a page of product listings might include a picture, name, and price for each product in a catalog, organized using a table with multiple rows (Chapter 6).

  As template builder, you may not know in advance how many products the page will eventually list, so you can't fully design the page. However, you can use Dreamweaver MX to define a row—or any selection of HTML—as a repeating region, so that page authors can add new rows of product information when needed.

- **Optional Regions and Editable Optional Regions.** *Optional regions* make templates even more flexible. They let you show or hide content on a page-by-page basis.

  Suppose you create a template for your company's products. When some products go on sale (but others remain full price), you could add an *optional* region on the template that displays a big "On Sale!" logo. When creating a new product page, you could *show* the optional region for products that are on sale and keep it *hidden* for the others.

  Editable optional regions are similar, but they have the added benefit of being editable. Maybe you're creating a template for an employee directory, giving each employee a separate Web page with contact information. Some employees (you know the type) also want their picture displayed on the page, while others don't. Solution: Add an editable optional region that would let you show the space for a photo and add a different photo for each page. For the shyer types, you would simply hide the photo area entirely.

Note: The way Dreamweaver creates templates has changed significantly in Dreamweaver MX—so much, in fact, that you can't use template pages you created in Dreamweaver 4. However, if you've created a site using Dreamweaver 4's Template tools, Dreamweaver MX does understand those, so you can continue using those templates to build new pages in Dreamweaver MX.

Furthermore, Dreamweaver MX adds the ability to create *nested* templates, which inherit design elements from a master template. In this way, you can create a general unified design that's shared by other templates; this feature is described on page 552.

But facilitating page creation is only one of the benefits of templates. You'll also find that templates can greatly simplify the process of updating the design of a Web site. Like Library items, pages based on templates retain a reference to the original Template file. Any changes made to the template can be automatically passed on to all pages created from it, which can save you hours of time and trouble when it comes time to update the look or structure of your site. Imagine how much time you'll save when your boss asks you to add "just one more" button to the site's navigation bar. Instead of updating thousands of pages by hand, you'll need to update only a few template files.

Create a Template

The first step in creating a template requires building a basic Web page and telling Dreamweaver you'd like to use it as a Template. You can go about this in two ways: build a Web page and turn it into a template, or create a blank empty Template file and add text, graphics, tables, and other content to it.

Turning a Web Page into a Template

The easiest way to create a template is simply to base it on a Web page in your current site folder. Although you can create templates based on Web pages that *aren't* part of the current local site, you may run into problems with links and paths to images, as described in a moment.

Once you've opened the Web page, just choose File→Save As Template or click the Make Template button on the Insert bar (see Figure 18-2). In the Save As Template window (Figure 18-3), the name of the current local site appears in the Site pop-up menu; you see all templates for that site listed in the Existing Templates field.

Note: At this point, you could theoretically use the Save As Template window to save a template into any local site folder you've defined (see Chapter 14 for a discussion of local sites), but be careful with this option. If your page contains images and links, and you save it as a template for another local site, Dreamweaver won't copy the images from the first site folder into the other one; as a result, the paths to the image files and links won't work correctly.

If you must use a page from one site as a template for another, copy the Web page *and graphics* into the new site's root folder, open the page from there, and then create a template as described here.

Finally, type a name for the new template, and then click Save. Dreamweaver saves the page in the Templates folder of your local site root folder. It adds the extension .dwt to the file to indicate that it's a Dreamweaver template. (For dynamic Web pages, Dreamweaver adds the .dwt *before* the file's extension. For example, an Active Server Page template might have a name like *maintemplate.dwt.asp*.)

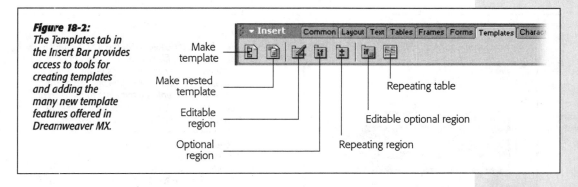

Figure 18-2:
The Templates tab in the Insert Bar provides access to tools for creating templates and adding the many new template features offered in Dreamweaver MX.

Make template

Make nested template

Editable region

Optional region

Repeating table

Editable optional region

Repeating region

Figure 18-3:
The Save as Template dialog box lets you save your template into any of the local site folders you've defined within Dreamweaver. Stick to your current local site to avoid broken links and related problems.

Building a Template from Scratch

It's easiest to create a Web page first and then save it as a template, but you can also build one from scratch. Open the Asset panel's Templates category by choosing Window→Assets and clicking the Template icon (see Figure 18-4). Then click the New Template button at the bottom of the Assets panel; once Dreamweaver adds a new, untitled template to the list, type a new name for it. Something descriptive, like "press release" or "employee page," will help you keep track of your templates.

After you've created a blank template for the site, you can open it by double-clicking its name in the Assets panel (or select its name and then click the Edit button at the bottom of the Assets panel). It opens just like any Web page, so that you can get busy designing it.

Define Editable Regions

Your next project is to specify which parts of your template are locked, and which are editable. By default, *everything* on a page is locked. After all, the main reason to use templates is to maintain a consistent, unchanging design and structure between pages. To make a template usable, you must define the area or areas you *can* change.

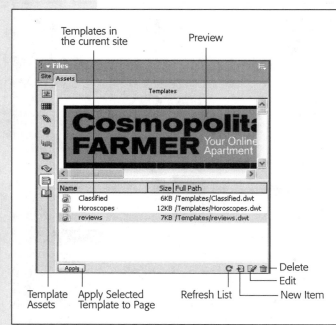

Templates in
the current site

Preview

Template
Assets

Apply Selected
Template to Page

Refresh List

Delete
Edit
New Item

Figure 18-4:
The Templates category of the Assets panel lists the name, file size, and location of each template in the current local site, and offers a number of controls for organizing them. The Apply button applies a template to the current open Web page. The Refresh Site List button updates the list of templates. (In general, Dreamweaver does a very good job of keeping the list up to date, so you'll rarely need this button.) The New Template button creates a new blank template in the Templates folder. Select a template from the list and click the Edit Template button to open the template for editing. To delete a template, select a template from the list and click the Delete button.

Adding a Basic Editable Region

To add an editable region to a template, start by selecting the part of the page you want to be able to change. You can incorporate anything in the document window (any HTML between the <body> tags).

Note: Dreamweaver 4 did not allow changes to the <head> of a page based on a template. Dreamweaver MX reverses that behavior. You can add custom style sheets, JavaScript, and meta tag information freely to any page created from a template (in fact, there's now no way to *prevent* users from doing this).

Drag across your page to select the elements you wish to make editable, or, for greater precision, you can use the tag selector (page 19) to make sure you select the exact HTML you want.

Now tell Dreamweaver that the selected elements are to be editable. You can use any of these techniques:

- Click the Editable Region button in the Templates tab of the Insert bar (see Figure 18-2).

- Choose Insert→Template Objects→Editable Region..

- Press Ctrl+Alt+V (Option-⌘-V).

- Right-click (Control-click) the selection and choose Templates→New Editable Region from the contextual menu.

When the New Editable Region dialog box appears, type a name for the region (you can't use the same name twice) and click OK. You return to your template, where the name you gave the region appears in a small blue tab above the editable region (see Figure 18-5).

Tip: If you use tables to lay out your pages (see Chapter 6), you'll often assign one table cell as the main area to hold the primary content of the page. For example, in the pages shown in Figure 18-1, the Frequently Asked Question and its answer appear in a single cell on the page. This cell makes a perfect editable region for a template. In the tag selector, just click the <td> tag associated with that cell and use any of the techniques discussed here to convert it to an editable region.

FREQUENTLY ASKED QUESTION

The Broken-Link Blues

Why aren't links in my templates working?

When you created the link, you probably *typed* a path into the Property inspector's Link field—a recipe for heartbreak. Instead, always select the target Web page for a link by clicking the folder icon in the Property inspector, or by pressing Ctrl+L (⌘-L). In other words, always link to pages within the site by *browsing* to the desired file.

Dreamweaver saves templates in the Templates folder inside the local root folder; all *relative* links need to be relative to this location. (Absolute links, like those to other Web sites, aren't a problem; see page 91 for the difference.) The reason you should browse to, rather than type in, your links is so that Dreamweaver can create a proper relative link.

Imagine this situation: You create a template for your classified ads. You'll store all classified ads for April 2001 inside a series of folders like this: *classifieds→2001→april,*

as shown in the site diagram here.

A link from a page in the april folder to the home page would follow the path marked 1 here. So when creating a link on your template, you might create a link to the home page by typing the path *../../../index.html.*

That's a logical choice if you're thinking about the page (in the *april* folder) you'll create *from* the template—but it won't work. Dreamweaver stores templates in the Templates folder, so the correct path would be path 2, or *../index.html.* When you create a new page *based on* the template and save it in the *april* folder, Dreamweaver, in its wisdom, automatically rewrites all paths in the page so that the links function correctly.

The beauty of Dreamweaver is that *you* don't have to understand how all this works. Just remember to use *relative* links in your templates and create them by clicking the folder icon in the Property inspector.

You may find that a single editable region is all you need. For example, the pages in Figure 18-1 have only one editable region—a single table cell where you can add a Frequently Asked Question and its answer. However, if you need to edit *multiple*

Repeating region   Tabs of editable regions   Template name

Figure 18-5:
This page is based on a template called Horoscope, as you can tell from the little tab in the document window's upper-right corner. You can modify editable regions, which are labeled with small tabs. In this example, the editable regions are called horoscope *and* signImage. *Additional editable regions appear within two repeating regions—labeled* RepeatCompatible *and* RepeatIncompatible—*which let you duplicate editable regions to form a list of items. The title of any page created from a template is also editable. All other parts of the page are locked; you can only make changes to the original template file.*

Under the Hood of Templates

Dreamweaver saves templates as HTML files in the Templates folder inside your current local site folder (see Chapter 14 for information on local sites). Each template bears the file name extension .dwt to distinguish it from regular Web pages. The program treats files in the Templates folder differently from normal Web pages, so don't save anything but .dwt files there. In addition, since Dreamweaver expects the Templates folder to be in the local root folder of your site, don't *move* the Templates folder. If you do, your templates won't work.

As with Library items, Dreamweaver uses HTML comment tags to indicate the name of the template. If you inspect a template-based document's HTML code (see Chapter 9), you'll see that, immediately following the opening <html> tag, Dreamweaver inserts a comment tag with the text

InstanceBegin template followed by the location and name of the template. Additional comment tags indicate areas of the page that you can modify, plus special template features like template parameters used for optional regions. For instance, the title of a page based on a template is always editable; its comment tag might look like this:

```
<!--InstanceBeginEditable
name="doctitle"-->
<title>My New Page</title>
<!--InstanceEndEditable-->
```

The first comment indicates the editable region's beginning and also includes the editable region's name. When editing pages based on the template, you can change only the HTML between these comment tags. Everything else on the page is locked.

areas of a Web page, add more editable regions to the template. For instance, when you create a template for an employee page, you might create editable regions for the employee's name, telephone number, and photo.

If you change your mind and want to lock a region again, select the editable region and choose Modify→Templates→Remove Template Markup. Dreamweaver removes the code that makes this region editable. This also works with the other types of template regions such as repeating and optional regions.

Warning: You can rename an editable region by clicking the blue tab on the template page and typing a new name into the Property inspector. However, if you've already built pages based on this template, it's not a good idea. Because template-based pages use the name to identify editable regions, Dreamweaver can lose track of where content should go when you rename a region. See Figure 18-18 for a workaround.

Adding a Repeating Region

Some Web pages contain lists of items. A catalog page might display row after row of product information—picture, name, price, and description. An index of Frequently Asked Questions might provide a list of questions and the dates they were posted.

FREQUENTLY ASKED QUESTION

Hindered by Highlighting

I'm distracted by the tabs and background colors that Dreamweaver uses to indicate Library items and Templates. How do I get rid of them?

When you use Library items or Templates, you'll see blue tabs and yellow backgrounds to indicate editable regions and Library items. Although these visual cues don't appear in a Web browser, they can still make your page harder to read while working in Dreamweaver. Fortunately, you can alter the background color of these items and even turn highlighting off altogether.

Choose Edit→Preferences or press Ctrl+U (⌘-U). In the Preferences Category list, click Highlighting. To change the background color for editable regions, locked regions, and Library items, use the color box (see page 34) or type in a hexadecimal color value. To remove the highlighting, turn off the Show box next to the appropriate item.

However, it's often useful to keep highlighting on; it's a good way to keep track of Library items and editable regions. If you want to turn off highlighting temporarily, simply choose View→ Visual Aids→Invisible Elements, or use the keyboard shortcut Ctrl+Shift+I (Shift-⌘-I) to toggle these visual cues off and on. This technique has the added benefit of hiding table borders, layer borders, and image maps, as well as other invisible elements.

If you were to make a template for either of these pages, you would add an editable region to the area of the page where these lists appear. Just creating an editable region, however, wouldn't give you any ability to enforce (or easily update) the design of these lists, because *everything* within an editable region can be changed on a page based on a template.

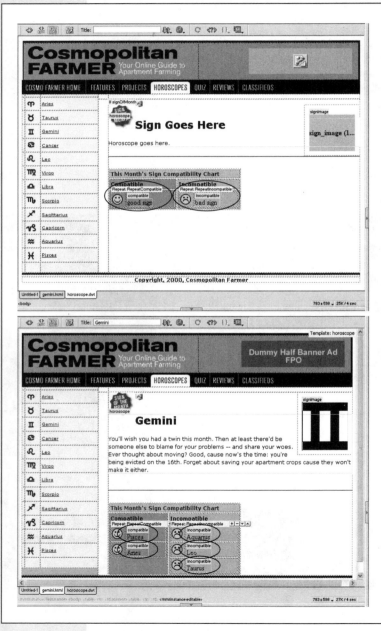

Figure 18-6:
A repeating region lets page authors add multiple selections of repeating information.

Top: In this example, the template has two repeating regions, labeled RepeatCompatible and RepeatIncompatible (circled).

Bottom: A complete page based on this template includes two repeated editable regions circled in the left column and three circled in the right column. If another page requires more compatibility listings, you could easily add additional rows to each list. However, the template still controls the basic design. Changing the background color of any of the repeating regions' cells in the template page automatically changes the same elements in all pages created from the template. From a design perspective, this also means that page authors can't mess around with the design of a repeating region—just the content marked as editable.

Fortunately, Dreamweaver MX provides a new pair of template tools to overcome this problem: *repeating regions* and *repeating tables*. Both let you create areas of a page that include editable (and uneditable) regions that can be repeated any number of times on any template-based page (see Figure 18-6).

Adding a repeating region is similar to adding an editable region. Select the area of the template page you wish to make repeatable, which usually contains at least one editable region. Most often, this will be a row in a table, so you could select the row (<tr> tag) with the information to be repeated. You could just as easily select a paragraph or a list item (<li> tag).

Tip: You can make a repeating region that doesn't include an editable region. For example, a template for a movie review Web page could include a repeating region that is simply a graphic of a star. A page author adding a new movie review could repeat the star graphic to match the movie's rating—4 stars, for example.

Now tell Dreamweaver that the selected elements are part of a repeating region. You can use any of these techniques:

- Click the Repeating Region button in the Templates tab of the Insert bar (see Figure 18-2).

- Choose Insert→Template Objects→Repeating Region.

- Right-click (Control-click) the selection and choose Templates→New Repeating Region from the contextual menu.

When the New Repeating Region dialog box appears, type a name for the region and click OK. You return to your template, where the name you gave the region appears in a small blue tab above the editable region (see Figure 18-6). (See page 558 for a discussion of using a repeating region when building a new template-based page.)

Warning: Dreamweaver MX lets you name a repeating region with a name already in use by an editable region. But don't—multiple template areas with the same name will cause Dreamweaver to act unpredictably.

Repeating Tables

The new *repeating table* tool is essentially a shortcut to creating a table with one or more repeating rows in it. You could, if you had a lot of time on your hands, achieve the same effect by adding a table to a page, selecting one or more rows, and applying a repeat region to the selection. To use the repeat table tool:

1. **Click on the template page where you wish to insert the table.**

   You can't insert a repeating table into an already defined editable, repeating, or optional region. You must be in an empty, locked area of the template.

2. **Click the Repeating Table button in the Templates tab of the Insert bar (see Figure 18-2).**

Alternatively, you can choose Insert→Template Objects→Repeating Table. Either way, the Insert Repeating Table window appears (Figure 18-7).

Figure 18-7:
The Insert Repeating Table dialog box lets you kill two birds with one stone: It adds a table to a page, turns one or more rows into a repeating region and adds editable regions into each table cell inside the repeating region.

3. **Fill out the basic properties of the table.**

The top part of the window lets you set up the basic structure of the table: rows, columns, cell padding, cell spacing, width, and border. This is the same information you'd provide when creating any table, as described on page 158. You usually start a repeating table with two rows—one for a heading, and another to contain the information you wish to repeat.

4. **In the Starting Row box, type the number of the row where the repeating region should begin.**

Often you'll just have one repeating row: one row of product information, for example. It's conceivable, however, that you might want each entry to take up two rows. The first would list Name and Description; the second would contain a cell for a photo and a cell for the price. You set up this effect in this step and the next.

5. **In the Ending Row box, type the number of the last repeating row.**

If you only wish to repeat a single row, this should be the same number you provided for step 4.

6. **Type a name for this repeating region.**

Don't use the same name as another template region. You'll run the risk of unpredictable results on template-based pages.

7. **Click OK.**

Dreamweaver inserts a table into the page. A blue tab with the name of the repeating region appears (see Figure 18-6), as do blue tabs in each cell of each repeated row. These tabs indicate new editable regions—one per cell.

Since these new editable regions have uninformative names like EditRegion4, you might want to rename them. Click the blue tab and type a new name in the Property inspector. (But do so *before* you create any pages based on the template—see the warning on page 539.)

To remove a repeating region, select it by clicking the blue Repeat tab and choose Modify→Templates→Remove Template Markup. A more accurate way to select a repeating region is to click anywhere inside the region and then click <mmtemplate:repeat> in the tag selector. (See page 19 for more on using the tag selector.)

Making a Tag Attribute Editable

An editable region lets you change areas of HTML on new pages you create from a template, areas such as a paragraph, image, or entire table. However, when you're creating a template for others to make pages from down the line, you may want to limit these page authors' editing abilities. You may want to allow budding Web designers to change the background color of a page, or the color of a table cell, without changing other properties like cell width or paragraph alignment. You can use Dreamweaver MX's new Editable Tag Attribute to specify *which* tag properties your successors can change.

Tip: Before making a tag attribute editable, first set that property to a default value in the template. Doing so inserts a default value and make the attribute appear in the Editable Tag Attribute window (see steps 3 and 7 that follow).

To make an tag attribute editable:

1. **Select the tag whose property you wish to make editable.**

Using the tag selector (see page 19) is the most accurate way.

2. **Choose Modify→Templates→Make Attribute Editable.**

The Editable Tag Attributes window opens (Figure 18-8).

3. **Select an attribute from the menu or add a new attribute with the Add button.**

Only properties you've already set for the selected tag appear in the Attribute menu. In other words, if you've selected an image, you'll probably see the Src, Width, and Height properties listed. But unless you've set the image's border, the Border property won't appear.

To add a property, click the Add button. In the window that appears, type the appropriate property name. For example, to add the <body> tag's background color property, you'd type Bgcolor. (If you're not sure of the property's name, check out Dreamweaver's built-in HTML reference, described on page 288.)

4. **Make sure the Make Attribute Editable box is turned on.**

If you decide that you no longer want to allow editing of this property, you can return to this dialog box and turn off editing, as described on the facing page.

Figure 18-8:
Dreamweaver provides detailed control for template pages. To make just a single property of a single tag editable when pages are later based on your template, use the Make Attribute Editable command.

5. **Type a name in the Label field.**

What you type here should be a simple description of the editable tag and property, which will help page authors correctly identify editable properties. For example, you could use *Page Color* as a label for the <body> tag's Bgcolor property, or *Product Image* when making a particular image's source (Src) property editable.

6. **Choose a value type from the pop-up menu.**

Your choices are:

Text. Use this option when a property's value is a word. For example, the image tag's Align property can be *top, middle, baseline,* and so on. Or, when using Cascading Style Sheets, you could make a tag's Class property editable to allow page authors to apply a particular custom style to the tag—*content, footer,* and so on.

URL. Use this option when the editable property is a path to a file, like an image's Src property or a link's Href property. Using its site management tools, Dreamweaver will keep track of these paths and update them correctly when you move your pages around your site.

Color. If the property requires a Web color, such as a page's background color, select this option. It will make Dreamweaver's color box available to people who build pages from the template.

True/False. You shouldn't use this option. It's intended for Dreamweaver's Optional Regions feature (discussed below), and it doesn't apply to HTML properties.

Number. Use this choice for properties that require a numeric value, such as an image's Height and Width properties.

7. **Type a default value into the Default field.**

This step is optional. The default value defines the initial value for this property, when people first create a page based on the template. They can then modify this value for that particular page. (If you have already set this property in the template, its value will appear automatically in this box.)

8. **Click OK to close the window.**

Dreamweaver adds code to the template page that allows page authors control of the attribute. Setting this attribute on pages created from the template is described on page 556.

If you later decide that you *don't* want a particular tag's property to be editable, Dreamweaver can help. Select the tag with the editable attribute and choose Modify→Templates→Make Attribute Editable. In the window that appears, turn off the "Make Attribute Editable" checkbox (Figure 18-8). Unfortunately, this doesn't remove *all* of the template code Dreamweaver added. Even after you turn off editing for an attribute, Dreamweaver leaves behind the parameter used to control the tag's property. To get rid of *this* extra code, see the box on page 551.

Adding Optional Regions

Templates provide consistent design. While that's generally a good thing, it can also become boring. Furthermore, there may be times when you'd like the flexibility to include information on some template-based pages but not on others.

Dreamweaver MX provides a new—and fairly foolproof—way to vary page design: *optional* regions. An optional region is simply part of a template page that can be hidden or displayed on each template-based page (see Figure 18-9). When creating a new page based on the template, a page author can turn the region on or off.

Creating an optional region is a snap. Just select the HTML code you wish to make optional, and then do one of the following:

• Click the Optional Region button in the Templates tab of the Insert bar (see Figure 18-2).

• Choose Insert→Template Objects→Optional Region.

• Right-click (Control-click) the selection and choose Templates→New Optional Region from the contextual menu.

In the New Optional Region window, type a name (see Figure 18-10). Make sure not to use the same name as any other region on the page, and—although Dreamweaver allows it—don't use spaces or other punctuation marks. (Following the rules for naming files as described on page 424 is the best method, and ensures that the optional region will work properly.) Click OK to close the window and create the new Optional region. Dreamweaver adds a light blue tab with the word "If" followed by the name you gave the region (Figure 18-9).

Figure 18-9:
Now you see it, now you don't. Optional regions let you show or hide content on a page-by-page basis. In these examples, the template page has an optional region containing a "Sign of the Month" button indicated by the blue tab with the label If signOfMonth (top). When creating a template-based page from this template, you can either display the optional region (bottom left) or hide it (bottom right).

Labels in figure: Template, Optional region, Template-based pages

Locking Optional Regions

An optional region can include editable and repeating regions *and* locked regions. For example, if you simply want to allow a page author to turn on or off a graphic ("This item on Sale!!!!"), insert the graphic into a locked area of the page and make it an optional region as described earlier. In this way, a page author won't be able to change the graphic or ruin its formatting—only make it visible or hidden.

Repeating Optional Regions

An optional region can also include repeating regions. For example, suppose you create a repeating region (page 539) that lets a page author add row after row of links to a list of related articles. You could then turn this repeating region into an optional region, as described earlier, so that if a particular page had no related articles, the author could simply hide the entire "related articles" section of the page.

Optional Editable Regions

Dreamweaver MX's Optional Editable Region command inserts an optional region with an editable region *inside* it. To use it, click in the template at the spot you'd like to add it, and click the Optional Editable Region button on the Templates tab of the Insert bar (see Figure 18-2). The New Optional Region window appears; give it a name and follow the same steps already outlined for an optional region.

This technique doesn't offer a lot of control; it's hard to insert HTML *outside* the editable region, for example. So if you want to have an image or table that is optional but *not* editable, it's usually better to just create the editable region as described on page 536 and turn it and any other HTML you wish to include into an optional region.

Figure 18-10:
The Optional Regions feature lets you show or hide specific content on template-based pages. Checking the Show By Default box tells Dreamweaver to display the region when a page author first creates a template-based page. Turn this box on if the optional region is going to show on most pages. You'll save someone the effort of turning the region on each time.

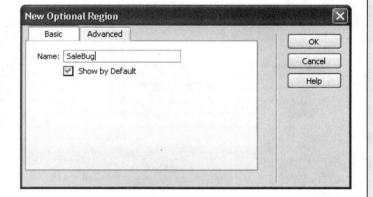

Advanced Optional Regions

Optional regions are rather simple affairs: They either appear or they don't. But Dreamweaver offers more complex logic for controlling optional regions. For example, maybe you want several different areas of a page to be either hidden or visible at the same time—perhaps an "On Sale Now!" icon at the top of the page *and* a "Call 1-800-SHAZBOT to order" message at the bottom of the page. When one appears, so does the other.

Because these objects are in different areas of the page, you have to create two separate optional regions. Fortunately, using Dreamweaver's advanced options for optional regions, you can easily have a single region control the display of one or more additional areas of a page. Here's how to do it:

1. **Create the first optional region using the steps on page 545.**

    Give the region a name using the Basic tab of the New Optional Region window (see Figure 18-10).

2. **Select the part of the page—an image, paragraph, or table—that you wish to turn into a second optional region.**

   In this case, you'll make the display of this region dependent on the optional region added in step 1. If the first region is visible on the page, this region will also show.

3. **Click the Optional Region button on the Templates tab of the Insert bar (see Figure 18-2).**

   The New Optional Region window appears.

4. **Click the Advanced tab.**

   The optional region's advanced options appear (see Figure 18-11). In this case, you want the first optional region you created to control the display of this new region. So instead of giving this region a name, you'll simply select the name of the first optional region.

Figure 18-11:
The Advanced tab of the New Optional Region window lets you provide more precise control over the display of an optional region. You can make the region display only when another region is visible, or use Dreamweaver's template expression language to create a more complex behavior. In this case, the selected region will only display when another region—named SaleBug—is NOT visible (the ! is a programming equivalent to "is not").

5. **Click the Use Parameter button and select the name of the first optional region from the pop-up menu.**

   This step is what makes the first optional region control this region. If a page author displays the first region, this second region will also display.

6. **Click OK to close the window and create the new optional region.**

   You can continue adding optional regions in this way, using the Advanced tab and selecting the name of the first optional region from the menu. This way, a single region can control the display of many other areas of the page.

Even fancier tricks

You can use these advanced controls for even more elaborate Web page stunts. For example, say your site comprises several sections. When a visitor is in one section of the site, its navigation button is highlighted and a secondary navigation bar miraculously appears with links to other pages in that section.

Using a template, you could add an optional region containing the highlighted section button. When you add the secondary navigation bar to the page, you'd make *it* an optional region controlled by the highlighted navigation button. Then, when you add a page to that section of the site, you would simply show the optional region containing the highlighted button, causing the secondary navigation bar to appear as well.

Controlling Regions with Expressions

You program these complex behaviors using a basic *expression language* that Dreamweaver understands. For example, instead of having an optional region appear when another optional region is visible (as in the above example), suppose you want to have a region appear when another region is *in*visible. This arrangement can come in handy when you're creating a navigation bar. When a page is in a particular section, for instance, the navigation button for that section is highlighted, but the button isn't highlighted if the page is in another section.

In other words, you could build a single template for all the sections of the site, but control the appearance of the navigation bar separately for pages in each individual section (see Figure 18-12).

Here's how you'd do that:

1. **Click in the page where you wish to insert the navigation buttons.**

2. **Insert the highlighted ("You are in this section") navigation button.**

   This could be a rollover image (see page 126) or just a single graphic. If you have multiple pages in the section, you'll probably also want to link this graphic to the main page for that section.

Figure 18-12:
These two pages were created from the same template, but an optional region on the page at left governs the highlighting of the top navigation button. A different optional region is turned on in the page at right.

3. **Click next to the highlighted button and insert the plain ("You can go here") navigation button.**

   This could also be a rollover image with a link to the main page for this section (for example, the main Products page).

4. **In the Property inspector, select the highlighted navigation button and link (if it has one).**

   This button will appear on any template-based page for this section.

5. **Click the Optional Region button on the Template tab of the Insert bar (see Figure 18-2).**

   The New Optional Region window appears. Make sure the Basic tab is selected.

6. **Type the name of the section into the Name field. Click OK to close the window and create the optional region.**

   For example, if this section of your site advertises your company's products, you might call it *products.* Don't use any spaces or punctuation other than hyphens (-) or underscores (_) for the name. Also make sure the Show by Default box is *not* turned on. Since you'll be building template-based pages for all the sections of your site, most pages you build will be in other sections of the site. Your work will go faster if this highlighted button starts out hidden. In the next steps, you'll make the plain nav button appear by default.

7. **Use the Property Inspector to select the plain button and link, and then click the Optional Region button on the Insert bar.**

   The New Optional Region window appears again, but this time you'll use the advanced options.

8. **Click the Advanced tab and turn on the Enter Expression radio button (see Figure 18-9).**

   You'll type an *expression* in the Expression field. An expression is a programming statement that is either true or false. (For an obvious example, the statement 2=2 is true, but the statement 2=4 is false.) The important thing to remember here is that when an expression is true, the optional region is visible; when it's false, it's hidden.

9. **Type an exclamation point (!) followed by the name you entered in step 6— *!products,* for example.**

   Dreamweaver's template expression language is based on the JavaScript programming language. An exclamation mark means "not," so this code means "not *products.*" A translation into non-caveman language: When the *products* region (remember, that's the highlighted button) is *not* displayed, this region (button) will appear on the page.

   The logic gets a little complicated, but have faith. When you add a new page based on this template, the optional region you added in step 6 is *not* visible (because you turned off the Show by Default box). In other words, because the region—*products* in this example—is *not* showing, this region, the one with the plain nav button, will by default appear on the page. Turning the *products* region on will therefore *hide* the plain nav button. In other words, the first optional region works like a light switch, alternately turning on one or the other navigation button.

10. **Click OK to close the window and add the additional optional region.**

Repeat this process for each button in the navigation bar. When you're finished, your template will be perfectly suited for displaying customized navigation bars for each section of your site. When you create a new template-based page, simply turn on the region for the particular section in which the page is located. (Hiding and showing optional regions is described on page 559.)

As you can see, optional regions are very powerful—and potentially confusing. But using even basic optional regions, you can exert a great deal of control over your template-based pages. For more information on template expressions and optional regions, take a look in Dreamweaver's built-in Help system. (Press F1; then, in the

---

POWER USERS' TIP

Understanding Template Parameters

When you insert an optional region, Dreamweaver adds special code called a *template parameter* to the head of the Web page. This code is responsible for showing or hiding an optional region.

In fact, Dreamweaver uses parameters when you make a tag attribute editable, too. A typical parameter for an optional region might look like this:

```
<!--TemplateParam name="SaleBug"
    type="boolean" value="true"-->
```

The *<!--*and*-->* are HTML comments that hide this code from a Web browser. *TemplateParam* tells Dreamweaver that the comment is actually part of the program's Template features—specifically, a template parameter.

A parameter has three parts: name, type, and value. The name is the name you gave the editable region. The type—Boolean—indicates that this parameter can be either true or false. Here, the value is "true," which means that the optional region called *SaleBug* will be visible. (Don't worry; you don't have to actually edit this code by hand to turn optional regions on and off, as you'll see on page 559.)

In programming jargon, a template parameter is known as a *variable*. In simpler terms, it's just a way to store information that can *vary*. Dreamweaver will react differently depending on this value: show the region if the parameter is true, or hide it if the parameter is false.

Editable tag attributes also use parameters to store the values you enter for the tag attribute. For example:

```
<!--TemplateParam
    name="PageColor" type="color"
    value="#FFFFFF"-->
```

On template-based pages, you can change the *value* of a parameter used for an editable tag attribute to change that tag's *property*.

Unfortunately, when you delete an optional region from a template, or remove the ability to edit a tag attribute, Dreamweaver often leaves these parameter tags hanging around in the head of the template document. Keeping in mind that Dreamweaver adds these parameter tags directly before the closing </head> tag, you can find and remove unused parameter tags in Code view (see Chapter 9).

---

window that appears, click the *Search* tab. Type *template expressions* in the box, and click the List Topic buttons. The Dreamweaver Help system then lists several articles related to templates and template expressions.)

Editing and Removing Optional Regions

After inserting an optional region, you can always return to the New Optional Region dialog box to change the region's name, alter its default settings, and use advanced options. To edit an optional region, first select it using one of these techniques:

- Click the region's blue tab in the document window (Figure 18-5).

- Click anywhere inside the optional region in the document window and click the <mmtemplate:if> tag in the tag selector (see page 19 for more on the tag selector).

When you select an optional region, an Edit button appears in the Property inspector. Click it to reopen the New Optional Region window. You can then change the region's properties.

To remove an optional region, select it using one of the techniques listed above and choose Modify→Templates→Remove Template Markup. Dreamweaver removes most of the code associated with the optional region (but see the box on page 551).

Nested Templates

Large sites may have many different sections or types of pages. Each section of the site or type of page may have its own unique look. A Frequently Asked Questions page may have distinct areas for a question, an answer, and links to further resources, while a product page may have a picture, a product description, and ordering information. You could create different templates for each type of page, but even that may be more work than necessary.

While many pages in a site may have subtle differences, they share very basic design features. The overall structure of every page, for example, may be the same: same logo, banner, and navigation bar. Even the basic layout may be the same. And there lies the problem with creating individual templates for each section. If you need to make a very basic site-wide change, such as adding a new button to the site's overall navigation system or altering the banner, you need to edit *each* template individually, adding extra time, effort, and risk of making a mistake.

Fortunately, Dreamweaver MX offers a new tool to solve just this problem: nested templates. A *nested template* is a template you make from another template, which then becomes the *master* template (see Figure 18-13). To imagine this in action, think of a basic software company Web site with three sections: Support, Our Products, and Downloads. Each section has its own brand of information and specific layout needs. However, all three sections share the same banner and navigation.

To create a template system for this site, you would first create a very basic template that includes elements, including editable regions, shared by all pages—the master template. You would then create a nested template based on the master. On the nested template, you could add further design refinements and additional editable regions for the areas that can be changed on pages created from the nested template.

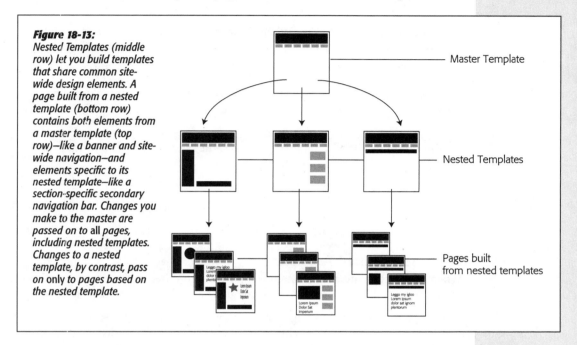

Figure 18-13:
Nested Templates (middle row) let you build templates that share common site-wide design elements. A page built from a nested template (bottom row) contains both elements from a master template (top row)—like a banner and site-wide navigation—and elements specific to its nested template—like a section-specific secondary navigation bar. Changes you make to the master are passed on to all pages, including nested templates. Changes to a nested template, by contrast, pass on only to pages based on the nested template.

Master Template

Nested Templates

Pages built from nested templates

Yes, this sounds complex—and yes, it is. But when the alternative is hours or days of manual template updating, you can see why serious Web designers are willing to spend the time to master any shortcut they can get.

To create a nested template:

1. **Build a template as described on page 534.**

   This page will act as the master template and control all nested templates. It should include the basic elements shared by all nested template pages, such as your logo and email links. This is also the time to add editable regions in the areas the nested templates can change, such as table cells to hold blocks of text and images.

2. **Close, name, and save this template (File→Save as Template).**

   Your template is safe on the hard drive.

3. **Choose File→New.**

   The New Document window opens (see Figure 18-14).

4. **Click the Templates tab. In the Templates For list, select the Web site you're working on.**

   You can open templates from any site you've defined in Dreamweaver.

5. **From the list of templates, select the name of the master template file you created in step 1.**

   Make sure the Update Page When Template Changes box is turned on. Otherwise, the nested template won't update when you edit the master template.

6. **Click OK.**

   Dreamweaver creates a new template-based page. At this point, it's simply a basic Web page based on the original template. Next, you'll turn it into a *nested template*.

7. **Choose File→Save as Template, or click the Nested Template button on the Templates tab of the Insert bar (see Figure 18-2).**

   The Save As Template window appears (see Figure 18-3).

8. **Type a name for the template and click the Save button.**

   Voila! A nested template.

Customizing Nested Templates

When you first create a nested template, there's no difference between it and the master template. They share the same design, content, and template regions.

The next step is adding the design elements that are specific to pages built from that template. For example, you might add a special type of table for displaying a product photo, description, price, and other information. This table will appear only in pages built from this nested template, not from the master template or any other nested template.

There are a few things you should keep in mind:

- When creating pages from templates, you can add content only to an editable region. That's true not only for template-based pages, but for nested templates, too. If the master template has *no* editable regions, you won't be able to change anything on the nested template created from it.

- When working on a nested template, you can insert an editable region only into an editable region supplied by the master template. For example, say you've created a master template to provide a consistent banner and navigation bar to the site, all in a locked region of the master template. Then you add a large empty area at the bottom of the page, and turn it into an editable region that you can customize to make specific layouts for each nested template. After creating a nested template from the master template, you can then add new editable regions to this open area. In fact, you can add any template region—repeating, optional, or editable—to this area.

• If, when working on a nested template, you insert a template region (editable, optional, or repeating) into an editable region supplied by the master template, pages based on the nested template can modify *only* those new regions. The rest of the editable region supplied by the master template is not editable on the pages based on the nested template.

Using the example in the above paragraph, let's say you next add a repeating table to your nested template (see page 541 for more detail about repeating tables). When you create a page based on this nested template, *only* the editable areas marked out in the repeating table can be changed. Of course, the other side of the coin is, if you add an optional region to the master template, and then refrain from adding any particular template regions, all of the HTML inside that region will be editable in the nested template *and* in all pages based on the nested template.

Using Nested Templates

Here's an example of how you might use nested templates. Suppose you want to create a uniform design for your site. Every page of the site should have a site logo and a site-wide navigation bar. Each page within one section of the site will also have a sidebar containing a *secondary* navigation bar, containing navigation buttons for just that section. Finally, every page will have a large content area to hold the information specific to that page.

Using nested templates, creating a Web site like this couldn't be easier. Create a master template containing the site banner and navigation bar. This template would also include editable regions for the sidebar and main content area.

Next, create a nested template for one *section* of the site, leaving the content area as it is. Since each page will have its own content in this area, you don't need to do anything to this region. Then add the secondary navigation bar to the sidebar area. To lock this region so no one can mess with the sidebar (in pages built from the nested template), add an empty editable region, or see the Tip below. If desired, you can build similar nested templates for the other sections of the site.

Now you're ready to start building the pages of your site. Create a new page based on one of the section templates. Add text or graphics to the editable content area of the page. Should you need to change the site logo or add a button to the site-wide navigation bar, open the master template, make the changes, save the file, and let Dreamweaver update all of the pages of your site with the new look. If you simply need to change the secondary navigation for one section of the site, then open the appropriate nested template, change the sidebar, save the template, and let Dreamweaver update all the section pages.

Tip: You can lock an editable region passed from a master template to a nested template, so that pages based on the nested template can't be changed in this region. In the nested template, go into Code view, locate the beginning of the editable region, which looks something like this <!--InstanceBeginEditable name="regionName"-->.

Then insert the text @@(" ")@@ directly after the -->.

If you need to do this often, think about creating a snippet (see page 515) of the text @@(" ")@@.

Building Pages Based on a Template

Building a template is only a prelude to the actual work of building your site. Once you finish your template, it's time to produce pages.

To create a new document based on a template, choose File→New to open the New from Template window (see Figure 18-14). Click the Templates tab and select the current site you're working on from the Templates For list. All templates for the selected site appear in the right column. Select the template you wish to use and click Create.

WORKAROUND WORKSHOP

Preventing Rollover Accidents

For a navigation bar to work effectively, the images used for a rollover must be *preloaded*; otherwise, there's a noticeable delay between the time a visitor moves the mouse over a button, and the highlighted button graphic downloads from the Internet and finally appears.

Unfortunately, Dreamweaver MX has a bug. If you add rollover images to a nested template, Dreamweaver fails to add the proper preloading code to pages created from the template. There is a workaround, but it's a bit complex:

1. Open the master template, and make the <body> tag's onLoad property editable. (Follow the steps on page 543 for creating an editable tag attribute.)

2. Open the nested template—the one based on the master template from step 1—and add all rollover images (the navigation bar, for instance) for this template.

3. Switch into Code view (View→Code) and locate the <body> tag. Look for the onLoad property

and copy everything from onload=" to the closing quotation mark. This is the *value* of the onLoad property, containing the code necessary to preload the rollover images. (Just copy the stuff *in between* the quote marks, not the quote marks themselves.)

4. Go back to Design view (View→Design) and choose Modify→Template Properties. The Template Properties window appears (see Figure 18-16).

5. Select the name of the editable tag attribute you created in step 1, and paste the onLoad code you copied from step 3 into the text field at the bottom of the window. Click OK.

Now when you create a page based on this template, the proper preload code is added to the page. The good news is, you only have to do this once. You can add other rollover images to this page, and Dreamweaver will correctly add their preload code as well.

Tip: If you don't want your new Web page linked to the template (so that changes to the template would also affect the Web page), turn off the "Update Page when Template Changes" checkbox. The result is a new page that looks just like the template, but has no locked regions; you can edit the entire page.

This is a useful tactic when, for example, you want to start with the general design and structure of a certain template when creating a brand-new design for another template. (Be aware that Dreamweaver remembers this choice the next time you create a new page. In other words, future pages you try to create from a template will *also* be unlinked—unless you remember to turn back on the Update Page box.)

Figure 18-14:
You can use the Templates For list to choose another site you've defined and reveal the list of templates it uses. However, choosing a template stored in a different site is not a good idea. Dreamweaver doesn't copy any images on the template to the current site and can't translate relative links correctly. The result is broken links aplenty.

A new Web page document opens, based on the template, bearing a tab in the upper-right corner that identifies the underlying template name. Dreamweaver outlines any editable regions in blue; a small blue tab displays each region's name (see Figure 18-5).

Dreamweaver makes it painfully obvious which areas you aren't allowed to edit; your cursor changes to a forbidden symbol (Ⓝ) when it ventures into a locked area.

To add content to an editable region, click anywhere inside it. You can type inside it, add graphics, or add any other objects or HTML you can normally add to a document. You can also change the document's title and add Behaviors (see Chapter 11), Cascading Style Sheets (see Chapter 8), and meta tag information (items that go in the <head> of an HTML document.

Note: Dreamweaver doesn't let you use the Layer tool to draw a layer into an editable region. That's because using this method, Dreamweaver tries to add the code for the layer at the very beginning of the page, which is usually a noneditable region. Instead, click somewhere in an editable region and choose Insert→Layer. You can then work with the layer as you normally would (see Chapter 12). (One exception: you can't add Timelines to template-based pages).

If you're designing sites to work with Netscape Navigator 4, it's best to not insert Layer code into a table cell, since Navigator 4 has trouble with that arrangement. The best solution is add a single paragraph to the template file, and mark *it* as editable. Then insert layers into this region of your template-based pages.

Working with Repeating Regions

Repeating regions work a bit differently from editable regions. In most cases, a repeating region will include one or more editable regions (which you can edit using the instructions on page 557). However, Dreamweaver provides special controls to let you add, remove, and rearrange repeating entries (see Figure 18-15).

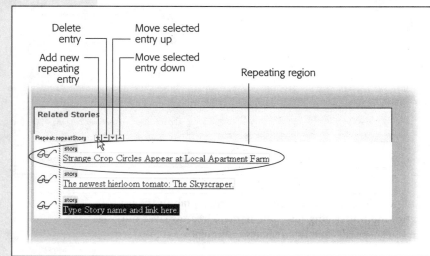

Delete entry — Move selected entry up

Add new repeating entry — Move selected entry down

Repeating region

Figure 18-15:
Repeating regions are a great way to quickly use lists in your Web pages. In this example, a list of links to related stories, you can add as many stories to the page as you'd like. Clicking the + button adds another row to this table complete with an icon (in a region locked by the template) and an editable story region.

These regions are intended to let a page author add repeated page elements—such as rows of product information in a list of products. To add a repeating entry, click the + button that appears to the right of the Repeat region's blue tab. You can then edit any editable regions within the entry. Click inside an editable region inside a repeating entry and click + again to add a new entry *after* it.

Deleting a repeating entry is just as easy. Click inside an editable region within the entry you wish to delete and click the – button.

To rearrange entries in this list, click inside an entry's editable region. Click the up or down arrows to move the entry in the list (to alphabetize a list, for example).

Changing Properties of Editable Tag Attributes

Unlike editable or repeating regions, an editable tag attribute isn't immediately apparent on template-based pages. There's no blue tab to represent it, as there are for editable regions; in fact, nothing appears in Design view to indicate that there are *any* editable tag properties on the page. The only way to find out is to choose Modify-→Template Properties to open the Template Properties dialog box (see Figure 18-16).

All editable tag attributes for this page appear in this window. (All parameters defined for this page, including optional regions, appear here, as discussed in the box on page 551.)

To change the value of a template property—in other words, to edit the property of an editable tag—select its name from the list and type a new value in the text field that appears at the bottom of the window. In the case of color properties, Dreamweaver thoughtfully lets you use the color box to pick a Web-compatible color.

Unfortunately, if the property is a path (such as a link or an image's source property indicating the graphic file's location in the site), Dreamweaver isn't as considerate. There is no folder icon that lets you browse to select the file, so you have to type the path by hand (see page 91 for a discussion of file paths).

Once, you've finished setting the editable properties for the page, click OK to close the window.

Figure 18-16:
The Template Properties window lets you control editable tag attributes and other parameters for optional regions. Depending on which parameter you select, the options at the bottom of the window change. In this case, since this page's Bgcolor property is editable, the PageBackground parameter lets you use Dreamweaver's color box to select a new color for the background of this page.

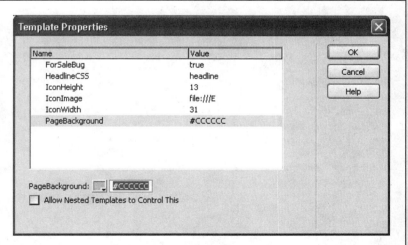

Hiding and Showing Optional Regions

As with Editable Tag Attributes, you use the Template Properties window to control the display of optional regions. On template-based pages, you can show or hide an optional region by choosing Modify→Template Properties to open this dialog box (see Figure 18-17). Next, select the name of the optional region. To make all page elements in the region appear, turn on the Show button at the bottom of the window. To hide the optional region, deselect this box.

Applying a Template to a Page You Already Made

What happens if you create a Web page and *then* decide you want it to share the look of a template? No problem. Dreamweaver lets you apply a template to any Web page in your site, as long as that page isn't already based on a template.

To apply a template to a page you've already created:

1. **Choose File→Open to open the page you want to alter.**

   The Web page opens.

2. **Choose Window→Assets and click the Asset panel's Templates button (see Figure 18-4).**

   The Assets panel appears and reveals a list of the site's templates.

FREQUENTLY ASKED QUESTION

Controlling the Nest

The Template Properties dialog box includes a checkbox labeled "Allow Nested Templates to Control This." What does it do?

Imagine that you create a template and add several optional regions and editable tag attributes to it. You then use this template as a basic design for more refined templates for each section of your site. When you create one of these nested templates based on the master template, it has access to the Template Properties window, where page authors can modify any of the template properties created by the original, master template.

For example, to better identify each section of a site, you might add a different background color to each section's pages: blue for the products section, orange for the support section, and so on. In the master template, you make the <body> tag's Bgcolor property editable. Now, when you create a nested template for the products section, you simply open the Template Properties dialog box and set the property to the blue color you desire. For the support section's nested template, set the property to orange. Now when you create a template-based page for the support section, its background will be orange, while a page for the products section will have a blue background.

However, to let your site's color palette go really wild, you might want *every* page in the site to have its own unique background color. (Disclaimer: Don't try this at home.) In this case, you'd want to let every page based on a nested template have an editable Bgcolor property.

To do so, open the nested template, open the Template Properties window, select the property that should be editable in pages built from this template (color in this case) and turn on the "Allow Nested Templates to Control This" checkbox. Now this property is *uneditable* in the nested template, but editable in all pages created from it.

You've probably realized by now that the phrase "Allow Nested Templates to Control This" doesn't make much sense. Turning it on actually *prevents* the nested template from controlling the property. A better way to think of it is "Allow pages *created from* this template to control this property."

The bottom line: Turning on this box makes the attribute uneditable on that page. If it's a nested template, it lets the Template property "pass through" to all pages based on this template. In other words, you can't set the background color in the template, but page authors can change it in pages created from the template.

Tip: You can also apply a template to a page by choosing Modify→Templates→Apply Template to Page. Select the name of the template from the window that appears and skip to step 5.

3. **Click a template in the list on the Assets panel, and then click Apply.**

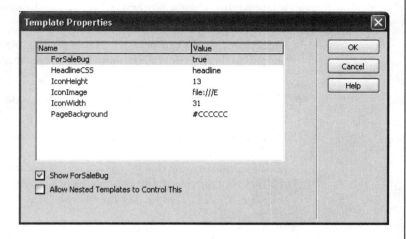

Figure 18-17:
A Template property for an optional region has either a value of "true" or "false." True means the contents of the region will be visible on the page, while false hides the region. (The "Allow Nested Templates to Control This" option is described in the box on the facing page.)

The clumsily named Inconsistent Region Names dialog box opens (Figure 18-18).

4. **In the list under Editable Regions, choose Document Body.**

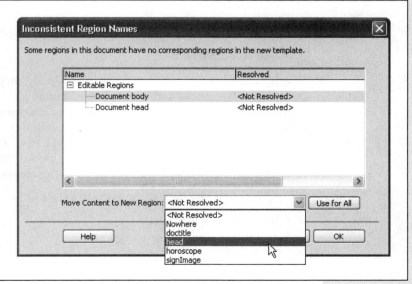

Figure 18-18:
When you apply a template to an existing page, you must tell Dreamweaver what to do with the material that's already on the page. Do this by selecting one of the template's editable regions from a pop-up menu. This window also appears after you've renamed an editable region in a template and are updating the template-based pages. In this case, you need to select the name of the old region in the top part of the window, then choose the renamed region from the drop-down menu.

To the right, in the Resolved column, you'll see <Not Resolved>. This is Dreamweaver's way of saying it doesn't know what to do with the contents of the current page. You need to pick one of the template's editable regions.

5. **From the Move Content to New Region menu, select an editable region.**

If you want to keep the material, select the name of an editable region from the list; otherwise, choose Nowhere, which, in effect, creates a new blank page based on the template.

Unfortunately, you can only select a single editable region; if several content regions are in the original, Dreamweaver merges them all into a single editable region.

6. **If Document Head also appears in the window, select it and choose, from the Move Content to New Region menu, *head*.**

Doing so will preserve any special information you added to the head of your page, such as Cascading Style Sheets, Metatags, custom JavaScript programs, and other information that goes in the <head> of the document. Unfortunately, the title of your original page is always replaced with the default title of the template. You'll have to reenter the title (see step 5 on page 32) after you apply the template.

Caution: If you apply a template to a page that has Dreamweaver Behaviors (Chapter 11) applied to it, be careful when selecting this option. If the same Behaviors already exist in the template code, Dreamweaver actually makes a duplicate copy of the JavaScript code in the <head> of the page. To get rid of this you'll need to go into Code view (Chapter 9) and manually remove it.

---

7. **Click OK.**

Your new page appears.

Update a Template

Templates aren't just useful for building pages rapidly; they also make quick work of site updates. Pages created from templates maintain a link to the original template file; you can automatically pass changes to a template along to every page built from it. If you used templates to build your site, you probably won't cry on your keyboard when the boss says you must add an additional button and link to the navigation bar. Instead of rebuilding every page, you can simply open the template file, update the navigation bar, and let Dreamweaver apply the update to all the pages.

You update a template (and all the pages based on it) like this:

1. **Choose Window→Assets.**

The Assets panel appears.

2. **Click the Templates button (see Figure 18-4).**

   This reveals a list of the site's templates.

3. **Double-click the template's name to open it.**

   Alternatively, you can select the template in the Assets panel and click the Edit button to open the original template (.dwt) file (see Figure 18-4).

   The template opens.

Tip: You can also open a template from the Site Files panel (see page 432.) Just double-click the appropriate template (.dwt) file in the Templates folder.

---

4. **Edit the template as you would any Web page.**

   Since this is the original template file, you can edit any of the HTML in the document, including Cascading Style Sheets, meta tags, timelines, and layers. You can also add additional editable regions to the page or remove editable regions (see page 539).

   Take care, however, to edit *only* the areas that you did *not* mark as editable regions. The reason: When you update your pages, any region marked as editable in a template file isn't passed on to pages based on that template. After all, the template is only supposed to dictate the design of those pages' *non*-editable regions.

Note: Be careful when you remove editable regions from a template. If you've already built some pages based on the template, Dreamweaver warns you when you save the template. As described in the following steps, you can either *delete* the content that was added to that region in each of the pages you created, or move it to another editable region in the page.

---

5. **Choose File→Save.**

   If you've already created pages based on this template, Dreamweaver opens the Update Template Files dialog box. It lists all the files that use the template.

6. **Click Update to update all files based on the template.**

   Dreamweaver automatically applies the changes you made to the pages based on the template. Then, the Update Pages dialog box opens and displays a log of all changes Dreamweaver made to the files in your site.

   On a large site, this automatic update feature can be an incredible timesaver, but you may *not* want to click Update, at least not right now. Perhaps you're just saving some of your hard work on the template, but aren't quite finished perfecting it—why waste your time updating all those pages more than once? In such a scenario, click the Don't Update button. You can always update the pages later (see the box on page 564).

7. **Click Close.**

The Update Pages dialog box closes.

You'll need to update all your files even if you make a simple change to the template, such as changing its name.

Updating Nested Templates

When you build a Web site using nested templates, you'll have multiple templates affecting your pages. The master template controls design elements of a nested template, which in turn controls pages based on the nested template. (You can even make nested templates *out of* nested templates, but for sanity's sake, you'd better not.) With this level of complexity, updates to nested templates can get confusing fast.

In a nutshell, here's how it works:

- If you edit a locked region in a master template and then update your site, not only will a nested template update, but also all pages built from that nested template.

- If you edit a locked region in a nested template and then update, those changes will pass on to pages built from that nested template.

POWER USERS' CLINIC

Wait to Update

Whenever you modify and save a Library item or a template, Dreamweaver gives you the option to update any pages in the site that are descended from it. Very often, you'll say Yes.

But there are times when you might wait to update the site. If you're making a lot of changes to multiple Library items or templates, for example, you may wish to wait until you've finished all your edits before letting the changes ripple through your pages. After all, it can take some time to update large sites that have lots of pages.

Dreamweaver lets you update pages that use Library items and templates at any time. Just choose Modify→Library→Update Pages or Modify→Templates→Update

Pages. Both menu options open the same dialog box.

At this point, you can update pages that use a specific Library item or template by choosing Files that Use from the Look In menu and then selecting the appropriate name from the pop-up menu. If you want to update all pages in the site, choose Entire Site, and select the name of the local site from the pop-up menu. Turn on both the Library Items and Templates checkboxes to update all pages.

When you click Start, Dreamweaver does its work, reporting the results of the update in the Log field at the bottom of the dialog box. If you find the log useless, just turn off Show Log to hide the report. Click Close after Dreamweaver finishes.

However, changes you make to an *editable* region of a master template do not pass on to any page. Neither do changes you make in editable regions of a nested template.

Unlinking a Page from a Template

If you're confident that you won't be making any further changes to a page's template, and you'd like to be able to edit the page's locked regions, you can break the link between a page and its template; just choose Modify→Templates→Detach from Template.

All of the HTML in the page is now editable, just as on a regular Web page—which is what it is. You've removed all references to the original template; changes to the template will no longer have any effect on this page.

Note: If you unlink a nested template from its master template, only the code provided by the original master template is removed. Any editable regions you added to the nested template itself remain.

Exporting a Template-Based Site

The good news about Dreamweaver's sophisticated templating features is that they let you build complex Web pages that are easy to create and update. The bad news is that a lot of behind-the-scenes code is necessary to achieve this ease of use. Dreamweaver's template features rely on HTML comment tags to identify editable, optional, and repeating regions, as well as nested template and editable tag attributes (see the box on page 551). Although this code is only for Dreamweaver's use and has no effect on how a Web browser displays the page, it can bog down your Web pages with unnecessarily longer download times.

Fortunately, Dreamweaver MX includes a new feature that lets you export an entire site into a new folder on your computer *without* any Template markup code. It's a good last step before transferring a freshly completed Web site to a Web server.

1. Choose Modify→Templates→Export Without Markup.

   Dreamweaver MX uses the currently active site, so make sure you've got the site you wish to export selected in the Site panel (see page 432). The Export Site Without Template Markup window appears (see Figure 18-19).

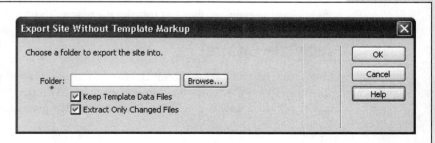

Figure 18-19:
Dreamweaver MX now lets you strip out bandwidth-hogging template code from template-based pages with the new Export Without Markup command.

2. **Click the Browse button and select a folder for the exported site.**

Select a folder *other* than the current local site folder. You'll always want to keep the original files in the local folder, since they're the ones that will keep the template markup making future updates possible.

3. **Turn on the export options you want.**

The Export window includes two options. The first, Keep Template Data Files, creates an XML file for each template-based page. In other words, when you export the site, there will be one HTML page (without any special template code) and an XML file (which includes all the template code as well as the page content).

(Theoretically, you could then go back and choose the File→Import→XML into Template to recreate the page, complete with the original Template information. However, in practice, you probably won't. For one thing, this process creates lots of additional files that you wouldn't want to move to the Web site. Also, when you want to work on the site to update and edit it, you should use the original files in the site's local folder anyway, since they still have the useful template code in them.)

The Extract Only Changed Files speeds up the process of exporting a large template-based site. It forces Dreamweaver to export only pages that you've changed since the last export. Unfortunately, it doesn't tell you *which* files it exported until after the fact. So, to make sure you get those newly exported files to the Web server, you'll have to keep track of changes by hand.

4. **Click OK to export the site.**

Dreamweaver goes through each page of the site, stripping out template code and exporting it to the folder you specified.

It's a fine idea to perform an export after you've completed your Web site and are ready to move it to the Internet. You can then move the lean, clean exported files to the Web server.

You can use Dreamweaver's FTP feature to do the uploading (see page 478), but you'll need to create a new site and define the folder with the *exported* files as a local root folder. Whenever you need to add or update template-based pages, use the original site files and then export the changed files. You can then switch to the site containing the exported files and transfer the new or updated files to the Web server.

Template Tutorial

In this tutorial, you'll create a template for the Horoscopes section of the *Cosmopolitan Farmer* Web site. Then you'll build a page based on that template and enjoy an easy site-wide update courtesy of Dreamweaver's templates feature.

Note: The tutorial in this chapter requires the example files from this book's Web site, *www.sawmac.com/dwmx/*. Click the Tutorials link to go to the tutorials page. Click to download <u>Template Tutorial–Mac Files</u> or <u>Template Tutorial–Windows Files,</u> depending on the kind of machine you're using.

After your browser downloads and decompresses the files, you should have a DWTemp (short for Dreamweaver Templates) folder on your computer, containing the Web pages and graphics needed for this tutorial. If you're having difficulties, the Web site contains detailed instructions for downloading the files you'll be using with this book.

Creating a Template

This tutorial guides you through the creation of a template, the creation of a page *based* on that template, and then an editing and auto-update procedure.

These instructions assume that you've downloaded the necessary tutorial files, as described on page 25, and defined a site using the DWTemp folder as your local root folder (for information on defining a site, see page 426).

1. **Open the Site window by pressing the F8 key.**

2. **In the Site window, find and double-click the page *horoscope.html* (it's in the root folder).**

   It's usually easier to start with an already-designed Web page and then save it as a template. For the purposes of getting to bed before midnight tonight, pretend that you've just designed this beautiful, half-finished Web page.

3. **Choose File→Save as Template.**

   The Save as Template dialog box opens.

4. **Name the template *Horoscope*; click Save.**

   Behind the scenes, Dreamweaver saves the file as Horoscope.dwt in the DWTemp→Templates folder, and a new template is born. You can see it in the Templates page of the Assets panel, as well as the new folder in the Site window.

   The template is a model for other pages. But although they'll be *based* on its design, they won't be identical. The next step is to identify those areas of the design that will change from page to page—the editable regions.

5. **Click the gray square labeled *sign_image*.**

   For placement purposes, you've put a dummy graphic on the page. When you add new horoscopes to the site, you can replace this graphic with a real astrological sign. To make it possible to replace it with a real image in the resulting Web pages, you need to mark this graphic as editable, like so:

6. **Choose Insert→Template Objects→Editable Region.**

   The New Editable Region dialog box appears.

Here, as in the following steps, you can also click the Editable Region button on the Templates tab of the Insert bar (see Figure 18-2) or press Ctrl+Alt+V (Option-⌘-V).

7. **Type *signImage*; click OK.**

   A small tab, labeled *signImage,* appears on the placeholder graphic. There is one more thing you'll want to replace every time you create a Web page based on this template: the horoscope text.

8. **Click before the "S" in the heading Sign Goes Here and drag down and to the right until you've selected the two lines of text.**

   At this point, the heading and the paragraph marked "Horoscope goes here" should be selected.

9. **Choose Insert→Template Objects→Editable Region, type *horoscope,* and click OK.**

10. **So far you've added two editable regions—the most basic type of template region. Next, you'll explore some of the new templating features Dreamweaver MX offers. Select the red "Sign of the Month" image.**

    Of course, only one sign each month can be the Sign of the Month, so you'll want this graphic to appear only on a single page each month. This is the perfect candidate for an optional region—an area of the page that you can hide or show on a page-by-page basis.

11. **Choose Insert→Template Objects→Optional Region.**

    The New Optional Region window appears.

12. **Type *SignOfMonth* in the name field, turn off the Show by Default checkbox, and click OK.**

    Since most pages *won't* display this graphic, you'll speed up your work by hiding it by default, and making it visible just on the one "Sign of the Month" page.

    Next you'll add two editable and two repeating regions to the Compatibility Chart at the bottom of the page.

13. **In the bottom-left table cell, select the words "good sign."**

    This cell will contain the name of a compatible sign. Each page will have a different list of compatible astrological buddies, so the cell should be turned into an editable region.

14. **Choose Insert→Template Objects→Editable Region and in the window that appears, type *compatible.* Click OK.**

    Dreamweaver inserts a new editable region with the familiar blue tab labeled "compatible."

15. **In the tag selector, click the last <tr> tag (see Figure 18-20).**

    Because a particular page may have more than one compatible sign, you'll turn this into a repeating region. In this way, when you create a new horoscope page, you can freely add as many compatible signs as your astrological charts require.

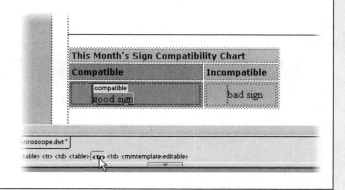

Figure 18-20:
It can be tricky to select HTML accurately in Dreamweaver's Design view, especially in a case like this, with lots of different tables. Using the tag selector is the most precise method of selecting a particular tag and its contents.

16. **Choose Insert→Template Objects→Repeating Region.**

    Alternatively, you can click the Repeating Region button in the Template tab of the Insert bar (see Figure 18-2). Either way, the New Repeating Region window appears.

17. **In the Name field, type *RepeatCompatible,* and click OK.**

    Above the editable "compatible" region, another blue tab appears with the label Repeat: RepeatCompatible. This is the tab for a repeating region.

18. **In the bottom-right table cell, select the words *bad sign,* and repeat steps 14–16.**

    This time, however, name the new editable region *incompatible,* and the new repeat region, *RepeatIncompatible.*

    There's one last item for this page: the banner ad. You'll notice that the ad there now is a placeholder. Because all ads that go in that location are the same size and require the same formatting, you don't need to make the entire graphic editable. You'll use Dreamweaver's editable tag attribute feature instead.

19. **At the top right of the page, click the graphic labeled Dummy Half Banner Ad. Choose Modify→Templates→Make Attribute Editable.**

    The Editable Tag Attributes window appears.

20. **Choose SRC from the Attribute menu. Turn on the Make Attribute Editable checkbox.**

    The other fields in the window become active (see Figure 18-21).

21. In the label field, type *adSrc*, choose URL from the Type menu, and leave the default value as it is.

   The window should look like Figure 18-21. The label helps you identify which particular property of which page element you're editing. *URL* in the Type menu informs Dreamweaver that this attribute is a path, enabling Dreamweaver's site management tools to accurately update links and paths to graphics files as you move template-based pages around your site.

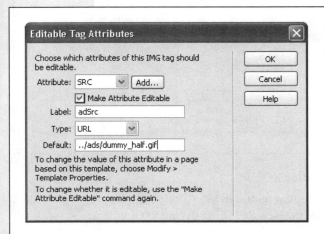

Figure 18-21:
The Editable Tag Attributes window lets you make a specific property of a selected tag editable on template-based pages.

22. Click OK to close the window.

   The graphic suddenly changes into Dreamweaver's broken-image icon. Don't worry; everything is just fine, as you'll see in the next section. (Note that in the real world, you'd also want to make the image's Alt property editable as well, so that you can add different alternate text for each ad on each page.)

23. Choose File→Save and then close the file.

   Congratulations! You've created your first template.

Creating a Page Based on a Template

Now it's time to get down to business and build Web pages. Look at the Site menu and make sure you've selected the site that you defined in step 1 at the beginning of this tutorial (page 567). Then proceed as follows:

1. Choose File→New.

   The New Document window opens.

2. Click the Templates tab.

   A list of all defined sites appears in the Templates For box at the left of the window.

3. **Make sure the site you defined for this tutorial is selected; also make sure the "Update Page when Template Changes" checkbox is turned on.**

   If you don't turn on the Update Page box, the new page won't be linked to the original template file—and won't update when you make changes to the template.

4. **Select Horoscope from the templates list and click Create.**

   And lo, a new, untitled Web page document appears, one that looks exactly like the template (Figure 18-22).

Figure 18-22:
In pages based on a template, blue tabs identify editable areas of the page, and a yellow tab appears in the upper-right corner of the document window to indicate that this page is based on a template. Notice that the repeat regions have small control buttons (+, -, and up and down arrows) and the optional region—the red graphic—is invisible. (Remember, you turned this off by default.)

5. **Choose File→Save. Save the file as *gemini.html* in the DWTemp→horoscopes folder.**

   (On the Mac, be sure to type in the *.html* extension; Windows adds it automatically.)

   To indicate that it's the offspring of your template, the document window has a yellow tab in the upper-right corner that reads Template: Horoscope. You can see your editable and repeating regions indicated by blue tabs.

6. **Make sure the document window's toolbar is visible (View→Toolbar); type** *Gemini* **into the Title field.**

You've just named your page, saving you from the ignominy of showing up in search engines as "Untitled." Next stop: Replacing the dummy sign image with a real one.

7. **Click the gray box labeled "sign_image" to select it. Press the Delete or Backspace key.**

It was useful to include placeholders for your text and graphics, like this image placeholder, in your templates, to give your page shape and make clear what the "real" content should look like.

You'll now replace this placeholder with a Gemini sign.

8. **Insert the Gemini image.**

Choose Insert→Image, for example. Navigate to the DWTemp→horoscope→ images folder; double-click the file called gemini.gif. When you return to your document, you'll discover that Dreamweaver has replaced the placeholder image with the sign's twins astrological symbol.

Now you'll add a proper horoscope.

9. **Select the words Sign Goes Here and type** *Gemini.*

You also want to add Gemini's unfortunate astrological forecast.

10. **Select the text "Horoscope goes here" and type the following:**

You'll wish you had a twin this month. Then at least there'd be someone else to blame for your problems and share your woes. Ever thought about moving? Good, 'cause now's the time: You're being evicted on the 16th. Forget about saving your apartment crops. They won't make it either.

Oh, well…There'll be other months for Gemini. However, it just so happens that Gemini is the Sign of the Month. (Remember, the optional region you created for this graphic in the previous tutorial?) It isn't currently displayed, because you turned it off by default. In the next step you'll magically make it reappear.

Note: This tutorial would like to apologize to those who have a true belief in and understanding of the zodiac. The astrological predictions included herein are purely fictitious and intended for entertainment purposes only.

---

11. **Choose Modify→Template Properties.**

The Template Properties window appears (see Figure 18-23). There are two items listed: The first is the editable tag attribute for the banner ad, and the second is the optional region you wish to make visible.

12. **In the properties list, select signOfMonth and turn on the "Show signOfMonth" checkbox.**

    This makes the optional region visible on the page. While you're here, you may as well also add a real banner ad to the page.

13. **Select adSrc in the Template Properties window and type ../ads/half_dr.gif in the adSrc field at the bottom of the window.**

    Unfortunately, you have to type the exact path yourself. In this case, Dreamweaver doesn't provide the usual "select file" button. (For a description of file paths and how they work, see page 91.)

14. **Click OK to close the window.**

    The red *Sign of the Month* button appears, as does an ad for Dr. Herbert's Amazing Plant Tonic at the top of the page. You're nearly done building this new page. The last task is adding a list of Gemini's compatible and incompatible signs.

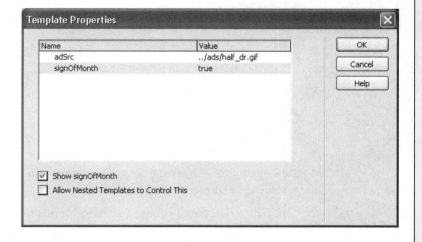

Figure 18-23:
The Template Properties window does double duty. Not only does it let you hide or show optional regions, but it's also the place to set values for editable tag attributes.

15. **At the bottom of the page, click the blue tab labeled "compatible."**

    This selects the text in that editable region.

16. **Type *Pisces*.**

    Gemini has other compatible signs. Fortunately, you can add additional entries using the repeating region controls.

17. **Click the + button just to the right of the blue Repeat:RepeatCompatible tab.**

    There are two + signs—one for the column of compatible signs and another for the column of incompatible signs. Make sure you click the first one. This adds another row to the page as shown in Figure 18-24.

Note: If a page has a lot of elements crowded together–tables, images, text–Dreamweaver sometimes can't display the small buttons that let you add and remove repeating entries. In this case, you can also use the Modify menu. Click inside a repeating region and choose Modify→Templates→Repeating Entries and select an action from the submenu, such as New Entry After Selection, to add another editable entry.

Figure 18-24:
The control buttons to the right of repeating regions (circled in this picture) let you add, remove, and rearrange repeating entries. In this example, clicking the + button adds another table row for adding an additional "compatible sign."

18. **Click the blue tab of the newly added Compatible editable region and type** *Aries.*

    Unfortunately for Geminis this month, there are more incompatible signs than compatible ones.

19. **Repeat steps 15–17 for the Incompatible repeating region. Add three incompatible signs:** *Aquarius, Leo,* **and** *Taurus.*

    OK. Gemini's received enough bad news for one month. This page is done.

20. **Choose File→Save and then close the gemini.html document window.**

    Congratulations! You've just created your first page based on a template. You could, of course, continue in this manner, building page after page based on this template.

Updating a Template

Now the fun begins. Remember, this page maintains a reference to the original template. In the final phase, you're going to make a few changes to the template. Choose Window→Assets to open the Assets panel, and click the Template button to reveal the templates for this site (see Figure 18-4).

1. **In the Assets panel, double-click the Horoscope template to open it.**

    The original template—the Horoscope.dwt file—opens. It would be nice to add a navigation bar to the left side of this page, so that visitors can quickly jump to a particular horoscope. Fortunately, there's a Library item already created for doing so (see Chapter 17 for more on Dreamweaver's Library tool).

2. **Click the Library icon in the Assets panel (directly below the Template icon).**

   There's one Library item listed, sidebar_nav.

3. **Drag the Library item from the Assets panel and drop it into the empty beige area on the left edge of template.**

   Alternatively, you could click inside the beige area in the document window, select the Library item in the Assets panel and then click the Insert button at the bottom of the Assets panel. Either way, a fresh new navigation system appears on the page.

   It would also be nice if the monthly compatibility chart was more attention-grabbing. You'll add some colorful icons to the chart.

4. **Click inside the empty cell to the left of the words "good sign."**

   This empty space is the perfect place for an icon.

Figure 18-25:
The finished tutorial page complete with banner ad, product information, and copyright notice. Feel free to compare the results of your work with the professionally completed version at www.sawmac.com/dwmx/tutorials/.

5. **Insert the icon image.**

   Choose Insert→Image, for example. Navigate to the DWTemp→images_global folder; double-click the file called *compatible.gif*. When you return to your document, you'll discover that Dreamweaver has inserted a smiley face.

   Now you'll add an unhappy face to represent an incompatible sign.

6. **Click inside the empty cell to the left of the words "bad sign." Insert the graphic** *incompatible.gif,* **as described in step 5.**

   Cute, huh?

7. **Choose File→Save.**

   The Update Template Pages dialog box appears, listing all of the pages in the site based on this template (this case just the lone gemini.html file).

8. **Click Update.**

   Dreamweaver opens the Update Pages dialog box and updates the appropriate Web pages, adding the new sidebar navigation and emoticons to each one. In this case, you based only one page on the template, so Dreamweaver updates only one page—as indicated by the list of changes Dreamweaver shows when it's finished.

9. **Click Close to close the Update Pages dialog box. Finally, open the file gemini.html, and press F12 to preview it in a Web browser.**

   Notice that the horoscope navigation bar now appears in the gemini.html document and smiley and sad face icons populate the sign compatibility chart (see Figure 18-25). All this happened because you changed the template to which it was genetically linked. Ah, the power.

Automating Dreamweaver

O ne of Dreamweaver's greatest selling points is that it makes you more productive. You've experienced this firsthand if you ever labored over tables in an HTML text editor. What once took many keystrokes now takes one click of the Insert bar's Table object.

If you're looking for even more ways to cut time off your day, Dreamweaver doesn't disappoint. In addition to its Snippets, Library, and Template features (see Chapters 17 and 18), the program offers two tools that let you automate common and time-consuming tasks: the History panel and the Find/Replace command.

The History Panel Revisited

As you work on a Web page, Dreamweaver keeps track of everything you do. You can see a list of your actions, or *history*, in the History panel. Each document has a separate history, which Dreamweaver discards when you close the document or quit the program.

You can use the History panel to quickly undo or redo multiple actions (page 60), but that's only the tip of the iceberg. You can also use it to replay and record a series of actions you wish to repeat. If you've ever used macros in Microsoft Word or actions in Adobe Photoshop, you'll probably get the hang of this feature quickly.

To open the History panel, choose Window→Others→History, or press Shift-F10 (see Figure 19-1).

Replay Your Steps

To replay a step in the History panel, click its name to highlight it. You can also select multiple steps by using one of these methods:

- To select a group of consecutive steps, drag over them. You can drag your mouse across either the labels or icons. Take special care not to move your cursor into the History slider on the left edge of the window; clicking there will undo or redo steps (page 61).

- You can also select consecutive steps by holding down the Shift key as you click down the list.

- To select steps that aren't consecutive, Ctrl-click (⌘-click) only the ones you want. For example, say you hit Return, typed *hello,* and then inserted a horizontal rule. If you wanted to omit the step where you typed *hello,* you could Ctrl-click (⌘-click) the other two. Dreamweaver ignores unselected steps.

Now, when you click Replay (see Figure 19-1), Dreamweaver replays the selected steps. Unfortunately, you can't re-order the steps; they always play from the top of the list to the bottom.

History slider

Replay selected steps

Copy steps

Save steps as a command

Figure 19-1:
The History panel lists every little step you've taken while working on the current document—even typos. You can replay one or more actions on the list, copy them for use in another document, or save them as a command in the Commands menu. If Dreamweaver can't replay an action, such as a mouse click, it appears with a red X next to it. The History slider indicates where you are in the document's history.

Once you've created a series of steps, you can reuse it. For example, say you format a paragraph as a bulleted list and apply a custom style to it. Once Dreamweaver records these steps in the History panel, you can select more text and replay those steps to format it the same way. Now imagine that instead of a two-step process, you have a ten-step chore that involves not only keystrokes, but multiple visits to the Insert bar and Property inspector…you can begin to see the power of this feature.

Tip: You probably know that you can repeat your last action by pressing Ctrl+Y (⌘-Y) or choosing Edit→Repeat. For example, if you type the word *hello* in the document window, pressing Ctrl+Y (⌘-Y) will type the word *hello* again. Unless you're Jack Nicholson's character in *The Shining*, this feature may sound less than useful, but used in combination with the History panel's Replay feature, it can be a real timesaver. When you use the History panel to replay several steps, you'll notice the last item in the History list is Replay Steps. Dreamweaver treats all of these steps as a *single action*. Now if you press Ctrl+Y (⌘-Y), you'll replay all of the steps again.

Exceptions and Errors

Unfortunately, Dreamweaver can't record and play back everything. The exceptions generally involve making changes in certain dialog boxes or moving objects with the mouse. For example, you can't record tasks you perform in the Modify Page Properties dialog box. And you're left to your own devices when you want to click, drag, or drop a graphic in the document window.

On the other hand, not everything you do with the mouse is off-limits to the History panel. It can track most common tasks, like clicking the Insert bar, choosing a menu item, or clicking in the Property inspector to set a property. Also, you can avoid using many mouse movements by using equivalent keystrokes, which Dreamweaver *can* record. (See the box below.)

If you take a step, such as a mouse drag, that Dreamweaver can't replay, a red X appears next to it in the History panel (see Figure 19-1). A line between two actions also indicates a step that can't be repeated. This problem usually arises when you've clicked in the document window (to deselect a selected image, for example). If you get into the habit of deselecting an object in the document window by pressing the keyboard's arrow keys instead, you'll find your History steps more fully replayable.

FREQUENTLY ASKED QUESTION

Keyboard to the Rescue

If Dreamweaver can't track mouse movements, how can I replay an action that involves selecting something?

It's easy to use the mouse to make selections and move items around the screen, but you can do much of the same with the humble keyboard. That's a good thing, because if you can type it, Dreamweaver can record it.

To move up one line, for instance, press the up arrow key; to move down a line, press the down arrow. You can move to the top or bottom of the document window with the Page Up and Page Down keys, or move to the beginning or end of a line by pressing Home or End. Press Shift while pressing the right or left arrow key to select the object or

letter to the right or left of the insertion point. Add the Ctrl (⌘) key to that combination to select one *word* at a time. Unfortunately, Dreamweaver doesn't record the keystrokes you use for moving between table cells (Tab and Shift-Tab). However, there's a workaround: To move from one cell to the cell on its right, press End, followed by the right arrow key. To move to the cell to the left, press Home, followed by the left arrow key; these are keystrokes the History panel can track.

(You don't have to memorize all of this. You can print out a complete list of keyboard shortcuts from within Dreamweaver, as described on page 605.)

Copying and Pasting Actions

Each document has its own history. Thus, if you work on one page and then switch to another, the History panel changes to reflect only the actions you performed on the new document. The biggest drawback of this quirk is that you can't make a series of steps in one document replay in another.

For example, while working on your home page, you might click the Date object in the Insert bar to insert the current date (see page 50) and then choose a format for the date in the dialog box. You want to place the date on another page using the same format. But when you switch to that page and click Replay on the History panel, your steps aren't there!

Fortunately, there's a workaround: ye olde copy/paste routine. Select the steps you want to copy (see "Replay Your Steps" on page 578, for selection techniques), and then click the Copy Steps button (see Figure 19-1) on the History panel. (The regular copy shortcut, Ctrl+C or ⌘-C, *doesn't* work in this situation.) Now switch to the new document, select an object (or click to place the insertion point), and then choose Edit→Paste or press Ctrl+V (⌘-V).

Dreamweaver responds by playing the copied steps.

Note: You can't reliably copy certain actions, most notably Copy and Paste. If the actions you wish to reuse include a copy or paste step, save the actions as a command instead (see below).

Save Steps as Commands

It's quick and easy to replay and copy steps to automate repetitive tasks, but if you close the document or quit Dreamweaver, your recorded actions disappear—and with them, any chance you had of replaying them in the future. What if you come up with a great sequence of steps that you'd like to use over and over again?

POWER USERS' CLINIC

Copy (and Study) Actions

Dreamweaver is relatively easy to customize, because the objects that appear in the Insert bar, the behaviors available from the Behaviors panel, and even the Property inspector are all, behind the scenes, combinations of HTML pages and JavaScript programs. If you understand JavaScript, you can add your own commands, behaviors, and objects.

When *learning* JavaScript, however, you may need all the help you can get. The History panel's Copy Steps feature is a good place to start.

To study how Dreamweaver's built-in commands, behav-

iors, and objects have been programmed, copy one or more actions using the method described above. Switch to another text-editing program like WordPad, TextEdit, or Microsoft Word and choose Edit→Paste. (In previous versions of Dreamweaver you could paste into Code View to see the JavaScript Code; that feature was removed in MX.)

What you see is the JavaScript code that Dreamweaver uses to carry out those actions. You'll find out, for example, that while you perceive adding a new paragraph to your Web page as a matter of hitting Enter, to Dreamweaver it looks like this: dw.getDocumentDOM().newBlock().

The solution: Before it disappears forever, turn it into a *custom command*. That way, Dreamweaver adds your command to the bottom of the Commands menu and you can choose it from there anytime.

To save steps as a command, select the steps you want to copy (see "Replay Your Steps" on page 578 for selection techniques), then click the Save Steps button (its icon looks like a little floppy disk) on the History panel.

The Save as Command dialog box pops open. (If you've selected steps that Dreamweaver can't replay, such as mouse movements, a warning appears. Click Yes to continue without those steps; the valid steps will work just fine.) Type a short, descriptive name and click OK. Now take a look at the Commands menu—sure enough, your command now appears at the bottom.

To use your custom command, simply select its name from the Commands menu.

Tip: If you decide you want to delete your command or change its name, choose Commands→Edit Command List. In the dialog box that appears, click the command's name to select it. Type a new name or click Delete.

Recording Commands

You can also create a command by telling Dreamweaver to watch and record your actions. This time, Dreamweaver won't *let* you perform mouse movements while you're recording, so you can be sure recorded commands will play back properly.

To record a command, make sure the relevant Web page document is frontmost, then choose Commands→Start Recording, or press Shift+Ctrl+X (Shift-⌘-X). The cursor turns into a cassette tape icon to indicate the command is recording; now's your chance to do whatever you want Dreamweaver to memorize. (If you try to use the mouse to move or select anything in the document window, Dreamweaver will complain via dialog box.)

When you're finished, choose Commands→Stop Recording, or press Shift+Ctrl+X (Shift-⌘-X). Your cursor returns to normal, and Dreamweaver saves the sequence as a command, which you can replay by choosing Commands→Play Recorded Command.

Note, however, that this command disappears when you quit Dreamweaver or record another command. (Dreamweaver can only save one recorded command at a time.) If you want to preserve it for posterity, you'll have to save it to the Commands menu, like this:

1. **Choose Commands→Play Recorded Command.**

   The History panel lists this action as Run Command.

2. **Choose the Run Command step from the History panel.**

   The step is highlighted to indicate you've selected it.

3. **Click the Save Steps button (its icon looks like a little floppy disk).**

The Save as Command dialog box appears.

4. **Type a name for the command; click OK.**

Dreamweaver adds your new command to the Commands menu, where it's ready for action in this or any future Dreamweaver session.

Create Web Photo Album

So you took your digital camera to your nephew's wedding. Your phone's ringing off the hook with family wanting to see those pictures. Using Dreamweaver's Create Web Photo Album command, you can quickly generate a simple showcase for your digital masterpieces. (This command works only if you have Macromedia Fireworks on your computer.)

WORKAROUND WORKSHOP

Pasting Bullet Points

All of this business about creating your own software-robot macro commands in Dreamweaver pays off in plenty of eccentric circumstances. Here's a prime example: When you copy and paste bulleted text from a word processing program (shown here at top) into Dreamweaver (bottom), you don't end up with a bulleted list. Instead, Dreamweaver pastes the list as a single paragraph. Each list item ends in a line break, and is preceded not with an HTML bullet, but with a bullet *character* (which won't display properly on the Web). If you use a Mac, you're even worse off—you get the Greek letter Sigma instead of a bullet character!

Fortunately, you can whip up a quick little command to get that text in shape. Here's how:

Click just before the first item in the list, and then choose Commands→Start Recording. As usual, the cursor turns into a cassette tape icon to show that Dreamweaver is recording.

Press Delete (Windows) or Del (Mac) to delete the bullet

symbol. (That's the *forward*-delete key; if your older Mac keyboard lacks one, press Shift-right arrow, then the regular Delete key.) Now press End to make the insertion point jump to the end of the line; then press Backspace (Windows) or Delete (Mac) to nuke the unnecessary line-break character.

Press End, and then Return, to create a new paragraph. Finally, choose Commands→Stop Recording.

Now you're ready to replay the newly created command: Click before the next problem line in the list, and then press Ctrl+P (⌘-P) to trigger the cleanup command. Continue until you've applied the command to each item in the list.

After you've gotten rid of the bad formatting, all you need to do is transform your information into a proper HTML bulleted list. Select the list items and click the Bulleted List button in the Property inspector (see Figure 3-2, page 65). You may want to save this command permanently to your Commands menu (see page 580 for instructions).

To create a photo album, put all the graphics you want featured into a single folder.
(It doesn't have to be in your site folder.) Then choose Commands→Create Web
Photo Album. The dialog box that appears (Figure 19-3) offers these controls:

- **Photo Album Title, Subheading Info.** The title you type will appear in a gray box
on the thumbnail page, and at the top of each photo page (Figure 19-2). If you
type a subheading, it will appear in smaller type on the thumbnail page, below
the title.

Figure 19-2:
*Use Dreamweaver's built-
in Create Web Photo
Album command to whip
up a set of Web pages
that showcase your
photos. The command
creates a simple index for
your photo album (left),
including clickable
thumbnail images. Each
opens up an individual
page that showcases a
larger version of the
photo (right).*

- **Other Info.** Use this optional box to provide a short description of the photos;
this text will appear as plain paragraph type below the subhead.

- **Browse.** Click the top Browse button (next to the Source Images Folder box) to
find and select your folder of graphics files. The graphics files themselves don't
have to be in a Web-ready format (GIF, JPEG, or PNG). Fireworks can take GIF,
JPEG, PNG, Photoshop (.psd), or TIFF files and convert them into a Web-friendly
graphics file format. (That's why you need Fireworks in order to generate Web
photo albums.)

  Click the lower **Browse** button (next to the Destination Folder box) to find and
highlight the folder where you want to store the converted graphics (and the
album Web pages). This should be an empty folder in your site folder.

  Dreamweaver creates a new *index.html* page for the album's thumbnail page, as
well as additional folders for the thumbnail images, larger images, and photo
pages.

- **Size pop-up menu.** You can choose from five preset sizes for the thumbnail images: 36 x 36, 72 x 72, 100 x 100, 144 x 144, or 200 x 200 pixels. These sizes represent the *maximum* size of the height and width of the thumbnail image. For
example, if a photo in its original format is 785 pixels wide and 405 pixels tall, the

100 x 100 option will create a miniature image that's 100 pixels wide by 52 pixels tall (Fireworks doesn't distort the image by turning it into a 100 x 100 pixel square.)

- **Columns.** Specify the number of columns you want for the thumbnail page layout. If you have nine photos, for example, type 3 in the column box. Dreamweaver produces a page that displays your images three across and three down.

- **Thumbnail Format pop-up menu.** Choose the graphics format for both the thumbnail images and larger photo images. Fireworks converts the photos in the folder you've specified into either JPEG or GIF images.

Figure 19-3:
The Create Web Photo Album dialog box lets you define the properties of your photo album. The Show Filenames box tells Dreamweaver to add the actual file name of the image under each thumbnail. If your images are from a photo CD or stock image disk, you'll probably get uninformative names such as DS3746F7.jpg.

- **Scale.** Here, you can type a percentage for scaling the original images. If the original photos are very large, for example, you might want to create smaller versions that fit on a Web page better and are small enough to download quickly. For example, say your original digital photos are 1000 pixels wide—really huge for a Web page— you might type *40* (percent) to bring the images on the resulting Web pages down to a reasonable size.

- **Create Navigation Page for Each Photo.** This useful option creates a separate page for each photo, complete with its title, file name, and previous/next links (Figure 19-2, bottom). If you turn off this box, Dreamweaver merely links the thumbnail images directly to each larger photo. When a visitor clicks the thumbnail, the full-size image will still appear, but without the title or navigation controls.

When you click OK, Fireworks opens and creates the thumbnail and larger photo images. This may take a few minutes depending on how many image files Fireworks must process (and how big they are). When it's done, Dreamweaver steps in and creates the pages themselves. An "album created" message appears when your new photo gallery is ready to preview; Press F12 to open it in your Web browser.

Find and Replace

You've probably encountered find and replace tools in word processing programs and even some graphics programs. As the name implies, the command finds a piece of text (*Webmaster,* for example) and then *replaces* it with something else (*Webmistress*). Like Microsoft Word, Dreamweaver can search and replace text in the body of your Web pages. But it also offers variations on this feature that enhance your ability to work within the tag-based world of HTML.

What's more, Dreamweaver lets you find and replace text on *every* page of your Web site, not just the current, open document. In addition, you can *remove* every appearance of a particular HTML tag, or search and replace text that matches very specific criteria. For example, you can find every instance of the word "aardvark" that appears within a center-aligned paragraph. These advanced find and replace options are some of the most powerful—and under-appreciated—tools in Dreamweaver's toolbox. If you learn how to use them, you'll be able to make changes to your pages in a fraction of the time it would take using other methods.

EASTER EGG HUNT

Would You Like to Play a Game?

As today's software programs go, Dreamweaver is delightfully brimming with Easter eggs (page 120). But there's one particular Easter egg that's never before been seen outside of Macromedia—a software surprise so delicious, it was revealed for inclusion in this book only on the promise that the actual trigger wouldn't be explicitly printed here. But experimenting until you find it is worth the time; the result is a full-fledged *color game,* a full-blown version of the old game Brainteaser—a fun little diversion when you want a break from the daily grind.

It goes like this: Summon the Create Web Photo Album dialog box. Type the secret, three-word password into the Photo Album Title box with no spaces. (And what's the password, you may well ask? Here's a hint: It's a key phrase in the 1983 Matthew Broderick movie *WarGames,* and it appears somewhere in this chapter.)

To play the game once it appears, your challenge is to guess the secret four-color pattern that Dreamweaver has dreamed up. Click each of the squares on the bottom left row; click repeatedly until it shows the color you want. When you've arranged the four rectangles in the colors that represent your guess, click Guess. The smaller squares at the right side show you how many of your guesses were "right colors, right positions" (black) and how many were "right colors, wrong positions" (white). Use these clues to guide you in your next guess—in the second row of left-side rectangles. Keep going until you've unveiled Dreamweaver's secret.

Tip: You can use Find and Replace to search an entire site's worth of files. This is powerful, but can also be slow, especially if some folders hold files you don't want to search—old archives for example. You can use Dreamweaver MX's new cloaking feature to hide files from find and replace operations. See page 492 for more detail.

Find and Replace Basics

To start a search, press Ctrl+F (⌘-F), or choose Edit→Find and Replace. (This command is only available if a document is open. Even a blank, unsaved document will work.) The Find and Replace window opens (see Figure 19-4). Now all you have to do is fill in the blanks and set up the search.

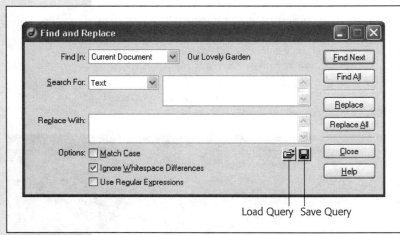

Figure 19-4:
Dreamweaver's Find and Replace feature lets you replace text and HTML quickly and accurately. By using the Load Query and Save Query buttons, you can even save complex searches to use in the future. (See the tip below.)

Load Query   Save Query

Whether you perform a simple text search or a complex tag-based search and replace, the procedure for using the Find and Replace command is basically the same. First, you need to tell Dreamweaver *where* to search (in a file, a folder, or an entire Web site). Next, tell it what to search for (text, HTML, or a particular tag with a specific attribute). Finally, you can decide what to replace the item with. This last step is optional; you can use the Find and Replace window as a way to locate an item on the page, or in your site, without actually changing it to anything.

Tip: After you've entered the Find and Replace criteria, click the Save Query button (see Figure 19-2). A Save dialog box appears; you can type in a name for your query, which Dreamweaver saves as a .dwr (Dreamweaver replace query) file. You can save this file anywhere on your computer. If it's a query you'll use for a particular site, you might want to save it with those files. If you plan to use the query you'll use frequently on different sites, consider saving it in the Dreamweaver MX→Configuration→Queries folder. To reuse a query, click the Load Query button and locate the .dwr file. The search and replace criteria load, and then you can click any of the four action buttons—Find Next, Find All, Replace, or Replace All.

Basic Text and HTML Searches

Dreamweaver can either search all of the HTML source code in a page or simply focus on text that appears in the document window. You'll choose one of these in Phase 2 below.

- A **source code** search lets you find and replace any character in the code of a page, including words, letters, and symbols.

- **Text** searches are more refined. They look only for text that appears within the body of a page. That is, Dreamweaver ignores HTML tags, properties, and comments when searching—in short, it ignores anything that doesn't appear as actual words in the document window. By using a text search when you want to change the word "center" to "middle," for example, you won't accidentally alter the center *alignment* option of a table cell—<td align="center">—by setting the alignment value of its HTML tag to "middle" (an invalid value that Web browsers would just ignore).

Figure 19-5:
The Find and Replace command is not limited to the current document. You can also search multiple Web pages or even an entire site.

If you've used Find and Replace in other programs, this routine will seem familiar:

Phase 1: Determine the scope of your search

Using the Find In menu (see Figure 19-5), choose any of these options:

- **Current Document.** Searches the Web page you're working on.

- **Entire Current Local Site.** Searches every Web page in the current site folder, including pages in folders *inside* the site folder. This option is invaluable when some basic piece of information changes throughout your site; for instance, when your boss's sex-change operation requires you to replace every instance of "Mark Jones" with "Mary Jones" throughout your company's site.

Warning: Using the Find and Replace command is one of the best ways to quickly make changes to an entire site, but it's also one of the easiest ways to *wreck* a site's worth of Web pages. Dreamweaver can't undo changes made by the Find and Replace command to files that aren't open on your computer. So be careful. If you plan on making extensive changes, make a backup copy of your files first!

- **Selected Files in Site.** Searches files you select in the Site window. This option assumes, of course, that you've opened the Site window and selected files in the local file list. (See page 460 for details.)

- **Folder.** Search all Web pages in a particular folder. Dreamweaver also searches Web pages in all folders *within* the selected folder. You can use this option to search pages that aren't part of the current site.

Phase 2: Specify what to search for

For your next trick, you'll tell Dreamweaver what you want to search for. Use the Search For pop-up menu to choose one of these two options:

- **Text.** This makes Dreamweaver search for a certain word or phrase of text that appears in the *body* of the documents you've specified. Type the text you want to find into the Search For field. If you're searching for a pattern in your text, enter a *regular expression* here and turn on Use Regular Expressions (see the box on the facing page).

- **Source Code.** Basic text searches are very useful, but they're limited to text that appears in the body of the page (what you see in the document window). If you want to search and replace code, you need the Source Code option.

Source code searches work identically to text searches. The only difference is that Dreamweaver searches *everything* within the file—text, HTML, JavaScript, Cascading Style Sheets (CSS), and so on—and replaces any part of the file. Using this option, you could search for any instance of the tag <img src="mark_jones_photo.jpg">, for example, and replace it with <img src="mary_jones_photo.jpg">.

(If you're in Code View, Dreamweaver automatically selects the Source Code option.)

As you fill in the Search For field, be aware that some plain-English words are also special words in HTML, JavaScript, or CSS. If you try to replace *table* with *desk* using a source-code find and replace, you'll completely destroy any <table> tags on the page.

You can also enter a regular expression to search for patterns in your HTML source code (see the box on the facing page).

Phase 3: Provide the replacement text

If you want to change the text that Dreamweaver finds, type the replacement text into the Replace With box. It may be the word or words you'd like to swap in if you chose a Text search as described above, or actual HTML code if you're performing a source-code search.

If you only want to find the text without replacing it, you can skip this step.

Tip: If you want to find the specified text and replace it with *nothing* (that is, deleting every occurrence of the text), leave the Replace With field blank and perform a replace operation, described below.

Phase 4: Choose the search settings

Dreamweaver gives you three options that govern its search and replace option; some of them are quite complex.

- The **Match Case** option limits the Find command to text that exactly matches the capitalization you used in the Search For field. If you search for the text *The End* with the Match Case box turned on, Dreamweaver will find a match in "The End is near," but not "You're almost at the end." Use this trick to find every instance of *web* and replace it with *Web*.

- The **Ignore Whitespace Differences** option treats multiple spaces, tabs, nonbreaking spaces and carriage returns as a single space when searching. For instance, if you search for *the dog* and turn on this option, Dreamweaver matches "the   dog" as well as "the dog".

The HTML of a page can contain lots of extra spaces, line breaks, and tabs that don't appear in a Web browser or in Dreamweaver's document window. For ex-

---

Turbocharge Your Searches

If you want to find the phone number 555-123-5473, no problem; just type *555-123-5473* into the search field. But what if you wanted to find any and *every* phone number—555-987-0938, 555-102-8870, and so on—on a Web page or in a site?

In such a case, you need to use *regular expressions,* the geeky name for a delightfully flexible searching language, carried over from early UNIX days, consisting of wildcard characters that let you search for patterns of text instead of actual letters or numbers. Each phone number above follows a simple pattern: three numbers, a dash, three more numbers, another dash, and four more numbers.

To search for a pattern, you use a variety of symbols combined with regular text characters to tell Dreamweaver what to find. For example, \d, in the world of regular expressions, stands for "any number." To find three numbers in a row, you could search for \d\d\d, which would find 555, 747, 007 and so on. There's even shorthand for this: \d{3}. The number between the braces ({}) indicates how many times in a row the preceding character must appear to match. To finish up the example of the phone numbers, you could use a regular expression like this: \d{3}-\d{3}-\d{4}. The \d{3} finds three numbers, while the hyphen (-)

following it is just the hyphen in the phone number.

Here are some of the other symbols you'll encounter when using regular expressions:

. (period) stands for *any* character, letter, number, space, and so on.

\w stands for any letter or number

* represents the preceding character zero or more times (and is always used after another character). This is best explained with an example: the regular expression *colou*r,* for instance, matches both *colour* and *color*—the * following the *u* indicates that the *u* is optional (it can appear zero times). This would also match *colouuuuur* (handy for those times when you've fallen asleep at the keyboard).

To see a complete list of the regular-expression characters Dreamweaver understands, launch the Dreamweaver online Help system (press F1) and search for the topic "About Regular Expressions." A full-length discussion of regular expressions could fill a book of its own—and does, in fact; check out *Mastering Regular Expressions* by Jeffrey E. F. Friedl. (To see an example of Regular Expressions in action, see page 596.)

---

ample, in the HTML of a document, it's possible to have two lines of code that look like this:

```
<p>This sentence will appear on one
line in a Web browser</p>
```

Even though this text would appear on a single line in the document window, a search for "one line" *without* the Ignore Whitespace Differences would find no match. The carriage return at the end of "one" is not an exact match for the space character in "one line." In other words, it's best to keep this option turned on.

• The **Use Regular Expressions** option is used for matching patterns in text. For a discussion of this advanced technique, see the box on page 589.

Phase 5: Take action

Finally, you're ready to set the search in motion by clicking one of the four action buttons in the Find and Replace window (see Figure 19-4):

• **Find Next** locates the next instance of the search term. If you're searching the current document, Dreamweaver highlights the matching text. If you're searching an entire Web site or a folder of pages, Dreamweaver opens the file *and* highlights the match. You can cycle through each instance of the search term by repeatedly clicking this button.

Note: In some programs (notably Microsoft Word), you can press Enter to repeat the Find Next function. Not so in Dreamweaver—even with the Find window open, Enter or Return starts a new paragraph. You must click Find Next. If you've clicked into the document window—or even closed the Find window—you can press F3 (⌘-G) to repeat the Find Next function.

• **Find All** locates every instance of the search terms, all at once, and shows them to you in a list in the Search tab of the Results panel (Figure 19-6). The name and location of each file (if multiple files are searched) appear to the left, and the matched text appears to the right.

Figure 19-6:
The green arrow button reopens the Find and Replace window, and so does the more succinct Ctrl+F (⌘-F). The red Stop button is useful when you've accidentally launched a search through your entire site for, say, the word "the." Click it to abort the current search and start over.

Unlike the Find Next action, Find All doesn't automatically open any of the Web pages containing matches. Instead, to open a matched page, double-click its name in the results list. Only then does the Web page open; Dreamweaver highlights the match.

- **Replace** locates the next instance of the search term *and* replaces it with the text in the Replace With field, leaving the replaced text highlighted for your inspection.

  You can use this button in combination with Find Next to selectively replace text. First, click Find Next. Dreamweaver locates and highlights the next match. Then, if you want to replace the text, click Replace. If not, click Find Next to search for the next match, and repeat the cycle.

- **Replace All** is the ultimate power tool. It finds every instance of the search term and replaces it with the text entered in the Replace With field. Coupled with the Find in Entire Local Site option, you can quickly make site-wide changes (and mistakes).

  When you click this button, Dreamweaver warns that you can't undo this operation on any closed files. You can erase mistakes you make with the Find and Replace in *open* documents by choosing Edit→Undo, but Dreamweaver *permanently* alters closed files that you search and replace. So be careful! (On the other hand, changes to open documents aren't permanent until you save those files.)

If you use the Find All or Replace All commands, the Find and Replace window closes displaying the results in the Search tab. To reopen it, click the green arrow on the Search tab—called the Find and Replace button—or press Ctrl+F (⌘-F).

Advanced Text Searches

If you want greater control over a text search, you can use the Find and Replace command's *advanced* text search option, which lets you confine a search to text either inside or outside of a specific tag.

For example, when Dreamweaver creates a new blank document, it sets the page's Title property to *Untitled*. Unfortunately, if you forget to change it, a site can quickly fill up with untitled Web pages. A basic text search won't identify this problem, because it searches only the body of a page; titles appear in the head. And a source-code search for *Untitled* would turn up the word "untitled" *wherever* it appeared in the page, not just inside the <title> tag.

In cases like this, an advanced text search is your best choice. Simply set the Find and Replace command to search for *Untitled* whenever it appears within the <title> tag.

To use the advanced text search, use the same general routine as described on the previous pages. But before using one of the action buttons, you can make a few additional setup changes to the dialog box.

Limiting the search by tag

Choose Text (Advanced) from the Search For pop-up menu to make the expanded, new controls appear (see Figure 19-7).

Figure 19-7:
Use an advanced text search to limit your search to text that appears within a particular HTML tag. Or, conversely, search for text that doesn't appear in a particular tag.

Now, from the menu next to the + and – buttons, choose either Inside Tag or Not Inside Tag. For example, consider this line of code: "Stupid is as <b>stupid</b> does." The first instance of "stupid" isn't inside the <b> tag, but the second one is.

Note: A more descriptive name for the first option would be *"Enclosed* By Tag"; Dreamweaver actually searches for text that's between opening *and closing* tags. In fact, an advanced text search using this option doesn't identify text that's literally inside a tag.

For example, it won't find "vegetable" in this line of code: <img src="cabbage.jpg" alt="Beware this vegetable.">, but it would find "vegetable" in this one: <b>Beware this vegetable.</b>. In the first example, *vegetable* appears as part of the <img> tag, while in the second, *vegetable* is enclosed by the opening and closing <b> tags.

Once you've specified whether you're looking for text inside or outside of tags, you can choose a specific HTML tag from the Tag menu identified in Figure 19-7.

The menu lists all qualifying tags—that is, those with both an opening and closing tag. For example, the image tag (<img>) is not included, since it has no closing tag.

Tip: A great way to search for text in both the title and body of a Web page is to choose the HTML tag from this menu. That way, you can search for any text that appears within the opening <html> and closing </html> of the page—which, since those tags start and end any Web document, is *all* text on a page.

Limiting the search by attribute

To limit the search further, click the + button (see Figure 19-8); yet another new set of fields appears.

Figure 19-8:
When you click the + button on the Find and Replace window, a new set of fields appears. Use these options to carefully hone your Find and Replace commands and zero in on text that matches precise criteria.

Tag Modifier menu

Using the tag modifier menu—next to the + and − buttons (Figure 19-8)—you can choose from any of six options that break down into three groups:

- **With Attribute/Without Attribute.** To limit the search, you can specify that a tag must either have (With Attribute) or not have (Without Attribute) a specific property.

  For example, say the following line of code appears throughout a Web site:

  ```
  <p>For assistance, please email
  <a href="mailto:mail@cosmofarmer.com">
  Cosmopolitan Farmer.</a></p>
  ```

  But you need to change it to say "For assistance, please email Customer Service." A basic text find and replace would incorrectly change the words "Cosmopolitan Farmer" to "Customer Service" *everywhere* on the site.

  However, an advanced text search using the With Attribute option would do the trick. You could look for the text "Cosmopolitan Farmer" wherever it appears inside an <a> tag whose *href* attribute is set to "mailto:mail@cosmofarmer.com." (To learn about the different HTML tags and attributes, use Dreamweaver's built-in code reference; see page 288.)

  After you choose With Attribute, use the menu on the right to select *which* of the tag's properties you want to find. (Dreamweaver automatically lists properties that are appropriate for the tag you've specified.) For example, if you search inside a <table> tag, the menu will list such properties as Align, Background, and so on.

Advance to the next pop-up menu to choose a type of comparison: = (equals), != (not equal to), > (greater than), or < (less than). These options are useful only when the property's value is a numeric amount, such as the Width property of an image. In this way, you could locate all images that are wider than 100 pixels (width > 100). (This setting has no effect on values that are words, such as *center* in this example: <td align="center">.)

Finally, type the value of the property in the last field. For instance, if you were searching for a black-colored background, the value would be #000000 (the hex value for black; see page 34).

You can also click the menu and choose [any value]—a useful option when you want to find tags that have a certain property, but you're not interested in the property's value. For example, if you want to find all <table> tags with a background color (no matter whether the color's #336699, #000000, or #FFFFFF), choose the *bgcolor* attribute and [any value].

- **Containing/Not Containing.** These options let you specify whether the tag contains, or does not contain, specific text or a particular tag.

  When you choose this option, a different set of fields appears. Choose either Text or Specific Tag from the menu to the right, and then either enter some text or select a tag in the last field in the row.

  For example, another solution to the problem above would be to search for the text "Cosmopolitan Farmer" wherever it appears inside a <p> (paragraph) tag that *also contains* the text "please email" (Figure 19-8).

- **Inside Tag/Not Inside Tag.** These last two choices are identical to those described on page 592. They let you specify whether the tag is inside or not inside a specific tag. Use these to limit a search, for example, to text that appears only within a <font> tag that's *inside* a Heading 1 (<h1>) tag.

If you like, you can add even more restrictions to your search, adding new rules by clicking the + button and repeating the setup just described. When you're really on a roll, it's even possible to add so many modifiers that the Find and Replace window actually grows past the bottom of your monitor. To remove a modifier, click the – (minus) button.

Advanced Tag Searches

If you find the number of options an advanced text search offers overwhelming, you haven't seen anything yet. Dreamweaver's tag search adds more choices to help you quickly search for, and modify, HTML tags. You can use a tag search to strip out unwanted HTML tags (for example, if you're migrating a site to CSS, you could remove the <font> tag), transform one tag into another (you could turn unreadable italics [<i>] into eye-catching bold [<b>]), and perform a host of other powerful actions.

In its basic outline, a tag search is much like the regular text search described on page 587. But this time, from the Search For menu, you should choose Specific Tag.

Now a tag menu appears next to the Search For menu, and the dialog box expands to display a new set of fields (see Figure 19-9). Some of them are the same as the controls you see when performing an advanced text search (page 591), such as the tag modifier menu and the + button that lets you add additional restrictions to the search.

Figure 19-9:
Remember the nasty old <blink> tag that makes text flash on and off like the outside of a Las Vegas casino? It's a snap to remove unwanted (or obnoxious) tags when you use the Specific Tag option in Dreamweaver's Find and Replace command. This option is also handy if you're replacing old-style text formatting with cascading style sheets; use it to strip out unwanted <font> tags.

But a key difference here is the Actions menu (Figure 19-10). This pop-up menu lets you specify the action Dreamweaver will perform on tags that match the search criteria when you click Replace or Replace All (if you intend to search but not replace, these options don't apply):

- **Replace Tag & Contents** replaces the tag, and anything enclosed by the tag (including other tags), with whatever you put into the With box to the right of this menu. You can either type or paste text or HTML here.

- **Replace Contents Only** replaces everything enclosed by the tag with text or HTML that you specify. The tag itself remains untouched.

- **Remove Tag and Contents** deletes the tag and *everything* inside.

- **Strip Tag** deletes the tag from the page, but leaves anything inside the tag untouched.

- **Set Attribute** *adds* an attribute to the tag. For example, you could set the Alt property of an image this way (see the example on page 596).

- **Remove Attribute** removes an attribute from a tag. For example, you could remove the not-so-useful *lowsrc* attribute from all image tags on your pages.

- **Add Before (After) Start (End) Tag.** The last four actions in the menu simply offer variations on the same theme. They each let you place content in a Web page just before or after the tag you're searching for.

To understand how these actions work, remember that most HTML tags come in pairs. The paragraph tag, for example, has an opening tag, <p>, and a closing tag, </p>. Say you searched for a paragraph tag; you could add text or HTML *before* or *after* the start tag (<p>) or *before* or *after* the end tag (</p>). For an example of this action at work, see "Convenient Copyright Notices" at the end of this chapter.

Figure 19-10:
Once Dreamweaver finds a specific tag, it can perform any of eleven different actions on the tag or its contents.

A Powerful Example: Adding Alt Text Fast

You've just put the finishing touches on the last page of your brand-new, 1,000-page site. You sit back and smile—and then snap bolt upright when you notice you forgot to add an Alt description for the site's banner graphic (page 114). This graphic, called *site_banner.gif*, appears on every single one of the 1,000 pages. With rising dread, you realize that you'll have to open each page, select the graphic, and add the Alt property by hand.

And then you remember Dreamweaver's advanced tag-based find and replace.

Here's what you do. Press Ctrl+F (⌘-F) to open the Find and Replace window. Set up the dialog box like this:

1. **From the Find In menu, choose Entire Local Site.**

   You want to fix *every* page on your site.

2. **From the Search For pop-up menu, choose Specific Tag; from the pop-up menu to its right, choose** *img.*

   You'll start by identifying every image (the <img> tag).

3. **On the next row, use the three pop-up menus to choose With Attribute,** *src,* **and the equals sign (=).**

   This tells Dreamweaver to look for specific images—in this case, images with a *src* attribute (the path that tells a Web browser where to find the image file on the Web server) with a specific value.

4. **Type** *.*site_banner\.gif* **in the box next to the = sign.**

   The name *site_banner.gif* is the name of the image file. The *.** is the magic, and it'll be explained in a moment.

5. **Click the + button.**

   Another row of tag modifier menus appears.

6. **From the new row of menus, choose Without Attribute and** *alt.*

   You've further limited Dreamweaver's search to only those images that don't already have the *alt* attribute. (After all, why bother setting the Alt property on an image that already has it?)

Figure 19-11:
The numbers shown here correspond to the steps in this fictional example, in which you want to add an <alt> tag—for the benefit of people who can't, or don't want to, see graphics in their browsers—to every occurrence of the banner logo.

7. **From the Action menu, choose Set Attribute; from the tag menu, choose** *alt.*

   You've just told Dreamweaver what to do when you click the Replace or Replace All button. When Dreamweaver finds an <img> tag that matches the search criteria, it will then *add* an Alt property to that tag.

In this example, you might type *Cosmopolitan Farmer* in the To field; you've just specified the Alt text that Dreamweaver will add to the image.

8. **Turn on Use Regular Expressions.**

Regular expressions, described on page 589, let you search for specific patterns of characters, and in this case, will help you accurately identify the banner graphic file everywhere it appears.

You know you're looking for the file *site_banner.gif*, wherever it appears in the site. Unfortunately, if you just type *site_banner.gif* as the value of the *src* property of step 3, Dreamweaver won't succeed in its task. That's because the *src* attribute, the part of the <img> tag that includes the name of the file, varies from page to page. Depending on where a page is relative to the graphic, the *src* might be *site_banner.gif, images/site_banner.gif,* or even *../../../images/site_banner.gif.* What you need is a way to match every *src* attribute that *ends* in *site_banner.gif.*

A simple regular expression, .*site_banner\.gif, does the trick. The period stands for *any* character (6, g, or even %, for example), while the * (asterisk) means "zero or more times." When you add these codes to the graphic name, *site_banner.gif,* you instruct Dreamweaver to find every *src* value that ends in *site_banner.gif.*

FREQUENTLY ASKED QUESTION

Convenient Copyright Notices

I want to add a copyright notice to the bottom of each page in my Web site. Is there a way to automate this process so I don't have to edit every page in my site by hand?

Of course there is. Use Dreamweaver's Find and Replace command to add text or HTML to the bottom of any Web page. The trick is knowing how to use the command's Specific Tag option.

First, choose Edit→Find and Replace to open the Find and Replace window. Next, choose Entire Local Site from the Find In menu, and choose Specific Tag from the Search For menu. Choose *body* from the tag menu. Remember, the <body> tag in HTML encloses everything that appears inside a browser

window; it's equivalent to what you see in the document window.

From the Action menu, choose Add Before End Tag. The end tag in this case is </body>. Since </body> marks the end of any content in a Web page, whatever appears *directly* before this closing tag will appear at the bottom of the Web page. (You can probably see where this is going.)

Now, in the text field next to the Action menu, type (or paste) the copyright notice you'd like to use on each. You may want to first design the copyright message using Dreamweaver, then copy and paste the HTML into this field.

Click Replace All. Dreamweaver handles the rest.

Note the backslash before the last period: \.*gif.* Since in the world of regular expressions a period means "any character," simply using *site_banner.gif* would not only match *site_banner.gif,* but also *site_banner1gif, site_bannerZgif,* and so on—in other words, any character between *site_banner* and *gif.* The backslash means treat the next character literally, as just a period with no special regular-expression power.

The dialog box should look like the one in Figure 19-11.

9. **Click the Replace All and sit back.**

In a matter of moments, Dreamweaver updates all 1,000 pages.

Customizing Dreamweaver

Whether you're a hard-core HTML jockey who prefers to be knee-deep in Code view, or a visually oriented, drag-and-drop type who never strays from the document window, Dreamweaver lets you work *your* way.

Not only are the tools built into the program incredibly flexible, the program *itself* can be customized. Dreamweaver gives you the power to add, change, and share keyboard shortcuts—a simple way to tailor the program to your needs. If that's not enough of an efficiency boost, you can add features that even Macromedia's engineers never imagined, from new Flash button designs to additional Behaviors. Dreamweaver's design allows amateur and professional programmers alike to write new features and functions using HTML, JavaScript, and XML (Extensible Markup Language). There are hundreds of these extras, called *extensions*, for you to explore. Best of all, you can try most them for free.

Keyboard Shortcuts

As you use Dreamweaver, you'll hit the same keyboard shortcuts and travel to the same palettes and menus time and again. Perhaps your site uses a lot of graphics and Flash movies; you're constantly using the keyboard shortcuts to insert them. But you may find that, after the 1,000th time, Ctrl+Alt+F (⌘-Option-F) hurts your pinkie and uses too many keys to be efficient. On the other hand, the things you do all the time (inserting text fields into forms, for instance) may not have shortcuts at all; you're forced to go to a menu.

To speed up your work and save your tendons, Dreamweaver comes with a keyboard-shortcut editor that lets you define or redefine shortcuts for most of the program's commands.

Dreamweaver stores keyboard shortcuts in sets. It's easy to switch between them—a useful feat when you share your computer with someone who likes different keystrokes.

Four sets come with the program:

- **Macromedia Standard.** When you first fire up Dreamweaver, this is the set that's turned on. The latest versions of Macromedia products, including Fireworks and Flash, share these shortcuts, meaning that you can switch between Macromedia programs without missing a keystroke.

- **Dreamweaver 3.** Some keyboard shortcuts have changed since Dreamweaver 3—for example, F8 instead of F5 now opens the Site window—so if you're comfortable with the older shortcuts, you may prefer this set.

- **BBEdit.** If you're a Mac user with a code-editing past, you may have spent a lot of time learning shortcuts for Bare Bones Software's popular BBEdit. If so, choose this set.

Export Set as HTML
Rename Set
Duplicate Set
Delete Set

Figure 20-1:
The Keyboard Shortcuts window lets you select or duplicate a shortcut set, as well as add and remove keyboard shortcuts for every menu item in Dreamweaver MX.

- **HomeSite.** Likewise, if you're adept at the Windows HTML text editor HomeSite, you may choose to use its keyboard shortcuts.

You can access the shortcut sets from the Keyboard Shortcuts window. Choose Edit→Keyboard Shortcuts. Be patient; it can take some time for the sets to load. Once the dialog box appears, you can switch sets by choosing a new one from the Current Set menu (see Figure 20-1).

Make Your Own Shortcut Set

What if you want a set that *combines* BBEdit shortcuts with your most-used Dreamweaver 3 ones? You can easily create keyboard shortcut sets that fit the way you work. Dreamweaver doesn't let you alter any of the four standard sets, so if you want to create your own, the first step is to make a copy of an existing one.

To do so, choose Edit→Keyboard Shortcuts; in the Keyboard Shortcuts window, use the Current Set pop-up menu to choose the set you wish to copy, and then click the Duplicate Set button (see Figure 20-1). Dreamweaver asks you to name the new set; do so, then click OK.

You can rename or delete any set you create, once you figure out that the button in the Shortcuts window with the cryptic icon is the Rename Set button (see Figure 20-1). The Trash can button, of course, lets you delete a set.

Note: Unlike Dreamweaver 4, Dreamweaver MX lets you delete the four main keyboard shortcuts. If you want one of them back, don't worry. The file isn't actually gone. You just need to edit a file called *mm_deleted_files.xml* in the Dreamweaver MX→Configuration folder. Remove the line that lists the keyboard shortcut you want to get back and save the file. Then quit and restart Dreamweaver. (Note that Windows XP, 2000, and NT, and Mac OS X maintain a separate Configuration folder for each account holder. See the box on page 605 for more.)

Changing Keyboard Shortcuts

Once you've created a new set, you can select any command and alter its shortcut. Start by choosing Edit→Keyboard Shortcuts to open the Shortcuts window, if it's not already open. Then:

1. **From the Commands pop-up menu, choose the command type.**

   Dreamweaver organizes shortcuts into three (Macintosh) or five (Windows) primary categories. These categories don't always make sense; for example, Copy and Paste appear under the Code Editing category, even though you use them at least as frequently while editing a document in the visual Design view. Browse to see which commands have (or could have) keyboard shortcuts associated with them.

   Menu Commands are the commands in Dreamweaver's menus, such as Insert→Image.

You might presumably use the **Code Editing** commands when editing HTML code. However, you could just as easily use them in Design view. They include Cut, Paste, and Move to Top of Page, to name a few.

Document Editing commands are for selecting text and objects on a page, as well as previewing a page in a Web browser.

Site Panel Commands (Windows only) are the commands available from the menus on the Site panel, such as Site→Change Link Sitewide. (On the Mac, these commands are listed with the others in the Menu Commands category.)

Site Window Commands (**Windows only**), available when working in the Site window, include Cancel FTP. On the Mac, these commands are listed in the Document Editing group.

2. **In the list below the Commands menu, click the command whose keyboard shortcut you want to change.**

You'll find menu commands grouped by menu name: commands available in the File menu, like Open and Save, fall under File. Click the + (Windows) or flippy triangle (Mac) next to the menu name to display the list of commands hidden underneath (see Figure 20-1). If the command already has a keyboard shortcut, it appears in the right-hand column. If it isn't assigned a shortcut, you see an empty space.

3. **Click inside the Press Key field, then press the new keystroke.**

Unless you're assigning the shortcut to an Fkey, you must begin your shortcut with the Ctrl key (⌘ key). For example, the F8 key is a valid shortcut, but the letter R is not. Press Ctrl+R (⌘-R) instead.

Note: Some keyboard shortcuts may already be in use by your operating system, so assigning them in Dreamweaver may have no effect. For example, in Windows XP, Ctrl+Esc opens the Start Menu.

Of course, many commands already have shortcuts. If you choose a key combination that's in use, Dreamweaver tells you which command has dibs. You can pick a different key combination, or simply click the Change button to reassign the shortcut to your command.

4. **Click the Change button.**

Dreamweaver saves the new shortcut in your custom set.

Repeat from step 1 if you want to make other keystroke reassignments; when you're finished, click OK to close the dialog box.

What if a command you use often doesn't have a shortcut at all? It's no problem to create one. As a matter of fact, Dreamweaver lets you assign *two* keyboard shortcuts to every command—one for you, and one for your left-handed spouse, for example.

To give a command an additional shortcut (or its first):

5. **Choose the command.**

   Follow the first two steps of the preceding instructions, for example.

6. **Click the + button next to the word Shortcuts.**

   The cursor automatically pops into the Press Key field.

7. **Press the keys of your additional shortcut, then click the Change button again.**

   Repeat from step 1 if you want to make other keystroke reassignments; when you're finished, click OK.

Deleting shortcuts is just as easy. Simply click the command in the list and then click the – button next to the word Shortcuts.

Create a Shortcut Cheat Sheet

Unless your brain is equipped with an 80-gig hard drive, you'll probably find it hard to remember all of Dreamweaver's keyboard shortcuts.

Fortunately, Dreamweaver offers a printable cheat sheet for your reference. At the top of the Shortcuts window, there's a handy Export Set as HTML button. (It's labeled with a cryptic icon; see Figure 20-1.) Click this button to name and save a simple HTML page that lists all of the commands and keyboard shortcuts for the currently selected set. Once you've saved the file, print it out or use it as an online reference—a great way to keep a record of your shortcuts for yourself or a team of Web page designers (see the box below).

FREQUENTLY ASKED QUESTION

Sharing Shortcuts

How do I share my keyboard set with other people?

Dreamweaver stores your keyboard shortcuts as XML files. With Dreamweaver MX, however, *where* these files are exactly stored has gotten a little trickier. Depending on the operating system you're using, these files are in different locations. For operating systems that don't support multiple users—Windows ME, Windows 98, and Mac OS 9—you'll simply find these in the Dreamweaver MX→Configuration→Menus→Custom Sets folder. Each keyboard set lives in an XML file; the file's name ends with the extension .xml.

In Windows XP, 2000, or NT, you'll find the custom keyboard set on your main hard drive in Documents and Settings→[Your Name]→Application Data→Macromedia→Dreamweaver MX→Configuration→Menus→Custom Sets. For Mac OS X, these files are squirreled even farther away in the Users→[Your Name]→Library→Application Support→Macromedia→Dreamweaver MX→Configuration→Menus→Custom Sets.

You can copy these files and place them in the Custom Sets folder on other computers. Once you've done so, the Dreamweaver users on those machines can use the Keyboard Shortcuts window (Edit→Keyboard Shortcuts) to select the new set, just as though it had been created in that copy of Dreamweaver.

Dreamweaver Extensions

While keyboard shortcuts provide an easy way to access frequently used commands, they're not much help if the command you want doesn't exist. Suppose, for example, that you use the Validate Form behavior to make sure visitors to your site fill out your forms properly (see page 313). However, you wish that in addition to just checking for an email address or number, it could check for phone numbers, Zip codes, and social security numbers. What's a Web designer to do? You could dash off a quick email to *wish-dreamweaver@macromedia.com,* asking the bustling team of programmers to add the command to the next version. But you'd have to wait (and there's no guarantee that Macromedia will do it).

The legions of hard-core Dreamweaver fans have taken this feature-wish-list issue into their own hands. As it turns out, amateur (and pro) programmers can enhance Dreamweaver relatively easily by writing new feature modules using the basic languages of the Web: HTML, JavaScript, and XML. (In fact, HTML forms, JavaScript programs, and XML documents constitute much of the program. The objects in the Insert bar, for example, are actually HTML pages stored within Dreamweaver's Configuration folder, and all of Dreamweaver's menus have actually been written as an XML file.)

Because of this open architecture, you can add new functions and commands, called *extensions,* to Dreamweaver by downloading the work of all those programmers. (Macintosh fans shouldn't confuse these plug-in software modules with *system* extensions, the kind that drop into Mac OS 9's System Folder and sometimes cause troubleshooting headaches.)

A Dreamweaver extension can take many forms and work in a variety of ways to change the way the program works. It can be an icon on the Insert bar, a behavior listed on the Behaviors panel, or a command in the Commands menu. It might even be an entirely new floating window, like the Property inspector, that you use to alter some aspect of your page.

Best of all, whereas programming ability may be required to *create* extensions, none is necessary to use them. You can download hundreds of extensions from the Web and install them on your computer for free. In addition, many sophisticated extensions, like those for creating e-commerce sites, are commercially available.

Note: Dreamweaver MX introduces some changes to the way extensions work. As a result, some extensions that worked in earlier versions may not work in MX. As this book went to press, Macromedia engineers were hard at work, testing existing extensions and working with their creators to help them with MX compatibility. One way to be sure an extension will work in MX is to click the Advanced Search link at the Exchange site (see Figure 20-2), select Dreamweaver MX from the Product Version pull-down menu, and click Search. This setup finds all extensions made for MX.

Browse the Exchange

The best spot to find Dreamweaver extensions is the Macromedia Exchange Web site, which offers hundreds of free extensions. Although some come from Macromedia itself, the majority are written by an army of talented Dreamweaver users.

Using the Exchange is a straightforward process.

1. **In your Web browser, go to *www.macromedia.com/exchange/*.**

   You can also get there from within Dreamweaver by choosing Commands→Get More Commands.

2. **Click the Dreamweaver link.**

   Macromedia offers extensions for many other programs too, including Flash, ColdFusion Server, and HomeSite. That's why you must specify that you're using Dreamweaver.

3. **Log in (see Figure 20-2).**

   You can *browse* the site without logging in, but to *download* any of the extensions, you need to get a Macromedia ID and sign in, using the Exchange Login form.

4. **Browse the extensions.**

   Once you've logged on to the site, the home page highlights new and popular extensions. Unfortunately, at this writing, the site is poorly organized; finding an extension takes some work.

Figure 20-2:
To take advantage of the Exchange, you must get a Macromedia ID and log in to the site. Fortunately, the information you need to provide for membership is rather benign: name, email address, and preferred password. You needn't fill out a long questionnaire about your high-tech shopping habits or submit a DNA sample.

Get an ID

You have two ways to look. First, near the top of each page, you'll see a pop-up menu that lists different categories of extensions: Accessibility, DHTML/layers, Navigation, Productivity, Flash media, Scripting, Tables, Text, eCommerce, and so on. When you choose a category, you go to a page listing all of the extensions within that category (see Figures 20-3 and 20-4).

If you're looking for a *particular* extension, the search command is your best bet. Type the extension's name, or a few descriptive words, into the Search Extensions field, then click Go. (Unfortunately, this is the only way you can direct someone to a particular extension. At this point, the Exchange doesn't provide each one a unique URL.)

5. **Click an extension's name to go to its Web page.**

On an extension's page, you'll find a description of it, a link for downloading it, as well as a discussion board where you can post questions, comments, compliments, and criticism (see Figure 20-3).

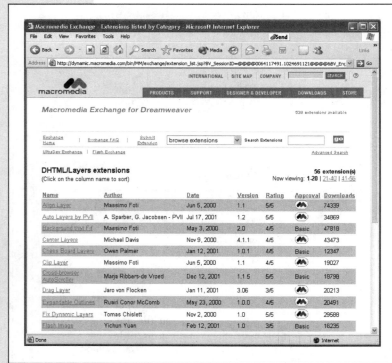

Figure 20-3:
At the Exchange, you can choose a category to see a list of extensions. Sort the list by clicking the headings at the top of each column. For example, click Date to sort the extensions by how recently they were posted.

Find a Good Extension

How do you figure out which extensions are worth checking out? First, you can find some recommendations of the best ones scattered through this book in special sidebars labeled Extension Alert (see page 128, for example).

The Exchange also provides information to help you separate the wheat from the chaff. Macromedia tests each new extension before posting it. Extensions that pass a basic set of tests—it installs OK, it works, it doesn't blow up your computer—are given a Basic approval rating. Some extensions also pass a more rigorous test that determines if the extension works in a way that's Dreamweaver-like. In other words, these extensions are designed to look, feel, and act like the program, so that you won't need to learn a new interface. These extensions get a Macromedia Approved rating, indicated by the Macromedia logo.

Of course, these approval ratings only let you know if an extension works; they don't tell you that it's *useful*. As an extra aid, Dreamweaver aficionados (including you) can rate each extension on a scale of 1 (worst) to 5 (best). An extension's average rating gives you a good indication of how handy it is. When you're browsing the Exchange, look for the column labeled Rating to the right (see Figure 20-3). Click the header to organize the extensions from most- to least-recommended.

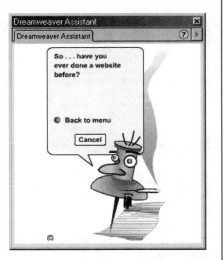

Figure 20-4:
If you ever need some destructive criticism, download the Dreamweaver Assistant extension. The assistant, a cigarette-smoking pushpin with a goatee and an attitude (and a stinging spoof of Clippy the Moronic Paper Clip in Microsoft Office for Windows), will gently comment on your site, ask for a beer, and make time with a paper clip. You'll find this amusing waste of time in, ironically, the Productivity category of the Exchange.

Download and Install Extensions

Once you've found a great extension, download it by clicking the link for your operating system: Mac or Windows. You can save the resulting downloaded file anywhere on your computer, but the Dreamweaver MX→Downloaded Extensions folder is a logical place.

A downloaded extension file's name ends with .mxp, which stands for Macromedia Exchange Package. That's a special file format that works with the Extension Manager—the program, described next, that actually installs the extension into Dreamweaver.

The Extension Manager

To add and remove a Dreamweaver extension, use the Extension Manager, a stand-alone program that's integrated with Dreamweaver. It's designed to manage extensions for Dreamweaver: install them, turn them on and off, and remove them. This feature can be quite handy if you also use Macromedia's Flash or UltraDev programs; you have a single access point for managing all of your extensions.

You can launch the Extension Manager from within Dreamweaver by choosing Commands→Manage Extensions (see Figure 20-5).

To add an extension:

1. **Download an extension package (.mxp file) from the Exchange.**

    See instructions on page 608.

Figure 20-5:
The Extension Manager window lists each extension you've installed along with its version number, type, and author. If you select an extension from the list, a description displays in the bottom half of the window.

The Windows and Macintosh versions differ slightly; the Windows version (top) includes four buttons for easy access to common tasks. The same functions can be accessed on the Mac (bottom) from the File and Help menus.

2. **From Dreamweaver, choose Commands→Manage Extensions.**

   The Extension Manager launches. It lists all currently installed extensions (see Figure 20-5).

3. **Choose Dreamweaver MX from the pop-up menu.**

   Since the Extension Manager handles extensions for several different programs, you need to specify which program you're using. Of course, if you don't have any other Macromedia products installed on your machine, Dreamweaver MX is the only option.

4 **Choose File→Install Extension.**

   If you're using Windows, you can also click the Install Extension button. The Select Extension window appears, listing the folders on your hard drive.

5. **Navigate to and select the extension package (.mxp file) you wish to add.**

   A disclaimer appears with a lot of legal text. In brief, it holds Macromedia free of liability if your computer melts as a result of installing the extension.

6. **Click Accept in the Disclaimer window.**

   A message may appear that asks you to quit and restart Dreamweaver. If so, follow the directions.

Tip: You can also install an extension simply by double-clicking the .mxp file after you download it, which saves you a few steps.

POWER USERS' CLINIC

The Secret Life of Extensions

Where do extensions go? The basic answer is: inside the Dreamweaver MX→Configuration folder. (This folder's location varies by operating system, as described on page 606.)

The Configuration folder holds many of the files that control the look and operation of the program. For instance, the entire menu structure, including menu items and submenus, is described in a file called *menus.xml*. When Dreamweaver starts, it reads this file and uses the information inside it to draw the menus on the screen.

The Configuration folder holds many subfolders, each with a special purpose. For example, the Objects folder contains files that tell Dreamweaver which icon buttons appear on the Insert bar and how each one works.

Depending on the type of extension you've downloaded—command, object, behavior, or whatever—the extension manager stores the file (or files) required by the extension in one or more folders inside the Configuration folder. Because all of the files inside the Configuration folder are crucial to the way Dreamweaver works, don't delete the folder or any of the files inside it. In fact, because the Extension Manager automatically makes any required changes to the Configuration folder, there's no reason for you to even look inside it.

(The only exception is when you want to copy your keyboard shortcut set to another computer. See page 605.)

To remove an extension, select it from the list and choose File→Remove Extension (or, in Windows, click the Trash can button).

Warning: If you install a lot of extensions, Dreamweaver may take longer than usual to load. It needs to process every extension file as it opens.

If you want to temporarily turn off an extension (as opposed to deleting it), open the Extension Manager and turn off the box next to the extension's name. To turn it back on again, simply turn on the box again. You may need to restart Dreamweaver to make the extension available again.

If you had downloaded and installed a bunch of extensions back when you used Dreamweaver 4, you can import them into Dreamweaver MX by choosing File→Import Extensions. Select Dreamweaver 4 from the menu and click OK; Dreamweaver MX will copy all installed extensions from Dreamweaver 4. (Again, not all Dreamweaver 4 extensions work in MX. Use this option with care.)

Make Your Own Extensions

The Exchange is a great resource for finding useful extensions. But what if you can't find the extension you need? Create your own.

Writing extensions involves in-depth knowledge of JavaScript and HTML. But when you create a command that lets you complete a weekly task in a fraction of the time it took before, the effort just may be worth it. For more information, choose Help→Extending Dreamweaver for an electronic reference, or visit the Extending Dreamweaver page on the Macromedia Web site: *www.macromedia.com/support /dreamweaver/extend.html.*

Part Six:
Dynamic, Database-Driven Dreamweaver

6

Getting Started with Dynamic Web Sites

The Web pages described in this book so far are straightforward HTML, which you can immediately preview in a Web browser to see a finished design. These are often called *static* pages: they don't change once you've finished them. For many Web sites, static Web pages are the way to go.

But imagine landing a contract to build an online catalog of 10,000 products. After the initial excitement disappears (along with your plans for that trip to Hawaii), you realize that even using Dreamweaver's Template tool (Chapter 18), building 10,000 pages is a lot of work!

Fortunately, Dreamweaver MX offers a better and faster way to deal with this problem. Its *dynamic Web site creation tools* let you take advantage of a variety of powerful techniques that would be difficult or impossible to implement with plain HTML pages. With Dreamweaver MX, you can build pages that:

- Display listings of products or other items like your record collection, your company's staff directory, or your mother's library of prized recipes.

- Search through a database of information and display the results.

- Require login so you can hide particular areas from prying eyes.

- Collect and store information from visitors to your site.

- Personalize your visitors' experience: "Hello Dave, it's been awhile since you've visited. Did you miss us?—Hal."

At Amazon.com, for example, you'll find more books than you could read in a lifetime. In fact, you'll find more products—DVDs, CDs, and even outdoor lawn furniture—than could fit inside a Wal-Mart. Do you really think Amazon hired an army of Web developers to create each Web page for every product they sell? Not a chance.

Instead, when you search for a book on Amazon, your search triggers a computer program running on an application server, which searches a large database of products. When the program finds products that match your query, it merges that information with the HTML elements that make up the page (banner, navigation buttons, copyright notice, and so on). You see a new Web page that's been created on the spot—perhaps for the first time ever (Figure 21-1).

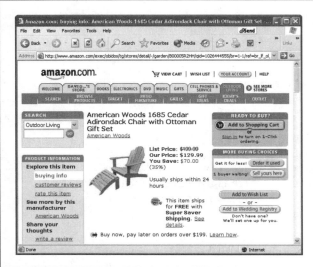

Figure 21-1:
An infinite number of monkeys couldn't create all the Web pages for the products Amazon sells. A dynamic Web site where pages are created by accessing information from a database is often the best choice for sites that present lots of similar information.

This is the *MX* part of Dreamweaver MX: the technologies that were added to this version. (Actually, it's what was *merged* with Dreamweaver from the former stand-alone product called Dreamweaver UltraDev, which no longer exists.)

In general, dynamic Web sites are the realm of professional programmers. This chapter and the next few, though, take a stab at teaching you the basics.

Pieces of the Puzzle

You may be thinking, "Yeah, that sounds fantastic, but so did that timeshare in the Bahamas. What's the catch?"

The catch is that dynamic Web sites are complex and involve more technologies. Static Web sites require only the machine you use to build them and a Web server to dish them out. You don't even need a Web server to preview them.

Dynamic Web pages, by contrast, require more (see Figure 21-2). Not only is there a Web server that handles requests for Web pages, there are also two other types of servers: an *application server* and a *database server*. And dynamic pages contain more than HTML; they also contain programming code. An application server processes this code and sends a complete HTML page to the Web server, which, in turn, sends that on to the visitor. Often, the programming code requires the application server to retrieve information from a database and then merge it with the HTML of a page.

Note: In this context, a *server* is software that dishes out particular types of information—Web pages, database queries, or the output of a program. It doesn't necessarily mean a separate computer; you can (and frequently do) have Web, database, and application servers all running on a single machine.

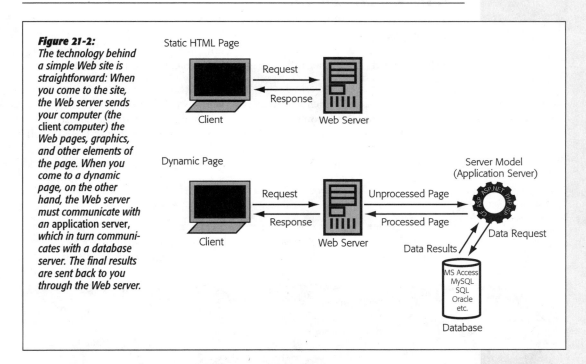

Figure 21-2:
The technology behind a simple Web site is straightforward: When you come to the site, the Web server sends your computer (the client computer) the Web pages, graphics, and other elements of the page. When you come to a dynamic page, on the other hand, the Web server must communicate with an application server, which in turn communicates with a database server. The final results are sent back to you through the Web server.

You can't just open a dynamic page on your own computer, before it's been posted online, as you can a regular Web page. You must view a dynamic page through a Web server that has an appropriate application server running. You must also set up a database and connect it to your application server. All of this *can* be quite complex, but it's not difficult to set up a basic Web server, application server, and database on your own computer. It's also easy to connect to other computers that are already configured to run dynamic, database-driven Web pages.

Once the Web server and other assorted components are in place, Dreamweaver MX can easily create complex Web pages that access databases and let you build powerful Web applications, all without your having to learn any programming.

Even so, there are hundreds of combinations of Web, application, and database servers, and Dreamweaver doesn't work with all of them. However, it is capable of working with five of the most popular and powerful combinations, using seven different programming languages!

Note: The term *Web application* refers to Web pages that work together to complete a task. For example, code that builds pages that let visitors search a database of products, view individual product pages, and add products to a shopping cart would be considered a Web application.

Understanding Server Models

In Dreamweaver MX lingo, the different application servers and programming languages are called *server models*. Dreamweaver recognizes several server models, including ASP and ASP.NET (pronounced "asp" and "asp dot net"), ColdFusion, PHP, and JSP. You use different methods to perform identical tasks on each one.

Which one you use depends on which type of Web server hosts your site, the operating system it uses, and which application server is available. For example, if you're hosting on Linux or UNIX, you'll most likely end up using PHP; if you're hosting on Windows NT or 2000, you've already got access to ASP and possibly ASP.NET. It all comes down to what you have on your computer, what your company uses, or (if you're using a Web hosting service) what the host computer understands. Here's a brief description of each.

ASP

ASP (Active Server Pages) is one of the most common ways to start building database-driven Web sites. This Microsoft technology is well established, so you'll find numerous help resources. In fact, if you're working on Windows 98, NT, 2000, or XP

FREQUENTLY ASKED QUESTION

The Dynamic Duo

How does a dynamic Web site differ from dynamic HTML?

Dynamic is a word that's thrown around a lot in Web circles, and it has a variety of uses.

For starters, *dynamic* sometimes refers to the power of JavaScript. For example, the animation effects you read about on page 390 use a combination of JavaScript and Layers to animate elements on a Web page. The result is often called "Dynamic HTML," because the elements on the page *change*.

However, in this section of the book, *dynamic* refers to any Web page that's processed by an application server—pages that undergo some form of transformation on the Web server's side of the Internet, like connecting to a database or collecting information from a form.

What's important to remember is that the JavaScript used for dynamic HTML and Dreamweaver Behaviors is a *client-side* programming language, meaning that it runs in someone's Web browser and is limited to only a handful of actions, like mouse rollovers or any of Dreamweaver's Behaviors (Chapter 11).

Dynamic Web sites, on the other hand, use *server-side* programs—those that run on an application server, out there on the Web somewhere. The visitors to your site never see the code, and their computers never have to run the program. They merely enjoy the results of the application server's hard work: a finished HTML page.

Professional, you already have the software you need: Personal Web Server (PWS) on Windows 98 or Internet Information Server (IIS) on Windows NT, 2000, or XP.

Note: Windows XP Home Edition and Windows ME can't run Personal Web Server. Microsoft, of course, recommends upgrading to Windows XP Professional (ka*ching!*).

Both PWS and IIS are Web servers with a built-in application server—the part that understands ASP code. In fact, it understands two different programming languages: *VBScript* and *server-side JavaScript,* both of which Dreamweaver MX speaks fluently. (You don't need to know either of these programming languages to get started, but you'll find many more resources for using VBScript with ASP pages. So if you plan to expand your knowledge of ASP beyond what Dreamweaver can do, you might want to use VBScript.)

If you don't have either the PWS or IIS software already set up on your computer, here's where to get them:

- You can download Personal Web Server from *www.microsoft.com/msdownload /ntoptionpack/askwiz.asp.*

- IIS is included on the Windows 2000 and XP Professional installation CDs.

- ASP can work with a variety of databases. For small projects, you can use Microsoft Access (the database program that comes with some versions of Microsoft Office), since it's fairly easy to use. For projects where lots of data needs to be stored and accessed by many users, Microsoft's SQL Server is a better choice.

.NET

.NET is the newest Microsoft server technology. It's actually an entire suite of technologies intended to integrate many activities over the Internet.

ASP.NET is more advanced and more powerful than ASP, but also harder to learn. Since it's a relative newcomer, you'll find fewer teaching resources available. You can program it in numerous languages, including Microsoft's VB.NET, C#, JScript.NET, and over 20 other languages. Dreamweaver MX recognizes C# and VB.NET.

Like regular ASP, ASP.NET runs in conjunction with a Microsoft's IIS Web server, which requires Windows 2000 or XP Professional. You also need to install the *.NET Framework,* downloadable from *www.asp.net.* Like ASP, ASP.NET works with many different databases.

ColdFusion

ColdFusion is a server application from Macromedia. It works in conjunction with several different Web servers, including IIS and Apache, and uses its own programming language, which resembles HTML. For this reason, some Web designers find it easier to learn than other programming languages.

Unfortunately, this server doesn't come cheap. You can download a free developer's edition that runs on your computer, but if you want to host the Web site on the

---

Internet, you have to buy the ColdFusion Server package or find a Web hosting company that offers ColdFusion hosting. (The Developer Edition of ColdFusion comes with the Macromedia Studio MX package. You can download it from *www.macromedia.com/software/trial_download/*.)

Like ASP and ASP.NET, ColdFusion works with many different databases.

JSP

JSP (Java Server Pages) is a server language based on Sun's popular Java programming language. It requires a Java application server, like Macromedia's JRun server.

This approach is not for the faint of heart; setting up a Java Server and connecting it to a database can be tricky. JSP isn't easy to learn, either.

A widely used version of JSP is Tomcat, available at *http://java.sun.com/products/jsp/tomcat/*. It's free, and it works with the Apache Web server and many databases.

PHP

PHP (Hypertext Preprocessor) is a programming language created specifically for building dynamic Web pages. It works in conjunction with the Apache Web server. Like Apache itself, it's available as a free download for Windows, Mac OS X, or any flavor of Unix or Linux (*www.php.net*).

While PHP can work with a variety of different database servers, Dreamweaver MX understands MySQL only—another free product, available at *www.mysql.com*.

Picking a Server Model

With so many choices, you're probably wondering which server model to choose. If you've never built a dynamic Web site before, your best bet is to start with ASP using a Microsoft Access database. You can create a database using Access (a relatively

---

FOR MAC USERS ONLY

Mac OS X and PHP

When it comes to dynamic Web site production, Mac fans have often had to rely on others for help, because ASP, ASP.NET, and Cold Fusion don't run on the Mac. If you use Mac OS 9, there's only one way to use Dreamweaver's database features: Connect, via network, to a Windows PC that has those technologies already set up and running.

But if you have Mac OS X, the news is much better. You can set up a complete database-driven Web development system right on your desktop. And now that Dreamweaver is OS X–compatible, you can even use it to build the site!

Since OS X is based on Unix, it can run many Unix-based programs, including the Apache Web Server, PHP application server, and MySQL database. In fact, Apache and PHP come with Mac OS X, and the MySQL server is free from *www.entropy.ch/software/macosx/mysql/*.

If the very thought of UNIX makes you squeamish, you can try a more user-friendly approach to installing MySQL: eSuite 4x, a commercial product that includes a graphic interface for setting up and administering MySQL databases. A free trial version is at *www.macosguru.de/*.

---

inexpensive program) and take advantage of either Personal Web Server (PWS) or IIS to run ASP pages. (Mac users, see the box on the facing page.)

In fact, since this is the easiest method, this book's tutorials will concentrate on ASP pages. Once you get the hang of Dreamweaver MX's dynamic Web-building properties, you can always try the other server models to build your sites. (However, switching a single site from one server model to another is difficult and not recommended.)

Of course, when you're building a real-world Web site, this decision may be out of your hands. You may be working for a company that's already using Cold Fusion for its Web site. Or, if you've already got a Web site running but want to add some database-driven material, you'll have to use what's already installed on that server. If your site is currently hosted at a Web hosting company, you should contact it to find out which operating system, Web server, and databases it uses.

Fortunately, the tools Dreamweaver MX provides for the different server models are largely the same. Once you learn Dreamweaver, you'll be able to build pages for any of the seven server models it works with.

Setting Up Dreamweaver for Dynamic Web Sites

Now that your head is spinning, and you're considering some noble career alternative like farmer, firefighter, or carpenter, it's time to set up Dreamweaver to work with an application server and database.

One approach involves using what Dreamweaver calls a *testing server*. Do you remember how you can create a Web site on your own computer (the *local site*) before posting it online for all to see (the *remote site*)? Here, the concept is similar. While your site is still a work in progress, you can create a *testing server* for storing and previewing dynamic pages in progress: a real Web server, application server, and database running on your computer.

Then, when you've finished the site, you can transfer the pages to the remote site using Dreamweaver's FTP feature (page 478). If you're working with other Web developers, the testing server can be on a machine that's part of your group's local network. Each developer can then connect to the testing server and retrieve files to work on. (Using the Check In/Check Out feature [page 494] is a good idea here.)

Note: You can always use your remote site as a testing server, as long as it has one of the application servers and databases that Dreamweaver offers. While this is an easy way to get started, contact your Web host to see what application server it uses and whether it can handle databases. You also need a fast Internet connection to the server; otherwise, testing your dynamic pages may just test your patience.

Finally, whenever you're working on dynamic files directly on a live Web server, be aware that mistakes you make along the way may affect a database that's used by *other* dynamic pages. For example, if, while hurriedly trying to complete your Web site, you accidentally create a page that deletes records from your database, important information may no longer be available on your Web site. So whenever possible, the testing server should be separate from the server where the finished and perfected site resides.

In the next three chapters, you'll be building a dynamic Web site using ASP and an Access database. The concepts, if not the details, will work for all of the other server models as well.

Setting Up a Testing Server

You can browse static HTML files on your computer without any special software. But dynamic data requires a Web server and database.

If you're using Windows 2000 or Windows XP Professional, you must install IIS on your local machine. To do so, insert your Windows 2000 Setup CD. (If the setup program doesn't start automatically, browse to the CD and double-click *setup.exe*.) Then proceed as shown in Figure 21-3.

Note: If you're using Windows 98, you must install PWS. Instructions and downloads are located at *www.microsoft.com/msdownload/ntoptionpack/askwiz.asp.*

After rebooting, open a Web browser and type *http://localhost/* in the Address bar. You see the default page for the Web server—a generic IIS welcome page. Voilà! A functioning Web server. But where are those Web pages kept? The root folder for your new Web server is *C:\\Inetpub\wwwroot* on your PC.

Note: If you're on a Mac, you must connect through a network to a Windows machine that's been set up as described above. If you're using Mac OS X 10.2 or later, you can use its built-in file-sharing command (Go→Connect to Server) to do so. Otherwise, Dave from Thursby Software *(www.thursby.com)* is one commercial software product that lets Macs network seamlessly with Windows machines.

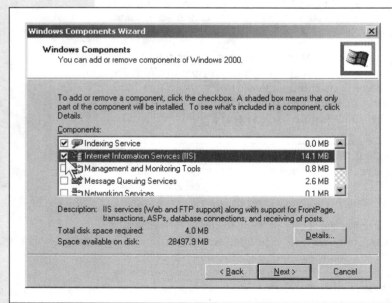

Figure 21-3:
In the Windows 2000 or XP Professional Setup program, choose Install Add-On Components (Windows 2000) or Install Optional Windows Components (Windows XP Pro).

In the resulting dialog box, turn on the Internet Information Services checkbox; click Next to begin the installation. (Click Details in the lower-right corner to remove unneeded options such as FTP Server or SMTP Server.)

After the installation is complete, you'll be asked to restart the PC.

Setting Up Dreamweaver

To learn Dreamweaver's dynamic features, you'll be building a small Web application for *Cosmopolitan Farmer* (see Figure 21-4). In fact, you'll turn the site's Classified Ads into dynamic Web pages that will retrieve information from a database and merge it with already-created HTML code.

Before you begin building the page, download the tutorial files. As always, you can find them at *www.sawmac.com/dwmx/;* click the Tutorials link to go to the tutorials page. Click either <u>Dynamic Set Up—Mac files</u> or <u>Dynamic Set Up—Win files,</u> depending on the kind of computer you're using.

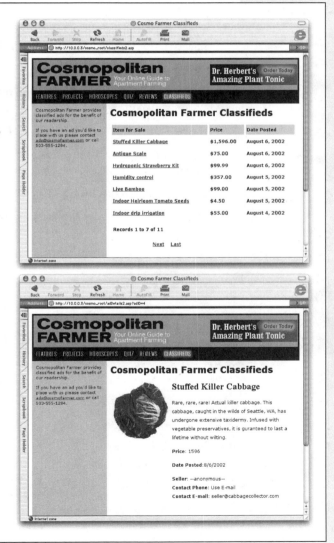

Figure 21-4:
Whenever you need to display lots of similar information, dynamic Web pages may be the answer. On Cosmopolitan Farmer, *dynamic pages list many different products in the form of classified ads. Because all the product information is stored in a database on* Cosmo Farmer's *Web site, the dynamic pages can display a list of products (top) and then individual product pages (bottom) by using the power of Dreamweaver's dynamic Web page building tools.*

After the download, you should have a folder named DWDynamic on your computer, containing a folder called *cosmo_root* (the root folder for this Web site) and a file called *cosmofarmer.mdb* (the Access database containing the classified ads).

To begin, move the *cosmo_root* folder into the newly installed Web server's root folder. If you followed the directions above, the root folder is at *C:\Inetpub\wwwroot* (assuming your Windows computer's main drive is the C:\ drive, of course). To make sure you've set this up right, open a Web browser and type *http://localhost/cosmo_root/* into the Address bar. If a Web page appears, your Web server is set up correctly.

Begin by defining a new site, like this:

1. **Choose Site→New Site.**

   The Site Definition window opens. Use the Site Wizard to help you set up this new site. If it isn't already selected, click the Basic tab at the top of the window.

3. **Type *Cosmo Classifieds* and click Next.**

   Now tell Dreamweaver whether you're building a static or dynamic Web site:

4. **Select "Yes, I want to use a server technology" and choose ASP VBScript from the pop-up menu (see Figure 21-5). Click Next to proceed.**

   In the next step, you'll tell Dreamweaver where your local files are and where you intend to put the files for the testing server.

5. **Select "Edit and test locally" (see Figure 21-6).**

   Dreamweaver provides four ways to work with dynamic Web page files and a testing server.

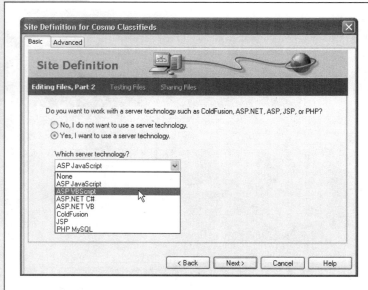

Figure 21-5:
When building a dynamic site, you must choose one of seven different server models. There are actually only five different application servers, but since Dreamweaver lets you use two different languages for both ASP and ASP.NET, there are two server models for each of those application servers.

Edit and test locally is a good choice when you've set up a Web and application server on your computer (as in this tutorial). Essentially, this means that you're working on a Web site located on a functioning Web server. In this way, you'll preview the pages running on a real Web server, so you can immediately test out all the nifty dynamic stuff.

Use the next three options only when the testing server is on another computer (maybe another PC on your network, or a full-fledged Web server on the Internet that you connect to using FTP).

Edit locally, then upload to remote testing server is a good option when you work with other designers. It lets you use the Check In and Check Out features (page 494), so that you won't accidentally overwrite other people's hard work when you transfer files back and forth between your computer and the test server.

Use the last two options when the testing server is on another computer but you're the only one working on the files. The only difference between the two is how you connect to the testing server: either a local network or FTP.

Note: If you're a Mac user who's following along with this tutorial, and you've set up a Windows machine to act as a testing server, choose "Edit directly on remote testing server using local network." Your Mac must be networked to the Windows server for this to work (see the note on page 622).

In the next step, you'll tell Dreamweaver where to find the files for the Web site.

6. **Click the folder at the right side of the middle of the window. Navigate to and select the *cosmo_root* folder on the Web server. Click Next.**

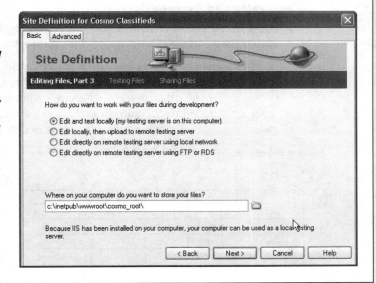

Figure 21-6:
If you don't have a working Web server on your computer, but do have an account with a Web hosting company that recognizes one of Dreamweaver's server models, you can use that server to test your files. Choose the last option: "Edit directly on remote testing server…" You can then connect to the server using FTP, as described on page 478. Although this method takes longer, since you must constantly upload and download files over your Internet connection, it's one way to get going with dynamic Web sites.

The *cosmo_root* folder is probably at *C:\Inetpub\wwwroot\cosmo_root*.

7. **In the box, type the URL of the test server; click Test.**

Dreamweaver may have already filled in this box. If the test server is on your PC, the URL begins with *http://localhost/* and ends with the folder containing the Web pages. In this case, the URL is probably *http://localhost/cosmo_root/*.

If you get an error message when you click Test, you've probably entered the wrong URL. This can happen when the folder following *localhost* in the URL is not actually on the Web server, or if you forget to add the trailing / in the URL.

8. **Click Next. Click No. Click Next one more time.**

If you were planning to move this site onto a Web server connected to the Internet, you would click Yes. But since this tutorial is just an exercise, you won't be putting it up on a live Web server.

9. **Click Done.**

Dreamweaver has set up your site! You're now ready to learn about databases and connect Dreamweaver to the *Cosmopolitan Farmer* classified ads database.

Databases Explained (in Five Minutes or Less)

A database is like an electronic filing cabinet that stores related information. You encounter them every day, whether charging a dinner on a credit card or calling Moviefone to get local movie listings. At home, you might have a low-tech database in the form of a filing cabinet containing folders for insurance statements, phone bills, car service records, and so on.

Tables and Records

Databases have an electronic equivalent to filing folders: *tables*. A table is a container for information about a set of similar items.

In the *Cosmo Farmer* classified ads database, a table stores information on a list of classified ads. It tracks the names of the products for sale, their prices, short descriptions, and a few other items. Each piece of information, like price, is stored in a column. All the information for each ad (all the columns taken together, in other words) make up a single *record,* which is stored in a row (see Figure 21-7).

Figure 21-7:
This diagram shows the structure of the Ads table, in which four records are stored. Each row in a table represents a single record *or item, while each piece of information for a record is stored in a single* field *or* column.

Column / Row

adID	adName	price	datePosted	description	imageURL
1	Hydroponic Strawberries	99.99	8/3/2002	Grow strawberr...	images/strawberry.jpg
2	Antique Scale	75.00	7/29/2002	This antique...	images/scale.jpg
3	Indoor Heirloom Tomato	4.50	8/5/2002	A taste of ...	images/tomato.jpg
4	Stuffed Killer Cabbage	1596.00	8/6/2002	Rare, rare, rare...	images/cabbage.jpg

If you were designing a database, you'd try to model a table on some real-world item you needed to track. In a database for generating invoices for your business, you might have a table called Invoices in which you'd store the invoice number, date, and so on. Your customers are another source of data that needs tracking, so you'd also create a table called Customers to store the information about them.

Note: If you track something on paper already, a good place to start is with the forms you use. For example, if your company uses a personnel form for collecting information on each employee, you've already got a ready-made table. Each box on the form is the equivalent to a category column in a table.

In addition to the Ads table, *Cosmo Farmer* also tracks the people who place the ads. (After all, the billing department needs an address to send the bill to, and the marketing department needs a telephone number to get their customers to place more classified ads.) Because an ad and a seller are really two different things, the database has a *second* table, called Sellers, that lists all those who place classified ads.

You might think, "Hey, let's just put all that information into the first table." After all, the seller's information is part of the information for each classified ad, isn't it?

But imagine this scenario: Bob X places an ad to sell his indoor irrigation system. All the ad information, including the product name and price, and Bob X's name, address, and telephone number, are put into a single table row. Next month, Bob X places another ad. But in the meantime, he moved! So now a different phone number and address goes into the ad database. When the marketing department tries to call Bob, they'll find two separate phone numbers for him.

Or worse: Suppose that whenever an item is sold, magazine employees delete the ad from the database (because they don't want to advertise something that's no longer for sale). Unfortunately, if they deleted Bob X's ad and it was the only ad he'd placed, his contact information would be gone. The billing department wouldn't have anywhere to send the bill, and *Cosmo Farmer* would soon be out of business.

Now you can see why it's prudent to keep separate classes of information in different tables. With two tables, when Bob X moves, you have to update his name and address only in the Sellers table, without touching the Ads table. This way, if the staff deletes an old ad (presumably *after* billing Bob X for it), the marketing department can still harass him mercilessly.

Relational Databases

You may be wondering, with a setup like this, how to tell which seller placed which ad. All you have are two distinct tables—one with just ad information and one with just seller information. How are they connected?

To connect information between tables, you create a *relationship* between them. In fact, databases that use multiple related tables are called *relational databases.*

The most common way to connect tables is by using what's called a *key* or *primary key*—a serial number or some other unique identifying flag for each record in the table. In the case of the *Cosmo Farmer* database, the Ads table includes a field named *adID* (see Figure 21-8). Whenever a classified ad goes into the database, it's assigned a new number. In a database that contains a table about employees, for example, you might use an employee's social security number as a primary key.

The Sellers table has a primary key named, not so creatively, *sellerID*. This key, too, is generated automatically whenever a new seller is added to the database.

To join these two tables, you'd add another column to the Ads table called *sellerID* (see Figure 21-8). Instead of storing *all* the contact information for a seller within the Ads table, you simply store the seller's ID number. To find out who placed an ad, you can look up the ad in the Ads table, find the seller's ID number in the sellerID column, and use that to find the seller in the Sellers table.

Ads table

Primary key   Foreign key

adID	adName	price	datePosted	description	imageURL	sellerID
1	Hydroponic Strawberries	99.99	8/3/2002	Grow strawberr...	images/strawberry.jpg	1
2	Antique Scale	75.00	7/29/2002	This antique...	images/scale.jpg	2
3	Indoor Heirloom Tomato	4.50	8/5/2002	A taste of ...	images/tomato.jpg	1
4	Stuffed Killer Cabbage	1596.00	8/6/2002	Rare, rare, rare...	images/cabbage.jpg	3

Sellers table

Primary key

sellerID	sellerName	sellerPhone	sellerEmail
1	Ado	510-555-1212	ado@cosmofarmer.com
2	Brian Alberta	408-555-3321	brian@cosmofarmer.com
3	--anonymous--	use e-mail	seller@cabbagecollector.com
4	Ellen Rigby	503-555-3838	ellen@cosmofarmer.com

Figure 21-8:
Each table should have a primary key—a column that contains a unique identifier for each record in a table. To relate information from one table to another, it's common to add an additional column with information pertaining to another table. In this case, a column called sellerID in the Ads table contains the primary key from the Sellers table. To determine who's selling the Stuffed Killer Cabbage, say, look at the last column in the Ads table, which identifies the seller's ID number as 3. When you check the sellers table, you see that seller 3 is "anonymous." When one column identifies the primary key of another table, it's referred to as a foreign key.

While this hopscotch approach is a bit confusing at first, it has many benefits. Not only does it prevent the kinds of errors mentioned earlier, it also makes creating a new ad simpler for the sales department. For example, when Bob X calls up to place another ad, the salesperson determines whether any of Bob's info has changed (by checking it against the Sellers table). If not, the sales rep simply adds the information for the new ad and leaves Bob's contact info untouched. Thus, relational databases not only prevent errors in your data, but also make data entry faster.

Databases, of course, can be much more complicated. It can take many tables to accurately hold the data needed to run a complex e-commerce site like Amazon.com. In some cases, you may already be working with a previously created database, so you won't have to worry about creating one, or even learning more than what's been described already. For the tutorials in this section of the book, you'll use the already created *Cosmo Farmer* database.

Connecting Dreamweaver to a Database

Dreamweaver MX works with a variety of different databases, from Access to the enterprise-level Oracle 9*i*. It connects to those databases in a variety of ways, depending on which server model you've chosen. For the PHP server model, for instance, Dreamweaver uses the MySQL database and connects directly to the MySQL server. In this tutorial, you'll work with the Access database you downloaded.

Databases, like server models, come in many shapes and sizes: Microsoft Access, SQL Server, Oracle, FoxPro, MySQL, and so on. Fortunately, something called the *ODBC protocol* (Open Database Connectivity) serves as a common language that lets different operating systems and programs communicate with various databases. Each database vendor can create ODBC drivers that let you connect to its database.

Windows comes with the proper ODBC drivers preinstalled for many popular databases, including Access. To further simplify the process, Windows PCs offer what's called a *Data Source Name* (DSN), a short nickname that lets you point to a particular database through a specific ODBC driver without having to remember a long complex series of codes to access your data. A DSN is one of the most common methods of connecting to a database on Windows. In fact, many Web hosting companies that provide Windows-based Web hosting services let you set up DSNs on their computers, making connecting to databases on remote Web servers much easier.

To set up a DSN, begin by opening the ODBC Data Source Administrator window (Figure 21-9) on the Windows PC hosting the Web site, like this:

- **Windows 98, NT, and 2000:** Open the Control Panel, and then open the ODBC Database Administrator icon.

- **Windows XP Pro:** Open the Control Panel→Administrative Tools folder, and then open the ODBC Database Administrator icon.

Figure 21-9:
In addition to having one of the longest names in Microsoft history, the Windows ODBC Data Source Administrator dialog box lets you register a database with your operating system. The point is to let Dreamweaver and the Web server communicate with a database.

Note: Mac users can follow these steps on a networked Windows machine. Copy the database file (cosmofarmer.mdb) onto the Windows server and follow these instructions for creating a DSN. Now you can connect to it from your Mac.

Once this window is open, the steps are the same for all Windows versions:

1. **In the ODBC Data Source Administrator, click the System DSN tab.**

   Now you're viewing all of the DSNs that are currently set up.

2. **Click Add to create a new DSN. In the Create New Data Source dialog box (Figure 21-10), choose Microsoft Access Driver.**

   Next, you'll tell Windows where the database is located and assign its DSN.

Figure 21-10:
The world is filled with different types of databases. So that Dreamweaver and the Web server can communicate with the information in the database, you must choose and use the proper ODBC driver—a translator that lets other programs speak the database's language. In this case, since you're using an Access database, you would use an Access driver.

3. **Click Finish to bring up the Microsoft Access Setup window.**

   You need to give this database connection a Data Source Name. This will act as shorthand so you can communicate with the database easily.

4. **Type *CosmoClassifieds* in the Data Source Name field (see Figure 21-11).**

   Next, you'll select the database file you downloaded earlier.

5. **Click Select. Navigate to the file cosmofarmer.mdb inside the DWDynamic folder you downloaded earlier. Click OK.**

   You've just told Windows which Access database it should use.

6. **Click OK to exit the Access Setup, and OK once more to close the dialog box.**

Clearly, setting up dynamic sites is much more complex than building static HTML sites. You're now set to build a real dynamic Web application.

Creating a Dynamic Page

Once you've set up an application server and database server, you're ready to connect to the database, retrieve information, and display it on a Web page. You already know how to take the first step: Design a page to display the database information—with HTML as its backbone. You can do this in a number of ways:

- Choose File→New to open the New Document window. Click the Dynamic Page category and double-click the appropriate dynamic page type: ASP, VBScript, Cold Fusion, PHP, or whatever. When you save the file, Dreamweaver automatically adds the proper extension: *.asp* for ASP, *.aspx* for ASP.NET, *.cfm* for Cold Fusion, *.jsp* for JSP, or *.php* for PHP pages.

  You can then use any of the page building tools described earlier in this book—tables, Cascading Style Sheets, Library items, and so on—to design the page. Even though the file may officially be, say, an ASP page, it still contains lots of HTML. Unlike a plain-vanilla HTML page, though, this one also contains the server-side programming code that lets the page communicate with a database.

- Right-click (Control-click) in the Site panel; choose New File from the contextual menu. Dreamweaver creates a file in the correct server model format and with the proper extension.

Note: Just renaming a file in the Site panel (from *about.html* to *about.asp,* for example) does *not* add the code at the beginning of the file necessary to apply the correct server model to the page. Changing the file's extension (from .asp to .php, for example) doesn't change the page to the new model, either, and will probably "break" the page.

You can edit the newly created page using either Design view or Code view. But before you can add dynamic content, you must create a connection to a database.

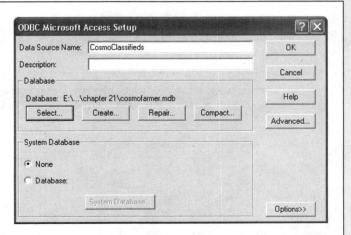

Figure 21-11:
Setting up an Access database to use with your testing server is easy. Just set up a name for the connection and select the proper Access (.mdb) file.

Connecting Dreamweaver to a Database

Once you've set up a DSN (page 629), connecting Dreamweaver to the database is straightforward. Start by opening a Web page—any page, even a blank one (because the database connection is stored with the site, not any particular page). Then:

1. **Open the Databases panel by choosing Window→Databases.**

   The Application panel group opens (see Figure 21-12).

2. **Click the + button at the top right of the panel. From the pop-up menu, choose the appropriate database connection.**

   The options you see depend on which server model you've selected. For example, if you're using Cold Fusion, you get a list of all *datasources* (ColdFusion's term for databases) defined in the Cold Fusion server. JSP developers see a long list of different database options. PHP developers see only MySQL Connection.

   In this tutorial, which uses ASP, your options are Custom Connection String and Data Source Name (DSN). Since you've already created a DSN, choose Data Source Name. The Data Source Name window opens (see Figure 21-13).

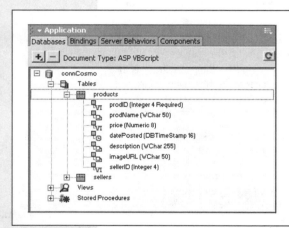

Figure 21-12:
The Application panel group contains four panels for working with dynamic database-driven Web sites. The Databases panel is described on page 634. (The Components tab contains advanced features for use with Cold Fusion, JSP and ASP.NET Web sites. It doesn't do anything in the ASP or PHP server models.)

Figure 21-13:
The Data Source Name dialog box lets you create a connection to a database using a predefined DSN connection on a Windows machine. The Define button lets you quickly open the Windows ODBC Data Source Administrator box to create a DSN, as described on page 629.

ASP.NET Note: Choose OLE DB Connection to open the OLE DB Connection dialog box.

---

3. **In the Connection Name box, type *connCosmo*.**

   You can actually use any name you want as long as it doesn't start with a number and doesn't contain any characters other than letters, numbers and underscores (_). In this case, *conn* reminds you that this is a database connection; it makes identifying it easier when you look into the underlying code of the page.

   Next, you'll connect to the database using the DSN you set up previously.

4. **From the DSN menu, choose *CosmoClassifieds.***

   The *Cosmo Farmer* database doesn't require a user name and password, so you can leave the User Name and Password boxes blank.

ASP.NET Note: In the Connection Name box, type:

Provider=Microsoft.Jet.OLEDB.4.0;Data Source=[path to database];

Replace the bracketed information–including the brackets–with a path to the .mdb (Access database) file. For example, if you downloaded the files to your C: drive, the path would be *C:\DWDynamic\cosmofarmer.mdb.* Skip to step 6.

---

5. **Make sure that the Using Local DSN button is selected.**

   (This option isn't available on the Mac, since a DSN and ASP testing server must reside on a Windows machine.) If you're using a database and testing server on another computer, select Using DSN on Testing Server instead.

6. **Click the Test button to make sure you've connected to the database.**

   The message "Connection made successfully" should appear. (If you got an error message, you can refer to page 145 of the *Getting Started with Dreamweaver MX* booklet or PDF file for help with troubleshooting database connections.)

7. **Click OK to close the dialog box.**

   Behind the scenes, Dreamweaver has created a small file, written in the selected server model's programming language and named after the connection name you gave in step 3 (here, connCosmo.asp). Dreamweaver adds this file to every page on the site that communicates with the database. It's in a folder called Connections in the root of the site.

Note: Don't delete this folder! If you throw this folder away while cleaning up your site, you'll break the database connection for all of your pages.

You're not limited to a single database connection. You can connect to multiple databases using the steps outline above. And once you've created a database connec-

---

tion, Dreamweaver makes it accessible to all pages in your site—you don't have to re-create the connection for each page.

Exploring the Databases Panel

The Databases panel (Figure 21-12) lets you do more than just connect databases to your site. It also lets you explore the structure and content of a database. By clicking the + buttons (flippy triangles), you can view any of three lists:

- **Tables** lists the tables in the database (see page 626); you can further expand this list to view the columns in each table. This is the option you'll use most often.

- **Views.** A list of all *views* stored in the database. A view is a selection of data in the database—a slice of its data. Unless you've created views using the database systems tools, this list is empty.

- **Stored Procedures.** A list of programs, stored in the database, that access and manipulate its information. Since they're stored within the database, they run faster than similar code stored in a Web page. (Some database systems—Access and MySQL, for example—don't recognize this feature.)

Note: To get a quick peak at the data in a database table, right-click (Control-click) the table's name in the Databases panel. From the contextual menu, choose View Data.

In this chapter, you've laid the foundation for a dynamic Web site. You're now ready to start adding data from a database—and building a real, dynamic Web application.

FREQUENTLY ASKED QUESTION

Parenthetical Puzzler

In the Databases panel, I see some weird information in parentheses next to the column names—Integer 4 Required, for example. What's that about?

You're right—there is a notation next to each column name. For example, Figure 21-12 shows a column called *datePosted*, which is followed by *(DBTimeStamp 16).*

The information in parentheses denotes the *type* of data in that column. In this instance, it's a database time stamp that's 16 characters long—in other words, it's a date. Every column in a database holds a specified kind of information: a number, a date, some text, or whatever. (In fact, within each of these categories are subtypes: integer, decimal number, and more.) Different databases recognize dif-

ferent data types, so the list of possible data types for all the server models Dreamweaver works with is quite long.

These notations may appear cryptic, but they occasionally come in handy. If you're creating a form for updating or inserting a record in a database (as described in the next chapter), the data type and length can help you determine what kind of information you're looking for and how long it should be.

For example, the prodName column pictured in Figure 21-12 contains text and is only 50 characters ("Char") long. So if you're creating a form element, you'll probably want to create a text field that accepts—at most—50 characters (see page 300 for details on form elements).

Adding Dynamic Data to Your Pages

W hat sets a database apart from a mere pile of facts is its ability to selectively retrieve information. After all, when you visit Amazon.com, you don't want to see every piece of information on every single book and product they sell. You probably want to see just a list of books on a certain subject or by a particular author, and then view more detail about the books that pique your interest.

This chapter shows you how to use Dreamweaver MX to display database information on your Web pages. Because these concepts can be tricky, you may prefer to get some hands-on experience by completing the tutorial on page 670 before reading the rest of the chapter.

Retrieving Information

Since databases can contain lots of information, you need a way to find just the data you need. Even though your company keeps information about its products, customers, suppliers, and so on, in a database, you may only be interested in, say, an alphabetical list of all your customers. After securing that list, you might want to look at a particular customer's contact information, or perhaps the list of products that person bought.

Understanding Recordsets

To retrieve specific information from a database, you start by creating what's called a *recordset*. A recordset—also called a database query—is a command issued to a database asking for particular information: "Hey Database, show me all the customers listed in the Customers table." It's the heart of many database operations you'll perform in Dreamweaver (and a piece of jargon you can't escape in the dynamic Web page business).

Recordsets let you retrieve specified columns in a database. They can also sort records alphabetically or in numerical order, as when viewing a list of products from least to most expensive. In addition, a recordset can zero in on a specific record based on information submitted by a visitor to the site, or based on information provided in a URL. In essence, recordsets let you winnow down massive amounts of database information in a fraction of a second—a powerful benefit, indeed.

ASP.NET Note: Dreamweaver uses the term *dataset* instead of recordset to refer to database queries in ASP.NET.

Creating Recordsets

Querying a database can be quite simple or extremely complex. Dreamweaver provides tools to get the novice database developer up and running quickly, while also supplying what's necessary to create more advanced recordsets. Whatever your level of expertise, you start by opening the Recordset dialog box using one of these methods (each of which assumes you've set up a server model as described in Chapter 21):

- Click the Recordset button on the Application tab of the Insert bar (see Figure 22-1).

- Choose Insert→Application Objects→Recordset.

- Click the + button on either the Bindings or Server Behaviors panels in the Application panel group (see Figure 21-13).

Whichever technique you choose, the Recordset dialog box opens (see Figure 22-2). This box lets you create a database query or recordset, and provides both simple and advanced modes of operation.

Insert Recordset   Dynamic Table   Recordset Navigation   Master-Detail Page Set   Record Update Form

Repeat Region   Dynamic Text   Recordset Navigation Status   Record Insertion Form

Figure 22-1:
The Application tab of the Insert bar provides one-click access to powerful application objects that automate common dynamic Web page-building tasks.

To create a simple query, make sure you're in the *Simple* mode. (If a button labeled Simple appears at the right edge of the dialog box, click it to make it say Advanced. Now you're in Simple mode.)

1. **In the Name field, type a name for the recordset.**

   You can use any name you want, as long as it doesn't start with a number and doesn't contain any characters other than letters, numbers, and underscores (_).

Tip: A common technique is to begin the name with *rs* (*rsAdsIndex,* for example). The *rs* helps identify the recordset when you're working in Code view.

---

2. **From the Connection menu, select a database connection.**

   The menu lists all of the database connections you've defined for the site. If you haven't yet created a connection, you can do so now by clicking Define and following the instructions for creating database connections on page 632.

3. **From the Table menu, select the table that will supply the data.**

   Information in a relational database is usually distributed among different tables, each of which holds information about a particular item, such as customer data or product data (see page 626). For example, to get a list of customers from a database, you'd select the Customers table (or whatever its name happens to be).

Note: To retrieve data from more than one table at a time, you need to create an *advanced* recordset (see page 646).

---

4. **To select columns from which you want to extract data, click the All or Selected button. If you choose Selected, click the columns you wish to select.**

   By default, Dreamweaver highlights the All button, but you may not want to get data from *all* columns. For example, suppose your table contains lots of detailed information for each product your company sells. You may want to create a basic index of all your products that simply lists its name, price, and description. For this index, you won't need all of the details like SKU number, sizes, inventory status, and so on. Therefore, just select the three columns you're interested in.

   To select multiple columns, Ctrl-click (⌘-click) their names in the list in the Recordset dialog box.

   It's always best to limit your recordset to just those columns whose information you need. The more data you retrieve, the more you make the application and database servers work and slow down your site, especially when the database is large.

5. **Choose a Filter option, if you like.**

In many cases, you don't want to retrieve *every* record in a table. For example, if you were looking for a phone number of a particular customer in your database, you wouldn't want the details on every one of your customers. *Filters* let you limit the records retrieved by a recordset. (Filters are described in more detail on the facing page.)

6. Choose a Sort option, if desired.

Data from a database may not appear in any particular order. Dreamweaver's sort options let you sort information based on a particular column. For example, maybe you're creating a recordset that gathers the title and release date for every CD you own. You might want to sort the results in alphabetical order by the title of the album, or chronologically by the date they were released.

To sort database records, choose a column to sort by from the first Sort pop-up menu (Figure 22-2). Then select the sort order: either Ascending (A-Z, 0-10, earliest to latest) or Descending (Z-A, 10-0, latest to earliest).

To view the results of the recordset, click Test to open the Test SQL Statement window, which contains all records that match that query. If there are more than 25 matches, you can see the next group of results by clicking Next 25 at the bottom of the window. When you're done looking at the test results, click OK to return to the Recordset window.

If the test results looked right, click OK to close the Recordset window and write the code into the currently opened page.

Figure 22-2:
The Recordset window lets you retrieve data from a database. The main window (pictured here) lets beginners search and sort databases for specific information. Advanced options let even seasoned database programmers take advantage of Dreamweaver's dynamic page-building abilities.

Note: Unlike a database connection, which is listed in the Databases panel and is available to every page on the site, a recordset is specific to a particular page. (See page 650 to learn how to reuse recordsets on other pages.)

Filtering Information

Although you may have selected a limited number of columns when creating a basic recordset, the final results of the recordset still include *all* of the records within the table. That's fine when you want a list of all items in a database, like as when you're creating an index of all your company's products. But it's not so useful when you want a particular subset of those records, like a list of just the red toupees your company sells, or when you want details on a *single* record—the "Flaming Inferno 78B toupee," for example.

To search a database table for specific records, use the Filter option in the Recordset window (see Figure 22-3). A *filter* lets you compare the information in one database column with a particular value and then select records that match. Suppose, for example, that your products database table contains a column named Price. To find all products that cost less than $10, you could create a filter that looked for all records where the price column held a value of less than 10.

Using the Filter feature in the Recordset dialog box takes only a few steps:

1. **Create a recordset as described on page 636.**

   To create a filter, you must fill out the four form fields of the Recordset window's Filter options—three menus and one text field.

Figure 22-3:
Filters let you limit the number of records retrieved by a recordset using information supplied in a URL or in a form submitted by a visitor to the site, among other ways. Using a filter, a recordset can identify and retrieve data for a single record in the database.

2. **From the first Filter pop-up menu, select a column name.**

This is the column that will be compared to a particular value. In the example above, you would select "price" from the menu to indicate the table's Price column (see Figure 22-3).

3. **From the next pop-up menu, choose a comparison operator (< or >, for example).**

To find products whose prices are less than $10, for example, you would use the < (less than) operator; to find an exact value (all products that are exactly $10), use the = (equal to) sign. Comparison operators are discussed below.

4. **Using the third Filter pop-up menu, select a source for the comparison value.**

A filter compares the information in a table column against some other value. There are many different sources for such a comparison value. For example, on a Search page, you could create a form that allows visitors to type in a search term and click a Search button. In this case, the comparison value would come from a form. To set up this arrangement, you, the designer, would select Form Variable from this menu.

For complete information on selecting a source for a comparison value, see "Getting Comparison Values" on the facing page.

5. **Into the lower-right Filter box, type a name or value.**

The value for this field depends on the source you selected in the last step; type in the name of the form variable, cookie, session variable, or whatever. The one exception: If you selected Entered Value in the previous step, type a specific value in this field. For instance, to compare the Price column to a specific value, you would select Entered Value and then type a number into the text field. The Recordset window would then look like Figure 22-3.

6. **Complete the Recordset window by choosing a sort option (if desired) and clicking OK.**

You can test the recordset and filter by clicking Test. If you selected anything other than Entered Value from the source menu, a message will prompt you to type in a test value for the source—URL Parameter, Form Variable, and so on.

Comparison Operators for Filters

Dreamweaver provides many different ways to compare information from a database column with information from another source, such as a form, cookie, or simply a value you type into the Recordset window. The type of comparison you choose also depends on the type of data you're comparing: text or numbers.

Comparing text values

You'll often want to create recordsets that find database matches to particular words. For example, a recordset could filter a list of products to find only those records whose descriptions contain the word "green," or you could filter a database of clients to search for a record for "Craig McCord." Dreamweaver provides the following types of text comparisons:

- **Equality.** To check if the information in a column is *exactly* the same as another value, select the = sign from the comparison menu.

- **Inequality.** To find records that don't match a particular piece of text, select the <> (not equal to) operator from the menu. You would use this, say, if you wanted to search a database of clothing items for ones that do *not* include a certain word (like "winter" in the Season column).

- **Begins With, Ends With, and Contains.** The last three comparison operators are ideal for locating one or more words within text. For example, a database of movies might have a column containing a short review of each movie. To locate reviews that included the words "horrible acting," you could choose the Contains option, which will find any movie that included the phrase "horrible acting" anywhere in its review.

  The Begins With and Ends With options are more selective. The former only finds records when the text at the very beginning of a particular record matches; the latter works only when the text appears at the end. You probably won't use these options very often.

The other comparison operators (<, >, <=, >=) aren't very useful for searching text in a database. They're intended for comparing numbers, as described next.

Comparing Numbers

Filters are particularly useful for numbers: finding products that cost less than $10, albums that were released in 1967, products with more than 3,000 items in stock. If you've taken basic algebra, these options for comparing numbers should be familiar: = (equal to), <> (don't match), < (less than), > (greater than), <= (less than or equal to), or >= (greater than or equal to).

Getting Comparison Values

By now it should be clear that the Filter option of the Recordset window lets you compare data from one column with some other value. But you're probably wondering where this "some other value" comes from. It depends on which option you selected from the source menu (see Figure 22-3).

The most straightforward option is the last item in the menu: Entered Value. After selecting it, you simply type the value into the field to the right of the menu. This could be a number, a letter, or one or more words. So, to create a recordset that will find a product whose price is more than $50, you'd select the Price column, the > (greater than) comparison symbol, and the Entered Value source option, and then type 50 into the value field.

Unfortunately, this kind of recordset is rather limited. The comparison value you specify (50) is hardwired into the recordset, making it very inflexible. What if a visitor wanted to see products that cost more than $15, $30, or $100? No joy. This recordset is limited to what you, the designer, entered as a value.

A better option would be to create the filter on the fly from information gathered when the page with the recordset is requested by the visitor's Web browser. In this way, you can create very flexible recordsets that are capable of searching databases for a variety of different pieces of information, not just the *one* value selected by a programmer. (After all, how good a of search engine would Yahoo be if the *programmers* determined what the search criteria were? No matter what you searched for—*Web Design, Used cars*—it would always find Web sites about Java, Burning Man, and Diet Coke.)

Dreamweaver can also draw a filter value from a form, cookie, or even the URL of a link. The process is always the same: From the filter's comparison value source menu (Figure 22-3), select the source you want, and then type the name of the appropriate source item. For example, if you select Form Variable from the source menu, type the name of the form field in the box to the right.

In most cases, you must depend on an additional Web page to provide the source of these values. For example, a search function on a Web site usually requires more than a single page: one (or more) containing a Search field and a Submit button to send the information, and another that displays the results of the search. In this example, the form on one page sends information (the search terms) to another page (the results page), which uses the form information to search the database. In essence, the words typed into the search form on one page are used to create the recordset on another page.

The two most common ways to pass information from one page to another are forms and URLs. (Three advanced sources—cookies, session variables, and application variables—are discussed on page 737.)

Form variables

A *form variable* is simply the information that a visitor types into a form field (or the value of a selected radio button, menu item, or checkbox). Forms are discussed in depth in Chapter 10, but their use in recordset filters is rather straightforward.

1. **Create a form page.**

   It can include a text field, pop-up menu, or some other form element (see page 300). Make sure you *name* the form element. For use in a Simple recordset filter, you're limited to a single form variable. Using an Advanced recordset (see page 646), you can use information from more than one form field to filter the data in a recordset.

   If you wanted to give your site's visitors a chance to look at differently priced products, for example, you could create a pop-up menu that included the values 10, 50, 100, 500, and so on. People could then choose one of those options to look at products below the selected price. (Also be sure to give the menu a name, such as "price," as described in step 3 on page 301.)

2. Set the Action property of the form (see step 6 on page 298).

You'll want it to point to the results page.

Note: For these steps to work, the form's method must be set to *Post* in the Property inspector (see step 7 on page 299). If *Get* is selected, the form information will appear in the URL when the form is submitted. What's more, form information won't be sent as a Form Variable. (You can, however, use the Get method in conjunction with the URL Parameters option discussed next.)

---

3. Open (or create) the results page.

This page will display the results of the recordset that's created using information from the form.

WORKAROUND WORKSHOP

Setting the Default Value for a Filter Source

There's a problem with using a variable source of information for a filter. If the filter requires information from a form or URL parameter, what happens if someone comes to the page without first filling out the form or clicking a link with a URL parameter? In most cases, the recordset will be empty and the page will display no records. You can, however, set a *default* value for the form variable or URL parameter, so that at least some records will always appear.

Using the steps outlined on these pages, create a basic recordset; include a filter using a form variable or URL parameter. Then click the Advanced button in the Recordset window.

Now you get a more complex view of the recordset. In the Variables, list, there's a single entry: the selected filter source (Form or URL). Click in the Default Value column and

change the 1 to something that will match records in your database.

One solution is to type a value that will match *all* the records in the database. For example, if the recordset is used to find products under a certain price, type a value (price) that's larger than the most expensive product in the database. This way, the recordset will retrieve all items under that price—in other words, all of the products.

(This trick also works for the other sources discussed on page 737: cookies, application variables, and session variables.)

One last word of warning: If you switch back to the basic recordset view by clicking the Simple button, Dreamweaver resets the recordset variable to the default value of 1. In other words, if you change the default value in the advanced view, *don't* switch back to the basic recordset view.

CHAPTER 22: ADDING DYNAMIC DATA TO YOUR PAGES

643

4. **Add a recordset to the page, using the directions on page 636.**

   You'll also create a filter using a form variable.

5. **From the Filter menu, select a database column. Then choose a type of comparison, as described on page 640.**

   All of this is the standard filter-creation routine.

6. **From the source pop-up menu, select Form Variable. In the box to the right of the source menu, type the name of the form field that contains the value for comparison.**

   In keeping with the above example, you would type *price* into the box, since that's the name of the menu on the form page.

7. **Add a sort option, if you like, and click OK to create the recordset.**

Remember that this kind of recordset's results depend upon information sent from a form. If a visitor just stumbles across the results page without using a form, the recordset will most likely produce no results. That's why you should link to this kind of page only by using a form's Action property (see step 6 on page 298).

URL parameters

In your Web travels, you've probably encountered URLs that look kind of strange, along the lines of *www.cosmofarmer.com/shopping.asp?prodID=34&quantity=4*. Everything up to the *?* looks fine, but you're probably wondering what the *?prodID=34&quantity=4* means.

Forms aren't the only way to pass information to a dynamic Web page; URLs can do it, too, thanks to information tidbits called *parameters*. Dynamic Web sites can read parameters and use them to create a recordset, among other things. (In fact, using the Get method for a form puts the form's information into the URL.)

By using the Recordset window's Filter option, you can use one of these parameters to search a database. To identify a single record in a database, for instance, the URL could contain a number identifying the record's *primary key* (see page 630 for a definition). You'll find an example of this trick in the tutorial on page 677.

The steps for using URL parameters to filter recordsets are similar to those for form variables. You need two pages, one with a link containing the URL parameter and another containing the recordset.

Tip: It's possible to add a link with a URL parameter on the *same* page as the recordset. For example, you could have several text links like "Products under $10" and "Products under $100" that link to the same page but have different URL parameters.

Creating a link with a URL parameter

Dreamweaver provides several ways to create a link that contains a URL parameter. The simplest way is to highlight the item you wish to turn into a link—usually text or a graphic. Then, in the Property inspector's link box, type the link followed by a ?, a parameter name, an =, and the value (for example: *classifieds.asp?prodID=7*).

However, you'll probably find it easier to browse for the file and let Dreamweaver write all the complex stuff. To do this, proceed as follows:

1. **Highlight the item you wish to turn into a link.**

   In other words, select a graphic or text on the page.

2. **Click the folder icon (Browse button) on the Property inspector.**

   The Select File window appears. (For more on creating links, see page 95.)

3. **Browse to and select the page containing the recordset.**

   This is the page that will display the results of the database search.

4. **Click the Parameters box in the lower-right corner of the Select File window.**

   The Parameters window appears (see Figure 22-4).

Figure 22-4:
The Parameters window lets you add URL parameters to a link. Recordsets can use these pieces of information to filter a database query.

5. **Click in the space below the Name column and type the name of the URL parameter.**

   Since this will be included in a URL, avoid spaces and any punctuation characters except hyphens and underscores. (Those characters aren't allowed in file names or links on the Web.)

6. **Click in the space below the Value column and type the value for the URL parameter.**

   This is the value that the filter in the recordset will use to match records in the database.

Unfortunately, here again, including spaces and other punctuation marks in the value will keep the recordset from working correctly. Therefore, you can't type a text value like *Bob Jones* in order to search for "Bob Jones" in the database. (To do that, you'd have to write some special code yourself.) In this situation, you'd be better off using form variables, because recordsets *can* read longer text (including punctuation marks) typed into form fields.

7. **Click OK to close the Parameters window. Click OK to close the Select File window and apply the link.**

Creating the recordset for the Results page

Once you've created the link, you need to create an appropriate recordset for the results page. Here's how:

1. **Open (or create) the results page.**

   This page will display the results of the recordset created using information from the form.

2. **Add a recordset to the page, using the directions on page 636.**

   You'll also create a filter using a URL parameter.

3. **From the Filter menu, select a database column. Choose a type of comparison, as described on page 640. From the source menu, select URL Parameter. In the box to the right of the source menu, type the name of the URL parameter.**

   This is the name supplied in step 5 of the previous instructions.

4. **Add a sort option, if you like; click OK to create the recordset.**

Like form variables, this recordset is dependent upon information included in the URL of a link. If a visitor just stumbles across the results page without using a link with a URL parameter, the recordset will most likely produce no results. Because of this, make sure you only link to this kind of page via a link with a parameter. Otherwise, modify the default value for the URL parameter in the recordset as described on page 643.

Advanced Recordsets and SQL

Sometimes you'll need more power than Dreamweaver's Simple recordset tool provides. For example, say you're building an online classified ads system. On one page, you want to present various pieces of information: the name of the sale item, its price, who's selling it, and how to contact the seller, for example. In order to store this kind of information, your database has two tables—one for products and one for sellers.

To present all this information, you must simultaneously access both tables. In addition, you need to connect the records of those two tables so that each product is associated with the correct seller—John Smith is selling the Whirligig 2003, for example. There's only one way to create this kind of complex query: using the advanced options of the Recordset window.

To display these options, insert a recordset, using the steps described on page 636. Then, in the Recordset window, click the Advanced button. The Advanced Recordset window should appear (see Figure 22-5). (If you see a Simple button, then you're in the advanced options.)

Unfortunately, putting together advanced database queries is not as easy as most other operations in Dreamweaver. The Advanced Recordset window is basically just a way of typing in commands, using a database programming language called *SQL* (Structured Query Language, pronounced *sequel*). SQL is a standard language used by many database servers to access, update, delete, and add information to a database.

To create an advanced recordset, type an SQL statement in the window's SQL box.

Figure 22-5:
The Recordset window's advanced options aren't for the uninitiated. You'll need to have a good grasp of SQL—the standard database program language—to make complex recordsets.

SQL: The very basics

SQL lets you communicate with a database by adding new records, deleting records, and creating new tables. In the context of the Advanced Recordset window, you only need to understand how SQL *retrieves* information. After all, a recordset is just a selection of data pulled from the database.

To make an SQL query (called an SQL statement), you must first specify:

• **Which columns of data you want to retrieve.** For example, product prices, product names, seller name, and seller contact information.

- **Which tables will supply this data.** In the example above, the information is stored in two tables: Ads and Sellers.

- **How the search should be limited.** You might just want products that are less than $10, or whose seller is Zachariah Smith.

- **The sort order.** You could sort items using the Price column to view a list of products from least to most expensive, for example.

Only the first two pieces of information are absolutely necessary. A very basic SQL statement would look like this:

```
SELECT adPrice, adName
FROM products
```

SELECT is an SQL keyword that specifies columns of data for retrieval; FROM indicates which database table contains it. This statement instructs the database server to look inside the Products table and retrieve the price and name of each product listed. The result is a list of the price and the name of each product in the database.

Of course, you may not always want *every* record in a table. You may want to limit the search to a select number or items, such as products under $10. The WHERE keyword lets you do just that.

```
SELECT adPrice, adName
FROM products
WHERE adPrice < 10
```

Now the SQL statement only retrieves the price and the name of products that cost less than $10. Finally, SQL can sort records into order. In this example, you could also sort all of the results from least to most expensive, like this:

```
SELECT adPrice, adName
FROM products
WHERE adPrice < 10
ORDER BY adPrice ASC
```

UP TO SPEED

Getting Your Feet Wet in SQL

SQL isn't difficult to pick up. While it is possible to create very complex SQL queries, a basic SQL statement is straightforward. Once you've reached the limits of Dreamweaver's basic recordset, you may want to expand your skills beyond this simple tool.

A great place to start learning how to write SQL statements is in Dreamweaver itself. After you create a simple recordset (see page 636), click the Advanced button. The SQL statement for the simple query appears in the SQL box.

This chapter introduces the very basics of SQL. For a more complete introduction, do a search at *www.google.com* for *beginning SQL* or *SQL tutorials*. Or pick up a book like *SQL in a Nutshell* by Kevin Kline or *Sams Teach Yourself SQL in 10 Minutes (2nd Edition)* by Ben Forta.

The ORDER BY keywords indicate which column should be used to sort the records. Specifying the adPrice column sorts the items by price. ASC is short for *ascending,* meaning that the records will appear in low-to-high price order.

Using the data tree view

Although you need to know SQL to use the Recordset window's advanced options, you can get a little help from the data tree in the Database Items list at the bottom of the window (see Figure 22-5). This area of the window functions just like the Databases panel, and lets you view the tables, columns, views, and stored procedures in the database (see page 632).

Click the + (arrow) button next to the word Tables heading to make a list of all tables in the database appear. Click the + (arrow) next to a table name to see all of the columns within that table. That's a very helpful technique when you're building an SQL statement, because you may not remember the exact names of every table and column in your database.

To build an SQL statement, you can select a column name and click one of the three buttons—SELECT, WHERE, or ORDER BY. The SQL command and column name then appear in the SQL box.

Suppose, for example, you wanted to create the following SQL statement:

```
SELECT adPrice, adName
FROM products
```

To build this statement using the data tree, click the + button next to the table named Products, which expands to show a list of all columns. Then click the column named adPrice and click SELECT. Next, click the adName column and click SELECT again.

Although these buttons can save you time, they don't check whether the SQL statement is valid. Unless you've got some grasp of SQL, you can easily create a statement that generates errors when run by the test server.

Note: Be careful when using multiple database tables that contain the same column name. For example, it's possible to have two tables—*Products* and *Sellers,* for example—that contain columns with the same name, such as sellerID. Dreamweaver won't make any distinction when inserting these columns using the Database Items tools. To correctly differentiate like-named columns in the advanced Recordset's SQL box, you must begin the column name with the name of the table, like this: *products.sellerID* or *seller.sellerID*.

Creating variables for filtering data

Variables let you filter data using information from sources such as forms, URLs, cookies, session variables, and application variables. If you use the filtering option in the basic Recordset window, Dreamweaver creates the variables for you—but in the Advanced Recordset window, you must create them yourself.

To add a variable for use in an SQL query, follow these steps:

1. **In the Recordset window, click the + button above the Variables box (see Figure 22-5). Click in the empty space below the Name column and type a name for the variable.**

   The name shouldn't include spaces or other punctuation marks.

2. **Press Tab to jump to the Default Value column. Type a default value for the variable.**

   A default value comes in handy when the form, URL, cookie, session variable, or application variable is empty. The recordset will use the default value to filter the database records.

3. **Press Tab to jump to the Run-Time Value column; type the appropriate code.**

   The exact code depends on the server model you selected. The best way to learn how to create variables is to use Dreamweaver's filter tool in the Recordset window (see instructions on page 639) and then switch to the Advanced Recordset window. The proper code for collecting information from forms, URLs, cookies, and so on will appear in the variables Run-Time Value column.

Note: Remember that if you add more than one SQL variable in the Advanced Recordset window, you won't be able to switch back to the Simple view.

Reusing Recordsets

Recordsets are created on a page-by-page basis. In other words, when you create a recordset, it's added only to the current document. If you create another Web page that requires the same recordset, you must add the proper code to the new page. You can do these either by recreating the recordset—a potentially laborious process—or by simply copying the recordset from one page and pasting it into another.

Here's how:

1. **Open the Server Behaviors panel by choosing Window→Server Behaviors.**

   Ctrl+F9 (c-F9) also works. You can also copy and paste from the Bindings panel.

2. **Right-click (Control-click) the name of the recordset you wish to copy; choose Copy from the contextual menu that appears.**

   In the Server Behaviors panel, recordsets appear like this: *Recordset (rsName)*, with the name of the recordset inside the parentheses. (If you're using the Bindings panel, this procedure won't work unless you actually select the name before right-clicking.)

Now switch to the document that will receive the pasted recordset. Right-click (Control-click) in the Server Behaviors panel and choose Paste from the contextual menu.

Tip: If you need a recordset that's similar to a recordset you've already created—but not identical—you can copy the original recordset, paste it into a new document, and then edit it, following the instructions below.

Editing Recordsets

What if you have to edit a recordset? Maybe you forgot an important column of information when you originally created the recordset, or perhaps you want to modify a recordset you copied from another page. The process is easy: Simply open either the Bindings panel (Ctrl+F10) or Server Behaviors panel (Ctrl+F9) and double-click the name of the recordset you wish to edit.

The Recordset window appears, looking just as it did when you first created the recordset (see Figure 22-2). Make any changes to the recordset, and then click OK.

Tip: If you change the name of a recordset while editing it, Dreamweaver displays a message indicating that you need to use Find and Replace to locate every instance of the recordset's name and change it to the new name.

But that's not efficient, and it may cause problems in your page, especially if the recordset's name is a common word used on the page (like Products or Ads). The safest way to change a recordset's name is to re-create it. Of course, that's extra effort—a good argument for making sure you're satisfied with a recordset's name when you *first* create it.

Deleting Recordsets

If you add a recordset to a page, and later realize that the page isn't using any of the information retrieved by the recordset, you should delete it. Each recordset forces the database server to do some work. Unnecessary recordsets only make your Web pages work harder and more slowly.

You can delete a recordset using either the Bindings or Server Behaviors panel. Just select the name of the recordset in either panel and click the – button at the top of the panel. (Pressing the Delete key on your keyboard has the same effect.)

Adding Dynamic Information

Once a recordset is created, it's a snap to add dynamic information to a Web page. In fact, Dreamweaver provides several techniques to go about it. Start in the document window by clicking the spot where you wish to add the dynamic information. Then do one of the following:

- Choose Insert→Application Objects→Dynamic Text.

- Click the Dynamic Text button in the Application tab of the Insert bar (see Figure 22-2).

Either way, the Dynamic Text window appears (see Figure 22-6), listing the record-sets on the current page. Pick the database column (also called *field*) containing the information you wish to add to the page. You can pick only one column at a time, but you can repeat this process to add multiple columns to the page.

Note: The term *Dynamic Text* is a bit of a misnomer. Using this tool, you can also insert dates, numbers, and dollar values—not just text.

The format menu lets you format the data, such as making a date appear as *January 17, 2004.* Formatting is discussed in depth on the facing page.

Figure 22-6:
After you select a database field to add to a page, Dreamweaver displays the code that it will add to the page in the Code field. This is the programming code used to make the data appear on the page. It's written in the programming language specified by the current server model.

Using the Bindings Panel

The Bindings panel (Figure 22-7) provides two other ways to put data from a recordset onto a page. Recordsets appear in the Bindings panel of the Application panel group. To open this panel, choose Window→Bindings or press Ctrl+F10 (⌘-F10).

To add data from the Bindings panel to a page, click in the document window where you wish to insert the dynamic data. Then select the column you wish to add and click Insert. Or, faster yet, just drag a column's name from the Bindings panel directly into the document window—into a paragraph or table cell, for example.

After adding dynamic information to a page, it looks something like {rsAdsIndex.adName}. The information in brackets indicates the name of the recordset (rsAdsIndex) and the name of the data column (adName). (You can make real data appear instead of this code using Dreamweaver's Live Data view, as described on page 660.)

Formatting Dynamic Information

Suppose a database includes a column for a product price, storing it as 8 or 10.99. But on your Web page, you want prices properly formatted with a dollar sign and two decimal places, like $8.00 or $10.99.

Figure 22-7:
A recordset listing in the Bindings panel includes the name of each column, plus three additional items: first record index, last record index, and total records. These can come in handy when you're only displaying part of a recordset, such as items 11–20 in a recordset of 149 items.

Dreamweaver MX includes many different formatting options for numbers, dates, and text. You can choose a formatting option when using the insert Dynamic Text window (see Figure 22-6). You can also apply, remove, or change a formatting option using the Bindings panel.

To set a format using the Bindings panel (Ctrl+F10), proceed as follows:

1. **In the document window, click the dynamic item you wish to format.**

   A down-pointing arrow appears under the Format column in the panel.

2. **In the Bindings panel, click the down-pointing arrow under the Format column and select a formatting option from the menu (see Figure 22-8).**

   Pick an option that's appropriate to the selected piece of data: currency formatting for the price of a product, for example. If you try to apply a formatting option that isn't appropriate for the selected item (currency to a text description, say), the page may produce an error when previewed on the testing server.

PHP Note: Dreamweaver doesn't include date, currency, or number formatting options for the PHP/MySQL server model.

You can also format selected dynamic data just as you would other text on a page by applying CSS styles, headings, bulleted lists, and so on.

Deleting Dynamic Information

Dynamic information added to a page behaves like a single object. Just click to select it. You can also drag it to another location on the page, copy and paste it, remove it from a page by selecting it and pressing the Delete key, and so on.

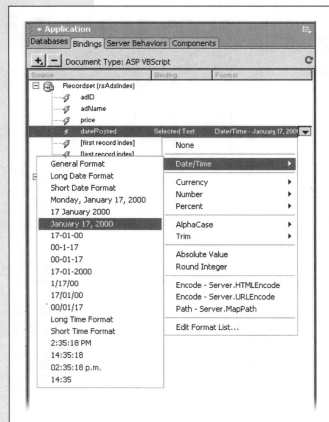

Figure 22-8:
Not all server models offer the same formatting options. The options displayed here are for the ASP/VBScript server model, and include a dizzying array of choices, including nineteen date and time formats. One of these options, Encode - Server.HTMLEncode, may come in handy if your database stores HTML code. For example, maybe you've created an online bulletin board that lets visitors post messages to the world, and these messages are stored in a database. When adding one of those messages to a page, applying the Encode - Server.HTMLEncode format will ensure that Web browsers won't render any code in a message as part of your page. Instead, any HTML in that dynamic text will appear to visitors as code. Similarly, if there's any chance a data field might store a bracket like this <, the Encode formatting option prevents a Web browser from thinking that the opening bracket is the start of an HTML tag.

If you remove all of the dynamic information from a page, and don't plan on using any information from the recordset, make sure you delete the recordset, too, as described on page 651. Even though you may not display any dynamic information on the page, if a page contains a recordset, it still must communicate with the database server, slowing down your pages.

Displaying Multiple Records

Often, you'll want to create a Web page that displays multiple records, such as a page that lists all of the products in your company's catalog.

However, so far you've learned how to insert dynamic data only from a single record. Fortunately, Dreamweaver provides two tools for displaying multiple records: the Dynamic Table and Repeat Region objects.

Creating a Repeating Table

HTML tables (see Chapter 6) were initially created to display data. The columns and rows of tables provide tidy compartments for individual pieces of information. It's not surprising, then, that in database terminology, *row* often refers to a single record in a database, and *column* indicates a single piece of information in a record.

Dreamweaver's Dynamic Table tool lets you display the results of a recordset in an HTML table. The top row of the table includes the name of each database column to identify the data in the rows below. The bottom row includes dynamic data—one database column per table cell (see Figure 22-9).

Figure 22-9:
The Repeat tab that appears above the row indicates that this row will repeat, once for each record in the recordset. To see the effect, use Live Data view (see Figure 22-13).

The magic of this tool is that it can duplicate the bottom row for each record in the recordset. In other words, the table will display multiple records, one per table row. Here's how to use it:

1. **Create a recordset as described on page 636. In the Application tab of the Insert bar, click the Dynamic Table object (see Figure 22-1).**

   You can also choose Insert→Application Objects→Dynamic Table. Either way, the Dynamic Table window opens (see Figure 22-10).

Figure 22-10:
The Dynamic Table tool lets you quickly create a table to display all or some of the records in a recordset. Unfortunately, this easy-to-use tool isn't available if you're using either of the ASP.NET server models.

2. **From the Recordset menu, choose the recordset you'd like to use.**

   Since a page can contain more than one recordset, you have to indicate which records you want to display.

3. **Using the Show radio buttons, specify the number of records you wish to display.**

   You can show all of the records on a single page by clicking the All Records button. However, if your recordset is huge—if your company has 10,000 employees, say—a single page with all of that information could be very large and difficult to navigate. In this case, you should display only a handful of items at a time.

   If you type *10* in this box, you'll see at most ten records when previewing the page. (If you choose this method, make sure to add a Recordset Navigation bar, as described on page 658, to let visitors page through the list of results.)

4. **Set the Border, Cell Padding, and Cell spacing values for the table.**

   These HTML table properties are described on page 144. All you're creating here is a plain old HTML table. You can dress it up later in Design view by changing the border, cell padding, cell spacing, background cell color, and other table properties.

5. **Click OK.**

   Dreamweaver inserts a table into the page. The top row contains the names of each column from the recordset—one name per table cell. You can, and probably should, edit these names to make them more understandable. After all, *adPrice, adName,* and *datePosted* may not mean anything to your visitors.

   The bottom row of the table contains the dynamic data from the recordset and represents one record. The table row has a Repeat Region object applied to it, which you can edit or delete as described in the next section.

Creating a Repeat Region

While the Repeating Table is easy to use, it doesn't provide the flexibility you might require. For example, what if your dynamic information was presented in a bulleted list (one record per bulleted item) or in individual paragraphs (one paragraph per record)? In these cases, you must create a *repeating region*—a chunk of HTML that repeats once for each record in a recordset.

Here's an example that can help you understand how to use the Repeat Region object. Imagine you're creating a page to list your company's staff directory. This page would include the name, telephone number, email address, and department of each employee. Of course, all of this information is stored in a table in a database—one column for each piece of information, and one record for each employee.

In Dreamweaver, you create the basic design of the page, and then add a recordset that retrieves the required information about each employee in the company. The page layout presents each employee's information in a single paragraph, so the finalized page has many paragraphs—one for each employee.

Since this is a dynamic page, you can't predict how many paragraphs will be needed. After all, your company may hire many new employees, which would add records to the database. To allow for this uncertainty, create a single paragraph by adding the dynamic information you want in it, following the steps on page 651. Then, tell Dreamweaver to *repeat* that paragraph using information from each record retrieved by the recordset.

Just follow these steps:

1. **Using the Bindings panel or one of the techniques described on page 651, insert dynamic text onto the page.**

   You should put these items together on the page, maybe in a single paragraph or in a bulleted or numbered list. Select the dynamic text and any HTML code you wish to repeat.

   For example, select the paragraph (click the <p> in the document window's tag selector) containing the dynamic data. If you're using a bulleted list to present this information, select the list item (<li> tag) containing the dynamic data. For data in a table row, select the table row (<tr> tag).

2. **In the Application tab of the Insert bar, click the Repeat Region button (see Figure 22-1).**

   You can also choose Insert→Application Objects→Repeated Region. Either way, the Repeat Region window appears (Figure 22-11).

3. **From the Recordset menu, choose the recordset you want the page to work with.**

   Since it's possible to have more than one recordset per page, be sure to select the recordset whose data is included in the area you are going to repeat.

4. **Choose the number of records you wish to display.**

   If you decide not to use the All option, make sure that you add a Recordset Navigation bar, as described on page 658, to let visitors page through the list of results.

Figure 22-11:
In a Repeat Region that reveals only a limited number of records at a time (in this case, 10), add a Recordset Navigation Bar (see page 658). Otherwise, visitors to the page will see the first ten records of a recordset, but will have no way to view additional records.

5. **Click OK.**

Dreamweaver adds the proper programming code to the Web page.

Editing and Removing a Repeat Region

If you selected the wrong recordset, or you want to increase the number of records displayed at a time, you can easily change a repeating region. Simply open the Server Behaviors panel (Ctrl+F9 or Window→Server Behaviors) and double-click Repeat Region from the list. In the Repeat Region window (Figure 22-11), make any changes and click OK.

To remove a Repeat Region, open the Server Behaviors panel. Select Repeat Region from the list and click the – button (or press the Delete key).

Recordset Navigation

Dreamweaver's Repeat Region tool lets you display multiple database records on a single Web page. But when recordsets retrieve large amounts of data—like 1,000 employee records—a Web page can quickly be overloaded. A large amount of information takes a long time to download and forces visitors to scroll for many screens to see all of it.

Fortunately, the tool also lets you limit the number of records displayed at one time. Of course, that presents its own set of problems: How do visitors see additional records, and how do you let them know where they are among all the records in the recordset?

FREQUENTLY ASKED QUESTION

A Little Less Repetition

I applied the Repeat Region object, and when I preview the page, the same record is repeated over and over. That's not what I wanted to do! What's going on?

This can happen when you apply a Repeat Region object and inadvertently select the wrong recordset from the Repeat Region window (see Figure 22-11)—a mistake that's easy to make if you've included more than one recordset on a page.

The Repeat Region object adds programming code that steps through each record of a recordset. So, in practice, the Repeat Region object should get the information from the first record in a recordset and write it to the Web page, then go to the second record and add *its* info to the page. This process should continue until it's either gone through all the records in the recordset or reached the limit specified

in the Records at a Time box.

However, if the information you want repeated is retrieved by a different recordset than the one selected in the Repeat Region window, this system breaks down. Instead, the code continues to cycle through each record from the selected recordset, but doesn't cycle through each record from the recordset containing the dynamic information you want repeated. The result: You get the same information over and over again. The first record of the recordset (the one you want repeated) is repeated for each record in the other recordset (the one you don't want repeated).

In other words, to ensure that Repeat Region works, select the recordset whose data is contained in the area you want *repeated.*

Fortunately, Dreamweaver comes with two handy commands for adding navigation to a recordset—and providing useful feedback about the recordset.

Recordset Navigation Bar

Suppose a page contains a recordset that retrieves 100 records from a database, but the repeating region on the page limits the display to ten records at a time. In this case, you should insert a Recordset Navigation Bar to add either text links or graphic buttons to a page. These navigation bars let your audience view the next ten records in the recordset, jump to the last records in the recordset (see Figure 22-12), jump back to the first record, or move to previous records in the recordset.

Figure 22-12:
Dreamweaver's Recordset Navigation Bar object prevents information overload by letting users step through easily digested pages of information. The Navigation Status message also keeps visitors informed of how many records are available.

To add a Recordset Navigation Bar, follow these steps:

1. **Click in the document window at the location you want to insert the navigation bar. In the Application Tab of the Insert bar, click the Recordset Navigation Bar button (see Figure 22-1).**

   You can also choose Insert→Application Objects→Recordset Navigation Bar. In either case, the Recordset Navigation Bar window appears.

2. **From the Recordset menu, select the recordset to navigate.**

   If the page contains more than one recordset, select the one that you used when creating the dynamic table or adding the repeating region.

3. **Select whether to use text or graphic buttons for the navigation bar.**

   If you select Text, Dreamweaver will propose the words First, Previous, Next, and Last to indicate the navigation controls. (You can edit them later.) The graphic buttons represent standard VCR controls, representing forward and backward. If you select this option, Dreamweaver copies the four .gif files into the folder containing the dynamic Web page. Later, you can replace these graphics with ones you created.

4. Click OK to insert the navigation bar.

Dreamweaver inserts a table into the document window, consisting of one row and four columns. Each cell contains one text or graphic navigation button. You can change the alignment and any other property of the table to fit your design.

Note: Dreamweaver uses various *server behaviors* to control the display of navigation bar buttons; see page 744.

Recordset Navigation Status

When you're viewing hundreds of records, it's nice to know where you are and how many records there are in total. The Recordset Navigation Status tool adds just such information to your pages, as shown in Figure 22-12. The status message is presented in the form of "Records 1 to 10 of 18," indicating which records the visitor is currently viewing and the number of total records.

Here's how to add a Recordset Navigation Status message:

1. **Click in the document window at the location you want to insert the status message. In the Application tab of the Insert bar, click the Recordset Navigation Status button (see Figure 22-1).**

   You can also choose Insert→Application Objects→Recordset Navigation Status. In either case, the Recordset Navigation Status window appears.

2. **Select a recordset from the pop-up menu.**

   If the page contains more than one recordset, you should select the one that you used when inserting the Recordset Navigation Bar.

3. **Click OK to close the window and insert the status message.**

The Recordset Navigation Status message is simply text with the three dynamic text items described in Figure 22-7. Change the words "Records," "to," and "of" to anything you like, such as "Products 1–10. 149 total products retrieved."

Viewing Live Data Within Dreamweaver

After you add dynamic information to a Web page, you see something like this in the document window: *{rsAdsIndex.adID}*. It gives you an idea of what the information is—in this example, the database column adID from a recordset named rsAdsIndex—but it doesn't show any real database information, which can make designing a page more difficult. You're especially far from seeing the actual result when a page contains a repeating region. What appears as a single row of dynamic text will actually appear as multiple rows or records when viewed in a Web browser.

Fortunately, you can preview a page with real database records directly in Dreamweaver. In addition to Design view and Code view, Dreamweaver includes one view expressly for working with dynamic information: Live Data view. When viewing a dynamic page in Live Data view, Dreamweaver contacts the testing server, retrieves recordset data from the database, and displays it in the document window (see Figure 22-13).

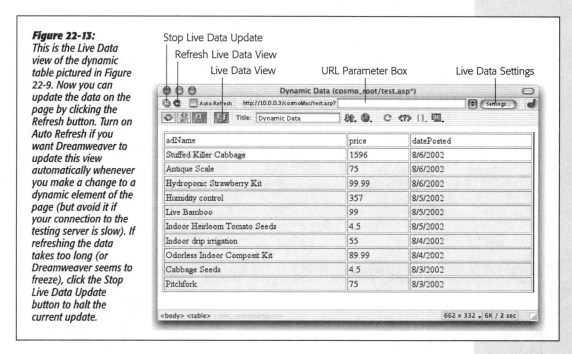

Figure 22-13:
This is the Live Data view of the dynamic table pictured in Figure 22-9. Now you can update the data on the page by clicking the Refresh button. Turn on Auto Refresh if you want Dreamweaver to update this view automatically whenever you make a change to a dynamic element of the page (but avoid it if your connection to the testing server is slow). If refreshing the data takes too long (or Dreamweaver seems to freeze), click the Stop Live Data Update button to halt the current update.

To turn Live Data view on or off, click the Live Data View button on the toolbar, choose View→Live Data, or press Shift+Ctrl+R (Shift-⌘-R). It may take a few seconds for the document window to change, since Dreamweaver must contact the testing server and retrieve information from the database. After a moment, the Live Data toolbar appears (see Figure 22-13), complete with tools for refreshing the displayed data, changing settings for Live Data view, and adding URL parameters to test recordset filters.

With Live Data view turned on, it's much easier to see what your page will look like when viewed on the Web. You can continue to work on a Web page in this view just as you would in Design view. You can add text and graphics, modify page properties, and even format dynamic data as described on page 653.

However, when you're working with a repeating region, you can only select, delete, or format the *first set* of dynamic data items. For instance, following Figure 22-13, a dynamic table displays repeating rows of database records. If you wanted to apply a Cascading Style Sheet style to the name of each ad listed, you would click the item in the first row of dynamic data—in this example, "Stuffed Killer Cabbage"—and apply the style to it. To see the style applied to the other records, click the Refresh button in the Live Data View toolbar.

Live Data View Settings

Some recordsets depend on information provided by a form or URL. When you use the filter option (see page 639), for instance, a recordset searches a database for records that match information from a form or URL.

This feature can come in handy for pages that provide detailed information about a single record. Frequently for these types of pages, the URL might appear something like this: *details.asp?prodID=38*, where the name of the page (details.asp) is followed by a URL parameter that includes a name (prodID) and value (38). The recordset then looks for the product whose ID (prodID) matches 38.

Because pages like this can't show up properly without a little help from the outside, you need to provide extra information in the Live Data View Setting window, like this:

1. **In the Live Data toolbar, click the Settings button (see Figure 22-13).**

   You can also choose View→Live Data Settings. Either way, the Live Data Settings window appears (Figure 22-14).

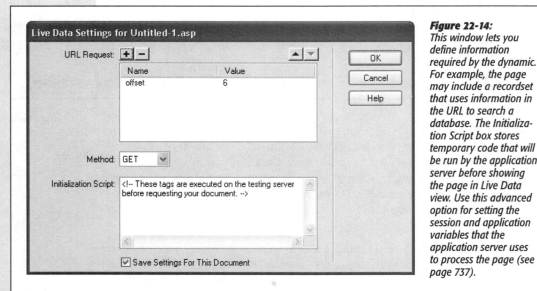

Figure 22-14:
This window lets you define information required by the dynamic. For example, the page may include a recordset that uses information in the URL to search a database. The Initialization Script box stores temporary code that will be run by the application server before showing the page in Live Data view. Use this advanced option for setting the session and application variables that the application server uses to process the page (see page 737).

2. **Click the + button to add a new name and value pair.**

   Dreamweaver refers to this as a URL Request, but essentially it means either a form variable (page 642) or a URL parameter (page 644).

3. **Click in the Name column and type a name for the new URL Request item.**

   If the URL Request is being used to filter data in a recordset, you would use the name you used when you created the filter in the Recordset window (see step 5 on page 640).

4. **Click in the Value column and type a value.**

   This may be a number or text, but the value must retrieve at least one record from the database, according to the filter options you set up in the recordset. For example, if you created a filter to find products under a certain price, you might type *price* as the name of the URL request and *10* as its value.

5. **From the Method menu, select either GET or POST.**

   If the filter in your recordset uses a form variable (page 642), select POST; if the filter uses a URL parameter, select GET.

6. **Click OK to close the Live Data Setting window.**

   If you haven't turned on the Auto Refresh button, you must click the Refresh button in the Live Data toolbar (see Figure 22-13) to see the new results. In addition, if you selected the GET method in step 5, a URL parameter box appears in the Live Data toolbar. You can change the values of the URL parameter directly in this box.

Tip: The Recordset Navigation Bar and Status message objects react differently depending on which records in a recordset are displayed. To see this effect in action, add a new URL request item named *offset* in the Live Data Settings window. Set the value to something other than 1. Click OK to return to the Live Data view. You can change this value directly in the URL parameter box in the Live Data View toolbar (see Figure 22-13) to see how the page reacts with different offset values.

Master Detail Page Set

A common task when building a database-driven Web site is providing your visitors with both an overview and detailed view of information. Usually, it takes two separate Web pages to do the job: one that lists limited information about all records in a recordset, and one which provides links to a page with detailed information about a single record. Dreamweaver calls these *master* and *detail* pages, and provides a tool for making quick work of this task (see Figure 22-15).

The Master Detail Page Set object automates the process of creating dynamic tables and recordset navigation bars, as well as adding many different server behaviors to your pages. In fact, there's nothing this tool does that you can't do (albeit more slowly) with the other tools you've learned in this chapter.

Note: The Master Detail Page Set object is not available for either the ASP.NET or PHP/MySQL server models.

To create a Master Detail Page set, follow these steps:

1. **Create two Web pages—one for the master page and another for the detail page.**

   They can be new, blank pages, or existing pages that just require the dynamic information from the database. It helps to use descriptive names for these pages, such as "productIndex.asp" and "productDetails.asp." (Save each page with an extension appropriate for the server model you're using: .asp, .cfm, or .jsp.)

Figure 22-15:
An example of Dreamweaver's Master Detail Page Set. The screen on the left represents a master *page—a list of items retrieved from a recordset. Clicking a link on this page opens a* detail *page (right), which displays the details of a single record.*

2. **Open the master page—the one listing all of the records—and add a recordset to it.**

   This recordset must include not only all of the columns to be displayed on the master page, but also all of the columns to appear on the detail page. Both pages use the same recordset, so *all* information you want on both pages must be retrieved by this one recordset.

3. **In the Application tab of the Insert bar, click the Master Detail Page Set button (see Figure 22-1).**

   You can also choose Insert→Application Objects→Master Detail Page Set. Either method opens the Insert Master-Detail Page Set window (see Figure 22-16).

4. **From the Recordset pop-up menu, choose the name of the recordset you created in step 2.**

5. **Select the fields (database columns) you wish to appear on the master page.**

   You'll most likely remove a bunch of columns from the Master Page Fields box, since most of the information is reserved for the detail page. To remove a column, click its name to select it and click the – button. (If you accidentally delete a column, click the + button to add it back.) You can also change the order of the columns by selecting a column name and clicking the up or down arrow buttons. The order the fields are listed in the box dictates the order they'll have on the master page.

6. **From the Link to Detail From pop-up menu, choose a column.**

You're determining which item on the master page is linked to the detail page. In Figure 22-15, the name of each ad has a link to the detail page. If you were creating a staff directory, you might select the column that contained each staff member's name. In this way, visitors could click a name to see a page with that staff person's details.

7. **Using the Pass Unique Key field, select a column.**

Choose a column that uniquely identifies a single record in the database, such as a product identification number or Social Security number. In most cases, this is the *primary key* in a database table (see page 627).

8. **Select how many records you wish to show.**

You can either type a number into the Records at a Time box or select All Records.

9. **Click Browse. Select the detail page you created in step 1.**

In this step and the next, you're defining the detail page and what information appears on it.

Figure 22-16:
The Insert Master-Detail Page Set window lets you quickly create two common types of dynamic pages: one that lists many records in a database, and another that shows detailed information about a single database record. Unfortunately, this tool is not available in the ASP.NET and PHP/ MySQL server models in Dreamweaver.

10. **Select the fields you wish to display on the detail page.**

The process is the same as step 5, but in this case, you'll probably include most, if not all, of the columns. After all, the detail page is where most of the information for an individual record shows up.

11. **Click OK to close the window and create the pages.**

It may take a few moments for Dreamweaver to complete this step. It's adding a lot of code to both the master and detail pages.

Once completed, you can (and should) modify the tables, format the dynamic items, and design the page to your liking. Because the Master Detail Page Set tool just automates the process of adding repeating regions, recordset navigation bars, and other server behaviors, you must edit those items individually on the page. In other words, you can't return to the Insert Master-Detail Page Set window (Figure 22-16) to alter items on either page. For example, if you decide to remove a piece of dynamic information from the detail page, you must make this change on the detail page itself.

While the Master Detail Page Set tool makes building these types of pages a snap, it does have its drawbacks. The primary problem is that Dreamweaver uses the same recordset for both the master and detail pages. This can slow down the works, because even though you may want to display only a few columns of data on the master page (the adName, price, and datePosted fields in Figure 22-15), the recordset added to the page must retrieve *all* of the information required by the detail page. The database server is doing a lot of extra work retrieving unused data.

Although the Master Detail Page Set tool makes quick work of creating these types of pages, you can do all the same tasks using the tools you've already learned—repeating regions, recordset navigation bars, and so on—with the added benefit of greater design flexibility. For an example of creating a more complex master and detail page set by hand, complete the tutorial at the end of this chapter.

Passing Information Between Pages

Every now and then, you'll want to pass a piece of information from one page to another. The Master Detail Page Set tool described in the previous section uses this concept: A link on the master page not only points to the detail page, but also passes along a unique ID used to create a filtered recordset on the detail page. In other words, the master page lists a bunch of records from a database. Each record not only links to the detail page, but also passes along its unique ID. The link might be something like *adDetails?adID=7.*

The information after the ? in the URL is a URL parameter, which the detail page uses to build a recordset. In this example, the detail page would find only one record—the one whose *adID* is 7—and display its details on the page. The key to the success of the master detail page set, then, is the ability to pass information to another page, and then use that information to filter a recordset (see page 639 for details on filtering database records).

Dreamweaver MX can pass information to other dynamic pages using either of two tools: the Go To Detail Page and Go To Related Page server behaviors.

Note: These two tools are only available for the ASP and JSP server models. For a description of server behaviors, see the box on page 693.

Go To Detail Page

A detail page, logically enough, is intended to provide more details on a single database record. To retrieve details on only one record, the detail page must include a recordset that filters the records of a database table based on some unique identifier, usually a record's primary key. For example, if every ad in a database of advertisements had its own unique ad ID, then a recordset could filter the date based on that ID number.

Note: The tutorial includes an example of this server behavior in action.

The Go To Detail Page server behavior provides a way to pass information to a detail page in the URL of a link. In this way, when the detail page loads, it can use this URL variable to filter the database to retrieve the requested record. (See page 644 for tips on using URL variable to filter recordsets.)

In many cases, you'll use this server behavior in conjunction with a repeating region (see page 656) on a page that lists multiple database records. In other words, you'll use this behavior on a master page. You'll then link each record in the list to the same page—the detail page—but pass along a different, unique ID for each record.

To use this server behavior, first add a recordset to the page. The recordset provides the information that's passed to the detail page (usually a record's primary key). Frequently, you'll also add a repeating region, or use Dreamweaver's Repeating Table command (page 655). Here's the whole process:

1. **Select an item on the page (graphic or text) that will serve as a link to a detailed page.**

   Since this server behavior is frequently used in conjunction with a repeating region, you could select a piece of dynamic text within the repeating region. For example, on a page that lists many products, you could select the name of the product.

2. **Make sure the Server Behaviors panel is open (Ctrl+F9). Click the + button; from the pop-up menu, choose Go To Detail Page.**

   The Go To Detail Page window appears (Figure 22-17). Skip the Link pop-up menu.

3. Click Browse and select the detail page.

You're choosing a dynamic page, of course.

Keep in mind that this server behavior doesn't actually *do* anything to the detail page, like adding a recordset to it. This behavior merely links to that page, passing along some additional information in the URL. In other words, to take advantage of the data passed along in the link, you'll need to add a recordset to the detail page that uses the URL variable. (You can also use the URL variable in other ways as described on page 738.)

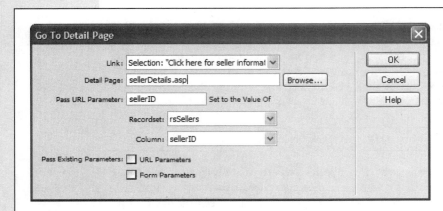

Figure 22-17:
The Go To Detail Page server behavior can pass information from a recordset to another page by adding a URL parameter to a link.

4. Type a name into the Pass URL Parameter box.

It's often best to use the same name as the database column whose value you're using. But at the very least, the name should contain only letters and numbers, without spaces or other punctuation (because it will be transmitted in the URL).

5. From the Recordset pop-up menu, choose a recordset.

This will be the recordset containing the information to be included in the URL.

6. From the Column pop-up menu, select a database column.

This should be a primary key field.

7. If you want to pass on URL variables and form variables already present on the page, turn on the URL Parameters and Forms Parameters boxes.

For a discussion of these options, read the following section.

8. Click OK to close the window and add the link.

Dreamweaver adds a link with all the programming required by your site's server model.

Once you've completed these steps, open (or create) the detail page and add a recordset that uses the URL variable.

Go To Related Page

The other Dreamweaver tool for passing information between pages is the *Go to Related Page* server behavior. It takes information that's been passed to a page (in the form of URL parameters or Form parameters) and passes it on to yet another page.

Here's how you might use this feature. Suppose your Web site sells expensive manufacturing equipment. On a detail page, which lists the specifications for a particular machine, you include a link to a page with a larger photo of the machine. When the visitor clicks the "click for larger photo" link, the photo page retrieves and displays the proper photo.

But how does the photo page know which photo to display? An easy way would be to pass along the ID for the product. Fortunately, this information is included in the URL on the detail page. After all, the detail page's own URL incorporates the product's ID number.

The Go To Related Page server behavior is ideal for this situation. It simply links to another page, passing along any URL parameters or form information already process by the page. To use it:

1. **Select the graphic or text that will serve as the link to another page.**

   Make sure the Server Behaviors panel is open (Ctrl+F9).

2. **Click the panel's + button; from the pop-up menu, choose Go To Related Page.**

   The Go To Related Page window appears (Figure 22-18). Ignore the Link pop-up menu.

Figure 22-18:
The Go To Related Page server behavior lets you link one page to another and pass along information contained in the URL, or information that had been sent to the first page as a form.

3. **Click Browse. Select the page to which you want to pass the URL or Form variables.**

   In order for the linked page to take advantage of these variables, you'll need to add a recordset and use the variables to filter the results. You can also add these variables to your Bindings panel, as described on page 737, and use them as dynamic text elements on the page, or even bind them to form elements.

4. **Turn on the appropriate boxes.**

The URL Parameters box will pass along any URL variables to the linked page. For example, suppose you add this behavior to a Details page, creating a link to page named *moreInfo.asp*. When someone comes to the detail page, the URL might be *adDetails.asp?adID=9* (depending on which record they're viewing). When the visitor clicks the link, the URL will become *moreInfo.asp?adID=9*. In other words, the *adID=9* from the detail page is sent along to the *moreInfo.asp* page.

The Form Parameters box does the same thing for form variables. For example, when someone fills out and submits a Search form, the information travels to a Results page, which displays the results of that search. You could then preserve the form information submitted to the results page, and pass it along to another page.

9. **Click OK to close the window and apply the server behavior.**

To edit one of these behaviors, double-click its name in the Server Behaviors panel; to delete one, select it in the panel and press the – button or your Delete key.

Tutorial: Displaying Database Information

In this tutorial, you'll continue the work you started in the last chapter. The classified ads section of the *Cosmopolitan Farmer* Web site requires two dynamic pages. The first will display a list of all classified ads currently running in *Cosmo Farmer*. From that page, visitors can jump to a detailed description of an item for sale by clicking its name. You'll learn how to create both basic and advanced recordsets and take advantage of some of Dreamweaver's built-in application objects.

To get started, download the files and complete the tutorial in Chapter 21. If you haven't yet done this, turn to page 621 and follow the instructions for preparing the application server, database, and Dreamweaver for this project.

Creating a Recordset

You'll start by opening an existing page and adding a recordset to it.

1. **Open *classifieds.asp* in the root folder of the local site you defined in the previous chapter.**

Either choose File→Open and navigate to and select classifieds.asp, or double-click the file name in the Site Files panel.

ASP.NET Note: You can follow along with this tutorial using the ASP.NET server model. Open the file called ASPNETclassifieds.aspx and follow along. Boxes like this one will appear when the instructions for .NET differ from ASP.

The basic structure of this page is already complete. It was built using tables, image rollovers, Cascading Style sheets, and the other HTML features you've already learned. There's nothing dynamic about this page yet, so you'll need to create a recordset and insert database information into the page.

2. **Choose Insert→Application Objects→Recordset.**

You can also click the recordset object on the Application tab of the Insert bar (see Figure 22-1), or click the + button on either the Bindings panel or Server Behaviors panel and select a recordset from the menu that appears. In any case, the Recordset dialog box should now be on the screen.

ASP.NET Note: In ASP.NET, a recordset is called a *dataset*. So choose Insert→Application Objects→ Dataset for this step.

Next, select the information you want to retrieve.

3. **Type *rsAdsIndex* into the Name box.**

Since Dreamweaver lets you connect to more than one database, you must now indicate *which* database connection it should use.

4. **From the Connections pop-up menu, select connCosmo.**

This is the name of the connection you created in the last chapter.

The Cosmo database contains two tables: one with ad information and one with seller information. For this page, you'll create an index of all the classified ads. That information is in the Ads table.

5. **From the Tables menu, choose "ads." Click Select.**

You don't need to retrieve *all* the information from the Ads table. Since this dynamic page will present a listing of all of the classified ads, you only need basic information like the name of the product, its price, and when it was listed for sale. More details about each ad will appear on a second page, to be created later in this tutorial.

6. **In the Columns list, Ctrl-click (⌘-click) adName, price, and datePosted.**

These are the columns of data you want to get from the database.

You won't have to filter this recordset—you can ignore these controls in the dialog box—but it would be nice if the ads appeared in chronological order, so visitors can see the newest ads first.

7. **From the first Sort pop-up menu, choose datePosted. From the second one, choose Descending.**

The Descending option makes certain the records start with the *latest* ad and end with the oldest.

8. **Click OK to close the Recordset dialog box. In the Bindings panel (Ctrl+F10 [⌘-F10]), click the + icon next to the Recordset icon.**

   The Bindings panel should look like Figure 22-19.

ASP.NET Note: The Bindings panel displays only adName, price, and datePosted. You won't see the last three items shown in Figure 22-19.

Note, too, that you'll have to place certain files on the Web server that Dreamweaver requires to build ASP.NET pages. To do this, choose Site→Deploy Supporting Files. The window that appears asks you to locate the *bin* directory of your testing server.

The bin directory is a folder for storing executable files—program files—that work with your Web site. In most cases, it's *C:\Inetpub\wwwroot\bin* (where *C:* is the name of the hard drive containing the Web site). You have to add these files only once per server (that is, once for your testing server, and once for your final production server).

Figure 22-19:
The Bindings panel provides a list of a page's recordsets and data fields. You can use these fields to add dynamic text to a page.

9. **In the document window, click inside the table cell directly below the one labeled Item for Sale.**

   In this cell, you'll add the name of the item for sale.

10. **In the Data Bindings panel, click adName and then click Insert.**

    You've just added dynamic data to the page. For the moment, it looks like {rsAdsIndex.adName}.

11. **Repeat steps 9 and 10, this time inserting *price* and *datePosted* into the remaining two cells.**

    You can also drag an item from the Data Bindings panel onto the page.

    At this point, your page should look like Figure 22-20.

Formatting Dynamic Information

Once you've added dynamic data to a page, you can format it so it looks like other text on your page. Dreamweaver lets you apply all of the formatting options available to regular text, including Cascading Style Sheets. In addition, Dreamweaver includes some formatting options specific to dynamic information, such as multiple formatting options for dates, currency, and numbers.

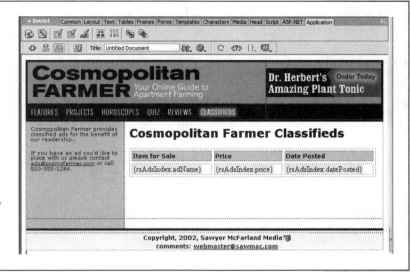

Figure 22-20:
After you add dynamic information to a page in Dreamweaver, it appears with a blue background. In this example, three pieces of dynamic data are added to the page ({rsAdsInex.adName}, for example). To change this background color, choose Edit→Preferences to open the Preferences window. Click the Highlighting category and change the Live Data View colors at the bottom of the window.

You'll start by adding some CSS formatting to the page.

1. **In the document window, click the ad name data ({rsAdsIndex.adName}).**

    You've just selected the data you want to format.

2. **Open the CSS Styles panel, if it isn't already open (Shift-F11). Make sure that the Apply Style button is selected, and then click the adName style.**

    The text is formatted in bold green.

3. **Repeat steps 1 and 2 for the other two data items, using the adInfo style in the CSS Styles panel.**

    Dreamweaver also includes special dynamic-text formatting options for dollar amounts, percentages, and more. That comes in handy now.

4. **Click the price data ({rsAdsIndex.price}) on the Web page.**

    Notice that the price is highlighted under the recordset. Before you proceed, make sure that the Data Bindings panel is open.

5. **In the Data Bindings panel, click the down-pointing arrow in the Format column. In the contextual menu that appears, choose Currency→2 Decimal Places (see Figure 22-21).**

You've just added a $ sign to the beginning of the price, and ensured that the price will always appear with two decimals, like this: $100.00. You can also pick from a variety of different formats for presenting dates.

ASP.NET Note: *Default* is the only choice for currency formatting in ASP.NET.

Figure 22-21:
Data in a database isn't always stored in a format that's attractive. Monetary values are usually stored as numbers— 9.9, for example. To get dynamic data into a more understandable format ($9.90), use the formatting options available from the Bindings panel.

6. **Click the date information ({rsAdsIndex.datePosted}) on the Web page. In the Data Bindings panel, click the Format arrow once again, but this time choose Date/Time and then select January 17, 2000.**

   Unfortunately, you can't see the effect of these formatting choices; you see only that cryptic {rsAdsIndex.datePosted} on the page. You'll get to see the actual data in the next section.

ASP.NET Note: Unfortunately, the date and time formatting options for ASP.NET are limited. Choose an option you think is appropriate.

Live Data View and Creating Repeating Regions

When you add dynamic data to a page, it doesn't look like much. All you see is the recordset and column name between braces ({rsAdsIndex.adName}, for example). Not only can this interfere with your design, it certainly doesn't give you a clear picture of what your page will look like.

Thank goodness for Dreamweaver's Live Data view.

1. **Click the Live Data View button in the document window's toolbar (see Figure 22-13).**

   Dreamweaver connects to the testing server and database to retrieve the data requested by the recordset (this may take a few seconds). For the first time, you get to see the page as it will appear on the Web (Figure 22-22). Notice the price and date formatting; it's just what you specified.

   But there's a problem: Only one item is listed. This page is meant to show listings for *all* classified ads. You have yet to create a repeating region—a part of the page that repeats for each record in a recordset.

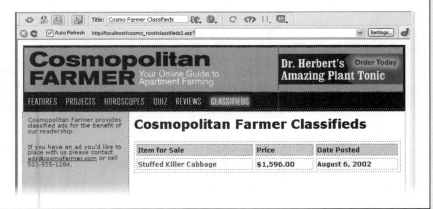

Figure 22-22:
When you click the Live Data View button in the document toolbar, Dreamweaver pulls data from the database and displays it in the document window. In addition, a second toolbar appears that lets you control various Live Data view settings.

2. **Move your cursor to the left of Stuffed Killer Cabbage until the right-pointing arrow appears, and then click.**

   That's how you select the bottom row of the table. (For other methods of selecting a table row, see page 161.) Since this row displays the info for a single ad, it's a perfect candidate for a repeating region. An additional row will appear in the table for each ad.

3. **On the Application tab of the Insert bar, click the Repeated Region button (see Figure 22-1).**

   The Repeat Region dialog box (Figure 22-11) appears, so that you can select which recordset to use (if the page has more than one) and how many records to display. In this case, since you have only one recordset, you just have to tell Dreamweaver how many records to show.

4. **In the Records at a Time box, type *7*. Click OK.**

   You don't know how many ads *Cosmo Farmer* will be running at a time. If it were a lot, you wouldn't want to show them all on a single page—a thousand listings would make a pretty long Web page. In this case, just list seven records at a time.

   If the database has more than seven ads, you need to provide a way for people to see the other ad listings. You'll do that next.

5. **Click the Live Data View button again to turn off Live Data.**

   The document window changes back to the original two-row column.

6. **In the Application tab of the Insert bar, click below the table that lists the ads; click the Recordset Navigation Bar button (see Figure 22-1).**

   The Recordset Navigation dialog appears. There's only one thing to do here.

7. **Make sure the Text button is selected; click OK.**

   Dreamweaver plops a table onto the page, containing four columns. They contain links that will let visitors navigate the classified ad listings.

   The table will look better if it's aligned to the left side of the page.

8. **In the document window, select the table. From the Align pop-up menu in the Property inspector, choose Default. Set the width of the table to 200 pixels.**

   For techniques on selecting a table, see page 161. (Tables *are* left-aligned by default, which is why you chose Default.)

9. **In the Application tab of the Insert bar, click directly above the new table; click the Recordset Navigation Status button (see Figure 22-1).**

   Dreamweaver inserts something that looks like this: *Records {rsAdsIndex_first} to {rsAdsIndex_last} of {rsAdsIndex_total}*. That's placeholder code for this notation: "Records 1-7 of 12."

   Now for a touch of formatting:

10. **Select the paragraph Dreamweaver just inserted. In the CSS Styles panel, click adInfo.**

    You've just formatted the paragraph with the adInfo CSS style. (While you're at it, apply the same style to the four parts of the Recordset Navigation Bar—First, Previous, Next, and Last, if you like.)

11. **Press F12 to preview the page in your Web browser.**

    The page opens in a Web browser displaying seven records (see Figure 22-23). You can click the Next link at the bottom of the page to jump to the next set of ads.

Editing a Recordset and Linking to a Detail Page

Tutorial: Showing Database Info

Now that the main Ads listings page is complete, you need to create a link to the name of each ad that, when clicked, will open a page with the details for that ad.

1. **Open the Server Behaviors panel by pressing Ctrl+F9 (⌘-F9), or clicking the Server Behaviors tab in the Application panel group.**

   A list of all the different *server behaviors* appears; these became available when you created a recordset, put dynamic text on the page, and used Dreamweaver's other dynamic page-creation tools. (Server behaviors are discussed in depth in Chapter 24.)

   Instead of adding another server behavior at this point, you can edit one you've already created: the recordset. When you first added this recordset, an important piece of information was left out—the ad's ID number. (Actually, it was omitted from the tutorial intentionally, so that you'd now have this engaging educational opportunity to learn how to edit a recordset.)

   Each ad has its own ID number, which you'll use to tell the Details page which ad to display.

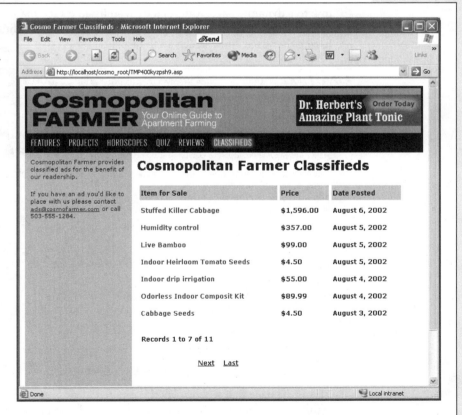

Figure 22-23:
Building dynamic Web pages in Dreamweaver is easy. In just a few short steps—all right, 28 steps—you can create Web pages that let you view database records.

2. **Double-click "Recordset (rsAdsIndex)" in the Server Behaviors panel to open the Recordset dialog box.**

ASP.NET Note: Double-click "DataSet (rsAdsIndex)" for this step.

---

3. **Ctrl-click (⌘-click) adID in the columns list, and then click OK.**

   You've just added one additional column (adID) to the recordset. Now the recordset will not only retrieve the name, price, and posted dates for each ad, but also its unique ID number.

4. **In the document window, select the dynamic data containing the ad's name—{rsAdsIndex.adName}.**

   A simple link won't work here. Instead, you need one of Dreamweaver's server behaviors.

5. **In the Server Behaviors panel, click the + button. From the pop-up menu, choose Go To Detail Page (see Figure 22-24).**

   The Go To Detail Page dialog box appears. This window lets you create a special link to a dynamic page. Although each ad listed on the main classified ads page will link to the same Details page, each link will include additional information letting that page know which ad to display.

ASP.NET Note: Unfortunately, Dreamweaver doesn't provide the Go To Detail Page behavior for ASP.NET. Instead, you must follow these steps:

1. Select {rsAdsIndex.adName} as in step 4.

2. In the Property inspector, click the Folder (browse for file) icon next to the Link box.

3. Select the file ASPNETadDetails.aspx in the site root. Don't close the Select File window yet.

4. In the Select File window, click the Parameters button at the bottom-right corner. The Parameters window opens.

5. Type *adID* into the Name column.

6. Click in the Value column to the right and click the lightning bolt icon. The Dynamic Data window opens.

7. Select adID from the recordset (you may need to click the + button to expand the list of database columns).

8. Click OK to close the Parameters window.

9. Click OK to close the Select File window.

10. Breathe a sigh of relief and jump to step 8.

---

6. **Click the Browse button. Select the file adDetails.asp.**

   This is the page that will display the detailed records of each ad. All of the other settings should already be filled out and should resemble Figure 22-25.

---

7. **Click OK to close this window.**

And now to make sure everything works:

8. **Press the F12 key to preview the page in your Web browser. Click the Stuffed
Killer Cabbage link.**

The detail page loads…without any details! You'll get to that step in a moment.
In the meantime, look at the URL in the Web browser's Address bar. It should be
something like this: *http://localhost/cosmo_root/adDetails.asp?adID=4*. Notice the
?adID=4 tagged onto the page *adDetails.asp*. That's the information the details
page will need to retrieve the proper ad information. In this case, the URL is
indicating that the page should retrieve info for an ad with the ID number of 4.

9. **Save and close this page.**

Figure 22-24:
*The Go to Detail page server behavior makes it easy to pass informa-
tion, such as a record ID number, to another page. In this way, you can
link from an item in a list to a Web page, containing more detailed
information on an item.*

Figure 22-25:
*The Go To Detail Page
server behavior makes it
easy to create a link that
passes URL parameters,
Form data, and other
necessary information to
a detail page. This
behavior is discussed in
depth in Chapter 24.*

Building the Detailed Ad Page

In this part of the tutorial, you'll build a detail page that will display all the details for a particular classified ad. In addition, you'll create an advanced recordset that combines information from two separate database tables.

1. **Open the file called adDetails.asp in the root folder of the site.**

   Either choose File→Open and navigate to and select adDetails.asp, or double-click the file name in the Site Files panel.

ASP.NET Note: Open the file ASPNETadDetails.aspx.

Since this page will display the details for an ad, it must retrieve data from the database. To set this up, start by creating a recordset.

2. **Choose Insert→Application Objects→Recordset.**

   You can also click the Recordset object on the Application tab of the Insert bar (see Figure 22-1). Or click the + button on either the Bindings panel or Server Behaviors panel, and then select *recordset* from the pop-up menu. In any case, the Recordset dialog box should now be open.

ASP.NET Note: Choose Insert→Application Objects→DataSet instead.

The *Cosmo Farmer* database contains two database tables—one for ad information, and one for information about the people who placed the ads. The detail page incorporates information from both tables, so that it can reveal both the description of the product and the contact info of the seller. Because the basic panel of the Recordset dialog box doesn't let you retrieve information from more than a single database table, you must use the advanced setting.

3. **Click the Advanced button on the right side of the window.**

   The Advanced Recordset dialog box appears.

   Unfortunately, this isn't one of the areas in which Dreamweaver is particularly user-friendly. It helps to understand SQL (see page 646)—or you can just take the following steps:

4. **In the Name field, type *rsDetails*. From the Connection menu, choose connCosmo.**

   In the next few steps, you'll create an SQL query—essentially a line of programming code that asks the database for particular information that matches specific criteria. In this case, it's the information for a particular classified ad.

5. **Click the + or flippy triangle next to the word "Tables" in the Database Items list (at the bottom of the dialog box).**

   It expands to reveal the two tables of the database: Ads and Sellers.

DREAMWEAVER MX: THE MISSING MANUAL

6. **Click the + (flippy triangle) to expand the Ads table.**

Your job is to select the information from this table that you want to display on the page.

7. **Select adName; click the Select button to the right.**

Notice that Dreamweaver writes *SELECT adName FROM ads* in the SQL box. This is SQL code for selecting a particular column of data from a table. You can now choose the other pieces of information.

ASP.NET Note: You'll see *SELECT ads.adName FROM ads* right in the SQL box.

---

8. **Repeat step 7 for the following items in the Ads table: price, datePosted, description, imageURL.**

These are all the items you need to retrieve from the Ads table. Now you can choose data from the Sellers table.

9. **Click the + (flippy triangle) to expand the Sellers table. Repeat step 7 for the following items from that table: sellerName, sellerPhone, sellerEmail.**

The dialog box should now look like Figure 22-26. Congratulations: You've just created a basic SQL query.

But there's a problem here: Because of the way this query is structured, it will retrieve *all* the records for both tables. To remedy the situation, you must do two things: First, combine information from two tables so that you get the seller

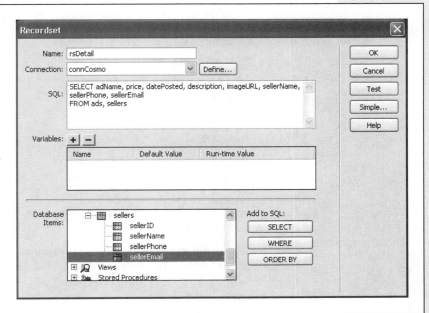

Figure 22-26:
The Advanced option of the Recordset window lets you use a data tree to build an SQL statement. By selecting a column name and clicking either the SELECT, WHERE, or ORDER BY buttons, you can get Dreamweaver to do some of the heavy lifting. Unfortunately, some understanding of SQL is still required to create functioning database queries using these advanced options.

information for the corresponding ad; and second, retrieve only that information for the particular ad specified by the link you created in the last part of this tutorial.

10. **Click inside the SQL box after the word "sellers." Press Enter or Return.**

    You'll have to dive into typing out SQL code.

11. **Type** *WHERE (ads.sellerID = sellers.sellerID).*

    This little bit of code is called a *WHERE clause,* and it helps filter information in a database. In this instance, you've created what's called a *join*—a statement that joins two or more tables together. You want to retrieve only the information for ads when a sellerID number (in the Ads table) matches the ID number of a seller in the Sellers table. In other words, this code retrieves the name and contact information for the seller of a particular ad.

    If your eyes are glazing over, go get a cup of coffee before plunging ahead.

12. **Click the + button to the right of the word "Variables."**

    You've just created a new SQL variable.

    You're about to expand on the WHERE clause you just wrote. Not only do you need to get the details of an ad (plus the seller's name and contact information), you also want to retrieve just a single record—the particular ad whose details the visitor wants to review.

ASP.NET Note: The process for creating an SQL variable is significantly different in ASP.NET. Follow these steps:

   1. Click the + button to the right of the word "Parameters" to open the Add Parameter window.
   2. Type *advert* in the name field.
   3. From the Type menu, choose SmallInt.
   4. Click the Build button to open the Build Value window.
   5. Type *adID* into the Name field.
   6. From the Source menu, choose URL parameter.
   7. Type *1* into the Default field; click OK to close the window.
   8. Click OK to close the Add Parameter window.
   9. Go to step 14 below.

---

13. **For the Name, type** *advert;* **for Default Value, type** *1;* **and for Run-time Value, type** *Request.QueryString("adID").*

    Look back to step 8 in the last part of this tutorial (page 681). Remember that the ID number for the ad is embedded in the URL. In other words, when someone clicks a link on the main ads listings page, the ID number for the ad is passed along like this: *adDetails.asp?adID=4.*

In this step, you're retrieving that information from the URL—that's the *Request.QueryString("adID")* part—and storing it in a variable that you'll use in the rest of the SQL query.

14. **Return to the SQL box. At the end of the WHERE clause (after the closing parentheses), type *AND ads.adID = advert*.**

The Recordset window should now look like Figure 22-27.

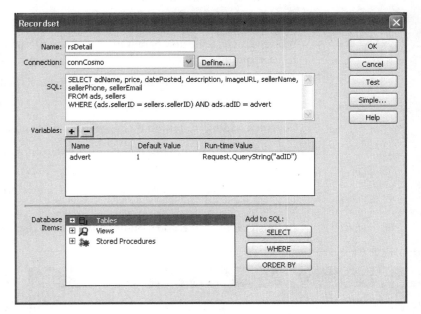

Figure 22-27:
In the Advanced settings of the Recordset window, you can create more detailed SQL queries that can retrieve and merge information from multiple database tables.

15. **Click the Test button.**

A Test SQL Statement window opens, containing a single record. Hallelujah! It includes not only ad details but also the seller's name and contact information.

ASP.NET Note: This testing procedure won't work for ASP.NET, but the final page will function correctly in Live Data view or when previewing from the testing server.

16. **Click OK to close the window. Choose File→Save to save your changes.**

Filling in the Details

Now all you need to do is add the information retrieved in the recordset to the page.

1. **In the document window, click in the empty space above the word "Price."**

You'll add the name of the "for sale" item here.

2. **Open the Bindings panel.**

   Either press Shift-F10 or click the Data Bindings tab in the Application panel group.

3. **In the Data Bindings panel, click the + (flippy triangle) next to the recordset to display all of the columns retrieved in the recordset. Select adName, and then click Insert.**

   That data appears in the document window.

4. **Press the right arrow key and hit the Return key.**

   You've just created a new paragraph below the ad's name where you'll insert an ad description.

5. **Insert "description" from the Data Bindings panel, as described in step 3.**

   The description is added to the page as well.

6. **Continue adding content to this page using these same steps.**

   Add the price, date posted, seller name, seller phone, and seller email in the appropriate places in the document window.

   If you like, you can also format the price and date items, as you did in steps 4–6 on page 673.

   To finish off this page, add a photo in the area to the left of the ad info like this:

Figure 22-28:
Paths for links and images needn't be hardwired into a Web page. You can retrieve paths for images and links from a database source. In this case, depending on which ad is currently on display, a different product image will appear on the page.

7. **Click in the empty table cell that's to the left of the cell with the ad information. In the Common tab of the Insert bar, click the Image button or choose Insert→Image.**

   The Insert Image window appears. You've encountered this dialog box many times before (see Chapter 5) when inserting a graphic. However, in this case, you'll retrieve the path to the image from the database.

8. **Click the Data Sources button.**

   The window should now look like Figure 22-28. A list of all of the different data items from the recordset appears. See the item labeled imageURL? The database stores the path to an image for each ad in the database. This is the path that the page will use when displaying the graphic.

9. **Select imageURL; click OK.**

   A little square icon appears in the document window.

10. **Click the Live Document View button. If everything looks good (Figure 22-29), choose File→Save.**

Figure 22-29:
You can preview additional records by modifying the URL that appears just below the document toolbar. In the box just to the right of adDetails.asp?, type: adID=3. the information for the classified ad with ID number 3 appears. Try other numbers to view other ads.

Congratulations! You've just built two powerful, complex dynamic Web pages (and probably watched three presidential administrations pass).

To see them in action, open the classifieds.asp page in Dreamweaver and press the F12 key to preview it in a browser. Now click a link to see the details for that product.

Note: If your local root folder isn't the same as your testing server, you'll need to move your files *from* the root folder *to* the testing server in order to preview these dynamic pages. See page 486 for more detail on transferring files.

Web Pages that Manipulate Database Records

Just *displaying* database information on a Web page is useful, but you may be more interested in using the Web to collect information about your site's visitors. Maybe something as simple as an online registration form will do the trick. Other times, you may have something more ambitious in mind—a full-fledged e-commerce system, for example, which doesn't pay the bills unless it provides a way to collect product orders and credit card numbers.

Once you've got data in the database, there'd better be a way to update and delete that information. After all, prices change, products are discontinued, and you may suddenly want to remove any record of Harvey the Wise Guy from your site's online guestbook. Thankfully, Dreamweaver makes changing information in a database simple and painless.

Adding Data

As noted in Chapter 10, the primary method of collecting information over the Internet is the *HTML form*. Its basic elements—text boxes, radio buttons, pop-up menus, and so on—can collect a wide assortment of data. But to put this information into a database, you need Dreamweaver's built-in tools. With its Record Insertion Form and Insert Record server behavior, Dreamweaver makes this a simple process.

Warning: You might not want just anyone adding, editing, or deleting database information. To control access to these types of pages—or any page, for that matter—use Dreamweaver's User Authentication server behaviors, as discussed on page 727.

Dreamweaver's Record Insertion Form

Dreamweaver's Record Insertion Form object is the quickest way to build a page for adding records to a database. It builds a form, creates a table, and adds all of the necessary programming code in just a couple of steps. To use it:

Figure 23-1:
Whether you're collecting credit card information for an e-commerce site or gathering signup information for an online newsletter, Dreamweaver MX simplifies the process of collecting information from a Web page and storing it in a database.

1. **Create a new Web page and save it to your site (or open a dynamic Web page that you've already created).**

   Make sure the page uses the extension (.asp, .aspx, .cfm, .php, .jsp) that matches the server model of your site. (See page 631 for creating new dynamic pages.)

2. **In the Document window, click where you want the insertion form to appear. Choose Insert→Application Objects→Record Insertion Form.**

You also can use the Record Insertion Form button on the Application tab of the Insert bar (see Figure 22-1). Either way, the Record Insertion Form window opens (Figure 23-2).

Figure 23-2:
When creating a form, it's a good idea to remove columns the database creates for its own use (by clicking the – button), such as record ID numbers. In this example, the column adID is a unique ID number created by the database whenever someone adds a new record. You wouldn't want anyone to tamper with this number, so leave it off the form (by deleting it from this list). If you accidentally delete a column, click the + button to add it back.

3. **From the Connection pop-up menu, select the database connection.**

   If your site works with several databases, select the connection for the database that this form will add information to. (Database connections are described on page 632.)

4. **Choose a table from the Insert Into Table pop-up menu.**

   A list of all tables available in the database appears in this menu. You can only insert data into a single table, and one page can hold only one Insert Record behavior. This means if you need to add records to multiple tables, you must create multiple Web pages, each with its own Record Insertion form.

   If you have a table for customers, and another for products, you'll need separate Add Customers and Add Products pages. You could then create a main Administration page that provides links to each of these table-updating pages.

5. **Click Browse. Navigate to and select a file from your Web site.**

   Choose the page your visitors will see after adding a record to the database. It could simply be a page saying, "Thanks for signing up with our Web site." Or if the insertion form adds a new employee to your company's employee database, you could choose the page that lists all of the employees (including the one just added to the database).

ASP.NET Note: On ASP.NET pages, you also have the option of specifying an Error page, which appears when the addition to the database fails for some reason.

You also can change how the menu item for each database column is formatted on the page, like this:

6. **In the Form Fields box, select a database column and change its settings, if you like.**

Your options include:

Label is the text Dreamweaver adds next to the form field on the page. It identifies what someone should type in the field, like First Name. Dreamweaver just uses the name of the column in the database—adID, for instance—so it's usually best to change this to something more understandable.

The **Display As** menu lets you select the *type* of form element you want to use to collect the column's information. For example, if the column is someone's first name, select Text Field. You'll add a text box to the form where visitors can type their names. On the other hand, if people are supposed to choose from a limited number of choices (U.S. Postal Service, FedEx 2 Day, and FedEx First Overnight, for example), you might select Radio Group instead.

Radio buttons or pop-up menus can also ensure consistency and rule out typos. On a form that asks visitors to indicate the state they live in, you could offer a pop-up menu that lists the 50 states; if you provided a text box instead, your visitors would be able to type in every conceivable abbreviation and misspelling. (For a description of the different types of form elements, see page 300.)

Tip: Dreamweaver can also create *dynamic* menus, which display data taken from a database. See page 704.

The **Submit As** menu is determined by how you've set up your database. It tells Dreamweaver what kind of data the field contains: text, number, date, and so on. In most cases, Dreamweaver figures this out correctly, so you won't need to change anything.

The **Default Value** lets you preload a form field with information; it's the same as a text field's *init value* described on page 303. You also can add a dynamic value generated by your server model's programming language. If you had a field called *date*, for example, you could add today's date to the field automatically by typing <%= *date* %> (in the ASP/VBScript server model).

In most cases, you'll change the label of every column. But for now, leave the other options alone.

7. **Click OK to close the window and create the form.**

Dreamweaver inserts a table, form, and all of the form elements you specified.

At this point, the page is complete and ready to accept information. Unfortunately, Dreamweaver doesn't let you return to this window to make any changes. (If you quickly realize that you made a mistake, you can always use Ctrl+Z [⌘-Z] to undo the operation and then reapply the Insert Record Form.)

To ensure that your form works correctly and doesn't produce any errors when it's submitted, add form validation (see the box below).

Caution: Once you've added the form, don't rename any form fields. You'll break the script responsible for inserting the record. If that happens, see page 694 for information on updating the Insert Record server behavior.

Using the Insert Record Behavior

Dreamweaver's Record Insertion Form tool makes quick work of adding the table, form, and programming code required to create a Web page for adding data to a table. At times, though, you might want a more customized approach. Perhaps you've already designed a form that you'd like to use or created a beautiful table design for

---

Validate That Form

You never know what someone might type into a Web form and try to submit to a database. Maybe the form field asks for the visitor's age. Aside from the fact you probably won't get an honest answer, the visitor may make an honest mistake by typing the wrong keys—*ew* instead of *32*, for example. If the database is set up to accept only numbers for the age column, the person submitting the form will receive a nasty error message.

In another situation, you may require a name and email address. However, someone could easily overlook or ignore these form fields. Dealing with missing and incorrect data is the bane of all database developers.

To circumvent these problems, it's a good idea to turn to *form validation.* You've already encountered Dreamweaver's Form Validation behavior on page 313. It prevents a form from being submitted if information is missing or in the wrong format—if the information in a field is not a number, for instance.

Better still, you can download the ultimate extension for validating forms from renowned extension developer Jaro Von Flocken: the Check Form MX extension. It can validate

not just text fields but menus, checkboxes, and radio buttons.

You can also make sure a value typed into a field is a date, or that two fields have the same value. (You'd want to check that two fields match, for example, in situations where you require visitors to register and make up a password before using your site. To rule out typos, you might require two Password fields—one labeled Password and another called Confirm Password.) To download the Check Form MX extension, visit *www.yaromat.com/dw/?t=Behavior&r=validation.*

Both Dreamweaver's built-in validation tool and Check Form MX are *client-side* JavaScript programs. That is, when someone submits the form containing a validation error, a JavaScript alert window pops up with the error message. Dreamweaver MX doesn't include any *server*-side validation features—programs that check the form after it's submitted to the Web server and then return a Web page listing the errors. This latter option is usually more attractive and professional looking, but requires knowledge of programming in VB Script, PHP, or whatever server language your site uses.

---

your form. Rather than relying on Dreamweaver's rather pedestrian table and form design, you can supercharge your own design with the Insert Record server behavior.

To build a page for adding database records, start by creating a Web page for your server model (ASP, PHP, ASP.NET, or whatever). Add a form to the page (see Chapter 10). Make sure the form has one form field per column that will accept data.

In some cases, you may not include a form field. For example, a database table's primary key (a unique identifier for each record) is usually generated automatically by the database for each new record. In this case, you wouldn't add a field for this column.

In other cases, you might add *hidden* fields (see page 310) that aren't set by someone filling out the form. Suppose someone signs up for your online newsletter and you want to store the date of registration. Instead of letting the visitor fill out the date, add a hidden form field with the current date (see step 13 on page 711.)

Once you've created the form, add the Insert Record server behavior like this:

1. **Choose Window→Server Behaviors to open the Server Behaviors panel.**

   The keyboard shortcut is Ctrl+F9 (⌘-F9).

2. **Click the + button on the panel and select Insert Record.**

   The Insert Record window opens. It's very similar to the Insert Record Form window (Figure 23-2), but one key difference is that you must manually associate a form element with the correct database column (see Figure 23-3). (Another difference is that you can't define default values for each form element in

Figure 23-3:
In this example, the form contains a field named "priceAd." To ensure that data typed into this field goes into the proper place in the database, you must select price from the Column menu. This tells Dreamweaver that whatever is typed into the priceAd field should be stored in the column named "price."

this window. You can, however, still apply default values to a form field using the Property inspector, as described on page 301.)

3. **Make your selections from the first three options.**

They're the same options described in steps 3–5 for the Insert Record Form tool (see page 689). You're telling Dreamweaver which database to use, which table to add data to, and which page to go to once the information is added to the database.

4. **Using the Get Values From pop-up menu, select the name of the form.**

Even though you can have only one Insert Record behavior per page, it's still possible to have multiple forms on a single page—a form for adding a record and a form for searching the site, for example. Select the name of the form used for adding data to the database.

5. **Select a form element from the list. Choose the matching database column from the Column pop-up menu.**

In order for the form's information to end up in the proper columns of the database, you must tell Dreamweaver which database column will store the selected form field's information. You can let Dreamweaver choose the proper type from the Submit As pop-up menu; as with step 6 on page 690, this choice depends on how your database is set up (which Dreamweaver can figure out).

FREQUENTLY ASKED QUESTION

Behaviors That Serve You Well

What's the difference between Dreamweaver Behaviors (Chapter 11) and a server behavior?

Both are simply prewritten programs created by Dreamweaver's engineers. They differ mainly in where the programs run and what they attempt to accomplish.

A Dreamweaver Behavior is a JavaScript program that runs in a Web browser. It usually affects the interaction between a visitor and a Web page; for instance, the Swap Image behavior causes the Web browser to change one image for another when a visitor moves the mouse over a link. The behavior itself runs inside the visitor's Web browser, and anyone can see the program by looking at the source code of the page in the browser.

A server behavior, on the other hand, can be written in a variety of different languages (ASP, PHP, C#, Java, and so on), depending on the server model your site uses. No matter what the language, however, server behaviors always run on the application server—that is, on the Web-server side of the Internet. They're the magic that lets you create connections to databases and display, edit, and delete information from databases—all without knowing any programming. In addition, since these programs run on the application server, they're never visible to your site's visitors. All they see if they look at the source of the page in their browser is regular HTML (the results of the server program).

In a nutshell, Dreamweaver behaviors add interactive elements to a Web page, like rollovers and JavaScript alert boxes. Server behaviors add the programming code needed to build sophisticated database-driven Web sites.

Tip: You need to perform step 5 only if the names of the form fields *differ* from the names of the columns in the database. If you name a form field adName, for example, and there's also a database column named adName, Dreamweaver automatically connects the two in the Insert Record window.

6. **Click OK to close the window and apply the server behavior.**

The page is now capable of adding information directly to the database.

If you change the name of a form field, add a form field, or wish to change any of the settings for this behavior, you can edit it by double-clicking Insert Record on the Server Behaviors panel. This opens the Insert Record window once again.

Updating Database Records

Maybe someone made an error while entering data into the database. Maybe the price of your product changes. Or maybe you want to provide a way for your Web visitors to update their email addresses. In any case, the time will come when you want to edit a record in a database.

Creating *Update Record Forms* in Dreamweaver is very similar to creating Insert Record forms. Both require a HTML form that your audience can fill out and submit. The primary difference is that an update form is *already* filled out with information from the database. It's like a combination of an Insert Record Form and a record detail page (such as the one created by the Master Detail Page set described on page 663).

The first step in creating an update form is to add a *recordset* to the update page (see page 636). The recordset will retrieve the data that appears in each field of the update form.

The recordset should contain only a single record—the one to be updated. Therefore, you must use a form or URL parameter to filter the recordset (see page 639 for more on filtering). For example, on a page listing company employees, you could add an Edit button that would link to the page containing the update form. If you added a Go To Detail Page server behavior (see page 667) to the employee listing page, you could then pass the ID for a specific employee to the update page. In turn, the update page would use that ID to filter the database for a single record and display the employee information in the form. (If all of this sounds confusing on paper, try the tutorial starting on page 708, which takes you step-by-step through the process.)

After you add the recordset to the update form page, you have two options for building an update form. You can either let Dreamweaver automate the process with its Insert Update Record form or build a form yourself and add the Update Record server behavior. The following pages cover both methods.

The Insert Update Record Form

Dreamweaver can automate most of the steps of creating an update form.

1. **Open a dynamic page (Chapter 22) with a recordset already added.**

   Remember, the recordset should only contain a single record—the one to be updated. So you must add a filter when you create the recordset (see page 639 for more on filtering recordsets).

Warning: Make sure the recordset used to retrieve the information for the update form is the *first* recordset added to the page. If it isn't, Dreamweaver won't automatically fill out the Default Value field for each form element (see Figure 23-4).

Figure 23-4:
A form field's default value is the information visible when the form first appears on the page. In the case of an update form, each form element will already be filled out with information from the database. After all, this page is meant for editing data that already exists, not for adding a new record. When using the Record Update Form tool, Dreamweaver is smart enough to fill out the default value for each form field with the proper information from the database (circled in this image). (See the warning above, however.)

2. **In the Document window, click where you want the insertion form to appear. Choose Insert→Application Objects→Record Update Form.**

   You can also use the Record Update Form button on the Application tab of the Insert bar (see Figure 22-1). Either way, the Record Update Form window opens (see Figure 23-2).

3. **From the Connection pop-up menu, select the database connection.**

   If your site works with several databases, select the connection for the database that this form will add information to. (Database connections are described on page 632.)

4. **From the Table to Update pop-up menu, choose a table to work with.**

   A list of all tables available in the database appears in this menu. You can edit data from just one table, and a page can hold only one Update Record behavior. (In fact, a single page can contain only one record-editing server behavior. Therefore, a single page can't be used to add, edit, or delete records; you must create a separate page for each operation.)

5. **Make sure the recordset you created previously is selected in the Select Record From menu.**

   The recordset should be selected already. If it's not, you must have created another recordset first. As a result, the Record Update Form command may function incorrectly (see warning on the previous page).

6. **Make sure the table's primary key column is selected in the Unique Key Column box. If the column contains a number—and it usually does—verify that the Numeric box is selected.**

   The Unique Key Column is used to identify which record to change during the update process. (For a description of primary keys, see page 627.)

7. **Click the Browse button; navigate to and select a file from the Web site.**

   This represents the page that will appear after a record has been updated. A good technique is to select a details page. Then, after updating the page, the visitor will immediately see a page showing the changes.

8. **If you like, change a column's settings.**

   After clicking a row in this box, you can change the Label, Display As Submit As, and Default Value properties of the database column, exactly as described on page 690.

   To delete a field so it doesn't appear in the form, click the Remove (–) button. You should *always* take this opportunity to remove the table's primary key—the column you selected in step 5. Since the key identifies the record, allowing someone to edit this could cause problems to your database, such as overwriting data for another record.

9. **Click OK to close the window.**

   Dreamweaver inserts a table, form, and all of the form elements you specified.

The Update Record Server Behavior

Dreamweaver's Record Update Form tool makes it delightfully easy to add the table, form, and programming code required to create a Web page for editing database records. But when you need more flexibility—if you've already designed a form that you'd like to use or created a table design for your form—the Update Record server behavior lets you keep your own beautiful design and give it more power.

You must start with a page that has a filtered recordset, as described on page 694. Then add a form to the page (see Chapter 10). Make sure the form has one form field for every database column that is to be edited. Don't include a form field for the database table's primary key. (Allowing anyone to change the primary key could have disastrous effects on your database.)

Tip: Giving your form fields the same names used for the database table's column will speed up the process of adding the Update Record server behavior.

At this point, the form is full of empty fields. If you preview the page, none of the data you retrieved from the recordset appears. To fill the form with data, you must *bind* data from the recordset to each form field, as follows:

1. **In the Document window, select the form field.**

   To select a form field in the document window, just click it.

Note: These instructions apply to text and hidden fields. Information on binding data to radio buttons, checkboxes, and menus appears on page 701.

---

2. **In the Property inspector, click the dynamic data button (the lightning bolt).**

   The Dynamic Data window appears (Figure 23-5).

Tip: You can also bind data from a recordset to a form field by dragging the database column from the Bindings panel (page 652) and dropping it on the form field.

Figure 23-5:
The Dynamic Data window lets you add information from a recordset to form fields so parts of a form can be pre-filled out. This is exactly what you want to do when updating information already in the database. In fact, the Dynamic Data window will display and let you use additional data sources (like URL variables) that you've added to the page (see page 737).

3. **Click the + button next to the recordset used for the update page.**

A list of all columns retrieved by the recordset appears.

4. **Select the name of the table column you want to bind to the form field. Click OK.**

You should ignore the Format menu and Code box. The form field is now set to display information from the recordset.

Once you've created the form and added recordset information to each field, add the Update Record server behavior.

1. **Choose Window→Server Behaviors to open the Server Behaviors panel.**

The keyboard shortcut is Ctrl+F9 (⌘-F9).

2. **Click the + button on the panel and select Update Record.**

The Update Record window opens (see Figure 23-6).

3. **Change the first five options, if you like.**

They're the same as described in steps 3–7 for the Record Update Form tool on page 695. They tell Dreamweaver which database to use, which table to update data to, which recordset the record information is coming from, which column is the table's primary key, and which page to go to once the edited information is added to the database.

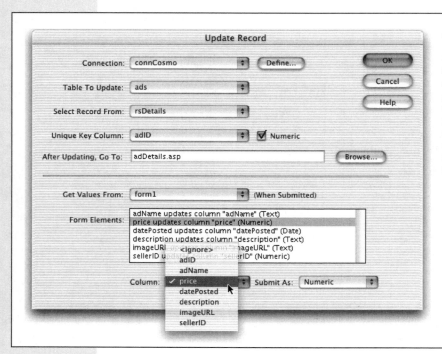

Figure 23-6:
The Update Record window is similar to the Record Update Form window (Figure 23-4). The main difference is that here you must manually associate a form element with the correct database column.

4. **From the Get Values From menu, select the name of the form.**

Even though you can have only one Update Record behavior per page, it's still possible to have multiple forms on a single page: a form for editing a record and a form for searching the site, for example. Select the name of the form used for editing data.

5. **Select a form element from the list, then select the matching database column from the Column menu.**

In order for the form's information to end up in the proper database columns, you must tell Dreamweaver which database column you want to store the selected form field's information.

Tip: If you use the name of your database columns to name the form fields too, Dreamweaver automatically associates the two, so you can skip this step.

Let Dreamweaver choose the proper type from the Submit As menu. As with step 6 on page 690, this choice depends on how your database is set up (which Dreamweaver can figure out).

6. **Click OK to close the window and apply the server behavior.**

The page is now capable of editing information from the database.

As with any server behavior, double-clicking its name on the Server Behaviors panel—in this case, Update Record—opens the behavior's dialog box so that you can make changes to its properties.

Dynamic Form Fields

Forms don't have to be empty. When a Web browser loads a form page, one or more fields may already be filled with information from a database.

You can use this feature for update forms on your site. It can also come in handy when, for example, you've created an Employee Directory section for your company's site. Suppose that, on the Insert New Employee page, you built a pop-up menu that lets the Human Resources department select a department for the new employee.

You, the designer, *could* create a menu like this by manually typing the name of each department. But what if the names of the departments change, or new departments are added? You'd have to reopen the page and edit the form field each time. If you opted for a dynamic menu instead, the page would build the Departments pop-up menu automatically by retrieving the current list of departments from the database (see Figure 23-7).

Dreamweaver's Insert Record Update Form object creates these kinds of dynamic form fields automatically. In essence, a dynamic form field is a form element whose value comes from dynamic data in the Bindings panel. The dynamic data can come from a recordset (as with an update form), a form or URL parameter, or even a cookie or session variable (see page 740).

Whenever you wish to use a dynamic form field, start by creating a form. Add all form fields that might include dynamic content. (Not all the fields have to be dynamic, however. In the previous example, only the menu would be dynamic. The other fields for entering an employee's information would be empty.) Then add a recordset, request variable, session variable, or application variable to the Bindings panel. (Request, session, and application variables are discussed on page 737.)

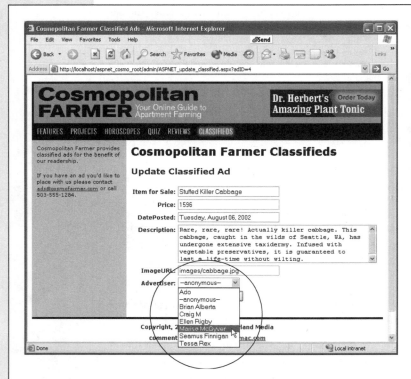

Figure 23-7:
Dynamic form fields come in handy with update forms. Form fields are already filled out with database information that's ready to be edited. The menus can also be dynamically generated from records in a recordset. In this case, the menu (shown open) lists records retrieved directly from a database table containing information on Cosmopolitan Farmer advertisers.

Dynamic Text Form Fields

Any form field that accepts typing—text, text area, and password fields—can be dynamic. For example, if a site requires a user login, you could include a "remember me" feature, so when a visitor who's previously signed in returns to the site, the user name and password will already be filled out.

You can add dynamic data to a text field (also called *binding* data to the field) using any of the methods described next. (Remember, you must first have added the form field to the page and added the dynamic data to the Bindings panel. This means adding a recordset to a page, as described on page 636, or creating additional data sources [like cookies or session variables] as described on page 737.)

- In Design view, drag the dynamic data item from the Bindings panel and drop it onto the form field.

- In Design view, select the text field. In the Bindings panel, select the dynamic data item and click the Bind button.

- Select the text field. In the Property inspector, click the dynamic data button (the lightning bolt). The Dynamic Data window appears (see Figure 23-5); select the dynamic data item from the list and click OK.

- In the Server Behaviors panel, click the + button and select Dynamic Form Elements→Dynamic Text. In the window that appears, you'll see a Text field menu. Select the text field you wish to add dynamic data to, then click the lightning bolt button to open the dynamic data window. Select the dynamic data item from the list and click OK.

Tip: You can bind dynamic data to a *hidden* field using the same steps.

After binding the data to the field, the name of the data item appears inside the field—{rsDetails.adName}, for example. If you're using Live Data view (see page 660), the actual data from the database appears inside the field.

Caution: Dreamweaver lets you format dynamic data in a form field just like dynamic text you add to a page (see page 653). Be careful with this option, though. If the form is submitting to a database, data may sometimes have to be in a certain format. For example, prices are often stored as numbers inside a database. But using Dreamweaver's currency format, you can make a price appear as $34.00 in a form field. When your visitor submits the form, the $ goes along for the ride, causing the database to spit out a horrible error message upon encountering this non-numeric character.

To remove dynamic data from a text field, just select the field and click the Unbind button in the Bindings panel. (Deleting the contents of the field's Init Value box in the Property inspector also works.)

Dynamic Checkboxes and Radio Buttons

With a text field, you can dynamically change the *value* of the field. With checkboxes and radio buttons, however, you can control only their status (checked or unchecked) dynamically.

You can use this value to select one radio button in a group based on a value in the database. For example, as part of a product ordering system, shoppers could select a particular shipping option: USPS, FedEx, or UPS. But after reviewing their orders, what if they change their minds and choose a different shipping option? When they return to the order page, you'd want the Shipping Option radio button selection to be updated. In other words, you want the page to read the shipping option for the order from the database and highlight the radio button that matches.

Dynamic radio buttons

You add dynamic radio buttons like this:

1. **Add a group of radio buttons to the page.**

   To add radio buttons, see page 305. You should have as many radio buttons as there are possible values stored in the database column. Note, too, that the value of each radio button must also exactly match the values stored in the database. For example, if a Shipping column in the database stores *USPS, FedEx,* or *UPS,* then the radio group should have three buttons, labeled exactly the same way: USPS, FedEx, and UPS.

2. **Open the Server Behaviors panel (Window→Server Behaviors). Click the + button and select Dynamic Form Elements→Dynamic Radio Buttons.**

   The Dynamic Radio Buttons window appears (see Figure 23-8).

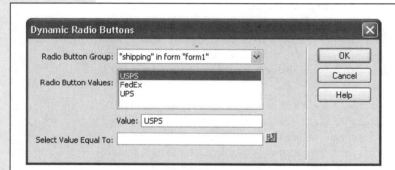

Figure 23-8:
The Dynamic Radio Buttons window lists the values of each button in the group. By selecting a button from the list, you can change its value in the Value field.

3. **From the first menu, choose the radio button group.**

   If your form has more than one group of radio buttons, select the one you wish to be dynamic.

4. **Click the dynamic data button (the lightning bolt) to the right of the Select Value Equal To field.**

   The Dynamic Data window opens (see Figure 23-5). Select the dynamic data item for this radio group. In a nutshell, the radio button whose value matches the dynamic data will be selected. If no radio buttons contain the same value, then no buttons will be selected.

Note: You set the Select Value Equal To field only once per radio group (not once per button in the group).

---

5. **Click OK to close the window.**

   Dreamweaver adds a Dynamic Radio Buttons server behavior to the page.

Dynamic checkboxes

Dynamic Checkboxes work almost the same way:

1. **Add a checkbox to the page.**

   This process is described on page 304.

2. **Open the Server Behaviors panel (Window→Server Behaviors); click the + button and select Dynamic Form Elements→Dynamic CheckBox.**

   The Dynamic CheckBox window appears (see Figure 23-9).

3. **If the form has more than one checkbox, select a checkbox from the first menu.**

   Select the checkbox you wish to control dynamically.

4. **Click the dynamic data button (the lightning bolt) to the right of the Check If field.**

   The Dynamic Data window opens (see Figure 23-5). Select the dynamic data item for this checkbox.

5. **Type a value into the Equal To box.**

   If the value from the dynamic data (step 4) matches the value you provide here, the checkbox will be selected. (If the checkbox is part of an update form, this should match the value you gave the checkbox from step 1.)

6. **Click OK to close the window.**

   Dreamweaver adds a Dynamic CheckBox server behavior to the page.

Figure 23-9:
The Dynamic CheckBox server behavior lets you control whether a checkbox is checked or not based on information from a database, cookie, URL parameter, or other piece of dynamic data.

To *remove* the dynamic properties from a group of radio buttons or a checkbox, open the Server Behaviors panel (Window→Server Behaviors panels). Among the list of server behaviors, you'll see the dynamic radio button or checkbox behavior. It looks something like Dynamic Radio Buttons(group_name) or Dynamic Check Box(checkbox_name)—where *group_name* or *checkbox_name* will be replaced with whatever name you gave the buttons or checkbox. Select it from the list and click the Remove (–) button. (Pressing the Delete key does the same thing.)

Dynamic Menus and Lists

Dynamic menus and lists are among the most-used form elements. They save you the effort of having to rebuild traditional menus or lists every time your company opens a store in a new state, adds a new employee department, or whatever.

To create a dynamic menu or list, proceed as follows:

1. **Create a form and add a menu or list to the page.**

   For example, choose Insert→Form, then Insert→Form Objects→List/Menu. This is the same process as adding a menu or list, as described on page 307. Don't add any items to the list, though. That's the whole point of this exercise: Dreamweaver will build the menu or list automatically.

ASP.Net Note: Dreamweaver doesn't provide a way to create a Dynamic List or Menu for the ASP.NET server model. However, it can create one when you use the Update Record Form tool (see page 695).

---

2. **Add a recordset to the page that includes the information you wish to appear in the menu or list.**

   Perhaps you want to create a menu listing the different categories of products your company sells—books, DVDs, CDs, lederhosen, clogs, and so on. If the database has a table containing the categories, you could then create a recordset that retrieves the name of each category. (In most cases, you'll also retrieve a primary key, like the category ID field. The name of the category will appear in the menu, while the primary key will be the value submitted with the form.)

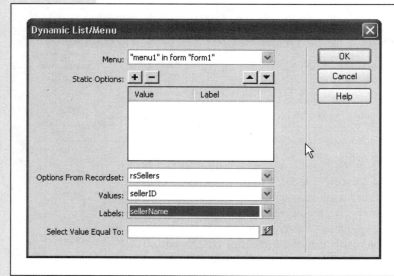

Figure 23-10:
Dreamweaver simplifies the process of creating automatically generated menus like the one pictured in Figure 23-7. Using information pulled from a database, you never have to create another menu by hand.

3. **In the Document window, select the menu or list and click the Dynamic button on the Property inspector.**

   The Dynamic List/Menu window opens (see Figure 23-10). The name of the menu or list you selected appears in the Menu box.

4. **If you like, add some static options to the menu or list.**

   A *static option* is simply a value and label that you enter by hand—unchanging menu or list items that appear at the top of the list. It doesn't come from the recordset you created.

   You could use this feature for options not likely to change—Amazon.com may begin to sell electronics, hors d'oeuvres, and dermatology services, but chances are good that Books will always be among its categories. You can also use it to provide clear instructions about operating this menu: "Pick a state," or "Choose an option from this list," for example. Of course, this step is optional. (Adding static options works just like a regular menu's List Values box, as described on page 307.)

5. **From the Options From Recordset menu, choose the recordset you created in step 2.**

   You've just told Dreamweaver where the items to be listed in the menu are coming from.

6. **Choose a table column from the Values menu; choose another column from the Labels menu.**

   Menu and list items consist of a *label*—what the user actually sees in the menu— and a *value*—the information that's transmitted when the form is submitted. Using the example in step 1, you would select *categoryID* (or whatever the name of the recordset's primary key is) from the Values menu and *category* from the Labels menu. If the label and value are the same, choose the same table column from both menus.

7. **If you want your menu to have one item preselected, then click the Dynamic data button (the lightning bolt.) In the Dynamic Data window (Figure 23-5), select a dynamic data item.**

   This step is optional and most frequently used for an update form. For example, suppose you create a form for updating information on your catalog of products. When the update page loads, all of the form fields would already be filled out with information about a particular product. The menu that lets you specify the product's category, therefore, should have the name of the category that matches the database record displayed and preselected.

8. **Click the OK button.**

   Dreamweaver adds a Dynamic List/Menu server behavior to the page.

You can remove the dynamic menu or list by selecting and deleting it. To leave the menu but remove its dynamic properties, open the Server Behaviors panel (Window→Server Behaviors). Here, you'll see the dynamic list/menu behavior; it will be listed as "Dynamic List/Menu(menu_name)," where *menu_name* is the name you gave the menu or list. Select it from the server behavior list and click the Remove (–) button or press the Delete key.

To edit the behavior, just select the menu in the Document window and once again click the Dynamic button in the Property inspector.

Deleting Records

Dreamweaver's Delete Record server behavior lets you build pages for removing records from a database. The setup is similar to using the Update Record server behavior, in that you must create a page with a recordset that retrieves a single record—the item to delete. This is just like a detail page, as described on page 663. Another page must link to the delete page and provide the proper key for filtering to a single record on the delete page.

One way to go about this is to add a link—Delete This Record, perhaps—on a record detail page. The link should pass the primary key for the condemned record to another page (the Go to Detail Page server behavior described on page 667 can help with this). This page—the Delete page—would include a recordset that retrieves the file to be deleted.

To confirm the deletion, the page might say something like, "Are you sure you want to delete this record?" (Adding some dynamic text from the recordset, such as a name column, will help identify the record.)

ASP.NET Note: The Delete server behavior for ASP.NET works differently. For an example of creating a delete function in ASP.NET, see the tutorial on page 708.

What makes a delete page differ from a regular detail page is that it also includes a form with a single Submit button and a Delete Record Server behavior.

To create a delete page, proceed as follows:

1. **Create a dynamic page containing a filtered recordset.**

   As noted above, the recordset should retrieve a single record—the one to be deleted.

2. **Add a form to the page with a single Submit button (see page 311).**

   Change the label of the button so that it reflects the action it will perform—Delete This Record, for example.

3. **Open the Server Behaviors Panel (Window→Server Behaviors). Click the + button and select Delete Record.**

The Delete Record window appears (see Figure 23-11).

Figure 23-11:
Dreamweaver's Delete Record server behavior simplifies the process of removing information from a database.

4. **Select a database from the Connection menu. From the Delete From Table menu, select the table with the record to be deleted.**

These steps should be familiar by now; the table you select should be the same one you used when creating the detail recordset for this page.

5. **Select the recordset you added to this page from the Select Record From menu.**

This specifies the recordset on the page (if there's more than one) that Dreamweaver should use for specifying the record to be deleted.

6. **Choose the table's primary key from the Unique Key Column menu. If it's a number, make sure the Numeric box is also checked.**

The Unique Key Column identifies which record to delete. (For a description of primary keys, see page 627.)

7. **Select the name of the form that contains the Delete button.**

Unless the page has more than one form, the name of the form you created in step 2 should appear here automatically.

8. **Click the Browse button; navigate to and select a file from the Web site.**

This represents the page that will appear after a record has been deleted. This could either be a page with a confirmation message—"The record has been successfully deleted"—or a page that lists the records of the database—a master page.

9. **Click OK.**

Dreamweaver inserts the code necessary to delete a record from the database.

As with any of the other server behaviors that change content in a database, you should carefully control who has access to the delete page. Going to work one morning and finding that someone has deleted all the products from your company's e-commerce site is enough to ruin your whole morning. Dreamweaver's User Authentication behaviors can help (see page 727).

If you ever need to change any of the properties of the Record Delete action, such as picking a different page to go to after a record is deleted, you can double-click Delete Record on the Server Behaviors panel. The Delete Record window opens; make any changes and click OK.

Tutorial: Inserting and Updating Data

In this tutorial, you'll continue working on the classified ads section of the *Cosmopolitan Farmer* Web site. You'll work on two administrative pages that allow employees of *Cosmopolitan Farmer* to add new classified ads to the database and to edit ads already in the database.

This tutorial assumes you've already completed the tutorials for Chapters 21 and 22. If not, turn to page 621 and follow the instructions for preparing the application server, database, and Dreamweaver for this project. Then turn to page 670 and build the classified ad pages.

Adding an Insert Ad Page

Start by opening a page that's already been created.

1. **Open the file named add_classifieds.asp in the *admin* folder of the local site you defined in Chapter 21.**

   Pages for adding and editing *Cosmopolitan Farmer*'s classified ads shouldn't be accessible to the public; you wouldn't want anyone adding ads without paying Cosmo Farmer. Accordingly, these pages are kept in a folder reserved for administrators of the Web site. (In the next chapter, you'll learn how to password protect these pages.)

ASP.NET Note: ASP.NET developers can follow along using the ASP.NET server model. Open the ASPNET_add_classified.aspx file and follow the instructions that follow. Throughout this tutorial, Note boxes like this one will point out differences in the procedures between .NET and ASP.

   One piece of information required for each new ad is an ID number for the person who placed the classified. The database for these ads actually contains two tables: Ads and Sellers. Information about each seller (name and contact info) is in the Sellers table, while information on each ad (price, description, and so on) is in the Ads table.

   To keep these two tables connected, so that you know which seller placed which ad, the Ads table includes a field containing the seller's ID number. Whenever you add a classified to the Ads table, you also need to insert the advertiser's ID number.

To make the process of selecting a seller easier, you should add a pop-up menu that lists all of the advertisers in the database. To make this kind of dynamic menu, start by creating a recordset.

2. **Choose Insert→Application Objects→Recordset.**

   The Recordset window opens. Make sure that the simple recordset options show up (see Figure 23-12). Next, you'll define the properties of this recordset.

ASP.NET Note: In ASP.NET, a recordset is called a *dataset*, so choose Insert→Application Objects→Dataset for this step.

---

3. **Type *rsSellers* in the Name box. Select connCosmo from the Connection menu. Select *sellers* from the Table menu.**

   These three steps set up the name, database, and table required for the recordset. For a recap of creating recordsets, turn to page 636.

4. **Click the Selected radio button; select sellerID and sellerName from the Columns list.**

   You can do this by holding down the Ctrl (Option) key while clicking the name of each column. Finally, pick an order for sorting the list of sellers.

5. **Choose *sellerName* from the Sort menu. Make sure *Ascending* is selected in the order menu.**

   The Recordset window should now look like Figure 23-12.

Figure 23-12:
When creating this recordset, make sure you're using the window's Simple options. If you see a button labeled Advanced, *you're in the right place. (If that button's missing, click the* Simple *button to access the basic recordset options.)*

6. **Click OK to close the window and insert the recordset in the page.**

   Now you're ready to add a form for inserting a new record.

7. **Click in the area directly below the headline "Add Classified Ad." Choose Insert→Application Objects→Record Insertion Form.**

   The Record Insertion Form window opens. Next, you'll tell Dreamweaver which database to connect to and which table will receive data from the form.

8. **From the Connection menu, choose *connCosmo*. From the Insert Into Table menu, choose *ads*.**

   You can insert data into only one table at a time. In this case, you've selected the Ads table because it holds all of the information for each classified ad. After information is added to the database, the visitor will be redirected to another page. You'll set this up next.

9. **Click the Browse button. Select the file *classifieds.asp*.**

   After adding a new classified to the database, your staff will be taken to the classified ads page (the one you created in the previous chapter). Since that page lists all ads with the most recent ones listed first, the newly inserted classified ad will show up immediately.

ASP.NET Note: In step 9, select the file ASPNETclassifieds.aspx.

Figure 23-13:
Although you can manually create a form and program it to insert a new record in a database, Dreamweaver's Record Insertion Form makes the task a snap to complete.

10. **In the Form Fields list, select *adID*. Click the Remove (–) button to remove this field.**

    In some cases, the database itself fills in certain fields. For instance, every ad in the database has its own unique ID—the table's primary key, which is generated by the database. When a new record is added, the database creates a new, unique number and stores it in the adID column. Because you don't want anyone entering the wrong information here, you should remove it from the form Dreamweaver is about to create.

11. **Select the adName column. Change the label in the Label field to *Item for Sale:*.**

    The label you type here doesn't affect your database in any way. It's just the text that visitors will see next to the form field.

    You can make entering new classified ads easier by teaching the database to enter the date automatically when the form is submitted. After all, the fewer fields someone needs to enter, the faster the process and the better the Web page. In this case, you should make DatePosted a hidden field—a form field that gets submitted with the other form data but doesn't actually appear on the page. (See page 310 for a description of hidden form fields.)

12. **Select the *datePosted* column. From the Display As menu, select Hidden Field.**

    But if the visitor doesn't see the field and can't change it, how is the proper date entered? We'll assume for this application that the day a classified is added to the database is the same day it should be posted. To accomplish this, you must use a little programming.

13. **In the Default Value field, type *<%= date %>*.**

    This is a little ASP programming code. In a nutshell, <% tells the application server that an ASP code is coming. The = means that the server should write something directly into the HTML of the page; *date* is a special command that generates the current date like, 3/20/2003. Finally, the %> tells the application server that the ASP code has ended and regular HTML follows. Taken together, this bit of code puts the current date into the default value property of the hidden field.

ASP.NET Note: Type *<%# String.Format("{0:d}", DateTime.Now) %>* into the Default Value field instead.

Next, you need to change the type of form field used for the ad description.

14. **Select the *Description* column. From the Display As menu, select Text Area.**

    Since the description may run several lines long, it's best to provide a large box to type into (the Text Area form field is described on page 301).

    Finally, create a dynamic menu to display the list of advertisers, like this:

15. Select the *sellerID* column, then change its label to *Advertiser*.

    This column only stores a number; the advertiser's name and contact information is stored in a different table. To make entering this information easier, you'll make a dynamic menu that lists all of the advertisers' names. When somebody chooses a name from the menu, the appropriate *sellerID* number will be submitted to the database.

16. From the Display As menu, choose *Menu*. Then click the Menu Properties button.

    The Menu Properties window opens (see Figure 23-14). Use this window to build the menu.

17. Click the From Database radio button. Make sure *rsSellers* is selected in the Recordset menu.

    You're telling Dreamweaver that the items to be listed in the menu are actually coming from a database query. In fact, they come from the recordset you created at the beginning of this tutorial—rsSellers.

Figure 23-14:
Dreamweaver MX can create dynamic menus—pull-down menus (also known as pop-up menus) that get their labels and values from a database.

18. From the Get Labels From menu, choose *sellerName*. Then, from the Get Values From menu, choose *sellerID*.

    The labels—the text that appears in the menu—will be the names of each advertiser. The value that's submitted with the form, meanwhile, will be the advertiser's ID number.

    You can skip the Select Value From field. It's useful if you want a particular value to be preselected when the form loads.

19. Click OK to close the window.

    At this point, the Insert Record Form window should resemble Figure 23-14.

ASP.NET Note: The form items may not be in the same order as they appear in Figure 23-14. Use the up and down arrows at the top right of the Form Field box to put them in the correct order.

20. **Click OK again to insert the form.**

Dreamweaver adds a table, a form, and all of the programming code necessary to add a new classified ad to the database.

21. **Choose File→Save.**

You're nearly finished. All that's left is to finish up the design and take it for a test drive.

Finishing the Insert Form

To make your form ready for primetime, you'll spruce up its appearance and prevent users from submitting bad data.

1. **Select the table containing the form.**

The fastest method is to click anywhere inside the table, then in the tag selector click the <table> tag (the one to the farthest right in the tag selector). For other table selection techniques, see page 161.

2. **In the Property inspector, from the Align pop-up menu, choose Default.**

The Default option aligns the table to the left without adding bandwidth-hogging HTML code.

It would be nice if the text looked more like the rest of the site, too; in the next step, you'll update the style of the text.

3. **Open the CSS Styles panel (Window→CSS Styles) and apply the adInfo style to the table.**

Make sure the Apply Style radio button is selected and then click "adInfo" in the list of styles. The text inside the table should now be formatted to better match the site's style.

Next, add form validation so that users can't submit the wrong kind of information.

ASP.NET Note: The Validate Form behavior does not work with ASP.NET Web control. For articles on Web form validation for ASP.NET, visit *http://msdn.microsoft.com/library/en-us/vbcon/html /vboriWebFormsValidation.asp.*

4. **Select the form by clicking the <form> tag in the tag selector.**

You can also click the red dashed line to select the form.

5. **Open the Behaviors panel by choosing Window→Behaviors.**

Shift-F3 does the same thing.

6. **Click the + button and select Validate Form.**

   The Validate Form window appears. In this case, you want to make sure that when this form is submitted, both an ad name and a price have been entered. It wouldn't make sense to have a classified ad without a name or price. In addition, you need to make sure that the user types a *number* (not alphabetic text) into the price field. Since the database expects a number for the price, you'll receive a nasty error if anything but a number is submitted.

7. **Select the first listing in the Named Fields box—"text "adName.""**

   This is the field used for collecting the name of the item for sale. There should be something in this box when the form is submitted.

8. **Check the Required box.**

   Notice that (R) appears next to the adName item. It tells you that a value is *Required* for this field. Set up the price field next.

9. **In the Named Fields box, select the "text "Price"" item. Turn on the Required box and the Number radio button.**

   The window should now look like Figure 23-15.

Figure 23-15:
The Validate Form behavior is a simple way to ensure that your Web forms don't generate any errors when you're attempting to insert data into a database.

10. **Click OK to close the window and apply the behavior. Choose File→Save; press F12 to preview the page in your Web browser.**

    The finished page should resemble Figure 23-16.

11. **Type information into each of the fields (use the file *images/nopicture.gif* for the ImageURL field) and click the Insert Record button.**

    If you filled out all of the fields correctly, you should see the classifieds page you built in the last chapter with the new item you just added listed at the top. Try filling out the form, except for the name and price, to see how the Validate Form behavior prevents you from submitting the form.

There are many ways to enhance this page. For example, there's currently no way to *add* an advertiser to the database. When you add a classified ad to the database using the form you just created, you're stuck selecting one of the names listed in the pop-up menu. To make this application more useful, you could add a button or link to the right of the Advertiser menu, call the link Add New Advertiser, and link it to another insert record page that would include form fields for inserting a new record into the Sellers table. With the steps you've learned in this tutorial, you could even make that form return you to the Add Classified Ad page after you've added an advertiser to the database.

Figure 23-16:
No database-driven site would be complete without some way to add new records to the database. Use forms like this one to collect newsletter signup information, collect order and payment details, or just create an online guest book.

Building a Page for Editing Database Records

If someone at *Cosmopolitan Farmer* typed in the wrong information for a particular classified ad and had no way to correct it, you'd be in a lot of trouble. That said, here's how to add an edit or update record page to the site.

Linking to the Update Page

An update page is very much like an insert record page; the only difference is that the form is already filled out with information about a particular record. The first step is to tell the update page which classified ad it's supposed to update. To do so, you must add a link to the ad details page you built in the last chapter.

1. **Open the file named adDetails.asp in the root folder of the local site.**

   This page lists details for a particular classified ad. As you may recall from the last chapter, this page is accessed from the classifieds.asp page, which displays a listing of all ads in the database. By clicking the name of an ad on that page, the adDetails.asp page retrieves and displays information on a single ad.

   Now you need to create a link on this page that, when clicked, takes a visitor to an update page for the particular ad.

ASP.NET Note: Open the file ASPNET_adDetails.aspx. Then skip to step 4.

---

2. **Open the Bindings panel (Ctrl+F10 [⌘-F10]). Click the + button and select Request Variable.**

   The Request Variable dialog box appears. In the next step, you'll add information from a URL parameter to the Bindings panel. Remember that the adDetails.asp page knows which ad to display because the link from the classifeds.asp page included a URL parameter—classifieds.asp?adID=4, for example. You're simply going to capture that parameter and pass it along to the update page.

Figure 23-17:
The Request Variable window lets you add information from a form field, URL parameter, or cookie to the Bindings panel. You can then add it to your page as dynamic text.

3. **From the Type menu, select *Request.QueryString*. Then type *adID* in the Name field. Click OK to close the window.**

   A new Request item labeled QueryString.adID appears in the Bindings panel. You'll use this information to create the link to the update page.

4. **Click in the empty space under Contact E-mail and type *Edit This Ad*. Select the text you just typed and click the Browse For File button (the little folder icon) in the Property inspector.**

   The standard Open File dialog box appears.

5. **Navigate to and select the file in the admin folder called *update_classified.asp*, but don't close the window yet.**

You need to add some additional information, which identifies the classified ad that needs updating, to the end of the URL.

ASP.NET Note: Navigate to and select the file ASPNET_update_classified.aspx instead.

---

6. **Click the Parameters button to open the Parameters window. Click in the name column and type *adID*.**

The Parameters button lets you add a URL parameter to the end of a link, allowing you to pass information on to another page. In this case, you're passing on a dynamic piece of data—the ad ID number for the ad currently displayed on the Ad Details page.

7. **Press Tab twice to hop to the value column. Click the dynamic data button (the lightning bolt).**

The Dynamic Data window opens. Here you can select data that you've already added to the Bindings panel, such as columns from a recordset or the URL parameter you added earlier.

8. **Select the item *QueryString.adID* and click OK.**

The link is nearly complete.

ASP.NET Note: Select the item "adID" from the rsDetails dataset instead.

---

9. **Click OK to close the Parameters window. Click OK once again to close the Select File window and apply the link.**

When you're all done, the link box in the Property inspector should look like this:

```
admin/update_classified.asp?adId=<%= Request.QueryString("adId")
%>
```

ASP.NET Note: The link box in the Property inspector should read: admin/ASPNET_update_classified.aspx?adID=<%# rsDetails.FieldValue("adID", Container) %>

---

10. **Choose File→Save.**

That was a lot of work, and you haven't even started building the update page yet.

Creating the Update Page

Now that the initial legwork is out of the way, you're ready to build the actual record update form. First, though, you'll borrow some of your work from a previous page.

1. **Open the file update_classified.asp in the admin folder.**

ASP.NET Note: Open the ASPNET_update_classified.aspx file.

---

2. **Choose Insert→Application Objects→Recordset.**

   The Recordset window opens. Make sure the simple options are displayed, as described in Figure 23-18.

ASP.NET Note: Keep in mind that ASP.NET uses the term *dataset* in place of recordset, so wherever you encounter *recordset* in these instructions, substitute *dataset*.

---

3. **Type *rsClassified* in the Name field, choose "connCosmo" from the Connection menu, and select "ads" from the Tables menu. Leave the All button selected.**

   Next, add a filter to the recordset. This will ensure that the recordset retrieves only a single record—the classified ad you wish to update.

4. **From the Filter menu, select adID. From the Comparison menu, select "=." From the Source menu, choose URL Parameter. Finally, in the last field in the Filter area of the window, type *adID*.**

   The Recordset window should now look like Figure 23-18. In essence, it instructs the recordset to retrieve only the record whose adID matches the number passed in the URL parameter adID.

Figure 23-18:
When you filter on a table's primary key (adID, in this case) using the = operator, the recordset never retrieves more than one record.

5. **Click OK to close the window and add the recordset to the page.**

   Next, you'll create a recordset listing all of the advertisers on the site. You'll use it to create a dynamic menu of advertisers, just as you did on the insert form.

6. **Follow steps 2–6 from the "Adding an Insert Ad Page" part of this tutorial (page 709) to create a new *rsSellers* recordset.**

   The hard part's behind you. You can now use Dreamweaver's Update Record Form tool to finish the page.

7. **Click in the empty area directly below the "Update Classified Ad" headline. Choose Insert→Application Objects→Record Update Form.**

   The Record Update Form window opens (see Figure 23-19). Next, you'll specify the recordset and fields the form should update.

8. **From the Connection menu, select connCosmo. Make these selections for the next three menus: "ads" in the Table to Update menu, rsClassified in the Select Record From menu, and "adID" in the Unique Key Column.**

   Next, you need to specify which page will appear after someone updates the record. Since the update page lets you edit a single ad, it makes sense that after submitting any changes, you should see the newly updated information on that ad's detail page.

9. **Click the Browse button. In the Select File window, navigate to and select the file adDetails.asp. Click OK to choose the file.**

   Now you must specify which fields will appear in the form. You also need to change which type of form element they should use and edit their labels. This process is very similar to the Insert Record form; it's summarized in the following steps.

ASP.NET Note: You'll have to follow a few more steps here:

1. In step 10, select the ASPNET_adDetails.aspx page, but don't close the Select File window.

2. Click the Parameters button.

3. In the Parameters window, click in the name column and type *adID*.

4. Press Tab twice to hop to the value column; click the dynamic data button (the lightning bolt).

5. Select the item "adID" from the rsClassifieds dataset.

6. Click OK to close the Parameters window; click OK again to close the Select File window.

---

10. **In the Form Fields list, select adID. Click the Remove (–) button to remove this field from the list.**

    Since adID is a primary key generated by the database, no one should be allowed to change it.

    Next, you'll change the text label that will appear next to the adName field.

11. Select the adName form field and change its label to *Item for Sale:*.

Next, you'll provide a little more room to the form for lengthy descriptions for each classified ad.

Figure 23-19:
Dreamweaver's Record Update Form makes very quick work of creating pages to update records in a database.

12. Select the Description column. From the Display As menu, choose Text Area.

In some cases, there may not be a picture for each classified ad. To rule out the possibility that an ad page will display an ugly broken image icon, you'll set a default value for the *imageURL* column.

8. Select imageURL and type *images/nopicture.gif* into the Default Value field.

This is the URL of a graphic file already present on the site.

9. Select the sellerID column, then change the label to *Advertiser*. From the Display As menu, choose "Menu"; click the Menu Properties button.

The Menu Properties window opens (see Figure 23-14).

10. Click the From Database radio button, make sure "rsSellers" is selected in the Recordset menu, then choose "sellerName" from the Get Labels From menu. Now, from the Get Values From menu, choose "sellerID."

Leave the Select Value Equal To field as is. Dreamweaver automatically selects the appropriate choice based on which advertiser placed the ad.

11. **Click OK to close the Menu Properties window.**

At this point, the Record Update Form window should look like Figure 23-19.

12. **Click OK to close the Record Update Form window.**

Dreamweaver inserts a table, form, form fields, and programming code to the update page. All that's left are some final cosmetic touches.

13. **Repeat steps 1–10 from the "Finishing the Insert Form" part of this tutorial (page 713).**

Doing so properly formats the form and adds the necessary form validation behavior. Your finished page should resemble Figure 23-20.

ASP.NET Note: See the note on page 713 for information on validating ASP.NET forms.

Figure 23-20:
When you're working in Design view, Dreamweaver highlights dynamic areas of the page—like this update form—in light blue. In Live Data view (see page 660), the same areas change to yellow. If you'd like to hide this coloring, open the Preferences window, select the Highlighting category, and turn off the two Live Data checkboxes.

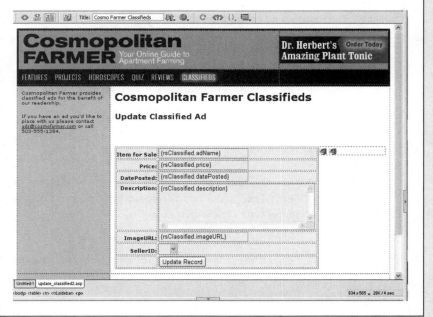

14. **Save this page and close it.**

To get a feel for what you've done, it's time to test your application.

15. **Open the *classifieds.asp* page. Press F12 to preview it in a browser.**

The page lists the ads in the database. Take a close look at one ad in particular.

ASP.NET Note: Open and preview the ASPNET_classifieds.aspx page instead.

---

16. **Click the name of any ad in the list.**

    A details page for that product appears.

17. **Click the Edit This Ad link near the bottom.**

    The Update Classified Ad page appears, complete with the form already completed.

18. **Change some of the information on the form and click the Update Record button.**

    Voilà! You're taken back to the details page for this ad, which proudly displays the freshly edited content.

Creating and Linking to the Delete Page

Once an item advertised in the classifieds sells—or the advertiser's contract expires—the staff at *Cosmo Farmer* will need a way to remove the ad from the database.

Adding a Link on the Details Page

To begin, you must provide a link to delete the ad. A good place for this would be on the details page of each ad. Since you've already added an Edit This Ad link to this page, you must now add a Delete This Ad link.

1. **Open the file adDetails.asp.**

    Add a link that leads to a Delete page.

ASP.NET Note: Open the file ASPNETadDetals.aspx file instead.

---

2. **Near the bottom of the page, click to the right of the text you added earlier: "Edit This Ad." Press the space bar, followed by the | character and another space; type *Delete This Ad*.**

    Now you'll link this type to the Delete page.

3. **Select the text "Delete This Ad" and click the Browse for File button in the Property inspector (the little folder icon). Navigate to and select the file *delete_classified.asp*, but don't close the window yet.**

    You need to tag on the information that will let the update form know which classified ad it should update.

ASP.NET Note: Navigate to and select the file ASPNET_delete_classified.aspx instead.

---

4. **Follow steps 6–9 in the "Linking to the Update Page" part of this tutorial (page 716).**

    Doing so creates a link that not only goes to the Delete page, but also passes along the ID number of the classified ad to be deleted.

There's one final step for this page: copying a recordset to use on the delete page.

5. **Open the Bindings panel. Select "Recordset (rsDetail)," right-click (Control-click) on it, and choose Copy from the contextual menu.**

   You've just copied the recordset information so you can use it on another page. (You can also copy a recordset from the Server Behaviors panel this way.)

6. **Save and close this page.**

Creating the Delete Page

You've just created a link to the Delete page; now you need to make the Delete page do its stuff.

1. **Open the file delete_classified.asp.**

   This is where you'll paste the recordset that you copied a moment ago.

ASP.NET Note: Open the file ASPNET_delete_classified.aspx. You'll notice that this page is blank! Don't worry, that's the way it should be. The Delete server behavior works a bit differently in ASP.NET.

---

2. **Make sure the Bindings panel is open. Right-click (Control-click) in the empty area of the panel; from the contextual menu, choose Paste.**

   Dreamweaver pastes all the programming code to create recordset from the Details page. This is a fast way to reuse a recordset.

ASP.NET Note: This page will simply delete the record. There isn't any intermediate "Are you sure you want to delete this record?" page. Skip to step 7.

---

3. **In the Bindings panel, expand the recordset listing by clicking the small + button to the left of the recordset.**

   Don't click the *large* + button, which lets you add additional recordsets. You just want to see an expanded listing of recordset columns so you can add some dynamic data to the page.

4. **Drag the adName column from the Bindings panel and drop it onto the Document window, just to the right of the text "Item to Delete." Click the B (bold) button on the Property inspector.**

   This inserts dynamic data into the page. When this page appears in a Web browser, the name of an ad will appear in bold type.

5. **Click in the empty space just below the text, "Are you sure you want to delete this ad?" Choose Insert→Form.**

   A red, dotted line—the boundaries of the form—appears on the page. Now you need to add a Delete button to the form.

6. **Choose Insert→Form Objects→Button. In the Property inspector, change the label to** *Delete*.

This button, when clicked, removes one classified ad from the database.

7. **Open the Server Behaviors Panel (Window→Server Behaviors). Click the + button and select Delete Record.**

The Delete Record window appears (see Figure 23-21).

Figure 23-21:
The Delete Record behavior adds all the necessary programming code to remove a record from the database. All that's needed to make it work is a recordset that retrieves a single record—and a form with a Delete button.

8. **From the Connection pop-up menu, choose "connCosmo."**

Dreamweaver should automatically fill in the next four menu items.

The Delete Record window should now look like Figure 23-22. Essentially, these four selections tell Dreamweaver which table the record is in, which recordset retrieved the record, which database column is the primary key, and which form has the Delete button. To finish filling out this window, you'll just tell Dreamweaver which page should appear after someone deletes the record.

ASP.NET Note: Make sure primary key value is selected in the first menu and that the other menus are similar to Figure 23-22.

---

9. **Click the Browse for File button in the Property inspector. Navigate to and select the file classifieds.asp.**

After removing an ad, the main ad listings page will reappear. The deleted ad, of course, will no longer be listed.

ASP.NET Note: Select ASPNET_classifieds.aspx instead.

---

10. **Click OK.**

    Dreamweaver adds the Delete Record server behavior to the page. You've done it! Now you need to test it out.

11. **Save and close this page. Open the *classifieds.asp* page. Press the F12 key to preview it in a browser.**

    The page lists the ads in the database. Take a closer look now at a specific ad.

ASP.NET Note: Open and preview the ASPNET_classifieds.aspx page instead.

Figure 23-22:
In ASP.NET, the Delete Record window is more complex than it is in ASP. Furthermore, the behavior doesn't require, or even provide, an "are you sure?" page that lets your visitors confirm their intention to delete a potentially valuable piece of data.

12. **Click the name of any ad in the list.**

    A details page for that product appears.

13. **Click the Delete This Ad link near the bottom.**

    The Delete Classified Ad page appears (see Figure 23-23). Notice that both the ad name and a Delete button appear.

ASP.NET Note: The record is automatically deleted and you're taken to the Classified ads listing page. If you want to create a confirmation page like the one shown in Figure 23-23, create a page that resembles it, and then add a link that passes the adID in the URL to the *ASPNET_delete_classified.aspx* page. Then simply change the link on the Delete This Ad link on the *ASPNET_adDetails.aspx page,* so that it points to the new confirmation page.

---

14. **Click the Delete button to remove the ad.**

    Don't worry: You can always insert more ads later!

    In any case, you'll note that that the ad is no longer listed in the Classified Ads listings.

Of course, in the real world, you wouldn't want just anybody deleting, adding, or editing *Cosmo Farmer's* classified ads. So in the next chapter, you'll learn how to keep prying eyes away from your coveted Insert, Update, and Delete pages.

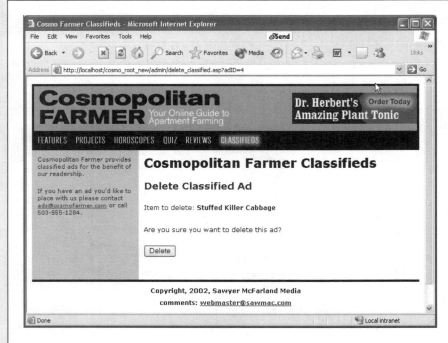

Figure 23-23:
This page is both a confirmation page and a Delete page. When visitors first accesses this page (from a link on an ad details page), they see the confirmation shown here. But when someone clicks Delete, the server reloads this page and sends a Delete command to the database. Once the deletion is complete, the Web browser displays another page—in this tutorial, the classified ad listings page.

Advanced Dynamic Site Features

Dreamweaver's basic database capabilities are impressive. But there may come a time when you need to dig deeper into the program to build successful Web applications. Dreamweaver's advanced features let you, the mere mortal, do things that the pros do every day, like password protecting pages, displaying content based on database results, and accessing information from forms, cookies, and URLs.

Password Protecting Web Pages

Although Dreamweaver MX lets you create Web pages that can add, edit, and delete records from a database, your e-business wouldn't last very long if just *anyone* could remove orders from your online ordering system or view credit card information stored in your customers' records. And certainly your company's executives wouldn't be happy if someone accessed the staff directory database, and changed their titles to things like, for example, Chief Bozo.

For these and other reasons, Dreamweaver provides a simple set of tools for locking your pages away from prying eyes.

For example, the User Authentication server behaviors can password protect any page on your site. With this feature, you can limit areas of your site to registered users only, allow customers to access and update their contact information, create maintenance pages accessible only to administrators, or personalize Web pages with customized messages ("Welcome back, Dave").

ASP.NET Note: Dreamweaver MX does not provide any User Authentication server behaviors for ASP.NET. If you want to add these to your ASP.NET pages, you'll have to do it yourself. Use the Web as a starting point—for example, *www.15seconds.com/issue/020220.htm* or *http://msdn.microsoft.com/library/en-us/cpguide/html/cpconaspnetauthentication.asp.*

Also, you can pick up a copy of *Programming ASP.NET,* by Jesse Liberty & Dan Hurwitz (O'Reilly & Associates, 2002). Check the Dreamweaver Exchange *(www.macromedia.com/exchange)* from time to time, too. Some enterprising programmer is bound to create a Dreamweaver extension for this much-needed feature—sooner or later.

PHP Note: Dreamweaver's PHP server model doesn't include any help for creating password-protected pages. Fortunately, you can buy a copy of PHP Login Suite. This commercial Dreamweaver extension gives you all of Dreamweaver's User Authentication server behaviors plus many additional features. For more information, go to: *www.dreamweavermxsupport.com/extensions/phploginsuite/.*

To password protect pages on your site, you'll need to get several elements in order:

- A database table containing user login information.
- A registration form for adding new users. (This is an optional step, but is frequently useful when you want to automate the process of adding user login information to the database.)
- A login form.
- One or more password-protected pages.

The Users Table

Your database must hold several pieces of information. Each user must have a user name and password. When a visitor attempts to log in, he types his user name and password into a form; if the user name and password match a record in the database, then he's logged into the site and can access password-protected pages.

Furthermore, it's frequently useful to include a field in the record for assigning an *access level* to each person. Dreamweaver provides tools not only to require a proper name and password, but also to allow access to only those with the proper clearance level. In this way, your site can have multiple sections accessible by different groups of people.

For example, if your site has a "members only" section that affords registered visitors extra content or special features, you could assign everyone who registers the level of "member" and give them access to these pages. However, you only want your site's administrators and staff to be able to update a product database or retrieve sales records. You would give these users a level of "administrator" for access to these areas.

At a minimum, then, your database needs a *users* table with three fields (user name, password, and access level). You can either use a stand-alone table or incorporate this information into another table. For example, if you require people to provide their name, address, email address, and so on when registering with your site, you could include the three login fields in this table. For an e-commerce system, login information could be stored in the table holding customer information.

Tip: Most database systems let you assign a *default* value to a column. That way, when someone creates a new record and supplies no information for the column, the application enters the default value instead.

For starters, it's a good idea to assign a default value for the access-level field. In other words, you can set your database to assign the lowest access level—"guest," for example—whenever someone creates a new user record. In this way, if you use a Web form for collecting and creating a new user, you can omit any form field for assigning an access level. This method is a good security precaution, because adept (and malicious) Web users could submit a fake form with a higher access level, potentially granting them access to sensitive areas of your site.

Creating a Registration Form

Once you've added a users table to your database, you'll need a way to add new users. If you plan to use password protection for sensitive pages that only your site's staff should access, you probably *shouldn't* create a Web form for adding new administrative users. You'd run the risk of someone finding the form and adding herself to the list of administrators. In such cases, you're better off adding the proper login records in the database system itself—in Microsoft Access, for example.

Tip: If you do create a Web form for adding new users with a high access level, password protect this form! Otherwise, anyone stumbling upon it could add new administrative users—and from there, Pandora's Box would be open.

On the other hand, if you want to let *lots* of people sign up as members of your site, you might want to add a registration form that *automatically* adds them to the list of users of the site. This setup would free you from the headache of assigning user names and passwords for everyone who wants to become a member.

If the site already includes a form for collecting visitor information, you can simply add the proper user fields to this form. Say your site includes a "Sign up for our email newsletter" page that collects a visitor's name, email address, and other contact information. You could add a field called "user name" and another called "password."

Tip: It's commonplace to use an email address as a person's user name for password-protected pages. In this case, if you're already collecting an email address, exclude the user name field from the form.

When the visitor submits the form, the Web application adds all of these fields to the database. (To add records to a database using a Web form, see page 687). While the process of creating a new user for password-protected pages is pretty much the same as adding a new record to a database, there's one additional step: You must make sure that every visitor has a unique user name.

Dreamweaver's Check New User Name server behavior ensures that each user name submitted in the form is unique. If the name already exists, the server won't add the new record to the database and will redirect the visitor to another page. To apply this server behavior, follow these steps:

1. **Add an insert record form to a dynamic page.**

   The form should include fields for a user name and password. You might also add a field for an access level, if that's how you've structured your site. However, for a form that's accessible to the public, it's best to use the database to set a default value for this; see the Tip on the previous page. (Creating record insert forms is discussed in depth on page 687.)

2. **Make sure the Server Behaviors panel is open (Window→Server Behaviors). Click the Add (+) button and, from the pop-up menu, choose User Authentication→Check New Username.**

   The Check New Username window appears (see Figure 24-1).

3. **Select the name of the database field that stores each user name.**

   Note that this is the name of the column in the *database,* not the name of the form field on the Web page. This field doesn't necessarily need to be named *username*. It could be *login* or something else. You could even use an email address as a user name.

4. **Click Browse and select a Web page.**

   Here, choose the page that will open if the user name is already assigned to someone else. This page (which you've created before applying this behavior) should include a note to your visitor, clearly spelling out the problem (the user name just supplied is already in use and therefore unavailable). To make re-entering information easier for your guest, you should include the insert form on this page as well, or provide a link back to the registration-form page.

5. **Click OK to close the window and add the server behavior to the page.**

   Now when someone fills out the registration form, this behavior will kick in and make sure that no one else registered has the same user name.

Figure 24-1:
When adding a new user to your database, the Check New Username server behavior lets you verify that the user name isn't already in use by another person.

Note: Unfortunately, registering a new user doesn't automatically log him into the site. He'll still need to go to a login page (described next).

After inserting the server behavior, Dreamweaver lists it in the Server Behaviors panel. If you wish to change any of its properties, just double-click its name in the panel to reopen the Check New Username window (Figure 24-1). To delete the behavior, select it in the Server Behaviors panel, and click the Remove (–) button.

Creating the Login Page

To access a password-protected page, your visitor must first log into the site using a Web form. This simple Web form should contain just two fields—a user name field and password field—and a Submit button.

When someone attempts to log in, the values she types into the form are compared with the user name and password columns in the database. If there's a match, then she's transported to another page—often the main page of a password-protected area of the site. If there is no matching record, then the visitor is carted away to a page of your creating—an "Access Denied!" page, or maybe just back to the login page.

To create a login page:

1. **Add a Web form to a dynamic Web page.**

   If your site includes password-protected pages aimed at a general audience of Web visitors, you could place this form on your home page. Or you could create a dedicated Login page (remembering to provide links to this page throughout your site). However, if you're creating a login for administrators, you might want to put the login form out of the way, so that it doesn't get in the way of the average visitor.

   Either way, the form should contain simply a user name field, a password field, and a single Submit button. Naming the fields "username" and "password" (rather than keeping Dreamweaver's default field names) will help with step 3.

2. **Open the Server Behaviors panel (Windows→Server Behaviors). Click the + button and choose User Authentication→Log In User.**

   The Log In User window appears (see Figure 24-2).

3. **From the first three pop-up menus, select the names of the login form, the form field for collecting the user name, and the password field, respectively.**

   You're telling Dreamweaver which form (if the page has more than one) and which fields to use for comparing to the users table in the database.

4. **From the Validate Using Connection pop-up menu, choose the name of the database connection.**

   This should be the database that contains the table with user login information.

5. **From the Table pop-up menu, choose the name of the users table.**

6. **Select the database column used to store user names from the Username Column. Select the database columns for passwords from the Password column.**

   This server behavior will search these two database columns for a record that matches the values your visitor types into the form.

Figure 24-2:
Dreamweaver's Log In User server behavior gives visitors a way to log into your Web site, so they can visit password-protected pages. There are quite a few items to fill out here, but they're all straightforward.

7. **To the right of the If Login Succeeds field, click the Browse button; navigate to and select a page from your site.**

   Most of the time, this will be the main page for a password-protected area of the site. If the site contains a members-only section, then, after logging in, the visitor would arrive at the Members page. If you're adding features for administering the site—adding, deleting, and editing database info, for example—create a main Administrators page with links to all of the database administration pages.

8. **Turn on the Go To Previous URL checkbox.**

   This option is a little confusing, but very convenient. Imagine a visitor stumbling across a password-protected page (you'll learn how to protect pages in the next section). He simply came across a link to a password-protected page and clicked it. Of course, since he hadn't logged in, he's denied access to the page and sent to another page. At this point, you're probably redirecting him to the login page, so he can log in and continue clicking his way through your site.

That's where this feature comes in handy. By checking this box, you permit the login form to take the visitor *back* to the page he couldn't get past at the outset. In other words, the visitor tries to access a password-protected page (*any* password-protected page in the site); he's not logged in, so he's sent to the login page; after successfully logging in, he's taken directly to the page he first tried to access (*not* the page you specified in step 7). This is very convenient for visitors who bookmark password-protected pages in your site—it saves them the hassle of having to log in, and click through the site to return to the page they wanted in the first place!

9. **To the right of the If Login Fails field, click Browse; navigate to and select a page from your site.**

    This page, which you've created in advance, should explain that the user name and password were not correct. Since the visitor may have just made a typo, it's polite to either include another login form on this page or provide a link back to the login page.

10. **If the database includes a column for storing an access level, select the Username, Password, and Access Level radio button.**

    This option not only lets folks log into the site, but also tracks their access levels. In this way, you can limit areas of your site to people with the proper access level—administrators, for example.

11. **From the Get Level From pop-up menu, select the name of the database column that contains users' access levels.**

    Dreamweaver lists all of the columns in the table you selected in step 5. If the table doesn't have a column for this information, go to your database application and add it, or deselect the Access Level radio button. (Even if you don't currently have plans for offering different levels of access, it's a good idea to keep this option in mind. In the future, you may very well want to add special pages for administrators, or Super Premium Members. Without an access level, anyone who has a user name and password will be able to visit those pages.)

12. **Click OK to close the window and apply the behavior to the page.**

The Log Out User Behavior

Dreamweaver's Log *Out* User server behavior lets somebody log out by clicking a link. Thereafter, her Web browser won't be able to load any password-protected pages in the site until she logs back in.

This setup is useful when a visitor shares her computer with others, maybe at the library or school, because it provides a sense of security to visitors who see that they have the ability to log out. (It's not technically necessary, though; her computer destroys the session variable used to keep track of her login status anyway, as soon as she quits her browser. Furthermore, if a certain amount of time passes without any activity—usually 20 minutes—the Web browser automatically logs out the user anyway. Again, though, a logout link can be reassuring to your audience.)

To add a Log Out server behavior:

1. **Open a dynamic page.**

   Note that since this adds programming code to the page, it works only on dynamic pages. You can't add a logout link to a static HTML page. So if you want to provide this option on all pages of your site, you'll have to save each page in your site as an ASP, PHP, JSP, or some other dynamic page that matches your server model.

2. **Click on the page where you'd like to add a logout link.**

3. **Open the Server Behaviors panel (Windows→Server Behaviors). Click the + button and, from the pop-up menu, choose User Authentication→Log Out User.**

   The Log Out User window appears.

4. **Select one of the two radio buttons.**

   There are several ways somebody can log out. You can log him out when the page loads or when he clicks a link. You'd use this behavior when you want to automatically log someone out when they reach a specific page. For example, say you create an online testing application, where students would sit at a computer and answer page after page of questions. When students reach the last page of the quiz—maybe a page summarizing their results—you could automatically log them out. The next student sitting down at the same computer would have to log in, preventing the testing application from thinking the new test taker is the same person as the previous student.

   Most commonly you'll just let users log themselves out by clicking a link. By default, the menu says, Create New Link: "Log Out," which adds a new link with the words "Log Out" to the page. After adding the behavior, you can then edit the page and change *Log Out* to any text you like, or even add a graphic button to the link.

Figure 24-3:
The Log Out User server behavior is generally an optional, but polite, addition to a Web site. It lets visitors log out after finishing viewing password-protected pages.

5. **Click Browse; navigate to and select a page from your site.**

Good choices for this page are the login page—so the next visitor can log in—or the home page.

6. **Click OK to apply the link and server behavior.**

Protecting Individual Pages

To password protect a Web page, you apply the Restrict Access to Page server behavior. You have to do this for each page you wish to protect, and you can only apply it to dynamic Web pages. (In other words, you can't password protect regular HTML files, text files, graphics, or any other file that isn't first processed by the application server.)

Note: Although some Web servers let you password protect an entire folder's worth of files, Dreamweaver doesn't provide any tools to do so.

The Restrict Access to Page behavior works like this: When someone attempts to load a password-protected page, programming code in the page sees if he's logged in already. If the page also requires a particular access level—administrators only, for instance—it checks to see if the user has the proper clearance; if so, then the browser displays the page. If the user isn't logged in or doesn't have the proper access level, however, then he's redirected to another page—such as an "Access Denied" page or the login page.

POWER USERS' CLINIC

Logging In: Behind the Scenes

The Log In User server behavior checks to see if the user name and password submitted by a form matches a user name and password in the database. If it does, the behavior generates two *session variables* (page 741): MM_Username and MM_UserAuthorization. The first one stores the user name of the logged-in visitor; the second stores the access level of that user. (The MM stands for Macromedia, since programs written by Dreamweaver engineers create these session variables.) The variables follow visitors from page to page of the site, until they log out, close the browser, or don't do anything on the Web site for at least 20 minutes.

The password protection scripts use these session variables to allow or deny access to a page. But you can take advantage of these variables in other ways. You can add MM_Username to the Bindings panel (see page 652), for example. You can then add it to your pages like other dynamic data for customized pages: "Welcome back, Kotter176@aol.com."

Furthermore, since each user name is unique—just like a primary key—you can use the session variable to filter records in a recordset (page 639). You could use this technique, for instance, when a logged-in user wishes to see all of his contact information. Create a recordset that filters the user table by the session variable.

You can also use either of these variables to control the display of certain areas of a page. For example, while regular visitors to your Web site might see a simple listing of products on a dynamic catalog page, administrators might see additional items like "Edit this product" and "Delete this product" buttons. The tutorial in this chapter has an example of this scheme in action (page 753).

To apply this server behavior, proceed as follows:

1. **Open the dynamic page you wish to protect.**

   It must be a dynamic page that uses the site's server model (page 618).

2. **Open the Server Behaviors panel (Windows→Server Behaviors). Click the + button and choose User Authentication→Restrict Access to Page.**

   The Restrict Access To Page window appears (see Figure 24-4).

Figure 24-4:
If you want to give access to more than one group, you can Ctrl-click (⌘-click) more than one level in this list to highlight them simultaneously.

3. **Turn on one of the two radio buttons.**

   To allow access to anyone in the users table, then select the Username and Password button. However, if you want to limit the page to users with a particular access level, then turn on the second button.

   The first time you use this behavior, you'll have to click Define and then type in each access level you use in the database—*admin, member,* and *guest,* for example. Capitalization counts. You need to define these levels only once; Dreamweaver remembers these settings for other dynamic pages in the same site.

Tip: At times, you may want to give access to more than one group. For example, a page intended for everyday access by registered members should also be accessible by administrators. (Otherwise, administrators would need two separate user names to see all the pages of the site!) Just Ctrl-click (⌘-click) the names of the levels who should have access, as shown in Figure 24-4.

---

4. **Click Browse; select the page people will see if they aren't logged in.**

   It's often a good idea to simply dump unregistered users onto the login page. That way, if they're legitimate customers, they can simply log on and return to the page. (Dreamweaver can help with this. See step 8 on page 732.)

5. **Click OK to apply the link and server behavior.**

   Dreamweaver adds the Restrict Access to Page behavior in the Server Behaviors panel. Double-click its name to change its properties, or use the – button to remove it.

Additional Data Sources

So far, you've been using Dreamweaver's dynamic page-building features to retrieve information from databases for building catalog pages, product detail pages, and other pages that require database-generated content. But at times, you'll want to collect data from other sources and add them to your page. For example, when someone logs into a site (see the Log In User server behavior on page 731), her user name travels along with her from page to page in what's called a *session variable*. Using the Bindings panel, you can capture this session name and then use it on a Web page.

Similarly, you can create *cookies* to store small pieces of information on a person's computer—such as a counter tracking how many times he's been to your site—and use Dreamweaver's Bindings panel to add that information to a Web page.

The Bindings panel lets you access these sources of data as well as information submitted from form fields and embedded in URLs. Each server model understands different types of dynamic data. But most recognize the ones listed below.

ASP.NET Note: Dreamweaver doesn't let you add any of these additional data sources to the Bindings panel.

Regardless of the type of dynamic data you wish to add, the process is pretty much the same. It differs only among server models.

For ASP

1. **Click the + button in the Bindings panel, and depending on the type of dynamic data you're interested in, select either Request Variable, Session Variable, or Application Variable.**

   In ASP, the Request Variable covers a wide range of data sources, including form variables, URL variables, cookies, and server variables. So there's an extra step you must perform after selecting Request Variable to open the Request Variable window (see Figure 24-5): choose a type of variable from the Type pop-up menu.

Figure 24-5:
The Request Variable window (for the ASP server model only) lets you add a wide variety of variable types for use in an ASP page. Request.QueryString is ASP's way of referring to a URL variable.

2. **Type the name of the variable into the Name field.**

   Capitalization doesn't matter. To ASP, *username, UserName, and USERNAME* are all the same.

3. Click OK.

Dreamweaver adds the variable to the Bindings panel.

For PHP and Cold Fusion:

1. **Click the + button in the Bindings panel and select the proper variable type: URL, Form, Cookie, or whatever.**

   A window appears for the particular type of data source.

2. **Type the name of the variable in the Name field.**

   This time, capitalization matters; *username, UserName, and USERNAME* are all different variables. Find a system you're comfortable with (all lowercase, all uppercase, or mixed case) and stick with it.

3. **Click OK.**

   The URL variable is added to the Bindings panel.

For JSP:

For JSP pages, Dreamweaver supplies tools for adding only form, URL, and session variables.

1. **Click the + button in the Bindings panel and select either Request Variable or Session Variable.**

   Depending on the choice, either the Request Variable or Session Variable dialog box appears.

2. **Type the name of the variable into the Name field.**

   Here again, capitalization matters, so *username, UserName, and USERNAME* are all different variables.

3. **Click OK.**

   Dreamweaver adds the URL variable to the Bindings panel.

After you add the variable to the Bindings panel, you can drag it to your Web page; any of the techniques for adding recordset data to a page also work (see page 636). Unfortunately, unlike recordsets, you can't copy and paste these variables from page to page.

Tip: You can drag data sources listed in the Bindings panel into Code view, as well. Once you've got your programming chops sharpened, this trick is helpful for quickly adding data to your own server-side programs.

URL Variables

Some URLs include information tagged onto the end of the name of a Web page like this: *www.sawmac.com/catalog.asp?prodID=4*. The information following the *?* is known as a *query string,* and it provides additional information to a dynamic page.

In most cases, this information comes in the form of one or more name/value pairs, which Dreamweaver refers to as *URL variables*. In this example, the name of the URL variable is *prodID,* and its value is *4.* URL variables are often used to transfer specific information for use in a recordset. You saw an example of this in the tutorial in Chapter 22: The number of a particular ad was passed in a URL to the adDetails page, which used this number to retrieve details on a particular ad.

You can also add a URL variable to the Bindings panel, and then include it in a Web page or use it anywhere you'd use a dynamic data source. (For example, you can use it as a parameter added onto the end of a link in order to pass the information along to another page. See the tutorial in Chapter 22 (steps 5-7 on page 678) for an example of this operation in action.

Keep in mind that a page that links *to* the page with the URL variable must include the proper query string in the link. For example, say you add a URL variable named *username* to the page *cabbage.html;* the page uses the query string to personalize the page: "Welcome, [username]." For this to work, you then need to link to the cabbage.html page with the query string attached to the URL like this: *cabbage.html? username=bob.*

You can add a URL variable to the Bindings panel using the methods described on page 737.

Form Variables

You can also add information from *forms* to the Bindings panel and use them on your page. If you add a form on one page, you can collect that information on the page the form submits to (the same page specified in the form's Action property, as described in step 6 on page 298). In other words, the page receiving the form data can display that information on the page *or* use it in some other fashion—such as inserting the information into the database, or creating a cookie or session variable.

If you're mainly using forms in conjunction with Dreamweaver MX's Insert Record and Update Record server behaviors, you won't generally take advantage of form variables. Those two behaviors work by collecting data from a form, adding or updating a database record, and then redirecting the Web browser to another page. The page the visitor finally sees never has access to the form information, so you can't add any form variables to that page.

However, adding a form variable to the Bindings panel can come in handy when you create a search page. For example, suppose you've created a page for searching a database. The search form lets the visitor type in a name—of an author or musician, for instance. You could then create a search results page that looks in the database for any records that match the search term. On that page, along with adding the database results, you could add text like "Search Results for: [search_term]," where *search_term* would be the word the visitor typed into the form. Just add the form variable to the Bindings panel and then drag it to the spot in the search page where you wish it to appear.

Note: If you use the GET method for submitting a form, the names and values of each form field are included in the URL. In this case, they are considered URL variables, so if you wish to add any of these fields to the Bindings panel, use the URL variable method instead. (For the difference between GET and POST, see step 7 on page 299.)

Cookies

One problem with Web servers is that they have no memory. Suppose a site has a particularly long and annoying Flash movie that welcomes visitors with an ear-pounding, seizure-inducing multimedia display. Even if the designer was kind enough to include a "Skip this nauseating display" button, the Web server won't remember that you clicked it the *last* time you were there.

To overcome this limitation, most Web browsers store *cookies*—small text files containing specific information—that Web servers can create and read. In the example above, the Web server could drop a cookie onto your computer when you clicks the "Skip intro" button. The next time you visit the site, the Web server reads the cookie and kindly ushers you past the Flash movie and directly to the home page.

You can use cookies to store information on visitors' computers, too. Cookies are a great way to store customer ID numbers and other bits of identifying information.

They play by a few rules:

• A single cookie is stored on just one browser and one computer at a time. If you log onto a site that adds a cookie to your computer, and then log on again later from the public library, that computer won't have access to the cookie. In fact, if you use a different Web browser on the *same computer,* the Web server won't be able to read the original cookie from the other browser. (A variation: In some corporations, a Web browser stores cookies on a network server. This kind of cookie *can* be accessed by a particular browser—Internet Explorer, for example—on different computers on the network.)

• Only the domain that created the cookie can read it. *You* can't create dynamic pages that read a cookie set by Amazon.com, for example. Fortunately, that means other Web sites can't read the cookies you set on your visitors' computers, either.

• Web browsers can only store 300 cookies total, and each cookie can be no larger than 4 K in size, so that your hard drive won't crumble under the weight of them.

You can add a cookie to the Bindings panel using the method described on page 737. Unfortunately, Dreamweaver MX doesn't provide any tools for creating cookies (send your feature requests for the next version of Dreamweaver to: *wish-dreamweaver@macromedia.com*). Several third-party developers have risen to the occasion, however, and created extensions for two of the server models:

• **PHP developers:** Dreamweaver Extension developer Felice Di Stefano has developed a free cookie extension for the PHP server model. It includes server behaviors for adding and deleting cookies from a PHP page. You can find it at the Macromedia Exchange or at *www.felixone.it*.

- **Cold Fusion developers:** Basic UltraDev distributes a free extension called CF_Cookie. You'll find it in the extensions section of their site: *www.basic-ultradev.com/extensions/index.asp*.

ASP Note: See the box below for information on how to add cookies yourself.

Session Variables

Not only do Web servers not recognize repeat customers, they generally don't track a user from page to page during the same visit. Web servers don't know or care whether the person requesting your company's home page just placed a $10 million

---

POWER USERS' CLINIC

Adding and Deleting Cookies Using ASP Pages

While Dreamweaver doesn't provide a tool for adding the scripts necessary to create and delete cookies with ASP pages, it isn't difficult to add the code yourself. (Dreamweaver can easily *retrieve* cookie information, as described on page 737.)

First, decide which page should add the cookie. The script will run when the page is requested, so that the cookie is sent to the visitor's browser before the page content. Thus, you could add a script like this at the beginning of a form-processing page. For example, if someone registers at your site, the name he enters in the registration form can be stored as a cookie on his computer. When he returns to the site, the home page could read the cookie and display "Welcome back, Bob"—assuming, of course, that his name is Bob.

To add a cookie, use this code:

```
<%
Response.Cookies("name_of_cookie")
    = "value_of_cookie"
Response.Cookies("name_of_cookie").Expires
    = Date + 30
%>
```

This code should go below the first line of code in Code view. Remember to include the opening <% and closing %>, which tell the application server that everything in

between is programming code and *not* HTML.

Replace *name_of_cookie* with whatever name you wish to give the cookie: *username*, for example. Also replace *value_of_cookie* with whatever you want to store *in* the cookie. In many cases, this will be a dynamic value—information from a recordset, a URL variable, or a form variable. Using the steps described on page 737, you could add the appropriate dynamic data to the Bindings panel, then drag it to the spot in the code directly following the = sign (in this case, omit the set of double quote marks : " ").

The next line of code sets an expiration date. In this case *Date + 30* means 30 days from today. You must set an expiration date; if you don't, the cookie will last only as long as the visitor's browser remains open.

You may also want to *delete* a cookie at some point. Just assign no value to the cookie you wish to delete, like this:

```
<%
Response.Cookies("name_of_cookie")
    = ""
%>
```

If you find yourself typing this code a lot, you can save yourself some time by turning the programming code into Snippets (page 515).

---

order, or is a first-time visitor. Of course, *you* probably care, and so do most Web applications, which need to follow visitors as they travel a site. For example, in a typical e-commerce site, people use a "shopping cart" to store items they're interested in purchasing. For this to work, however, you need to track each shopper's movement from page to page.

To make this possible, most Web servers recognize what are called *session variables.* A session variable is created by the Web developer (or more accurately, by a dynamic Web page that creates the variable) and follows the visitor from page to page. This type of variable lasts, logically enough, for a single *session:* If the visitor closes the browser, the session ends and the variable disappears. Most Web servers also add a limited time that the variable sticks around—usually 20 minutes. In other words, if you don't visit any page in the site for 20 minutes, the Web server assumes that you're no longer around and destroys the session variable.

Note: Session variables take up resources from the Web server. That's why a Web server gets rid of them as soon as it can. Creating lots of server variables for a busy Web site can slow down the server.

When it creates a session variable, the Web server sends a cookie to the visitor's machine. The cookie contains a unique number (not the actual data contained in the variable), which the server uses to keep track of each visitor. When that person requests a page, the Web server reads the cookie with the unique ID. It can then retrieve session variables for that individual. For this reason, session variables won't work if the visitor's Web browser doesn't accept cookies.

Note: Dreamweaver itself creates session variables when you use the User Authentication server behaviors. See page 735 for a discussion of these session variables and how you can use them.

You may be wondering how cookies and server variables differ and when you'd want to use one over the other. The difference is that cookies can last between visits. If you want to have access to a piece of information when a visitor comes back tomorrow, or next week, or next month, use a cookie. For example, you'd use a cookie to remember a selection someone made from a previous visit—such as "Skip this crazy Flash intro."

Session variables, on the other hand, provide better security. The actual information stored in the session variable stays on the Web server, while cookies exist as text files on a computer and can be opened and read by anyone with access to the computer. Accordingly, if you need to keep track of a confidential piece of information (someone's bank account password, for example), you'd use a session variable.

You can add a session variable to the Bindings panel using the method described on page 737.

Unfortunately, as with cookies, Dreamweaver MX doesn't provide any tools for creating or destroying session variables. To find third-party extensions that work with session variables, try the Macromedia Exchange (*www.macromedia.com/exchange/*). Click the Dreamweaver link, and search using the term *session.*

PHP Note: Felice Di Stefano has developed a free session extension for the PHP server model. It includes server behaviors for adding and deleting session variables from a PHP page. You can find it at the Macromedia Exchange or at *www.felixone.it.*

Server Variables

Web servers collect and produce lots of information, much of which is hidden from the everyday Web surfer (and even the everyday Webmaster). Some of that information is obscure, but some can come in handy. For example, you can find out which Web browser the visitor is using, or which language the browser uses. While the exact list of server variables varies by Web server, here are some useful variables that work on many Web servers:

- **HTTP_USER_AGENT.** Information about the browser visiting the page. Unfortunately, you don't get a neat little summary like *Microsoft Internet Explorer 6 for Windows.* Instead, browser information is usually rather long-winded: *Mozilla/4.0 (compatible; MSIE 6.0; Windows NT 5.1; Q312461; .NET CLR 1.0.3705).*

POWER USERS' CLINIC

Adding and Deleting Session Variables Using ASP Pages

While Dreamweaver doesn't provide a simple wizard for adding the code necessary to create and delete session variables with ASP pages, it isn't difficult to add it yourself. (Dreamweaver does, however, make quick work of *retrieving* session variables; see page 737).

The procedure is much like the one for adding cookies (see the box on page 741)—for example, here again, the script will run when a visitor requests the page. When people register at your site, therefore, the email address they enter in the registration form could be stored as a session variable.

To add a session variable, use this code:

```
<%
Session("name_of_variable") =
   "value_of_variable"
%>
```

This code should go below the first line of code in Code view.

Replace *name_of_variable* with whatever name you wish to give the server variable: *email,* for example. Also re-

place *value_of_variable* with whatever you want to store in the session variable. In many cases, this will by a dynamic value like information from a recordset, a URL variable, or a form variable. Using the steps described on page 373, you could add the appropriate dynamic data to the Bindings panel, and then drag it to the spot in the code above directly following the = sign (in this case, omit the set of double quote marks: " ").

You may also want to delete a session variable to conserve server resources. (Dreamweaver's Log Out User server behavior uses this method to log a user out of a site.) To delete a server variable, add this code to the beginning of a page:

```
<%
Session.Contents.Remove("name_of_variable")
%>
```

To delete *all* session variables for a particular individual in one fell swoop, use this code:

```
<%
Session.Abandon
%>
```

- **REMOTE_ADDR.** The IP address of the computer requesting the Web page. It'll look something like 65.57.83.12. Depending on the visitor's setup, this could be the exact address of the computer. (Big Brother, where art thou?)

  Knowing this address has its uses. If someone frequently causes problems on your site—posts phony information to registration forms, submits offensive messages to a message board—one potential solution is to prevent submissions to your database from that particular IP address.

- **HTTP_REFERER.** The URL of the page that *leads* to the current page. For example, say you click a link on page A to get to page B. Page B's HTTP_REFERER server variable would be A.

  You could use this knowledge to create the ultimate Back button. Simply add the HTTP_REFERER server variable to the Bindings panel. Then add a link to whatever you wish to be the Back button—graphic or text—and use the server variable as the link. When visitors click this link, it will take them back to whichever page brought them there in the first place.

For a list of server variables supported by Microsoft's IIS Web server, visit *http://msdn.microsoft.com/library/en-us/iisref60/htm/ref_vbom_reqocsv.asp*. For a list of server variables for use with the Apache Web server, visit *http://hoohoo.ncsa.uiuc.edu/cgi/env.html*.

Advanced Server Behaviors

In addition to the server behaviors described already, you'll find two other sets of behaviors that can come in handy on dynamic Web pages.

Tip: You can also download many more third-party server behaviors from the Macromedia Exchange. Click the + button in the Server Behaviors panel and choose Get More Server Behaviors. Dreamweaver launches your Web browser and connects to the UltraDev Exchange site. UltraDev is the earlier dynamic Web site version of Dreamweaver, so not all extensions listed here work with Dreamweaver MX. Your best bet is to click the Advanced Search link, and search for extensions that work with Dreamweaver MX.

Recordset Paging

This set of five different behaviors lets you add links for jumping to different records in a recordset. In fact, Dreamweaver makes use of these same behaviors as part of its Recordset Navigation Bar object. You'll use these for moving through a long list of records, like a complete listing of products in a database.

To begin, add a recordset to a page. It should contain multiple records (jumping to the *next* record when there's only one doesn't make much sense). The page could also contain a repeating region, so that several records appear.

- **Move To First Record** adds a link that jumps to the first record in the recordset.

- **Move To Previous Record** adds a link that jumps to the record before the current record. If you use a repeating region, it jumps to the previous *set* of records. For example, say you create a repeating region that displays five records at a time. If the page currently displays records 6–10, clicking a link with this server behavior applied to it causes records 1–5 to appear.

- **Move To Next Record** adds a link that jumps to the next record in the recordset. If you use a repeating region, it jumps to the next *set* of records.

- **Move To Last Record** adds a link that goes to the last record in the recordset.

- **Move To Specific Record** adds a link that goes to a single record based on information passed in the URL.

Using any of the first four behaviors involves the same steps:

1. **Create a recordset and add dynamic content to the page.**

2. **Click the page where you wish to insert the link.**

   You can also select an item on the page—text or a graphic—that you'd like to turn into a link.

3. **From the Server Behaviors panel, click the + button. Select Recordset Paging, and then choose a behavior from the submenu.**

   The window for the particular server behavior appears (see Figure 24-6).

Figure 24-6:
Dreamweaver is about to create a new link on the page (or to text or a graphic that you had selected before applying the behavior). You can also use the Link menu to select any link already on the page. This usually isn't a good idea, however, since Dreamweaver will erase whatever link was previously applied.

4. **Choose a recordset from the Recordset pop-up menu.**

   This is the recordset the behavior will move through.

5. **Click OK.**

   Dreamweaver adds the server behavior to the page and adds its name to the Server Behaviors panel.

The Move to Specific Record Behavior works a bit differently. It doesn't add a link to the page; it simply forces the page to display a particular record when the page is requested. It does this by looking for a URL parameter that specifies a particular record in the recordset. In general, this isn't a good approach, since it requires the database server to retrieve many records just to display a single item from the database—a waste of server resources, and on a busy site, that could mean a slowdown. You're better off creating a detail page (page 667), which simply retrieves one record from the database.

Show Region Server Behaviors

At times, you'll want to display different information on a page based on the results of a recordset. For example, if a visitor searches your site's database of products for a product you don't sell, the search results page should say something like, "Sorry, we don't carry alligator skin bicycle seats." But if someone searches for a product you do sell, then the page should present the relevant details for that product. The Web page displays different text depending upon whether the search item was in the recordset.

Dreamweaver provides three sets of server behaviors that let you display any selection of HTML based on the results of a recordset.

- **Show If Recordset Is Empty.** If the recordset retrieves no records, this behavior will make the selected HTML appear in the browser window.

- **Show If Recordset Is Not Empty.** If the recordset retrieves *any* records, this behavior will cause the selected HTML to appear in the browser window: a list of search results or details on a specific database record, for example.

- **Show If First Record.** This server behavior, like the next three, works in conjunction with recordset paging behaviors. It makes the selected HTML appear when the page displays the *first* record of a recordset, which comes in handy when you want to let people step through several pages of records.

- **Show If Not First Record.** This behavior is the opposite of the previous one. If the page *does not* contain the first record in a recordset, then the selected HTML appears.

  Dreamweaver makes use of this behavior in its Recordset Navigation Bar (see page 658). In that case, if the page displays anything *except* the first item in a recordset, the First Item and Previous Page links appear. If the page *does* display the first item in a recordset, those links are hidden. (After all, you can't very well view the previous page if you're on page 1.)

- **Show If Last Record.** This behavior functions just like the Show If First Record behavior, but for the last record in a recordset.

- **Show If Not Last Record.** This behavior functions just like the Show If Not First Record behavior, but for the last record in a recordset. Dreamweaver uses this behavior to hide or show the Next Page and Last Item links in the Recordset Navigation Bar (see page 658).

You can use these behaviors to show any selected object on the page—a paragraph of text, an image, a table, and so on. Your page can contain any combinations of these behaviors, and you can use any behavior two or more times to display multiple areas of a page.

For example, maybe you'd like two things to appear when the recordset successfully retrieves a record: a graphic in the page's sidebar and a message in the main area of the page. You'd apply a Show If Recordset Is Not Empty server behavior to both selections of HTML (the graphic and the message).

To apply any of these behaviors:

1. **Create a dynamic page containing a recordset.**

   This could be a search results page, or a master page that lists many records from the database.

2. **Select the HTML you wish to show based on a recordset outcome.**

   For example, when applying a Show If Recordset Is Empty server behavior to a search results page, select the message that should appear if the search returns no results.

3. **Open the Server Behaviors panel (Window→Server Behaviors). Click the + button, select Show Region, and choose one of the six behaviors from the submenu.**

   A window like Figure 24-7 appears. While the title of the window varies depending on which behavior you selected, each of the six behaviors has just this one option.

Note: The last four behaviors—Show If First Record, Show If Not First Record, Show If Last Record, and Show If Not Last Record—work only on pages that also have one of the recordset paging server behaviors applied.

---

4. **Select the name of the recordset from the menu and click OK.**

   The recordset you select should be the one whose results you're interested in. For example, on a search results page, you'd select the recordset you created to perform the search.

Figure 24-7:
Regardless of which of the Show Region server behaviors you apply, there's only one option to choose: the recordset whose results control the display of the region.

After applying one of these behaviors to a selection of HTML, a gray line appears around the selection, and a gray tab appears bearing the words "Show If." That's the area that will appear if the given recordset condition is met (for example, if the page is displaying the last record of the recordset).

To remove a Show Region server behavior, select its name in the Server Behaviors panel and click the – button (or press the Delete key). Doing so removes the gray tab and outline. Now the affected HTML will appear regardless of the recordset results.

Tutorial: Authentication

In the tutorial at the end of Chapter 23, you created Web pages that could add, delete, and update records in the *Cosmopolitan Farmer* database. You wouldn't want to allow just anyone who visits the Web site to access these pages, let alone delete ads from the site.

ASP.NET Note: Unfortunately, Dreamweaver doesn't include any tools for adding password protection to ASP.NET pages. For a list of resources covering how to add password protection using ASP.NET, see page 728.

The following steps assume that you've worked through the tutorial in Chapter 23, and have all of the completed files ready to go. You'll build on them in the following steps.

Building a Login Page

The first step is to create a login page—a simple form with fields for a user name and password. After a successful login from this page, an administrator will be able to access the administration pages.

1. **Open the file *login.asp* in the admin folder of the site.**

   This page will contain the form for typing in an administrator's user name and password. You'll add the form next.

2. **Choose Insert→Form.**

   Dreamweaver adds a red dashed line to the page, indicating the beginning and ending <form> tags.

3. **In the Property inspector, type *login* as the name of the form.**

   While this step isn't required, it's good to get into the habit of giving your forms helpful names.

4. **In the document window, click inside the red dashed lines and type *Username:***

   This is the label for the form field you'll add next.

5. **Choose Insert→Form Objects→TextField. In the Property inspector, name this field *username*.**

   Next, because a login requires both a user name and password, you need to also add a form field for capturing a password.

6. **Click to the right of the form field you just inserted and press the Enter (Return) key to add a new paragraph. Type *Password*.**

7. **Choose Insert→Form Objects→TextField. In the Property inspector, name this field** *password* **and select the Password radio button.**

   By turning this form element into a password field, anything your visitors type in the field will be displayed like this **** or this ••••, hiding the secret password from nosy passersby watching over your shoulder.

   To complete the form, you'll add a Submit button.

8. **In the document window, click to the right of the password field and press the Enter (Return) key. Choose Insert→Form Objects→Button.**

   The form is complete. Now it's time to let Dreamweaver do its magic.

9. **Choose Window→Server behaviors to open the Server Behaviors window.**

   Alternatively, you can use the keyboard shortcut: Ctrl+F9 (⌘-F9).

10. **Click the + button and choose User Authentication→Log In User.**

    The Log In User window appears (see Figure 24-8). The first three items should already be filled out: the name of the form, the name of the user name field, and the name of the password field. If you had more than one form on the page, or additional fields inside the one form, you'd have to tell Dreamweaver which form and which fields to use for collecting the login information.

Figure 24-8:
Before visitors can access password-protected pages, they first need to log in to the site. Dreamweaver MX's Log In User server behavior makes adding this feature a snap.

11. **From the Validate Using Connection pop-up menu, select connCosmo.**

    This indicates which database contains the login information. You also need to specify which table and columns contain the user name and password.

12. **Select users from the Table menu; select userName from the Username Column pop-up menu; and select userPwd from the Password Column pop-up menu.**

    You've just set up the basic logic of the login behavior: Whatever a visitor types into the two form fields is compared with data stored inside the "users" table in the *Cosmo Farmer* database.

    Next, you need to specify what happens when there's a match—when your visitor types a valid user name and password into the form—and what happens when the visitor types in an invalid user name or password.

13. **Click the Browse button to the right of the "If Login Succeeds, Go To" field. In the Select File window, navigate to and select the file admin.asp inside the admin folder. Click OK.**

    You've just chosen the page that will appear if the login is successful; the visitor will be taken to an administration page.

14. **Click the Browse button to the right of the "If Login Fails, Go To" field. In the Select File window, navigate to and select the file denied.html inside the admin folder. Click OK.**

    This, of course, is the Access Denied page that will appear when somebody types in an invalid user name or password.

    Because this section of the site is for administrators only, you'll add an additional layer of security by restricting administrative pages using an access level as well as a password and user name. In this way, you'll also be able to have other password-protected pages—such as a special "paid subscribers" section—for registered visitors, without letting them access administrative areas of the site.

15. **Select the Username, Password, and Access Level button. From the "Get Level From" pop-up menu, choose userAccess.**

    The database table includes a special field for defining the access privileges of each registered user. For example, each administrator record in the *users* table also includes the value *admin* in the userAccess field.

16. **Click OK. Save this file. Press F12 to preview it in your Web browser.**

    You'll now try out your newly created login page.

17. **In your Web browser, type anything you want in the two fields; click Submit.**

    Unless you've just made an incredible guess, you just typed in a user name and password that doesn't exist in the database. If the technology gods are smiling, an Access Denied page appears.

Now try it again:

18. Click the "Try logging in again" link to return to the login page. Type *bigcheese* in the Username field and *sesame* in the Password field; submit the form.

This time, you're in: the browser takes you to the main administration page. Here you can jump to the pages you created earlier for adding, updating, and deleting classified ads.

The login script works just fine—you end up at the right page when you type in a valid user name and password. However, none of those other pages is protected yet. You can go to any of them, even if you haven't logged in. In the next part of this tutorial, you'll lock down each admin page, so only logged-in administrators can access them.

Password Protecting the Administration Pages

Dreamweaver's password protection features require you to add a server behavior to each page you wish to protect.

1. Open the file *admin.asp* in the admin folder.

This page is the main jumping-off point for adding, deleting, and updating classified ads. It should only be accessible to administrators, so you'll add password protection to it.

2. Make sure the Server Behaviors window is open (Window→Server behaviors). Click the + button and choose User Authentication→Restrict Access To Page.

The Restrict Access To Page window appears (see Figure 24-9). Since you want to limit access to administrators only, you'll make sure the page is restricted to those with the proper access level.

Figure 24-9:
Administrative pages can be reserved for those with the access level "admin," while regular subscribers of Cosmopolitan Farmer will have access to pages intended for subscribers.

3. Select the Username, Password, and Access Level radio button.

You want to specify which type of user has access to this page, but first you must tell Dreamweaver what the different levels *are*.

4. **Click Define to open the Define Access Levels window. In the Name field, type** *admin*; **then click OK to close the window.**

The word *admin* appears in the Select Levels box. If you had other areas of the site with different access privileges, such as a subscriber area of the site only paying subscribers could access, you could continue to add levels by repeating this step.

5. **Click Browse; select the denied.html file in the admin folder and click OK. Click OK again to close the Restrict Access To Page window.**

The window should look like Figure 24-9. To finish this page, you'll add a "Log out" link.

6. **Click in the empty area directly below the "To delete a classified ad" bullet point.**

You'll put the logout link here.

7. **On the Server Behaviors panel, click the + button and select User Authentication→Log Out User.**

The Log Out User window appears (see Figure 24-10).

Figure 24-10:
The Log Out User server behavior lets you offer visitors the polite option of logging out from your site. In essence, this behavior destroys the session variables used to track the login status of a visitor.

8. **The first radio button should already be selected. The text** *Create New Link:* **"***Log Out***" appears in the menu.**

These are the proper settings; you're simply adding the words *Log Out* to the page. They'll link to the logout script.

Next, you'll tell Dreamweaver which page to go to after the user logs out.

9. **Click the Browse button; navigate to and select the file** *classifieds.asp* **in the root folder of the site.**

When people log out, they'll simply end up at the main Classified Ads page. Since they'll will no longer be logged in as administrators, they won't be able to access any of the administrative pages without logging back in. The window should now look like Figure 24-10.

10. **Click OK to close the window.**

Now it's time to test the result.

11. **Choose File→Save; press F12 to preview the page in your browser.**

    One of two things will happen: Either you'll end up on the Access Denied page, or you'll see this administration page.

    If you quit your Web browser after the previous section of this tutorial, or never logged in to begin with, the Restrict Access To Page server behavior is working: It doesn't recognize you as a registered administrator and denies you access to this page. Click the "Try logging in again" link to go to the login page. Type *bigcheese* in the Username field and *sesame* in the Password field, and submit the form. You're now logged in and sent to the admin page.

    However, if you logged in following the instructions from the previous section in this tutorial, and you haven't quit your Web browser in the meantime, you're still logged in. In this case, the Restrict Access To Page server behavior is again doing its job. You're allowed onto this admin page, because you *are* a registered administrator.

12. **Click Log Out.**

    The site logs you out and takes you to the main classified ads page. To make sure you really are logged out, you'll open the administration page again.

13. **Return to Dreamweaver and the admin.asp page. Press F12 to preview the page again.**

    You're immediately redirected to the Access Denied page. You're not logged in, so you can't see the administration page. Hooray! The page is successfully protected from snoops.

    Of course, the most vulnerable pages (the update, delete, and ad pages) are still accessible to everyone. You need to lock down those pages as well.

14. **Open the page *add_classified.asp* and repeat steps 2–5 on the preceding pages.**

    If you want, you can also add a Log Out link to each of these pages by following steps 7–10.

    Repeat this step for the delete_classified.asp and update_classified.asp pages.

Now all of the administrative pages in the site are password protected. Only authorized administrators who log into the site can add, edit, or delete records from the database.

Displaying a Portion of a Page to Logged-In Users

Even though unauthorized users can't access any of the pages that can change the database, they can still see the links on the Ad Details page—"Edit this Ad" and "Delete this Ad." Nothing particularly earth-shattering will happen—unauthorized users will just end up at the Access Denied page—but even that's not very elegant. Wouldn't it be tidier if those links didn't even *show up* except to people logged in as administrators?

You'll set that up next.

1. **Open the adDetails.asp page.**

   You'll be doing a little painless programming in the Code view at this point.

2. **In the document window, click inside the text "Edit this Ad"; in the tag selector, click the <p>.**

   You've just selected the paragraph containing the two links. This paragraph should appear only to administrators.

3. **Choose View→Code.**

   The document window switches into Code view (see Figure 24-11).

Figure 24-11:
When you enter Code view, whatever you had selected in the document window is highlighted in the code. Here a paragraph (and everything inside it) is selected.

4. **Click at the beginning of the selection, just before the opening <p>.**

   The insertion point is now the start of the paragraph. You'll add some programming code here.

5. **Type <% IF Session("MM_UserAuthorization") ="admin" THEN %>.**

   The opening <% tells the application server that some ASP code is coming; in other words, this isn't HTML, it's a program that the application server must process. The IF and THEN parts of this code indicate what's called a *conditional statement*. In this case, it means, "*if* this person is logged in with an access level of 'admin,' *then* the paragraph will appear on the page."

   To determine if the user is logged in with the proper access level, the code sneaks a peak at a session variable called MM_UserAuthorization. As mentioned on page 735, the server behavior creates this session variable when someone logs into a site. This bit of code follows the user around the site and contains a word that indicates what level of access the user has. In this case, if the authorization is "admin," then the user is logged on as an administrator, and the paragraph appears.

6. **Click to the right of the last paragraph and type <% *END IF* %>.**

   This code concludes the conditional statement. In other words, all of the HTML between the first line of code you added in the previous step and this final <% END IF %> will appear *only* if the user is logged in as an administrator.

   The code should now look like Figure 24-12.

Figure 24-12:
The finished code. Here the paragraph you wish to hide from unregistered users is wrapped in ASP programming code.

```
101              <strong>Contact Phone</strong>:<%=(rsDetail.Fields.Item(
       "sellerPhone").Value)%> <br>
102              <strong>Contact E-mail</strong>: <%=(rsDetail.Fields.Item(
       "sellerEmail").Value)%></p>
103          <% IF Session("MM_UserAuthorization") = "admin" THEN %><p><a
       href="admin/update_classified.asp?adID=<%= Request.QueryString("adID") %>"
       >Edit
104              this Ad</a> | <a href="admin/delete_classified.asp?adID=<%=
       Request.QueryString("adID") %>">Delete
105              this Ad</a></p> <% END IF %>
106          <p> </p>
107          </td>
108      </tr>
```

7. **Choose File→Save; press F12 to preview the page.**

   Because you logged out earlier, the links should now be invisible. To see them, you must log in and return to the ad details page.

8. **In the Web browser, click the Administrator link on the left side of the page.**

   You go to the Access Denied page because you're not yet logged in.

9. **Click the "Try logging in again" link to go to the login page. Type *bigcheese* in the Username field and·*sesame* in the Password field. Click Submit.**

   You're now logged in and sent to the main administration page. If you return to the ad details page, the links will miraculously return.

10. **Click the Classifieds button in the top navigation bar on the page to go to the classified ads listings. Click the name of an ad to see the details for that ad.**

    Voila! The links are back. You can freely edit or delete any ad in the database. If you return to the administration page and click the Log Out button, you won't see these links until you log back in.

Part Seven: Appendix

Getting Help

7

Getting Help

Hard as it may be to believe, even this book may not answer all your questions about Dreamweaver. Fortunately, a wide range of other resources awaits when a particular feature doesn't work for you.

Getting Help from Dreamweaver

There's plenty of assistance built right into the program, from beginning tutorials to a complete browser-based help system. The new Answers panel (see Figure A-1) provides access to tutorials, articles, extensions, and technical notes—all of which are routinely updated (over the Internet) with new material. You can also access Dreamweaver's electronic help system and online support center from the Help menu.

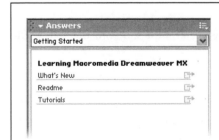

Figure A-1:
The new Answers panel provides introductory material on the program. Using the menu at the top of the panel, you can choose different answer categories to see most requested technical notes, featured articles, and the newest Dreamweaver extensions.

Getting Started

If you're brand new to Dreamweaver, see the What's New presentation, and follow the six step-by-step tutorials that cover specific Web-creation tasks. These range from creating an image map to using Dreamweaver's dynamic page-building tools. You'll find them fairly basic (this book's tutorials cover most of the same ground more thoroughly), but you can never have too much practice. Both of them await in either the Help menu or the Answers panel (choose Window→Answers).

Detailed Assistance

For detailed information on specific features of the program, turn to the Using Dreamweaver reference. This electronic help system includes information on all features of the program, although its coverage, alas, can be spotty and often lacks detailed explanations. Choose Help→Using Dreamweaver or press F1 to open this help system.

If you're getting into writing your own Web code, Dreamweaver's Reference window (Help→Reference, Window→Reference, or press Shift-F1) provides in-depth information on HTML, CSS, JavaScript, ASP, JSP, Cold Fusion, and Web accessibility.

The Answers panel delivers constantly updated material, organized into categories that you select from a pull-down menu near the top of the panel (see Figure A-1).

One of its best features lies in the Tech Notes category. Just type a word or two about your question into the Search box, and then click the right-pointing arrow. Dreamweaver goes online to the Macromedia Web site and pulls up any technical notes related to your question. Click one of these notes, which are actually links, to launch your Web browser and view the entire technical note. (Unfortunately, the search engine isn't very sophisticated; if you type in *MySQL access error,* you'll get every tech note that includes "MySQL," "access," or "error." You'll get better results if you keep your search terms short—"MySQL," for example.)

Getting Help from Macromedia

You can also get more up-to-date and personalized support offerings from Macromedia, ranging from technical notes posted on the Macromedia Web site to pay-as-you-play support plans.

Free Help by Email

www.macromedia.com/support/email/complimentary/

As a registered owner of Dreamweaver, you're entitled to 90 days of free help by email *and phone,* although Macromedia doesn't advertise this last option. The clock starts ticking when you make your first request for help, and it's available only if you've registered your copy of the software first (by choosing Help→Register Dreamweaver).

To post a question, go to the Web site whose address appears above, where you'll find a Web-based support form to fill out. Macromedia says it will usually send you an answer within one business day.

For phone assistance, call this *not* toll-free number: (415) 252-9080. Expect to wait on hold, but the support staff is usually very helpful and knowledgeable.

Tip: Dreamweaver users outside the United States should visit Macromedia's International Support page at *www.macromedia.com/international/support/*.

Paid Support

www.macromedia.com/support/programs/

Once your free email-help period expires, you can turn to four levels of personalized fee-based support, ranging from $65 for a single incident to the whole-hog luxury of the $1,750 Gold Support program. For more information on these programs, go to the Web page whose address appears above, or call (800) 457-1774 within the United States and Canada.

If you just have a single nagging question, the single-incident help program gets you a Macromedia technician who will work with you until the issue is resolved. Customers in the U.S. and Canada call (800) 470-7211 to order this service. (More information on this option, and choices for international customers, should visit *www.macromedia.com/support/programs/singlesupp.html*).

Macromedia Web Site

www.macromedia.com/support/dreamweaver/

If you don't mind hunting around for the right information, you'll find plenty of good, *free* information on Macromedia's Web site. If you've got a question or problem, the best place to start is at the site's Dreamweaver support area . Here you'll find useful tips, techniques, and tutorials, along with a searchable archive of tech notes (short articles on specific, tweaky problems) that may just hold the answer you're seeking.

Macromedia's relatively new Designer and Developer Center features articles and tutorials. The Dreamweaver MX portion of the site includes sample database applications, video tutorials, and in-depth articles. This is one site worth checking out frequently: *www.macromedia.com/desdev/mx/dreamweaver/*.

Quick Reference Guide

http://www.macromedia.com/support/dreamweaver/documentation/dwmx_shortcuts/

Cheat sheets are always a blessing when learning a program. Macromedia supplies Mac and Windows reference guides in PDF format (and in multiple languages). Keyboard shortcuts are neatly organized by topic in this handy two-page reference.

Newsgroups

news://forums.macromedia.com/macromedia.dreamweaver
news://forums.macromedia.com/macromedia.dreamweaver.appdev

The Macromedia *newsgroup* (Internet bulletin board) is a terrific source of information, offering almost real-time answers on Dreamweaver and related Web-design techniques. Macromedia sponsors two newsgroups—the regular Dreamweaver newsgroup for basic questions and the Appdev group, where people discuss Dreamweaver's dynamic Web-page features. A popular newsgroup like Macromedia's can generate hundreds of replies-to-replies a day. Using a newsgroup reader like the one in Outlook Express, you can post questions here. Odds are one of the many knowledgeable experts who always seem to be hanging around will come back with an answer, sometimes within minutes. (If you're new to newsgroups, *www.macromedia.com/support/forums/using.html* explains how to use them. You'd be wise to visit *www.macromedia.com/support/forums/etiquette.htm,* too, to learn the proper etiquette for using newsgroups.)

Tip: If newsgroups aren't your cup of tea, Macromedia also offers a Web version of the Dreamweaver forums, accessible through any Web browser at *http://webforums.macromedia.com/dreamweaver/.*

If you're a little late to the party, you can search previous forum questions and answers in an online archive at *http://groups.google.com/groups?oi=djq&as_ugroup= macromedia.dreamweaver.*

Help from the Real World

If Macromedia doesn't have the answer, there's probably a Web site somewhere that does. In fact, you're likely to find more honest critiques of the program at some of these sites. Here are a few of the best non-Macromedia sites for answers.

Dreamweaver FAQ and Resource Site

www.dwfaq.com

The Dreamweaver FAQ and Resource Site is a compendium of fabulously useful links to Dreamweaver tutorials and information. It's the best place to start for answers to most routine questions about Dreamweaver.

The Dreamweaver Zone

www.dwzone.net

The Dreamweaver Zone includes tutorials, extensions, and Macromedia-related news.

Newsgroup FAQs

www.cauzway.net/dreamweaver/faq.asp

This site's FAQ list holds the answers to some very common Dreamweaver questions.

Help with Extensions

If you're excited by the possibilities of Dreamweaver extensions discussed in Chapter 20, you'll find plenty of sites dedicated to extension development. On the Web, you'll be able to find hundreds of extensions to supercharge your copy of Dreamweaver; most are free. Here's a sampling of some of the best Dreamweaver extension sites.

The Exchange

www.macromedia.com/exchange/dreamweaver

Of course, the most comprehensive source of extensions is Macromedia's own Exchange Web site. It's dedicated to providing Dreamweaver users access to hundreds of (mostly) useful add-ons; see page 606 for more detail.

Massimo's Corner

www.massimocorner.com

Massimo Foti, one of the premier extension developers in the Dreamweaver community, hosts this site full of useful extensions, tips, and tricks.

Yaromat

www.yaromat.com/dw

Another great developer, Jaro van Flocken, provides his extensions at this site.

Project Seven

www.projectseven.com

Project Seven has developed some truly remarkable, very advanced extensions especially for animation and interactivity. This site also offers tutorials and a line of commercial (as in, you have to pay for them) Dreamweaver templates.

Creating Your Own Extensions

If you've got the programming bug and are well-versed in JavaScript, you might want to take a crack at creating your own Dreamweaver Extensions. To help you out, Dreamweaver includes a *detailed* electronic help system covering every aspect of extension development. Choose Help→Extending Dreamweaver. Your Web browser opens, and the first page of the reference appears.

After creating an extension, you can learn how to prepare it for public consumption by choosing Help→Creating and Submitting Extensions. You get an electronic help system explaining how to prepare your extensions in the .mxp format (the format used by the Extension manager), and how to submit them to the Macromedia Exchange for review.

Index

Colophon

The book was written in Word 2000 and 2001, whose revision-tracking features made life far easier as drafts were circulated from authors to technical and copy editors.

The screen images in this book were captured by Ambrosia Software's Snapz Pro *(www.ambrosiasw.com)* on the Mac and TechSmith's SnagIt *(www.techsmith.com)* on Windows. Adobe Photoshop and Illustrator *(www.adobe.com)* were called in as required for touching them up.

The book was designed and laid out in Adobe PageMaker 6.5 on a Power Mac 8500, Power Mac G3, and Power Mac G4. The fonts include Formata (as the sans-serif family) and Minion (as the serif body face). To provide the ⌘ symbol, a custom font was created using Macromedia Fontographer.

The book was generated as Adobe Acrobat PDF files for proofreading, "beta reading," and final transmission to the printing plant.

Yes, it's a big book—but it's a big program.